南宁非遗

CATALOGUE OF INTANGIBLE CULTURAL HERITAGE OF NANNING CITY

南宁市非物质文化遗产图录

南宁市民族文化艺术研究院 出品

毛小雨 李德山 主编

北京时代华文书局

图书在版编目（CIP）数据

南宁市非物质文化遗产图录 / 毛小雨，李德山主编. — 北京 : 北京时代华文书局, 2023.4
ISBN 978-7-5699-4937-7

Ⅰ. ①南… Ⅱ. ①毛… ②李… Ⅲ. ①非物质文化遗产－南宁－图录 Ⅳ. ①G127.671-64

中国国家版本馆CIP数据核字(2023)第034786号

拼音书名 | NANNING SHI FEIWUZHI WENHUA YICHAN TULU

出 版 人 | 陈　涛
选题策划 | 周海燕
责任编辑 | 周海燕
执行编辑 | 胡元曜
责任校对 | 陈冬梅
封面设计 | 程　慧
版式设计 | 王艾迪
责任印制 | 訾　敬

出版发行 | 北京时代华文书局 http://www.bjsdsj.com.cn
北京市东城区安定门外大街138号皇城国际大厦A座8层
邮编：100011　电话：010-64263661　64261528
印　　刷 | 北京盛通印刷股份有限公司　010-52249888
（如发现印装质量问题，请与印刷厂联系调换）
开　　本 | 635 mm × 965 mm　1/8　　印　　张 | 71.5　　字　　数 | 1145千字
版　　次 | 2023年6月第1版　　印　　次 | 2023年6月第1次印刷
成品尺寸 | 235 mm × 300 mm
定　　价 | 860.00元

主　编

毛小雨　李德山

副主编

马旭苒　潘雨茜

编写人员

方　宁　马旭苒　周俊洁　杨　楠　张　帆　李　航　许燕滨　王建坤

英文翻译

毛沐霖　未　名

摄　影

毛小雨 等

图片编辑与翻译

毛小雨

Chief Editor

Mao Xiaoyu　Li Deshan

Deputy Editor in Chief

Ma Xuran　Pan Yuqian

Author

Fang Ning　Ma Xuran　Zhou Junjie　Yang Nan　Zhang Fan　Li Hang　Xu Yanbin　Wang Jiankun

English Translation

Mao Mulin　Wei Ming

Photography

Mao Xiaoyu, etc

Picture Editing and Translation

Mao Xiaoyu

前言

Introduction

南宁，简称“邕”，是广西壮族自治区首府，自治区政治、经济、文化、教育、科技和金融中心，是中国—东盟博览会永久举办地，北部湾经济区中心城市，素有“中国绿城”“天下民歌眷恋的地方”等美誉，是“联合国人居奖”获得城市、全国文明城市、国家生态园林城市、全国双拥模范城、国家卫生城市、国家森林城市、美丽山水城市。南宁市总面积2.21万平方千米，2020年末，常住人口约874.16万，其中少数民族人口逾400万，是一个以壮族为主的多民族城市。

南宁的历史颇为悠久，秦代为桂林郡辖地，东晋大兴元年（318）设晋兴郡，郡治南宁，为南宁建置之始，至今已有1700多年的建城史。唐置南晋州，贞观六年（632）改称邕州。唐咸通三年（862）设岭南西道，邕州为岭南西道治所，管辖今广西所属地区，是当时这一地区的政治、军事中心。元设邕州路，泰定元年（1324）改为南宁路，南宁名称始于此时。明清时期，广西的最高政治、行政中心移至桂林，但南宁作为广西最高军事中心的地位未变。民国初期，旧桂系军阀陆荣廷统治广西，将省府移至南宁，1936年省府又迁往桂林。1949年解放，同年设市。1950年2月南宁成为广西省会。1958年广西僮（壮）族自治区成立，南宁成为自

Nanning, abbreviated as “Yong”, is the capital of Guangxi Zhuang Autonomous Region, and the political, economic, cultural, educational, scientific and financial center of the region, the permanent venue of China-ASEAN Expo and the core city of Beibu Gulf Economic Zone. It is known as “China’s Green City” and “the place where the world’s folk songs are attached to”. It is a city that has won the UN Habitat Award, National Civilized City, National Ecological Garden City, National Model City of Double Support, National Health City, National Forest City and Beautiful Landscape City. Nanning, with a total area of 22,100 square kilometers and a permanent population of 8,741,600 until the end of 2020, including more than 4 million ethnic minorities, is a multi-ethnic city dominated by Zhuang.

The history of Nanning is quite long. In Qin Dynasty, Nanning was under the jurisdiction of Guilin County. In the first year of Daxing in the Dongjin Dynasty (318), Jinxing Prefecture was set up, and the prefecture governing area including Nanning. Since its creation, the city of Nanning already has over 1700 years of history. In Tang Dynasty, the city was named Nanjinzhou. In the sixth year of Zhenguan (632), the city was renamed Yongzhou. In the third year of Xiantong in Tang Dynasty (862), Lingnan West Road was established, and Yongzhou was the administration of Lingnan West Road. It governed the area to which Guangxi is now. It was the political and military centre of the region at that time. In Yuan Dynasty, Yongzhou Province was established, but in the first year of Taiding (1324) was changed to Nanning Province, and the name of Nanning began at this time. During the Ming and Qing Dynasties, the highest political and administrative centre of Guangxi moved to Guilin, but Nanning's status as the highest military centre in Guangxi has not changed. In the early years of the Republic of China, the old Guangxi warlord Lu Rongting ruled Guangxi and moved the provincial government to Nanning. In 1936, the provincial government moved to Guilin. Liberated in 1949 and set up the city in the same year. In February 1950, it became the provincial capital of Guangxi. In 1958, the Guangxi Zhuang Autonomous Region was established and Nanning became the capital of the autonomous region.

Nanning has not only a long history, but also a unique natural environment. The city is located within the Nanning Basin, and the northeast and northwestern parts of the city are the Daming Mountain hilly area, with a maximum altitude of 1760 meters. The central branch of Daming Mountain stands tall, and its highest peak, Shihen Peak, is 487 meters above sea level. The urban area of Nanning is located on the south

治区首府至今。

南宁是一座历史悠久的边陲古城，拥有得天独厚的自然条件。它地处南宁盆地，东北、西北部系大明山山地丘陵地带，最高海拔达1760米。中部大明山支脉高峰岭耸立，其最高峰石痕峰海拔为487米。市区位于高峰岭南侧。南部、西南部为低山丘陵地带，海拔在150—300米。东南部以低丘及邕江冲积平原为主。高峰岭南北两侧是沉积盆地，以平原台地为主，是农业生产水平较高的地带。南宁属亚热带湿润季风气候，年平均温度21.7℃，年降水量1300毫米左右，全年无霜期约360天。境内水网密布，邕江流经市区，左、右江在市区以西40千米处汇合流入邕江，大小河流均属西江水

系，水资源较为丰富。主要矿产资源有锰、铁、铜、钨、铝、重晶石、石灰石、煤等20多种。森林资源丰富，现有森林面积约30万公顷，木材蓄积量达470万立方米，植物种类多样，仅乔木树种就近150种，其他各类植物多达3000种。

南宁交通四通八达，是一座枢纽之城。南宁的水陆空交通十分便利，是桂南地区商贸中心和农副土特产品的集散地，商业贸易繁华。近年来，各种类型的商业、服务业发展较快，市场容量不断扩大，对外贸易发展迅猛。

总的说来，南宁区位优势突出，是一座开放之城；南宁产业发展迅猛，是一座奋进之城；南宁生态环境优美，是一座宜居之城；南宁投资土壤肥沃，是一座兴业之城。

邕江景色　摄影 李辉
View of Yongjiang River　Photo by Li Hui

side of the peak ridge. The south and southwest are low hills with altitudes between 150 and 300 meters. The southeast are mainly low hills and alluvial plains of the Yongjiang River. The north and south sides of the peak ridge are the lacustrine sedimentary basins, which are mainly plain terraces and are areas with high agricultural production levels. Nanning has a subtropical humid monsoon climate, with an annual average temperature of 21.7 °C, and its annual precipitation is about 1300 mm. Throughout the year, the frost-free period is about 360 days. And in Nanning's territory, the water network is densely distributed. The Yongjiang River flows through the urban area, its left and right branches meet 40 kilometers west of the city. All streams and rivers belong to the Xijiang water system, and the water resources are abundant. The city also has more than 20 kinds of mineral resources including manganese, iron, copper, tungsten, aluminum, barite, limestone and coal. And it is also rich in forest resources. The existing forest area is about 300,000 hectares, and the wood stock is around 4.7 million cubic meters. There are various plant species, not only 150 species of arbor trees but also 3,000 species of other plants.

Nanning is a hub City. Nanning's water, land and air transportation are very convenient. Nanning has always been a distribution centre for commercial and trade centres and agricultural and sideline products in southern Guangxi, and commercial trade is prosperous. In recent years, various types of commercial and service industries have developed quickly, market capacity has been expanding, and foreign trade has developed rapidly.

Generally speaking, Nanning has outstanding geographical advantages and is an open city. Nanning's industry is developing rapidly and is a city of endeavor. Nanning has a beautiful ecological environment and is a livable city. Nanning has fertile investment soil and is a city of prosperity.

With its long history and unique geographical environment, as well as the pluralistic ethnic composition, Nanning is rich in cultural resources and owns a unique and magnificent intangible cultural heritage resource. According to the Convention for the Safeguarding of Intangible Cultural Heritage, issued by UNESCO in 2003, the concept of "intangible cultural heritage" refers to each practices, performance, expressions, knowledge, skills, and related tools, objects, crafts, and cultural venues culturally inherited by community groups, and sometimes individuals. Intangible cultural heritage has been passed down from generation to generation and has been continuously re-created in the interaction of communities and groups with the environment and with nature as well as history, providing a sense of identity and continuity to these communities and groups, thereby enhancing respect for cultural diversities and human creativities. The greatest feature of intangible cultural heritage is that it does not deviate from the special way of life production of the nation, and it is the manifestation of "living" of the national personality and the national aesthetic habits. It exists on the basis of the human being, and uses sound, image and skill as the means of expression, and continues to be passed down as a cultural chain by the oral tradition.

According to the Law of the People's Republic of China on Intangible Cultural Heritage, the intangible cultural heritage shall mean various traditional cultural manifestations which are handed down by the people of all ethnicities from generation to generation and regarded as a constituent part of their cultural heritage, and physical objects and premises related to the traditional cultural manifestations, including:

(1) Traditional oral literature and the language as a carrier thereof;

(2) Traditional fine arts, calligraphy, music, dance, drama, folk art and acrobatics;

(3) Traditional artistry, medicine and calendar;

(4) Traditional rituals, festivals and other folk customs;

(5) Traditional sports and entertainment;

(6) Other intangible cultural heritage.

Accordingly, the book is divided into nine chapters according to the classification of intangible cultural heritage items, namely, folk literature, traditional music, traditional dance, traditional drama, traditional art, traditional sports, entertainment and acrobatics, traditional crafts, traditional medicine and folk customs. It covers 166 items of Nanning in the national, autonomous and municipal level intangible cultural heritage lists by 2021. At the same time, on the basis of investigation and predecessor's data, basic information such as element name, alternative name, geographical location and range, element inscribed list, competent body involved in safeguarding and representative inheritor are set up for each element. The historical origin, main contents and characteristics, development status and problems of inheritance of each intangible cultural heritage are also introduced in detail.

Intangible Cultural Heritage of Nanning has profound resources. Its basic characteristics, mainly in the following six aspects: uniqueness, liveliness, inheritance, rheology, Ethnic Group and regionality.

悠久的历史和独特的地理环境，以及多元的民族构成，让南宁拥有丰富的文化资源，形成了独具特色且蔚为大观的非物质文化遗产资源。根据联合国教科文组织于2003年颁布的《保护非物质文化遗产公约》，“非物质文化遗产”这一概念，是指被各社区、群体、有时为个人视为其文化遗产的各种实践、表演、表现形式、知识和技能及其有关的工具、实物、工艺品和文化场所。非物质文化遗产世代相传，在各社区和群体适应周围环境以及与自然和历史的互动中，被不断地再创造，为这些社区和群体提供认同感和持续感，从而增强对文化多样性和人类创造力的尊重。非物质文化遗产的最大的特点是不脱离民族特殊的生活生产方式，是民族个性、民族审美习惯的“活”的显现。它依托于人本身而存在，以声音、形象和技艺为表现手段，并以口耳相传形成文化链延续下去。

按照《中华人民共和国非物质文化遗产法》的规定，非物质文化遗产是指各族人民世代相传并视为其文化遗产组成部分的各种传统文化表现形式，以及与传统文化表现形式相关的实物和场所，它包括：（一）传统口头文学以及作为其载体的语言；（二）传统美术、书法、音乐、舞蹈、戏剧、曲艺和杂技；（三）传统技艺、医药和历法；（四）传统礼仪、节庆等民俗；（五）传统体育和游艺；（六）其他非物质文化遗产。据此，本书按照非物质文化遗产项目之分类共分为九章，分别为民间文学，传统音乐，传统舞蹈，传统戏剧，传统美术，传统体育、游艺与杂技，传统技艺，传统医药，民俗，涵盖南宁市截至2021年的国家级、自治区级、市级非物质文化遗产名录项目166项，可谓丰富翔实。同时，本书在继承前人研究与资料的基础上，为每个项目设置了项目名称、别称、分布范围、入选名录、保护单位、代表性传承人等基本信息，也详细介绍了每个非物质文化遗产项目的历史源流、主要内容与特色、传承发展现状和面临的问题等。

邕剧《芦花荡》
Yongju Opera *Reed Catkins Marsh*

南宁非物质文化遗产资源深厚，内容丰富。其基本特征主要有以下六个方面：独特性、活态性、传承性、流变性、民族性和地域性。

一、独特性。南宁的非物质文化遗产项目，一般是作为艺术或文化的表达形式而存在的，体现了本地区内各民族人民独特的创造力，这种创造力或表现为物质的成果，或表现为具体的行为方式、礼仪、习俗，这些都是独特而不可复制的。而且，它们间接体现出来的思想、情感、意识也都有其独特性，是其他地区或其他族群难以模仿的。例如：壮族刺绣艺术既是我国少数民族美术中特有的一种艺术样式，也是民间表达情感的手段，其独特性足以令人叹为观止。就刺绣艺术来说，它用途广泛，或用于制衣的绣花图样，或用于日常的装饰，或用于节日的庆贺。而它又是一种象征符号，蕴含着丰富的意义，是壮族人民特有的祈福和祝福的方式，有独特的审美价值。任何民族的文化都含有独特的传统的因

1. Uniqueness. Intangible cultural heritage elements in Nanning usually exist as an expression of art or culture, reflecting the unique creativity of the peoples of the region. This creativity or performance is material achievement, or manifested as specific behavior, manners and customs. These are unique and cannot be duplicated. Moreover, their indirect thoughts, feelings and consciousness also have their own characteristics, which are difficult to imitate in other areas or other ethnic groups. For example, the embroidery art of Zhuang is not only a unique art form in China's Minority Fine Arts, but also a means of expressing emotions among the people. And its uniqueness is acclaimed as the peak of perfection. As far as embroidery art is concerned, it has a wide range of uses, either for embroidery patterns in garment making, or for daily decoration, or for festival celebrations. It is also a symbolic symbol, which contains rich meanings. It is a unique way of praying and blessing for the Zhuang people and has unique aesthetic value. Every nation's culture has unique traditional factors, certain cultural genes and national memory, which is the basis for the existence and development of a nation. If we lose these, we will lose our own characteristics and the driving force of sustainable development. For instance, the March three of the Zhuang ethnic minority was originally the ancestor worship festival of the ancestors of the Zhuang ethnic minority, the ancient Luo Yue people. Later, it became a traditional festival of the Zhuang. On the 3rd day of the third month of the Chinese lunar calendar each year, it holds a grand folk event such as offering sacrifices to ancestors, Mother Dragon, and singing folk songs. It bears rich and unique national memory, which is deeply connected with tradition. Intangible Cultural Heritage is the unique creativity of the people of this region, the national memory is manifested, and it is also the crystallization of collective wisdom of the generations.

2. Liveness. The intangible cultural heritage attaches great importance to the value of human beings, to the living, dynamic and spiritual factors, to the superb, exquisite and original technology and skills, to the creativity of human beings, and to the significance and its national emotion and expression, wisdom, way of thinking, world outlook, values and aesthetics reflected through it and its value factor. Although intangible cultural heritage has material factors and carriers, its value is not mainly reflected through physical form. It belongs to the category of human behavior activities. Some need action to show it, and some need superb and exquisite skills to be presented and inherited. The expression and inheritance of intangible cultural heritage require language and action, which is a dynamic process. Specifically,

traditional music, dance, drama and other types of performing arts are completed in the dynamic performance, folk customs, festivals and other rituals are also dynamic process. Crafts and other production techniques are also reflected in the dynamic process. As a folk culture, the existence of intangible cultural heritage must depend on the actual participation of the inheritance subject, which is embodied as a three-dimensional and complex dynamic activity in a specific space-time. If we leave this activity, its life will not be realized. This animation is also reflected in the changes of intangible cultural heritage, and in the interaction with nature, reality and history, they are constantly emerging, changing and innovating. For example, a variety of temple fairs spread in the city, such as Ban Shan temple fair, Luo Bo temple fair and Fu Bo temple fair, were originally sacrificed to pray for rain or to commemorate the ancestors, and gradually evolved into colorful folk activities. Although it is held regularly every year and passed down in an orderly manner, its form of expression is not fixed. The specific content changes with the times. Every activity is fresh and lively, showing different characteristics from the past. It is constantly being enriched and developed by people, reflecting the characteristics of living conditions.

3. Inheritance. The inheritance of intangible cultural heritage is mainly preserved by generations. Moreover, the way of inheritance is often transmitted by mouth and mind. Once heritage activities are stopped, it means that intangible cultural heritages will gradually disappear. Inheritance often depends on the family or ethnic group. Within a family, the selection and determination of the successor mainly focuses on the intimate relationship with the selected person. Usually these skills are passed from one generation to the next. It is this inheritance that makes the preservation and continuation of intangible cultural heritages possible. For example, the traditional medicine of the Zhuang ethnic minority, which is based on the life experience of the ancestors of the Zhuang, has summed up a set of national medical experience, adapted to local conditions, local materials and formed a unique medical system. It has been passed down from generation to generation through family members, and has been widely recognized by the people of the region for its clinical practical value. In a nation, people form a collective because of their common language, culture, life customs and even beliefs, and the intangible cultural heritage among them has become the witness of national history. If there were no such inheritance activities, there would be no such dynamic expression activities, let alone intangible cultural heritage. For example, the legendary story of One Hundred Birds' Clothes of the Zhuang, which was produced by the social life of the Zhuang

素、某种文化基因和民族记忆，这是一个民族赖以存在和发展的根本。如果失去了这些，也就失去了自己的特性和持续发展的动力。再比如：广西壮族的三月三，原是壮族先民古骆越人的祭祖节，后来演变成为壮乡的传统节日，于每年农历三月初三举行祭祖先、拜龙母、办歌圩等盛大民俗活动。它承载着丰富而独特的民族记忆，民族记忆又与传统深刻地联系在一起。非物质文化遗产是本地区人民独一无二的创造力的具体表现，将民族记忆表现出来，也是世世代代人民集体智慧的结晶。

二、活态性。非物质文化遗产重视人的价值，重视活态的、动态的、精神的因素，重视技术、技能的高超、精湛和独创性，重视人的创造力，以及通过其反映出来的该民族的情感及表达方式、智慧、思维方式、世界观、价值观、审美观等。非物质文化遗产虽然有物质的因素、物质的载体，但其价值并非主要通过物质形态体现出来，它属于人类行为活动的范畴，有的需要借助于行动才能展示出来，有的需要通过某种高超、精湛的技艺才能被呈现和传承下来。非物质文化遗产的表现、传承都需要语言和行动，这是一个动态的过程。具体来说，传统音乐、舞蹈、戏剧等表演艺术都是在动态的表现中完成的，民俗、节庆等仪式的表现也都是动态的过程，手工艺等制作技艺也是在动态的过程中得以表现的。非物质文化作为民间文化，它的存在必须依靠传承主体的实际参与，体现为特定时空下一种立体的、复合的能动活动，如果离开这种活动，其生命便无法实现。这种活态性还体现在非物质文化遗产的变化中，在与自然、现实、历史的互动中，它们不断生发、变异和创新。例如流传于广西壮族自治区南宁市的多种庙会活动，如斑山庙会、罗波庙会、伏波庙会等，原为祭祀求雨或纪念先人，后逐渐演变成为丰富多彩的民俗活动。虽然每年定期举办，传承有序，但其表现形式并非固定不变，具体内容也随着时代发生变化，每一次活动都是新鲜的与活泼的，展现出不同于以往的特色，在传承中不断被人们丰富和发展，体现出活态性的特质。

三、传承性。非物质文化遗产主要依靠世代相传保留下来，而且，传承方式往往是口传心授，一旦传承活动停止，也就意味着非物质文化遗产在逐渐消亡。传承性往往依托家族或者民族。在一个家族内，传承人的选择和确定主要着眼于与被选择者的亲密关系。通常这些技能由上一代流传到下一代，正是这种传承才使非物质文化遗产的保存和延续有了可能。比如，壮族的传统医药，它是在壮族先民生活经验的基础上，总结出一套民族医学经验，因地制宜，就地取材，形成了独特的医药体系，并通过许多单个家族世代传承的形式流传至今，又因其临床的实用价值，受到本地区人民的广泛认可，得以延续下来。在一个民族中，人们因共同的语言文化、生活习俗乃至信仰而组成一个集体，从中产生的非物质文化遗产也就成了民族历史的见证。假使没有了这些传承活动，就不存在这些动态的表现活动，也就更谈不上非物质文化遗产了。例如，壮族民间传说故事百鸟衣，它是由壮族人民在封建时期的社会活动中通过丰富的想象力创造的，记录了壮族人繁衍生息的自然环境、历史变迁、民俗民风，其情节内容又随着历史的变迁不断发展，依靠民间口耳相传的方式得以一代代保存和传承。正因如此，这些宝贵的非物质文化遗产才需要我们去抢救、整理，从而让更多类似的壮族民间传说故事完整地保存下来，使其为全面认识壮族历史发挥独特的作用。

四、流变性。非物质文化遗产或通过一方有意识地学习、另一方悉心传授，或通过人们之间自发地相互学习等方式得以传播到其他区域、民族和国家。这种传播呈现出活态流变的性质，使非物质文化遗产的共有共享成为可能，而且这也是它与物质文化遗产的重要区别之一。通常来说，物质文化遗产的传播通过复制就可以完成，但非物质文化遗产的传播是一种活态流变，是继承与变异、一致与差异的辩证结合。在传播过程中，它常常与当地的历史、文化和民族特色

in the feudal period and the rich imagination of the Zhuang people, has been circulating among the people, recording the natural environment, historical changes, folk customs of the Zhuang ethnic minority's life and reproduction. Its plot content has been continuously developed with the change of the history, and can be preserved and passed from generation to generation by relying on the oral of the folk. Because of this, these precious intangible cultural heritages need us to rescue and sort them out, so that more similar folk tales of the Zhuang can be preserved intact and play a unique role in understanding the history of the Zhuang ethnic minority in an all-round way.

4. Rheology. Intangible cultural heritage can be spread to regions, countries and other nations through conscious learning by one side, careful teaching by the other side, or spontaneous learning between people. This kind of communication shows the nature of dynamic change, which makes it possible to share the intangible cultural heritage, and it is also one of the important differences between it and the tangible cultural heritage. Generally speaking, the transmission of material cultural heritage can be completed by copying, but the transmission of intangible cultural heritage is a kind of dynamic change, a dialectical combination of inheritance and variation, consistency and difference. In the process of its dissemination, it often merges with the local history, culture and national characteristics, so as to present the coexistence of inheritance and development. For example, Guangxi Cantonese Opera, as a product of Lingnan culture and Bagui culture, not only has its unique Southern art characteristics, but also has the similarities with Guangdong Cantonese Opera, which is of great significance to the study of the evolution and development of Cantonese Opera in history. It is this change and development that makes intangible cultural heritage projects show different cultural characteristics in different regions. However, we should also see that although there are changes and developments, intangible cultural heritage projects still show basic consistency. If they are completely different, they will lose their characteristics. For example, as a traditional delicacy, zongzi can be seen everywhere in China. However, the shape of zongzi in Hengzhou City is different from that in other places. Because of the Zhuang Ethnic Group's custom, zongzi is endowed with more beautiful meaning. There is a stress on when to eat and when to send zongzi in daily life, which makes this intangible cultural heritage project of precious folk value.

5.Ethnicity. The Ethnic Group of intangible cultural heritage refers to the uniqueness of a certain ethnic group, deeply imprinted on the brand of the nation, reflecting the unique thinking mode, world outlook, values, aesthetic consciousness, emotional expression and so on. The characteristics of a particular nation are manifested in all aspects from form to content. From the perspective of the form characteristics of the nation, ethnic language, production and lifestyle, customs and habits, etc., are mostly formed naturally, and are greatly influenced by natural ecology. From the perspective of deeper national characteristics, world views, beliefs, ways of thinking, values, cultural and psychological structure of the nation, aesthetic taste, national identity, etc., these factors have long been formed, manifested in all aspects of daily life and behavior, with strong stability and are not easy to change. For example, Nanning is one of the important origins of paddy cultivation. Many intangible cultural heritage items, such as rice noodle making skill, five color glutinous rice making skill, rice god sacrifice, grain supplement and longevity, are related to paddy cultivation closely. All these are the concrete embodiment of the Ethnic Group of intangible cultural heritage.

6. Regionality. As far as a nation is concerned, each nation has its own specific area of life and activity. The natural environment of the region has a great influence on the nation. Generally, intangible cultural heritage is generated in a certain region, which is closely related to the environment. The unique natural ecological environment and social ecological environment, which formed different characteristics and inheritance ways. Without the region, it will lose the soil and conditions on which it depends. There is no protection, inheritance and development. The intangible cultural heritage elements in Nanning are all based on the local natural geographical environment and national cultural tradition. Meanwhile, they are subjected to the regional environment of the region and change their own living conditions with the change of the environment. For example, song fair events are distributed in all regions of Nanning, they are born because of the good natural environment and people's living habits and agglomerate regional characteristics, which is a concentrated reflection of regional characteristics. Nowadays, folk song duet is still an indispensable element in various folk activities of Nanning. It can be seen that regional characteristics reflect the typical feature of intangible cultural heritages.

Nanning's intangible cultural heritage is an integral part of life in all ages. It is a product of era, environment, culture and spirit, and inevitably has a long-standing relationship with the social history of Nanning. Therefore, Nanning's intangible cultural heritage has many functions, allowing people to

相互融合，从而呈现出继承和发展并存的状况。比如广西粤剧，作为岭南文化与八桂文化共同孕育的产物，既有其独特的南派粤剧艺术特色，又有与广东粤剧一脉相承的相似之处，且对研究粤剧在历史上的流变发展有着重要意义。正是这种变化与发展，让非物质文化遗产项目在不同的地域显示出不同的文化特色。不过，我们也应该看到，虽然有变化和发展，非物质文化遗产项目仍然展现出基本的一致性，如果完全不同，也就失去了其特质。比如横县[①]大粽制作技艺，粽子作为传统美食在中国大地上随处可见，但是横州市的大粽在形态上又与其他地方有所不同，且因壮族的习俗被赋予了更多美好的意义。横州市的大粽在日常生活中何时吃、何时送都有讲究，也赋予了这一非物质文化遗产项目宝贵的民俗价值。

五、民族性。非物质文化遗产的民族性是指其为某一民族独有，深深地打上了该民族的烙印，体现了特定民族独特的思维方式、世界观、价值观、审美意识、情感表达等。特定民族的特性表现在从形式到内容的各个方面。从民族的形式特征方面看，民族的语言、生产生活方式、风俗习惯等，这些大都是自然而然形成的，受自然生态的影响较大。从更深层的民族特性来看，世界观、信仰、思维方式、价值观、民族的文化心理结构、审美趣味、民族认同等，这些因素是长期以来形成的，表现在日常生活和行为的方方面面，有很强的稳定性，不太容易改变。比如，南宁是稻作文化的重要起源地之一，许多非遗项目如米粉制作技艺、五色糯米饭制作技艺、稻神祭、添粮补寿等传统技艺或传统习俗，都与稻作文化息息相关。这些都是非物质文化遗产民族性的具体体现。

① 编者注：横县，自2021年起撤县立市，改为横州市。因书中大量项目列入非物质文化遗产名录时录为横县，故项目名称不做修改，其他处均为横州市（横县文化馆亦不做修改）。

“三月三”歌圩活动
March 3rd of Lunar Calendar Song Fair

六、地域性。就一个民族来说，每一个民族大都有自己生活和活动的特定地域，该地域的自然环境对该民族有很大影响。通常，非物质文化遗产都是在一定的地域内产生的，与该环境息息相关，该地域独特的自然生态环境和社会生态环境形成了不一样的特点和传承方式；离开了该地域，非物质文化遗产便失去了其赖以存在的土壤和条件，也就谈不上保护、传承和发展。南宁的非物质文化遗产项目无不是依托本地的自然地理环境与民族文化传统而产生的，同时受制于本地区的地域环境，随着环境变化而发生自身的活态变化。比如南宁各区域均有歌圩活动，因自然环境与人民的生活喜

know, appreciate, entertain, educate and even consume. Therefore, Nanning's intangible cultural heritage has rich value significance. Its value is mainly reflected in six aspects of history, culture, spirit, aesthetics, education and economy.

One is historical value. The intangible cultural heritage of Nanning bears the history and culture of Nanning. It is the wealth that has been passed down from the past. We can learn about history and experience history in a lively way. The intangible cultural heritage formed in history conveys specific historical information to people, and none of them has specific historical value. The historical value of Nanning's intangible cultural heritage is mainly manifested in the fact that no matter what type of intangible cultural heritage, there are always certain historical conditions that it produces, always with the historical characteristics of a particular era. Through the intangible cultural heritages such as Nanning folk songs, ballads and Zhuang faith songs, we can know the production and development level, social organization structure and production and life style, as well as the relationship between people, religious belief, moral pursuit or life taboo in the specific historical period of Nanning. Generally speaking, the intangible cultural heritage of Nanning reflects the history of local people and long-term collective life, which has historical value that cannot be ignored. For example, through Zhuang people's Folk Song Promoting Ethics and Morality and carrying forward songs, people use moral poems with mottoes, proverbs and common sayings to expose the filthily behavior of the ruling class in squeezing the people, discuss the moral norms and obligations of life, and how to deal with the internal relations of the family. Through the construction techniques of the Ganlan building of the Zhuang in Nanning, people can understand the natural geographical environment of Nanning in history, and the history of the ancestors using their wisdom and dexterous hands to create a living home. Intangible cultural heritage, in its folk, oral, simple and living form, can make up for the lack of official history, and help modern people to understand the past history and the cultural tradition of their own nation more truly, more comprehensively and more closely. The intangible cultural heritage reflects the nation's world outlook and living conditions, and reflects the nation's group mentality and behavior mode. Some intangible cultural heritage elements in Nanning are old and some are young. They accumulate the essence of different historical times, retain strong national characteristics, and are the living inheritance of national history. They have profound value significance for us to dynamically understand history and study historical changes today.

The second is cultural value. The intangible cultural heritage of Nanning contains rich cultural resources, which vividly records the ingenuity of the people of each groups in Nanning. These elements are the living fossils for understanding the cultural history of various ethnic groups. They are a huge cultural spiritual wealth and extremely precious. Whether Han or Zhuang, or other ethnic minorities, in their intangible cultural heritage, all contain the essence of the traditional culture of the ethnic group, which reflects the characteristics of the ethnic group and reflects the way of thinking of the nation. The aesthetic method, etc., reflects the unique cultural development traces of the nation and shows distinct cultural values. For example, Nuo dance in Nanning is a kind of dance with national characteristics. It was originally

好而生，凝聚着地域特色，这就是地域性的集中体现，而今山歌对唱仍然是南宁各种民俗活动中不可或缺的项目，可见地域性是非物质文化遗产的一个典型特征。

南宁的非物质文化遗产是其各个时代人们生活的有机组成部分，它是时代、环境、文化精神的产物，必然与南宁的社会历史有着千丝万缕的关系。因此，南宁非物质文化遗产具有多方面的功能，可以供人们认识、欣赏、娱乐、教育甚至消费，因此，南宁非物质文化遗产具有丰富的价值意义。它的价值主要体现在历史、文化、精神、审美、教育和经济六个方面。

其一是历史价值。南宁非物质文化遗产承载着南宁的历史和文化，是过去时代流传下来的财富，我们可以从中了解活态的历史、感受历史。历史中形成的非物质文化遗产，都

壮族“三月三”节庆
March 3rd of Lunar Calendar of Zhuang Ethnic Minority

向人们传递着特定的历史信息，没有一种不具有特定的历史价值。南宁非物质文化遗产的历史价值主要表现在，无论是何种类型的非物质文化遗产，总有其产生的特定历史条件，总带有特定时代的历史特点。通过南宁民歌、民谣、壮族信歌这些非物质文化遗产，我们就可以了解到南宁特定历史时期的生产发展水平、社会组织结构和生产生活方式，乃至人与人之间的关系、宗教信仰、道德追求或生活禁忌等。总的来说，南宁非物质文化遗产反映了本地区民众长期集体生活的历史，具有不容忽视的历史价值。例如，通过壮族传扬歌，人们用格言、谚语及俗语连缀的道德诗篇，来揭露统治阶级压榨百姓的丑恶行为，论述做人的道德规范和应承担的义务，以及如何处理好家庭内部关系。通过南宁壮族干栏建筑营造技艺，人们能够了解到历史上南宁的自然地理环境，以及先民运用聪明才智和灵巧的双手，创造出适于生存的家园的历史。非物质文化遗产以其民间的、口传的、质朴的、活态的存在形式，可以弥补官方正史的不足，有助于现代人更真实、更全面、更接近本质地去认识本民族过去的历史和文化传统。非物质文化遗产反映了民族的世界观及生存状况，折射了民族的群体心态和行为模式。南宁的非物质文化遗产项目有些是古老的，有些是年轻的，它们蓄积了不同历史时代的精华，保留了浓郁的民族特色，是民族历史的活态传承，对我们今天动态地认识历史、研究历史变迁有着极其深刻的价值意义。

其二是文化价值。南宁非物质文化遗产包含着丰富的文化资源，鲜活生动地记录了南宁各民族人民的聪明才智。这些项目是认识各个民族文化史的活化石，是巨大的文化精神财富，极其珍贵。无论是汉族还是壮族，或者其他少数民族，在它们的非物质文化遗产中，都包含着该民族传统文化的精髓，反映着该民族的特色，折射出该民族的思维方式、审美方式等，体现出该民族独具特色的文化发展踪迹，展现出鲜明的文化价值。例如，南宁傩舞就是一种具有民族特色

used for the religious ceremony of exorcising ghosts and eliminating epidemics, praying for blessings and eliminating disasters. The dance action is primitive and simple, bold and straightforward. It is the representative of Nuo culture in Nanning and even in Guangxi. Its representative work Da Choulei completely reflects people's logging, production tools, farming, harvest and other production processes, as well as the ceremony of Nuo dance in Nanning. Dance, mask and other elements contain rich cultural connotations. In fact, the process of social development is the process of cultural accumulation. The culture accumulated from generation to generation has become the source and symbol of the development of all ethnic groups in the region. At the same time, these intangible cultural heritages constantly collide with each other, exchange and merge in the process of communication among different ethnic groups, and burst out new cultural values. Cultural diversity is not only an important aspect of human cultural characteristics, but also an important aspect of the cultural value of intangible cultural heritage. The diversity of human culture itself promotes the emergence and development of intangible cultural heritage, while the uniqueness of intangible cultural heritage element shows its unique cultural tradition and cultural value. Therefore, to safeguard and inherit these intangible cultural heritage elements is to protect and develop cultural diversity, which is to promote the overall development of local culture.

The third is spiritual value. The intangible cultural heritage of Nanning vividly inherits rich history and culture. It is the vitality of the nation, the spiritual home of the people and the emotional support. It is the source of the rejuvenation of national culture and the overall sustainable development of national culture, and has the important role and value of inheriting national spirit. The intangible cultural heritage deeply contains the cultural gene and spiritual characteristics of the nation, which maintain the national blood, in turn, they shape and continue the same life attitude and social behavior of ethnic groups, and form the unique spiritual heritage of the nation. The national spirit accumulated in the long-term productive labor and social practice is the accumulated experience of development and wisdom of survival, the national consciousness with cohesion and appeal formed historically, the ideological essence and cultural concept of the nation passed down from generation to generation, and the group including the national values, psychological structure, temperament and emotion. Consciousness and group spirit are the soul and essence of national culture. Therefore, as a vivid preservation of the living cultural heritage of the national culture with regional characteristics, intangible cultural heritage inherits the essence of national culture and national spirit, and makes the spiritual heritage value of national culture recognized in the world in its multicultural world. Although some intangible cultural heritages no longer have their original status and functions, their significance and value will not pass away with the passage of time as the historical witness of the formation process of the nation and as the living remains of the precious spiritual feelings of the nation. For example, in Bishan Village, Pinglang Township, Hengzhou City, and its surrounding areas, there are a series of unique and traditional folk customs of the local culture – the life etiquette of Bishan, which has been reported for more than 500 years. In Bishan, local people hold special ceremonies during important aspects of life, such as birth, adulthood, and birthday. The life etiquette with rich connotation not

的舞蹈，它最初用于驱鬼驱疫、祈福消灾的宗教仪式，舞蹈动作原始古朴、豪放粗犷，是南宁乃至广西地区傩文化的代表，其代表作大酬雷，完整地反映了人们伐木、制作工具、耕田、丰收等生产过程，南宁傩舞的仪式、舞蹈、面具等要素都蕴含着丰富的文化意蕴。实际上，社会发展的过程原本就是文化积累的过程，世代积累的文化又成为本地区各民族发展的源泉和标志。同时，这些非物质文化遗产又在不同民族的交往过程中不断地相互碰撞，交流融合，迸发出新的文化价值。文化的多样性是人类文化特性的一个重要方面，也是非物质文化遗产文化价值的一个重要方面。人类文化的多

宾阳甘棠镇彩凤表演
Gantang Color Phoenix Performance in Binyang County

样性本身促进了非物质文化遗产的产生和发展，而非物质文化遗产项目的独特性又展现出其独特的文化传统和文化价值。因此，保护、传承这些非物质文化遗产项目，就是保护和发展文化的多样性，就是在促进本地区文化的整体发展。

其三是精神价值。南宁非物质文化遗产鲜活生动地传承着丰富的历史文化，是民族的生命动力，是人民的精神家园和情感依托，也是民族文化复兴、民族文化整体可持续发展的源泉，具有传承民族精神的重要作用和价值。非物质文化遗产中深深蕴藏着维系民族血脉的文化基因、精神特质，反过来，这些又塑造并延续了该民族一脉相承的生活态度和社会行为，形成民族特有的精神传承。这些在长期的生产劳动、社会实践中积淀而成的民族精神，是积累起来的发展的经验、生存的智慧，是历史地形成的具有凝聚力与号召力的民族意识，是世代相传沉积下来的民族的思想精髓、文化理念，是包含了民族的价值观念、心理结构、气质情感等在内的群体意识和群体精神，是民族的灵魂、民族文化的本质和核心。因此，作为一种丰富地保留了富有地域特色的民族文化的活态文化遗存，非物质文化遗产传承了民族文化、民族精神的精华，使民族文化的精神传承价值在多元文化世界中因其独特性得到了世界的认可。尽管某些非物质文化遗产已不再具有当初的地位与功能，但它们作为民族形成过程的历史见证，作为民族珍贵的精神情感的活态遗存，其意义和价值不会随着时间的流逝而逝去。例如，在横州市平朗乡笔山村及其周边地区，流传着一系列独特的、极具地域文化色彩的传统民间习俗——笔山人生礼仪，据传已有500多年历史。在笔山，每逢生育、成年、寿诞等人生重要环节，当地人均会举行特定的仪式。有着丰富内涵的人生礼仪，既体现了生育、家庭、宗教等社会制度对个人地位的规定和角色的认可，也体现着特定的文化规范对个体的人格塑造。它连接了个人与群体的关系，也丰富了当地人的精神文化生活。可

only embodies the regulations and roles of the social system of fertility, family, religion and so on, but also reflects the individual personality shaping of individual cultural norms. It connects the relationship between individuals and groups, and also enriches the spiritual and cultural life of the local people. It can be seen that the national spirit is often rooted in the unique development process of a nation and is the crystallization of the nation's own generation and creation. The national and regional cultural spirit requires people to continue to inherit innovation. It is through the inheritance of national spirit with each nation's own characteristics and cultural characteristics that the situation of all ethnic cultures competing for splendor and all kinds of flowers competing for splendor is formed, and the cultural diversity and diversity pattern are formed. This kind of spiritual value is continuously accumulated, and is constantly recognized by the people of the region in the process of inheritance. Therefore, only by developing and inheriting intangible cultural heritage elements, can its spiritual value be recognized by the new generation, and continue to accumulate this valuable spiritual value on the basis of predecessors.

The fourth is aesthetic value. Most of the handicrafts and performing arts in the intangible cultural heritage of Nanning have a very high aesthetic value and artistic value. They are valuable resources for art research and even guide to a new art creation. The rich and colorful intangible cultural heritage shows the national life style, aesthetic taste and artistic creativity, with high aesthetic value. On the one hand, there are a large number of works of art in the intangible cultural heritage of Nanning, such as Zhuang brocade works, Nanning pottery works, Binyang oil paper umbrella and bamboo works of art. They are the crystallization of the labor and wisdom of people of different times and nationalities in history, and they are artistic products created according to the aesthetic fashion and standards at that time. They can be passed on to today, in addition to a certain use value, it also shows that its ability to create beauty has been recognized by people in different eras in history, and thus has a very high aesthetic value, and is worthy of today's people to understand, appreciate and study. In these intangible cultural heritage elements, there are not only many works of art, but also many talented artistic creations. They have exquisite art skills, unique art forms, which can deeply impress people's hearts and are the crystallization of wisdom of generations of inheritors. From present day's perspective, there are many things in the intangible cultural heritage that really belong to artistic creation and even artistic masterpieces. Artists at that time expressed their attitude, understanding and evaluation of the world through these works of art, and revealed and reflected the living conditions and social relations at that time. Through these works of art in the intangible cultural heritage, we can vividly see the historical events, people's living conditions and ways of life, the lives and customs of different groups, their thoughts and feelings, their artistic creation methods, artistic characteristics and artistic achievements. In any time, as one part of the intangible cultural heritage, the works of art are not only the original creation of individual genius, but also have distinctive characteristics of the times, the nation and the region.

The fifth is the value of education. The educational value of intangible cultural heritage is determined by its nature, because it contains rich historical and cultural knowledge, a large amount of scientific knowledge, and many fine art products with great aesthetic value. It is worthwhile to use this content for school education and social education. In order to make intangible cultural heritage education an important part of education, education has become an important way to protect the inheritance of intangible cultural heritage. In order to fully realize the educational value of intangible cultural heritage, the Law of the People's Republic of China on Intangible Cultural Heritage states: "Schools shall carry out relevant intangible cultural heritage education in accordance with the regulations of the competent department of education under the State Council. " Because the intangible cultural heritage itself covers a large number of various aspects of knowledge and is an important source of knowledge for education. There are a large number of unique skills in intangible cultural heritage that can be taught, which also constitutes an important content and aspect of educational activities. There are many inheritors of intangible cultural heritage. The process of imparting their unique and valuable skills is the process of educational activities, while the process of students accepting knowledge and skills is the one of learning. Learning the knowledge related to intangible cultural heritage can not only understand the rich and colorful history and culture of the nation and the region, receive aesthetic education, scientific education and even physical education, but also acquire practical skills, so as to lay the foundation for the continuous promotion and development of traditional culture.

To make full use of and give full play to the educational value of intangible cultural heritage, it is necessary to carry out extensive education on intangible cultural heritage and its protection in school education and social education. With the development of the times, intangible cultural heritage has gradually entered the public's vision. Then, the public, especially young people and students, should have a

见，民族精神往往植根于一个民族独特的发展历程之中，是民族自身代代相传和创造的结晶。民族和地域文化精神需要人们不断传承创新。正是通过每一个民族富有自身特色、具有文化特性的对民族精神的传承，才形成了全国各族文化竞相开放、百花争艳的局面，才构成了文化的多样性和多元化格局。这种精神价值是不断积累的，在传承过程中不断得到本地区人民认同，因此，只有发展传承好非物质文化遗产项目，才能让其精神价值得到新生代的认同，同时在前人基础上继续累积这种宝贵的精神价值。

其四是审美价值。南宁非物质文化遗产中的手工艺品、表演艺术等，大部分都具有很高的审美价值和艺术价值，是可以进行艺术研究的宝贵资源，甚至能够指导新的艺术创造。丰富多彩的非物质文化遗产，展示了民族的生活风貌、审美情趣和艺术创造力，审美价值很高。一方面，南宁非物质文化遗产中存在大量的艺术作品，比如壮族织锦艺术作品、南宁制陶作品、宾阳油纸伞及竹编艺术品，它们都是历史上不同时代、不同民族的人民劳动和智慧的结晶，是按照当时审美风尚和标准创作的艺术产品。它们能流传到今天，除了具有一定的使用价值，还说明其创造美的能力得到了历史上不同时代人们的认可，因而具有很高的审美价值，也值得今天的人们去认识、欣赏和研究。在这些非物质文化遗产项目中，不仅有许多艺术作品，而且有许多天才的艺术创造，它们具有精美的艺术技巧、独特的艺术形式，能深深打动人心，是一代代传承人智慧的结晶。以今天的眼光来看，非物质文化遗产中有很多东西确实属于艺术创造乃至艺术杰作。当时的艺术家通过这些艺术作品形象地表达了他们对世界的态度和认识、评价，形象地揭示并反映了当时的生活状况、社会关系。通过这些非物质文化遗产中的艺术作品，我们可以形象地看到当时的历史事件、人的生存状态和生活方式、不同人群的生活与风俗，以及他们的思想与感情，他们的艺术创作方式、艺术特点和艺术成就。在任何时代，作为

非物质文化遗产的一部分，艺术作品往往既是富有原创性的个人创造，同时又具有鲜明的时代特点、民族特性和地域特征。

其五是教育价值。非物质文化遗产的教育价值是由其性质决定的，因为其包含丰富的历史文化知识、大量的科学知识，还有许多极富审美价值的艺术精品，这些内容值得用于学校教育与社会教育。并且，我们要使非物质文化遗产教育成为教育的一个重要组成部分，使教育成为非物质文化遗产保护传承的一条重要途径。为充分实现非物质文化遗产的教育价值，《中华人民共和国非物质文化遗产法》规定："学校应当按照国务院教育主管部门的规定，开展相关的非物质文化遗产教育。"因为非物质文化遗产本身涵盖了大量的各方面的知识内容，是

correct understanding of the value, status and importance of intangible cultural heritage. It is very important to carry out the universal education of intangible cultural heritage, because it can make the whole society fully realize the value and importance of intangible cultural heritages, and form a good social atmosphere for the safeguarding and inheritance of intangible cultural heritage in the whole society. In this way, we have qualified talents with special knowledge and technology in the protection, inheritance, research, management and development of intangible cultural heritage.

The sixth is economic value. Intangible cultural heritage also contains rich economic value. As a part of the value system of intangible cultural heritage, under the condition of market economy, economic value has become a very important value of intangible cultural heritage. If we transform the cultural resources in intangible cultural heritage into real economic resources and cultural productivity, we can bring economic benefits. In this way, the intangible cultural heritage will be brought a lasting and more profound foundation of inheritance. Negative protection of intangible cultural heritage is hard to last, only positive protection is lasting protection. The policy of intangible cultural heritage protection is "protection first, rescue first, rational utilization, inheritance and development". Therefore, on the premise of rescue and protection, it is very necessary to develop the economic resources of intangible cultural heritage reasonably and make scientific use of its economic value under the background of market-oriented era. According to the Law of the People's Republic of China on Intangible Cultural Heritage, the State encourages and supports the development of intangible cultural heritage resources with special advantages. On the basis of effective protection, the representative intangible cultural heritage projects should be rationally used to develop cultural products and services with local, national characteristics and market potential. To encourage the productive protection of intangible cultural heritage, we should explore and promote the way of production driven inheritance for qualified intangible cultural heritage resources and projects, and ask local governments to give appropriate support.

In fact, the productive protection of those craft and technology elements in intangible cultural heritage can not only provide employment opportunities and economic benefits, but also bring sustainable development to the element. In recent years, relying on the location advantage of the ASEAN countries, Nanning has carried out a lot of relevant events to promote the intangible cultural heritage elements in the region, such as diet, handicrafts, traditional art, traditional drama and other works at home and abroad, and has received gratifying economic benefits. These benefits complement the inheritance of intangible cultural heritage in the region. Some intangible cultural heritage elements that were on the brink of extinction, stimulated by policy support and economic benefits, are once again rejuvenated, attracting more people to participate in the inheritance, forming a virtuous circle. It can be seen that rational utilization of the economic value of intangible cultural heritage and scientific protection of production are promising.

The intangible cultural heritage contains precious memories of the traditional culture of all ethnic groups. It is the spiritual and cultural home of people's endless life. It has unique value for the survival and development of human beings. Protecting intangible cultural heritage, for inheriting the excellent human cultural traditions of different ethnic groups, groups and regions, for maintaining the diversity of human culture, for giving full play to the imagination

教育的重要知识来源，非物质文化遗产中又有大量的独特技艺技能可传授，这也构成教育活动的重要内容和方面。非物质文化遗产有许多传承人，他们传授自己独有的宝贵技能的过程就是教育的过程，而学生接受知识技能的过程就是学习的过程。学习非物质文化遗产相关知识，既可以了解本民族、本地区丰富多彩的历史文化，受到审美教育、科学教育乃至体育教育，也可以获得实际的技能，为继续弘扬和发展传统文化奠定基础。

要充分利用、发挥非物质文化遗产的教育价值，就要在学校教育、社会教育中广泛开展有关非物质文化遗产及其保护相关内容的教育。随着时代的发展，非物质文化遗产逐渐走进公众的视野，那么，民众尤其是青年人和学生，对非物质文化遗产的价值、地位、重要性就要有正确的认识。开展非物质文化遗产的普及教育非常重要，这是因为它能使全社会充分认识到非物质文化遗产的宝贵和重要，能在全社会形成保护、传承非物质文化遗产的良好社会氛围。这样，我们在保护、传承、研究、管理、开发非物质文化遗产方面，就有了具有专门知识、专门技术的合格人才。

其六是经济价值。非物质文化遗产中也蕴藏着丰厚的经济价值。作为非物质文化遗产价值体系的一部分，在市场经济条件下，经济价值成为非物质文化遗产的一种非常重要的价值。如果我们将非物质文化遗产中有条件的文化资源转化成为现实的经济资源，转化成为文化生产力，就可以带来经济效益。这样，才会为非物质文化遗产带来持久的、有更深厚基础的传承。对非物质文化遗产消极的保护难以长久，只有积极的保护，才是持久的保护。非物质文化遗产保护工作的方针是"保护为主，抢救第一，合理利用，传承发展"。因此，在做好抢救与保护的前提下，对非物质文化遗产中的经济资源加以合理开发，科学利用其经济价值，在市场化的时代背景下就显得非常必要。《中华人民共和国非物质文化遗产法》规定："国家鼓励和支持发挥非物质文化遗产资源的特殊优势，在有效保护的基础上，合理利用非物质文化遗产代表性项目开发具有地方、民族特色和市场潜力的文化产品和文化服务。”鼓励开展非物质文化遗产生产性保护工作，就有条件的非物质文化遗产资源和项目，进行探索、推行借助生产带动传承的方式，并要求地方政府给予适当的支持。

实际上，对那些非物质文化遗产中的工艺性、技艺性项目进行生产性保护，既可使其成为提供就业机会和产生经济效益的生产行业，又会给项目带来可持续的发展。近年来，南宁依托靠近东盟国家的区位优势，开展了不少相关的活动，将本地区的非物质文化遗产项目，如饮食、手工艺品、传统美术、传统戏剧等推广到海内外，收到了可喜的经济效益。这些收益又反哺本地区非物质文化遗产的传承，有些原本濒于灭绝的非物质文化遗产项目，在政策支持和经济效益的刺激下，再次焕发青春，吸引更多人投身到传承事业中去，形成良性循环。可见，合理利用非物质文化遗产的经济价值，科学进行生产性保护，大有可为。

非物质文化遗产蕴含着各民族传统文化的宝贵记忆，是人们生生不息的精神文化家园，它对于人类的生存与发展具有独特的价值。保护非物质文化遗产，对于传承不同民族、群体、地域的优秀人类文化传统，对于维护人类文化的多样性，对于充分发挥各民族人民的想象力和创造力，对于社会的可持续发展以及人们的相互沟通、相互了解、相互团结协作等，都具有十分重要的意义。然而，在高速发展的现代社会里，由于经济全球化的影响，人们的生存环境和生产生活方式发生了翻天覆地的变化，各类非物质文化遗产赖以生存的土壤日渐萎缩，它们的生存遇到了前所未有的危机。每个族群的文化传统促使形成某种人类文化的有机整体，非物质文化遗产即是其中的重要组成部分。因此，发掘、抢救和保护那些处于生存困境中的非物质文化遗产，已成为时代赋予我们的紧迫历史使命，也是我们义不容辞的责任。非物质文

壮族服饰制作
Zhuang Costume Making

and creativity of the people of all ethnic groups, for the sustainable development of society and for people. It is of great significance for the mutual communication, mutual understanding, mutual solidarity and cooperation of people. However, in the high-speed development of modern society, due to the impact of economic globalization, people's living environment and production and life style have changed dramatically, and the soil all kinds of intangible cultural heritage relyed on is shrinking day by day, their survival has encountered an unprecedented crisis. The cultural tradition of each ethnic group encourage to form an organic whole of human culture, and the intangible cultural heritage is an important part of it. Therefore, discovering, salvaging and protecting the intangible cultural heritage in the predicament of survival has become an urgent historical mission entrusted to us by the times and is our unshirkable responsibility. Intangible cultural heritage is precious, and the national spirit contained in it is of great value. The latecomers of each local nation should not only attach importance to the spiritual legacy and explore, but also increase the gold content of these heritage through their own efforts.

Finally, as an overview of intangible cultural heritage in Nanning, the book hopes to enhance readers' understanding of intangible cultural heritage elements of Zhuang, Han and other ethnic groups in Nanning, and deepen readers' understanding of intangible cultural heritage safeguarding and inheritance. At the same time, this book can also be used as Nanning's cultural representative to show the colorful national culture and history of Nanning to the outside world. It has not only strong readability, but also ornamental value and collection value. It is hoped that the publication of this book will make more people pay attention to the inheritance and protection of intangible cultural heritage, and make many ancient skills shine again in the new era.

化遗产是宝贵的，蕴藏其中的民族精神更是具有无上价值，每一个本地区本民族的后来者，不仅要重视并发掘这些精神遗产，更要通过自身的努力来增加这些遗产的含金量。

最后，本书作为南宁非物质文化遗产的概览，期望增进读者对南宁市壮、汉等民族非物质文化遗产项目的了解，加深读者对非物质文化遗产保护传承的认识。同时，本书也可以作为南宁的文化名片，向外界展现南宁异彩纷呈的民族文化与历史，既有很强的可读性，也有观赏价值和收藏价值。期望本书的出版能够让更多人关注非物质文化遗产的传承与保护，让众多古老的技艺在新时代重新焕发光彩。

目　录
Contents

第一章　民间文学
Chapter One　Folk Literature

第二章　传统音乐
Chapter Two　Traditional Music

第三章　传统舞蹈

Chapter Three　Traditional Dance

第四章　传统戏剧

Chapter Four　Traditional Opera/Drama

第八章　传统医药

Chapter Eight　Traditional Medicine

第九章 民俗

Chapter Nine Folk Customs

第一章　民间文学

Chapter One　Folk Literature

壮族百鸟衣故事

The Story of Hundred-bird Dress of Zhuang Ethnic Group

项目名称：壮族百鸟衣故事

别称：无

分布范围：横州市校椅镇及周边地区

入选名录：2014年第四批国家级非物质文化遗产名录

2007年第一批自治区级非物质文化遗产名录

2007年第一批市级非物质文化遗产名录

保护单位：横县文化馆

代表性传承人：韦其本

Element name：The Story of Hundred-bird Dress of Zhuang Ethnic Group

Alternative name：None

Geographical location and range：Xiaoyi Town in Hengzhou City and the surrounding areas

Element inscribed list：In 2014 on the Fourth National List of Intangible Cultural Heritage

In 2007 on the First Autonomous Region List of Intangible Cultural Heritage

In 2007 on the First Municipal List of Intangible Cultural Heritage

Competent body involved in safeguarding：Hengxian Cultural Centre

Representative inheritor：Wei Qiben

百鸟衣故事雕塑
Sculpture of The Story of Hundred-bird Dress

广西丘陵广布，山水秀丽，物产丰饶，长期的山林生活培养了壮族人勇猛机智的性格，催生出壮族独有的民间传说。壮族百鸟衣故事，就是流传于南宁市横州地区的壮族民间故事。故事形象地展现了土司统治时期壮族人民的社会生活，讴歌了珍贵的爱情，表达出壮族百姓不畏强权、勇敢追求幸福生活的精神。

传说，青年张亚原自幼丧父，以上山打柴、打猎，给土司做苦工为生。某日，张亚原挑柴回家途中，偶遇一只大公鸡，便好心将公鸡带回家，并精心饲养。半年后，这只神鸡为报恩，化作一位貌美的姑娘嫁给了他。土司得知此事后，欲霸占其妻为妾，对张亚原夫妇百般刁难，却一直未得逞。情急之下，土司便强取豪夺，将亚原的妻子掳走。妻子临走时嘱咐张亚原去山上射一百只鸟，做成一件百鸟羽衣，一百天后穿上“百鸟衣”到衙门。妻子被抢走后，家中老母被活活气死，张亚原带着悲愤走进深山射鸟，被困在衙门的妻子

Guangxi is covered by mountains and hills, with beautiful scenery and abundant resources. Zhuang people's long history of living in the mountains has nourished their braveness and cleverness, therefore lead to the creation of unique folklore of Zhuang Ethnic Group. The story of Hundred-bird Dress of Zhuang Ethnic Group is a Zhuang folklore being circulated among the Hengzhou area of Nanning city. It vividly portrays Zhuang people's life during the Tusi (Chieftain) rule period, praises precious love, and shows Zhuang people's spirit of not being threatened by the ruling power and actively pursuing for a happy life.

According to legend, a young man named Zhang Yayuan lost his father since he was a kid, he has to cut firewood, hunt or do hard labour for Tusi to support himself. One day, on Zhang's way home after cutting firewood, he meets a rooster, and he brings the rooster home out of kindness, then takes good care of it. Half a year later, to pay the debt of gratitude, the rooster turns into a beautiful girl and marries Zhang. Then Tusi wants to take Zhang's wife as a concubine after he finds out about this story. He creates all kinds of obstacles for Mr. and Mrs. Zhang but never succeeds. Out of temper, Tusi chooses the hard way and takes Mrs. Zhang away. Mrs. Zhang, before going away with Tusi, tells Zhang Yayuan to shoot a hundred birds on the mountain, to make a hundred-bird dress and wear it to the Yamen (mansion where Tusi lives). Zhang Yayun goes into the mountains to shoot with grief, and his wife becomes dispirited in Yamen. Finally, after a hundred days, Zhang shoots 100 birds and wears the hundred-bird dress that he made to Yamen. His wife, suddenly, turns her sad face into a big smile when she sees Zhang, and Tusi wants to own the hundred-bird dress, he promises Zhang that he will trade a fine horse for the dress, and Zhang agrees. When Tusi is changing his robe to the dress, Zhang seizes the chance and kills Tusi with a knife. In the end, Zhang and his wife escapes with a fine horse, then lives happily afar.

The story of Hundred-bird Dress of Zhuang Ethnic Group starts from Song Dynasty, spreads through Tusi rule time till now, and keeps covering more and more region, also receives great compliments from Zhuang people. The story has hundreds of years history of being told. In 1950s and early 1960s, Wei Qilin, a writer wrote a long narrative poem

愁容满面，日渐憔悴。张亚原不畏艰险，翻山越岭，终于到了第一百天，他射落了一百只鸟并且将制成的“百鸟衣”穿在身上，来到衙门。妻子见到亚原身着“百鸟衣”，满脸愁容转为笑容，土司见状便想将“百鸟衣”据为己有，并答应亚原以骏马交换。当土司脱下官袍与亚原换穿“百鸟衣”的时候，亚原趁机用利刃将土司刺死。最终，张亚原和妻子骑着骏马逃出衙门，去远方过上了美好的生活。

壮族百鸟衣故事始于宋朝，自土司统治时期流传至今，从横州市校椅镇流传至周边乡村，流布范围不断扩大，深受壮族百姓喜爱。百鸟衣故事有着千百年漫长的流传历史，20世纪50年代至60年代初，作家韦其麟撰有叙事长诗《百鸟衣》，使百鸟衣故事走出相对封闭的壮族村寨，以百鸟衣故

大型舞剧《百鸟衣》
Dance Drama *The Story of Hundred-bird Dress*

事为题材创作的戏剧、歌舞以及电影相继问世，百鸟衣故事的流传进入兴盛时期。

壮族百鸟衣故事依托壮族封建时期社会生活及壮族人丰富的想象力产生，记录了壮族人生息繁衍的自然环境、历史变迁、民俗民风、伦理道德，其情节内容随着历史的变迁不断发展，既有历史感又有时代性。它一方面歌颂了青年男女坚贞不渝的爱情，另一方面批判了土司统治对老百姓的压迫，真实地反映出阶级社会中壮族底层百姓的悲苦生活，以及壮族人反抗压迫、追求美好生活的强烈愿望。故事融合了现实主义与浪漫主义两种创作方法，以丰富的想象力将神话与现实生活结合，情节引人入胜、魅力无穷，对研究壮族历史有一定的参考价值。同时，壮族人勤劳淳朴、不畏强权的民族品质也凝聚其中。故事历经世代传承及流变，衍生出多个版本，直至今日，依旧以追求真善美的精神内核，鼓励着壮族人乐观生活，积极奋进。

为积极推动百鸟衣故事的传承，横州市党委、政府在横州市校椅镇建立壮族百鸟衣民间故事传承基地，中、小学开设以百鸟衣故事为内容的民间文学故事会课程以及演讲比赛活动。2014年，经国务院批准，壮族百鸟衣故事列入第四批国家级非物质文化遗产名录。

Hundred-Bird Dress, which let the hundred-bird dress story known to the outside world. After that, movies, plays, songs, and dances based on the story were made one after another, and the story became more well-known than ever.

The Story of Hundred-bird Dress of Zhuang Ethnic Group is created with Zhuang people's rich imagination based on their life during the feudal times. It recorded the living environment, history, tradition, moral values of Zhuang people. The plot of the story changes through time, therefore the story not only is historic but also modern. It not only praises loyal love but also criticizes Tusi ruling power's oppression to civilians, and realistically reflected ordinary people's rough life within a class society, moreover, Zhuang people's strong wishes for resisting the power and pursuing a better life. The story emerged two styles of writing including realism and romanticism and combined the legend with real-life using rich imagination. The plot of the story, therefore, is very engaging, and on some level, helpful for the research of Zhuang history. In the meantime, Zhuang people's hard-working spirit and character of defying against the power also got integrated into the story. After a long time of passing and changing, multiple versions of the story have been created. Now, however, the story's core remains to be the spirit of pursuing truth, love, and kindness, which encourages Zhuang people to stay happy and work hard.

In order to actively promote inheriting the Hundred-bird Dress story, Hengzhou City Party Committee and Government has established Zhuang Ethnic Group Hundred-bird Dress Story Inheritance Base at Xiaoyi Town, Hengzhou City. Middle schools and Primary schools established folklore classes and speech competitions based on the Hundred-bird Dress story. In 2014, with approval from the State Council, the Hundred-bird Dress story has been inscribed on the Fourth National List of Intangible Cultural Heritage.

南宁五象传说

The Legend of the Five Elephants in Nanning

项目名称：南宁五象传说

别称：无

分布范围：南宁市市辖区

入选名录：2014年第五批自治区级非物质文化遗产名录
2013年第五批市级非物质文化遗产名录

保护单位：南宁市民族文化艺术研究院（南宁市非物质文化遗产保护中心）

代表性传承人：莫炜

Element name: The Legend of the Five Elephants in Nanning

Alternative name: None

Geographical location and range: Nanning Municipal Districts

Element inscribed list: In 2014 on the Fifth Autonomous Region List of Intangible Cultural Heritage
In 2013 on the Fifth Municipal List of Intangible Cultural Heritage

Competent body involved in safeguarding: Nanning Ethnic Culture and Art Research Institute (Nanning Intangible Cultural Heritage Protection Centre)

Representative inheritor: Mo Wei

五象传说是南宁流传已久的民间神话传说故事，它至迟起源于明代，以南宁市良庆区为发源地，流布于南宁市全境。南宁五象传说是人们以古代南宁人驯象、以象耕田及治理水患等历史为基础，结合丰富的想象力创造而成。

传说很久以前，天上有五头神象经过邕州（南宁的古称），发现此处土地富饶、山水秀丽，百姓淳朴善良、勤恳热情，便下凡帮助百姓翻耕土地，收粮割稻。久而久之，神象与邕州百姓建立起真挚的感情。后来邕江洪水泛滥，土地被淹，民不聊生。为了抵挡水患，五头神象便化作五座高山，堵住洪水，拯救了南宁百姓。从此，这五座山被视为南宁的守护神。

古代邕州植被茂盛，水源充足，气候温和，野芭蕉、瓜果类植物生长繁茂，适宜大象栖居。自古以来，大象与南宁民众的生产生活联系密切，五象传说虽情节传奇，但内容与情感却都来自南宁特殊的历史文化背景，反映了南宁五象岭农耕文化的浓郁地方色彩。明朝曾在南宁府设立驯象卫，据《南宁府志》记载："邕江南岸那五座相连不断的土坡，山势雄峻，拱向成廊，为邕之砥障，五峰相倚，如五象饮

The legend of Five Elephants is a folklore being known for a long time. It originated in the Ming Dynasty at the latest, from Liangqing District, Nanning City, and circulated through entire Nanning. The story is based on Nanning people's tradition of training elephants to help farm and control flood in the ancient times, then combined with people's rich imagination.

Long time ago, according to the legend, five holy elephants pass through Yongzhou (Nanning's former name) in the sky, and discover that this place has abundant resources, beautiful mountains. Also the people are kind and hard-working, then decide to descend to the world to help the people to farm and harvest. As time passes, the holy elephants and people of Yongzhou establish close relations. After, Yongzhou experiences flood, farm land gets submerged and people's life suffers. In order to stop the flood, the five holy elephants turn into five huge mountains to block the flood in order to save the people. Since then, these five mountains have been treated as Nanning's guardian saints.

Ancient Yongzhou was covered by flourishing plants, and had abundant water. The climate was mild. The region also grew a lot of wild bananas, melon and fruit plants luxuriantly, where it was suitable for elephants to inhabit. Since ancient times, elephants have been close to Nanning people's daily life. Although the legend of Five Elephants is a bit extreme, its content and emotions came from Nanning's unique cultural background and history. Also, the legend reflected the special farming culture at Five-elephant Mountain ridges, Nanning.

南宁五象广场
Five Elephants Square in Nanning

In the Ming Dynasty, elephant-taming district was established in Nanning Prefecture. According to *Annals of Nanning Prefecture*, it was recorded that "The five contiguous slopes on the south bank of the Yongjiang River, with steep mountains forming like arched galleries, are barriers to Yongzhou and five peaks are interdependent, such as the five elephants drinking water in the river." The five peaks have different postures, some are squatting, some are crawling, and some are running forward, all surrounded by smoke fog and clouds. Five-elephant mountain ridge has always been famous for its tourist attraction, which also carries some holy flavor because of the legend. Yongzhou people see these five peaks as their guarding gods, with their unique shapes and rich imagination, they created the legend. Nanning got its nickname "Five-elephant City" because of the legend. Literatures including *Annals of Nanning Prefecture, Lingwai Dai Da* all have related records of the legend of five holy elephants. Nanning people are diligent and kind. The five elephants are close to Nanning people, reflecting Nanning people's wish to have a nice home, pursue kindness, and unite together.

Before 1949, the legend of Five Elephants was mainly spread through oral literature. In the process of oral transmission, the content of the legend of Five Elephants has been enriched and many versions have been formed. After the recession of 1966-1976, the legend started to circulate again. However, under the big environment of transitioning from traditional agricultural society to modern industrial and commercial society, the legend gradually lost its basis to survive, the people who can tell the story became fewer and fewer, and related research was weak as well. As for now, Nanning city integrates five-elephant elements with urban construction, uniting myths with modern construction designs. Some of the sites, such as five-elephant sculpture fountain, five-elephant design street lights, five-elephant forest park, have been built. The legend of Five Elephants features Nanning's regional culture, shows Nanning's treasure of intangible cultural heritage. In 2014, with the approval of Guangxi Zhuang Autonomous Region Government, The Legend of the Five Elephants in Nanning was inscribed on the Fifth Autonomous Region List of Intangible Cultural Heritage.

江。”五座山岭形态各异，犹如五象有蹲、有匐，有欲往前奔之态，山色朦胧，云气缭绕。自古以来，五座山岭以风景秀丽驰名，传说故事也为其平添了不少神话色彩。邕州百姓以此五座山岭为保护神，结合其形貌特征，发挥想象力，创造出五象传说，南宁的别称“五象城”也因五象岭而来。《南宁府志》《岭外代答》等多部文献中均有五象传说的相关记述。南宁人勤劳朴实，五象对南宁人亲善友好，折射了南宁人建设美好家园、追求善与美的心愿，凝聚了南宁人真挚的情感。

1949年以前，南宁五象传说主要以民间口头文学的形式流传，在口耳相传的过程中，五象传说内容不断丰富，形成了多个版本。在经历了1966—1976年的凋敝期后，五象传说开始重新流传。但是，在传统农业社会向现代工商业社会转型的大背景下，南宁五象传说逐渐失去了生存的土壤，能生动讲述五象故事的人越来越少，相关研究也异常薄弱。目前，南宁市将五象元素有机地融入南宁城市建设，将历史神话故事与现代建筑设计相结合，相关建筑或设计有五象雕塑泉、五象造型路灯、五象森林公园等。五象传说凸显出南宁的地方文化特色，是展示南宁独特魅力的非物质文化遗产宝藏。2014年，经广西壮族自治区人民政府同意，南宁五象传说列入第五批自治区级非物质文化遗产名录。

《南宁府志》中关于五象的记载
Documents of Five Elephants in *Annals of Nanning Prefecture*

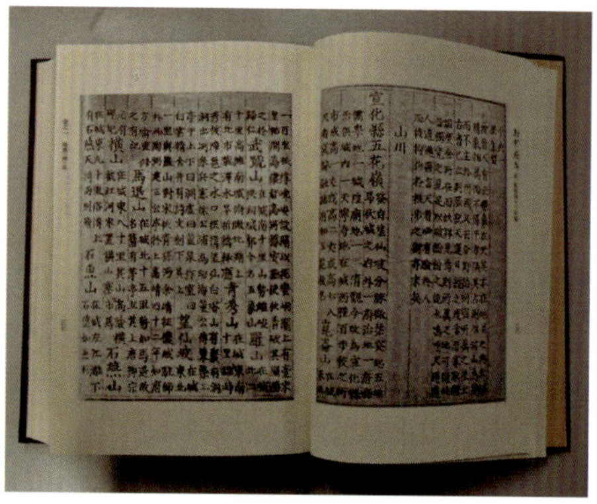

妈勒访天边传说

The Legend of Ma Le's Visit beyond the Horizon

项目名称：妈勒访天边传说

别称：无

分布范围：南宁市、百色市、崇左市、河池市等

入选名录：2014年第五批自治区级非物质文化遗产名录

2013年第五批市级非物质文化遗产名录

保护单位：南宁市民族文化艺术研究院（南宁市非物质文化遗产保护中心）

代表性传承人：罗世周

Element name：The Legend of Ma Le's Visit beyond the Horizon

Alternative name：None

Geographical location and range：Nanning City, Baise City, Chongzuo City, Hechi City and others

Element inscribed list：In 2014 on the Fifth Autonomous Region List of Intangible Cultural Heritage

In 2013 on the Fifth Municipal List of Intangible Cultural Heritage

Competent body involved in safeguarding：Nanning Ethnic Culture and Art Research Institute (Nanning Intangible Cultural Heritage Protection Centre)

Representative inheritor：Luo Shizhou

The legend of Ma Le's visit beyond the horizon, an oral literature, is a Zhuang folklore. The story circulates within the Zhuang area in Guangxi. After three thousand years of changing and elevating, the content of the story has been more enriched than ever. Once upon a time, the Zhuang people lived within caves that were cold and dark, they yearned for light and warmth. Adults, kids, and elders all wanted to find the sun at the edge of sky. A young pregnant lady volunteered to represent her people to find the sun, she said: "I might not reach the beautiful place, but the baby I bear will keep going for me until the sun is reached." On her way to find the sun, the lady gave birth to "Le" (Zhuang word for "son") and told him to keep going to find the sun, no matter what happened. Le kept his mom's word and eventually reached where the sun rises.

By judging from interviewing the inheritor and investigating content details, the legend started from primal times and then thrived from the late Song Dynasty till the Republic of China. After 1949, the story went into a reborn and prosperous era, then experienced a dim from 1966 to 1978. After that, the legend slowly recovered. In 1984, Zhuang writer Wei Qilin published a long narrative poem *Mother Who Finds the Sun*. The legend of Ma Le's visit beyond the horizon has been collected in books including *Zhuang Folklore Collection*, *Chinese Minor Ethnic Group Folklore Collection*,

妈勒访天边传说是壮族民间传说故事，属于壮族口头文学。它流传于广西壮族聚居地，历经数代流变，内容不断丰富充实，形成至今已有近3000年的历史。故事讲述很久以前，壮族先民生活在阴暗寒冷的山谷中，他们渴望光明和温暖，青年人、老人、孩子都希望去寻找天边的太阳。一位年轻的孕妇也主动请求代表族群去寻找太阳，她说："也许我走不到那美丽的地方，可我有腹中的娃仔，他会继续阿妈的路，一直走向太阳。"孕妇在寻找太阳的途中生下"勒"（壮语意为"儿子"），并教育他继续越过艰难险阻，完成寻访太阳的使命。勒谨记母亲的嘱托，一直坚持走向太阳升起的地方。

从采访传承人、调查传说的情节内容来判断，妈勒访天边传说起源于原始社会，兴盛于宋代末期到民国时期，1949年后进入新生和繁荣时期，继而经历1966—1978年的低迷期。此后，传说逐渐复苏，1984年，壮族作家韦其麟出版了叙事长诗《寻找太阳的母亲》。妈勒访天边传说相继被《壮族民间故事选》《中国少数民族神话选》《中国少数民族民间文学丛书选·故事大系·壮族卷》《中国少数民族文学作

舞剧《妈勒访天边》第一幕：孕妇怀着孩子在大地的怀抱中，森林花草为她开道相送

Act One of Dance Drama of *Ma Le's Visit beyond the Horizon*: A pregnant woman in the arms of the earth, forest flowers and plants to see her off

舞剧《妈勒访天边》第一幕：妈妈怀着儿子勒时载着族人的希望去寻找太阳

Act One of Dance Drama of *Ma Le's Visit beyond the Horizon*: The mother is carrying the hope of her son Le to find the sun

品选》等书籍收录。1999年，壮族第一部史诗性舞剧《妈勒访天边》诞生，进一步推动了传说的传承。

妈勒访天边传说发源于邕江、左江、右江和红水河流域，流传于广西南宁、百色、崇左、河池等壮族聚居地，流传地域广。这些地区石灰岩分布广泛，多为喀斯特地貌，具有石林、岩洞、伏流等奇特景观，山岭连绵，河流交错。壮族人民依山傍水而居，所处环境气候温和，雨量充沛，土壤肥沃，有利于农业、林业、牧业的发展。特殊的自然环境与特定的生产方式，使得壮族民间文学饱含着壮族人勤劳淳朴、勇于探索的精神特质。

妈勒访天边传说诞生于远古时期，与壮族的历史文化和社会生活有着密切的关系。传说故事融入壮族特有的民族心理，并随着时代的发展流传广泛，内容逐渐充实，表现出壮族人勤劳勇敢、勇于探索、团结友爱、甘于奉献以及坚忍不拔的民族精神，承载着壮族生存繁衍、历史发展以及社会制度、伦理道德等重要信息。同时，传说具有瑰丽多姿的神话色彩，故事生动，构思奇巧，想象力丰富，具有无穷的艺术魅力，凝聚了壮族文化的精华，是非常珍贵的文化宝藏。

历史上，妈勒访天边传说主要以口头文学的形式在民间流传。1949年后，叙事长诗《寻找太阳的母亲》以及壮族舞剧《妈勒访天边》的诞生，使妈勒访天边传说的社会影响力不断提高，其传承价值越来越被重视。2013年，南宁市民族文化艺术研究院将其申报为市级非物质文化遗产。2014年，经广西壮族自治区人民政府同意，妈勒访天边传说列入第五批自治区级非物质文化遗产名录。

Chinese Minor Ethnic Group Folklore Series · Story Series · Zhuang Volume, *Chinese Minor Ethnic Group Literature Collection*. The first Zhuang epic dance drama, *Ma Le's Visit beyond the Horizon*, was created in 1999. The creation of the drama further promoted the heritage of the legend.

The legend of Ma Le's visit beyond the horizon started from Yongjiang River, Zuojiang River, Youjiang River, and Hongshui River Basin, circulated through Zhuang cities like Nanning, Baise, Chongzuo, and Hechi. Limestones are widespread within these areas, the region carries karst landform, which has beautiful sights including stone forests, caves, and waterfalls. Also, the region is covered by mountains and rivers. Zhuang people live by mountains and rivers, so the weather is warm and comfortable, rain is abundant, and the soil is rich. This kind of environment is good for farming, forestry, and stock raising. The unique environment and way of living have made Zhuang literature containing Zhuang people's hard-working and exploring spirit.

The legend of Ma Le's visit beyond the horizon was created in ancient times and has close relations to Zhuang history and society. The story incorporated Zhuang people's special mentality and got circulated through time. The content of the story got more and more detailed through time, showing Zhuang people's braveness, will to give, exploration spirit and kindness. Therefore, the content bears important information on social structures, moral standards, and historical developments. In the meantime, the legend is very vivid, vibrant, and well organized. It has a rich imagination and endless charm of aesthetics. Also, it combines the essences of Zhuang culture and becomes a priceless treasure of culture.

In the past, the legend was mainly spread through oral literature. After 1949, the long narrative poem *Mother Who Finds the Sun* and Zhuang Dance Drama *Ma Le's Visit beyond the Horizon* was created. Then, the legend's social impact began to increase, and its inheritance value got appreciated more. Nanning Ethnic Culture and Art Institute declared the story as city-level intangible cultural heritage in 2013. Later in 2014, with the approval from Guangxi Zhuang Autonomous Region Government, *Ma Le's Visit beyond the Horizon* got inscribed on the Fifth Autonomous Region List of Intangible Cultural Heritage.

起凤山传说

The Legend of Qifeng Mountain

项目名称：起凤山传说

别称：无

分布范围：武鸣区

入选名录：2015年第六批市级非物质文化遗产名录

保护单位：武鸣区文化馆

代表性传承人：曾麒璋

Element name：The Legend of Qifeng Mountain

Alternative name：None

Geographical location and range：Wuming District

Element inscribed list：In 2015 on the Sixth Municipal List of Intangible Cultural Heritage

Competent body involved in safeguarding：Wuming District Cultural Centre

Representative inheritor：Zeng Qizhang

起凤山传说是广泛流传于壮族聚居地的传说故事，共由十多个传说故事组成，包括镇江岩传说、广德公主传说、读书岩故事、通天洞故事、太极洞“凤”字由来、起凤山庙历史等，这些故事均来源于香山河畔的起凤山。其中，镇江岩传说讲述了远古时期玉皇大帝使用“镇江法”震慑恶魔的故事；广德公主传说是明永历帝次女广德公主于顺治初年下嫁到起凤山的史话；读书岩故事讲述明末进士黄锡衮隐居于起凤山读书，并在此题字的故事；通天洞故事讲述五代时期，大明山剑师干将抽剑朝天捅出通天洞的故事。

起凤山位于武鸣区夏黄村的香山河畔，因其形似展翅欲飞的凤凰，故又名凤凰山。武鸣区位于广西壮族自治区中南部，地形以盆地、河谷为主，是壮族的发源地之一，被誉为

The legend of Qifeng Mountain is a folklore widely spread in the Zhuang people's settlements. It consists of over ten stories, including Zhenjiang Rock legend, Princess Guangde legend, Dushu Rock story, Tongtian Cave story, origin of Feng character of Taiji Cave, and the history of Qifeng Mountain Temple. All these stories came from the Qifeng Mountain on the side of Xiangshan River. Within these stories, the Zhenjiang Rock legend tells the story of Yuhuang emperor taming demons in the ancient times. Princess Guangde legend is a historical story of Yongli Emperor's second daughter, Princess Guangde's marriage at Qifeng Mountain in the Qing Dynasty. The Dushu Rock story tells a story of Huang Xigun, a scholar of the late Ming Dynasty, who lived in seclusion in Lifeng Mountain to study and inscribed here. And Tongtian Cave story is about one of Daming Mountain Sword Troop's soldiers' story of using his sword to create the Tongtian Cave during the Five Dynasties.

Qifeng Mountain is located at the side of Xiangshan River at Xiahuang Village, Wuming District. Due to the

起凤山全景
Overall View of Qifeng Mountain

mountain's unique shape of a flying phoenix, the mountain is also named as Phoenix Mountain. Wuming District is located within the south-central area of the Guangxi Zhuang Autonomous Region. The land is mainly consisted by basins and rivers, and it is one that the main origin places of Zhuang people, so Wuming District is honored as the Zhuang homeplace of China. Although the body of the mountain is small, but it contains a lot of Taoist and Buddhism temples. These places are filled by joss sticks and candles, serving Guanyin, Wenchang, and Guandi. According to *Records and Maps of Wuyuan County*, Qifeng Mountain is one of the old eight sights of Wuming. Educated people in the past would come here to write poems or engrave. Engraving are everywhere on cave walls and cliffs. Among these engravings, cliff engraving CHAOYANG MINGFENG is made by the late Ming Dynasty Jinshi Huang Xigun. Wang Yuanren, County Magistrate of Yangshuo in Qing Dynasty engraved a big letter FENG, 4 meters high and 3 meters wide, which is among the three biggest single letter he has ever engraved. The letter corresponds with the big letter DAI on the Bi Lian Hill of Yangshuo. One on the north, and one on the south, the two characters created a magnificent view. Moreover, Qifeng Mountain Temple was built in 1844, consisted by Guanyin Temple and Wenchang Pavilion. The temple is very aesthetic since it was built by grey bricks and decorated by all kinds of engraving and drawing. All these works are strong evidence of the Qifeng Mountain legend.

Although the story of Qifeng Mountain is a legend, most of the names, locations, and plots are closely tied to Qifeng Mountain engravings, carrying rich local elements. These stories not only record Qifeng Mountain's long history and culture, but also carry people's moral standards, including praising Princess Guangde's kindness, which is appreciated by Zhuang people. The legends came from vast working people, they not only have some historical basis, but also have the presence of Chinese traditional culture, and bear Zhuang people's moral standards and ethnic spirits. The stories have been inherited generation after generation and possess high value in research. As a big part of the cultural resources of Zhuang ethic group, the legend of Qifeng Mountain adds cultural flavors to the natural sights, and lifts the cultural standard of the tourist attractions.

As time goes on, the legend of Qifeng Mountain has gradually faded from people's memories, some youth might not even know about the legend. Therefore, it now faces a situation of not having people to inherit it. Plus, the legend has not been documented, but has been passed on through

起凤山大『凤』字
Big Character "Feng" of Qifeng Mountain

“中国壮乡”。起凤山山体虽小，却汇集了古道观和寺庙，供奉有观音、文昌、关帝等，香火缭绕。据《武缘县图经》记载，起凤山是武鸣旧八景之一，历代文人墨客游山赋诗、题词刻字，山体四处洞壁、崖壁石刻颇为丰富。其中“朝阳鸣凤”大字是明末进士黄锡衮隐居崖刻。清朝阳朔知县王元仁的巨刻“凤”字，高4米，宽3米，是其在广西所书三个独体大字之一，与阳朔碧莲峰上巨刻“带”字南北呼应，奇丽壮观。另有建于1844年的起凤山庙，由观音阁和文昌阁组成，青砖砌筑，雕梁画栋，甚为美观。这些都是起凤山传说的有力见证。

起凤山故事虽为传说，但大多数都有明确的人名、地名，故事情节也与起凤山石刻内容紧密相关，带有浓郁的地域色彩。这些故事不仅记载着起凤山悠久的历史文化，还寄寓着民众的道德观念，其中广德公主传说即以表现壮族人仁爱的美好品德闻名遐迩。传说来自广大劳动群众，不仅具有一定的历史依据，展现了中国传统文化的深厚底蕴，还承载着壮族百姓的道德品质与民族精神，世代相传，经久不衰，具有较高的研究价值。作为壮族文化资源的重要组成部分，起凤山传说为自然景观增添了人文色彩，提升了旅游景区的文化品位。

随着时间的推移，起凤山传说逐渐淡出人们的记忆，许多青年人对其了解甚少，传播面临后继乏人的困境。又由于传说没有被整理为文字记录下来，一直以口耳相传的方式传播，因此很多故事会因老一辈的去世而失传。针对这一问题，武鸣区政府采取了一系列保护措施，如普查传承人、组织专家学者对起凤山传说的相关资料进行抢救性发掘整理、举办相关文化活动以及加强对起凤山文化旅游的扶持等。2015年，经南宁市人民政府同意，起凤山传说列入第六批市级非物质文化遗产名录。

people's mouths and ears. The legend might be lost after the pass of the last generation. To deal with this situation, Wuming district government implemented a series of protection actions, including interviewing inheritors, organizing experts to salvage related materials, holding related cultural events to increase the effort of improving Qifeng Mountain area's culture and tourism. In 2015, with approval from Nanning people's government, the legend of Qifeng Mountain has been inscribed on the Sixth Municipal List of Intangible Cultural Heritage.

南宁民谣

Nanning Folk Ballads

项目名称：南宁民谣

别称：无

分布范围：南宁市

入选名录：2014年第五批自治区级非物质文化遗产名录
2013年第五批市级非物质文化遗产名录

保护单位：兴宁区文化馆

代表性传承人：谢桂友

Element name：Nanning Folk Ballads

Alternative name：None

Geographical location and range：Nanning City

Element inscribed list：In 2014 on the Fifth Autonomous Region List of Intangible Cultural Heritage
In 2013 on the Fifth Municipal List of Intangible Cultural Heritage

Competent body involved in safeguarding：Xingning District Cultural Centre

Representative inheritor：Xie Guiyou

南宁民谣是流传于南宁民间，由南宁人创作、吟诵的一系列民间口头文学，主要包括生活民谣、时政民谣、游戏民谣、爱情民谣和童谣等。其中，生活民谣主要表现各种日常生活情景和人们的生活感悟；时政民谣多针砭社会现象，或对历史故事和民间传奇加以褒贬；游戏民谣表现生活中的逸闻趣事以及百姓的喜怒哀乐；爱情民谣以男女青年传送心语为主要内容；童谣为儿童在生活中所哼唱，又分为游戏谣、教诲谣、绕口令等，富于想象力和童趣。南宁民谣内容丰富，包罗万象，反映出南宁社会历史风貌，且语言通俗，唱起来朗朗上口。

南宁民谣在南宁百姓社会生活的基础上提炼而成，题材多样，表现内容与社会生活、时代发展息息相关，是南宁社会历史发展的真实反映。南宁民谣主要运用南宁本土白话、平话以及壮话方言吟唱，句式长短不一，多为三言、四言、五言句式，讲究押韵，内容通俗风趣。作为民间口述传统文化的重要组成部分，南宁民谣多源于偶发事件或闲聊，具有随意性和娱乐性。由于南宁民谣大部分在民间流传，少有文字记载，因此它的起源时间难以稽考，早期作品也难以被全

Nanning folk ballads are a series of folk oral literatures written and sung by Nanning people. They mainly include daily life folk ballads, political folk ballads, game folk ballads, love folk ballads and nursery rhymes. Among them, the daily life folk ballads mainly represent various daily life situations and people's perceptions of life. The political folk ballads often criticize social phenomenon or praise or disparage historical events and folk legends; the game folk ballads express the anecdotes in life, also joys and sorrows of the people; the love folk ballads mainly express love between young men and women. Nursery rhymes are sung for children in their activities. They are also divided into games, teachings, tongue twisters, etc., which are full of imagination and childishness. Nanning folk ballads are rich in content and reflect all aspects of Nanning's social history and language.

Nanning folk ballads are refined on the basis of the social life of the people in Nanning. The subject matter is diverse, and the content is closely related to social life and development of the city. It is a true reflection of the social and historical development of Nanning. Nanning folk ballads mainly use Nanning native vernacular, Pinghua and Zhuang dialect to sing, the length of sentences are different, mostly three-word, four-word, five-word sentence style, all pay attention to rhyme, the content is popular and interesting. As an important part of the folk oral culture, Nanning folk ballads are mostly from trivial matters or chats, which are casual and entertaining. Since most of the folk ballads in Nanning are circulated among the people, there are only few written records, so its time of origin is difficult to check, and early works are difficult

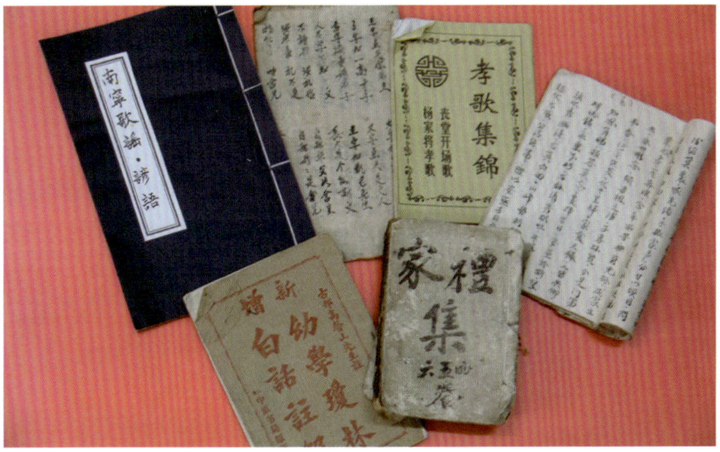

南宁民谣分类别歌本
Classification of Songbook of Nanning Folk Ballads

《南宁市歌谣》歌本
Songbook of *Nanning Folk Ballads*

to collect. In recent years, the cultural department of Nanning has collected Nanning folk ballads and compiled *the Nanning Folk Songs*, *Nanning Sanjiangkou · Folk Idioms*, *Nanning Classic Vintage Folk Songs* and so on. Although the Nanning folk ballads are mainly from the streets, it is like a mirror, reflecting all aspects of life in Nanning. It is a summary of life wisdom of the people of Nanning. It has an interesting philosophy being simple and vivid, which also encourages and educates people in the subtleties. The folk ballads are the treasure of Nanning folk literature.

Since the Nanning folk ballads have been circulated orally among the people, there are few written records. Some people cannot help but thinking that the folk ballads are difficult to be elegant, and some folk ballads are even banned from singing because of the content. In recent years, the excavation and protection of Nanning folk ballads have gradually gained the attention of relevant departments. With the launching of series of folk ballads contests, young people are keen to sing Nanning folk ballads in new forms. The addition of Western-style instruments such as guitars and jazz drums allowed Nanning folk ballads to be on stage and be interpreted in new ways. At present, Nanning has a number of Nanning folk ballad bands, such as Nanning Folk Guitar Street Group, New East and West Band, Focus Band, and Nanning folk guitar training business is going strong as well. The participation of modern bands has made Nanning folks renew their vitality. In 2014, with the consent of the People's Government of Guangxi Zhuang Autonomous Region, Nanning folk ballads were inscribed on the Fifth Autonomous Region List of Intangible Cultural Heritage.

面采集。近年，南宁市文化部门征集南宁民谣并汇集编纂了《南宁民谣》《南宁三江口 · 民谣谚语》《南宁经典怀旧民谣集》等。南宁民谣虽为里巷歌谣，但它却像一面镜子，映射出南宁人生活的方方面面，是南宁百姓生活智慧的结晶，凝聚着丰富的生活哲理，质朴生动，于细微处鼓励、教育人们，成为南宁民间文学的宝藏。

由于南宁民谣一直以口头传唱的方式流传于民间，少有文字记载，一些人不免认为民谣难登大雅之堂，部分民谣甚至因内容针砭时弊被禁止传唱。近年来，对南宁民谣的挖掘和保护逐渐得到相关部门的重视，随着征集和创作民谣比赛活动的展开，年轻人热衷于以新的形式传唱南宁民谣。吉他、爵士鼓等西式乐器的加入，使南宁民谣登上舞台，被全新演绎。目前，南宁市有南宁民谣吉他街唱小组、新东西乐队、焦点乐队等一批南宁民谣原创乐队，南宁民谣吉他培训业务也如火如荼，现代乐队的参与使南宁民谣焕发出新的活力。2014年，经广西壮族自治区人民政府同意，南宁民谣列入第五批自治区级非物质文化遗产名录。

白话童谣

Vernacular Nursery Rhymes

项目名称：白话童谣

别称：无

分布范围：广西白话地区及百色市等

入选名录：2014年第五批自治区级非物质文化遗产名录
　　　　　2013年第五批市级非物质文化遗产名录

保护单位：南宁市民族文化艺术研究院（南宁市非物质文化遗产保护中心）

代表性传承人：万立仁、刘子林

Element name：Vernacular Nursery Rhymes

Alternative name：None

Geographical location and range：Guangxi Vernacular Language Region, Baise City and others

Element inscribed list：In 2014 on the Fifth Autonomous Region List of Intangible Cultural Heritage
　　In 2013 on the Fifth Municipal List of Intangible Cultural Heritage

Competent body involved in safeguarding：Nanning Ethnic Culture and Art Research Institute (Nanning Intangible Cultural Heritage Protection Centre)

Representative inheritors：Wan Liren, Liu Zilin

Guangxi has a superior natural environment and has been a multi-ethnic mixed place with abundant language varieties since ancient times. The vernacular nursery rhymes are based on Cantonese language. Although the specific time period of origin cannot be verified, the development history of the rhymes is similar to the development history of vernacular. The distribution of vernacular accounts for one-third of the area in Guangxi, and there are more than 30 counties and cities within the area, such as Nanning, Yongning, Hengzhou, Guigang, Guiping and Pingnan. "Vernacular" is Cantonese, and the vernacular nursery rhymes are folk oral literatures circulating in the Cantonese-speaking area. It is the earliest literary style of children in the vernacular area. The nursery rhymes are rich in content, diverse in subject matter, and more in the life of things, such as *A Lot of Ants, Tiny Insects, Moonlight, Radish Head, Chicken Figurine and Bended Tail* and so on. The vernacular nursery rhymes are the enlightenment literature of children in the vernacular area. The language is plain and easy to understand, the rhythm is free and lively, the sentence pattern is short, witty and vivid, and the imagination is peculiar.

Children's nursery rhymes belong to the folk song category. They are one of the oldest and most basic genres of children's literature. They start with the singing of mothers and the growth of children. Children's nursery rhymes help children to derive perception from imitation, obtain beauty from singing, understanding affairs, tempering temperament, and cultivating good habits. Every nation regards nursery rhythms as the gentlest memory and the purest life. Most of the children's nursery rhymes are made of folk customs and folk songs. They are spoken in the dialects and sung by children. They represent the region well, high in historical value and rich in cultural connotation. They are the coordinates of childhood memories, the red line of emotions, and the symbol of cultural identity.

The vernacular nursery rhymes are rich in content, diverse in subject matter, and have strong regional characteristics. To a certain extent, they reflect social phenomena and the living conditions of the vernacular people. A sense of humor is the main feature of the vernacular nursery rhymes. Since the nursery rhymes are plain and interesting, they are very popular among children. The nursery rhymes are designed for children, the language is simple and easy to understand, also pays attention to rhythm and phonology, and attracts children to learn about music. The rhymes are short and vivid, sometimes with three words, five words, or seven words, etc. Compared with poetry, the form is more flexible,

广西自然环境优越，自古以来就是多民族杂居地，语言种类丰富。白话童谣以白话为基本依托产生，虽然产生的具体年代已无法考证，但发展历史与白话发展史相近。白话分布范围占广西地域的三分之一，境内通行白话的县市有30多个，如南宁、邕宁、横州、贵港、桂平、平南等。“白话”即粤语，白话童谣是流传于粤语区的民间口头文学，是白话地区儿童最早接触的文学样式。童谣内容丰富，题材多样，多取材于生活事物，有《蚂蚁多多》《点虫虫》《月光光》《萝卜头》《鸡公仔，尾弯弯》等。白话童谣是白话地区儿童的启蒙文学，语言平白易懂、声韵自由活泼，句式短小，俏皮生动，想象奇特。

童谣从属于民歌，是儿童文学最古老、最基本的体裁之一，它从母亲抚拍乳儿的吟唱开始，伴随着儿童的嬉耍成长。童谣使孩子从模仿中获得感知、从诵唱中获得美感，从而明白事理、陶冶性情、培养良好的习惯。每个民族无不视童谣为最温存的记忆、最纯美的生命。童谣大多以民风民俗为素材，以方言为载体，传唱于儿童之口，地域性强，历史价值高，文化内涵丰富，是童年记忆的坐标、维系情感的红线、文化认同的标志。

白话童谣内涵丰富，题材多样，具有浓厚的地域特征，一定程度上反映了社会现象以及白话人的生活状态。富有幽默感是白话童谣内容的主要特征，虽平白如话却意趣十足，十分受儿童欢迎。童谣专为儿童创作，语言质朴易懂，讲究节奏和音韵，以音乐性吸引儿童学习吟唱。童谣句式短小生动，有三言、五言、七言等，与诗歌相比，形式更加灵活，有的只用两句歌词反复吟唱，易于儿童接受。作为岭南地区民间文学的重要组成部分，白话童谣以独特形式反映岭南地区百姓生活，对研究古代社会生活具有重要的价值。它拥有特殊的艺术魅力以及重要的教育意义，是壮、汉民族文化互动的载体，是民族和谐共处、文化融合的象征。

当今社会，尽管白话童谣依然被白话人熟知，但是有些传统童谣因为内容不符合现代社会而逐渐失传。因此，南宁市非物质文化遗产保护中心着力于挖掘整理白话童谣资料，同时白话童谣也成为南宁市多数中小学特色教学科目并进行针对性授课。2014年，经广西壮族自治区人民政府同意，白话童谣列入第五批自治区级非物质文化遗产名录。

and some use only two lyrics to sing repeatedly, which is easy for children to accept. As an important part of folk literature in Lingnan area, the vernacular nursery rhyme reflects the life of the people in Lingnan in a unique way. It has important values for studying ancient social life, also special artistic charm and important educational significance. It is the interaction of Zhuang and Han national cultures; the symbol of harmonious ethnic coexistence and cultural integration.

In today's society, although the vernacular nursery rhymes are still well known by the vernacular people, some traditional nursery rhymes have gradually lost their content because they do not conform to modern society. So Nanning Protection Centre for Intangible Cultural Heritage focused on excavating the information on the vernacular nursery rhymes. At the same time, the vernacular nursery rhymes also became the most suitable primary and secondary school teaching subjects in Nanning. In 2014, with the consent of the People's Government of Guangxi Zhuang Autonomous Region, the vernacular nursery rhymes were inscribed on the Fifth Autonomous Region List of Intangible Cultural Heritage.

小学生演出的《白话童谣》参加2016年南宁市第十一个文化遗产日
Children's Ballad in Vernacular Performed by Primary School Students Participated in the 11th Cultural Heritage Day of Nanning in 2016

壮族信歌

Epistolary Style Ballad of Zhuang Ethnic Group

项目名称：壮族信歌

别称：无

分布范围：平果市、武鸣区、马山县、上林县、宾阳县、忻城县、都安县、大化县等

入选名录：2014年第五批自治区级非物质文化遗产名录

2013年第五批市级非物质文化遗产名录

保护单位：南宁市民族文化艺术研究院（南宁市非物质文化遗产保护中心）

代表性传承人：无

Element name: Epistolary Style Ballad of Zhuang Ethnic Group

Alternative name: None

Geographical location and range: Pingguo County-Level City, Wuming District, Mashan County, Shanglin County, Binyang County, Xincheng County, Du'an County, Dahua County and others

Element inscribed list: In 2014 on the Fifth Autonomous Region List of Intangible Cultural Heritage

In 2013 on the Fifth Municipal List of Intangible Cultural Heritage

Competent body involved in safeguarding: Nanning Ethnic Culture and Art Research Institute (Nanning Intangible Cultural Heritage Protection Centre)

Representative inheritor: None

壮族信歌是由方块壮字写成的歌体书信，流传于壮族民间，既具有信函的称谓和寄发对象，又以歌代信，保留着歌谣的形式，非常独特，因此它既是信又是歌。壮族信歌流布于广西马山县及其周边的武鸣、平果、上林、宾阳、忻城、都安、大化县等壮族聚居地。信歌内容极为丰富，从篇幅来看，最长可达400多行，多是对壮族社会生活的反映。其内容大致分为三类：一是反映生产劳动和生活习俗，如“耙田盼下雨，怕天不如意”“八月谷穗垂，才想起筑坝”等；二是表达青年男女爱恋之情，壮族青年男女从相识到交往、定情、成婚都可借助信歌传情达意；三是封建社会中，劳动人民倾诉生活中的苦难。壮族信歌既有特定的倾诉对象，又极擅于传递情感，因此成为壮族人交流信息的重要方式。

从调查访问及收集到的壮族信歌文本判断，壮族信歌最迟产生于清代，是土著文化和流官文化结合的产物，与思恩府的统治密切相关。其流布区域属历史上明、清时期思恩府的管辖范围，地形多石山和丘陵，物产丰富，河流众多，人群流动频繁，壮、汉文化交流密切。明代思恩府建立于今平果市的旧城乡，其间两次搬迁，分别位于马山的乔利乡和武鸣的府城，目前大部分保存较完好的壮族信歌文本都是在这些地方发现的。

壮族信歌有着深厚的历史文化内涵，是思恩府文化的一部分，它在汉文化向南方少数民族传播的历史中产生，折射出汉文化强大的辐射力。信歌内容涵盖社会生活、地方风俗等多方面，世代相承，是马山县及周边地区壮族历史文化的有力见证。壮族信歌将信与歌结合，交流信息的方式独特，是研究壮族社会历史的重要文献资料。信歌通常被保存在歌手的歌书里，是民间歌谣的有机组成部分，具有特殊的艺术价值与欣赏价值。

目前，民间原有信歌文本流失严重。随着社会的发展，民间聚会中的对歌传统逐渐弱化，信歌使用的社会文化空间

The epistolary style ballad of Zhuang Ethnic Group is a kind of letter written by the square Zhuang characters in the form of ballad, which is popular among Zhuang people. Although it has the appellation, sender and addressee, it uses ballads to express the content of the letter, also maintaining the form of ballad. The epistolary style ballad of Zhuang is very unique due to its mixed form of both ballad and letter. The epistolary style ballad is popular in Mashan County and its surrounding areas like Wuming, Pingguo, Shanglin, Binyang, Xincheng, Du'an and Dahua counties and other settlements for Zhuang Ethnic Group. The contents of epistolary style ballad are very colorful. In the length of the ballad, the longest one has nearly 400 lines, most of them reflecting the social life of Zhuang people. The content of epistolary style ballad can be divided into three categories. The first category reflects the productive labor and life customs, such as "harrowing the field and waiting for the rain, only fearing the god to go against my prayer", "the ears of grain hanging down in August, then I just remember to build the dam" and so on. The second category is used to express love of young men and women. The young men and women of Zhuang can use epistolary style ballads to convey love from interaction to engagement and marriage. The third category is used by laboring people to pour out their suffering in feudal society. The epistolary style ballad of Zhuang is good at conveying emotions and feelings with specific themes, thus it has become an important way to exchange information for Zhuang people.

Based on the investigation, interview and text of collected ballads, it can be speculated that the epistolary style ballad appeared in the Qing Dynasty at the latest. The ballad was a product of both indigenous and official cultures, which was closely related to the rule of the Si'en government. The regions where the epistolary style ballad spreads were under the administration of Si'en government in the Ming and Qing dynasties. The major terrain of these areas is rocky mountain and hill. They are abundant with natural resources and rivers. People here flow frequently, thus the cultural exchange between Zhuang and Han cultures are close. The site of Si'en government was built on the ancient site of today's Pingguo County-Level City, which once was moved to Qiaoli Township of Mashan County and Fucheng Town of Wuming County respectively. At present, most well-preserved epistolary style ballads were found in these areas.

The epistolary style ballad of Zhuang bears profound historical and cultural connotations, which is a part of Si'en government culture. It came into being during the history of Han culture's spreading toward ethnic minorities in the south, reflecting powerful radiation of Han culture. Passing on from generation to generation, the content of the epistolary style ballad covers various aspects like social life and local customs, which is a great witness of the history and culture of Zhuang in Mashan County and its surrounding areas. The epistolary style ballad of Zhuang combines both letters and ballads to communicate information in a unique way, which is an important document for studying the social history of Zhuang. The epistolary style ballads are often preserved in ballad books of singers. This is a positive part of folk ballads and bears great artistic and appreciation values.

At present, the original folk epistolary style ballads have suffered a serious loss. With the development of society, the tradition of antiphonal singing on folk parties has been weakened, leading to the loss of the social and cultural space for epistolary style ballads, thus it is hard to create new ballads in general. All sectors of the society should strengthen the awareness of the value of epistolary style ballads. Most of the ballad texts are preserved by the old artists, and the inheritance of them are hard to continue. In 2012, Nanning Ethnic Culture and Art Research Institute established a group to protect the ballad by investigating and exploring epistolary style ballads and surveying its inheritors and inheritance situation. In 2014, with the approval from the People's Government of the Guangxi Zhuang Autonomous Region, the epistolary style ballad of Zhuang Ethnic Group was inscribed on the Fifth Autonomous Region List of Intangible Cultural Heritage.

不复存在，基本上无法催生新的信歌。社会各界对信歌价值的认识有待提高，信歌文本多存于老艺人手中，传承难以为继。2012年，南宁市民族文化艺术研究院成立了壮族信歌保护工作小组，调查、挖掘壮族信歌，普查传承人及传承现状。2014年，经广西壮族自治区人民政府同意，壮族信歌列入第五批自治区级非物质文化遗产名录。

壮族祭台
An Sacrificial Altar of Zhuang Ethnic Group

壮族传扬歌

Zhuang Folk Song Promoting Ethics and Morality

项目名称：壮族传扬歌

别称：无

分布范围：武鸣区、马山县、上林县、忻城县、都安县等

入选名录：2014年第五批自治区级非物质文化遗产名录
　　　　　2013年第五批市级非物质文化遗产名录

保护单位：马山县文化馆

代表性传承人：蓝日茂

Element name：Zhuang Folk Song Promoting Ethics and Morality

Alternative name：None

Geographical location and range：Wuming District, Mashan County, Shanglin County, Xincheng County, Du'an County and others

Element inscribed list：In 2014 on the Fifth Autonomous Region List of Intangible Cultural Heritage
In 2013 on the Fifth Municipal List of Intangible Cultural Heritage

Competent body involved in safeguarding：Mashan County Cultural Centre

Representative inheritors：Lan Rimao

Zhuang Folk Song promoting ethics and morality are actually long poems of folk ethics and morality. In the hand-copied version of the ancient Zhuang characters, the title of the song collection is written as "Zhuang Zi Huan Chuan Yang", which means songs and poems promoting ethics and morality. They are also called "Fwencienzyiengz" in Zhuang language. These folk songs are composed of mottos, proverbs and folk adages. By using philosophical language, they expose the immoral conducts of the ruling class in oppressing and exploiting common people, discuss the moral standards and obligations that one should observe and fulfill, and give the methods to deal with the internal family relations. Zhuang folk songs promoting ethics and morality are long ethical poems integrating the traditional moral thoughts of Zhuang Ethnic Group.

The contents of these folk songs can be divided into three categories, including personal cultivation, family ethics and social morality. The personal cultivation part comprehensively elaborates the moral norms in interpersonal relationship of Zhuang people, and puts forward detailed methods for improving moral education and cultivation. Family ethics emphasizes filial piety and clarifies the relationship between family members and their rights and obligations in the family. The social morality part advocates "the officials should help the plain citizens" and "the government rights should serve the people", firmly opposing corruption, exploitation and oppression. Zhuang folk songs promoting ethics and morality reflect the Zhuang people's distinct attitude toward good and evil, beauty and ugliness, as well as the righteous spirit of observing social morality.

Zhuang Folk Song promoting ethics and morality is popular in Mashan, Shanglin, Xincheng, Wuming, Du'an and other counties. Mashan County in central Guangxi is boasting of convenient transportation. Its unique geographical advantages allow it to create this folk literature of Zhuang Ethnic Group. These folk songs have a long history. *Folk Song Promoting Ethics and Morality I* is one of the representatives among the songs. According to the place and official names mentioned in the song, it was created in the Sui and Tang dynasties at the latest, and was finalized in the Ming Dynasty. *Folk Song Promoting Ethics and Morality II* was written by song master Meng Tingshou in the Qing Dynasty, in which it mentioned four specific years of Wuxu, Guimao, Wushen and Dingyou. The earliest one of these four years was in the reign of Emperor Shunzhi and the latest on was in the reign of Emperor Qianlong in the Qing Dynasty. *Folk Song Promoting Ethics and Morality III* spreads in areas like Mashan County and Shanglin County, which was the work finalized in the reign of Emperor Qianlong in the Qing Dynasty. *The Song of Longevity* and *Never Forgetting the Upbringing of Parents* are popular in Pianlian and other towns of Mashan County, whose contents are based on storytelling and singing works in the

壮族传扬歌是壮族民间伦理道德长诗，在民间古壮字手抄本中写作“壮字欢传扬”，壮语叫作Fwencienzyiengz，意为传播弘扬伦理道德的歌。它以格言、谚语及俗语连缀创作而成，通过哲理性的语言，揭露统治阶级压榨百姓的丑恶行为，论述做人的道德规范和应承担的义务，以及如何处理好家庭内部关系等，是集壮族传统道德思想之大成的伦理长诗。

壮族传扬歌的内容主要包括个人修养、家庭伦理道德和社会道德三个方面。个人修养类全面阐述了壮族人际关系中应遵守的道德规范，提出了道德教育和修养的具体途径和方法；家庭伦理道德类强调孝道，阐明家庭成员之间的关系以及个人在家庭中的权利和义务；社会道德类主张“以上补下”“掌印为民”，反对腐败和剥削压迫。壮族传扬歌反映出壮族人对善、恶、美、丑的鲜明态度，以及坚守社会道德的正义精神。

壮族传扬歌流传于马山、上林、忻城、武鸣、都安等县区。广西中部的马山县交通便利，得天独厚的区位优势使这里孕育出这一壮族传统民间文学。壮族传扬歌历史悠久，《传扬歌一》是壮族传扬歌的代表，从诗中提到的地名和官名来推断，最迟产生于隋唐，定型于明代。《传扬歌二》由清代歌师蒙廷守创作，其中提到戊戌、癸卯、戊申、丁酉四年，最早在顺治时期，最晚在乾隆年间。《传扬歌三》流传于马山、上林一带，为乾隆时期作品。《百岁歌》和《不忘父母恩》都流传于马山片联等乡，内容均来源于清代的说唱作品。20世纪60年代至80年代，《壮族道德经——传扬歌》被整理出版，分别为《传扬歌一》《传扬歌二》《传扬歌三》《百岁歌》《不忘父母恩》，共计430首，分别收集于马山古寨、金钗、里当、林圩等乡镇。

壮族传扬歌不同于一般故事传说，没有情节及人物塑造，专门以富含哲理的语言劝人向善，修身立德，具有直接的教育、警示功能。它多以格言、谚语及俗语连缀而成，精炼且寓意深长，被誉为“壮族的道德经”。它不仅用于歌师吟唱，其中的名言警句还经常出现在各种交际场合，深受壮乡群众喜爱，成为当地民众生活中不可或缺的精神食粮，在壮族节日、婚丧嫁娶、集会等场合都有传扬歌的身影。传扬歌历史悠久且随着时代的发展不断更新，延续至今，已逐渐成为壮族古老又独具特色的文化品牌，对其之保护与传承为打造马山特色旅游文化品牌以及丰富壮族民间音乐、歌舞、戏曲的创作素材提供了有利条件。

随着社会娱乐方式与教育方式逐渐多元化，壮族传扬歌应用面逐步萎缩。历史上，壮族传扬歌曾被当作封建迷信山歌搜查烧毁严重，目前原始手抄本毫无踪迹，传承人出现断代现象。2013年，在开展非物质文化遗产普查的基础上，马山县制订了《马山壮族传扬歌五年保护计划》，同年，古寨乡古寨村建立了壮族传扬歌传承基地，传扬歌五部长诗的出版使得传扬歌得到了保护与发展。2014年，经广西壮族自治区人民政府同意，壮族传扬歌列入第五批自治区级非物质文化遗产名录。

马山县古寨村传承人蓝日茂整理的传扬歌手抄本

Manuscripts of Zhuang Folk Song Promoting Ethics and Morality Compiled by Lan Rimao, Inheritor of Guzhai Village, Mashan County

Qing Dynasty. From the 1960s to the 1980s, *The Scripture of Ethics of Zhuang Ethnic Group: Folk Song Promoting Ethics and Morality* were compiled and published, including *Folk Song Promoting Ethics and Morality I*, *Folk Song Promoting Ethics and Morality II*, *Folk Song Promoting Ethics and Morality III*, *The Song of Longevity* and *Never Forgetting the Upbringing of Parents*, with a total of 430 small pieces. These folk songs are now collected in villages and towns such as Guzhai, Jinchai, Lidang and Linxu.

Zhuang folk songs promoting ethics and morality have no plots and characters, which makes them different from common stories and legends. They use philosophical languages to encourage people to be good and cultivate their morality, which bear direct function of education and warning. As most of the folk songs are composed of mottos, proverbs and folk adages, they are often concise in language and profound in meaning, with a reputation of “Tao Te Ching of Zhuang Ethnic Group”. The folk songs promoting ethics and morality are not only used for singing, their famous sayings and aphorisms are also often used in various social occasions. These folk songs are deeply loved by Zhuang people and have become an indispensable part of local people. There are folk songs pomoting ethics and morality in Zhuang festivals, weddings and funerals, gatherings and other occasions. Folk songs promoting ethics and morality have a long history and are constantly updated with the development of the times. They have gradually become an ancient and unique cultural brand of the Zhuang Ethnic Group. The protection and inheritance for folk songs promoting ethics and morality, providing favorable conditions to build a tourism cultural brand with Mashan characteristics and enriching the creative materials of Zhuang folk music, song and dance, and drama.

With the gradual diversification of social entertainment and education, the application of Zhuang folk songs promoting ethics and morality has gradually shrunk. In history, Zhuang folk songs promoting ethics and morality were once regarded as feudal superstitious folk songs, which were searched and burned seriously. At present, there is no trace of the original manuscript, and the inheritors are lost by generations. In 2013, based on the general survey of intangible cultural heritage, Mashan County formulated *The Five-year Protection Plan for Mashan Zhuang Folk Songs Promoting Ethics and Morality*. In the same year, Guzhai Village, Guzhai Township established a heritage base for Zhuang folk songs promoting ethics and morality, and the publication of five long poems of the folk songs promoting ethics and morality protected and developed the folk songs. In 2014, with the consent of the People's Government of Guangxi Zhuang Autonomous Region, Zhuang folk songs promoting ethics and morality were selected into the Fifth Autonomous Region List of Intangible Cultural Heritage.

宾阳“老窍”的故事

Binyang's Story of "Laoqiao"

项目名称：宾阳“老窍”的故事

别称：无

分布范围：宾阳县

入选名录：2010年第三批自治区级非物质文化遗产名录
　　　　　2010年第三批市级非物质文化遗产名录

保护单位：宾阳县文化馆

代表性传承人：黄红新（已故）

Element name：Binyang's Story of "Laoqiao"

Alternative name：None

Geographical location and range：Binyang County

Element inscribed list：In 2010 on the Third Autonomous Region List of Intangible Cultural Heritage
In 2010 on the Third Municipal List of Intangible Cultural Heritage

Competent body involved in safeguarding：Binyang County Cultural Centre

Representative inheritor：Huang Hongxin (Late)

宾阳"老窍"的故事是民间传说系列故事，以民间曲艺的形式流传于南宁市宾阳县16个乡镇，属于口头文学。故事以聪慧机敏的"老窍"为主人公，讲述了小人物一段又一段有趣的传奇经历，在宾阳县家喻户晓。老窍系列故事有100多个，均取材于农村百姓的社会生活，由当地劳动群众创作而成。

"老窍"的故事大致分为笑话类，劫富济贫、整治贪官类，斗智类。笑话类主要以幽默的故事情节讽刺吝啬贪财之人，有《捅菜篮》《学跳神舞》《打老鼠》等。《捅菜篮》讲述老窍的岳父万世昌是当地财主，此人极为吝啬虚伪，每次老窍登门拜访，他便将鱼肉之类的好吃饭菜藏起来，只留一些清淡的素菜在桌子上，不料老窍早已看穿岳父的诡计。一日，老窍又上门拜访，岳父急忙将一盘刚炒好的腊肉藏在了菜篮里，悬挂于高处的钩子上。老窍进屋闻到肉味飘香，而桌子上只有一盘青菜，便知岳父故伎重演。于是，在岳父的一番热情询问之后，老窍便说这次是为献艺而来，不等岳父点头，他便抄起扁担舞弄起来，故意装作不小心将悬空高挂的菜篮捅落在地，眼见冒着热气的炒腊肉撒满一地，岳父不由得羞愧万分。劫富济贫、整治贪官类的故事有《龙麟玉锅》《灵筒测》《智毁灵筒》等。《龙麟玉锅》讲述某年宾州大旱，粮食颗粒无收，佃户便求老窍想办法减免万家佃租。老窍与妻子阿莲设计以祖传"龙麟玉锅"为代价，迫使贪财的岳父岳母在众人面前立下减缓一年佃租的字据，帮助百姓渡过了饥荒难关。斗智类故事有《选婿》《分牛》《智擒偷鸡贼》《五斤肉》等。其中，《选婿》讲述财主万世昌为三女儿选婿：谁能三天之内摘完万家榄子树的榄子就可娶三小姐为妻。万家院中的榄子树又高又大，三日之内摘完榄子难度堪比摘天上的月亮，众人知难而退，只剩下竹篙鬼、火炭鹊和老窍三人自告奋勇。竹篙鬼和火炭鹊各执一长竹竿，各自选了一棵榄子树左右打起来，只有老窍在一旁若有所思。待到半夜，老窍和阿莲偷偷将两桶盐水灌进一棵榄子

Story of "Laoqiao" is a series of stories spread among people. It is spread in 16 towns and villages of Binyang County and Nanning City in the form of folk art, and belongs to oral literature. Laoqiao is the protagonist of the oral stories that are about various interesting experience about normal people. They are well known in Binyang County. There are more than 100 Laoqiao stories and all of them are from the social life of rural people and are created by local people.

The topics of stories about "Laoqiao" could be categorized into joke, assistance to poor people and punishment to corrupted officers, wisdom. Jokes use humorous stories to satire people who are mean and greedy. This kind of stories include *Overthrow Food Basket, Learn God Dance, Catch Mouse* etc. *Overthrow Food Basket* is a story about Laoqiao's father-in-law Wan Shichang who is very rich but mean and hypocrisy. Every time Laoqiao visits his father-in-law, Wan Shichang will hide delicate food away, like fish and meat, and only leave plain food like vegetables on the table. However, Laoqiao has seen through the tricks. One day, he visits his father-in-law and Wan Shichang hides a newly cooked bacon in the food basket in a hurry and hanged the basket on a hook. Laoqiao immediately figures out what happen when he smells the flavor of bacon after walking in the room and sees there is only one plate of vegetable on the table. Wan Shichang asks him what he comes for and Laoqiao says he comes to performance. Before father-in-law nods, he starts to dance with a pole. He pretends to overthrow the food basket carelessly. Seeing the freshly fried bacon falling on the ground, father-in-law feels great shame. Stories about assistance to poor people and punishment to corrupted officers include *Dragon Scale and Jade Pot, Wisdom Scroll, Destroy of Wisdom Scroll* etc. *Dragon Scale and Jade Pot* happens in a year struck by drought. Tenant farmers beg Laoqiao to help them reduce the land rent from landlords Wan for they harvest nothing due to the drought. Laoqiao and his wife Alian set a trap. They use so-called dragon scale and jade pot which are inherited from ancestors to lure Laoqiao's greedy parents-in-law. Eventually, the greedy landlords are forced to reduce land rent for one year in a written form. In that case, poor people survived the drought. Stories about wisdom include *Choose Son-in-Law, Divide Cows, Catch Chicken Thief with Wisdom, Five Jin of Meat. Choose Son-in-Law* talks about the rich landlord Wan Shichang picking up a son-in-law for his third daughter. The one who is able to knock down all of the olives from olive trees within three days will be the husband of landlord's lovely daughter. The olive trees are very tall and knocking downing all of the olive is as difficult as picking the moon in the sky. Many candidates quit and only three, Laoqiao, Zhuhaogui

民间讲述“老窍”故事
Folk Story Telling of “Laoqiao”

and Huotanque, come forward. Zhuhaogui and Huotanque find poles and start to knock olives immediately but Laoqiao remains thinking. In the midnight, Laoqiao and the daughter of landlord Alian water the tree with salty water secretly. The next day Wan Shichang went to the orchard only to find that all of the olives are on the ground and Laoqiao is picking the olives. He has no choice but to allow his daughter to marry Laoqiao. From then on intelligent Laoqiao becomes the son-in-law of the rich landlord and leads a happy life with Alian.

When these stories were born is hard to figure out for there's no historical record. However, based on the written document provided by late old artist Shi Caichun and oral information from other artists, it can be concluded that the stories are originated from Hongwu period in the

树根底。第二天，万世昌到果园巡查，见老窍正在忙着捡满地的榄子，再看榄子树上的榄子一颗不剩，惊奇万分，最终不得已将女儿许配与老窍。足智多谋的老窍从此成了大财主的三姑爷，与阿莲过上了幸福美满的生活。

宾阳“老窍”的故事源于何时，并没有史料记载，但是根据老艺人施彩春（已故）提供的资料，并结合10多位老艺人的口述，可以推算宾阳老窍故事自明代洪武元年（1368），即艺人祖宗落籍宾阳时已有流传。宾阳地区人杰地灵，历史悠久，老窍天资聪颖，善良睿智，虽出身贫寒，却不贪钱财，屡施巧计救助穷人，惩治恶霸，侠肝义胆。有关老穷的故事很多，且都幽默诙谐、奇趣无穷，不仅在宾阳境内各地流传，还流传至周边的上林、横州、来宾、武鸣等地。20世纪90年代，长篇小说《老穷》《老穷续传》相继问世，并被福建电视台拍摄成电视连续剧《穷哥》。

以老穷这一主要人物贯穿系列故事，牵引出宾阳农村生活中形形色色的人物事件，反映家庭、婚姻、商贸、反封建、惩治污吏等世俗百态，“老穷”故事可谓描绘宾阳地区风土人情的生动画卷。每个小故事都是当地劳动群众生活经验与智慧的结晶，宣扬了愤世嫉俗、惩恶扬善、仗义疏财、劫富济贫等人生观与价值观。老穷的机敏聪慧和高尚品德是宾阳百姓善良淳朴、机智勇敢等可贵品质的凝聚，时至今日依旧具有极强的教育作用。故事传奇生动，自成系列，逻辑清晰，情节结构合理，富于想象力，趣味十足。讲述宾阳“老穷”的故事多用宾阳本地方言，有的只以一句与故事相关的方言为主线，就可构成一个引人哄堂大笑的小故事，故事流传至不同的方言地区，内容被不断充实丰富。

受现代多元文化的冲击，传统民间故事的吸引力日益减弱，宾阳“老穷”的故事的传承遇到了很大的难题。为了加大保护力度，宾阳县文化部门一方面搜集整理故事，一方面鼓励老艺人积极开展传承工作，或将故事内容改编，或创作剧本，将之改为舞台剧，巡回演出。2010年，宾阳“老穷”的故事列入第三批自治区级非物质文化遗产名录。

Ming Dynasty (1368) when the ancestor of these artists first moved to live in Binyang. Binyang enjoys glories of natural environment and talented people and has a long history. Laoqiao is intelligent and kind-hearted. He is born in poverty but never greedy for money. He uses his wisdom to help poor people and punish bullies. He has the heart of a hero. There are many funny and interesting stories about Laoqiao and they are widely spread in neighboring areas like Shanglin, Hengzhou, Laibin and Wuming. In the 1990s, the novel *Biography of Laoqiao* and *Second Biography of Laoqiao* were published and Fujian TV station also made TV series named *Brother Qiao*.

The stories about Laoqiao reflect various characters in rural areas of Binyang. They show different social sectors including family, marriage, business and commerce, anti-feudalism, punishment to corrupted officials and assistance to poor people. They are vivid pictures of folklore in Binyang. Every story is the crystallization of life experience and wisdom from local people. Outlooks on life and values about cynicism, praising virtue and punishing vice and spreading money to poor people are promoted. The intelligence and high virtue, as well as the kindness, honesty, witness and bravery are of great importance in education. These stories are vivid, reasonsble, imaginatine and interesting, and have clear logic. The stories about Laoqiao are mostly told in Binyang local dialect. Some of them only have a sentence ralated to the story as the main clue, which can form a small story-chat makes peple laugh. The stories have been spread to different dialect areas, and the contents are still enriching.

Due to the impact of modern multi-culture, traditional folk stories have limited attraction to people. The inheritance of Laoqiao stories in Binyang is faced with many obstacles. In order to better protect these stories, cultural department select and categorize stories while it encourages old artists to inherit or adapt these stories. Some of them are adapted into stage performance and go on touring performance. In 2010, Laoqiao stories were inscribed on the Third Autonomous Region List of Intangible Cultural Heritage.

青山流米洞故事

Qingshan's Story of Running Rice Cave

项目名称：青山流米洞故事

别称：无

分布范围：青秀区、兴宁区、江南区、西乡塘区、邕宁区等壮、汉民族聚居地

入选名录：2018年青山流米洞故事与龙象塔故事合并列入第七批自治区级非物质文化遗产名录
2017年第七批市级非物质文化遗产名录

保护单位：青秀区文化馆

代表性传承人：梁代竹

Element name: Qingshan's Story of Running Rice Cave

Alternative name: None

Geographical location and range: Qingxiu District, Xingning District, Jiangnan District, Xixiangtang District, Yongning District and other settlements for Zhuang and Han peoples

Element inscribed list: In 2018 Qingshan's Story of Running Rice Cave and of Dragon-Elephant Tower Merged on the Seventh Autonomous Region List of Intangible Cultural Heritage
In 2017 on the Seventh Municipal List of Intangible Cultural Heritage

Competent body involved in safeguarding: Qingxiu District Cultural Centre

Representative inheritor: Liang Daizhu

青山流米洞故事起源于南宁市青秀区，属于民间口头文学。传说故事流传至今已有近400年，内容和该地区民众生产、生活息息相关，深受民众喜爱。

青山流米洞讲述古时南宁青山上有座寺庙，寺旁有一神奇的流米洞，此洞每天都会流出米粒，但是每天流米量只够寺中老和尚吃一天。老和尚虽吃斋念佛多年，却红尘未脱，常下山赊账喝酒，欠了邻村酒铺很多酒钱。他想拿洞中流出的米去换酒，但又嫌流米洞中流出的米太少。于是他用斧头将洞口劈开，劈至水桶般大，将手伸进洞内，想把米扒出来，不料却扒出来一堆沙子。从此，流米洞不再流米，只流清泉，形成了后来的董泉。

故事发源地为南宁市青秀山。青秀山又名泰青峰，俗称“青山”，位于南宁市区东南方向的邕江江畔，是南宁市十大景观之一，有“绿城翡翠”之称。青秀山历史悠久，气候宜人，古代已是邕南著名的避暑胜地，现存明、清时期古建筑和名人雅士题吟颇丰，很多民间故事流传于此，游客络绎不绝。据《南宁府志》记载，早在东晋时期就已有关于青秀山的史料。明代刑部主事董传策被贬至邕州，发现流米洞泉眼，将其命名为“混混泉”。后有南宁郡守方瑜及兵备徐浦，十分敬佩董传策的为人，便命石工在泉眼旁石壁上刻“董泉”两字为之纪念。惩恶扬善的青山流米洞神话故事产生于明代，随着社会的发展不断丰富，广泛流传于南宁周边壮、汉民族聚居地，世代相传，至今魅力不减。

青山流米洞故事是劳动人民集体创作的结晶，鞭挞贪得无厌、唯利是图的丑恶现象，宣扬人与自然和谐相处。故事内容涉及神话传说、社会生活、伦理道德等多方面，反映当地劳动人民生活状况以及人生观、价值观，具有鲜明的民族特色和宝贵的历史研究价值。流米洞故事历史悠久，内容随着社会的发展不断丰富完善。故事内容生动，诙谐幽默，乡土气息浓厚，给口头文学增添了娱乐性和趣味性，不仅流传

The story of Running Rice Cave originated from Qingxiu District in Nanning city and was an oral story. It has existed for more than 400 years and is closely related with production and life of local people, which earned people's love.

This story is about a miracle cave named “Running Rice” near a temple on Qingshan Mountain near Nanning. Every day rice would flow out of the cave, but the rice was only enough for an old monk in the temple. Although the old monk eats fast and recites Buddha for many years, he is not far away from secular life and often goes down the mountain to drink on credit. He usually drank liquor but couldn't pay in time so that he owed much to the liquor stores. He tried to exchange liquor with rice from the cave, but the amount of rice was insufficient. With an axe he expanded the entrance of the cave to the size of a bucket and put his hand into the cave for more rice but only found sand. From then on, this cave would never flow rice but clear water. And the water is called “Dongquan” spring nowadays.

This story originated from Qingxiu Mountain in Nanning, which is also called Taiqing Peak and Qingshan Mountain. It stands on the river bank of Yongjiang River which is in southeast part of the city. The mountain ranks among “Top 10 sights” of Nanning and enjoys the reputation as “The Jade of Green City”. Qingxiu Mountain has a long history and agreeable climate. In ancient time it is a famous summer resort in south Nanning. There are many ancient buildings of the Ming and Qing dynasties as well as inscriptions from celebrities. Many folk stories are widely spread there and many tourists visit the mountain. The record of Qingxiu Mountain could be found back to the Eastern Jin Dynasty according to *Annals of Nanning Prefecture*. Dong Chuance, director of Criminal and Punishment Department was demoted to Yongzhou city and he found the cave. He named it “Hunhun Spring”. The chief of Nanning Fang Yu and military director Xu Fu admired the virtue of Dong Chuance so that they commanded stonemasons to curve “Dongquan Spring” on the cliff near the spring in memory of Dong Chuance. This story which praised goodness and punished greediness was created in the Ming Dynasty and was enriched with the development of society. It was widely spread in habitats of Zhuang and Han Nationalities and was passed among different generations of people with long-lasting charm.

The story of Running Rice Cave was the crystallization of the collective wisdom of labor people. It criticized greed and money-oriented rascality while it praised the harmony between

董泉
Dongquan Spring

people and the nature. The story covered myths, legends, social life, ethic values and other sectors. It reflected the local people's attitudes on life and value and had prominent ethnic characteristics. It was valuable in history research. The story of Running Rice has a long history, and its content is constantly enriched and improved with the development of society. The content was vivid and humorous with great local features, which increased entertainment to the oral literature. This story was told not only in Nanning but in neighboring areas. Charms of folklore were well shown. It was also important in folklore culture research. Later generations also found inspiration and raw materials from this story.

Although the story is accepted by people and is convenient to spread due to its oral form, it is hard to record and save. In 2009, Nanning municipal government and Qingxiu District government started a survey about Running Rice Cave and other stories. In 2011, Guangxi People's Publishing House put out *The Legends of Qingxiu Mountain* which included Qingshan's Story of Running Rice Cave. In 2018, Qingshan's Story of Running Rice Cave and of Dragon-Elephant Tower were merged into the Seventh Autonomous Reigon List of Intangible Cultural Heritage.

至南宁市全境，还辐射到周边地区，展现出当地民间文化的风采，具有一定的民俗文化研究价值，也为后人进行艺术创作提供了素材。

以口头文学形式传承的青山流米洞故事，虽具有一定的群众基础和方便简捷的传播途径，但长期以来保存困难。2009年南宁市政府、青秀区政府启动了对青山流米洞等故事的项目普查，2011年广西人民出版社出版了包含青山流米洞故事在内的《青秀山的传说》。2018年，青山流米洞故事与龙象塔故事合并列入第七批自治区级非物质文化遗产名录。

青山龙象塔故事

Qingshan's Story of Dragon-Elephant Tower

项目名称：青山龙象塔故事

别称：无

分布范围：青秀区、兴宁区、江南区、西乡塘区、邕宁区等壮、汉民族聚居地

入选名录：2018年青山龙象塔故事与流米洞故事合并列入第七批自治区非物质文化遗产名录

2017年第七批市级非物质文化遗产名录

保护单位：青秀区文化馆

代表性传承人：梁代竹

Element name: Qingshan's Story of Dragon-Elephant Tower

Alternative name: None

Geographical location and range: Qingxiu District, Xingning District, Jiangnan District, Xixiangtang District, Yongning District and other settlements for Zhuang and Han peoples

Element inscribed list: In 2018 Qingshan's Story of Dragon-Elephant Tower and of Running Rice Cave Merged on the Seventh Autonomous Region List of Intangible Cultural Heritage

In 2017 on the Seventh Municipal List of Intangible Cultural Heritage

Competent body involved in safeguarding: Qingxiu District Cultural Centre

Representative inheritor: Liang Daizhu

Qingshan's story of Dragon-Elephant Tower is a folk legend about traditional customs and beliefs, which spreads in Nanning and its surrounding areas. The story is originated from Qingxiu Mountain (Mount Qing or Qingshan in Chinese) with a certain mythological color. It records the natural environment where the local people live and develop and ethnic customs and ethics, which is deeply loved by the local.

Qingshan's story of Dragon-Elephant Tower has a history of more than 400 years. This story has many different versions and most of them are related geomancy. This story tells a Taoist priest in ancient times trudging through mountains on foot so as to choose a good place to bury his father. When he arrived at Mount Qing, he found that auspicious clouds hovering around the mountain, which made the mountain seem like a phoenix ready to fly. On seeing this, the Taoist priest went back to his hometown and brought his father's bone to Nanning. During his journey, he stayed overnight at Xiao Shengchang's home at the foot of Mount Qing. After three cups of wine, the Taoist priest told Xiao the purpose of his journey. At that night, Xiao played tricks to change his own father's bone into the golden cinerary urn. In the next day, the Xiao's family accompanied the Taoist priest to bury the urn in the Phoenix Hill. Since then, Xiao's family gained fame and fortune while the Taoist priest's family began to come down to the world. Several years later, the Taoist priest learned the truth and came to Nanning again. He told Xiao Shengchang that the phoenix on the Phoenix Hill would fly away. If the Xiao's family wanted to secure official positions for generations, they needed to build a tower on the hill to suppress the phoenix. Actually, the Taoist priest's suggestion to retain the phoenix by building a tower was aimed to poke the phoenix's wing so as to achieve the purpose of revenge.

Qingxiu Mountain is located at the river bank of Yongjiang River, which is one of the ten great landscapes of Nanning. It is a national 5A class scenic spot with beautiful scenery and the reputation of "the giant lung of Nanning". According to *Annals of Nanning Prefecture*, the earliest historical record of Qingxiu Mountain appeared in the Eastern Jin Dynasty. The Dragon-Elephant Tower was built by a government official named Xiao Yunju during the reign of Emperor Wanli in the Ming Dynasty. The name of this tower is originated from the sentence "dragon is the most powerful creature in the water and elephant is the most powerful creature on the land" from the Buddhist Scripture. It can be inferred from the construction history of the tower that the story of Dragon-Elephant Tower can be originated in the reign of Emperor Wanli in the Ming Dynasty. The story gradually spreads in Nanning's surrounding Zhuang and Han settlements with the development of society.

青山龙象塔故事是有关风俗信仰的民间故事，流传于南宁周边地区。故事发源于青秀山，具有一定的神话色彩，记录了当地人民生息繁衍的自然环境以及民族习俗和伦理道德，深受当地人喜爱。

青山龙象塔故事已有400多年的历史，有多个版本流传于世，多与风水信仰有关。故事讲述古时一位外地道士徒步踏山，择地葬祖，寻觅至青山一带，见祥云缭绕，山势犹如一只展翅欲飞的凤凰，便回原籍将父骨运至南宁，投宿于青山脚下肖盛昌家。酒过三巡，道士将此行目的告诉了肖盛昌。当晚，肖盛昌施计将自己父亲的骨骸偷偷换入道士的金坛。次日，一家人与道士将金坛埋葬在青山凤凰岭上。此后，肖家发迹，道士则家道中落，穷困潦倒。多年后，道士得知真相，便再次来到南宁，告知肖盛昌凤凰岭上的凤凰会飞，需做法事留住凤凰才能保肖家代代做官，并建议肖家在青秀山凤翅岭上建造宝塔镇压凤凰。道士以建塔留凤为名，实则设钉戳凤，以达到报复肖家的目的。

青秀山位于邕江江畔，是南宁十大景观之一，国家5A级景区，景色宜人，有“南宁市巨肺”的美称。据《南宁府志》记载，关于青秀山的史料最早出现于东晋时期。龙象塔始建于明万历年间，由时任吏部左侍郎的南宁籍进士肖云举所建，因佛经“水行龙力大，陆行象力大”而得名。从龙象塔建造的历史可以推断，青山龙象塔故事产生于明代万历年间，随着社会的进步发展，故事逐渐流传至南宁周边壮、汉民族聚居地。

青山龙象塔故事记录了骆越先民长期以来生息繁衍的自然环境、人文环境以及历史变迁、民族习俗、伦理道德等，反映出壮、汉民族的价值观念和思维方式，集中体现了南宁周边地区的民族文化与地域文化，为了解和研究南宁及周边地区的历史提供了珍贵的资料。青山被认为是“龙脉”的象征，龙象塔因传说故事被赋予了深刻的文化内涵。故事将人物神仙化，情节玄幻，具有传奇色彩，引人入胜。故事内容虽围绕风水信仰展开，却更多地反映了当地民众对风水信仰的怀疑与否定，并蕴含了惩恶扬善的朴素观念，进而升华出追求仁爱和谐的思想意义，具有一定的教育功能，为后人进行艺术创作提供了文学素材。

在《南宁史志》等史料中，只记载了龙象塔建塔历史，对其背后的故事鲜有记载，因此，青山龙象塔这一口头文学的传承需加大力度。2010年，南宁市委宣传部、市文联对青秀山民间故事进行收集整理，2011年编辑并出版了《青秀山的传说》。2004年，南宁市粤剧团根据青山龙象塔故事创编大型神话粤剧《龙象塔奇缘》，于2013年赴新加坡演出，进一步推动了龙象塔故事的传承。2018年，青山龙象塔故事与流米洞故事合并列入第七批自治区级非物质文化遗产名录。

粤剧《龙象塔奇缘》
Yueju Opera *Romance of Dragon-Elephant Tower*

Qingshan's story of Dragon-Elephant Tower records the natural environment, humane environment, historical changes, ethnic customs and ethics of Luoyue ancients who lived here for a long time. It reflects the value orientation and thinking mode of Zhuang and Han nationalities, collectively representing the national and regional culture of Nanning and its surrounding areas, which provides valuable information to understand and study the history and culture here. Mount Qingxiu is regarded as the symbol of "dragon vein" and the legend of the tower has been endowed with profound cultural connotation. The story deifies the characters and plots with legendary atmosphere, which is very fascinating. Although the story is about geomancy, it reflects more about the local's suspicion and denial toward geomancy and contains the simple concept of protecting the good and fighting against the evil. This story further sublimes people's pursuit of love and harmony, which can not only educate people, but also provide literary material for later generations to carry out artistic creation.

In the historical materials such as *Historical Record of Nanning*, in addition to the construction history of Dragon-Elephant Tower, there are few records about the stories of it. Therefore, the inheritance of this oral literature needs to be strengthened. In 2010, the Publicity Department of Nanning Municipal Committee of CPC and The Federation of Literary and Art Circles collected and sorted out the folk stories of Qingxiu Mountain, and edited and published the book *The Legends of Qingxiu Mountain* in 2011. In 2004, Nanning Cantonese Opera Troupe created a large-scale mythological Cantonese opera *Romance of Dragon-Elephant Tower* based on the story. In 2013, the troupe performed the opera in Singapore, further promoting the inheritance of the story of Dragon-Elephant Tower. In 2018, Qingshan's Story of Dragon-Elephant Tower and the Story of Running Rice Cave were merged into the Seventh Autonomous Reigon List of Intangible Cultural Heritage.

龙象塔
Dragon-Elephant Tower

壮族特掘传说

The Legend of Tejue of Zhuang Ethnic Group

项目名称：壮族特掘传说

别称：无

分布范围：武鸣区、上林县、马山县、宾阳县等

入选名录：2018年第七批自治区级非物质文化遗产名录

2017年第七批市级非物质文化遗产名录

保护单位：武鸣区文化馆

代表性传承人：陆祖汉

Element name：The Legend of Tejue of Zhuang Ethnic Group

Alternative name：None

Geographical location and range：Wuming District, Shanglin County, Mashan County, Binyang County and others

Element inscribed list：In 2018 on the Seventh Autonomous Region List of Intangible Cultural Heritage

In 2017 on the Seventh Municipal List of Intangible Cultural Heritage

Competent body involved in safeguarding：Wuming District Cultural Centre

Representative inheritor：Lu Zuhan

特掘传说是流传于南宁市武鸣区壮族聚居地的民间神话传说。“特掘”指从蛇化身而来的秃尾龙，传说以“三月三，龙拜山”为主要内容，属于龙母文化的一部分，并与环大明地区壮族人忌讳吃蛇、杀蛇等民俗相关，距今已有千年的历史。

特掘传说讲述一个叫“娅迈”（壮语意为寡妇）的妇女在野外捡到一条小蛇，将其带回家中喂养。小蛇逐渐长大，由于茅棚装不下它了，娅迈只好将它的尾巴砍掉一截。壮语把秃尾巴称作“掘”，于是她给小蛇取名“特掘”。人们按照壮族的习惯把娅迈叫作“乜掘”（“乜”在壮语里意为母亲）。娅迈死后，狂风大作，雷雨交加，一条金光闪闪的巨龙昂头摆尾，凌空而下，把“乜掘”抬到大明山安葬。每年三月三前后，特掘都会上大明山为“乜掘”扫墓。特掘扫墓之时，大明山地区风雨大作，电闪雷鸣。风雨过后，连绵的大明山脉瀑布飞泻而下，这是特掘为母亲高悬的白色挽幛；瀑布奔流的轰鸣声，是特掘在为祭奠养母举行闹龙殿的仪式。

特掘传说主要流传于环广西大明山地区的武鸣、上林、马山、宾阳等县、区，其中武鸣的两江、马头、罗波、陆斡等镇为核心区域。专家认为武鸣马头一带是骆越方国的古都，壮族人信仰的图腾就是特掘龙的化身。特掘传说历史久远，《武缘县图经》载有“武缘水即古骆越水”“大明山庙在县东八十里，八月十五日祭；龙母庙，县境乡村多有之，祀秦女龙母温夫人……”。许多特掘、龙母故事都和真实的地名相联系，如大明山上有“莫乜堀”山，即龙母坟山；罗波潭在清代被称作龙窟，即掘尾龙的龙宫。1966年至1976年，特掘传说的传承遭到破坏，故事被禁讲、禁唱、禁演，龙母村的龙母庙、罗波庙等庙宇均被拆除。1978年后，特掘传说虽得以恢复传承，但很快又受到现代文化的冲击，出现生存危机。

The legend of Tejue is a folk tale spreading in the settlement of Zhuang Ethnic Group in Wuming District. “Tejue” refers to the bald-tailed dragon incarnated from the snake. With a history of thousands of years, the legend is based on “the dragon visiting its mother’s grave on the 3rd day of the 3rd lunar month”, which is a part of the Dragon Mother culture and related to the customs of the Zhuang people living near Daming Mountain, such as the taboo of eating and killing snakes.

The legend of Tejue tells a story of a woman named “Yamai” (means widow in Zhuang language) who found a small snake in the wild and brought it home to feed up. As the small snake growing up, it became so big that the cottage could not shield it, thus Yamai had no choice but to cut off a piece of its tail. In Zhuang language, an animal without tail is often called “jue”. Therefore, Yamai gave a name to the small snake “Tejue”. According to the Zhuang custom, people began to call Yamai “Niejue” (“Nie” means mother in Zhuang language). After Yamai’s death, the heavy gale began to blow with storms accompanied by peals of thunder. Suddenly, a golden dragon dived from the high air and buried “Niejue” in Daming Mountain. Around the 3rd day of the 3rd lunar month every year, Tejue would come to Daming Mountain to commemorate “Niejue”. At this time, the storm would burst in all its fury with lightning and thunder. After the storm, water would cascade everywhere from the high mountain, just like large white elegiac scroll hung by Tejue for its foster mother. The roaring sound of the waterfall symbolized the ceremony to commemorate “Niejue”.

The legend of Tejue is spread in districts and counties like Wuming, Shanglin, Mashan, Binyang and so on, with towns in Wuming District like Liangjiang, Matou, Luobo and Luwo as the core areas. Some experts believe that Matou area in Wuming District was the capital of Luoyue city-state in the history and the totem of the Zhuang people was the incarnation of the dragon Tejue. The legend of Tejue has a long history. The book *Records and Maps of Wuyuan County* contains the words “the water of Wuyuan is the water of the ancient Luoyue”, and “the temple of Daming Mountain is located 40 kilometers east of the county, offering sacrifice on the 15th day of the 8th lunar month; Longmu Temples are often seen in villages of the county, offering sacrifice to Dragon Mother, Madam Wen…” Many stories of Tejue and Dragon Mother are related to real place names, such as Momiejue Hill on Daming Mountain, also named “Mountain of Dragon Mother’s Grave”. Luobo Pond once was named Dragon Cave in the Qing Dynasty, that is, the palace of the bald-tailed dragon. From 1966 to 1976, the inheritance of the legend was destroyed. Stories were forbidden to be told, sung or performed. The Temple of Mother Dragon and Luobo Temple in Longmu Village were demolished. After 1978, the legend of Tejue resumed its inheritance, but it is soon suffered the impact of modern culture, confronting a new round of crisis.

The legend of Tejue distinctly represents the traditional culture of the Zhuang Ethnic Group, It reflects the belief and value orientation of Zhuang people and bears special value of anthropology, ethnology and folklore research, which has attracted the attention of academic circles at home and abroad. The legend of Tejue is originated from Zhuang areas and is deeply rooted in people's heart, which is rich in both local and ethnic characteristics with precious folk literature value. The holding of sacrificial activities and folk song fairs plays a positive role in promoting national unity. The "kind mother and filial son" is the core of the legend. On this basis, the plot keeps bringing forth the fresh and the whole legend represents a vigorous situation. At present, the legend of Tejue has been widely known in Daming Mountain area, Pearl River basin and even the whole country and the Southeast Asia. Due to its longtime and wide spread, the legend has been continuously influenced by regional cultures and has gradually acquired various cultural accumulation, becoming a living fossil of national culture with multiple spiritual connotations.

Influenced by the trend of global economic integration, the young generation is keen to pursue fashion, and their enthusiasm to inherit ancient legends is fading, which leads to a big crisis of the legend inheritance. The government of Wuming District has carried out a comprehensive investigation. In 2018, The Legend of Tejue was inscribed on the Seventh Autonomous Reigon List of Intangible Cultural Heritage. In the future, the legend will be paid more attention by relevant departments and better developed and inherited.

特掘传说突出表现了壮族传统文化，体现了壮族人的信仰和价值取向，具有人类学、民族学、民俗学研究的特殊价值，已受到国内外学界关注。特掘传说产生于壮族地区，并深深扎根于民间，富有地方特色和民族特色，具有极其珍贵的民间文学价值，其流传区域内举办的祭祀活动、歌圩活动等对促进民族团结起到一定作用。"母慈子孝"是特掘传说的核心内容，在此基础上情节不断出新，整个传说故事呈现生机蓬勃的状态。目前，特掘传说在环广西大明山地区、珠江流域乃至全国和东南亚都有流传，可谓家喻户晓、老幼皆知。长期广泛的流传，使特掘传说不断地受地域文化影响，逐渐具备多方面的文化积淀，成为具有多重精神内涵的民族文化的活化石。

受当代全球经济一体化思潮的影响，年青的一代热衷于追求时尚潮流，特掘传说的传承面临巨大危机，武鸣区政府已经开展全方位的调查工作。2018年，特掘传说列入第七批自治区级非物质文化遗产名录。今后，特掘传说将受到有关部门重视，得到更好的发展传承。

良庆壮族嘹啰山歌

Liangqing's Liaoluo Folk Song of Zhuang Ethnic Group

项目名称：良庆壮族嘹啰山歌

别称：无

分布范围：良庆区、邕宁区等

入选名录：2014年第五批自治区级非物质文化遗产名录
2013年第五批市级非物质文化遗产名录

保护单位：良庆区文化馆

代表性传承人：无

Element name: Liangqing's Liaoluo Folk Song of Zhuang Ethnic Group

Alternative name: None

Geographical location and range: Liangqing District, Yongning District and others

Element inscribed list: In 2014 on the Fifth Autonomous Region List of Intangible Cultural Heritage
In 2013 on the Fifth Municipal List of Intangible Cultural Heritage

Competent body involved in safeguarding: Liangqing District Cultural Centre

Representative inheritor: None

Liangqing's Liaoluo folk song of Zhuang Ethnic Group is popular among Liangqing, Yongning districts of Nanning City, and it originated from Zhuang-inhabited villages in Liangqing where there once prevailed a custom of throwing a hen and selecting husband. Specifically, it mainly circulates among 5 towns in Liangqing District, such as Liangqing, Nama, Datang, Nachen and Nanxiao.

Generations of Zhuang Ethnic Group settle in Liangqing, a fascinating district with a long history and profound civilization. Just as a geographical masterpiece *Ling Wai Dai Da* (by Zhou Qufei, Southern Song Dynasty) recorded "Most people in Guangxi, no matter citizens or countrymen, can hum tunes. They hum for sacrifice, for marriage, for funeral, for laboring in farmland and... you name it." Even today, the custom of singing folk songs is still remained by the locals. Another custom having an affinity with singing folk songs is throwing hens and selecting husband. As it implies, a girl finds her Mr. Right by throwing a hen like throwing an embroidery ball (a Chinese traditional custom that helps ancient girls to find their husbands), the fellow who grabs the ball will be her husband. In this process, candidates will scramble to catch the precious "love token", and will attract the girl's attention by shouting, "Liaoluo... Liaoluo" (meaning "see me" and "enjoy it"). As time goes on, such shouting of "liaoluo" had been fixed down to be a custom that performed before folk singing, and such song is called Liaoluo folk song.

As the content of the folk songs covers a wide range including love, friendship, and ties of kinship, it is a key way for Zhuang people to disclose love and entertain friends. It is a two-part folk song with a beautiful melody, which is sung by two or more people, and lining words like "Liao" "Luo" will be used in the beginning, middle and end of songs. Liaoluo folk song, is also called "Jia" in Zhuang language, which is echoed by many melodies' name including Jianuo, Jiaquqiao, Jiayiai, Jiate, Jiahuale. Most of the lyrics are in the form of "four or three" with seven words and four sentences. In addition, accompanied by the Liaoluo folk songs are all kinds of concerts, which are generally produced on the basis of visiting relatives and friends between different villages. According to statistics, there are 437 concerts in Liangqing District alone, of which the "Qiusi Song Fair" is the most typical one.

As a distinctive art of high value, Liaoluo folk song is supposedly a dynamic epic of Zhuang Ethnic Group, since it not only records the time-honored history and culture, but also reflects all aspects of their life. As we can see, singing folk songs can both meet the need of a better cultural life and

良庆壮族嘹啰山歌是流传于广西南宁市良庆区、邕宁区等地壮族民间的一种歌谣，源自良庆区壮族村寨曾经流行的一种抛鸡选婿风俗。嘹啰山歌在良庆及其周边地区广为流传，其中良庆区所辖的良庆镇、那马镇、大塘镇、那陈镇、南晓镇这5个乡镇是这种山歌最主要的流传区域。

南宁市良庆区是一个壮族先民世代聚居、具有悠久历史和深厚文化底蕴的城区，南宋周去非《岭外代答》记载："广西诸郡，人多能合乐，城郊村落，祭祀婚嫁喜葬，无不用乐，虽耕田亦必口乐相之。"直至今日，当地的壮族人民也一直保持着唱山歌的习俗。据说，良庆壮族嘹啰山歌与当地村落曾经流行的一种抛鸡选婿的风俗有关。抛鸡选婿，顾名思义就是女子把鸡当作绣球抛向人群，抢到者即为如意郎君。每逢此时，待选的后生们都争先恐后地想要抓到那个珍贵的"爱情信物"，他们高呼"嘹啰""嘹啰"（壮话"嘹"，汉语为"看""笑"，"嘹啰"意为"看啊""笑啊"），以此来吸引女孩子的注意。这种在热闹欢腾的气氛中伴随着"嘹啰"二字起头的演唱形式，后逐渐固定下来形成了良庆壮族嘹啰山歌。

良庆壮族嘹啰山歌是壮族民众"以歌传情、以歌会友"的主要方式，它所表达的内容十分丰富，爱情、亲情、友情等都是其歌咏和传唱的素材。它曲调优美，以"嘹啰"开唱，是一种二声部山歌，一般为两人或多人对唱，在歌唱时，首、中、尾部都出现"嘹"与"啰"的衬词。当地壮话中嘹啰山歌叫"加"，其曲调主要有"加喏""加曲巧""加衣嗳""加特""加华乐"等，歌词多为七言四句的"四三"格式。此外，与嘹啰山歌相伴而生的是各种歌会，这种歌会一般是在不同村落之间访亲会友的基础上产生的，据统计，仅良庆区就有歌会437个，其中以"毬丝歌会"最为典型。

作为一种形态独特、艺术价值颇高的艺术形式，嘹啰山

嘹啰山歌歌谱
Music Score of Liaoluo Folk Song of Zhuang Ethnic Group

歌不仅记录了壮族悠久的历史文化，也反映了壮族人民生产生活的方方面面，可以称得上是一部动态的壮族历史文献。唱山歌对于壮族人民来说不仅是精神文化生活的需要，更是一种情感表达的寄托。

良庆壮族嘹啰山歌作为地方民族传统文化之一，得到了地方有关部门的重视。据统计，全城区有嘹啰山歌基地10个，嘹啰山歌协会1个，嘹啰山歌歌队50多支，嘹啰山歌歌手1万多人，是南宁民间歌队最多的城区之一。之后，文艺培训实习基地、嘹啰山歌合唱团、山歌协会相继成立，让“中国嘹啰山歌之乡”的歌声唱得更响、传得更远。2014年，良庆壮族嘹啰山歌经广西壮族自治区人民政府同意，列入第五批自治区级非物质文化遗产名录。

bridge the gap of interrelationship for Zhuang people.

Liangqing's Liaoluo folk song of Zhuang Ethnic Group, as one part of the traditional culture of Nanning, has got addressed by the local authorities. According to statistics, there are 10 bases,1 association, more than 50 teams, and more than 10,000 folk singers promoting Liaoluo folk songs in Liangqing district which holds the biggest number of folk singers among Nanning. And these songs were brought further by the establishment of the practice base of literary and artistic training, the chorus of Liaoluo folk Song and the Folk Song Association. In 2014, Liangqing's Liaoluo Folk Song of Zhuang Ethnic Group was inscribed on the Fifth Autonomous Region List of Intangible Cultural Heritage after the approval of People's Government of Guangxi Zhuang Autonomous Region.

隆安壮族排歌

Long'an Pai Song of Zhuang Ethnic Group

项目名称：隆安壮族排歌

别称：潘

分布范围：隆安县都结乡、布泉乡、城厢镇、那桐镇、乔建镇、丁当镇等

入选名录：2012年第四批自治区级非物质文化遗产名录

2011年第四批市级非物质文化遗产名录

保护单位：隆安县文化馆

代表性传承人：陆金席

Element name: Long'an Pai Song of Zhuang Ethnic Group

Alternative name: Pan

Geographical location and range: Dujie Town, Buquan Town, Chengxiang Town, Natong Town, Qiaojian Town, Dingdang Town and others of Long'an County

Element inscribed list: In 2012 on the Fourth Autonomous Region List of Intangible Cultural Heritage

In 2011 on the Fourth Municipal List of Intangible Cultural Heritage

Competent body involved in safeguarding: Long'an County Cultural Centre

Representative inheritor: Lu Jinxi

排歌是壮族山歌的一种，属于民间音乐的范畴。在当地，隆安壮族排歌被称为“潘”，分为高腔排歌和低腔排歌，主要分布在隆安县的都结乡、布泉乡、城厢镇、那桐镇、乔建镇、丁当镇等壮族聚居区。自古以来，隆安人民以排歌吟唱生产生活，并以此来抒发内心情感、歌唱祖国山河、赞颂田园风光，同时也用来贺喜悼亡、祭祀神灵等。

隆安壮族排歌“潘”的产生和发展历史久远。根据相关研究与骆越文化历史证明，隆安是壮族稻作文化的发祥地之一，近年来在此出土的大石铲也可以充分证实这一点，由此可见，隆安的传统文化根基深厚，而根植于隆安地区传统文化的隆安壮族排歌具体起源于何时，已无详细的史料记载。另据有关史料记载，分布于武鸣、隆安等地的壮族歌圩在明清时期是最为兴盛的，明代邝露在《赤雅》中就记载了壮族歌圩的动人景象。隆安县广大壮族地区自古以来就是歌舞之乡，盛行歌圩活动，人们纷纷在歌圩上传唱“潘”，使其不断继承发展、流传至今。

作为一项历史悠久的民族文化，隆安壮族排歌在民族民间音乐中独具特色。由农耕文化衍生的隆安壮族排歌，直接

Paige, one of folk songs of Zhuang Ethnic Group, is mainly sung among Zhuang-inhabited areas of Dujie, Buquan Townships; Chengxiang, Natong, Qiaojian, and Dingdang Towns of Long'an County. The locals call the song "Pan" either, which is divided into types of Paige with high pitch and Paige with low pitch. By singing, ancient Zhuang people record what they saw and heard in daily life, such as celebrating, mourning and worshipping, and pour their passion for magnificent land and rural scene.

Paige, or Pan, is boasting of its time-honored history. According to some studies and the development of Luoyue Culture, Long'an is one of the birthplaces of a rice-cultivating culture of Zhuang Ethnic Group, which can be fully proved by stone shovel unearthed recently. Traditional culture of Long'an does have a profound accumulation, as it mentioned above, but there is no detailed historical materials help us trace the original time of the Paige, which deeply rooting on Long'an culture. Nevertheless, it is inferred from some records that the blossom time of folk song fair (people gather together to sing folk songs on festivals) is in the Ming and Qing dynasties. For example, Kuang Lu (Ming Dynasty) described a stirring folk song fair in his book *Chi Ya*. As a heaven of songs and dances, Zhuang-inhabited areas in Long'an have been supporting folk song fair where people give performances of Pan, so as to promote the development and inheritance of Pan Culture.

The Paige folk song formed its unique traits throughout the course of its long history. As a derivative culture of cultivation civilization, it is of high study value because what

歌手林碧与女歌手共同演绎排歌
Lin Bi, An Singer is Singing Pai Song with a Female Singer

it reflects includes productive practices, local customs, love and marriage and daily trivialities. In addition, every Pai folk song narratives a rough story, as if it were an exquisite and touching literature that reanimate the locals' cultural life. Pan, with abundant content and diversified expression, has been an excellent folk art form shining in front of the world.

The folk songs encountered great obstacles caused by modern culture; as a consequence, its impartment was much hindered in its declining trend. In order to improve the situation, an editorial board called Santao Jicheng compiled few works of folk literature under the aegis of the authorities of Long'an County, such as *the Collection of Long'an Folk Ballads* and *the Collection of Long'an Folk Stories*. The efforts they took were paid off, a lot of intangible cultural heritages, including Paige folk songs have been rescued in time. In September 2007, the Long'an County Cultural Centre reconducted a general survey of folk cultures and took more efforts to protect them. At the same time, the government made a decision to place the Paige folk songs into the list of intangible cultural heritage of county level. In 2012, Long'an Paige of Zhuang Ethnic Group was inscribed on the Fouth Autonomous Region List of Intangible Cultural Heritage.

反映出了一个民族的劳动生产、风土人情、爱情婚姻以及日常生活等，具有很高的研究价值。此外，隆安壮族排歌属于叙事山歌，每一首排歌都有一个相对完整的故事情节，一首首排歌犹如一部部细腻动人的文学作品，生动形象地反映了当地的社会文化生活。内容丰富、多姿多彩的隆安县壮话排歌“潘”，已然成为一种优秀的民间艺术形式，闪亮地展现在世人面前。

随着现代文化对民间传统文化的严重冲击，排歌有着逐渐衰落的趋势，其传承受到阻碍。因此，1987年，在县委、县政府的支持下，隆安县民间“三套集成”编委会编撰了《隆安民间歌谣集》《隆安县民间故事集》等，阶段性地抢救了包括排歌在内的一大批非物质文化遗产。2007年9月，隆安县文化馆对包括排歌在内的民间传统文化再次进行普查并挖掘保护。同时县政府做出决定，明确把排歌列入县级非物质文化遗产名录进行保护。2012年，隆安壮族排歌列入第四批自治区级非物质文化遗产名录。

隆安排歌演出现场
Performance of Long'an Paige Song

上林瑶族山歌

Shanglin's Folk Song of Yao Ethnic Group

项目名称：上林瑶族山歌

别称：无

分布范围：上林县镇圩瑶族乡等

入选名录：2012年第四批自治区级非物质文化遗产名录

保护单位：上林县文化馆

代表性传承人：卢成

Element name: Shanglin's Folk Song of Yao Ethnic Group

Alternative name: None

Geographical location and range: Zhenxu Town of Yao Ethnic Group in Shanglin County and others

Element inscribed list: In 2012 on the Fourth Autonomous Region List of Intangible Cultural Heritage

Competent body involved in safeguarding: Shanglin County Cultural Centre

Representative inheritor: Lu Cheng

As a blossom dazzling on the branch of the Ethnic Group music in China, Shanglin's folk song of Yao Ethnic Group has been one of the representatives of Yao culture, because it sounds resonant and clear, sweet and agreeable, fine and smooth. In ancient times, a visitor who called on a Yao-inhabited village, would knock three times on the bamboo tube placed in the col at the village entrance, which would then be echoed by the-chief-of-the-village' ox horn, then all villagers would sing to extend their welcome. Besides, folk songs occupy in every aspect of their life, such as productive practices and folk life (such as marriage and funeral, sacrifice, migration and festivals). They actually express how they feel and what they aspire in such a special way.

Yao people have been famous for their talent to compose and sing songs that eulogize history, reflect daily life and changes of social psychology. According to *A New Encyclopedia of Guangdong* (by Qu Dajun, Qing Dynasty) "folk songs are popular among Yao people, men and women gathering get all ready to sing with a leading singer at any moment", we can see clearly how popular folk songs could be. In addition, Yao in Shanglin, with Yao in neighboring counties including Dahua, Bama and Du'an, belongs to Bunu Yao, which is the second biggest branch after Pan Yao. And the first four prominent family names of Yao in Shanglin are Lan, Meng, Luo and Wei. From oral information and family trees of the locals, we learned that Shanglin's Yao Ethnic Group with its songs has existed for more than 300 years.

Shanglin's folk songs have been fixed with recognized tunes and accepted lyrics, thanks for the transmission and improvement of generations of Yao people. The sentences in songs have never been restricted, longer one or shorter one, whatever. As for the content of the songs, it is all-encompassing from the rules of the universe to trivial matters in the mundane. In terms of tunes, they are full of ethnic flavor and moving blend of undecorated features and aesthetic feeling, granting the songs a magic power to express happiness and sorrows. Besides, these tunes have a strong national and local color, both simple and artistic beauty. At the same time, many of Shanglin Yao folk songs are featured by their lining words, and *the Song of Liquor* is one of the best examples.

Shanlin's folk songs of Yao Ethnic Group are passed down oraly from generation to generation, recording and preserving the scenes of Yao people's life and promotion, such as marriage and funeral, welcome, sacrifice, migration, etc. The folk songs are not only precious materials for studying folk customs and cultures, but also the essence of Yao culture of Guangxi, as they are handed down for ages and sung for

上林瑶族山歌是我国少数民族音乐中一朵艳丽的奇葩，因其演唱风格高亢嘹亮、委婉流畅、细腻优美而深入人心，成为瑶族文化的代表之一。自古瑶寨如有到访的客人，必在寨口山坳处摆放的竹筒上敲打三声，寨主听到竹筒声后便吹起牛角以回应，并召集乡亲唱着山歌欢迎客人的到来。除了迎客仪式，在生产劳动、民俗生活（如婚丧、祭祀、迁徙、节庆等活动）中，瑶族儿女都会借歌抒情、以歌言志，用这样一种独特的形式来表达自己的心声与情感。

瑶族人民一直都以能编善唱著称，他们以歌来传颂本民族的悠久历史，反映他们的生活状况，记录他们的情感变迁。清朝屈大均在《广东新语》中记载："瑶俗最尚歌，男女杂沓，一唱百和"，由此可以看出瑶族山歌传唱之盛况。此外，上林瑶族与邻近的大化、巴马、都安的瑶族同属布努瑶支系，是瑶族众多支系中仅次于盘瑶的第二大支系。如今居住在上林县境内的瑶族主要有四大姓，即蓝、蒙、罗、韦，根据当地人口述及家藏的谱系计算，瑶族和瑶族山歌在上林县已有300多年的历史。

经过瑶族人民的传唱、加工和完善之后，如今的上林瑶族山歌已经成为具有固定曲谱、随文可唱、词韵合拍的民间音乐。上林瑶族山歌在句式上以长短句为主，体例自由，没有固定的章法。传唱内容上至天文地理，下至凡人琐事，几乎无所不包。从曲调上看，上林瑶族山歌十分擅长用曲调来诠释人们的各种心情，喜、怒、哀、乐都能展现得贴切而又富有感染力。此外，这些曲调都具有浓厚的民族性和地方性色彩，既有质朴之感，又兼具艺术之美。同时，上林瑶族山歌的许多歌谣都以其衬词而得名，《酒歌》就是明显的例子。

上林瑶族山歌是由祖辈代代口头传承下来的，记录、保存了上林瑶家儿女婚丧、迎宾、祭祀、迁徙等生活和生产劳动的情景，是研究上林瑶族生活习俗、劳动生产以及民间文

齐唱瑶族山歌
Singing Folk Song of Yao Ethnic Group Together

化的珍贵史料，也是广西瑶族文化之精华。挖掘和保护上林瑶族山歌，对研究瑶族文化和推动民族地区文化发展都具有深远的意义。

如今，在日益丰富的现当代文化冲击下，上林瑶族山歌遭受冷落。愿意拜师学唱瑶族山歌的人越来越少，瑶族老艺人也相继离世，会唱、会教学徒唱瑶族山歌的人屈指可数，上林瑶族山歌的传承面临后继乏人的困境。对此，上林县委、县政府委派文化馆负责该项目的管理与保护工作，并派专门人员开展对瑶族山歌的收集、整理工作，进一步建立、健全上林瑶族山歌项目资料和档案，不断加大对该项目的保护力度。上林镇圩乡政府组织镇马剧团筹办上林瑶族山歌专场演出，并重视利用上林山歌开展民族文化交流工作。同时，《瑶山歌》还唱出了国门，分别在马来西亚和泰国中央中文台播出，使得上林瑶族山歌能够继续传承和发展。2012年，广西壮族自治区人民政府将上林瑶族山歌列入第四批自治区级非物质文化遗产名录。

every aspect of their life. More exploration and protection for these folk songs is of great significance to study Yao culture and promote cultural development in ethnic group areas.

Under the impact of ever-growing modern culture, the folk songs seem to face a gloomy future. Fewer and fewer people are willing to learn these folk songs, and the successive death of sophisticated artists causes few people can teach folk songs, all these got the inheritance of the songs into trouble. To address this challenge, authorities of Shanglin County took in charge of the protection of these songs by collecting and rearranging songs, establishing and improving relevant data files. The township government organized a special performance of the folk songs showed by Zhenma Troupe; it also paid great attention to uphold ethnic cultural exchanges by promoting the folk songs. Meanwhile, *The Folk Song of Yao* was brought further, once performed on the Central Chinese Radio of Malaysia and Thailand. In 2012, the government of Guangxi Autonomous Region approved Shanglin Yao folk songs to be inscribed on the Fourth Autonomous Region List of Intangible Cultural Heritage.

上林四六联民歌

Shanglin's Siliulian Folk Song

项目名称：上林四六联民歌

别称：无

分布范围：上林县各乡镇

入选名录：2012年第四批自治区级非物质文化遗产名录

保护单位：上林县文化馆

代表性继承人：无

Element name: Shanglin's Siliulian Folk Song

Alternative name: None

Geographical location and range: Towns of Shanglin County

Element inscribed list: In 2012 on the Fourth Autonomous Region List of Intangible Cultural Heritage

Competent body involved in safeguarding: Shanglin County Cultural Centre

Representative inheritor: None

四六联在万寿节中表演
Siliulian Folk Songs Performed in Longevity Festival

上林四六联民歌是流传于上林县各乡镇的壮族民歌，是壮族先民在壮族民歌的基础上吸收中原文化、借鉴魏晋南北朝的骈赋文体创作出的一种民歌样式。

上林是壮族集居之地，生活于此的壮族先民能歌善舞、淳朴厚道、好客好学，尤其善于吸收外民族特别是汉民族的文化精华。在历史上汉人先后几次向壮族地区迁移，汉族的商贾也随之来到此地，尤其是唐武德四年（621）置上林县，隶南方州，京官、州官、学者也常到县地巡查，无形中促进了各种文化的交流。当楚辞汉赋以及魏晋南北朝的骈赋传播到上林时，聪明好学的壮族先民便将其中优美的四六、

Shanglin's Siliulian folk song is popular among Zhuang people living in towns of Shanglin County. Originating from primitive Zhuang songs, it was recreated by the ancestors of Zhuang people by absorbing the culture of central China and drawing on the style of poems prevailed in Wei-Jin and the Southern and Northern dynasties, which characterized by parallelism and ornateness.

Zhuang people are concentrated in Shanglin where the ancient Zhuang is famous for their kind, honest, and hospitable characters. They are also good singers, dancers and learners for absorbing external cultures, particularly Han culture. Actually, Han people migrated to the Zhuang-inhabited areas several times, among which one worth mentioning is the migration in the years of Wude. In the fourth year of Wude in Tang Dynasty (621), Shanglin County was set up, governing Nanfang Zhou. Since then a growing number of people, including capital officials, provincial officials and scholars, swarmed into Shanglin and unexpectedly promote culture exchanges. When ancient Zhuang learned Han literature including songs of Chu, essays of Han, and poems in Wei-Jin and the Southern and Northern Dynasties, they appreciated sentences of Siliu and Siqi style and creatively applied them into folk songs. With continuous improvement and innovation, Shanglin Siliulian folk songs whose middle part and end part are in rhyme came into being.

A precious Siliulian folk song, the *Liuhe Strong Mansion Monument* [be founded in the first year of Yongchun, Tang Dynasty (682)], can still be found craved on a stale by Qingshui river in Chengtai township:

"Oppressive tax makes us have food without ploughing"

"We have many fine woods even the best wood from Zhongnan Mountain"

"Wealth pouring like spring which is the grace of the fading descendants"

"I shall use brief words to express my gratitude to our ancestors"

This is one of the precious inscriptions recording the form of Shanglin Siliulian Folk Songs in Shanglin County. It truly reflects the popularity and development of the folk songs in Shanglin Zhuang Ethnic Group area during the Tang Dynasty. There was no written language in ancient Zhuang Ethnic Group, so many beautiful folk songs were spread and popular by oral and heart teaching, and few folk songs were recorded in written form. Restricted by this mode of transmission, the number of the folk songs handed down is far less than that of the past, which shows the value of *Liuhe Strong Mansion Monument*.

What the folk songs talk about actually stemmed from people's productive practices and daily life. For example, people's inner feelings and fleeting musings were poured into songs, through which they convey their passion for magnificent mountains and rivers; or tranquil rural scene. Besides, the songs can also be written for offering sacrifice, entertaining friends, celebrating wedding and uncovering crimes and so on. The songs have the following characteristics: Firstly, they are recorded by Han characters while sung in Zhuang language. Secondly, they are composed by recognized tunes. In addition, sentences in songs are made of lines of four-words or six-words. The third characteristic is that there are four characters in the first part of one line and six in

四七句式吸收过来，融进丰富多彩的壮族民歌文化中，再经过不断的创作加工，形成了腰尾互韵的上林四六联民歌。

在澄泰乡清水河畔的唐《六合坚固大宅颂碑》[唐永淳元年（682）立]上，就刻有珍贵的四六联民歌：

回波所利，不耕□获之□；

和之所多，未乏南山之有。

若地之流，……祚者欤？！

卿达短辞，用申之曲云尔。

这是上林县境内记载四六联民歌形式的珍贵碑刻之一，它真实地反映了唐朝时四六联民歌在上林壮族地区的流行发展情况。古代壮族没有文字，因此许许多多优美的民歌都是以口传心授的方式传播，很少有以文字形式记载下来的。受这种传播方式的制约，流传下来的四六联民歌在数量上远不如从前，由此可见《六合坚固大宅颂碑》之珍贵。

上林四六联民歌在内容方面多跟人们的生产、生活有关，人们以歌唱的形式表达心中的快乐与苦衷，将情感融入歌曲，伴随着动人的旋律，歌唱祖国山河，赞颂田园风光。除此之外，祭祀神灵、交友传情、联谊求婚、批判丑恶等也都是四六联民歌中能够体现的内容。四六联民歌的特点：一是记以汉字，唱以壮音；二是固定曲谱，随文可唱；三是句式字数为前四后六，四六两句合十，为前半节，符合完满吉数，下半节亦为四六相对，两半节合为一小节，节数多少根据内容而定；四是尾腰共韵，错落优美。上半节首句尾字，即四六联的首句第四字起韵，押第二句，即“六”中的第四字作腰韵；第二句末，即第六字又起韵，押第三句尾字韵，即第四字韵；第三句第四字韵又押第四句第四字腰韵。如此一来，上林四六联民歌整体上庄重悦耳、朗朗上口、韵味无穷。

上林四六联民歌是众多壮族民歌中一种独具特色的艺术形式，同时也是中原文化对少数民族地区社会文化渗透和影响的有力见证，它对于保护、传承壮族丰富多彩的民间文学具有重要意义和价值。为保护和传承上林四六联民歌，上林县政府采取有力措施，加大调研力度，全面系统整理四六联民歌的歌词、曲调，开设歌手文化传习班，进一步推动四六联民歌文化的传承与发展。2012年，上林四六联民歌经广西壮族自治区人民政府同意，列入第四批自治区级非物质文化遗产名录。

the last part. Ten characters in one line is one chapter. Ten characters mean fortunate in traditional culture. Every chapter will have ten characters and the number of characters will be decided by the content of songs. The fourth character is that the end part rhymes of the middle part. The last character of the first line shares the same rhyme as the fourth character of the second line of six words. And the last character (the sixth character of the line) of the second line rhymes with the fourth character (the last character of the line) in the third line, and so on. In this way, the folk songs are full solemn with long-lasting charm and easy to sing.

As a unique branch of folk songs of Zhuang, the Siliulian folk song witnessed how central China culture had infiltrated and influenced ethnic group culture, and it is of enormous significance for protecting and inheriting diversified folk literatures. Accordingly, the government of Shanglin has taken effective measures to promote more studies to collect and rearrange lyrics and tunes. Cultural training courses for folk singers were also set up, so as to bring further the development and impartment of folk songs. In 2012, Shanglin's Siliulian folk song was inscribed on the Fourth Autonomous Region List of Intangible Cultural Heritage, after the approval of People's Government of Guangxi Zhuang Autonomous Region.

第二章　传统音乐

Chapter Two　Traditional Music

壮族三声部民歌

The Folk Song with Three Vocal Parts of Zhuang Ethnic Group

项目名称：壮族三声部民歌

别称：欢哈

分布范围：马山县古零镇、加方乡、古寨乡、里当乡等

入选名录：2008年第二批国家级非物质文化遗产名录
2007年第一批自治区级非物质文化遗产名录
2007年第一批市级非物质文化遗产名录

保护单位：马山县文化馆

代表性传承人：温桂元（已故）、莫花美

Element name：The Folk Song with Three Vocal Parts of Zhuang Ethnic Group

Alternative name：Huan Ha

Geographical location and range：Guling Town, Jiafang Town, Guzhai Town, Lidang Town and others of Mashan County

Element inscribed list：In 2008 on the Second National List of Intangible Cultural Heritage
In 2007 on the First Autonomous Region List of Intangible Cultural Heritage
In 2007 on the First Municipal List of Intangible Cultural Heritage

Competent body involved in safeguarding：Mashan County Cultural Centre

Representative inheritors：Wen Guiyuan (Late), Mo Huamei

2013年8月，马山壮族三声部民歌、壮族打扁担到维也纳参加“2013中国蒲公英维也纳金色大厅夏季音乐会”演出
In August 2013, Mashan Zhuang Folk Songs with Three Vocal Parts and Zhuang People Playing Shoulder Pole Went to Vienna to Participate in the Performance of "2013 China Dandelion Vienna Golden Hall Summer Concert"

壮族三声部民歌起源于广西壮族自治区南宁市马山县的加方乡、古零镇、古寨乡、里当乡以及周边壮族地区，当地壮族群众称其为“欢哈”，意思是“和声山歌”。顾名思义，壮族三声部民歌在演唱时分为三个声部，且声部间相互协调、风格统一。由于产生时间较早、传播地区广泛，因此，壮族三声部民歌被称作壮族民歌的“活化石”。

早在唐朝末年，壮族三声部民歌就在马山县东部的大石山区开始传播，成为人们交流感情、传递信息的重要方式。在劳动生产、婚丧嫁娶、迎神祭祖等活动中，唱山歌是人们主要的娱乐和交流形式，由于一人独唱不足以烘托气氛，于是变为多人附唱，将一声部变为多声部，壮族三声部民歌便由此产生。根据《岭南录异》记载，从唐末开始，随着山歌

The folk song with three vocal parts of Zhuang Ethnic Group originated from Jiafang Town, Guling Town, Guzhai Town and Lidang Town of Mashan County and its surrounding Zhuang areas. This folk song with three vocal parts is called "Huan Ha" by local Zhuang people, which means "singing folk songs together". As the name implies, the folk song of three vocal parts can be divided into three parts when singing. The three parts are coordinated with each other and unified in style. Due to its early appearance and wide spread, the folk song with three vocal parts has been recognized as the "living fossils" of folk songs of Zhuang.

As early as in the late Tang Dynasty, the folk song with three vocal parts began to spread in Dashishan mountain area in the east of Mashan County, becoming an important way for people to exchange feelings and convey information. No matter in activities like labor production, weddings and funerals or ancestor worship, singing folk songs is a main form of entertainment and communication for people. As one person singing alone was not enough to heighten atmosphere, the song was gradually sung by more than one person and the only one vocal part was added to more than one parts, thus the folk song with three vocal parts came into being. According to the *Record of Strange Things in Lingnan* (a note of geography and custom in Lingnan areas), from the late Tang Dynasty, with the popularity of folk songs, the folk song developed from one vocal part to two vocal parts. From the Ming Dynasty, the two vocal parts developed to three vocal parts, and began to spread in Guling Town, Jiafang Town, Guzhai Town, Lidang Town, Jinchai Town and other areas. Then, on this basis, the folk song with three vocal parts of Zhuang Ethnic Group continued to spread to surrounding areas, bringing a great impact on the production and life of the local minorities. According to the legend, in the middle Ming Dynasty, the folk song with three vocal parts was in full flourish in Mashan County. On the third day of the third lunar month in a certain year, people in Mashan County held a party of folk song with three vocal parts at Jinlun Cave. People who participated in the party sang this kind of folk song to make friends and express affection for three days and nights. Huge crowds of people filled inside and outside the cave with the singing rising one after another, which was very bustling. The singing party attracted not only song masters and young men and women from villages in the county, but also many people from other places to participate in it. This grand gathering of folk songs not only achieved the aim to make friends and express affection, but also created a favorable condition for the folk song with three vocal parts of Zhuang people to spread out of the county. Since then, this kind of folk song began to be popular in the surrounding areas of Mashan County.

The songbook of folk song with three vocal parts of Zhuang Ethnic Group is relatively fixed, but it also contains some improvisations according to daily life. Most of these songs reflect the Zhuang people's love and pursuit of a better life in spite of the harsh living condition, which represents Zhuang people's unremitting self-improvement and optimism. In addition, the folk song with three vocal parts of Zhuang Ethnic Group was created on the basis of Zhuang people's social life. Its development process also represents the vicissitudes of production, life, tradition and customs as well as the cultural feature like psychological characteristics and religious beliefs of Zhuang people, which carries information of regional social life and economic development. In singing, Zhuang language, a minority language, integrates with the tunes of folk songs in complete harmony, making the songs rich in connotation and be of great appreciation and study values. At present, this kind of folk song has had a wide range

的盛行，壮族民歌从一声部发展到二声部；明代开始，二声部又变为三声部，并开始在古零镇、加方乡、古寨乡、里当乡、金钗镇等地区传播，随后在此基础上，壮族三声部民歌不断向周围地区传播，并对当地少数民族的生产和生活产生了巨大影响。相传在明代中期，壮族三声部民歌在马山县境内盛极一时。某年的农历三月初三，马山县民众在金伦洞举行壮族三声部民歌歌会，人们以歌会友、以歌传情，连唱三天三夜，洞内洞外人山人海，歌声此起彼伏，热闹非凡。歌会不仅吸引了县内各村寨的歌师以及青年男女，还吸引了不少外地民众前来参赛和观看。这次的山歌盛会，不仅起到了以歌会友、以歌传情的娱乐目的，还为壮族三声部民歌走出县境、传播四方创造了重要条件。此后，壮族三声部民歌便开始在马山周边地区广泛地传播开来。

壮族三声部民歌的演唱歌本有相对固定的，也有根据日常生活即兴创作的，大多是反映壮族人民在恶劣的生存条件下仍然不失对美好生活的热爱与追求，体现了壮族人民自强不息、乐观向上的精神品质。另外，壮族三声部民歌取材于壮族社会生活的方方面面，它的发展历程中处处显示着壮族人民生产生活、风俗习惯等社会变迁，体现了壮族人民的心理特征、宗教信仰等文化特质，承载了区域社会生活、经济发展等信息。在演唱中，壮语这一少数民族语言和山歌的曲调水乳交融，使作品艺术内涵丰富，具有很高的欣赏价值和研究价值。目前，壮族三声部民歌的作品种类繁多，其中主要有：男女新婚时陪娘们所唱的《欢雅娜》、表现孤儿悲苦的《孤儿欢》、歌颂父母恩情及表达儿女孝心的《孝儿欢》，以及用来求子的《花婆欢》。此外，还有《季节欢》《花欢》《送别欢》《迎客欢》等曲目，都收集在《壮族三声部民歌歌集》当中。

1981年，壮族音乐家范西姆在马山县采风时发现了壮族三声部民歌，随后发表了有关壮族三声部民歌的调查报告，在世界音乐界引起不小的轰动，经美国《华侨周报》转载后，壮族三声部民歌更是在国内外引起了广泛的关注。它的发现，推翻了国外某些专家关于“东方少数民族没有多声部民歌”的定论。

但是，随着社会经济的发展，唱山歌的娱乐形式已逐渐被其他丰富多彩的文化娱乐方式取代。三声部民歌的传唱者多为中老年人，年轻人越来越少，保护工作任重而道远。为全面保护这一宝贵遗产，马山县委、县政府采取了积极的保护措施：深入开展普查工作，全面了解壮族三声部民歌的历史和现状，建立相关档案；组织开展新歌曲创作工作，为壮族三声部民歌的传扬提供优秀素材；为充实传承人队伍，在古零镇安善村建立壮族三声部民歌传承基地文化生态保护村，组建壮族三声部民歌专业和业余演唱队伍，并开办壮族三声部民歌业余学校，广泛培养传承人，开展壮族三声部民歌进校园活动，在部分中、小学教授壮族三声部民歌；拨出专款编辑出版壮族三声部民歌音像、文字资料，并创编排练壮族三声部民歌专题歌舞剧目，开展巡回演出活动，积极开展宣传工作。2008年，壮族三声部民歌经国务院批准，列入第二批国家级非物质文化遗产项目名录。

壮族三声部民歌进入校园课堂
The Folk Songs with Three Vocal Parts of Zhuang Ethnic Group Enter the Classroon

of categories, including the song sung by bridesmaids on wedding, *Huan Ya Na*; the song to represent the hardship of orphans, *Song of Orphans*; the song to praise the upbringing of parents and express children's filial piety, *Song of Dutiful Son* and song to pray for newborn, *Song of Huapo*. Besides, folk songs like *Song of Season*, *Song of Flowers*, *Song of Farewell* and *Song of Welcoming* are all collected in the *Collection of Folk Songs with Three Vocal Parts of Zhuang Ethnic Group*.

In 1981, Fan Ximu, a Zhuang musician discovered the folk song with three vocal parts of Zhuang Ethnic Group while collecting folk songs in Mashan County. Then he published the survey report on his discovery, which created much of a stir in music circle. After being reprinted by *Overseas Chinese Weekly*, the folk song with three vocal parts attracted more attention at home and abroad. The discovery overturns the conclusion made by some foreign experts that "oriental minorities do not have multiple-part folk songs".

However, with social and economic development, folk songs have been gradually replaced by other colorful entertainment forms. Most of the singers of the folk song with three vocal parts are middle-aged and old people, with less and less young people to sing it. Therefore, the protection of the folk song of three vocal parts is an arduous task. In order to fully protect this precious heritage, the committee and government of Mashan County have taken the following steps: comprehensively carrying out a survey to understand the history and present situation of the folk song with three vocal parts and building relevant archives; developing new songs to provide excellent material for the spread of folk songs with three vocal parts of Zhuang Ethnic Group; establishing the cultural and ecological inheritance and protection base in Anshan Village of Guling Town to enlarge the inheritance team; organizing professional and amateur performance group of folk song with three vocal parts of Zhuang Ethnic Group and setting up relevant schools for amateur singers so as to train inheritors; carrying out activities of folk songs with three vocal parts in schools and teaching this kind of folk song in primary and secondary schools; allocating special funds to compile and publish related audio, video and text information; creating and rehearsing relevant songs and dances with special themes, holding touring performances and implementing publicity work. In 2008, with the approval of the State Council, the folk songs with three vocal parts of Zhuang Ethnic Group was inscribed on the Second National List of Intangible Cultural Heritage.

南宁壮族哭嫁歌

Nanning's Song of Crying Marriage of Zhuang Ethnic Group

项目名称：南宁壮族哭嫁歌

别称：无

分布范围：兴宁区三塘镇，江南区吴圩镇、苏圩镇、江西镇，良庆区大塘镇、南晓镇、那陈镇等壮族及壮汉杂居地区

入选名录：2012年第四批自治区级非物质文化遗产名录

保护单位：兴宁区文化馆

代表性传承人：黄翠荣

Element name: Nanning's Song of Crying Marriage of Zhuang Ethnic Group

Alternative name: None

Geographical location and range: Santang Town of Xingning District; Wuxu Town, Suxu Town and Jiangxi Town of Jiangnan District; Datang Town, Nanxiao Town and Nachen Town of Liangqing District; Zhuang areas and areas of mixed inhabitation of Zhuang and Han peoples

Element inscribed list: In 2012 on the Fourth Autonomous Region List of Intangible Cultural Heritage

Competent body involved in safeguarding: Xingning District Cultural Centre

Representative inheritor: Huang Cuirong

哭嫁是一种流行于广西各地的壮族婚姻风俗，广泛分布于南宁市兴宁区的三塘镇，江南区的吴圩镇、苏圩镇、江西镇以及良庆区的大塘镇、南晓镇、那陈镇等壮族及壮汉杂居地区。作为当地壮族青年极为隆重的结婚仪式，吟唱哭嫁歌是姑娘出嫁时，以“哭”代说，倾诉衷肠，表达离情，它生动、形象地描绘出女性命运与婚姻的关系。

追溯南宁哭嫁歌的流传历史，具体的文字记载难以考究，而哭嫁歌的起因，大概是源于古代妇女尤其是壮族妇女无法用文字记录自己的故事，只能以诉说和吟唱的方式表达心情，从而形成了长久以来传承不断的南宁哭嫁歌。若从深层次追本溯源，正如一些学者所提出的：哭嫁歌既是古代掠夺婚姻的遗留，又是封建买卖婚姻“盲婚”制度的产物，因此罪恶的封建买卖婚姻制度，无疑是催生哭嫁歌的重要原因之一。还有一种观点认为，哭嫁歌最原始的起因是“抢婚”，因此，一些学者认为“哭嫁最早起源于古代的抢掠妇女时的呼救声”。到了近代，哭嫁歌的悲情色彩大大减退，随之而来的是新婚的喜庆和欢乐，时代的变迁、经济的发展，也给古老的文化赋予了新的内涵。

南宁哭嫁歌是新娘在伴娘的伴唱下通宵达旦地跪唱，一般是从结婚的头天开始，一直持续到第二天上轿后才结束，有些地区甚至要唱三天三夜。它的内容相对固定，但非常丰富，主要有《十姐妹歌》《唱歌堂》《花烛歌》《十拜歌》《上轿歌》《骂媒歌》《叹女身》《哭爹娘》《骂舅爷》《哭弟弟》《哭妹妹》《骂轿夫》等。由于哭嫁歌的主要作用是表情达意，所以一般都以“爷呀——娘”这种句式开头，多为七言。

在我国诸多民族的婚姻风俗的产物中，南宁哭嫁歌可谓是独具特色，它多元的文化特征，对于研究南宁婚俗和历史文化具有重要的参考价值，对展示南宁婚俗文化特色、丰富南宁历史文化内涵都有重要意义，其音乐素材、演唱形式和

Crying marriage is a popular marriage custom of Zhuang Ethnic Group in Guangxi. It spreads widely in Santang Town of Xingning District, Wuxu Town, Suxu Town and Jiangxi Town of Jiangnan District, Datang Town, Nanxiao Town and Nachen Town of Liangqing District, Zhuang areas and areas of mixed inhabitation of Zhuang and Han peoples. As an important part of the wedding ceremony of Zhuang Ethnic Group, sing the song of crying marriage, which uses crying to replace saying, is a way for women to express their sad feelings at separation with parents when they get married. It vividly depicts the relationship between women's fate and marriage.

It is hard to date back the specific history of the song of crying marriage according to written records. The origin of the song was probably from ancient women, especially women of Zhuang who could not write down their experiences and stories could only express their feelings by telling or singing, thus the song of crying marriage came into being and passed on for a long time. If we trace the source of the song of crying marriage at a deep level, just as many scholars have put forward, the song of crying marriage is the remnant of ancient capture marriage as well as the product of mercenary marriage and blind marriage. Therefore, it is undoubted that the dark feudal mercenary marriage system was the reason for the creation of the song of crying marriage. Another view takes the ground that the song of crying marriage originated from the primitive capture marriage, thus some scholars believe "the song of crying marriage stemmed from the cry for help when women were captured". In modern times, the sad feelings of the song of crying marriage have been greatly reduced, and the marriage are often filled by joy and delight. The vicissitudes of times and the development of economy also put new atmosphere to this ancient culture.

Nanning's song of crying marriage is often sung by bride kneeling on the ground with the vocal accompaniments of bridesmaids. The song usually starts from the first day of the wedding and lasts until the second day after the bride getting into the sedan chair. In some areas, the song even lasts for three days and nights. The contents of the song of crying marriage is relatively fixed yet colorful. The major songs include *Song of Ten Sisters*, *Singing Hall*, *Song of Flowers and Candles*, *Song of Ten Kowtows*, *Song of Sedan Chair*, *Song to Blame Matchmaker*, *Song to Sigh Being a Woman*, *Crying for Parents*, *Crying for Uncles*, *Crying for Brothers*, *Crying for Sisters*, *Song to Scold Sedan Chair Bearers* and so on. Since songs of crying marriage are mainly used to express feelings, thus most of them begin with sentences like "oh father-mother" and most of the beginning sentences include seven words.

Among the production of the marriage customs in many ethnic minorities of China, Nanning's song of crying marriage is unique. Its diversified cultural characteristics have important reference value for the study of wedding customs and historical cultures in Nanning. It is also of great significance to represent the characteristics of Nanning's wedding customs and enrich the historical and cultural connotation of Nanning. Its music materials, singing forms and works not only retain strong national and folk colors, but also have distinct features of the times, which bear high both appreciation and research values of music. In addition, it can also provide rich creative materials for folk music.

With the change of social customs, the song of crying marriage is hard to find in the folk marriage customs today, and the people who can sing it are also becoming less and less. The inheritance and development of the song of crying marriage in Nanning has been hindered. Therefore, the local government and relevant departments have taken a series of measures to save and protect it. On the third day of the third lunar month every year, a grand song festival will be held. Various folk song singers, including those singers of the song of crying marriage, will gather together and carry out a singing competition. At the same time, the performance of the song of crying marriage will be held on various festivals so that this ancient cultural tradition can survive and pass on. In 2012, with the approval of the People's Government of the Guangxi Zhuang Autonomous Region, Nanning's song of crying marriage was inscribed on the Fourth Autonomous Region List of Intangible Cultural Heritage.

作品，既保留了浓厚的民族民间色彩，又具有鲜明的时代特征，蕴含较高的音乐欣赏价值和研究价值，除此之外，它也为民间音乐提供了丰富的创作素材。

随着社会风俗的变化，哭嫁歌在民间婚俗中已难觅踪迹，会唱哭嫁歌的人也越来越少，南宁哭嫁歌的传承和发展受到了阻碍。为此，当地政府及相关部门采取一系列措施，对其进行抢救和保护。每年的农历三月三，举行盛大的三月三歌节，各路山歌歌手，包括哭嫁歌歌手汇集到一起，开展歌手擂台赛。同时利用各种节庆开展哭嫁歌展演活动，让古老的文化传统得以生存和延续。2012年，南宁壮族哭嫁歌经广西壮族自治区人民政府同意，列入第四批自治区级非物质文化遗产名录。

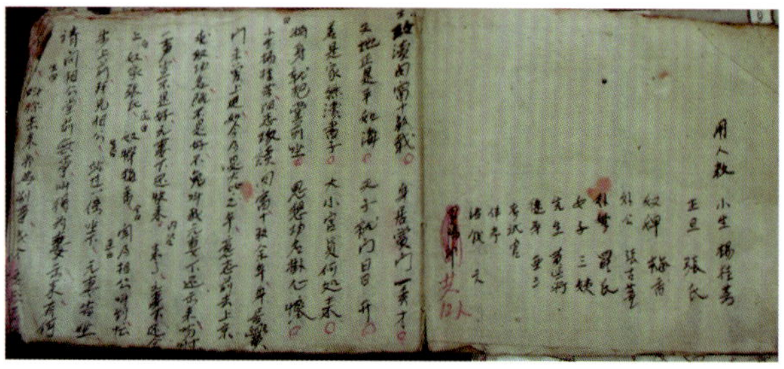

哭嫁歌歌本　摄影 潘城任
"Zhuang's Song of Crying Marriage" Photo by Pan Chengren

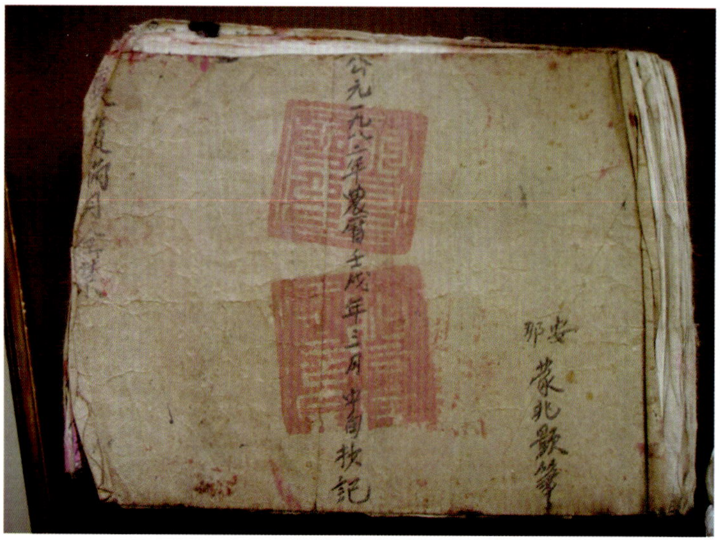

哭嫁歌歌本封面　摄影 潘城任
Cover of "Zhuang's Song of Crying Marriage" Photo by Pan Chengren

南宁平话民歌

Nanning's Folk Song in Ping Language

项目名称：南宁平话民歌

别称：无

分布范围：南宁市武鸣区、横州市、宾阳县、隆安县及百色市、崇左市等

入选名录：2010年第三批自治区级非物质文化遗产名录

2010年第三批市级非物质文化遗产名录

保护单位：江南区文化馆

代表性传承人：梁世华

Element name: Nanning's Folk Song in Ping Language

Alternative name: None

Geographical location and range: Wuming District, Hengzhou City, Binyang County, Long'an County of Nanning City; Baise City, Chongzuo City and others

Element inscribed list: In 2010 on the Third Autonomous Region List of Intangible Cultural Heritage

In 2010 on the Third Municipal List of Intangible Cultural Heritage

Competent body involved in safeguarding: Jiangnan District Cultural Centre

Representative inheritor: Liang Shihua

Folk song in Ping language, as it implies, is sung in Ping dialect that spreads in Guangxi Zhuang Autonomous Region. Gathering the essence of Ping language culture, it has been passed from mouth to mouth, generation to generation, for more than 400 years. The folk songs are mainly spread in Wuming District, Hengzhou City, Binyang and Long'an counties of Nanning City, as well as Baise City and Chongzuo City, especially in Baihe and Mashan of Hengzhou City. Cultural features initially exist in these folk songs are still remained today.

Dialect Pinghua is a complex language system and took its shape amidst aborigine and Central China people, who experienced the southward migration and had intermarriage with local people. Tingzi Pinghua spoken in Jiangnan District of Nanning has been regarded as the most authentic Pinghua, due to its pure flavor surpassing any other Ping language in south Guangxi. About 300 thousand people use Pinghua as their mother language. Meanwhile, Pinghua culture also has a deep-root and self-contained system in Jiangnan District and neighboring habitants.

As a monophonic music, Nanning's folk song in Ping language puts emphasis on rhyme. The songs follow the rules of ancient regulated poems to compose lyrics. More than 20 kinds of rhymes are frequently used in songs, such as Jinyin, Jiaoqing, Jiaolian, Jiaorong, Jiaomei, Tixi, Disi, Qiaozhang, Qiaozhuang, Pengcui, Pengguai, Qing guai, Qingjiao, Pengjiao, Pengge, Jiao'e, Tuosu, Liaodiao, Laodao, Masha, Tuosha, Guailiu, Tanshen, Ludu, etc. The rhyme will be decided based on whom the song written for. For example, songs for lovers will use Qingguai as the rhyme words while songs for friends will use Pengguai. In terms of songs' form, folk song in Ping language can be divided into Seven-Word Verse and Family Letter. The former, with particular rhythm, is composed of four sentences each one and seven words each sentence. In contrast, the latter has a relatively free form and has 7 words in the first and last sentences. The other lines may have three, five, six or eight words.

Extracting all brilliant elements of Ping language culture, Nanning's folk song in Ping language played the main entertainment role of the locals in history, and it still remains essential in recreational time of many senior locals. Folk songs sung in parties is often seen as an indispensable game, or even unacquainted Ping language speakers, once co-hear a folk song in Ping language, would bear a favorable impression for each other just for the local accent. In addition, as a comprehensive record of Ping language speakers' daily life, folk song in Ping language is of great research value in terms of sociology,

平话是流传于广西壮族自治区的一种汉语方言，平话民歌是用平话所唱的歌，它汇聚了平话文化的精髓，依靠口传在平话人中代代相传，至今已有400多年的历史。南宁平话民歌主要流传于南宁市的武鸣区、横州市、宾阳县、隆安县以及百色市、崇左市等地区，其中尤以南宁市郊县以及横州市的百合镇、马山乡等地的平话民歌较为集中，流传至今一直保持着原生态平话民歌的文化特色。

平话是中原人南迁与当地原住民“杂居通婚”后，由于长时间生活在一起而衍生出的一种特殊的汉语方言。其中，南宁市江南区的亭子平话是桂南最纯正的平话群体，一直被南宁平话人视为平话语言之正宗，这里约有30万人以平话为母语，同时，平话文化也在江南区及周边的平话人聚居区根深蒂固且自成体系。

南宁平话民歌属单声部民歌，在歌唱时比较讲究韵律，歌词属于古律诗的一种，常用的有金银、娇情、娇连、娇容、娇眉、啼西、的思、乔张、乔妆、朋崔、朋乖、情乖、情娇、朋娇、朋哥、娇娥、陀苏、寥刁、劳刀、麻沙、陀沙、乖流、潭深、卢都等二十几种韵律，每首歌采用的韵要根据对象的不同进行选择，如对象是情人则用“情乖”韵，对象是朋友则用“朋乖”韵。在形式上有七言家、家信（家书）两种。七言家每句七言，每首四句，讲究押韵，似七言诗。家信的句式相对比较自由，这种句式前后七言，中间的韵律有三、五、六、八字不等。

南宁平话民歌汇聚了平话文化之精髓，在历史上它是平话人主要的娱乐形式，现在依然是很多中老年平话人文娱生活的重要内容。在聚会时，山歌常常是平话人必不可少的一项活动，素昧平生的平话人听到平话民歌就会因浓烈的平话乡音认同感而亲热起来。此外，平话民歌全面记录了平话人的日常生活，对社会学、历史学、语言学、民俗学等诸多学科都有宝贵的研究价值。

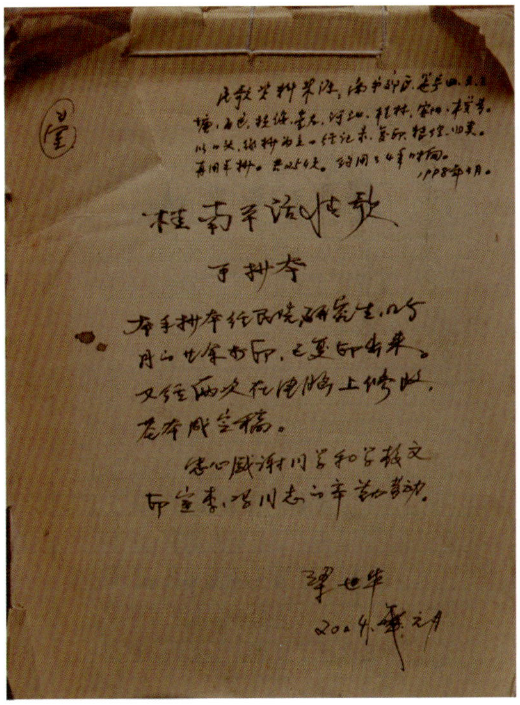

南宁平话民歌传承人梁世华
Liang Shihua, Inheritor of Nanning's Folk Song in Ping Language

桂南平话民歌手抄本
Manuscripts of Guinan's Folk Song in Ping Language

由于平话民歌是农耕时代的产物，时至今日，它所生存的土壤已经发生了巨大的变化。目前，平话区青少年已经很少用平话来交流了，没有了方言的大环境，平话民歌也就失去了生存的土壤，如果不加保护，平话民歌就会陷入无法传承的危险境地。近年来，相关部门不仅组织力量对平话民歌进行了系统性挖掘整理，建立了数据档案，汇编成资料留存，还组织平话民歌老艺人到学校开展传承教学活动，培育更多的传承人，挽救和保留原生态平话民歌，使平话民歌能够薪火相传，生生不息。2010年，南宁平话民歌经广西壮族自治区人民政府同意，列入第三批自治区级非物质文化遗产名录。

historical sciences, linguistics, and folklore.

Folk song in Ping language was once embedded in the age of farming. Times change however, nowadays few teenagers in Ping-dialect area use Ping language to communicate. It keeps struggling facing the plight of less and less practice of Ping dialect and could be in jeopardy of no adherence if more action is not taken. To address this challenge, relevant authorities called for all-out efforts to systematically excavate and study the existing folk songs, establish data files and compile them into data for preservation. They also organized sophisticated artists to schools for teaching folk songs, more inheritors will be prepared to save and retain these pristine folk songs in Ping language from generation to generation. In 2010, Nanning's folk song in Ping language was inscribed on the Third Autonomous Region List of Intangible Cultural Heritage, with the approval of People's Government of Guangxi Zhuang Autonomous Region.

松柏汉族多声部平话山歌

Songbai's Pinghua Folk Song with Multiple Vocal Parts of Han Ethnic Group

项目名称：松柏汉族多声部平话山歌

别称：无

分布范围：兴宁区三塘镇、五塘镇、昆仑镇等

入选名录：2008年第二批自治区级非物质文化遗产名录
2007年第一批市级非物质文化遗产名录

保护单位：兴宁区文化馆

代表性传承人：潘英雄

Element name: Songbai's Pinghua Folk Song with Multiple Vocal Parts of Han Ethnic Group

Alternative name: None

Geographical location and range: Santang Town, Wutang Town, Kunlun Town and others of Xingning District

Element inscribed list: In 2008 on the Second Autonomous Region List of Intangible Cultural Heritage
In 2007 on the First Municipal List of Intangible Cultural Heritage

Competent body involved in safeguarding: Xingning District Cultural Centre

Representative inheritor: Pan Yingxiong

歌师在田间演唱松柏汉族多声部平话山歌
The Singers Are Singing Songbai's Pinghua Folk Songs with Multiple Vocal Parts of Han Ethnic Group in the Field

松柏汉族多声部平话山歌，是流传于广西南宁市兴宁区三塘镇、五塘镇、昆仑镇等汉族居住地及周边地区的原生态汉族歌种。由于民歌发源地为三塘镇松柏村，故得名松柏汉族多声部平话山歌。松柏村地处壮、汉杂居之地，受语言及其民间风俗习惯的影响，形成了独特的民歌演唱风格。

松柏村位于广西壮族自治区南宁市兴宁区三塘镇壮族聚居区，是三塘镇唯一的汉族村落，全村以汉族平话为日常交流用语。据说明万历年间，南宁虎邱村黄氏两兄弟（兄黄金、弟黄钰）迁居三塘，此后汉族平话就逐渐传播开来。南宁市兴宁区所辖乡镇多杂居着壮、汉两个民族，在长期的共存中，由于两个民族之间的文化及风俗习惯相互交流、相互影响，遂形成了民歌风格上的许多共同点。据《邕宁县志》记载：“县境水陆交通、五方辐辏、流寓过客、言语不一……所谓官、平、土、白是也。”南宁松柏汉族平话多声部山歌，就是在这种多元而复杂的环境中产生的。

南宁松柏汉族平话多声部山歌是在单声部平话民歌的基础上，融入壮族双声的元素发展而成的，属双声支声版复调。它主要分为“逗引高腔”和“平腔”两部分。逗引高腔二声部平话山歌，是民歌歌手在歌会之前召集歌手到歌场唱歌的信号，一般由两个召集的歌师来高声唱，其他歌手听到

Songbai's Pinghua folk song with multiple vocal parts of Han Ethnic Group, with its pristine flavor, is spread by Han people in and around areas like Santang, Wutang, and Kunlun Towns, Xingning District, Nanning City, Guangxi. It is so called because of its birthplace, Songbai Village, Santang Town where there are Zhuang and Han nationalities live together. And it is diversified languages and folk customs there that endow folk songs with unique singing style.

Sitting in Zhuang Ethnic Group ghetto in Santang Town, Songbai Village remains to be the only Han Ethnic Group hamlet where villagers daily speak in Han language. It is said that during the Emperor Wanli reign of Ming Dynasty, two brothers of Huang family (older brother Huang Jin and younger brother Huang Yu) moved from Huqiu Village to Santang Town, henceforth, Ping language had got about. As the Zhuang and Han people live together in towns of Xingning District, folk songs there share quite a lot of common features attributing to mutual communication and reciprocal relations by two nationalities throughout their co-existing. According to *Annal of Yongning County*, "Thousands of passing travelers converge in the county through river and land transportation… they speak in different languages including mandarin, Ping language, Cantonese and countryside dialect." Naturally, Songbai's Pinghua folk song with multiple vocal parts of Han Ethnic Group came into being under such complex and pluralistic social context.

Originating from Pinghua folk song of mono-voice, Songbai's Pinghua folk song with multiple vocal has developed by integrating with bitonal elements of Zhuang Ethnic Group music. It is one kind of polyphony of bitonal heterophony consisting of Douyin High-pitched Tune and Gentle Tune. Pinghua folk song of Douyin High-pitched

Tune, as a prelude of a song party, is usually performed by two singers, through which other singers could get the call and join in the performance. Such bitonal folk song played by two singers is considered as the polyphony of heterophony. Based on five-tone scale, its basic tune is made of leading part ("hard" part named by local folk singers) and chorus part ("soft" part named by mountain singers), also known as the "starting" and "replying" part respectively. Such folk songs are mainly composed of lining words, with resonant and evocative tones, so "Pinghua folk song of Douyin High-pitched Tune" (Douyin meaning summoning in Chinese) it is. Songs can be classified into 16 kinds of rhymes including Jinyin, Qiaozhuang, Jiao'e, Jiaolian, Qiaozhang, Tusu, Masha, Chuiliu, Liaodao, Leidui, Tixi, Chenguai, Laodao, Yexie, etc.

Singing folk songs is not only a recreation for Songbai villagers, but also a way of expressing and communication. Just as a folk song singing, "Sing a family letter, relish my cheer." The locals prefer to call folk songs family letter, which seems like a tie bringing people closer to each other. The contents of the folk songs usually cover a wide spectrum including love melodies sung by couples, paeans for harvest and hard-working, and odes to profitable policies implemented by the Communist Party and so on. Songbai's folk songs are popular among the people for they are concise, vivid, and easy to understand. Their unique rhythmic structure and singing form bear high value of art, aesthetics and appreciation. And it is of great significance in studying traditional Chinese folk music. Besides, such folk songs are supposedly rare among the pristine songs of Han Ethnic Group, which provides valuable chance for studying cultural amalgamation between Zhuang and Han peoples.

As people's living standards improved, culture of folk songs developed among countryside and mountains has been replaced by emerging recreation in cities. Worse still, the number of folk singers gradually reduced for some are in their declining years, some even dead. In order to better protect intangible cultural heritages, authorities of Xingning District has declared two intangible cultural heritages of the city-level and of autonomous region level. Meanwhile, Central Primary School of Santang has been designated as the base of intangible cultural heritage of both city-level and autonomous region-level, which help pass and develop the culture of Songbai's folk songs. In 2008, Songbai's pinghua folk song with multiple vocal parts of Han Ethnic Group was inscribed on the Second Autonomous Region List of Intangible Cultural Heritage, after the approval of People's Government of Guangxi Zhuang Autonomous Region.

歌声时则纷纷赶到歌场集合来对歌，其含意是歌会开始了，众知音闻声，速来聚会。这种二声部山歌一般由两人演唱，属支声复调，曲调结构以五声音阶作为调式的基础，主唱部分（上声部）被当地民歌手称为“硬”声部，合唱部分（下声部）被山歌手称为“软”声部，也称“起”腔和“答”腔。此山歌以衬词为主，腔调高亢洪亮，有召集力，故称“逗引高腔平话山歌”。平腔二声部平话山歌，是根据平话单声部民歌的方言韵律发展的山歌。平话单声部民歌的歌词有16个韵律，如金银韵、桥庄韵、娇娥韵、娇连韵、桥张韵、图苏韵、麻沙韵、垂留韵、撩刀韵、雷堆韵、啼西韵、陈乖韵、劳刀韵、爷些韵等。

平话山歌既是松柏村当地百姓的娱乐活动，也是他们抒发情感、交流情感的一种方式，正如山歌中的歌词所唱：“唱支家词解心乐”，当地百姓把山歌称为“家词”，就像“家书”一样。平话山歌对歌的歌词内容非常广泛，天南地北，斗智斗艺，无所不唱，有男女之间交流情感的情歌，有庆丰收时劳动人民对劳动的歌颂，有对党的富民政策的歌颂等。松柏平话山歌因内容通俗易懂、自然朴实、比喻生动而深受群众喜欢，其独特的韵律结构以及演唱形式，具有很高的艺术价值、美学价值和欣赏价值，对研究中国传统民间音乐具有重要意义。此外，松柏汉族多声部平话山歌在中国汉族原生态歌种中实为罕见，为研究当地壮族文化与汉文化的交融提供了宝贵的材料。

随着生活水平的提高，新的娱乐与街市文化逐渐代替了原来的山乡文化，有的歌师已老或去世，民歌歌手也渐渐减少。为了挖掘和保护非物质文化遗产，兴宁区已先后成功申报了市级、自治区级非物质文化遗产，三塘镇中心小学已定为南宁市、自治区级非物质文化遗产松柏汉族多声部平话山歌传承基地，为其传承与发展而不断努力。2008年，松柏汉族多声部平话山歌经广西壮族自治区人民政府同意，列入第二批自治区级非物质文化遗产名录。

南宁壮族高腔民歌

Nanning's Folk Song with High Pitch of Zhuang Ethnic Group

项目名称：南宁壮族高腔民歌

别称：无

分布范围：南宁市及周边地区

入选名录：2016年第六批自治区级非物质文化遗产名录

保护单位：南宁市民族文化艺术研究院（南宁市非物质文化遗产保护中心）

代表性传承人：陆锦福

Element name：Nanning's Folk Song with High Pitch of Zhuang Ethnic Group

Alternative name：None

Geographical location and range：Nanning City and the surrounding areas

Element inscribed list：In 2016 on the Sixth Autonomous Region List of Intangible Cultural Heritage

Competent body involved in safeguarding：Nanning Ethnic Culture and Art Research Institute (Nanning Intangible Cultural Heritage Protection Centre)

Representative inheritors：Lu Jinfu

Nanning's folk song with high pitch of Zhuang Ethnic Group is a traditional music that widely spreads among Zhuang-inhabited area of Nanning. It was much loved by the locals on account of time-honored inheritance, rich variety and peculiar enchantment as a national music. There are no clear written records giving us a hint of its original time, but it does have a long history in the light of its inheritance course. And another thing we can certain is that the folk song has grown up with the emergence of the folk song fair.

The folk song with high pitch has never lost its distinctive local characteristics throughout the whole course of development, such as stirring melody, high-pitched tune, and wide diapason, free and changeable rhythm. When it is performed with deep breath, few words and diversified tunes from low to high pitch will cast listeners into a feast of lyrical sentiment. Because of its wide spreading and multiple integration with different cultures, the folk songs can mean different types in different areas including Yongzhou high-pitched tunes of Mashan, two-part high-pitched tunes of Wuming, Long'an high-pitched tunes, Xiyan high-pitched tunes of Shanglin, Tanluo high-pitched tunes of Xixiangtang, etc. The content of these songs mostly focuses on people's daily life, covering a high range of topics, such as labor, love, marriage, family relationship. Besides, most of the songs are of four lines of seven words each, or of five words each. As for singing forms including monophonic part, two-part, solo, duet and chorus, will bring audience a variety of audio-visual experience. And there are quite a few classical pieces: *Sweet Eighteen, Blooming Girl Herein, Fragrance Lingering over*

南宁壮族高腔民歌是广泛流行于南宁壮族地区的传统音乐，传承时间悠久，种类多样，再加上具备民族音乐的独特魅力，所以曾经在当地十分受欢迎。从民间的传承情况来看，南宁壮族高腔民歌的历史相当久远。它究竟起源何时，因为没有明确史料记载，目前无从考证，但可以认定的是，高腔民歌是随着壮族歌圩的出现而逐渐兴盛的。

南宁壮族高腔民歌在整个的传承和发展过程中，一直保持着浓郁的地方特色，旋律激昂，音调高亢，嘹亮奔放，音域较宽，节奏自由而富于变化，在演唱时字少腔多，气息悠长，歌唱时歌腔从低音一直到高音，一气呵成，抒情性极强。由于流传广泛，又和多地文化相互融合，南宁壮族高腔民歌形成了不同的种类，包括马山永州高腔、武鸣二声部高腔、隆安高腔、上林西燕高腔、西乡塘坛洛高腔等。歌唱的内容多以人们的日常生活为主，涵盖劳作、爱情、婚姻、亲情等许多方面。此外，南宁壮族高腔民歌多为五言四句和七言四句，吟唱形式有单声部、二声部、独唱、对唱、多人组合等，不同的形式会呈现出不同的效果，给人以变幻多彩的视听感受，经典曲目主要有《妹子十七八》《这里姑娘娇》《园中果芳香》《难分离》《三月花儿红》等。

安路小学老师蓝雅婷在教授学生唱南宁壮族高腔民歌
Lan Yating, Teacher from Anlu Primary School Teaches Pupils to Sing Nanning's Folk Song with High Pitch of Zhuang Ethnic Group

传承人在对歌
The Inheritors Are Singing in Antiphonal Style

对歌
Singing in Antiphonal Style

作为一项历史悠久、独具特色的民族音乐形式，南宁市壮族高腔民歌对民族、民俗学研究有着非常重要的意义，并且它将传统民歌的表现手法和现代演唱技巧恰到好处地融合在一起，既有传统之美，又不失现代之力，因此具有很高的欣赏价值和研究价值。除此之外，南宁壮族高腔民歌对推动我国少数民族民歌内容和形式的研究以及传承壮族的传统文化都具有重要意义。

近几年，在非物质文化遗产保护工作的努力下，南宁高腔民歌得到较好的保护、传承，南宁壮族高腔民歌中的“马山永州壮族高腔民歌”已多次在南宁国际民歌艺术节开幕式上亮相，得到了进一步的推广。南宁壮族高腔民歌在各地开展专项传承活动，组织高腔民歌走进社区和学校，培养新的传承人。2016年，南宁壮族高腔民歌经广西壮族自治区人民政府同意，列入第六批自治区级非物质文化遗产名录。

Orchards, Hard to Farewell, Fiery Flowers in March, etc.

As a national music with a long history and unique characteristics, the folk song with high pitch counts for much in studying Ethnic Group and folklore. Integrating the form of traditional folk songs with contemporary singing techniques, it is boasting of perfect blend of conventional and modern beauty, and of high value in appreciation and research. All in all, it is of great significance, not only in promoting the study of the folk songs of ethnic minorities, but also in inheriting the traditional culture of the Zhuang Ethnic Group.

In recent years, the folk songs have been well protected and developed, thanks to the efforts for preservation of intangible cultural heritage. For instance, Yongzhou high-pitched tune of Mashan has been admired by more and more people, after its performances for the opening ceremonies of International Art Festival of Folk Songs in Nanning. The folk songs even have been promoted and brought to communities and schools, and more inheritors will be prepared. In 2016, Nanning's folk song with high pitch of Zhuang Ethnic Group was inscribed on the Sixth Autonomous Region List of Intangible Cultural Heritage after the approval of People's Government of Guangxi Zhuang Autonomous Region.

武鸣壮族山歌

Wuming's Folk Song of Zhuang Ethnic Group

项目名称：武鸣壮族山歌

别称：欢

分布范围：武鸣区

入选名录：2012年第四批自治区级非物质文化遗产名录

保护单位：武鸣区文化馆

代表性传承人：韦秋岑

Element name: Wuming's Folk Song of Zhuang Ethnic Group

Alternative name: Huan

Geographical location and range: Wuming District

Element inscribed list: In 2012 on the Fourth Autonomous Region List of Intangible Cultural Heritage

Competent body involved in safeguarding: Wuming District Cultural Centre

Representative inheritor: Wei Qiucen

武鸣区是壮族文化的发源地，素有“壮乡”“歌海”之称，武鸣壮族山歌在壮语中被称作“欢”，土生土长的武鸣壮族人民，不论男女老少，几乎人人能歌善唱，无处不飞歌，几乎到了“以歌代言”的地步。

武鸣壮族山歌历史悠久、源远流长，它产生于民间，兴盛于民间，流传于民间，是武鸣区一方水土独特的产物，与壮族歌圩有着十分密切的联系。据说以宁明花山为代表的左江崖壁画，展现的便是秦以前壮族先民骆越举行盛大歌圩的场面。南宋周去非所撰的《岭外代答》记载，壮人“迭相歌和，合情凄婉……皆临机自撰，不肯踏袭，其间仍有绝佳者”，明朝天顺进士刘大厦在南宁写的《闻从者谈土俗写怀柬王宪佥》诗中也提到“男女歌谣成卺礼”等，皆描绘了壮族歌圩上男男女女对歌不断的情景。清光绪年间编成的《武缘县图经》记载，清光绪年间，思恩知府李彦章喻令禁歌，但“答歌之日，武缘（今武鸣）仙湖、廖江二处有之，每年三月初一日至初十日，沿江上下，数里之内，士女如云”。由此可见武鸣壮族山歌之盛行。

武鸣壮族山歌按照调式可分为宫、商、徵、羽四种。按区域划分，主要有东、西、南、北、中五部区歌种，它们虽然都属于武鸣壮族山歌，但特点各异，其中东部山歌源于大明山脚下的两江、陆斡、罗波、马头等镇，旋律婉转抒情，优美缓慢；西部山歌源于锣圩、灵马等镇，曲调旋律高昂，唱腔嘹亮；南部山歌源于甘圩镇，旋律悠扬柔和；北部山歌源于府城、仙湖等镇，曲调高亢明快；中部山歌源于城厢、太平、双桥、宁武等镇，旋律流畅，情绪高亢。一般来说，武鸣壮族山歌的歌词是五字四句，有严格的腰脚韵，歌唱时以对唱和喊山为主。

作为一种独特的壮族文化活动，武鸣壮族山歌具有深厚的壮族历史文化底蕴，对研究壮族历史文化有着重要的研究价值，重视和发展武鸣壮族山歌不仅能够弘扬壮族的优秀文

Wuming District is the cradle of Zhuang cultures, which is known as “the hometown of Zhuang Ethnic Group” and “sea of songs”. In Zhuang language, Wuming’s folk song of Zhuang is called “Huan”. The native Zhuang people living in Wuming District, regardless of men or women, the elder or children, are almost good at singing and can sing at any moment in any place, nearly replacing speaking by singing.

Wuming’s folk song of Zhuang has a distant origin and a long development. It originated from the people and also flourished among people. It was a unique product of Wuming District, which was closely related to the song fair of Zhuang Ethnic Group. Represented by Huashan Mountain in Ningming County, it is said that what the cliff paintings of Zuojiang River shows is the scene of ancients of Zhuang holding the grand song fair in Luoyue state before Qin Dynasty. Zhou Qufei, a writer of Song Dynasty, wrote a famous geographical book *Ling Wai Dai Da*, in which it records that “Zhuang people sing songs one after another sadly and mildly and these songs are all improvisations without repetition, among which there are some excellent works indeed”. A scholar of Tianchun in Ming Dynasty Liu Dasha wrote a poem *Lister to the Fellomers Talking About Local Customs and Write a Letter to Wang Xianqian* in Nanning, in which he mentioned that “people sing songs on the wedding ceremony”, depicting the scene of singing in antiphonal style of men and women of Zhuang Ethnic Group on song fairs. *Records and Maps of Wuyuan County* compiled during the reign of Emperor Guangxu in Qing Dynasty records that during the reign of Emperor Guangxu, Li Yanzhang, the magistrate of Si’en, tended to forbid people from singing songs. However, “on the day of song fair, that is, from the first to the tenth day of the third lunar month every year, young men and women would gather together at Xianhu Lake in Wuyuan (today’s Wuming District) and Liaojiang River, with the row of people stretching a few miles long”. This shows the prevalence of Wuming’s folk song of Zhuang.

Wuming’s folk song of Zhuang Ethnic Group can be divided into four categories according to the tones: Do, Re, Mi and La. It can also fall into five classes according to geographical positions: folk songs of the east, west, south, north and central region. Although they all are Wuming’s folk song of Zhuang Ethnic Group, they have different characteristics. The folk song of the east originated from towns like Liangjiang, Luwo, Luobo and Matou at the foot of Daming Mountain, which is mild in melody and slow in rhythm. The folk song of the west was stemmed from towns like Luoxu and Lingma with high melody and clear music voice. The folk song of the south is mild and melodious, which originated from Ganxu Town. The folk song of the north was derived from towns like Fucheng and Xianhu, which is loud and sonorous. The folk song of the central region was popular in towns such as Chengxiang, Taiping, Shuangqiao, and Ningwu. The folk song of this place is full of melodic fluency and exciting mood. Generally, the lyrics of Wuming's folk song are composed by four lines with five words of each line. They have strict rhymes and the major forms are antiphonal singing and singing toward mountains.

As a unique cultural activity of Zhuang Ethnic Group, Wuming's folk song of Zhuang bears profound historical and cultural connotations, which has an important value in studying history and culture of Zhuang people. Paying more attention to develop Wuming's folk song of Zhuang can not only carry forward excellent national cultures, but also play a significant role in exploring, rescuing, protecting and inheriting intangible cultural heritage of Zhuang.

To carry forward the essence of Wuming's culture of Zhuang Ethnic Group and build a brand of folk song of Zhuang, the county government began to hold song fairs since 1980. The song fairs have become more and more grand especially after 1985. The number of participants of the folk song galas, folk song contests and antiphonal singing contests of folk song can reach 100,000 every year. In 2010, the county government formulated *The Plan for Inheritance and Training of Folk Song in Wuming County* and *The Plan of Building Inheritance Base of the Intangible Cultural Heritage Folk Song in Wuming County*. Later in 2011, the Folk Song Associations were established in Wuming County and other 13 towns. Nowadays, learning, singing and teaching folk songs have become a routine for Zhuang people living in Wuming District. Students of primary and secondary schools and even all the people of Wuming District have been immersed in "an atmosphere of folk songs". Wuming District of Zhuang Ethnic Group have become a veritable "sea of songs". In 2012, with the approval of the People's Government of the Guangxi Zhuang Autonomous Region, Wuming's Folk Song of Zhuang Ethnic Group was inscribed on the Fourth Autonomous Region List of Intangible Cultural Heritage.

化传统，且对发掘、抢救、保护与传承壮族非物质文化遗产起到了极其重要的作用。

为弘扬武鸣壮族文化精髓，打造壮族山歌文化品牌，自1980年起，县政府开始筹办歌圩，特别是1985年以来，歌圩盛况空前，每年参与山歌晚会、歌王大赛、山歌对唱等活动的群众多达10万。2010年，武鸣县政府制定了《武鸣县山歌传承与培训活动方案》《武鸣县非物质文化遗产山歌传承基地实施方案》。2011年，武鸣县成立了山歌协会，另外有13个镇也成立了山歌分会。如今，武鸣壮族人民学山歌、唱山歌、教山歌成了家常便饭，中小学生乃至武鸣区全民中间都弥漫着浓厚的“山歌之风”，武鸣壮乡成为名副其实的“歌海”。2012年，武鸣壮族山歌经广西壮族自治区人民政府批准，列入第四批自治区级非物质文化遗产名录。

武鸣妮达尼山歌合唱团
Wuming Nidani Folk Song Chorus

上林壮族八音

Shanglin's Music with Eight Instruments of Zhuang Ethnic Group

项目名称：上林壮族八音

别称：无

分布范围：上林县白圩镇、大丰镇、明亮镇、澄泰乡等

入选名录：2012年第四批自治区级非物质文化遗产名录

保护单位：上林县文化馆

代表性传承人：王志新

Element name：Shanglin's Music with Eight Instruments of Zhuang Ethnic Group

Alternative name：None

Geographical location and range：Baixu Town, Dafeng Town, Mingliang Town, Chengtai Town and others of Shanglin County

Element inscribed list：In 2012 on the Fourth Autonomous Region List of Intangible Cultural Heritage

Competent body involved in safeguarding：Shanglin County Cultural Centre

Representative inheritor：Wang Zhixin

八音班在表演
The Band of Eight Musical Instruments Is in the Performance

Shanglin's music with eight instruments of Zhuang Ethnic Group is a traditional folk music prevalent in towns such as Baixu, Dafeng, Mingliang and Chengtai in Shanglin County. Its profound history can be dated back to the reign of the Emperor Daoguang in the Qing Dynasty. At that time, music with eight instruments was popular in Foshan of Guangdong Province. A large number of music houses and music troupes playing eight instruments gathered in the areas of Changshengshu, Malang and Panxiang. For the purpose of doing business, people from Foshan of Guangdong Province migrated to Guangxi Province along the waterway

上林壮族八音是盛行于上林县的白圩镇、大丰镇、明亮镇、澄泰乡等地区的传统民间音乐，其悠久的历史可追溯到清朝道光年间。当时广东佛山八音广泛盛行，乐行会馆林立，有着大量的八音班汇聚于长生树、马廊、潘巷一带。出于经商的目的，不少广东佛山一带的人民沿水路一路迁徙到广西，逐渐开始在上林定居，随后广东粤剧班频繁进入广西，使当地的本土音乐受到了一定的影响。因此，上林壮族八音在富有壮民族和民俗特色的吹打乐的基础上，兼收并蓄广东音乐精华，又与上林当地的音乐相互融合，逐渐发展为极具壮族特色的上林壮族八音，并在上林及周边广大地区盛行不衰。

上林壮族八音，原本是古代吹打乐器的统称，其表演的乐器有两套：演奏福禄寿的乐器有大锣、大镲、唢呐、谷、啧、大鼓、小鼓，或箫、琴、笛、二胡、秦琴、长管；演奏八音的乐器有大鼓、小鼓、谷、啧、大锣、大镲、唢呐、二管。在风格上，上林壮族八音以豪迈粗犷为突出特色，这种特色的形成主要取决于演奏所采用的乐器，正因为它的吹打性质非常突出，所以其乐曲常常使用大跳音程及刚健有力的节奏，抑扬顿挫极为鲜明，加上大锣、大镲的击奏以及唢呐的深吐运气法，音色更优美、高亢，撼人心旌。在演奏内容方面，上林壮族八音分为喜乐和丧乐两大部分，在结婚、贺寿、节日等喜庆场合主要演奏喜庆的曲目，在老人逝世等丧事中以演奏哀乐曲目为主。另外，演奏形式分为武场和文

八音乐器
Eight Instruments

and gradually settled in Shanglin County. Later, Cantonese opera troupes began to frequently enter Guangxi and to some extent affected the style of local music. Therefore, on the basis of an ensemble of Chinese wind and percussion instruments with folk characteristics of Zhuang, Shanglin's music with eight instruments absorbed the essence of Cantonese music and integrated with the local music of Shanglin, gradually developing into the music with eight instruments of strong Zhuang characteristics and prevailing in Shanglin and its surrounding areas.

Shanglin's music with eight instruments of Zhuang once was the general designation of the ancient wind and percussion instruments. It includes two sets of performance instruments: one set for playing music about happiness, wealth and longevity and another one set for playing music with eight instruments. The former includes instruments like big gong, big cha, suona horn, gu, ze, big drum, small drum, or xiao, Chinese zither, bamboo flute, erhu, Qin zither and long wind instrument. The later includes instruments like big drum, small drum, gu, ze, big gong, big cha, suona horn and the instrument with two pipes. The music of eight instruments are rough and firm in style. The formation of such a characteristic depends on the instruments used in performance. It is because of the prominent nature of wind and percussion instruments, the music often uses skipping intervals and powerful rhythm to represent a distinct cadence. Coupled with the percussion of the big gong and big cha and deep breathing method of suona horn, the timbre becomes more beautiful, sonorous and breathtaking. In terms of performance content, the music of eight instruments can be divided into two major parts: music of happiness and music of lament. On marriage, birthday banquet for the elder, festival and other joyful occasions, music for happiness will be performed. On the contrary, on the funeral of the elder and other sorrowful occasions, music of lament will be played. In addition, the performance forms can also be divided into Wu (intense in style) and Wen (soft in style). On Wu performance, the music will be played mainly by suona horn and accompanied by cymbals, drums, gongs and other percussion instruments. On Wen performance, in addition to wind and percussion instruments, there are also Zhuang and Cantonese accapella accompanied by orchestral instruments, mainly including *the Eight Immortals Coming to Offer Birthday Congratulations*, *the Immortal Sending the Child*, *Music on Getting into Bridal Sedan Chair*, *Music on Welcoming the Bride*, etc.

With the rapid development of modern society and influenced by the modern film and television cultures and music, the music with eight instruments has suffered serious hit and challenges. Therefore, the Culture and Sports Bureau of Shanglin County and Shanglin Culture Centre have carried out an in-depth survey and research on Shanglin's folk music of eight instruments and recorded its performance in the form of video and audio. What's more, the bureau and the culture centre have collected and sorted out the traditional music scores (gongchepu, a traditional Chinese musical notation) of the music with eight instruments of Zhuang. They have also surveyed the situation of the representative inheritors and performers. In addition, the bureau and the culture centre also organized the troupe for folk music performance to participate in activities like the opening ceremony of Shanglin Ecological and Healthy Tourism Festival and the Exhibition of Rural Culture of Nanning, so as to further carry forward and inherit Shanglin's music with eight instruments of Zhuang. In 2012, with the approval of the People's Government of the Guangxi Zhuang Autonomous Region, Shanglin's music with eight instruments of Zhuang Ethnic Group was inscribed on the Fourth Autonomous Region List of Intangible Cultural Heritage.

场，武场八音用的乐器以唢呐吹奏为主，以钹、鼓、锣等打击乐为辅；文场八音在使用吹打乐器外，还有壮语清唱、粤曲清唱，并配以多种管弦乐器伴奏。演奏的主要曲目有《八仙贺寿》《仙姬送子》《大开门》《小开门》等。

随着现代社会发展步伐的加快，受现代影视文化音乐的影响，八音音乐也受到了很大的冲击与挑战，对此，上林县文体局和文化馆对壮族八音进行了深入的调查与研究，将八音的演奏做成了录像、录音并存档。更重要的是，上林县文体局和文化馆对壮族八音演奏的传统曲牌乐谱（工尺谱）做了收集和整理，并对代表性传承人和演奏员情况做了调查统计。除此之外，上林县文体局和文化馆还组织了壮族八音表演队进行演出活动，例如参加上林县原生态养生旅游节开幕式表演、南宁市乡村和谐文化大展演活动等，借助这些平台，进一步弘扬和传承上林壮族八音。2012年，上林壮族八音经广西壮族自治区人民政府同意，列入第四批自治区级非物质文化遗产名录。

宾阳八音

Binyang's Music with Eight Instruments

项目名称：宾阳八音

别称：文武场

分布范围：宾阳县芦圩镇、新桥镇、邹圩镇等

入选名录：2020年第八批自治区级非物质文化遗产名录
　　　　　2009年第二批市级非物质文化遗产名录

保护单位：宾阳县文化馆

代表性传承人：无

Element name：Binyang's Music with Eight Instruments

Alternative name：Civil and Military Music (Wen Wu Chang)

Geographical location and range：Luxu Town, Xinqiao Town, Zouxu Town and others of Binyang County

Element inscribed list：In 2020 on the Eighth Autonomous Region List of Intangible Cultural Heritage
In 2009 on the Second Municipal List of Intangible Cultural Heritage

Competent body involved in safeguarding：Binyang County Cultural Centre

Representative inheritor：None

八音引路

The Band of Eight Musical Instruments Leads the Way

Binyang's music with eight instruments, also known as "Civil and Military Music" (Wen Wu Chang), is a kind of traditional wind and percussion music originated from Luxu Town of Binyang County of Nanning, which is also popular in towns like Xinqiao, Zouxu and other places. The major instruments include drum, gong, cymbal, suona horn and erhu. Binyang's music with eight instruments is often played on festivals, temple fairs, sacrificial ceremony, weddings, funerals and other occasions.

Although there are no specific documents recording the emergence and formation of Binyang's music with eight instruments, according to the local folk artists, Binyang's music with eight instruments may emerge at the same time

宾阳八音又称“文武场”，是一种起源于南宁市宾阳县芦圩镇，后广泛流传于新桥、邹圩等地的传统吹打乐曲，其乐器主要以鼓、锣、钹、唢呐、二胡组成，一般用于节日庆典、庙会祭祀、红白喜事等场合。

宾阳八音的产生和形成虽无具体文献资料记载，但据当地的民间艺人介绍，宾阳八音与炮龙应该产生在同一时期——北宋皇祐五年（1053）左右。按照当地的一般习俗，宾阳人舞炮龙总是会用锣鼓开道，以此来营造热闹欢腾的气氛，吸引观众的注意，这就是现代宾阳八音的雏形。另外还有一个有趣的传说：相传在清朝咸丰年间，宾州南街的黄土剑担任知县时，恰逢这年正月十一舞炮龙，街上一位擅长扎灯彩的师傅扎了一只白鸽，本想引起知县的重视，不料知县黄土剑并没有留意。第二天，陈宾聚写了一首打油诗贴在黄家屋外："白鸽扎得好，放在鼓架边。知府看不见，宾聚气几天。"这里所提到的鼓架，正是八音所用的鼓架。由此可以看出宾阳人舞炮龙与八音之间的密切关系。在逐渐的发展过程中，宾阳八音形成了如今有曲牌、有套路、有文场、有武场的格局，并广泛运用于各种庆典和活动中。

被称为"文武场"的宾阳八音有两种形式。以唢呐配民族器乐演奏的，称为"文场"，主要是以勾锣、小钹、凸锣来演奏，演奏出来的乐曲连贯性强，适合情感的倾诉和表达，时而哀怨凄楚，令人肝肠寸断，时而悦耳动听，令人心旷神怡。"武场"主要指以唢呐配锣鼓演奏，演奏出来的曲牌气势雄浑、热烈奔放。

无论文场或武场，宾阳八音所演奏的曲牌均以事先规定的曲牌或是由掌板（文场敲勾锣者，武场为击鼓者）而定，

宾阳八音参加游行活动
Bingyang's Music with Eight Instruments Takes Part in the Parade

with dragon firecracker around the fifth year of the reign of Emperor Huangyou in Northern Song Dynasty (1053). According to the local customs, people of Binyang County used gongs and drums to clear the way before performing dragon firecrackers so as to create a jubilant atmosphere and attract the attention of the audience. This was the prototype of modern Binyang's music of eight instruments. Actually, there is also an interesting legend. It is said that during the reign of Emperor Xianfeng in Qing Dynasty, when Huang Tujian held the post of the magistrate of the south street of Binzhou County, it happened to be the eleventh day of the first lunar month for performing dragon firecrackers. A craftsman named Chen Binju who was good at making colored lanterns made a white dove-shaped lantern, tending to attract the attention of the magistrate, but Huang didn't notice it. On the second day, Chen Binju wrote a doggerel sticking outside the house of Huang Tujian, in which he wrote "The white dove is made well, being put beside the drum stand. The magistrate didn't notice it, making Binju depressed for days." The drum stand mentioned in the doggerel was the very drum stand used in Binyang's music with eight instruments. From this we can see the close relationship between the dragon firecracker performance and the music with eight instruments. In the process of development, Binyang's music with eight instruments has gradually formed a pattern with repertoire, fixed patterns, civil division and military division. It has also been widely used in various celebrations and activities today.

Binyang's music with eight instruments, which is also called "civil and military music" (Wen Wu Chang), has two major forms, that is, civil and military ones. Civil music is often performed by suona horn and folk instruments, with hook gong, small cymbal or convex gong to beat the rhythm. The music of civil division is suitable for expressing emotions. It is sometimes sorrowful and sad with deep grievance, and sometimes melodious and relaxing. The music of military division mainly refers to the music played by suona horn and accompanied by gong and drum, which is forceful and enthusiastic in style.

No matter performing music of civil division or military division, the performed music will be selected beforehand or be determined by hook gong performer of civil division or drum player of military division. Binyang's music with eight instruments can be divided into local music and Cantonese music. The local music mainly consists of excellent music of both local ethnic groups and that is introduced from other places while Cantonese music mainly includes music of Guangdong and Guangxi. In the performance, the music played in civil division generally includes *Music of Victory*, *A String of Beads*, *Shuangjinqian*, *Mantra of Buddha* and *Music of Fukurokuju*. The major music of military division includes *Music on Getting into Bridal Sedan Chair*, *Music on Welcoming the Bride*, *Music of Victory*, *Dimness*, *Sigh for Yanhui* and *Shou Tuo*. In general, the civil division will be performed at first and military division next.

As a unique traditional art form, Binyang's music with eight instruments is graceful and fluent in melody and simple and natural in style. With the development of society, the inheritance of Binyang's music with eight instruments has been confronted with various difficulties. Therefore, the party committee and government of Binyang County have paid attention to the inheritance of this kind of music. They have organized teams to comprehensively collect and sort out Binyang's music with eight instruments. The large-scale festivals and celebrations also invite performance troupes to play Binyang's music with eight instruments, which both represents the charm of this music and promotes the inheritance and development of it. In 2020, with the approval of the People's Government of Nanning, Binyang's Music with Eight Instruments was inscribed on the Eighth Autonomous List of Intangible Cultural Heritage.

所演奏的曲牌分本地曲牌和广式曲牌。本地曲牌以本地民族和引进的其他地方的优秀曲目为主，广式曲牌则以两广音乐的曲目为主。在演奏时，文场所演奏的曲目一般为《得胜令》《串联珠》《双金钱》《普庵咒》《福禄寿》等，武场所演奏的曲目主要有《大开门》《小开门》《得胜令》《朦胧》《叹颜回》《手托》等。在一般情况下，均为先奏文场，后奏武场。

作为一项独具特色的传统艺术形式，宾阳八音曲调优美流畅、质朴自然。随着社会的发展，宾阳八音的传承也面临一些困境。对此，宾阳县委、县政府十分重视，组织人员展开全面的收集、整理工作，在每次大型节日庆典活动中，都会邀请宾阳八音的表演队参加，向社会各界展示八音魅力的同时，也推动了宾阳八音艺术的传承和发展。2020年，宾阳八音经南宁市人民政府同意列入第八批自治区级非物质文化遗产名录。

三津八音

Sanjin's Music with Eight Instruments

项目名称：三津八音

别称：吹哒嘀、座堂八音

分布范围：广西左右江壮族地区及桂东南汉族地区

入选名录：2015年第六批市级非物质文化遗产名录

保护单位：江南区文化馆

代表性传承人：黄树华

Element name：Sanjin's Music with Eight Instruments

Alternative name：Playing Dadi, Music with Eight Instruments of Jubilance

Geographical location and range：Zhuang areas along Zuojiang River and Youjiang River and Han areas in southeast Guangxi

Element inscribed list：In 2015 on the Sixth Municipal List of Intangible Cultural Heritage

Competent body involved in safeguarding：Jiangnan District Cultural Centre

Representative inheritor：Huang Shuhua

Sanjin's music with eight instruments is a traditional folk art prevailing in Zhuang areas along Zuojiang River and Youjiang River and Han areas in southeast Guangxi. Due to its jubilant nature, it is good at heightening delight atmosphere. Therefore, Sanjin's music with eight instruments is often used in various local celebrations. As an art form with distinctive characteristics, this kind of music is popular in Nanning and its surrounding areas, among which Sanjin's music with eight instruments of jubilance in the settlement of people who speak Pinghua (a kind of dialect of Guangxi) on both sides of Yongjiang River, especially in Shajing area of Jiangnan District, is the most famous one.

Sanjin's music with eight instruments was flourished in the late Qing Dynasty and the early Republic of China. It was influenced by percussion music with eight kinds of gongs and drums of Guangdong Province and integrated with the cultural elements of Zhuang Ethnic Group, then gradually developing into wind and percussion music with distinctive local characteristics. Sanjin's music with eight instruments is also called music with eight instruments of jubilance and commonly known as "playing Dadi". It is subordinate to traditional "large ensemble of Chinese wind and percussion instruments". The major instruments include small drum, suona horn, gong, cymbal, woodblock, high-low crapper and small gong. Sanjin' music with eight instruments is often used on occasions such as marriage, moving into the new house, ceremony for baby's completion of its first month of life, birthday celebration for the elder and business-starting ceremony to created the jubilant atmosphere. It is noticeable that Sanjin's music with eight instruments is never played on funerals. In the 1920s, the music troupe of Sanjin's music with eight instruments was established in Shajing, which was composed by Huang Shaofeng, Huang Tai and other folk artists. The first and second generations of artists imparted the music by gongche notation (a traditional Chinese musical notation). Until the third generation of artists taking over the troupe in 1970, the young generations with art expertise simplified the traditional notation into numbered musical notation, which has been used until today.

The repertoire of Sanjin's music with eight instruments is mainly adapted from the music score of the traditional operas, which is usually played into wind and percussion music and short folk tunes, such as *Water Dragon Chant*, *Shang Xiao Liu*, *Welcoming the Bride*, etc. There are over 40 kinds of specific repertoire for festivals, marriage, birthday for the elders and other delight activities, including *Music on Getting into Bridal Sedan Chair*, *A Godsent Marriage*, and

三津八音是盛行于广西左右江壮族地区及桂东南汉族地区的传统民间艺术，由于其热闹喜庆，善于烘托欢乐的氛围，因此多用于当地的各种庆贺活动。作为一项特色鲜明的艺术形式，三津八音广泛流行于南宁市及周边地区，其中以邕江两岸的平话人聚居区特别是江南沙井片区的三津喜庆八音最为著名。

三津八音兴盛于清末民初，起初受广东“八音锣鼓”影响，同时融汇了壮族民间文化元素，逐渐发展并形成富有本地特色的八音吹奏艺术。三津八音又被称作座堂八音，民间俗称“吹哒嘀”，属于传统的“大吹打乐”，乐器主要有小鼓、唢呐、锣、钹、木鱼、高低梆、小锣等。一般来说多用在如婚嫁、新居入宅、小孩满月、祝寿、企业庆典等喜庆活动中，以营造场面热闹气氛，但值得注意的是，三津八音从不参加白事活动。20世纪20年代，沙井三津喜庆八音乐队组建成立，由三津村黄少凤、黄泰等民间艺人组成，第一、二代都是以工尺老谱传教，直到1970年第三代接传后，有文艺专长的青年一代把老谱编译成现在的简谱，一直沿用至今。

三津八音的曲目主要以戏班的曲谱调律改编，通常将戏班的曲谱调律改编后吹打成乐；除此之外也有流传于民间的简短曲调，如《水龙音》《上小流》《接新娘》等；而年例时节、嫁娶、贺寿等喜庆节日时，会专门演奏《大开门》《天赐良缘》《大朝臣》等共计40多首牌曲。三津八音的调式和板式并不是十分繁复、华丽，而是呈现出一种特有的简约美和质朴美，从而构成调式、板式的简朴性特征。各种乐器都在各种牌曲段落里按照节调吹奏、击打，可谓一场和谐悦耳的听觉盛宴。

作为一项具有悠久深厚的历史文化渊源、鲜明的艺术特征的独特表演技艺，三津八音根植于当地的自然条件和当地居民的生产生活方式、民俗习惯及特殊信仰，是依托于多种需求产生和发展起来的一种集休闲娱乐、表演等元素于一

八音乐器
Eight Musical Instruments

婚礼表演现场
Performance for Marriage

体的民间音乐形式，有着十分丰富的文化内涵，且兼具地方性、依附性和娱乐性。同时，它见证着社会的发展，蕴含着劳动人民特有的生活理念、思维方式和民族情感，是南宁民间传统文化不可忽视的一部分，也是民众十分喜爱的传统音乐项目。

现在，三津八音共有5个分队，每队每年应邀参加50场以上的喜庆活动，很受广大群众的喜爱。此外，南宁市江南区文化馆还扶持老艺人定期开办三津喜庆八音吹奏兴趣班，教授喜庆八音演奏技艺，并初步建立传承人传承机制，为三津八音的传承与发展而不断努力。2015年，三津八音经南宁市人民政府同意，列入第六批市级非物质文化遗产名录。

the Great Courtier. The mode and type of metre of Sanjin's music with eight instruments are not complicated or gorgeous, but simple and unadorned, thus constituting the simplicity of the mode and type of metre. All kinds of wind and percussion instruments are played in accordance with the tunes of repertoire, which provides a harmonious and pleasant auditory feast for people.

As a unique performance art with profound history and distinct art characteristics, Sanjin's music with eight instruments is rooted in the local natural conditions, production methods and lifestyle of local people and their customs and beliefs. It is a kind of musical form integrated with entertainment and performance that is developed due to various demands. Sanjin's music with eight instruments is filled with rich cultural connotation and local, dependent and entertainment features. At the same time, it has witnessed the development of society, and contained the unique life concepts, ways of thinking and national emotion of laboring people. Sanjin's music with eight instruments is a part of Nanning's traditional folk culture that cannot be ignored, as well as a popular traditional music form for people.

Nowadays, there have been 5 troupes for Sanjin's music with eight instruments. Each troupe will be invited to participate in more than 50 festival activities every year and is popular among people. In addition, Jiangnan District Cultural Centre also supports old artists to regularly hold classes to teach Sanjin's music with eight instruments and relevant skills. The inheritance mechanism of inheritors has been initially established. In 2015, with the approval of the People's Government of Nanning, Sanjin's music with eight instruments was inscribed on the Sixth Municipal List of Intangible Cultural Heritage.

上林瑶族鼓乐

Shanglin's Drum Music of Yao Ethnic Group

项目名称：上林瑶族鼓乐

别称：无

分布范围：上林县镇圩瑶族乡

入选名录：2015年第六批市级非物质文化遗产名录

保护单位：上林县文化馆

代表性传承人：无

Element name：Shanglin's Drum Music of Yao Ethnic Group

Alternative name：None

Geographical location and range：Zhenxu Town of Yao Ethnic Group in Shanglin County

Element inscribed list：In 2015 on the Sixth Municipal List of Intangible Cultural Heritage

Competent body involved in safeguarding：Shangling County Cultural Centre

Representative inheritor：None

瑶山鼓演奏
Performance of Yaoshan Drum

“瑶山鼓”是上林县镇圩瑶族乡的传统瑶族鼓乐，它是一种历史悠久的少数民族艺术形态。从宋朝流传至今，已有上千年的历史。“瑶山鼓”源于古时瑶民区的赶猴子：瑶族人民一直居住在深山，他们所种的粮食经常被猴子偷食，每到收获季节，为了赶跑偷粮食的猴子，瑶族人民便以敲鼓、呐喊的方法来吓跑猴子。由于猴子下山的时间不确定，人们便在山寨的制高点放置了一面大鼓，并派人轮流看管。如果发现猴子下山就敲打大鼓，寨中不管男女老少，听到鼓声就随即跟着敲鼓呐喊。在家的人就敲起放置在家中的中鼓，在外面干活的人就打起随身携带的小鼓，如果身边没有鼓就以脚跺地跟着大家呐喊，喧腾热闹的气势吓跑了前来偷食的猴子。后来这种被瑶家人戏称为“赶猴鼓”（猴鼓舞）的打鼓方式就慢慢演变成为各种节奏的鼓点，经过瑶族人民一代又一代传承，并且不断地加工、完善，形成了一种激励人们奋发图强、追求美好生活的独特艺术形式。“瑶山鼓”也一直流传至今。

As one of traditional drum music of Yao Ethnic Group, Yaoshan Drum has a time-honored history of ethnic art for more than a thousand years since the Song Dynasty. It actually originated from an ancient custom of dispersing monkeys. It is said that the ancient Yao people lived in remote mountains where their crops were often stolen by monkeys. The clever villagers then resorted to beating drums and shouting to scare monkeys off in harvest season. In order to cope with monkeys' irregular downhill stealing, a huge drum of alarming was placed on the highest spot of the village and watched over by villagers in turn. Anyone who, whether he or she at home or outside, hear the alarming drumbeat should beat his drums at hand or shout and stamp. As a consequence, the monkeys already in readiness would be frightened away by the noisy sound. Such drumbeating, jokingly called expelling-monkeys drum (monkey drum-dance) by the locals, has developed to drumbeats with regulated rhythms after generations. And it finally became an inspiring art via continuous modification and still goes on up these days.

Yaoshan Drum remains original and ethnical though its drumbeats are simple. The drum performance begins with a tenor drum that beats on the side and awakens the bass drum. Then side drums perform to the beats while the tenor and the bass drums beat times. Next, side drums echo the other two drums and follow the rhythm of the bass drum that hits the main beat. Along the performing, the rhythm runs from strong to small and then goes in reverse. If men hit and women dance, wooden shoes on the women's feet will jump agilely to the rhythm. The dance is changeable and graceful thanks to professional movements, such as foot hook, beating after turning over and beating and dancing around drums while shouting. Generally, the Yaoshan Drum performance is given in harvest celebrating, sacrifices offering, festivals, temple fairs and so on.

The impartment of drum music of Yao Ethnic Group is threatened by less and less senior artists who are able to make and play Yao drums. If more efforts are not taken, the drum music may be reduced to the predicament of no adherence. To address the challenge, the authorities of Shanglin County called for all-out efforts to systematically excavate and rearrange relevant information of Yaoshan Drum, establish data files and compile them into data for preservation. They also set up an inheritance base of Yaoshan Drum where there are senior artists teach drum making, so as to pass down the craft making art. Meanwhile, Yaoshan Drum has been also brought into school classes imparting traditional Yao culture. In 2015, Shanglin' drum music of Yao Ethnic Group was inscribed on the Sixth Municipal List of Intangible Cultural Heritage, after the approval of People's Government of Nanning city.

“瑶山鼓”的鼓点虽然简单，但原汁原味，富有民族特色。瑶山鼓表演一般先由中鼓敲边，击鼓三声，唤醒大鼓；再由中鼓和大鼓打拍，然后众小鼓按拍表演；接下来由大鼓打主拍，中鼓引路，小鼓跟着大鼓的节奏来表演。节奏从大到小、从小到大、由强到弱、由弱到强。若是男击女舞，则由男子单独击打，女子脚上的木鞋跟着鼓点跳出相协的节奏。舞蹈里有瑶族擅长的勾脚动作，还有翻身打鼓、转着鼓边打边跳、边敲打边呐喊等，变幻多姿、轻盈灵动。一般来说，瑶山鼓表演适用于庆祝丰收、祭祀神灵、节日庆典、庙会等活动。

目前能够掌握瑶鼓制作和表演技艺的瑶族老艺人已经为数不多，上林瑶族鼓乐的传承也受到了威胁，若不及时加强保护，就有可能出现人去艺绝的危机。对此，上林县委、县政府开展对“瑶山鼓”的收集整理，健全保护档案材料，组建瑶山鼓传承基地，通过“师传徒学”的方式，培养年轻的瑶族鼓手，还定期举办“制鼓手艺班”，请精通制鼓的瑶族艺人教授瑶鼓制作工艺，让制鼓手艺代代相传。同时，当地还开展了瑶山鼓进校园活动，把学习击鼓作为一门传承传统瑶族文化的课程。2015年，上林瑶族鼓乐经南宁市人民政府同意，列入第六批市级非物质文化遗产名录。

制作大鼓　摄影 蒙健
Making a Large Drum Photo by Meng Jian

瑶族剪刀歌

Song of Scissors of Yao Ethnic Group

项目名称：瑶族剪刀歌

别称：无

分布范围：马山县古寨乡、加方乡、里当乡、金钗镇，忻城县遂意乡、北更乡，都安县龙湾乡、菁盛乡、百旺乡等

入选名录：2018年第七批自治区级非物质文化遗产名录
2015年第六批市级非物质文化遗产名录

保护单位：马山县文化馆

代表性传承人：陆建情

Element name：Song of Scissors of Yao Ethnic Group

Alternative name：None

Geographical location and range：Guzhai Town, Jiafang Town, Lidang Town, Jinchai Town in Mashan County; Suiyi Town, Beigeng Town in Xincheng County; Longwan Town, Jingsheng Town, Baiwang Town in Du'an County and others

Element inscribed list：In 2018 on the Seventh Autonomous Region List of Intangible Cultural Heritage
In 2015 on the Sixth Municipal List of Intangible Cultural Heritage

Competent body involved in safeguarding：Mashan County Cultural Centre

Representative inheritors：Lu Jianqing

传承人陆建情在教授村民唱剪刀歌

Inheritor Lu Jianqing Teaches Villagers to Sing Songs of Scissors

Song of Scissors of Yao Ethnic Group, a traditional art originated from Gutang Village, Guzhai Township, Mashan County, is popular in Yao-inhabited areas among Guzhai, Jiafang, Lidang Townships and Jinchai Town in Mashan County; Suiyi, Beigeng Townships in Xincheng County; Longwan, Jingsheng, Baiwang Townships in Du'an County. Gutang Village, located in the eastern Dashishan Mountains of Mashan County and at the northern foot of Damingshan Mountain, was around by beautiful scenery and pleasant environment and given unsurpassed natural conditions to enrich its folk cultural deposits. In ancient times, the area around Gutang was densely forested with mountains and long distances, even the traffic was blocked either. as the information inside and outside the mountain could not be exchanged, the song of scissor has long been unknown to the world, until July 2012, it was discovered by cultural workers in Mashan County.

There is a legend about how the song spreads to Gutang Village. It is said that there was a talented woman named Fairy Lanmei who was in a rich family. She was a good singer with no rivals. She had made a vow to marry whoever, rich or poor could win her in singing. The news came to Gutang Village

瑶族剪刀歌是发源于马山县古寨乡古棠村的瑶族传统艺术形式，分布于马山县古寨乡、加方乡、里当乡、金钗镇，忻城县遂意乡、北更乡，都安县龙湾乡、菁盛乡、百旺乡等瑶族地区。古寨瑶族乡古棠村景色秀丽、环境怡人，地处马山县东部大石山区，大明山北麓，得天独厚的自然环境丰富了这一地区民族民间文化底蕴。古时，古寨乡古棠村一带山高林密，交通十分闭塞，山内外信息无法交流，因此古棠村的剪刀歌长期以来一直不为世人所知，直至2012年7月才被马山县文化工作者发现。

剪刀歌传到古棠村时还有一个传奇的故事。传说当年都安县百旺土司辖区内有一才女，叫蓝美娘，家境颇丰，聪颖过人，善唱山歌，特精于盘歌，在当地无人是她对手。她曾立下誓言，谁能唱赢她的歌就嫁给谁，不论贫富。消息传到古棠村，恰巧村里有一年青小伙子名叫陆道康，他天资聪颖、机智过人，唱山歌远近闻名，但由于他是瑶族人，长期受社会歧视，生活十分贫苦。当得知这一消息后，陆道康立即前去对歌，双方对唱一天一夜，正在难解难分时，陆道康突然亮出剪刀歌，蓝美娘听到前所未闻的剪刀歌，顿时哑言。最终陆道康赢得了这场对歌的胜利，美娘不负誓言与陆道康结为连理，过上了美满幸福的日子。陆道康用剪刀歌打破了壮瑶不能通婚的先河，被后人传为佳话。从此，剪刀歌在古棠村扎下根基，在陆姓人家代代相传，不曾断绝。

剪刀歌的歌词结构独特，读法为五三五言六句式，因为中间那三个字不是横写而是竖写唱的，所以记字为五一五言四句式。唱的顺序是：第一段的第一句先唱第一行的前五言句，接竖写中间三言句的头一个字，后接第二行后五言句的词；第二句唱第二行前五言句，接竖写中间三言句的末尾那个字，后接唱第一行后五言句的词，唱完一首歌的第一段，这种顺序唱法为剪刀形走向，人称为“剪刀歌”。如：

阳春三月里　好　鹧鸪叫声喧

踏青多逍遥　天　桃李开满山

　　　　　　气

其歌唱顺序为先唱“阳春三月里，好天气，桃李开满山”；后唱“踏青多逍遥，气天好，鹧鸪叫声喧”。其歌词押韵是脚脚腰韵，即第一行的前五言句末的“里”字（脚）和中间三言句末的“气”字（脚）相押韵后再和第二行后五言句中的“李”字（腰）押韵；第二行的前五言句末的“遥”字（脚）和中间三言句的“好”字（脚）相押韵后再和第一行后五言句中的“叫”字（腰）押韵。

现在剪刀歌还用于日常生活中的婚嫁、宗教活动、庆典活动及配合政府中心工作宣传演唱。并且，马山古寨乡瑶族剪刀歌歌词结构独特，唱法、押韵独特，是瑶族先人创造力

where there was a young man named Lu Daokang. He was born an intelligent man and also well-known for singing folk songs. However, he lived a hard and poor life because he was a Yao Ethnic Group that was discriminated against by the society for that time. When he heard the news, Lu Daokang went to take this challenge with no hesitance. The two did not stop singing and competing with each other until the battle is locked, Lu Daokang suddenly played his trump card, the song of scissors, which cast Fairy Lanmei in silence as she had never heard before. In the end, the winner, Lu Daokang got married with the girl and they lived a happy life. The story then became a much-told tale for the courage that made Lu Daokang broke the old custom in which Zhuang people could not marry Yao people. Since then, the song of scissors has taken root in Gutang Village and has been handed down from generation to generation in Lu family.

Scissor songs have unique structures. There are six lines in one song and three phrases in one line. In every line, the first and third phrases have five characters while the middle one only has one character. The one in the middle should not be sung horizontally like the other two but should be sang vertically with other middle characters in following lines. The order of singing is also unique. In the beginning people will sing the first five characters in the first written phrase of the first line. Then people should sing three middle characters and finally the last written phrase in the next line. This is the first oral line of scissor songs. As for the second oral line, people will start from the first phrase in the second written line, then sing the middle three characters backward and finally sing the last phrase of the first written line. Different lines cross with each like a scissor. For example:

Sunny Spring in Beautiful March...Agreeable...Lovely Francolin is Singing Happily (Another five characters)... Bright...(Another five characters)

How Leisurely is Spring Walking...Refreshing...Peaches are Blooming on Mountains

The oral form of beginning of this scissor song should be "Sunny Spring in Agreeable March, Agreeable Refreshing Bright, Peaches are Blooming on Mountains". Next, people will sing "How Leisurely is Spring Walking, Bright Refreshing Agreeable, Lovely Francolin is Singing Happily". In Chinese, the fifth character in the first written line, the seventh character in the second written line and the middle character in the third written line are in rhyme. The fifth character in the second line, the ninth character in the first line and the middle character in the first line are in rhyme.

The song is still sung for weddings, funerals, religious

剪刀歌表演
The Performance of Song of Scissors

rites, ceremonies, and even for policy promoting. The distinctive structure of the lyrics and rhyming lines symbolize the creativity and wisdom of the ancient Yao. It deserves deeper discussion on its delicate artistic features.

Though the songs have been passed down for hundreds of years, they are almost completely lost due to various restrictions, singers' gap and difficulties in compiling lyrics. In order to better protect the song of scissors, authorities of Mashan County have made a written plan, *The Five-Year Protection Plan of Song of Scissors of Yao Ethnic Group in Mashan,* carried out a survey on intangible cultural heritage to grasp information including the development history, distribution, inheritance and existence status of the Yao scissors song in Mashan, and compiled all of them into a book. In 2014, an inheritance base for the song was established in Gutang Village. A new epoch of the song has been unveiled, seeing that more than 30 students have been trained by representative inheritors Pan Liguo and Lu Jianqing. In 2018, Song of Scissors of Yao Ethnic Group was inscribed on the Seventh Autonomous Region List of Intangible Cultural Heritage, after the approval of People's Government of Nanning City.

和智慧的结晶，其中所包含的精巧的艺术特色，值得后人探讨其中的奥妙。

马山瑶族剪刀歌虽然传唱了几百年，但由于各种条件的限制，并且在编造歌词方面难度很大，再加上歌师断层，如今邻近县的过山瑶地区的剪刀歌几乎已全部失传。为了保护瑶族剪刀歌，马山县制订了《马山瑶族剪刀歌五年保护计划》，开展非物质文化遗产普查，初步掌握了马山瑶族剪刀歌的发展历史、分布状况、传承方式以及生存环境等情况，并编印成册。2014年，马山县在古寨乡古棠村建立了瑶族剪刀歌传承基地，由代表性传承人潘立国、陆建情负责培训剪刀歌手工作，已培养了30余名学员，给瑶族剪刀歌的传承与发展带来了新的契机。2018年，瑶族剪刀歌经南宁市人民政府同意，列入第七批自治区级非物质文化遗产名录。

第三章　传统舞蹈

Chapter Three　Traditional Dance

南宁傩舞

Nanning's Nuo Dance

项目名称：南宁傩舞

别称：无

分布范围：西乡塘区及周边地区

入选名录：2012年第四批自治区级非物质文化遗产名录

保护单位：西乡塘区文化馆

代表性传承人：陈亚弟

Element name: Nanning's Nuo Dance

Alternative name: None

Geographical location and range: Xixiangtang District and the surrounding areas

Element inscribed list: In 2012 on the Fourth Autonomous Region List of Intangible Cultural Heritage

Competent body involved in safeguarding: Xixiangtang District Cultural Centre

Representative inheritor: Chen Yadi

南宁傩舞是一种具有民族特色的舞蹈形式，流行于南宁市西乡塘区及周边地区。它最初是一种驱鬼逐疫、祈福消灾的宗教仪式，在明末清初最为盛行。

“傩”产生于上古时期，有着悠久深厚的历史积淀，是各种文化艺术元素的融合。傩祭早在4000多年前的商周时期就已经盛行，广西的傩祭活动也有2000多年的历史，据《南宁府志》记载：“乡间则于元宵节前三日举行春傩，演尸公，其喜若狂。”这充分说明南宁的傩祭活动早已成为民间习俗。南宁市的傩祭活动分布于当时南宁市的陈东村、友爱村、万秀村、秀厢村、大岭村、苏卢村、石埠村、大灵村、乐洲村、义平村、上林村、下椤村、北湖村、连畴村等14个村。在这14个村当中，以陈东村为代表的傩祭活动，得到了很好的传承与发展，并逐步演变为民间师公傩舞，每年农历三月初二至初六进行表演。其中，古傩“大酬雷”是该村第二十二代传承人陈健民任陈东村古傩艺术团团长后，经过深入挖掘整理以及相关专家指导，进而创作出的一种舞蹈表现形式。

傩舞的舞蹈动作原始古朴，以马步、弓步、摆拳、跳跃

Nanning's Nuo Dance, with rich ethnic features, is popular in and around Xixiangtang District, Nanning City. Once flourishing during the late Ming and early Qing Dynasty, it was initially one of many religious rites through which people believe can drive ghost away, end disasters and pray for good fortune.

As an art fusion of all kinds of cultural elements, Nuo Culture embodies a profound civilization and can be traced back to the ancient times. Nuo exorcism prevailed as early as Shang and Zhou Dynasties more than 4000 years ago. Even in Guangxi, such activities have been carried on for more than 2000 years. According to *Annals of Nanning Prefecture*, an official recording of local culture and history, "Spring Nuo, held in the countryside on the third day before the Lantern Festival, usually performed about Shigong (a local wizard) and brings uproar of joy to people." It fully shows that Nuo exorcism has already become a folk custom in Nanning. Similar activities about Nuo exorcism could be found in 14 villages then, including Chendong, Youai, Wanxiu, Xiuxiang, Daling, Sulu, Shibu, Daling, Lezhou, Yiping, Shanglin, Xialuo, Beihu and Lianchou. It is worth mentioning that Nuo exorcism in Chendong Village has especially been well inherited and developed into Nuo Dance of Shigong, which is performed every year from the second day to the sixth day of March in the lunar calendar. A traditional Nuo Dance called Da Choulei (meaning praying for spring rain and celebrating the harvest) is a quintessential one that elevates above all evolving from previous dances, owing to the guidance of experts

陈东村古傩『大酬雷』
Ancient Nuo Dance Da Choulei in Chendong Village

and the efforts of Chen Jianmin, the head of the Ancient Nuo Art Troupe of Chendong Village, and also the 22nd generation inheritor of the village.

Nuo dance is primitive and simple, with horse step, bow step, swing boxing and jump as its main dancing movements. Sometimes it is also studded with rolling, body pyramid, blessing words patterning, etc. The uninhabited and bold expression that the dancing movements deliver, along with the strong rhythm of gongs and drums, to achieve the purpose of dispelling the evil. Nuo masks, worn by Nuo dancers during their performances, are usually made by wood carvings with painting features representing different figures, evil or merciful. Da Choulei, as the representative art of Nanning Nuo Dance, also one of the representatives of Nuo culture in Guangxi, demonstrates the whole process of farm work, such as lumbering, making farm tools, plough, sowing, transplanting, cultivating, fertilizing, harvesting, threshing, grinding, cooking, celebrating bumper harvest, and feasting guests.

In order to better inherit this folk art, the government of Xixiangtang District has made unremitting efforts for deeper exploration of Nuo Culture. Shigong art troupes have been reestablished, such as the tropes in Xinwei, Youai, Shibu, Xialing, Gangde and Wulian. Among these troupes, Shigong Art Troupe of Chendong is set as a key example to link all troupes up for cultural protection. At the same time, experts and staff are sent to found Ancient Nuo Art troupe of Chendong Village and improve rehearsal and reorganization work. More young performers are attracted into troupes to revitalize the traditional art. Female performers, once were excluded from conventional Shigong Dance, are also absorbed in performances to enrich the meaning it conveys. In addition, interest-oriented classes of national culture are also held in primary and secondary schools to teach Nuo-mask dance and percussion music with ethnic flavor. The Ancient Nuo Art Troupe nowadays is supposedly an art flower flourishing on the stage of folk culture, weather-beaten but of great vitality to nourish the development of the Nuo Dance. In 2012, Nanning Nuo Dance was included into the Fourth Autonomous Region List of Intangible Cultural Heritage, after the approval of People's Government of Guangxi Zhuang Autonomous Region.

为主，有时还穿插翻滚、叠罗汉、排字等，在锣鼓的强烈节奏中展现出豪放粗犷的舞姿，以此达到驱除邪恶的目的。傩舞人表演时戴的傩面具，是傩文化的显著特征，形象或凶恶或温婉，分别代表不同的神像，一般用木雕刻彩绘而成。作为广西傩文化的代表之一，南宁傩舞的代表作“大酬雷”，反映了人们上山伐木、制作农具、耕田犁地、播种、插秧、耘田、施肥、收割、打谷、磨谷、做饭、喜庆丰收、宴请贵宾等水稻劳作的全部生产过程。

为了传承这一民间传统艺术，西乡塘区政府不断开展全面而深入细致的挖掘工作，并重新组建心圩、友爱、石埠、下灵、刚德、五联等师公艺术团，同时，以陈东师公团为重点，以点带面在全辖区展开保护工作。除此之外，还派专家与工作人员亲临指导团内的排练和组建工作，成立陈东村古傩艺术团，加大传承力度，吸收年轻演员加入师公团，为这一传统艺术形式注入新鲜活力。在表演方面，大胆突破师公传统习俗，吸收女演员参加演出活动，壮大演员队伍，丰富演出内容；还在中小学举办了民族文化兴趣班，教授傩面舞蹈及民族打击乐。现在的古傩艺术团，是活跃在民间舞台上的一朵古老而年轻的花朵。南宁傩舞正得到不断的传承和发展。2012年，南宁傩舞经广西壮族自治区人民政府同意，列入第四批自治区级非物质文化遗产名录。

“大酬雷”表演
Performance of Da Choulei

良庆区香火龙舞

Liangqing District's Spark Dragon Dance

项目名称：良庆区香火龙舞

别称：无

分布范围：良庆区缸瓦窑村及周边地区

入选名录：2010年第三批自治区级非物质文化遗产名录
　　　　　2007年第一批市级非物质文化遗产名录

保护单位：良庆区文化馆

代表性传承人：罗新有

Element name：Liangqing District's Spark Dragon Dance

Alternative name：None

Geographical location and range：Gangwayao Village of Liangqing District and the surrounding areas

Element inscribed list：In 2010 on the Third Autonomous Region List of Intangible Cultural Heritage
In 2007 on the First Municipal List of Intangible Cultural Heritage

Competent body involved in safeguarding：Liangqing District Cultural Centre

Representative inheritor：Luo Xinyou

香火龙舞表演
Performance of Spark Dragon Dance

Liangqing District's spark dragon dance is a folk dance of Zhuang Ethnic Group spreading in Gangwayao Village of Liangqing District and the surrounding areas. Different from the traditional dragon dance, Liangqing District's spark dragon dance has a set of unique dance movements and props. This dance has graceful movements with strong rhythms and contains profound meanings.

The spark dragon dance once was a celebration before firing the "Huolong kiln". The dance originated from Shiwan Town (an ancient town of crockery making) of Foshan City in Guangdong Province and was introduced to Wayao Village of Liangqing Town in Nanning and the surrounding areas from the Qing Dynasty, with a history of nearly 300 years until today. Due to the advantageous water transportation and suitable soil condition, the crockery industry was prosperous in the village. Therefore, the Wayao Village got a reputation of "the village of crockery". To obtain the blessing from god and make the crockery live up to expectation, people made the spark dragon in the shape of a line of Huolong kiln with one next to another. At the moment of firing the kiln, people would prepare some sacrificial offerings and burn incense to worship in the Earth Temple. Then people would begin to beat gongs and drums and perform the spark dragon dance excitedly. The long spark dragons would pass through the

良庆区香火龙舞是一种壮族民间舞蹈，分布于南宁市良庆区缸瓦窑村及周边地区。与舞龙民俗不同的是，良庆区香火龙舞有一套独特的舞蹈动作和道具，舞姿优美，节奏感强，寓意深刻。

香火龙舞原为“火龙窑”点火前奏的庆典，它源自广东佛山市的石湾镇（制陶瓷的古镇），自清代传入南宁市良庆镇瓦窑村一带，距今已有近300年的历史。瓦窑村因为水路畅通，且土质非常适合烧制陶器，因此制陶业十分兴旺，被誉为“缸瓦村”。为了在冥冥之中求得神的护佑，使得烧制的陶器能够达到最好的预期效果，人们就按照那一孔紧挨一孔、排成长长一列的火龙窑形状制成香火龙，在点火窑的时刻，准备好祭品，先到土地庙焚香祭拜一番，然后鸣锣击鼓，欢天喜地地狂舞香火龙。长长的香火龙在良庆镇缸瓦窑村及周边地区穿圩过巷，在烟花爆竹和锣鼓声中激舞，再加上耀目的火光、缭绕的烟雾，犹如龙腾云中，气氛热烈，场面壮观。这种在点火窑前祈祷龙神保佑烧陶成功的祭

香火龙舞表演
Performance of Spark Dragon Dance

祀舞蹈，后来由娱神慢慢发展成为一项祈求平安吉祥的民间舞蹈，每逢农历八月十四至十六晚，就会进行香火龙舞的表演。

缸瓦窑村的香火龙舞，火龙制作十分讲究，整个火龙由龙头、龙身、龙尾、龙珠、龙灯五个部分组成。由于香火龙舞多在夜晚表演，因此走街串巷时，以大排灯为前导，四盏小排灯依次相随，后面是舞珠者引一条香火龙（舞龙头者一人，舞龙身者一节一人，舞龙尾者一人，另有两人分别替换龙头龙尾）成一行，打击乐队紧跟龙尾伴奏，以增加气氛。整个表演过程有游龙、滚珠和摆龙三个部分，在广场表演时，三种表演形式可顺序也可随机反复进行，表演完毕后，香火龙走街串巷，这称为“游龙”，接着来到邕江边，人们纷纷割下一段“龙筋”（连接龙节的麻绳）拿回家收藏，最后将火龙抛入江中，以示龙归大海。

良庆区香火龙舞从产生到成熟，一直都是民间的礼俗活

streets and alleyways in Gangwayao Village of Liangqing District and people would dance in the sound of firecrackers, gongs and drums. Coupled with the dazzling flare of the flame and the curling smoke, the spark dragon seemed like speeding across the sky, which is an exciting yet spectacular scene. The spark dragon dance, which is performed for the dragon's blessing of successful burning of crockery before firing the kilns, later gradually developed from entertaining gods dance into a folk dance to pray for peace and good fortune. From the 14th day to the 16th day of the eighth lunar month, spark dragon dance will be performed in Gangwayao Village and its surrounding areas.

The production of the spark dragon used in spark dragon dance of Gangwayao Village is very exquisite. The whole spark dragon is composed of dragon head, dragon body, dragon tail, dragon ball and dragon lanterns. As the spark dragon dance is often performed at night, thus the spark dragon will follow a leading large row of lights and four small rows of lights with the guidance of the performer who holds the dragon ball (one performer holds the dragon head; several performers hold the dragon body with each person holding one section of the body; one performer holds the dragon tail; two performers are prepared to replace the head holder and tail holder respectively). The percussion band will follow the dragon tail to heighten the atmosphere. The whole performance can be divided into three major parts, including dragon touring, playing dragon ball and posing, which can be performed repeatedly or randomly during the performance. After the performance, the spark dragon will pass through the streets and alleyways, which is also known as "dragon touring". Then, the spark dragon will come to the bank of Yongjiang River. People will cut sections of "dragon vein (the hemp rope used to connect the dragon body)" and bring them home for collection. Finally, the spark dragon will be thrown into the river, indicating the dragon going back to the sea.

From its emergence to the maturity, Liangqing District's spark dragon dance has always been an indispensable performance in folk ritual activities. It has been continuously adjusted in accordance with people's preference. Up until the modern times, it has formed a relatively fixed music and dance routines. Although its drumbeat, mode and type of meter for music are not very complicated and gorgeous, it can represent unique beauty of simplicity that is loved by people.

In recent years, with the prevailing of new cultural forms, changes have taken place on the social base of the development of Nanning's spark dragon dance. Its inheritance and development are also confronted with head wind. Under such condition, the Culture Department of Liangqing District has taken a series of measures to protect and inherit this dance. For example, the department has organized investigation team to explore and collate related information of spark dragon dance in Gangwayao Village of Liangqing District and upgraded the village's dance troupe that has 25 dancers. It also established Spark Dragon Art Festival on the Mid-Autumn Festival and the Theory Seminar of Spark Dragon Dance. Through these events, Liangqing District's spark dragon dance has been revitalized and developed to a certain extent, thus representing a vibrant scene again. In 2010, with the approval of the People's Government of the Guangxi Zhuang Autonomous Region, Liangqing District's spark dragon dance was inscribed on the Third Autonomous Region List of Intangible Cultural Heritage.

动必不可少的舞蹈项目，它根据人们的喜好不断进行调整，演变到近代，已形成了相对固定成套的乐曲和舞蹈套路，其鼓点、调式和板式，虽不是十分繁复华丽，但却能显出一种特有的简约美和质朴美，深受人们喜爱。

近年来，各种新的文化形式盛行，南宁香火龙舞赖以发展的社会基础发生了变化，香火龙舞的传承和发展状况并不乐观。为此，南宁市良庆区文化部门采取了一系列的措施：如组成香火龙舞调查组深入良庆缸瓦窑村，对香火龙进行全面的发掘整理，并完善了缸瓦窑村25人的香火龙舞表演队伍；举办中秋香火龙文化艺术节和香火龙舞理论研讨会等。通过这些活动，良庆区香火龙活动得到一定程度的振兴和发展，重新呈现出生机勃勃的景象。2010年，良庆区香火龙舞经广西壮族自治区人民政府同意，列入第三批自治区级非物质文化遗产名录。

扎制香火龙
Making Spark Dragon

青秀区壮族芭蕉香火龙

Bajiao Spark Dragon Dance of Zhuang Ethnic Group，Qingxiu District

项目名称：青秀区壮族芭蕉香火龙

别称：无

分布范围：南宁市青秀区、邕宁区、兴宁区、良庆区，钦州市等

入选名录：2010年第三批自治区级非物质文化遗产名录
2009年第二批市级非物质文化遗产名录

保护单位：青秀区文化馆

代表性传承人：李武康

Element name：Bajiao Spark Dragon Dance of Zhuang Ethnic Group，Qingxiu District

Alternative name：None

Geographical location and range：Qingxiu District, Yongning District, Xingning District, Liangqing District of Nanning City; Qinzhou City and others

Element inscribed list：In 2010 on the Third Intangible Cultural Heritage List of Autonomous Region
In 2009 on the Second Municipal List of Intangible Cultural Heritage

Competent body involved in safeguarding：Qingxiu District Cultural Centre

Representative inheritor：Li Wukang

Bajiao spark dragon dance of Zhuang Ethnic Group is a traditional folk dance of Zhuang that has a history of over 300 years. It is mainly popular in Qingxiu District, Yongning District, Xingning District, Liangqing District in Nanning and Qinzhou City in Guangxi, among which Changtang Town of Qingxiu District is the most representative one.

Bajiao spark dragon dance of Zhuang Ethnic Group originated from an ancient legend. It was said that more than 300 years ago, there was a village at the foot of Junshan Mountain, which faced today's Changtang Town of Qingxiu District across the river. Due to the inconvenient transportation, people in this village had lived an enclosing yet tranquil lifestyle. One day, with the violent shaking of the mountain and the earth, the whole village suddenly collapsed with a crash. The village, home to hundreds of people, was destroyed in a flash with only a few villagers surviving. People believed that it was the fairy dragon who control the fortune abandoning the village that caused this disaster. At this time, people who sank into the superstitious mood happened to see a strange thing up and down with many floating Bajiao (Banana) trees in the Huishui Bend of Yongjiang River. Then, people salvaged it and believed it should be a prostrate statue of Bodhisattva. The floating Bajiao trees in the river were just like the fairy dragon lingering in the Huishui Bend. People believed that it was the fairy dragon escaped from the village on the other side of the river that wanted to settle down in this place. Therefore, the local people built a temple for the Bodhisattva and burned incense to comfort the fairy dragon, setting up a home for both of them. That day happened to be the 19th day of the sixth lunar month, thus it later became the celebration day of the foundation of Changtang Street. At the beginning of the establishment of the village, there was only a sparse population. However, the Bajiao trees clustered round and winded into a street, thus people gave the name "Bajiao Street" to it.

One year, due to the severe drought and crop failure, people can only live on bananas. After bananas being eaten out, people began to eat the banana pith inside the stems or even the roots of the trees. The banana trees in this village sacrificed themselves and saved the villagers during the hardest times. Since then, out of the appreciation for the grace of Bajiao Dragon (Banana Tree Dragon), people decided to make a Bajiao Dragon model with large banana leaves and put incense on the whole dragon body on the birthday of the local guardian god (the 2nd day of the 2nd lunar month) and on the celebration day of the foundation of Changtang Street (the 19th day of the 6th lunar month) every year. Accompanied by

壮族芭蕉香火龙是一种属于舞蹈范畴的壮族传统民俗表演，距今已有300多年的历史，主要流传于广西南宁市的青秀区、邕宁区、兴宁区、良庆区以及钦州市等地，其中尤以南宁市青秀区长塘镇最具代表性。

壮族芭蕉香火龙源于一个古老的传说。相传300多年前，在与现南宁市青秀区长塘镇隔江相望的军山脚下，有个古老的村子，因交通不便，村里的人们一直过着闭塞而又静谧的生活，突然有一天，“轰隆”一声巨响，随着山体和大地的剧烈震动，整个村子轰然陷落，数百人的村子顷刻间村毁人亡，只有几人侥幸逃生。人们认为这是主宰旦夕祸福的神龙弃村遁逃之故，陷入迷信情绪的人们，恰巧看到对面邕江的回水湾内浮泛着许多芭蕉树，其中有个奇怪的东西随波沉浮，于是人们划船将其捞起，竟是一尊俯伏于水的菩萨塑像。那些漂浮水中的芭蕉树，正如神龙流连于回水湾不肯离去，人们认为这是从对面村子遁逃的神龙要在此登岸安居。于是当地民众便在岸上为菩萨建庙，焚香安龙，结寮安居。这一天是农历六月十九，此后这一天便成了长塘街的建街吉日。因为当时新村初建，居民稀少，到处蕉林簇簇，逶迤成街，便起名“芭蕉街”。

某年大旱，庄稼颗粒无收，缺粮断炊的人们便以芭蕉为食，吃完芭蕉，又吃芭蕉杆里的芭蕉心，还挖掘芭蕉根充饥。在人们最困难的时候，芭蕉舍身相救，它牺牲自己保住了众生，出于铭感芭蕉龙的恩泽，人们于每年农历二月初二土地神诞日、六月十九街庆日，选择高大的芭蕉扎成龙形，在龙身上遍插香火，并配以吹打乐和舞蹈，举行欢乐而盛大的舞芭蕉龙活动，祈请神龙保佑生活美满、幸福平安。

壮族芭蕉香火龙最初由一根芭蕉树构成，芭蕉根作龙头，芭蕉叶作龙尾，制作简单，造型简易。之后由于生产力水平的发展，人们也越来越追求造型上的美感，于是就取龙飞九天之意，将芭蕉龙制作成九节龙，每节以竹子编织，再用芭蕉绳捆扎连成一体，饰上芭蕉壳，扎上芭蕉叶，于龙头、龙身处密插点燃的香火，就成了新颖别致、熠熠生辉的芭蕉龙。壮族芭蕉香火龙舞龙的主要套路有醒龙、纳礼、龙巡、播雨、除害、撒福、交合、舞乐、谢龙等。由于壮族芭蕉香火龙源自壮族师公舞，以师公麒麟舞步、九罡舞步为独特的舞蹈表现形式，演出时有游龙、滚珠和摆龙等舞法。

以芭蕉香火龙巡游为核心，舞狮、唱山歌、演师公戏、斗竹马等一系列民俗活动也竞相开始。而除了每年农历的正月外，壮族芭蕉香火龙也在壮族二月二龙抬头节、三月三歌节等活动中占有重要的地位，进而构成了一个独特的壮族芭蕉香火龙文化活动空间。

近年来，在青秀区政府的大力支持下，壮族芭蕉香火龙得到了较大的发展：壮族芭蕉香火龙在长塘镇楞仲村建立了壮族芭蕉香火龙传承基地；2011年6月，长塘镇壮族芭蕉香火龙舞队代表广西到浙江宁波参加了第十届中国民间文艺山花奖舞龙大赛，喜获金奖。这条绿色的巨龙在不断传承和发展的同时，也向世界展示了独具特色的壮族原生态文化。2010年，壮族芭蕉香火龙经广西壮族自治区人民政府同意，列入第三批自治区级非物质文化遗产名录。

壮族芭蕉香火龙
Bajiao Spark Dragon Dance of Zhuang Ethnic Group

wind and percussion music and dance, people would hold a joyful and grand dance of Bajiao Dragon so as to pray to the fairy dragon for contented life, happiness and safeness.

At the very start, the Bajiao spark dragon was made by a large banana tree with the root as the dragon head and the crown as the tail, which was easy to make due to its simple shape. Later, with the development of productivity, people began to look at the aesthetics of the model. Therefore, taking an idea of "the dragon flying onto the Ninth Heaven (the highest of heavens)", people then made the Bajiao dragon into nine sections with bamboo canes weaving first and banana ropes binding next. Then decorated with plantain leaves and burning incense on the dragon head and body, a novel and sparkling Bajiao Dragon is finished. The main routines of the Bajiao spark dragon dance of Zhuang include awakening dragon, offering sacrifices, dragon touring, commanding the rain, removing the evil, spreading blessing, making friends, dancing and playing music, and thanking for the dragon. As Bajiao spark dragon dance is developed from Shigong dance of Zhuang, its unique dance steps include Shigong Kylin step and Nine Gang step. The performance mainly consists of dragon touring, playing dragon ball and posing.

With the parade of Bajiao spark dragon dance as the core, a series of folk activities such as lion dance, folk song singing, Shigong dance and bamboo hobby horse competition also begin to develop. In addition to performing in the first lunar month each year, Bajiao spark dragon dance also plays an important role on the Dragon-Head-Raising Festival (the 2nd day of the 2nd lunar month) and the Song Fair of Zhuang Ethnic Group (the 3rd day of the 3rd lunar month), thus further forming a unique space for the development of Bajiao spark dragon dance of Zhuang Ethnic Group.

In recent years, with the great support of the government of Qingxiu District, Bajiao spark dragon dance has gained substantial development. The inheritance base of Bajiao spark dragon dance of Zhuang Ethnic Group has been established in Lengzhong Village of Changtang Town. In 2011, representing Guangxi Zhuang Autonomous Region, the dance troupe of Changtang Town went to Ningbo of Zhejiang Province to participate in the Tenth Mountain Flower Award for Chinese Folk Art — Dragon Dance Competition and won the gold award. While continuing to inherit and develop, the green Bajiao spark dragon also represents the unique culture of original Zhuang Ethnic Group. In 2010, with the approval of the People's Government of the Guangxi Zhuang Autonomous Region, Bajiao spark dragon dance of Zhuang was inscribed on the Third Autonomous Region List of Intangible Cultural Heritage.

南宁壮族春牛舞

Nanning's Spring Cattle Dance of Zhuang Ethnic Group

项目名称：南宁壮族春牛舞

别称：春牛舞

分布范围：江南区苏圩镇及周边地区

入选名录：2010年第三批自治区级非物质文化遗产名录

保护单位：江南区文化馆

代表性传承人：奚均仁（已故）

Element name: Nanning's Spring Cattle Dance of Zhuang Ethnic Group

Alternative name: Spring Cattle Dance

Geographical location and range: Suxu Town of Jiangnan District and the surrounding areas

Element inscribed list: In 2010 on the Third Autonomous Region List of Intangible Cultural Heritage

Competent body involved in safeguarding: Jiangnan District Cultural Centre, Nanning

Representative inheritor: Xi Junren (Late)

壮族春牛舞
Spring Cattle Dance of Zhuang Ethnic Group

春牛舞是广泛流传于壮族地区的民间传统表演形式，是春节习俗中的一项重要内容，于春节期间由春牛贺年队到各村表演，由于演出活动越来越受群众欢迎，进而形成各类喜庆日子必不可少的庆祝活动，主要分布于南宁市江南区苏圩镇及周边地区。

古代南方百越族群以种植水稻为生，耕牛则为必不可少的农用牲畜。早在新石器时代，壮族先民就形成了崇拜牛的思想，为表达对牛的崇拜和敬奉，壮族地区有“敬牛节”“牛倌节”“脱轭节”等传统节日，春牛舞也是其中之一。广西的土牛迎春活动之起源，要追溯至唐宋时期，当时在中原地区即有鞭春活动并流传开来。据明代《南宁府志》记载：“立春先一日，府州县排列彩亭，设土牛，迎村于东郊。”“是日办理迎春仪仗甚盛，凡距城二十里内，男女老少相竞追逐来观，至为热闹。”由此可见，土牛迎春的习俗最晚在明代即已盛行于广西。

春牛舞表演有固定的套路和故事情节，分为四个部分：

Spring cattle dance is a traditional folk performance widely spreading in Zhuang areas, which is also one of the important customs of the Spring Festival. During the Spring Festival, the spring cattle dance troupe will perform in each village. As the performance is increasingly popular among the masses, the spring cattle dance, which is mainly popular in Suxu Town of Jiangnan District of Nanning and the surrounding areas, has become an indispensable celebration activity on festive days.

In ancient times, people of Baiyue (also known as Guyue) Ethnic Group in south China made a living by planting rice, thus cattle were a kind of essential agricultural animal. As early as in the Neolithic Age, the ancestors of Zhuang had formed the idea of cattle worshipping. To express their reverence toward the cattle, there are traditional festivals such as “Cattle Worship Festival”, “Cowherd Festival”, “Cattle King Festival” and so on, among which Spring Cattle Dance is also one of the activities to worship cattle. The origin of welcoming the spring with clay cattle can be traced back to the Tang and Song Dynasties. At that time, the activity of whipping the clay cattle to welcome the spring in Central China began to spread to other places. According to the *Annals of Nanning Prefecture* in the Ming Dynasty, “People would arrange colored pavilions (a kind of sacrificial offerings made of paper) and set clay cattle the day before the Beginning of Spring so as to welcome the spring in the eastern suburbs” and “all people regardless of age and sex living within a circumstance of 20 miles would come to the Spring Welcoming Activity, which would be a bustling and splendid occasion”. These records verify that the custom of welcoming spring with clay cattle had been popular in Guangxi in the Ming Dynasty at the latest.

The performance of spring cattle dance has four parts of fixed routines and plots. In the first part, the male peasant first comes to the stage and sings the song *Wishing for a Harvest This Year*. Then a farm cattle performer comes to the stage and makes movements such as “getting out of the shed”, “browsing”, “scratching the itch”, “mooing” and “whisking flies away”. At this time, the peasant will shoulder a bamboo pole to pretend to drive the cattle to plough and will sing the *Song of Driving Cattle* to perform the plots of cattle-taming and sowing. In the second part, a female peasant and a female clown will come to the stage to perform the scenes of pulling up seedlings, rice transplanting and caring the rice seedling field. During the performance, the female clown will speak in Chinese while others will speak in Zhuang language, which will cause funny misunderstandings, enabling people to burst out laughing. The third part is the laboring scenes of the peasant couple and other villagers, representing an idyllic scene of harmonious relationship among people of Zhuang Ethnic Group. In the last part, the villagers will perform laboring scenes like harvesting and carrying, intending to celebrate the bumper harvest. Then, the child cowherd will ride cattle onto the stage and drive the cattle to fight for fun, which forms a jubilant atmosphere. The dance part of this performance can be divided into three parts. The first one is cattle dance, which aims to simulate the movements and habits of the cattle. The second part of dance is to simulate the scene of laboring through using colorful fans and other props. The third part is to represent the stylized tea-picking steps.

The spring cattle dance is rich in forms. It artistically processes the movements of people and animals and beautifies the laboring scene, such as using the opening and closing of colored fans to symbolize sowing and planting, which provides people a familiar aesthetic feeling. The activities and singing contents are plentiful. Both male and female tea pickers will perform in accordance with the lyrics. Each of them usually performs as multiple characters with implicit yet humorous improvisations, which will win bursts of applause from the audience. The costumes and props of the spring cattle dance are very exquisite and particular. The performers such as tea pickers, cowherd and the performers of cattle are required to wear in accordance with the convention. The spring cattle is made by wires and bamboo strips with a piece of yellow velvet covered on it. With meaningful connotation, the whole activity of welcoming the spring not only represents the diligence and simplicity of Zhuang people, but also embodies the unique artistic conception of folk artists, expressing people's sincere wish for bumper harvest and happy life. In 2010, the spring cattle dance of Zhuang Ethnic Group was inscribed on the Third Autonomous Region List of Intangible Cultural Heritage.

1.耕田郎上，唱《都想今年五谷好》。接着春牛上，做出“出栏”“吃草”“搔痒”“鸣叫”“赶牛虻”等动作。耕田郎扛一根竹子做套牛“犁田”动作，同时唱《十二月使牛歌》，表演驯牛、播种等劳动情节。2.插秧娘及丑旦那连婆相继出场，表演拔秧、插秧、护理秧田等劳动情节。丑旦表演时用汉语对话，其他人用壮语对话，对答之间，误会迭出，令人捧腹大笑。3.表演耕田郎夫妻及村民的劳动场景，反映壮民和睦相处的田园风景。4.众乡亲表演收割、挑谷等劳动情节，意在庆丰收。放牛娃们骑牛上场，并驱牛相斗，场面热闹非凡。春牛舞中舞蹈分为三个部分：一是牛舞，模仿牛的动作、习性、各种状态；二是借助彩扇等道具模仿农业生产动作的舞蹈；三是展示程式化的采茶步。

春牛舞舞蹈形式多样，将模拟动物、人物生活场景等动作进行艺术加工，如彩扇一开一合象征播种和插秧，赋予了舞蹈丰富的含义，美化了劳动场景，给人以亲切的审美感受，活动演唱内容丰富，茶公茶娘随着歌词内容进行表演，往往是一人多角，即兴发挥，含蓄幽默，赢得观众的阵阵掌声和喝彩。春牛舞服饰、道具十分讲究，茶公、茶娘、牛仔与舞牛者都需按规定穿戴，春牛道具由铁丝和竹篾等扎起，并蒙上彩绘的赭黄色平绒。整个迎春活动内涵丰富，既体现出壮族劳动人民勤劳且朴实的性格特征，又凝聚了民间艺人独特的艺术构思，表达人们对新的一年粮食丰收、生活美满的真诚祈愿。2010年，春牛舞列入第三批自治区级非物质文化遗产名录。

壮族麒麟舞

Kylin Dance of Zhuang Ethnic Group

项目名称：壮族麒麟舞

别称：无

分布范围：青秀区长塘镇及周边地区

入选名录：2012年第四批自治区级非物质文化遗产名录

保护单位：青秀区文化馆

代表性传承人：谭景威

Element name: Kylin Dance of Zhuang Ethnic Group

Alternative name: None

Geographical location and range: Changtang Town of Qingxiu District and the surrounding areas

Element inscribed list: In 2012 on the Fourth Autonomous Region List of Intangible Cultural Heritage

Competent body involved in safeguarding: Qingxiu District Cultural Centre

Representative inheritor: Tan Jingwei

麒麟舞
Kylin Dance

Kylin is a kind of strange animal in ancient Chinese legend, which is composed of the dragon's head, the deer's body, the horse's hoofs, the bull's tail and the wolf's forehead and covered by multicolored scales. Embedding good wishes, people regard kylin as a symbol of auspiciousness and happiness. Kylin dance of Zhuang is one of the folk dances that is popular in Changtang Town of Qingxiu District and the surrounding areas such as Liangqing District, Jiangnan District and Hengzhou City. Its major dance step, Sangang low step, is to simulate the movements of animals, such as frogs jumping into the water, crabs creeping out of the hole, lobsters crawling to the bank and Zhenfu (a deity in Taoism) treading the turtle and the snake. With the careful observation of life, people of Zhuang give full play of their imagination and constantly enrich the movements and connotations of the dance, gradually creating the kylin dance that embodies Zhuang people's wishes for good weather, prosperity and peace.

Kylin dance of Zhuang Ethnic Group was introduced from Guangdong Province in the Ming Dynasty, which has a history of over 500 years. This dance usually has 12 main dancers and several supporting dancers. The 12 main dancers, half male and half female, represent the 12 months in a

麒麟是我国古代传说中的一种奇异动物，它的整个形象是龙头、鹿身、马蹄、牛尾、狼额，身披五彩鳞甲，人们在其身上寄予了美好的祝愿，是吉祥和幸福的象征。壮族麒麟舞是流传于以青秀区长塘镇为中心，并辐射至周边的良庆区、江南区、横州市等地的一种民间舞蹈形式。它以三罡矮步为主要步调，模拟动物的动作特征，如青蛙落水、螃蟹出洞、龙虾爬岸、珍妇踏龟蛇等，人们在认真观察生活后又充分发挥自己的想象，不断丰富舞蹈的动作与内涵，形成了麒麟舞这样一种凝聚着壮族人民对风调雨顺、国泰民安等美好期盼的民间习俗。

壮族麒麟舞于明代从广东传入，距今已有500多年的历史。表演时有主要演员12人，次要演员若干。主要演员中男女各半，分别代表一年12个月，寓意四季平安。在表演麒麟舞的舞台两旁，放置火球来驱邪去晦。壮族麒麟舞表演中有金麒麟和蓝麒麟，各代表一雌一雄，金麒麟寓意祖国繁荣富强，蓝麒麟则寓意人们和谐共处、生活幸福美满。当麒麟出场时一对“金童玉女”端坐高台，旁边是手舞足蹈“风情万种”的“花婆娘”，队列后面是乐手与歌手方阵，包括2名唢呐手、3名锣鼓手和3名歌手。每头麒麟由两个人来表演，一个舞动麒麟头，另一个钻进麒麟身体内部，以腰腿运动演绎麒麟尾，随着音乐节奏，它们时而摇头摆尾，时而狂欢嬉耍，有绝活，有互动，生动活泼，舞态多姿，将喜怒哀乐的情绪表露无遗。

作为壮族地区独特的舞蹈艺术形式，麒麟舞兼收并蓄了壮族师公舞蹈等各种民族舞蹈、武术之精华，又融合了一些说唱艺术的元素，整体上别具一格，具有很高的审美价值和研究价值。同时，壮族麒麟舞的保护和发展，还能够促进南宁及周边地区民族文化的传承，对推动地方旅游业发展、打造旅游文化名片，都有积极作用。

为了传承和发展壮族麒麟舞这一文化遗产，青秀区政府、长塘镇政府及有关部门都对此予以高度重视，并通过资金投入、技术指导等方式给予大力支持。在2011年农历二月初二的“土地诞”日，由青秀区政府、城区文化馆组织，对壮族麒麟舞进行了一次全面而深入的文字、摄影、摄像采录工作，使这项古老的民间舞蹈能够更广泛地传播和发展。2012年，壮族麒麟舞经广西壮族自治区人民政府同意，列入第四批自治区级非物质文化遗产名录。

year with an implication of being well throughout the year. Fireballs were placed on either side of the stage to ward off evil spirits. In the performance of kylin dance of Zhuang, there are dancers to perform golden male kylin and blue female kylin respectively. The golden one symbolizes the prosperity and strength of the motherland while the blue one symbolizes the harmony between people and happiness in life. When the kylins appear on the stage, a pair of golden boy and jade girl (immortal boy and girl in waiting of a divine house) will sit on the high platform, next to the fascinating “Hua Po Niang (a women)” who is dancing. Behind the dancers are musicians and singers, including two suona horn players, three gongs and drums players and three singers. Each kylin is performed by two people, with one waving the head and the other getting into the body of the kylin costume to control the tail with his waist and legs. Accompanied by music rhythm, the kylins sometimes shake their heads and tails and sometimes make fun together. With unique skills and interaction, the dance vividly represents the four moods (pleasure, anger, sorrow and joy) of kylins with various dance movements.

As a unique dance art of Zhuang Ethnic Group, kylin dance has absorbed the essence of various ethnic dances and martial arts such as Shigong dance of Zhuang Ethnic Group, and it integrated some elements of storytelling and singing. It is special on the whole and bears great aesthetic and research values. At the same time, the protection and development of kylin dance can promote the inheritance of the ethnic cultures in Nanning and the surrounding areas and play a positive role in promoting the development of local tourism and establishing tourism and cultural brand.

To inherit and develop the cultural heritage of kylin dance of Zhuang, the governments of Changtang Town and Qingxiu District and relevant departments have attached great importance to this dance. They have provided strong support to its inheritance through financial aid and technical guidance. On the second day of the second lunar month in 2011, that is, the “birthday of the local guardian god” in south China, the government of Qingxiu District and the culture centre organized a comprehensive work to collect and collate writing materials, photos, and video records about kylin dance so as to promote a wider spreading and development of it. In 2012, with the approval of the People’s Government of the Guangxi Zhuang Autonomous Region, kylin dance of Zhuang was inscribed on the Fourth Autonomous Region List of Intangible Cultural Heritage.

壮族九莲灯

Jiulian Lantern Dance of Zhuang Ethnic Group

项目名称：壮族九莲灯

别称：佛手莲花舞

分布范围：以隆安县雁江镇为中心，广泛流传于隆安县那桐镇、乔建镇、屏山乡、布泉乡、南威镇及百色市、平果市等

入选名录：2010年第三批自治区级非物质文化遗产名录
2010年第三批市级非物质文化遗产名录

保护单位：隆安县文化馆

代表性传承人：何方仕

Element name: Jiulian Lantern Dance of Zhuang Ethnic Group

Alternative name: Dance of Buddha's Hand with Lotus

Geographical location and range: Taking Yanjiang Town in Long'an County as the centre, widely spreading in towns of Long'an County such as Natong, Qiaojian, Pingshan, Buquan, Nanwei, as well as cities like Baise, Pingguo and others

Element inscribed list: In 2010 on the Third Autonomous Region List of Intangible Cultural Heritage
In 2010 on the Third Municipal List of Intangible Cultural Heritage

Competent body involved in safeguarding: Long'an County Cultural Centre

Representative inheritor: He Fangshi

2013年6月，在文化遗产日上隆安县"壮族九莲灯"进行表演
In June 2013, on the Day of Cultural Heritage, the "Jiulian Lantern Dance of Zhuang Ethnic Group" Performed in Long'an County

壮族九莲灯亦称佛手莲花舞，是以隆安县雁江镇为中心，广泛流传于隆安县那桐镇、乔建镇、屏山乡、布泉乡、南威镇及百色市、平果市等地区的风格独特的壮族民间舞蹈。

作为一种历史悠久的民间舞蹈，壮族九莲灯曾是道公为逝者超度亡魂的道场中一段极具特色的舞蹈，是在为有儿有女、子孙满堂、福禄寿全的老人去世后或二次葬的固定祭祀舞蹈。现在的壮族九莲灯，仍然活跃在民间法事活动中，还成为一种独特的艺术形式，在大众舞台上大放异彩。

Jiulian lantern dance of Zhuang Ethnic Group is also known as the dance of Buddha's hand with lotus. With Yanjiang Town in Long'an County as the centre, this unique folk dance of Zhuang Ethnic Group is widely spreading in towns of Long'an County such as Natong, Qiaojian, Pingshan, Buquan, Nanwei as well as cities like Baise and Pingguo.

As a folk dance with a long history, Jiulian lantern dance of Zhuang used to be one of the highly distinctive dances in Taoist rites when the Taoist released the soul of the deceased from purgatory. It was a fixed dance for the funeral or the secondary burial for the elders who had both sons and daughters, children and grandchildren as well as happiness and longevity. Nowadays, Jiulian lantern dance is still active in folk ritual activities and has become a unique art yielding brilliant results on stage.

Since ancient times, it was popular to invite Taoists to conduct religious rites in folk funerals of Zhuang in Yanjiang County. As early as in 1774, the Yanjiang County established the market and quickly became a famous commercial port of Long'an County due to its convenient land and water transportation and advantageous geographical location. Then it got the reputation of "Mini Nanning" and "Mini Hong Kong". With the development of commercial and trade activities, cultural exchanges became increasingly frequent. At that time, based on local customs and later absorption of foreign culture essence, the local Taoists created the ritual dance named Jiulian lantern dance of Zhuang.

As a ritual dance, the movements of Jiulian lantern dance are choreographed in accordance with sacrificial offerings, including incense, flower, lamp, perfume, food and music. The dancers will vary poses and make flower-shaped gestures through changes on hand movements, wrists and fingers during singing. The movements and gestures include rotating fingers into flower shape, turning wrists outward or inward to make flower shape, Buddha's hand, dharma's hand, monk's hand, incense gesture, flower gesture, lamp gesture, perfume gesture, food gesture, music gesture, turning wrist into Buddha's hand, turning wrist into sword shape, turning wrist and making figure snap, holding hands flatly and flicking finger, Qianri finger flower, finger flower of mercy, finger flower of Triratna and so on. In addition, the Jiulian lanterns can be divided into three categories: top level, middle level and bottom level. The incense, flower, lamp, perfume, food and music in Jiulian lantern dance will be distributed to filial men and women through Buddhas, dharmas and monks so as to bless them with bumper harvests, thriving domestic animals and smooth life. It also plays a role in teaching people that only doing good deeds can they get the true happiness and embark onto a happy, wealthy and healthy life.

The distribution areas of Jiulian lantern dance of Zhuang Ethnic Group are originally limited, and today its influence has been further shrinking. In addition, some excellent dancers have gradually retired from the stage due to their advanced ages, leading to an increasingly serious shortage of dancers. Under such condition, the culture department of Long'an County made positive efforts to make in-depth exploration, collation and improvement of Jiulian lantern dance of Zhuang Ethnic Group in the 1980s, making it become an excellent stage art. These efforts have also aided in the dance's spreading and improved its influence, thus enabling this art form with distinctive ethnic characteristics to be continuously inherited and developed.

自古以来，在雁江镇的壮族民间丧事中，就一直盛行请道公做法事的习俗。早在1774年，雁江镇开圩，由于雁江镇水陆交通便利，地理位置独特，很快便成为隆安县远近闻名的商埠，有着“小南宁”“小香港”的美称。由于商业贸易活动发达，文化的交流也逐渐频繁起来。这时候当地道公以本地风俗为基础，吸收外来文化精华，创造了祭典舞蹈——壮族九莲灯。

作为一种祭祀舞蹈，壮族九莲灯围绕“香、花、灯、涂、果、乐”等内容，边唱边通过手、腕、指来变化造型，做出各种花手舞，它的动作及手位包括：翻腕轮指花、外内腕花、佛手、法手、僧手、香手、花手、灯手、涂手、果手、乐手、腕花佛手、腕花剑指、腕花响指、端掌弹指、千日指花、慈悲指花、三宝指花等。除此之外，“九莲灯”的花灯分上、中、下三品，通过“佛、法、僧”将“九莲灯”中的“香、花、灯、涂、果、乐”赐予孝男孝女，祝福他们日后种植业五谷丰登、养殖业六畜兴旺，生活顺顺利利，教诲众人只有行善积德才能修成正果，迎来福、禄、寿的美满生活。

壮族九莲灯本身的传播区域有限，如今所能活动的地域更是日渐缩小。此外，一些有造诣的壮族九莲灯舞师由于年事已高，逐渐退出舞台，人才青黄不接的状况日趋严重。基于这种状况，隆安县文化部门做出了积极的努力，于20世纪80年代对壮族九莲灯进行深入的挖掘整理和艺术加工，使之成为一种优秀舞台艺术形式，拓宽其传播范围，提高其影响力，使壮族九莲灯这一极富民族特色的艺术形式得以不断传承和发展。

瑶族蚩尤舞

Chiyou Dance of Yao Ethnic Group

项目名称：瑶族蚩尤舞

别称：无

分布范围：马山县里当乡、古寨乡、白山镇瑶族村屯，忻城县北更乡，上林县镇圩瑶族乡等

入选名录：2014年第五批自治区级非物质文化遗产名录

保护单位：马山县文化馆

代表性传承人：蓝秀神（已故）

Element name：Chiyou Dance of Yao Ethnic Group

Alternative name：None

Geographical location and range：Lidang Town, Guzhai Town, Villages of Yao Ethnic Group in Baishan Town of Mashan County; Beigeng Town of Xincheng County; Zhenxu Town of Yao Ethnic Group in Shanglin County and others

Element inscribed list：In 2014 on the Fifth Autonomous Region List of Intangible Cultural Heritage

Competent body involved in safeguarding：Mashan County Cultural Centre

Representative inheritors：Lan Xiushen (Late)

Chiyou dance of Yao Ethnic Group is a traditional dance to extol and commemorate Chiyou (a mythological warrior engaged in fighting with the Yellow Emperor) with a long history about over 700 years. It is performed to worship gods and celebrate the festival during the 27th to 29th of the fifth lunar month each year, that is, the festival of redeeming the vow to gods of Yao. The Chiyou dance is mainly popular in Lidang Town, Guzhai Town and villages of Yao Ethnic Group in Baishan Town of Mashan County, Beigeng Town of Xincheng County as well as Zhenxu Town of Shanglin County.

Chiyou was the leader of the Jiuli clan tribal alliance in the ancient times. He was brave and wise and later was known as "the God of War". According to *The Record of Yuejue* (the local chronicles of Wu and Yue areas), there is a record said that Chiyou once helped Shaohao to govern the western areas. There is another record in this book said that Chiyou was an assistant of Shaohao as well as the leader of Jiuli clan. After researching, it is found that Chiyou was the very ancestor of Miao, Yao and other ethnic minorities in China. After the Battle of Zhulu, Chiyou and his subordinates were hunted down by Emperor Yan and Yellow Emperor, thus they fled the central plains and migrated to the south for living. In order to escape the wars, they lived in high mountains, hunting birds and animals for food and opening up wasteland for farming. Through their diligence and efforts, they were able to live a relatively stable life. Therefore, they rehabilitated and bred here, gradually forming a unique culture of Ethnic Group. People of Yao designated the days from 27th to 29th of the fifth lunar month as the festival of redeeming the vow to gods. On these days, they would choreograph sacrificial dance to worship Chiyou. This is the origin of the name of "Chiyou Dance".

Chiyou dance mainly includes seven parts: opening channel, hunting, cutting millet, threshing, winnowing, making merry on the field and carrying millet. The performer of Chiyou will first come to the stage and blow the horn. Then he will shout for three times of "time to opening wasteland". Later, other performers will respond him with "hullo" and the sound of drum and music will begin. Then the clansman will come to the stage with a long knife in his hand and the clanswoman will come with a bag of seeds of five grains on her back. Next, the male actors holding spears, bows and arrows, bird traps and other props will come to the stage following the clansman and the female actors with bamboo baskets, dustpan, hoe and sickle will be on the stage following the clanswoman. All the dance movements are designed in accordance with the

瑶族蚩尤舞是瑶族的传统舞蹈，为歌颂和纪念先贤蚩尤，在每年旧历五月二十七日至二十九日还愿节，敬奉神灵和庆祝节日时表演。蚩尤舞主要流行于马山县里当乡、古寨乡、白山镇瑶族村屯，忻城县北更乡，上林县镇圩乡等地区。它历史悠久，迄今已有700多年的历史。

蚩尤是上古时代九黎氏族部落联盟的首领，他骁勇善战，有"战神"之称。据《越绝书》记载："少昊治西方，蚩尤佐之，使主金。"又载："蚩尤是少昊之末，九黎之君。"经过研究发现，蚩尤就是中国少数民族中苗、瑶等民族的始祖。由于逐鹿一战，蚩尤被炎、黄二帝合擒杀之，其部下惨遭追杀，于是纷纷逃离中原祖地，迁徙到南方以求生存。为躲避战乱，他们在高山峻岭之中，捕鸟猎兽、开荒种地，通过自己的勤奋和努力，过上了较为安定的生活，并在此休养生息，繁衍后代，形成了一种独特的少数民族文化。每年的旧历五月二十七至二十九，瑶族人民定为还愿节，编排祭祀舞蹈来敬奉蚩尤，"蚩尤舞"因此得名。

蚩尤舞主要分为七个部分：开渠、狩猎、割谷、打谷、扬谷、闹场和背谷。表演先由"蚩尤"出场，吹起强劲的牛角号，随后高呼三声——"开荒啰"，众应："呼喂"，然后鼓乐声起。紧接着，男族人带着长刀、女族人带着一包五谷种子上场，众男演员手握长矛、弓箭、捕鸟器等道具跟男族人上场，众女演员背竹篓，拿簸箕、锄头、镰刀等道具，随女族人上场。整场表演的舞蹈动作都是以蚩尤舞的七个主要部分来设计，内容丰富，形式优美，场面古朴粗犷，体现出了瑶族人勤劳勇敢的精神。

作为凝聚了瑶族历史文化的舞蹈形式，瑶族蚩尤舞采取现实主义的创作方法编排舞蹈，展示了原生态的民族文化，不仅有很强的欣赏价值，还对研究瑶族历史文化、社会生活变迁有重要参考价值。

2013年11月，参加第二届全区基层群众文艺会演舞蹈比赛获三等奖
In November 2013, Winning the Third Prize in the Second Grassroots Mass Art and Dance Competition

由于人民群众文化娱乐方式日益丰富多彩，对原始古朴的民族文化逐渐失去兴趣，瑶族蚩尤舞的传承也受到了一定的影响。1982年，经过马山县文化工作者的挖掘整理，曾一度失传的瑶族传统舞蹈蚩尤舞，再次呈现在人们面前。2008年，马山县展开非物质文化遗产普查，初步掌握了瑶族蚩尤舞的发展历史、分布状况、传承方式以及生存环境等情况，并编印成册，作为资料留存。2009年，马山县政府在白山镇民族村弄着屯建立了瑶族蚩尤舞传承基地，由传承人教授蚩尤舞。2014年，瑶族蚩尤舞经广西壮族自治区人民政府同意，列入第五批自治区级非物质文化遗产名录。

seven parts of Chiyou dance, which are colorful in content, beautiful in form as well as simple and unsophisticated in scene, vividly representing the industrious and brave spirit of people of Yao Ethnic Group.

As a dance that embodies the history and culture of Yao, Chiyou dance is choreographed with realistic approaches, which represents the original ethnic cultures. It not only has strong appreciation value, but also has important reference value for studying the history, culture and vicissitudes of social life.

As ways of entertainment becoming increasingly diverse, people has begun to lose interest in the primitive ethnic cultures, which to some extent has affected the inheritance of Chiyou dance of Yao. In 1982, with the exploration and collation of art workers in Mashan County, the Chiyou dance that once was lost reappeared in front of people. In 2008, Mashan County carried out a survey of intangible cultural heritage and initially grasped the information about Chiyou dance's development history, distribution, inheritance and living environment, which has been complied into books and retained as data. In 2009, the government of Mashan County established an inheritance base of Chiyou dance of Yao Ethnic Group in Nongzhuo Village of Baishan's Ethnic Group's villages, where the Chiyou dance can be taught by the inheritors. With the approval of the People's Government of the Guangxi Zhuang Autonomous Region, Chiyou dance of Yao Ethnic Group was inscribed on the Fifth Autonomous Region List of Intangible Cultural Heritage in 2014.

马山壮族踩花灯

Mashan's Caihuadeng Dance of Zhuang Ethnic Group

项目名称：马山壮族踩花灯

别称：踩朝

分布范围：马山县古寨乡、加方乡、里当乡、古零乡、白山镇、林圩镇、周鹿镇、乔利镇、永州镇等

入选名录：2012年第四批自治区级非物质文化遗产名录

保护单位：马山县文化馆

代表性传承人：潘庆福（已故）

Element name：Mashan's Caihuadeng Dance of Zhuang Ethnic Group

Alternative name：Cai Chao

Geographical location and range：Guzhai Town, Jiafang Town, Lidang Town, Guling Town, Baishan Town, Linxu Town, Zhoulu Town, Qiaoli Town, Yongzhou Town and others of Mashan County

Element inscribed list：In 2012 on the Fourth Autonomous Region List of Intangible Cultural Heritage

Competent body involved in safeguarding：Mashan County Cultural Centre

Representative inheritors：Pan Qingfu (Late)

壮族“踩花灯”，壮语叫“踩朝”，是一种民间宗教活动，其作用主要是超度亡魂、祈愿祝福。这种传统民间宗教活动流行于马山县古寨、加方、里当、古零、白山、林圩、周鹿、乔利、永州等壮瑶族乡镇，至今已有数百年的悠久历史。正因为其活动是围绕花灯踩步跳踏，所以得名“踩花灯”。

当地风俗认为，人死后阴魂要离开自己原来的家庭，告别兄弟父老踏上新的旅程，于是，点“花灯”就可以说是亲人为逝者照亮路途，之后会由师公、道公手握法器，脚踏舞步，围绕花灯敲锣打鼓，引领逝者冲开迷阵，尽快到达极乐世界。传说“踩花灯”是海龙王与八仙抢夺“花魁”的一个过程，最终八仙代其主家争到了此花，寓意逝者以后就能与仙人住在一起，主人家今后的生活也会顺顺利利。

“踩花灯”祭祀活动的时间一般是从午夜开始。舞蹈前，先在逝者棺木前的地面上摆上九盏或十二盏花灯，接着师公、道公们穿着华丽的道服出场，围着花灯阵站立，先由领头的师公念念有词，高声唱念，同时，众道公也高声附和，随之进行“踩花灯”的仪式。首先由领头师公手执宝

Caihuadeng dance of Zhuang Ethnic Group, also known as "Cai Chao" in Zhuang language, is a religious folk activity, which is mainly performed for tranquilizing the dead and praying for blessings. This traditional folk religious activity is popular in towns of Yao Ethnic Group in Mashan County, such as Guzhai, Jiafang, Lidang, Guling, Baishan, Linxu, Zhoulu, Qiaoli and Yongzhou, which has a long history of hundreds of years. It is because this activity is to tread and dance around Huadeng (a kind of festival lantern) that it gets the name of "Caihuadeng (treading and dancing around Huadeng)".

According to the local customs, when a person passes away, its ghost will leave his family and embark on a new journey. Therefore, people will light "Huadeng" to illuminate the road for the deceased. Then, the wizard-like masters, holding musical instruments used in Taoist mass, will dance and beat drums and gongs around the Huadeng so as to lead the deceased to break through the maze and reach the paradise as soon as possible. It is said that "Caihuadeng" once was a competition between the Dragon King and the Eight Immortals for getting the "flower queen". Finally, the Eight Immortals won the competition. This means that the deceased would be able to live together with the immortals and the life of his or her family would also live in peace.

The sacrificial activity of Caihuadeng often starts from midnight. Before the dance, people will place nine or twelve Huadeng (festival lanterns) on the ground in front of the coffin of the deceased. Then, the wizard-like masters

2011年11月，大同村庙会活动踩花灯场面
In November 2011, Performance of Caihuadeng Dance at the Temple Fair of Datong Village

will come on the stage in their ornate costumes and stand around the Huadeng. The leading master will first mutter incantations and sing loudly. Other masters will echo with him subsequently. Then, the Caihuadeng activity will begin. At the beginning, the leading master will walk into the Huadeng array with sword in his hand and one of the deceased's family members will follow the leading master with a memorial tablet of the deceased. The other masters will follow the family member with spirit tablets, memorial, gongs, drums, cymbals and other props in turn. The last one will hold a bowl of water in his left hand and a leafy branch in his right hand so as to drip the water by the branch. When the gongs and drums are beating, people will dance following the leading master. At first, they will dance slowly around each Huadeng. Later, with the gradually intense rhythm, their paces will become more and more urgent. The props will also be waved up and down rhythmically until the whole process is complete. Finally, one of the masters will raise the central Huadeng high and turn around excitedly, implying that they have got the Huadeng for the family and the deceased person can be immortal.

The dance steps of "Caihuadeng" are choreographed in accordance with the movements of bees when collecting honey. The whole dance is filled with climax and excitement, which fully reflects the delicate observation and colorful imagination of people of Zhuang Ethnic Group. As an ancient folk culture, Mashan's Caihuadeng dance of Zhuang bears great academic value for the studies of ethnic archaeology, folklore and ethnic religion.

With the development of social economy, the traditional folk culture has suffered a great hit. The number of troupes and performers of Caihuadeng dance has been decreasing and the scale of the activity has also been shrinking. Under such condition, the relevant departments of Mashan County have carried out a series of protection work toward Caihuadeng dance. They have surveyed and collated relevant information, established data base, organized three relatively stable performance troupes in the distribution areas, and held various activities and performances so as to promote people's understanding about Caihuadeng dance, improve the dance's influence as well as provide new opportunities for its inheritance and development. In 2012, with the approval of the People's Government of the Guangxi Zhuang Autonomous Region, Mashan's Caihuadeng dance of Zhuang Ethnic Group was inscribed on the Fourth Autonomous Region List of Intangible Cultural Heritage.

剑，走进花灯阵，主家手捧着逝者灵牌紧跟在他身后，其他师公、道公们手上捧着神主牌位、表文、小锣、小鼓、小钹等道具依次排列其后，最后的一位师公左手端一碗清水，右手拿一根带叶子的树枝，并用树枝边走边沾上清水抛洒。在锣鼓敲响的同时，大家就跟着领头师公舞动起来，舞步由开始围着每一盏花灯慢慢行走，到后来随着鼓点的逐渐加快，步伐越来越急，师公们手上的道具也有节奏地上下挥动，直到整个踩花灯程序完成。最后，其中的一个师公把放在中间的花灯高高举起，兴奋地原地转圈，寓意是替主家争到此花灯，逝者就可以成仙成佛了。

“踩花灯”在花灯阵中的步伐，是参照蜜蜂采花时飞舞的动作编排的。整个舞蹈高潮迭起、热闹非凡，充分体现了壮族人民细腻的观察力和丰富的想象力。作为一项古老的民俗文化，马山壮族的“踩花灯”对于民族考古学、民俗学以及民族宗教学有着重要的学术价值。

随着社会经济的发展，传统的民俗文化受到了极大的冲击，“踩花灯”队伍和表演人员逐渐减少，“踩花灯”活动有逐步萎缩的趋势。为此，马山县有关部门对“壮族踩花灯”舞蹈开展了一系列的保护工作，普查整理相关资料、建立数据库，并在该项目集中分布的区域组成了三个相对稳定的民间“踩花灯”表演队伍，举办各类展演活动，增进人们对民间舞蹈“踩花灯”的了解，提高影响力，为其传承与发展提供新的契机。2012年，马山壮族踩花灯经广西壮族自治区人民政府同意，列入第四批自治区级非物质文化遗产名录。

横县百合茅山舞

Hengxian's Baihe Maoshan Dance

项目名称：横县百合茅山舞

别称：无

分布范围：横州市百合镇、马山乡及周边地区

入选名录：2014年第五批自治区级非物质文化遗产名录

保护单位：横县文化馆

代表性传承人：无

Element name：Hengxian's Baihe Maoshan Dance

Alternative name：None

Geographical location and range：Baihe Town, Mashan Town of Hengzhou City and the surrounding areas

Element inscribed list：In 2014 on the Fifth Autonomous Region List of Intangible Cultural Heritage

Competent body involved in safeguarding：Hengxian Cultural Centre

Representative inheritor：None

百合茅山舞表演
Performance of Baihe Maoshan Dance

Hengxian's Baihe Maoshan dance is a popular folk dance for sacrifice in Baihe Town and Mashan Town of Hengzhou City and the surrounding areas, which has a history of more than 200 years. As a traditional dance with unique ethnic characteristics, its dance movements are classical and natural with colorful forms, orderly steps and rhythmical features, which has become a popular dance material for art workers. This dance is often performed in various large-scale artistic performances and it is welcomed by local people.

Baihe Maoshan dance originated from Daogong dance and was introduced from Fuwang Village of Pubei County over 200 years ago. Its emergence and inheritance came from a fairy tale. It is said that there was a lady Chen in the Tang Dynasty whose brother was captured by the demons and imprisoned in the iron cage. Unfortunately, the person who wanted to rescue the brother was swallowed by the demons. Therefore, Mrs. Chen determined to kill those demons and save her brother. Then, she went to Maoshan Mountain with her sworn sisters to learn magic arts. After going through all kinds of difficulties and dangers on the way, they finally arrived at Maoshan Mountain. However, it was unfortunate that the magic arts had been learned by the believers of Taoism and Buddhism, only with two treasures, a fire tube and a paring knife, being left. Being touched by Mrs. Chen's story, the master in Maoshan Mountain gave her these two treasures. Then the three ladies went back to fight against the devil. To their surprise, the paring knife turned into a sharp golden

横县百合茅山舞是一种流行于横州市百合镇、马山乡及周边地区的民间祭祀舞蹈，距今已有200多年的历史。作为独具民族特色的传统舞蹈，其舞姿古朴自然，语汇丰富，舞步规整而富有韵律，已成为广大文艺创作者青睐的舞蹈素材，在各种大型文艺演出中，深受当地群众喜爱。

百合茅山舞源自道公舞，相传在200多年前从浦北县福旺村传入，其产生和传续有一个神话故事：相传唐代有位陈氏夫人，其兄长被妖魔抓走囚于铁笼，前去搭救者也不幸被妖魔所噬，陈氏夫人下定决心救兄除魔，于是与结拜姐妹林、李两位姑娘同去茅山学法。在途中历尽艰险之后，终于到了茅山，但事不凑巧，法术都给先到的道教、佛教学完了，只剩下一只火筒和一把瓜刨，茅山师父怜其救兄心切，将火筒、瓜刨两件宝物相赠。三人回去与妖魔斗法，瓜刨变成了锋利的金刀，吹两下火筒，便有天兵天将前来助阵，最终她们战胜妖魔，救出了兄长。为了表达心中的喜悦，大家一起跳舞欢庆。后来，茅山师父又派唐文明、葛文都、周文干三位将军与三姐妹一起，共保人间太平。自此，民间就把三夫人和三大将军尊奉为神，每逢三月三、中元节、重阳节或丰收喜庆，便请师公艺人跳“茅山舞”，以祈风调雨顺，岁岁平安。随着时间的推移，百合茅山舞逐渐成为一种为观众所喜爱的艺术形式，成为一种独具特色的舞蹈项目，活跃于民间舞台。

在百合茅山舞中，“行罡步”“三台罡步”“五星步”“七星罡步”等步法极富特色，且每段舞蹈中都会出现。整个舞蹈共分四段，每段表演前必须四响牛角，表演者右手转动牛角，左手舞弄令刀，有节奏地碰击使之发出“叮当叮当”的响声。整个舞蹈过程围绕着一个神话故事开展，大意就是三夫人从求法、学法，到战胜妖魔，最后与三位将军一起共保人间太平。这四段分别是“请师”“三夫人”“三将军”“罗帏”，舞蹈由七个人表演，分别装扮为使者、三夫人和三将军，前三段表示他们施展法术、驱邪除恶，最后一段“罗帏”即以罗网把所有妖魔鬼怪一网打尽，使乡村得以太平安宁。

百合茅山舞是从道公娱神舞蹈中分离出来的极富艺术魅力的一朵奇葩，除了参加市县举行的各项大型文艺活动展演外，还常活跃在一些民间宗教活动中，如庙会、上刀山过火海、添粮祝寿等，为繁荣和丰富当地的文艺事业做出了重要的贡献。2014年，横县百合茅山舞经广西壮族自治区人民政府同意，列入第五批自治区级非物质文化遗产名录。

knife and divine troops descending from Heaven would come to help them after slightly blowing the fire tube. Finally, they defeated the demons and rescued the brother. They were so happy that they began to dance to express their joy. Later, the master of Maoshan Mountain sent three marshals, Tang Wenming, Ge Wendu and Zhou Wengan to guard the peace of the world together with the three sworn sisters. Since then, the three ladies and three marshals began to be respected as gods by the people. On the third day of the third lunar month, the Hungry Ghost Festival, the Double Ninth Festival and days to celebrate bumper harvest, people will invite Shigong to perform Maoshan dance so as to pray for good weather and safeness. As time goes by, Baihe Maoshan dance has gradually become an art form welcomed by audience as well as a unique dance being active in civil.

In Baihe Maoshan dance, the special dance steps like “Xing Gang step”, “Santai Gang step”, “Wuxing step” and “Qixing Gang step” are always used in every part of the dance. The whole dance can be divided into four parts. Before the performance of each part, the performers will sound the horns for four times. Their right hands will turn the horns and left hands will brandish swords, making the sound of “tinkle” with rhythmical collision. The whole dance develops around the fairy tale that tells the story of the three sworn sisters’ pursuit and learning of magic arts, their success to defeat the demons as well as their efforts to protect the world with three marshals. The four parts of the dance are “seeking master”, “the three sworn sisters”, “the three marshals” and “capturing the demons”. The dance is usually performed by seven dancers. Each of them will perform as the envoy, the three sworn sisters, and the three marshals respectively. The first three parts of dance represent the scene that they cast spells to drive away demons. The last part demonstrates their capture of demons by the net and the peace of village.

Baihe Maoshan Dance, which is separated from Daogong Yushen dance, is a wonderful work with artistic charm. In addition to participating in various large-scale performances in cities and counties, it is also performed in folk religious activities, such as temple fairs, the performance of the unique skill “climbing mountain of swords or plunging into sea of flames”, and the birthday of the elders, which has made a great contribution to the enrichment of the local arts. With the approval of the People’s Government of the Guangxi Zhuang Autonomous Region, Hengxian’s Baihe Maoshan Dance was inscribed on the Fifth Autonomous Region List of Intangible Cultural Heritage in 2014.

百合茅山舞法器
Musical Instruments of Baihe Maoshan Dance

上林壮族师公舞

Shanglin's Shigong Dance of Zhuang Ethnic Group

项目名称：上林壮族师公舞

别称：调筛、古筛

分布范围：上林的大丰镇、三里镇、乔贤镇、西燕镇、巷贤镇、澄泰乡、塘红乡、镇圩瑶族乡等

入选名录：2012年第四批自治区级非物质文化遗产名录
2012年第四批市级非物质文化遗产名录

保护单位：上林县文化馆

代表性传承人：雷桂丰

Element name: Shanglin's Shigong Dance of Zhuang Ethnic Group

Alternative name: Diaoshai, Gushai

Geographical location and range: Dafeng Town, Sanli Town, Qiaoxian Town, Xiyan Town, Xiangxian Town, Chengtai Town, Tanghong Town, Zhenxu Town of Yao Ethnic Group and others of Shanglin County

Element inscribed list: In 2012 on the Fourth Autonomous Region List of Intangible Cultural Heritage
In 2012 on the Fourth Municipal List of Intangible Cultural Heritage

Competent body involved in safeguarding: Shanglin County Cultural Centre

Representative inheritor: Lei Guifeng

上林壮族师公舞是流传于壮族地区的一种宗教祭祀舞蹈，在上林县一带十分流行，主要分布在大丰、澄泰、三里、乔贤、塘红、镇圩、西燕、巷贤等各乡镇，起先主要是用于师公教的祭祀活动中，而后渐渐从祭祀活动中独立出来，与古骆越巫文化相互交融，形成一种独立的具有审美价值的舞蹈形式。在壮语中，师公舞被称为“调筛”或“古筛”，是壮族民间舞蹈的重要组成部分。

上林壮族师公舞起源于原始巫舞，但具体起源于何时，民间流传着不同的说法。一种说法是源于周代，因为在师公舞的唱本中有“周朝唱师传下来”“三元三圣号真君，周兴幽厉作谏臣，辞职参师为正教，究竟五行秘密文”等唱词；一种说法是源于黄帝时代，认为黄帝就是运用梅山教密文战

Shanglin's Shigong dance of Zhuang Ethnic Group is a dance related to religion and sacrifice. It is popular in Shanglin County and its surrounding areas, such as towns like Dafeng, Chengtai, Sanli, Qiaoxian, Tanghong, Zhenxu, Xiyan and Xiangxian. It was first used in the sacrificial activities of Shigong Religion and later became independent from the sacrificial activities. Then it integrated with the Wu (Witch) culture of ancient Luoyue state, becoming an independent dance with unique aesthetic value. In Zhuang language, the Shigong dance is called "Diao Shai" or "Gu Shai", which is an important part of folk dances of Zhuang.

Shanglin's Shigong dance of Zhuang originates from the original Wu dance, but there are different views upon the specific time of its emergence. One view believes that the dance originates from the Zhou Dynasty, because there are lyrics in the libretto of Shigong dance like "the singers of Zhou Dynasty passed it down", and "the sages of San Yuan and San Sheng can be called the men of moral integrity; the King You

师公在龙母节时给观众表演师公舞步踩花灯
The Masters Perform Stepping on Louts Lanterns at the Dragon Mother Festival

and King Li of the Zhou Dynasty encouraged rational debate; they all learned religions from the masters to figure out the secret of the five elements". Another view takes the ground that the dance was derived from the Yellow Emperor times. This view also believes that the Yellow Emperor used the secret writing of Meishan Religion to defeat Chiyou (a mythological warrior engaged in fighting with the Yellow Emperor). Another legend said that Tang, Ge and Zhou beat the drums and danced before the emperor's mother to drive away evil spirits and cure diseases. Then the emperor designated them as "San Yuan". Since then, the "San Yuan Religion (Meishan Religion)" began to widely spread. In addition, it is also said that the Shigong dance originated in the Han Dynasty. When Zhuge Liang marched to the south to fight against the Shidong Manwang, believers of Meishan Religion followed him. Later, they were stranded in the mountain, which led to the appearance of Shigong. Although all of the above are oral legends, they also reflect that the Shigong dance originated from the ages ago to some extent, which was related to the ancient Wu dance and Nuo dance in Lingnan areas.

As a traditional dance for sacrifice, Shanglin's Shigong dance of Zhuang is mostly performed in folk activities such as "pacifying the dragon vein", "worshiping the gods of land and grain", "worshiping ancestors", "marriages", "funerals", "redeeming the vow to gods" and "inviting gods for protection". Due to the long history and influenced by the ancient Wu dance and Nuo dance, Shanglin's Shigong dance of Zhuang has maintained the basic characteristics of the two dances, such as playing the role of gods and inviting gods by dancing. For example, the performance is always accompanied by bee-shaped drums and the dancers must wear "Xiang (masks)" on their faces. The common dances subordinated to Shigong dance include Sanyuan dance, Tianshi dance, Gongcao dance, Liangwu dance, Thunder dance, Pan Gu dance, Lu Ban dance and dance of the land. The contents of the dances are mainly about "four marshals", "the supernaturalism of five elements", "the King Moyi" and "the Father of Heaven and the Mother of Land" who send good fortune and descendants for people. Shanglin's Shigong dance of Zhuang Ethnic Group has fixed dance movements, in which solo dance is the most representative one. When performing solo dance, the dancer will wear a mask on his face with props in his hands. Then the dancer will dance toward the east, west, south, north and the centre respectively. The trembling of the knee, the flexing of the wrist, the twiddling of the shoulder, the twisting of the hip and the waggling of the body show the distinctive style of the dance of Zhuang Ethnic Group.

2015年师公舞出师度界仪式（中间人为出师人）
The Ceremony of Finish One's Apprenticeship of Shigong Dance (Middle, Apprentice)

胜蚩尤的；一种说法称唐、葛、周为皇帝母亲击鼓舞蹈，驱邪治病，皇帝封其为三元，从此之后“三元教”（即梅山教）广为流传；还有一种说法称壮族师公舞起源于汉代，诸葛亮南征十洞蛮王时，有梅山教徒随征，后流落于十万大山传教，由此出现师公。以上种种，虽说均属口头传说，但也在一定程度上反映出“师公舞”起源甚古，与岭南古代巫舞、傩舞有着一定的渊源关系。

作为民间传统祭祀舞蹈，上林壮族师公舞多用于民间活动中的“安龙”“庆社”“祭祖”“红喜”“白喜”“还花还愿”“游神”等仪式，由于历史悠久，且受到了古代巫舞、傩舞的一定影响，上林壮族师公舞一直保持了楚巫舞以巫扮神、以舞降神的基本特点，例如表演时用蜂鼓伴奏，跳神时必须戴“相”（面具）等。三元舞、天师舞、功曹舞、梁吴舞、雷神舞、盘古舞、鲁班舞、土地舞等是上林师公舞的常用舞目，舞蹈内容有“四帅”“五雷”“莫一大王”以及表现给人间送福赐子的“天公”和“地母”。上林壮族师公舞有固定舞姿，其中最具代表性的舞蹈形式是独舞，即一个头戴面具的师公，手执道具，在神台前对着东、西、南、北、中五个方向舞蹈，舞蹈中膝部的颤、腕部的转、肩部的绕、胯部的扭和上身的晃，显示出了壮族舞蹈的独特风格。

上林壮族师公舞，作为古代舞蹈的现代遗存，不仅为研究中国舞蹈史提供了丰富的形象资料，而且对综合研究和探索古代舞蹈的源流、特点、形态功用、活动方式等有着重要意义。此外，在壮族传统节日里，师公舞的表演还能够活跃气氛，极大地满足了人们的精神需求。

随着时间的推移、社会的不断发展，许多手抄唱本及珍贵资料大量遗失，蜂鼓制作技艺已趋于简单化等，使上林壮族师公舞的传承和发展也受到了一定的冲击。为此，上林县有关部门对其境内的壮族师公舞进行全面的普查和整理，扶持业余团队，举办各种民间宣传活动，还在西燕等乡镇初步建立了壮族师公舞传承基地。随后，上林县政府及有关部门继续加大资金和人员投入，为保护和传承古代祭祀舞蹈的“活化石”——上林壮族师公舞做出了努力。2012年，上林壮族师公舞经广西壮族自治区人民政府同意，列入第四批自治区级非物质文化遗产名录。

As a relic of ancient dance in modern society, Shanglin's Shigong dance of Zhuang Ethnic Group not only provides rich image materials for the study of Chinese dance history, but also has great significance for the comprehensive study and exploration of the origin, characteristics, forms and functions of ancient dances. Besides, in the traditional festivals of Zhuang, the performance Shigong dance can also heighten the atmosphere and greatly meet people's spiritual needs.

With the passing of time and the continuous development of the society, a lot of hand-copied transcripts and precious materials have been lost and the production technique of bee-shaped drums has been simplified, which has also impacted the inheritance and development of Shanglin's Shigong dance of Zhuang Ethnic Group. To this end, the relevant departments of Shanglin County have conducted a comprehensive survey and sorted out related materials of the dance. The departments have also supported the establishment of amateur troupes, held various popularization activities and initially built up the inheritance base of Shigong dance in Xiyan and other towns. Later, the government of Shanglin County and relevant departments have continued to increase investment in funds and personnel to protect and inherit the "living fossil" of ancient sacrificial dance, that is, Shanglin's Shigong dance of Zhuang Ethnic Group. In 2012, with the approval of the People's Government of the Guangxi Zhuang Autonomous Region, the dance was inscribed on the Fourth Autonomous Region List of Intangible Cultural Heritage.

上林瑶族猴鼓舞

Shanglin's Monkey-like Drum Dance of Yao Ethnic Group

项目名称：上林瑶族猴鼓舞

别称：无

分布范围：以镇圩瑶族乡为中心，流传于上林县与马山县交界一带的布努瑶山区

入选名录：2012年第四批自治区级非物质文化遗产名录
2012年第四批市级非物质文化遗产名录

保护单位：上林县文化馆

代表性传承人：罗延武

Element name：Shanglin's Monkey-like Drum Dance of Yao Ethnic Group

Alternative name：None

Geographical location and range：With Zhenxu Town of Yao Ethnic Group as the centre, spreading in Bunuyao mountainous areas at the border of Shanglin County and Mashan County

Element inscribed list：In 2012 on the Fourth Autonomous Region List of Intangible Cultural Heritage
In 2012 on the Fourth Municipal List of Intangible Cultural Heritage

Competent body involved in safeguarding：Shanglin County Cultural Centre

Representative inheritor：Luo Yanwu

上林瑶族猴鼓舞是一种与鼓相关的瑶族原始舞蹈，它以镇圩瑶族乡为中心，广泛流传于上林县与马山县交界一带的布努瑶山区。瑶族猴鼓舞历史悠久，其产生和发展一直都与瑶族人民有着密切的联系，可谓记录瑶族历史生活的风俗画卷。

历史上，瑶族地区战乱不断。宋朝时，北方的金兵进犯，瑶族人民为了躲避灾祸，只能在山洞中过着异常艰苦的生活。瑶族英雄卜努为了抗击侵略，号召各寨瑶胞联合起来抵御金兵。一天，瑶胞们在森林里迷了路，所幸得到老猴王引路，帮助他们摆脱了困境。为了迷惑金兵，瑶胞隐蔽在丛林中，迂回打起皮鼓，而猴王也带着猴子猴孙们在一旁帮腔，声音似千军万马，让金兵不寒而栗，一时间不知所措。于是，瑶胞们趁机出击，以寡敌众大获全胜。在农历五月二十九这天，瑶家各路兄弟凯旋。为了感谢猴王的帮助，英雄卜努带头敲起皮鼓狂歌欢跳，用生动的歌舞和热闹的气氛来表达对猴王的感激，遂形成了猴鼓舞的雏形。此后，人们把五月二十七至二十九日这三天定为瑶家最盛大的节日——达努节（正万瑶族称“排玖”）。每到这天，人们就会跳起热闹欢腾的猴鼓舞，以慰藉神灵、感恩先祖。随着时代的变迁，猴鼓舞慢慢演变为布努瑶欢庆丰收和纪念祖先的一种活动，并流传至今。

作为一项重要的祭祀舞蹈，上林瑶族猴鼓舞气氛欢快、形神兼备。它的基本动作是脚抬腿跳，上身微微扣胸，双手曲肘且双腿自然弯曲，上步抬腿顿足，双肘和双手同时抖动，以此来模仿动物的形态。一般来说，跳猴鼓舞的人数为四人，此外还有乐队和伴唱。表演者出场时都装扮成猴子模样，一人扮身背酒葫芦的猴王，负责打鼓，一人打小钹，两人手持扇子。舞蹈开始时，猴王先模仿猴叫，之后密擂皮鼓，打钹者应声而起，紧接着乐队随鼓声演奏，打钹和持扇子的“猴子们”同时出场，伴随节奏围绕猴王开始舞蹈，猴王围着场子中央的大皮鼓用手和肘敲鼓，众小猴随着鼓钹声

Shanglin's monkey-like drum dance is a primitive dance of Yao Ethnic Group related to the drum. With Zhenxu Town of Yao Ethnic Group as the centre, it widely spreads in Bunu Yao mountainous areas at the border of Shanglin County and Mashan County. Monkey-like drum dance has a long history. Its emergence and development are closely related to people of Yao Ethnic Group, which can be described as a genre picture that records Yao people's historical life.

In the history, the area where people of Yao Ethnic Group located was often plagued by warfare. In the Song Dynasty, the soldiers of the Jin Dynasty invaded Yao people's settlement from the north. To elude the invasion from Jin, people of Yao Ethnic Group can only live an austere life in the caves. In order to fight against the aggression, the hero of Yao Ethnic Group Bunu called on all the villagers to come together against the intruders. One day, people of Yao Ethnic Group lost their way in the forest. Fortunately, they got the guidance of the old Monkey King and got out of trouble. To confuse soldiers of the Jin Dynasty, people of Yao Eyhnic Group hid themselves in the jungle and beat the leather drums. At the same time, the Monkey King, with its children and grandchildren, helped Yao people with voices like thousands of troops and horses, which made Jin soldiers begin to tighten up without knowing what to do. Therefore, people of Yao Ethnic Group took this opportunity to attack the intruders, defeating the enemy troop with a force inferior in number. In order to thank the Monkey King for its help, the hero Bunu took the lead to beat the leather drum, singing and dancing. They used vivid songs and dances as well as the jubilant spirits to express their appreciation for the Monkey King, which created the embryonic form of monkey-like drum dance. Since then, the three days from 27th to 29th of the fifth lunar month have been designated as the grandest festival of Yao Ethnic Group, that is, Danu festival (also known as "Pai Jiu" of Yao Ethnic Group in Zhengwan County). On these days, people will perform the monkey-like drum dance to worship gods and thank ancestors. With the vicissitudes of the times, the dance has gradually turned into an activity for Bunu Yao Ethnic Group to celebrate harvest and worship ancestors till today.

As an important dance for sacrifice, Shanglin's monkey-like drum dance of Yao Ethnic Group is cheerful and in unity of both form and spirit. In dancing, the performers will jump with their feet lifting. Their upper bodies slightly inward with elbows bending and legs naturally curving. Then the dancers lift their feet up and their elbows and hands will shake at the same time so as to imitate the shape of monkey. Generally, there are four dancers in the dance. In addition, there are also a band and some vocal accompanies (singers). All of the dancers will dress up as monkeys at the beginning. One of the dancers will perform as the Monkey King with a gourd-shaped wine container on his back and be responsible for beating the drum. One of the other three dancers will play the cymbals and the other two need to hold fans in their hands. When the dance begins, the performer of Monkey King will imitate the sound of the monkey at first and then beat the leather drum in a strained speed. Then the band will play the music in accordance with the drum rhythm and the other three monkey performers will come onto the stage and dance around the "Monkey King". The "Monkey King" will dance around the big leather drum at the centre of the stage and use his hands and elbows to beat the drum. The other three small monkeys dance up and down according to the sound of cymbals, sometimes making faces, sometimes fanning the Monkey King, sometimes getting around the Monkey King and sometimes steal the wine from the king's wine gourd. The performance vividly represents the sanguinity and agility of the monkeys. At the same time, the accompanied singers will sing songs to extol the Monkey King and describe the life of Yao Ethnic Group.

This unique dance of imitating monkeys reflects ancient people's worship toward nature and their desire to be as clever and agile as monkeys so as to protect themselves and live without worries. As time goes by, the connotation of Shanglin's monkey-like drum dance has been constantly enriched. It is not only an important form and link for Yao people to recall their ancestors, but also an expression of their wishes for stable society and harmonious life. This dance is also a symbol of the coexistence between people of Yao Ethnic Group and the Mother Nature.

To inherit and develop this significant cultural heritage of monkey-like drum dance, Shanglin County established Zhenma Art Troupe in 1989 to carry out exhibition and performance of the dance. In addition, this dance has been regarded as a signature of Shanglin ethnic culture. The government of Shanglin has increased capital investment to further explore, collect and sort out related materials of monkey-like drum dance, and made constant efforts to protect and inherit this intangible cultural heritage. In 2012, with the approval of the People's Government of the Guangxi Zhuang Autonomous Region, Shanglin's monkey-like drum dance of Yao Ethnic Group was inscribed on the Fourth Autonomous Region List of Intangible Cultural Heritage.

上下起舞，时则扮鬼脸，时则帮猴王扇扇子，时则缠住猴王，时则偷喝猴王葫芦里的酒……将猴子的活泼与灵性表现得淋漓尽致。在跳猴鼓舞的同时，还会有歌者伴唱，主要内容是对猴王的歌颂以及瑶族的生活风情。

这种模仿猴子进行舞蹈的独特形式，体现出了古代人类对自然的顶礼膜拜，渴望像猴子一样聪慧灵巧、机智敏捷，能够保护自己，生存无忧。随着时间的推移，上林瑶族猴鼓舞的内涵和意蕴不断丰富，它既是瑶族人民缅怀先祖的重要形式，也是瑶族人民追求社会安定、生活和谐之愿望的表达，更是瑶家与大自然和谐共存的象征。

为传承和发展猴鼓舞这一重要的文化遗产，上林县于1989年在镇圩乡成立镇马艺术团，开展猴鼓舞的展演活动。此外，上林县将瑶族猴鼓舞列为上林民族文化名片，并加大资金投入，进一步挖掘、收集、整理猴鼓舞的相关资料，为保护和传承这一非物质文化遗产不断努力。2012年，上林瑶族猴鼓舞经广西壮族自治区人民政府同意，列入第四批自治区级非物质文化遗产名录。

猴鼓舞表演

Performance of Monkey-like Drum Dance

壮族骆垌舞

Luodong Dance of Zhuang Ethnic Group

项目名称：壮族骆垌舞

别称：无

分布范围：武鸣区城厢镇、锣圩镇、陆斡镇、两江镇、马头镇、玉泉乡等

入选名录：2010年第三批自治区级非物质文化遗产名录

保护单位：武鸣区文化馆

代表性传承人：潘腾宗（已故）

Element name：Luodong Dance of Zhuang Ethnic Group

Alternative name：None

Geographical location and range：Chengxiang Town, Luoxu Town, Luwo Town, Liangjiang Town, Matou Town, Yuquan Town and others of Wuming District

Element inscribed list：In 2014 on the Third Autonomous Region List of Intangible Cultural Heritage

Competent body involved in safeguarding：Wuming District Cultural Centre

Representative inheritor：Pan Tengzong (Late)

Luodong dance of Zhuang Ethnic Group is a sacrifice dance of ancient Luoyue state, which is popular in towns such as Chengxiang, Yuquan, Luoxu, Luwo, Liangjiang and Matou in Wuming District today. In Zhuang language, "Luodong" was the title for the generals of ancient Luoyue state, later its meaning developed into "mask". Actually, Luodong dance was a folk dance of ancestors of Zhuang Ethnic Group that was performed by Shigong (master) with masks during grand ceremonies like praying for rain in drought, thanking god for bumper harvest, exorcising evil spirits and funerals.

As an art form with profound history and culture, the emergence of Luodong dance of the Zhuang Ethnic Group is closely related to the ancient state of Luoyue. It is said that there was a famous ancient state named Luoyue in history, whose capital city and environs were located in the southwestern foot of Daming Mountain, that is, in today's areas like Luwo, Liangjiang, Matou and Yuquan of Wuming District. In 111 B.C., Luoyue state demised. Although its former glory disappeared, its profound history and culture were cherished by millions of people. Therefore, Luodong dance of Zhuang Ethnic Group, which embodied the essence of the history and culture of the ancient Luoyue state and

壮族骆垌舞是流行于武鸣的城厢、玉泉、锣圩、陆斡、两江、马头等乡镇的古骆越祭祀舞蹈，属于师公舞的一种。在壮语中，“骆垌”是古代骆越将军的称号，后来演变为“假面具”的意思，因而骆垌舞就是壮族先民在天旱求雨、丰收酬神、驱鬼逐邪或料理丧事时所举行的盛大仪式中师公戴着面具所跳的一种民间舞蹈。

作为一种凝聚了深厚历史文化的艺术形式，壮族骆垌舞的产生和骆越古国有着密不可分的联系。据传，在历史上曾名盛一时的骆越古国，其国度和京畿就位于大明山西南麓，即今武鸣县境内的陆斡、两江、马头和玉泉一带。公元前111年，骆越古国灭亡，昔日之辉煌虽已荡然无存，但其长久以来的历史和丰富多彩的文化为万千臣民历久怀念。于是，凝聚着骆越古国历史文化遗留之精华的壮族骆垌舞，便通过祭祀的形式，由师公舞派生而成，并以其经久不衰的生

祈丰节开场仪式舞
Opening Ceremony Dance of Festival of Praying for Good Harvest

命力，在骆越国都的那片土地——现武鸣区玉泉乡一带上演和传播。

壮族骆垌舞反映的内容是骆越人的祭祀过程，包括出征、点兵、行军、打仗、筹粮、存粮、养兵、招魂、驱邪，祈求风调雨顺、国泰民安等。表演时舞者头戴三元帽，身着长红袍，手持独特响棍，还戴着所饰之神的面具。整个舞蹈由打击乐伴奏，通常是先歌后舞，舞时不歌，鼓舞相随，且边舞边发出“呗……”的震唇音，舞姿落落大方、庄重古朴。另外，壮族骆垌舞中一个舞者在一场活动中可以扮几个角色，但即使是女舞，也只能男扮女装，绝无女子参演的先例。

作为一种古老的祭祀舞蹈，壮族骆垌舞不仅较全面而富有特色地展现了古骆越的文化风貌，而且保存了许多鲜为人知的壮族远古信息，堪称壮族远古文化的活化石。

对于这种极富特色又承载了重要历史文化价值的艺术形式，武鸣区文化部门十分重视，一直致力于挖掘、整理、保护和弘扬这一特色文化，举办了壮族骆垌舞展示会，建立保护传承基地，壮大壮族骆垌舞队伍，不断完善壮族骆垌舞的服装道具等。从2009年开始，中国壮乡武鸣三月三歌圩和灵水旅游风景区及农村文艺汇演中，壮族骆垌舞以舞台表演形式完整地展现于世人面前，充分展示了它作为古骆越文化之缩影的魅力与价值。2010年，壮族骆垌舞经广西壮族自治区人民政府同意，列入第三批自治区级非物质文化遗产名录。

was derived from Shigong dance, continued to be performed and spread on the site of ancient Luoyue state, that is, today's Yuquan Town of Wuming District with its enduring vitality and in the form of sacrifice dance.

Luodong dance of Zhuang Ethnic Group reflects the sacrifice process of Luoyue people, including going on expeditions, recruiting soldiers, marching, fighting, raising grain, saving grain, raising soldiers, summoning souls, exorcising evil spirits, praying for good weather and health as well as praying for prosperity and peace for the country and people. During performance, the dancers will wear Sanyuan hats and long red robes with special clanging sticks in their hands and masks on their faces to simulate the god. The whole dance is accompanied by percussion music with singing firstly and dancing next. When the performers are dancing, they cannot sing at the same time and the dance is often accompanied by the sound of drums. The dancers will make a lip vibration of "bei" while dancing. Their dance movements are graceful, solemn and simple. In addition, a dancer in Luodong dance is allowed to play several roles in the performance. However, it is noticeable that even in the female dance, the performers are only males who dress up as women. The female dancers never appear in this dance from ancient times till now.

As an ancient dance of sacrifice, Luodong dance of Zhuang Ethnic Group not only comprehensively and distinctively represents the culture of ancient Luoyue, but also preserves many little-known ancient information of Zhuang Ethnic Group, which is deserved to be the "living fossil" of the ancient culture of the Zhuang Ethnic Group.

For the special art forms that bear important historical and cultural values, the cultural department of Wuming District always attaches great importance to them. The department has been committed to exploring, sorting out, protecting and carrying forward this unique culture. It also has held the exhibition of Luodong dance of Zhuang Ethnic Group, built protection and inheritance base, strengthened Luodong dance troupe and improved the props and costumes of the dance. Since 2009, in activities like Wuming song fairs on the third day of the third lunar month and the art shows of Lingshui scenic spot and rural areas, Luodong dance of Zhuang Ethnic Group has been full presented to the world in the form of stage performance, representing its charm and value as an epitome of ancient Luoyue culture. In 2010, with the approval of the People's Government of the Guangxi Zhuang Autonomous Region, Luodong dance of Zhuang Ethnic Group was inscribed on the Third Autonomous Region List of Intangible Cultural Heritage.

壮族打扁担

Dance with Pole Carriers of Zhuang Ethnic Group

项目名称：壮族打扁担

别称：无

分布范围：南宁市马山县、上林县，河池市都安县等

入选名录：2010年第三批自治区级非物质文化遗产名录

保护单位：马山县文化馆

代表性传承人：蒙雪凤

Element name：Dance with Pole Carriers of Zhuang Ethnic Group

Alternative name：None

Geographical location and range：Mashan County, Shanglin County of Nanning City, Du'an County of Hechi City and others

Element inscribed list：In 2010 on the Third Autonomous Region List of Intangible Cultural Heritage

Competent body involved in safeguarding：Mashan County Cultural Centre

Representative inheritor：Meng Xuefeng

2007年马山县千人打扁担表演
摄影 李海瑛
Performance of Dance of Carrying Pole by Thousands of People in Mashan County in 2007
Photo by Li Haiying

打扁担是流行于广西南宁市马山县和上林县、河池市都安县部分壮族乡村的一种民间舞蹈，主要反映壮族人民从春种到秋收的劳动过程。

据记载，壮族打扁担源于“打舂堂”，与壮族打榔有相通之处，同时又存在区别。首先它们工具各异，打榔较为厚重，而打扁担比较轻便；打榔多为男性，而打扁担者多为女性。唐人刘恂的《岭表录异》云：“广南有舂堂，以浑木刳成槽舩，皆有偏拍。槽声若鼓、闻于数里。”民国《隆山县（原马山县）志》中记载：“打舂堂之习，相传已久，今犹未衰，每逢正月初一至元宵为自由娱乐期，妇女三五成群，作打舂堂之乐。其意预祝来年风调雨顺，五谷丰登，人畜安康，盛世太平。”故有谚云：“正月舂堂声轰轰，今年到处禾黍丰。”在早期，“扁担舞”是专属女性表演的、用来自娱自乐的民间舞蹈。每逢农历正月初一至十六，包括各种红事、喜事，都是打扁担最盛行的日子，到处可见壮家妇女为了烘托喜庆气氛而欢跳“扁担舞”的身姿，铿锵的锣鼓声，敲打竹筒的咚咚鸣响声，“嗨嗨”的叫喊声，伴随着清脆悦耳的扁担碰击声，在圩镇和乡间、晒场和檐下，处处回荡不绝。

Dance with pole carriers of Zhuang Ethnic Group is a folk dance that is popular in Mashan County and Shanglin County of Nanning as well as in Du'an County of Hechi, which mainly reflects the working process from spring sowing and autumn harvest of people of Zhuang Ethnic Group.

According to the records, the dance with pole carriers is originated from “Da Chong Tang (a dance with carrying pole and bench)”, which is similar to “Dalang dance” of Zhuang Ethnic Group. At the same time, there are also some differences. First of all, they use different tools in performance, which means that “lang (a kind of wood trough)” used in Dalang dance is heavier and thicker than carrying pole used in dance with pole carriers. Besides, the performer of Dalang dance mainly are men while the performers of dance with pole carriers mainly are women. Liu Xun, a writer of the Tang Dynasty, wrote in *Ling Biao Lu Yi* (a geographical note of Lingnan areas) that “there is Chong Tang in the south of Guangxi, which was made by wood and cut into trough shape. The sound of the wood trough is like the sound of drum that can spread even for miles.” According to the *Records of Longshan (Mashan) County* written in the Republic of China (1912-1949), “the tradition of Da Chong Tang has a long history and is still popular nowadays. From the New Year's Day to the Lantern Festival are days for entertainment, during which three to five women will gather together to dance Da Chong Tang so as to celebrate pleasant weather, bumper harvest, good health and peaceful time.” Therefore, there is a saying goes that “so long as there is rumbling sound of Chong Tang, the rice will welcome a bumper harvest this year”. In the early days, the performers of “dance with pole carriers” were only females. It is a kind of folk dance used to amuse people themselves. From the New Year's Day to the sixteenth day of the first lunar month, as well as on marriages and celebrations, dance with pole carriers will be performed by women to heighten the jubilant atmosphere everywhere. The clanging sound of gongs and drums, the beating of bamboo tubes, the shouting of "hai hai" and the pleasant sound of the carrying pole striking echoed everywhere in the town, in the drying ground and even under the roof.

The number of performers in the dance with pole carriers of Zhuang Ethnic Group is often four, six, ten, twenty or other even numbers. In performance, the dancers will hold the carrying pole in hand and stand face to face around a trough or bench with the length of more than one Zhang (a Chinese unit of length, about 10/3 meters) and the width of one Chi (a Chinese unit of length, about 1/3 meter). They use their flexible wrists to put the poles up and down and pound them with each other. They sing and dance to simulate the posture of harrowing, planting, bailing, harvesting, threshing and husking, which is agile and vigorous. If there are numerous performers, people will play a drum to guide the dance movements so that people's speed, rhythm and movements can maintain consistency. Sometimes the performers will dance in pairs or four, or dance in a row with many people. The postures include standing, squatting, step bowing and turning. With alternation of light and heavy strength, strong and weak dynamics, as well as fast and slow speed, the dancers' movements are complex, changeable yet natural.

For inheriting and developing this cultural activity with folk characteristics, the relevant departments of Mashan County have carried out an in-depth survey. While understanding and exploring the origin of dance with pole carriers, they also try to understand its distribution and inheritance condition. The relevant departments have also organized three relatively stable performance troupes composed by local farmers in its distribution areas, and 1000 sets of props and costumes have been funded and produced. As a unique brand of traditional culture, the dance with pole carriers of Zhuang Ethnic Group have taken an active part in various activities to improve the understanding and influence of this art form inside and outside the district. In 2010, the dance with pole carriers participated in the performance of Guangxi Theme Activity Week in Shanghai Expo, showing the artistic charm and cultural value of the dance with pole carriers of Zhuang Ethnic Group.

壮族扁担舞在演出时表演者有四人、六人、十人、二十人不等，且均取双数，一般多是妇女。出场表演时，舞者手持扁担，相向而立，围着一条长一丈多、宽一尺的木槽或板凳，运用灵活的双腕，使扁担上下飞舞，左右碰击，且边打边唱边舞，模拟农事活动中的耙田、插秧、戽水、收割、打谷、舂米等动作，敏捷矫健、轻松自如。如果打扁担的人数众多，就会配上一面鼓来对整个场面进行带动和指挥，使大家打扁担的速度、节奏和动作保持一致。打扁担的舞者时而双人对打，时而四人交叉对打，时而多人连打；有站、蹲、弓步、转身打等，轻重、强弱、快慢错落有致，动作复杂多变、优美自然。

为了传承和发展这一民间特色文化活动，马山县相关部门开展深层次普查，在了解挖掘壮族打扁担起源的同时，掌握其分布地区和生存状况，并在该项目集中分布的区域，组成了三个相对稳定的农民打扁担表演队伍，筹资制作了1000多套道具和演出服装。作为一个独具特色的传统文化品牌，壮族打扁担积极参加各类活动，增进区内外对这项艺术活动的了解，提高其影响力。2010年，壮族打扁担参加了上海世博会广西活动周的表演，向世界展示了壮族打扁担的艺术魅力与文化价值。

打扁担训练班
Training Class of Dance of Carrying Pole

壮族打砻（榔）舞

Rice Hulling (Dalang) Dance of Zhuang Ethnic Group

项目名称：壮族打砻（榔）舞

别称：打舂堂

分布范围：马山县古寨乡、加方乡、里当乡、古零乡等

入选名录：2010年第三批自治区级非物质文化遗产名录

保护单位：马山县文化馆

代表性传承人：陆荣艳

Element name：Rice Hulling (Dalang) Dance of Zhuang Ethnic Group

Alternative name：Da Chong Tang (a dance with carrying pole and bench)

Geographical location and range：Guzhai Town, Jiafang Town, Lidang Town, Guling Town and others of Mashan County

Element inscribed list：In 2010 on the Third Autonomous Region List of Intangible Cultural Heritage

Competent body involved in safeguarding：Mashan County Cultural Centre

Representative inheritor：Lu Rongyan

Dalang dance of Zhuang Ethnic Group was called "Da Chong Tang (a dance with carrying pole and bench) in ancient times. It is popular in Guzhai Town, Jiafang Town, Lidang Town and Guling Town of Mashan County of Nanning and the surrounding areas. At festivals and celebrations, local people of Zhuang and Yao ethic groups will perform this dance to entertain themselves. Many self-organized amateur folk troupes in related villages will also make touring performances in different villages, which is welcomed by local people.

Mashan's folk Dalang dance is originated from the Tang Dynasty. Liu Xun, a writer of the Tang Dynasty, wrote in *Ling Biao Lu Yi* (a geographical note of Lingnan areas) that "there is Chong Tang in the south of Guangxi, which is made by wood and cut into trough shape. The sound of the wood trough is like the sound of drum that can spread even for miles. Although the sound of pounding cloth in washing is loud and clear, it is still inferior to that of Chong Tang." The tradition of Da Chong Tang has a long history and is still popular nowadays. From the New Year's day to the Lantern Festival are days for entertainment, during which three to five women will gather together to dance Da Chong Tang so as to celebrate a bumper harvest this year. Therefore, there is a saying goes that "so long as there is rumbling sound of Chong Tang, the rice will welcome a bumper harvest this year". In addition, it is said that there were many tigers living in the mountains in ancient times. They often cruelly injured or killed people in villages at night. To drive the tigers away, people began to scare the tigers away by beating the "lang (a kind of wood trough)", so that the tigers would not dare to enter the village and people can live in peace.

The dance movements of Dalang are derived from people's daily work, which mainly reflects the working process from spring sowing to autumn harvest. The performers sometimes beat the trough or each other's langs, and sometimes turn around or jump. Coupled with the shouting of "heehaw", the performance is often at a hectic pace and in a jubilant atmosphere. The props used for Dalang include the lang, the stick to beat the head of the lang, the stick to beat the middle of the lang, gong and drum. Generally, Dalang dance is performed on occasions like worship ceremonies, festivals, entertainment, marriages, celebrations and competitions. As an ancient and traditional dance with ethnic characteristics, Dalang dance of Zhuang Ethnic Group is of wide influence, which bears important values for studying traditional dance and customs of Zhuang Ethnic Group. The protection of the folk Dalang dance is not only beneficial to promote the traditional culture of Zhuang Ethnic Group, enrich people's

壮族打榔古称“打舂堂”，是流行于南宁市马山县古寨、加方、里当、古零乡等乡镇及其周边地区的民间舞蹈。每逢节庆，当地村村寨寨的壮族、瑶族群众便会以此自娱自乐，还有很多村寨自发组织业余民间文艺队，在各村寨巡回演出，深受广大人民群众欢迎。

马山民间传统舞蹈打榔起源于唐朝，唐人刘恂的《岭表录异》云：“广南有舂堂，以浑木刳成槽舡，皆有偏拍。槽声若鼓、闻于数里，虽思妇之巧弄秋砧，不能比浏亮也。”打舂堂之习，世代相传，每逢正月初一至元宵为自由娱乐期，其时妇女三五成群，作打舂堂之乐，其意预祝丰年。故有谚云：“正月舂堂声轰轰，今年到处禾黍丰。”另外，传说古时候当地深山里有很多老虎，到了晚上经常出没于村庄残害人类，人们为了赶走老虎，就通过打榔发出咚咚的声音吓走老虎，这样老虎不敢进村，村民就可以平安生活了。

壮族打榔的动作来源于人们的日常劳作，主要反映劳动人民从播种到收获的劳动过程。在表演时舞者时而击槽，时而交击，时而转身，时而跳跃，有时候配合舞蹈作“嚯嗨”的呼喊，场面紧凑，气氛热烈。打榔所用的道具包括榔身、榔头棒、榔中棒以及锣、鼓等。一般来说，打榔用于敬神仪式、节庆娱乐、红事喜事、大型庆典、竞技比赛等场合。作为古老且富有民族特色的传统舞蹈，壮族打榔具有广泛的影响力，对研究壮族传统舞蹈和壮族民俗等有着重要的参考价值。保护民间舞蹈打榔，不仅有利于推广壮民族传统文化、丰富人民群众生活、构建和谐社会，对展示壮族民间特色文化、增强壮民族精神文化自信心和凝聚力也具有重大的现实意义。

如今在马山县东部山区，有许多村寨长期保持着这一特有的习俗，每逢节庆之日，打榔便成了村村寨寨壮族、瑶族群众自娱自乐的形式，有些村寨还自发组织业余农民剧团，在各村寨间巡回演出，很受广大群众的欢迎。特别是古寨瑶族乡的古寨村农民剧团，每逢乡庆或民间重大群众活动，打榔是必须上演的节目，这一剧团还曾晋京演出，受到首都观众的一致好评。

随着现代娱乐方式的增多，打榔还是在一定程度上受到了影响，活动范围逐渐萎缩，打榔队伍日益减少，传承人也出现断代失传的现象。另外，打榔乐谱也濒临失传，目前能找到的就是古寨乡兰氏婆有打榔十二套打法谱。对此，马山县文化部门采取了相应的措施，如在项目集中分布地区古寨乡建立打榔文化生态保护点；广泛培养传承人，组织特色表演队伍，增强传承队伍和表演队伍力量；开展试点普及工作，选择基础好、具有一定影响力的学校作为试点，传授打榔技法，并通过学校和业余表演团队逐步向全县推广，使之成为全县性的民间舞蹈项目。除此之外，还创编民间舞蹈打榔专题歌舞剧，开展巡回演出，并利用各种演出平台展示壮族打榔的文化魅力。2010年，壮族打榔经广西壮族自治区人民政府同意，列入第三批自治区级非物质文化遗产名录。

打砻（榔）表演　摄影 李海瑛
Performance of Dalang Dance Photo by Li Haiying

life and build a harmonious society, but also of great practical significance to represent the folk culture of Zhuang Ethnic Group and enhance self-confidence and cohesion of Zhuang spirit and culture.

At present, many villages in the eastern mountainous areas of Mashan County still maintain this unique custom. On festival day, Dalang dance will become an entertainment form for people of Zhuang and Yao ethnic groups in the villages. Some villages have also spontaneously organized amateur troupes composed by local farmers to make touring performance among villages, which has been welcomed by local people. The farmer troupe of Guzhai Village of Guzhai Autonomous Town of Yao Ethnic Group, in particular, will perform Dalang dance on township celebrations every year and on each major folk mass activities. This troupe once also performed in Beijing, which was praised by the audience.

With the increase of modern entertainment forms, the inheritance of Dalang dance has been affected to a certain extent. The number of areas where Dalang dance is popular has become less and less and the number of Dalang dance troupe is gradually decreasing. The dance has failed to be handed down from past generations. In addition, the music notation of Dalang is also on the verge of being lost. At present, the existing notations are only the twelve sets of notations from an old lady named Lan in Guzhai Town. In this regard, the cultural department of Mashan County has taken corresponding measures, such as establishing Dalang cultural and ecological protection point in Guzhai Town and other distribution areas; widely cultivating inheritors, organizing special performance troupes and strengthening the team of inheritors and performers; carrying out pilot popularization work in schools with good foundation and influence so as to impart skills of Dalang dance to students; popularizing Dalang dance to the whole county through schools and amateur troupes so as to make it a popular folk dance in the county. Besides, the relevant department has created and composed folk dance drama with the theme of Dalang dance. The department has also conducted touring performances and used performance platforms to represent the cultural charm of Dalang dance of Zhuang Ethnic Group. In 2010, with the approval of the People's Government of the Guangxi Zhuang Autonomous Region, Mashan's Dalang dance of Zhuang Ethnic Group was inscribed on the Third Autonomous Region List of Intangible Cultural Heritage.

壮族竹竿舞

Dance with Bamboo Sticks of Zhuang Ethnic Group

项目名称：壮族竹竿舞

别称：无

分布范围：武鸣区

入选名录：2015年第六批市级非物质文化遗产名录

保护单位：武鸣区文化馆

代表性传承人：无

Element name：Dance with Bamboo Sticks of Zhuang Ethnic Group

Alternative name：None

Geographical location and range：Wuming District

Element inscribed list：In 2015 on the Sixth Municipal List of Intangible Cultural Heritage

Competent body involved in safeguarding：Wuming District Cultural Centre

Representative inheritor：None

“三月三”活动现场，众人唱着山歌跳起欢快的竹竿舞
At the Festival of the Third Day of the Third Lunar Month, People Sang Folk Songs and Danced Happily with Bamboo Poles

壮族竹竿舞，是少数民族竹竿舞的一种，其形式活泼灵动，气氛热闹欢腾，是壮族人民在传统节日三月三中必不可少的节目之一。由于壮族竹竿舞娱乐性很强，因此也是壮族人民和众多前来庆祝节日的宾客共同欢度佳节的重要表演形式。

三月三是多个民族的传统节日，对于壮族而言，一方面它是壮族人民踏青、举办歌会等活动的日子，另一方面也是壮族祭祖的重要节日。壮族竹竿舞就是在每年的“三月三上巳节”中一代接着一代流传下来的。据说，这种舞蹈在过去是有福分的老人死后跳的，随着时间的推移逐渐演变成了壮族三月三或是其他重要节日与宾客共舞的娱乐性较强的表演形式。中华人民共和国成立初期，壮族竹竿舞曾在武鸣区民间的城厢镇、锣圩镇、两江镇等地进行过演出，并参加过自治区、南宁市各类比赛活动。一度，壮族竹竿舞被禁止。改

Dance with bamboo sticks of Zhuang Ethnic Group is a kind of bamboo dance of the minority nationalities. It is lively in form and joyous in atmosphere, which is one of the indispensable programs of the traditional festival of the third day of the third lunar month for Zhuang people. Due to its strong nature of entertainment, dance with bamboo sticks has become an important performance form for the Zhuang people and guests to celebrate the festival together.

The third day of the third lunar month is a traditional festival for many ethnic groups. For the Zhuang people, it is a day for activities like spring outings and song fairs. On the other hand, it is also an important festival for the Zhuang people to worship their ancestors. Dance with bamboo sticks of Zhuang Ethnic Group has been passed on from generation to generation from the annual “Shangsi festival on the third day of the third lunar month”. It is said that this kind of dance was performed after the death of the blessed elders in the past. As time goes by, it gradually developed into an entertaining performance form to dance with guests on the third day of the third lunar month and other important festivals of Zhuang Ethnic Group. During the initial period of the People’s

千人竹竿舞
Thousands of People Dance with Bamboo Poles

Republic of China, dance with bamboo sticks was popular in Chengxiang Town, Luoxu Town and Liangjiang Town of Wuming district. It was also performed in competitive activities at autonomous region and municipal level. Then, the bamboo dance was prohibited during one period. After the implementation of reform and opening-up, this kind of dance was allowed to re-perform. Then, it was spread out of the towns and had an even broader stage. Since 1985, guided by the local government, the competitive activities of the dance with bamboo sticks began to be held on the third day of the third lunar month with thousands of participants. Its style, "the pure uncouthness and the colorful folklore", has attracted numerous people to participate in every year. Thousands of young men, women and guests all celebrate their own festivals by dancing with bamboo sticks, creating a spectacular view of bamboo dance.

The bamboo dance performance needs to place two long and thick parallel bamboo sticks with an interval around nine units of length. Six to ten thin bamboo sticks will be

革开放后，壮族竹竿舞又重新恢复了演出，并且走出村寨，有了更广阔的舞台。1985年起，由政府引导的传统壮族竹竿舞，在每年壮族三月三活动中都举办千人竹竿舞表演比赛，其“土得精粹，俗得亮丽”的风格年年都吸引许许多多的人参与其中，千名壮家青年男女和宾客以跳竹竿舞来庆祝自己的节日，形成了千人齐跳竹竿舞的壮观景象。

竹竿舞的表演是将两根长粗竹竿平行排放，两竿之间相距约9尺，其间横放6—10条竹竿，击竿者两人一组，有3—5对不等，在表演过程中，表演者位于细竿的两端，双膝跪地，臀部后坐，相对的两人手执一对竿，按照节奏敲击竹竿。竹竿舞的跳法分单人跳、双人跳和多人跳，单人跳的方式是表演者在竹竿中间，沿竹竿之间的四个空隙边跳边舞，时而向前，时而向后，往复不止。双人跳、多人跳是两人或多人一组，每组人员的动作必须高度协调，彼此相互照顾，根据一对竹竿的开合变化，在间歇中配合优美的舞姿巧妙地跳动，跳完上个空格后，又返回重复，变幻多姿，乐趣无穷。

作为一项传统节日中必不可少的带有民族特色的演出形式，壮族竹竿舞气氛欢乐，节奏感强，不仅有着很强的审美价值，而且对研究壮族三月三文化以及壮族文化的产生、发展有着重要的参考价值，同时对壮族的历史、民俗的研究也有积极的推动作用。

为做好壮族竹竿舞的传承和保护工作，南宁市武鸣区成立了壮族竹竿舞保护工作领导小组，开展壮族竹竿舞传承保护工作的组织、协调、实施等工作。多年来，以“政府主导、民间主体、群众参与”的方式，举办每年一度壮族三月三节，其间也会举办壮族竹竿舞展演和竞技比赛，整个场面热闹非凡。2010年，千人壮族竹竿舞荣获自治区“八桂群英奖”。2012年，壮族竹竿舞成为武鸣区第一批县级非物质文化遗产代表性项目。目前，壮族竹竿舞传承保护状况良好，民间自发组织跳壮族竹竿舞的群众热情高潮，并已成为武鸣区非物质文化遗产进校园主要项目之一。2015年，壮族竹竿舞经南宁市人民政府同意，列入第六批市级非物质文化遗产名录。

placed vertically on the two long and thick ones. One group of the bamboo stick holders consists of two people and the whole bamboo dance performance need three to five groups of holders. During the performance, the bamboo stick holders will sit on the heels at the two ends of the thin sticks respectively and beat the rhythm with two sticks in their hands. The ways of bamboo dance can be divided into single dance, double dance and multiple dance. The way of single dance is that the performer dances forward and backward repeatedly in the interspaces of the four thin bamboo sticks. Double or multiple dance with two or more performers require high coordination and mutual consideration between performers. According to the opening and closing of the bamboo sticks, performers will dance with beautiful postures in the interspaces repeatedly, which is of great interest with various postures.

As an essential performance form with national characteristic in traditional festivals, dance with bamboo sticks of Zhuang Ethnic Group has joyous atmospheres and strong rhythms. It not only bears strong aesthetic value, but also has great reference value for study of Zhuang culture of the third day of the third lunar month, as well as the emergence and development of Zhuang culture. Dance with bamboo sticks has also promoted the study on history and customs of Zhuang Ethnic Group.

To properly inherit and protect dance with bamboo sticks of Zhuang Ethnic Group, protection group has been established in Wuming District to organize, coordinate and implement the work of bamboo dance protection. For many years, the Zhuang festival on the third day of the third lunar month has been held in the form of “the government taking the lead, the non-government as the main body and the mass as the major participants”. During the festival, the performances and competitions of dance with bamboo sticks will also be held with a boisterous scene. In 2010, bamboo dance with a thousand of performers won “Guangxi Talent Prize”. In 2012, dance with bamboo sticks of Zhuang Ethnic Group became the first batch of representative intangible cultural heritage in Wuming District. At present, the inheritance and protection of dance with bamboo sticks is in good condition. There are also folk people to perform bamboo dance of Zhuang Ethnic Group spontaneously and enthusiastically. Dance with bamboo sticks of Zhuang Ethnic Group has become one of the programs of intangible cultural heritage entering schools. With the approval of the People’s Government of Nanning, it was inscribed on the Sixth Municipal List of Intangible Cultural Heritage in 2015.

隆安壮族狮舞

Long’an Lion Dance of Zhuang Ethnic Group

项目名称：隆安壮族狮舞

别称：无

分布范围：隆安县城厢镇及周边地区

入选名录：2018年第七批自治区非物质文化遗产名录
2017年第七批市级非物质文化遗产名录

保护单位：隆安县文化馆

代表性传承人：苏庆安

Element name: Long’an Lion Dance of Zhuang Ethnic Group

Alternative name: None

Geographical location and range: Chengxiang Town of Long’an County and the surrounding areas

Element inscribed list: In 2018 on the Seventh Autonomous Reigon List of Intangible Cultural Heritage
In 2017 on the Seventh Municipal List of Intangible Cultural Heritage

Competent body involved in safeguarding: Long’an County Cultural Centre

Representative inheritor: Su Qing’an

隆安壮族狮舞是发源于隆安县城厢镇的壮族传统舞蹈。作为一种集传统舞蹈、传统体育与民俗文化于一体，集南狮、北狮典型动作自成一格的艺术形式，隆安壮族狮舞在众多壮族传统舞蹈中独具特色。

隆安壮族狮舞的产生，与人们崇拜瑞兽狮子有关。古代，隆安县壮族人民依赖“那文化”，先于周边许多地区栽种了水稻，但常常遇上旱涝、禽兽抢食，以及各种不可预测的意外，人民因此饱受煎熬、苦不堪言。有些年景，眼看地里的粮食丰收在望，却因突如其来的灾害而颗粒无收。由于狮子被人们当作可以驱邪避害的瑞兽，便借鉴外地舞狮的做法，用篾条、砂纸、彩布等扎成狮子，以舞狮作为一种外力的鼎助，表达人民内心的愿望。每逢重大节庆活动，还会以舞狮来烘托气氛，到了春节，舞狮拜年也是必不可少的。

Long’an lion dance of Zhuang Ethnic Group was a traditional dance originated from Chengxiang Town of Long’an County. As an art form combined both traditional dance, sports and folk culture, as well as typical dance movement of lion dance in the south and the north, Long’an lion dance is very unique among many traditional dances of the Zhuang Ethnic Group.

The emergence of Long’an lion dance of Zhuang Ethnic Group was related to Zhuang people’s worship of lion, an auspicious animal in Zhuang culture. In ancient times, the Zhuang people in Long’an County relied on "Na culture (land culture)". They planted rice in the county’s surrounding areas, but the field often suffered droughts, floods, animal’s scrambling for food and other unpredictable accidents, which made people unspeakably suffering. In some years, due to the sudden disasters, anticipated bumper harvests finally turned into nothing at all. As the lion was regarded as an auspicious animal that can expel evil influences and avoid harm, people began to learn lion dance from other places. They used bamboo strips, sandpaper and colored cloth to tie the lion

隆安县大王庙广场，隆安壮族舞狮团正在表演
Lion Dance Troupe of Zhuang Ethnic Group Is Performing in Dawangmiao Temple Square of Long’an County

as a generous help to express their wishes. On each major festival and celebration, people will use lion dance to foil the atmosphere. This kind of dance is also indispensable on the Spring Festival.

Long'an lion dance is the same as lion dances in other areas, which can foil a jubilant atmosphere. The basic dance movements include stunning, fearing, delighting, climbing, squatting, backing and rolling. There are also various footwork accompanied with the above-mentioned movements, such as pouncing, falling, turning, rolling, jumping and scratching. With the movement of the eyes, mouth and ears, the lions seem to be vivid and lifelike. In the process of continuous inheritance, Long'an lion dance of Zhuang Ethnic Group has broken through the traditional skills of lion dance in the south and integrated with the essence of both lion dance in the south and the north, creating representative performances with local ethnic characteristics such as "golden lion climbing the mountain of swords", "golden lion climbing the bridge on the sky" and "three lions playing on the tower". These representative performances not only represent the skills of lion dance, but also reflect the novelty and uniqueness of national culture, thus gaining wide popularity among people.

As an art form that transcends the traditional dance category, Long'an lion dance of Zhuang Ethnic Group is of obvious ornamental value. Its major function of livening things up is indispensable in some festival activities. In addition, it has its own style and various dance movements, which is of great significance for the study of traditional culture and dance of Zhuang Ethnic Group.

Like many other traditional dances, Long'an lion dance has also been confronted with various difficulties in its development. With the impact of modern dances and young people's migrating to cities, Long'an lion dance once was in trouble due to the lack of performers. With the support of the government, the lion dance troupe of Long'an has consolidated itself and continued to innovate performances. Long'an lion dance troupe has developed from ordinary events like just performing lion dance and paying a New Year call, to a star troupe in Guangxi that has won prizes in lion dance competitions both at home and abroad. While communicating with the lion dance troupes from other places, Long'an lion dance troupe has also spread the influence of this art to more places. With the approval of the People's Government of Nanning, Long'an lion dance of Zhuang Ethnic Group was inscribed on the Seventh Municipal List of Intangible Cultural Heritage in 2017 and inscribed on the seventh Autonomous Reigon List Intangible Cultural Heritage in 2018.

隆安壮族狮舞和许多地区的舞狮习俗一样，能将整个表演场面烘托得热闹欢腾、喜气洋洋，舞狮的基本动作有愕、怕、喜、爬、蹲、退、滚等，表演时还会配合多种多样的步法，做出扑、跌、翻、滚、跳跃、搔痒等动作，伴随着眼、嘴、耳的活动，整个狮子活灵活现、惟妙惟肖。在不断传承的过程中，隆安壮族狮舞突破了南狮传统技法，集南狮、北狮之精粹，打造出“金狮上刀山”“金狮登天桥”“三狮戏楼台”等极富地方民族特色的代表性节目，既有普通舞狮的技艺技巧，又有民族文化的新颖独特，因而广受观众喜爱。

作为一项超越传统舞蹈范畴的艺术形式，壮族隆安狮舞的观赏性不言而喻，其最主要的助兴作用更是在一些节庆活动中必不可少。此外，它自成一格、动作丰富，对于研究壮族传统文化以及壮族传统舞蹈都有着重要意义。

隆安壮族狮舞也如其他传统舞蹈一样，从产生到发展的过程中遇到许多困难。因受现代多姿多彩的舞蹈活动形式的冲击、年轻人进城务工等原因，曾导致狮队缺员而陷于困境。在政府的扶持下，隆安壮族狮舞团巩固了队伍，并进行节目创新，从当年“舞舞狮”“拜拜年”的简单活动，精进为广西魅力十足的明星团队，在国内、国际舞狮比赛中荣获大奖，与各地舞狮艺术交流的同时，也将这一艺术的影响力传递到了更多、更远的地方。2017年，隆安壮族舞狮经南宁市人民政府同意，列入第七批市级非物质文化遗产名录；2018年列入第七批自治区级非物质文化遗产名录。

第四章 传统戏剧

Chapter Four Traditional Opera/Drama

粤剧

Yueju Opera

项目名称：粤剧

别称：下四府粤剧、南派粤剧

分布范围：广西壮族自治区南宁市、贵港市、钦州市、北海市、梧州市等粤语方言区，广东省、香港、澳门等

入选名录：2014年第四批国家级非物质文化遗产扩展项目名录

保护单位：南宁市民族文化艺术研究院（南宁市非物质文化遗产保护中心）

代表性传承人：冯杏元、梁素梅、黄俊成、颜怡、钟晓俊、姚艳、刘希瑛

Element name: Yueju Opera

Alternative name: Xiasifu Yueju Opera, Southern Yueju Opera

Geographical location and range: Yue Dialect Areas in Nanning, Guigang, Qinzhou, Beihai, Wuzhou cities of Guangxi Zhuang Autonomous Region; Guangdong Province, Hong Kong, Macao and others

Element inscribed list: In 2014 on the Fourth Extended List of National Intangible Cultural Heritage

Competent body involved in safeguarding: Nanning Ethnic Culture and Art Research Institute (Nanning Intangible Cultural Heritage Protection Centre)

Representative inheritors: Feng Xingyuan, Liang Sumei, Huang Juncheng, Yang Yi, Zhong Xiaojun, Yao Yan, Liu Xiying

粤剧流布于广西粤方言区，是岭南文化与八桂文化共同孕育的产物。明万历年间，就有戏班在广西梧州演出。清末民初到20世纪40年代，粤剧演出在广西非常兴盛。广西粤剧的舞台表演和题材内容具有鲜明的广西地域特色，流行地区在地理上和古代下四府接近，又称下四府粤剧或南派粤剧。

广西粤剧的形成，与弋阳腔、昆腔、梆子腔和皮黄腔的传入关系密切。今保留的例戏《六国大封相》《天姬送子》等在历史文献中早就有记载。另据麦啸霞考证："皮黄乱弹……南流之线由湖南、广西而入广东。"认为徽班向南传播系经湘至桂而后再入粤。所以广西粤剧在孕育过程中大抵也是这样一条线路。自清始，广西戏曲兴盛。清代晏商端的《粤游纪程》载："……署中演戏，为郁林土班，不广不昆，殊不耐听。"这说明广西班已入粤演出。1906年，演员走盘珠在南宁演出，开始了广西粤剧的一个新时代。20世纪20年代，粤剧日趋旺盛。抗日战争时期，粤剧戏班猛增。中华人民共和国成立后，广西粤剧勃兴，南宁、梧州、玉林、

Spawned by Lingnan culture and Bagui culture, Yueju Opera is popular among Yue dialect areas of Guangxi. It appeared in Wuzhou of Guangxi as early as Wanli years of the Ming Dynasty and flourished from the late Qing Dynasty and early Republic of China to the 1940s. It is also called Xiasifu Yueju Opera or Southern Yueju Opera, seeing that it has distinctive regional characteristics in terms of performing and theme performing and its regions are close to Xiasifu area.

The birth of Yueju Opera was tightly bound to the introduction to Yiyang Opera, Kunqiang Opera, Bangzi Opera and Pihuang Opera. Repertoires still remained today, such as *The Prime Minister of Six Countries* and *The Cowherd and The Weaving Maid*, could be found in early historical materials. According to Mai Xiaoxia's textual research, "Pihuang Opera is ... and it was brought southward from Hunan province, then through Guangxi, and then to Guangdong." It shows how Pihuang Opera was introduced into Guangdong, and Yueju Opera was probably disseminated along the same route. The opera was supposedly flourishing since the Qing Dynasty. As it described in *The Journey in Guangdong* (Eleven Years of Yongzheng, Qing Dynasty), "a stage performance was played by a Yulin troupe in the state office, it sounds strange because it's neither similar to Guangqiang opera nor Kun Opera." Troupes from Guangxi

《白蛇传》
The White Snake

《六月飞霜》
Snowing June

(Yulin is a city in Guangxi) had already spread in Guangdong then. In 1906, an actor called Zoupanzhu played Yueju Opera in Nanning, unveiling a new epoch of Guangxi Yueju Opera. The opera was increasingly popular in the 1920s and numbers of the opera troupes insurged during the War of Resistance against Japan. Even after the foundation of the People's Republic of China, relevant troupes were widely distributed in Nanning, Wuzhou, Yulin, Beihai, Liuzhou and Baise etc.

The Yueju Opera is featured by bright color of Lingnan and Bagui cultures. It initially had ten types of roles including elderly male roles, middle-aged male roles, young male roles, elderly female roles, demure female roles, lively female roles, painted roles, clown roles, negative painted roles, and walking-on roles. And now the roles have been simplified into fewer types, such as male roles, demure female roles and clown roles. It was once performed by using official stage language and later the language was changed for Cantonese in the late Qing Dynasty and early Republic of China. The music used in the opera belongs to one branch of Pihuang music though, some of them still retain high-pitched tune, which was inherited from Yiyang and Kun Operas at early period. It is matched with a great variety of tunes and euphonic melodies, and the music played by gongs, cymbals and Suona horn is much

北海、柳州、百色等市都有粤剧团。

广西粤剧具有鲜明的岭南和八桂地域特色。广西粤剧分十大行当：末、净、生、旦、丑、外、小、贴、夫、杂。现时则以文武生、花旦、丑生行当较为常见。清代以“戏棚官话”为其舞台语言，清末民初改用粤语白话演唱。广西粤剧的音乐属皮黄系统，但早期受昆腔和弋阳腔的影响，也保留了一些高腔牌子的剧目，曲牌较多，唱腔优美。其伴奏音乐突出大锣、大钹、唢呐，声音高亢激越。总体来说，表演既有火爆的南派武打，又有动人的生旦戏。广西粤剧以武戏见长，武打出自南拳套路，风格古朴粗犷，讲究硬桥实马，与其他剧种迥异，许多身段、造型以至出手等都来源于桂西南一带壮、汉两族人民共同喜爱的民间舞蹈、武技和造型。“变脸”“耍牙”“跳台铲椅”“吊辫”“过山”“吐血”“三上吊”“踩跷”“甩发”等武功特技展现了广西粤剧的特点。舞台美术简练质朴，并有少数民族风格。其代表剧目有《西河会妻》《目连救母》《七状纸》《芦花河》等。

广西粤剧是植根于八桂大地上的民族民间艺术，对研究粤剧的流变具有重要价值。广西粤剧是少数民族地区各族集体创造的结晶，从业者不仅有汉族，还有壮族、京族等少数民族，他们进行过用壮语演出的尝试。因此，研究广西粤剧也对研究粤剧与少数民族文化的融合有参考意义。再者，粤剧是连接东盟的一条文化纽带，历史上有些粤剧团体就是从东南亚迁回内地的，现在广西的粤剧团体经常到东盟国家演出，因此，广西粤剧发挥着中国与东南亚国家联系和交流的文化纽带作用。

目前，广西粤剧传承中的主要问题是：老资料散失，新剧目匮乏。传统剧目大量失传，文字、实物、音像资料等得不到妥善保存，大部分传统特技绝活难以继承，濒临失传。从业人员减少，行当不齐。针对这些问题，南宁市政府积极应对，举办传统粤剧排场展演及青年粤剧比赛。在南宁新会书院定期演出，使其成为粤剧展示、传承的基地，以创作促进粤剧的动态保护。近年来，广西南宁粤剧共获得了国家级、自治区级和地市级的各类文艺奖项达90余项（次）。2014年，经国务院批准，粤剧列入第四批国家级非物质文化遗产扩展项目名录。

《玉蜻蜓》
Jade Dragon Fly

resonant. Generally speaking, it has been famous for acrobatic fighting dramas and moving dramas that have demure females as leading roles, especially the former. Its movements in acrobatic fighting performance, drawing lessons from southern pugilistic art, are primitive and rough but with real fighting skills, which is totally different with other operas. The dancing postures, movements, roles' modeling in operas are all designed by emulating the elements of folk art that are popular among Zhuang and Han people in the southwest Guangxi. The characteristics of the opera are vividly displayed in acrobatic fighting skills, such as Mask-changing, teeth-playing, jumping and kicking chairs, plait-hanging, hands-raising over heads, blood-spitting, hanging for three times, walking on stilts and hair-swaying. Besides, the aesthetic feeling of the stage performance is simple and plain with Ethnic Group style. Representatives of the plays include *Meeting Wife alongside the West River*, *Mulian Saves Mother*, *Seven Pieces of Written Complaint* and *Luhua River*.

Guangxi Yueju Opera, deeply rooted in the folk art of Bagui areas, has great value in studying the evolution of Yueju Opera. It is a common fruit made by nationalities including Han, Zhuang and Jing, and it was even performed in Zhuang language. In this sense, it is of great significance in studying cultural integration. In addition, some Yueju Opera groups from Southeast Asia once joined in the tropes of mainland in history, and now Guangxi Yueju Opera groups often perform overseas in ASEAN countries. Hence it is not difficult to see that Yueju Opera serves as cultural bound connecting China and Southeast Asian countries.

At present, what hinders the development of the opera is that many old recordings of it were lost or hard to preserve, less and less people engaged in the performing leads a dilemma of no inheritance. To address these challenges, the government of Nanning takes all-out efforts to better protect Yueju Opera, such as arranging Yueju Opera performance, holding relevant exhibitions and promoting youth competition of Yueju Opera in Xinhui Academy of Nanning, which was set as the base for performing and inheriting Yueju Opera. Recently, Guangxi's Yueju Opera has won more than 90 literary and art awards of national, municipal and autonomous region level respectively. In 2014, Yueju Opera was included in the Fourth Extended List of National Intangible Cultural Heritage, after the approval of the State Council.

邕剧

Yongju Opera

项目名称：邕剧

别称：广戏、老戏、五六腔

分布范围：南宁市宾阳县、贵港市、北流市、玉林市等

入选名录：2008年第二批国家级非物质文化遗产名录
2007年第一批自治区级非物质文化遗产名录
2007年第一批市级非物质文化遗产名录

保护单位：南宁市民族文化艺术研究院（南宁市非物质文化遗产保护中心）

代表性传承人：洪琪、冯杏元、蒋耀明（已故）、梁克俭（已故）、李传湘、杭彪（已故）
黄学超、梁素梅、宁靖、张铁锋、何惠临、郝芸

Element name：Yongju Opera

Alternative name：Guangxi Opera, Laoxi Opera, Wuliuqiang Opera

Geographical location and range：Binyang County of Nanning City, Guigang City, Beiliu City, Yulin City and others

Element inscribed list：In 2008 on the Second National List of Intangible Cultural Heritage
In 2007 on the First Autonomous Region List of Intangible Cultural Heritage
In 2007 on the First Municipal List of Intangible Cultural Heritage

Competent body involved in safeguarding：Nanning Ethnic Culture and Art Research Institute (Nanning Intangible Cultural Heritage Protection Centre)

Representative inheritors：Hong Qi, Feng Xingyuan, Jiang Yaoming (Late), Liang Kejian (Late), Li Chuanxiang, Hang Biao (Late), Huang Xuechao, Liang Sumei, Ning Jing, Zhang Tiefeng, He Huilin, Hao Yun

邕剧《芦花荡》
Yongju Opera *Reed Catkins Marsh*

邕剧是广西四大地方剧种之一，旧时习称为“广戏”“老戏”“五六腔”，主要流布在广西壮族自治区的南宁市、宾阳县、贵县、北流、玉林等地，以南宁为中心，波及广西的左右江、西江一带，流传至广东、云南、贵州等省及越南、柬埔寨等国家。它属于皮黄声腔系统，因活动中心在古邕州（南宁的古称）一带，且用邕州官话演唱，中华人民共和国成立后将之定名为“邕剧”。

邕剧的起源向有三种说法：一说是清道光、咸丰年间，祁剧艺人来桂南传艺，始有本地班的产生，初为宾州、武鸣班的丝弦戏，至同治年间，受广班的影响，发展成为以邕州班为代表的本地班；一说是清咸丰年间李文茂的起义军从广东带来红船子弟兵，兵败后，流落广西民间，以演出谋生；另一说是在祁、桂剧的基础上吸收民间艺术，形成广班，其支系流入广东而为粤剧。诸说迄今无定论，但多数认为第一种说法较接近于历史事实。祁、桂、邕、粤剧同为皮黄系统，相互之间有着十分密切的关系。光绪年后，常与丝弦

Yongju Opera, one of the four main operas in Guangxi, had been called Guangxi Opera, Laoxi Opera or Wuliuqiang Opera for a long time. It is popular among Binyang County of Nanning City, Guigang, Beiliu and Yulin and other cities. Originating from Nanning, it then spread along southwest to the areas surrounding Zuojiang, Youjiang, and Xijiang rivers in Guangxi, and then to Guangdong, Yunnan, Guizhou provinces, Vietnam, Cambodia and other countries. It belongs to one branch of Pihuang music though, it was named Yongju Opera after the founding of the People's Republic of China, seeing that it is sung in the official language of Yongzhou and mainly performed in Yongzhou (the old name of Nanning).

There exist three arguments about the origin of Yongju Opera. The first is that it was initially brought to Guangxi by artists singing Qiju Opera (an opera prevailed in Hunan province) during the years of Daoguang and Xianfeng of the Qing Dynasty, and was once performed as Sixian Opera in Binzhou and Wuming. Having been affected by Guangdong troupes, it finally formed Yongzhou troupes singing Yongju Opera during the reign of Emperor Tongzhi of the Qing Dynasty. The second argues that it was brought here from Guangdong by uprising soldiers that once led by Li Wenmao, who were reduced to singing opera as the last resort after defeats. The last believes that it was based on Qiju and Guiju

邕剧《五台会兄》
Yongju Opera *Meet Brother in Wutai Mountain*

邕剧《三进士》
Yongju Opera *Three Imperial Candidates*

operas and then developed into Guang opera that hatched out Yueju Opera in Guangdong. Most people approve that the first one is closer to the fact, although there is no definite conclusion yet. The reality is that Qiju, Guiju, Yongju and Guang Operas are all parts of Pihuang clans and are closely bound to each other. For example, they have many similarities in music, repertoire, performing style and customs, because they learnt from each other by sharing actors of their troupes after Emperor Guangxu years. Yongju Opera, rooted in the folk, has gradually matured under the elaborate creation by generations of artists. It has a huge number of audiences of all nationalities in and around Nanning, owing to its strong country flavor and ethnic characteristics in tunes, procedures and repertoire. In general, Yongju Opera distinguishes itself with its exquisite and mature artistic skills, graceful and unique performing style and quick-witted stage lines.

The roles of Yongju Opera can be roughly divided into four types: sheng (male roles), dan (female roles), jing (painted roles) and chou (clown roles), and it can be more than ten types in subdivision. It was initially performed by elderly male roles, young male roles, female roles and face-painted roles, and then gradually young male roles and female roles became the main actors of Yongju Opera. The stage lines of it are mainly official language of Yongzhou, studded with idioms, vocabularies and proverbs from languages of Cantonese, Kejia, Ping, and Zhuang. The aria is Pihuang tunes, supplemented by Anqing tune, Qijuban tune (Luoluo tune), Bugang tune and other local tunes. As for the accompanying music, it is played by gongs, cymbals, erxian and houguan. As a combination of Southern martial arts and flavors of West

班、老广班相互参班演出，师承和流布地域相互交错，在剧目、表演、音乐、演出习俗等方面有许多近似之处。邕剧扎根民间，在历代艺人的精心打造下逐步完善成熟，形成了一整套带有浓郁乡土气息和民族特色的音乐唱腔、表演程式、演出剧目，在民间拥有庞大的观众群体，深为南宁及周边地区各族人民所喜爱。邕剧以其精美圆熟的艺术技巧、优美典雅的独特风格、机智的戏剧语言而独具特色。

邕剧的行当有生、旦、净、丑四大类，细分则有十余行之多，最初以小武、武生、散发花旦、花脸四行当家，后来逐渐演变成以小武和散发花旦为主。邕剧的舞台语言用邕州官话，并含有大量的白话、客家话、平话和壮话的民间习语、词汇、谚语、歇后语等。其唱腔绝大多数以皮黄声腔为主，安庆调、七句半（罗罗腔）、补缸调及地方小调为辅。音乐伴奏以大锣、大钹、二弦、喉管为主。邕剧的表演风格古朴、粗犷，是南派武功和粤西风骨的结合。武打粗犷激昂，表演夸张、泼辣，讲究硬桥实马，拳、刀、枪、叉、棍、牒各有套路，与其他剧种迥异，其传统变脸、要獠牙、跳台铲椅等武功特技深受广大观众的欢迎。而许多身段、造型以至出手、投足等都来源于桂西南一带壮、汉两族人民共同喜爱的民间舞姿、武技和美术造型，在某些方面体现了壮族的雄浑粗犷的民族风格。其文戏表演则非常细腻，注重人物内心感情的抒发。邕剧的传统剧目有600多个，移植改编剧目及创作剧目近百个。其中代表剧目有《拦马过关》《天门阵》《李槐卖箭》《红布恨》《春满柜台》《百鸟衣》《十五贯》《阮文追》等。

邕剧有着深厚的文化积淀和良好的群众基础。曾涌现出许少康、李名扬、黄少金等名伶，以及全新凤、合新凤、寿新凤、乐尧天等班社。南宁市人民邕剧团于1951年成立，20世纪50年代末60年代初，中央领导多次观看《拦马过关》《泗水关》《五台会兄》等优秀邕剧剧目，给予高度评价。其影响力远播至东南亚，剧团在为越南、缅甸、柬埔寨、新加坡等东南亚国家领导人和代表团演出时，也同样获得高度赞誉。为了使邕剧得到更好的传承和发展，从1987年开始，南宁市的有关部门对邕剧展开了一系列的抢救工作，使得邕剧观众爱好者不断增多，市场不断扩大。2007年，南宁市邕剧团建制得到恢复。2008年6月7日，邕剧经国务院批准，列入第二批国家级非物质文化遗产名录。

邕剧排场《打闭门》
Yongju Opera Classical Fragment *Combat Fighting in the Room*

Guangdong, it is played in primitive and rugged style. It has a series of real aerobatic fighting skills in using pugilistic art, swords, spears, forks and sticks which provide exciting aerobatic scene and evocating performance that varies from other operas. The dancing postures, movements, roles' modeling in operas are all designed by emulating the elements of folk art that are popular among Zhuang and Han people in the southwest Guangxi. In addition, singing plays of the opera stress the expression of the inner feelings of characters, making the whole play touching. There are more than 600 traditional repertoires of Yongju Opera, among which nearly 100 operas are adapted. Representatives of the plays include *Get Away by Stopping the Horse, Against Tianmen Formation, Lost in Red Cloths, Li Huai Selling Arrows, Booming Business, The Hero in Thousands-Feathers Gown, The Story of Fifteen Strings of Coppers* and *Ruan Wenzhui.*

Yongju Opera with its profound cultural civilization is deeply rooted in the foundation of people. A number of famous actors including Xu Shaokang, Li Mingyang and Huang Shaojin have emerged, as well as troupes such as Quanxinfeng, Hexinfeng, Shouxinfeng and Le Yaotian. Nanning People's Yongju Opera Troupe, founded as far back as 1951, provided the central leadership with excellent Yongju Opera repertoires at the end of 1950s and received their high praises, such as *Get Away by Stopping the Horse, Sishui Pass*, and *Meeting the Brother at Wutaishan Mountain*. And its charm was also tasted by southeastern countries when the opera troupes performing for leaders and delegations from Vietnam, Myanmar, Cambodia, Singapore and other countries. In order to better protect and help inherit Yongju Opera, the authorities of Nanning have launched a series of rescue work, which makes the audience increasing and the market expanding. In 2007, Nanning Yongju Opera Troupe successfully resumed its running. On June 7th, 2008, Yongju Opera was included into the Second National List of Intangible Cultural Heritage after the approval of the State Council.

南宁平话师公戏

Nanning Shigong Opera in Pinghua Language

项目名称：南宁平话师公戏

别称：尸公

分布范围：兴宁区、西乡塘区、江南区、邕宁区、高新技术开发区等

入选名录：2014年第五批自治区级非物质文化遗产名录

保护单位：南宁高新技术开发区文体局

代表性传承人：无

Element name：Nanning Shigong Opera in Pinghua Language

Alternative name：Shigong

Geographical location and range：Xingning District, Xixiangtang District, Jiangnan District, Yongning District, High-Tech Development Zone and others

Element inscribed list：In 2014 on the Fifth Autonomous Region List of Intangible Cultural Heritage

Competent body involved in safeguarding：The Culture and Sports Bureau of High-Tech Development Zone of Nanning City

Representative inheritor：None

南宁平话师公戏是南宁市的地方戏之一，广泛流传于广西平话人居住地区，活动在南宁市六城区及周边县的壮、汉族杂居处，以兴宁、西乡塘、高新、江南、邕宁等区演唱最频繁。

南宁平话师公戏源于古代的巫傩祭祀活动，是一种逐鬼驱疫、婚娶发丧的仪式。装师公的人，戴假面具，边跳边舞，以表现“请神驱鬼”“祈福消灾”“丰收酬神”的内容。经过长期的发展，这种舞仪不断地演变，到了清末开始发展成为一种戏曲——“师公戏”。从明清时期起，师公在桂林、柳州、南宁和钦州就有演唱。清末民初到20世纪40年代，师公用不同的语言唱“尸”“跳岭头”，在广西非常兴盛。广大的农村、庙宇成为师公演出的重要场所。随着社会的进步和时代的发展，南宁“平话师公戏”在表演的题材方面广泛地吸收了当地流传的民间故事、传说，逐渐具有了唱、做、念等形式和生、旦、净、丑等戏剧角色，形成了独特的唱腔和舞蹈套路，并从最初的娱神向娱人转变。

平话师公戏，又称“尸公”、它属于傩戏系统。其宗旨是消灾纳福，服务于壮、汉各民族。南宁平话师公戏采用平话与本土壮话相结合的说唱形式，间或插有桂柳话和白话。在表演的题材方面广泛地吸收了当地流传的民间故事、传说。在发展过程中逐渐成为具有唱、做、念的形式，以唱为主，也有道白。道白为演员上台后根据唱词前后内容的呼应而加的过渡语。角色行当也分为生、旦、净、丑，独特的唱腔和舞蹈。在表演上，南宁平话师公戏一般以丰富的故事内容、生动易懂的唱词吸引观众，并不着意刻画戏剧人物。表演动作一般有“三元指”“丁字步”“碎步”“跳跃步”“旋转”“颤步”等，并且以颤步为主要动作。另外，南宁平话师公戏已以化装代替了过去的木面具和纸面具。剧本题材既有神目类，如《请师科》，也有正本戏，如传统剧目《大酬雷》《七仙女下凡》等。

Shigong Opera in Pinghua Language is one of local operas of Nanning and popular in Liucheng district and neighboring regions where Zhuang and Han people co-inhabit. It is most frequently performed in Xingning, Xixiangtang, Jiangnan and Yongning Districts and High-Tech Development Zone.

The opera was originated from ancient sacrificial activities which served for weddings, funerals, and driving ghost and diseases away. The actor who plays as Shigong (the local wizard) will dance and sing with a mask on his face, expressing people's hope for banishing ghosts, praying for good fortunes and their appreciation for harvest granted by the god. During a long period, such activity developed into one kind of opera, Shigong Opera, which appeared among people in Guilin, Liuzhou, Nanning and Qinzhou during the Ming and Qing Dynasties. It later sprouted out branches with different languages and once flourished in Guangxi villages and temples from the end of the Qing Dynasty and the beginning of the Republic of China to the 1940s. It absorbed varies folk stories and legends with the time to enrich its contents. Gradually, it has formed the procedures of singing, acting, speaking and fixed roles such as male roles, female roles, painted roles and clown roles.

Shigong Opera, or Shigong, belongs to a branch of Nuo opera to pray for blessings for Zhuang and Han people. It is sung in Pinghua and Zhuang languages, sometimes in Guiliu dialect and Cantonese. It has enriched topic subjects by absorbing folk stories and legends and formed the procedures of singing, acting, speaking, among which singing is essential with Daobai (transitional words added by the actors according to the content of the around the libretto) as a supplement. In terms of acting, it is appreciated with its lively story and easy libretto rather than stressing character sketch. Its basic movements are including "Sanyuan Pointing", "T-Step", "Quick and Short Step", "Squat Step", "Jump Step", "Rotation Step", "Tremble Step"and"Swing Step", among which Tremble Step is the main steps on the stage. Besides, the wooden or paper masks wore on actors' faces in the past were replaced by hand makeup. The theme of the opera includes Taoism topic such as *Invite Taoist Immortal* and story plays, such as the traditional drama *Dachoulei* (meaning praying for spring rain and celebrating the harvest) and *Seven Goddess Down to Earth*.

The Shigong Opera, with distinctive characteristics in style and contents, has great value of both appreciation and art and is much loved by people speaking in Pinghua Language. It keeps a primitive flavor in singing style. Nuo dance, music

八仙贺寿
Eight Immortals' Congratulations on Life

天姬送子
Goddess Delivers Children

of gongs and drums, especially the dance figure, the action of exorcising both stem from the folk dance popular among Zhuang and Han people. As time goes by, it has changed its purpose from entertaining gods to entertaining people. Although Shigong Opera is still performed for funerals and harvest in the folk, it has been more reformed into a modern opera. For example, in some places it was transcribed into folk song opera equipped with music of gongs and drums, performing modern content with elements existing today. However, the inheritance of Shigong Opera in Pinghua Language has been facing a gloomy future due to little troupes that engage in performing. To address the problem, the government of Nanning's High-tech Zone attaches great importance to the protection of the opera. They allocate special funds to support the construction of the art troupe of Shigong Opera, and call for all-out efforts to collect and rearrange relevant data. In 2014, Nanning's Shigong Opera in Pinghua Language was inscribed on the Fifth Autonomous Region List of Intangible Cultural Heritage, after the approval of People's Government of Guangxi Zhuang Autonomous Region.

平话师公戏的表演和题材内容具有鲜明的广西地域特色，既有观赏价值又有艺术研究价值，是平话人喜闻乐见的剧种。其演唱、傩舞、锣鼓风格保留古朴风味，特别是舞的造型、做法事的动作等都来自本土壮、汉两族人民共同喜爱的民间舞蹈。随着时代的发展，南宁平话师公戏已经从最初的娱神向娱人转变，在民间虽然在“丧葬习俗”“年例”上依然盛行师公戏，但更多的已被改革成现代师公戏，有些地方还被改为山歌剧，配有音乐和锣鼓，融入了现代文化元素，传统的师公戏被注入现实主义色彩，表演现代内容。但是，近年来，师公戏传承也面临断层现象，现存的师公团体本来就很少，师公团员能够坚持参加演出的所剩无几。为此，南宁市高新区政府高度重视平话师公戏的保护工作，划拨专项资金支持师公艺术团建设，组织力量开展南宁平话师公戏相关资料的收集和整理工作。2014年，南宁平话师公戏经广西壮族自治区人民政府同意，列入第五批自治区级非物质文化遗产名录。

上林壮族师公戏

Shanglin Shigong Opera of Zhuang Ethnic Group

项目名称：上林壮族师公戏

别称：无

分布范围：上林县巷贤镇、大丰镇、西燕镇、乔贤镇、镇圩瑶族乡、塘红乡等

入选名录：2012年第四批自治区级非物质文化遗产名录

保护单位：上林县文化馆

代表性传承人：周宗美

Element name：Shanglin Shigong Opera of Zhuang Ethnic Group

Alternative name：None

Geographical location and range：Xiangxian Town, Dafeng Town, Xiyan Town, Qiaoxian Town, Zhenxu Town of Yao Ethnic Group, Tanghong Town and others of Shanglin County

Element inscribed list：In 2012 on the Fourth Autonomous Region List of Intangible Cultural Heritage

Competent body involved in safeguarding：Shanglin County Cultural Centre

Representative inheritor：Zhou Zongmei

师公戏做祭祀活动时演唱祭文
Shigong Masters Sing Sacrificial Texts during Ritual Events

Shanglin Shigong Opera of Zhuang Ethnic Group, a traditional folk art based on exorcising practice, is much appreciated by Zhuang people in Xiangxian, Dafeng, Zhenwei, Xiyan, Qiaoxian, Tanghong and other townships of Shanglin County. Absorbing quite a few folk stories and legends, it developed its characteristics of both story play and Caidiao Opera and finally turned to a simple drama art deeply rooted in countryside during a long period.

Since the most stage lines of the opera were mainly taught from mouth to mouth, no written records could help us trace the actual time of the opera's origin. One thing we are sure is that it was spawned by religious sacrificial activities among the people. From *Shanglin Annals* written in the years of Emperor Kangxi of the Qing Dynasty, however, we can know relevant sacrificial activities about Shigong appeared at least 200 years ago. It was recorded that "people in sickness will take no medicine but ask wizards to dance and pray for them, such activity is called exorcising", "the sixth day of the June was designated as the day holding Crop Fair, wizards of towns would dance for Tiangong and Tiangmu (the god in charge of people's harvest in Chinese folklore). Such activity is

上林壮族师公戏是在跳神的基础上发展而来的，是上林壮族人民喜闻乐见的传统民间艺术，主要分布在上林县巷贤、大丰、镇圩、西燕、乔贤、塘红等乡镇。在长期的流传过程中，上林壮族师公戏广泛吸收了当地流传的民间故事、传说，兼具故事剧和彩调的特点，逐步发展成为一种根植于乡土的较简单的戏剧艺术形式。

师公戏是从民间宗教祭祀活动中脱胎出来的，很多师公唱词多是靠口传心授，没有确切的文字记载师公戏的起源年代。康熙年间的《上林县志》载：“或遇疾病，不服医药，辄延鬼师歌舞祈祷，谓之跳鬼。”又有“六月六日为‘青苗会’。各乡延巫诣管苗庙祀田公、田母，以祈有年，谓之‘调庙’”，以及“十月收成，延巫就社坛建平安醮，禳灾除疫。俗以是月初一日定风色，旬内俱南风者主来岁大熟”。由此可见，至少在200多年前，上林就有师公宗教祭祀活动。《广西百科全书》中也提到，广西师公戏是在师公跳神的基础上发展起来的，原是师公在法事活动中戴上各种神灵面具跳娱神舞仪，唱酬神故事。清同治年间，其发展成为分角色演唱民间故事的剧种，称为师公戏。

早期的上林壮族师公戏具有故事剧、彩调的优点，是一种较简单的戏剧艺术形式。近代以来，由于师公的宗教活动受到严格的限制，师公戏遂与宗教祭祀活动脱离，成为独立的表演形式。上林壮族师公戏有独特的唱腔和舞蹈，以唱为主，少有道白，偶有道白则是演员上台后，根据唱词前后内容的呼应，而临时自由发挥所加的过渡语。唱词分师腔与欢腔两种，均使用本地壮语。师腔唱词固定七言，二句一段，段中押脚韵或腰韵，每段唱完时要击鼓打锣踩台过门。欢腔唱词源自壮族山歌“欢”，五言四句一首，用唱腔，但在押韵上又有讲究：第二句前三字要有一字押首句末字的韵，二、三句同脚韵，第四句前三字有一字押二、三句脚韵。表演方面一般不按人物刻画加以表情动作，它主要以丰富的故事内容、生动易懂的唱词吸引观众，不太讲究角色行当。上林壮族师公戏有固定的动作贯穿全剧表演，一般为“三元指”“青蛙指”“腕子功”“腕臂功”“臂功”“丁字步”“碎步”“蹲步”“跳跃步”“旋转”“颤步”“大甩步”，并以颤步为师公戏表演的主要台步。上林壮族师公戏以木质面具代替化装，所戴面具多是诸神形象，酬什么神戴什么面具，如玉女娘、土地公、土地婆、特兴、特凸、猴神、雷神、农婆等，大都是驱鬼镇妖之神。上林师公戏的传统剧目共有300多出，如《布伯与雷王》《甘王》《花婆》《四值公曹》《莫一大王》等，也有移植改编的剧目，如《大闹天宫》《唐三藏西天取经》《梁山伯与祝英台》和《孟姜女》等。

上林壮族师公戏是环大明山原生态文化的重要成分，是了解和探析民族传统文化的一个重要窗口。1949年之后，上林壮族师公戏曾一度兴起，但1966年至1976年又遭受到严

called sacrifice offering” and “when in the harvest in October, wizards will be asked to build sacrificial altar and praying for no disasters and diseases. People believe that the next year will be a harvest year if south wind blows throughout the first ten days of October”. According to the *Encyclopedia of Guangxi*, Shigong Opera developed on the basis of exorcising activity, which was originally a sacrificial dance performed by Shigong (the local wizard) with masks. and the sacrificial dance developed into an opera called Shigong that sings folk stories by roles during the years of Tongzhi of the Qing Dynasty.

The early Shigong Opera was a simple drama art that integrates the merits of story play and Caidiao Opera. It has gradually separated itself with sacrificial and became a more independent performance as the consequence of strict limits imposed on religious activities recent days. The Opera has a unique singing and dance form and is sung essential with Daobai as a supplement, which is transitional words added by the actors according to the content of the around the libretto. The libretto is divided into two types: Shi tune and Huanqiang tune, both of which are in local Zhuang language. The former is fixed with seven words in a sentence and two sentences made for one paragraph with rhymes or assonance. Whenever a paragraph is finished, the performers should re-step on the stage over the sound of drums and gongs. Huanqiang tune is so called because it stems from Huan folk songs of Zhuang Ethnic Group. Every Huan song is composed of four lines with five words each, and they are rhymed in a more rigid way: it is regulated that one of the first three words of the second lines must rhyme with the last word of the first line, the second and third lines should have the same foot rhyme, and one of the first three words of the last line should either rhyme with the last word of the two lines above. In terms of acting, the opera is performed with no fixed roles, which is totally different from other operas that stress character portrayal and expression. Or rather, it is appreciated with its graphic story and easy libretto and studded with basic movements that used for a long time. The basic movements include “Sanyuan Pointing”, “Frog Pointing”, “Wrist Motion”, “Wrist-Arm Motion”, “Arm Motion”, “T-Step”, “Quick and Short Step”, “Squat Step”, “Jump Step”, “Rotation Step”, “Tremble Step”and“Swing Step”, among which Tremble Step is the main steps on the stage. The performers of the opera wear wooden masks rather than painted ones. Most of the masks are the images of their gods that help drive ghost away, such as Yunu Goddess, the God and Goddess of the land, Texing, Teluo, the Monkey God, Thunder God and the God of Agriculture. There are more than 300 traditional repertoires of Shanglin Shigong Opera, such as *Bubo and King Lei, King*

Gan, Huapo, Four Immortal Watching the Time and *King Moyi*. Adapted operas are also popular transplanted from folk stories including *Create A Tremendous Uproar, Journey to the West, Liang Shanbo and Zhu Yingtai* and *Lady Meng Jiang*.

Shanglin Shigong Opera of Zhuang Ethnic Group is an essential part of original ecology culture around the Damingshan Mountain, providing a chance for us to explore and study traditional ethnical culture. It once had its flourishing time after 1949 (the year of the foundation of the People's Republic of China), but then unluckily crashed during 1966-1976 (10 years of the Great Cultural Revolution of China), and attached significance after the 1980s. Due to the change of mechanism and the large number of young people working outside, the number of actors decreased day by day, and the writers and directors of the opera are even scarcer. All these factors pushed the Shigong Opera in a predicament which urgently needs to be supported and protected. Recent years the opera is under better protection, thanks to the efforts of the government of Shanglin County. In 2008, a competition of Shigong Opera performing was held in Mingliang Town, and a number of actors are rewarded. At the same time, various folk publicity events for Shigong Opera, such as performance and drama exchanges, were also run around towns, so as to encourage the society to heed the art and extend its influence. In 2012, Shanglin Shigong Opera of Zhuang Ethnic Group was included into the Fourth Autonomous Region List of Intangible Cultural Heritage, after the approval of People's Government of Guangxi Zhuang Autonomous Region.

厉打击。进入20世纪80年代后，上林壮族师公戏得到一定的重视。由于机制的改变和青年大批外出打工，上林壮族师公戏的演员队伍日益减少，壮族师公戏的编剧、导演人员更为紧缺，以上诸多因素使得上林壮族师公戏处于濒危状况，亟须加以扶持培养。近年来，上林县政府采取了各种积极的措施，使壮族师公戏得到了有效的保护。2008年，上林县在明亮镇开展上林壮族师公戏展演比赛，奖励了一批师公戏戏班和演员，同时发动和鼓励社会对上林壮族师公戏的重视和关注，举办各种民间宣传活动，组织上林壮族师公戏戏班到县城和周边县乡进行交流演出，以扩大上林壮族师公戏的影响力。2012年，上林壮族师公戏经广西壮族自治区人民政府同意，列入第四批自治区级非物质文化遗产名录。

新编师公戏
Newly-adapted Shigong Opera

古潭邕剧

Gutan Yongju Opera

项目名称：古潭邕剧

别称：无

分布范围：隆安县古潭乡

入选名录：2016年第六批自治区级非物质文化遗产名录
　　　　　2015年第六批市级非物质文化遗产名录

保护单位：隆安县文化馆

代表性传承人：毕加良

Element name：Gutan Yongju Opera

Alternative name：None

Geographical location and range：Gutan Town of Long'an County

Element inscribed list：In 2016 on the Sixth Autonomous Region List of Intangible Cultural Heritage
In 2015 on the Sixth Municipal List of Intangible Cultural Heritage

Competent body involved in safeguarding：Long'an County Cultural Centre

Representative inheritor：Bi Jialiang

正在排练中的古潭邕剧传承人　摄影 李晶
The Inheritors of Gutan Yongju Opera in Rehearsal　Photo by Li Jing

古潭邕剧的道具与服装展示　摄影 李晶
The Props and Costumes of Gutan Yongju Opera　Photo by Li Jing

Gutan Yongju Opera, a branch of Yongju Opera in Guangxi, widely spread in Gutan Township, Long'an County. It had its heyday with the establishment of Yongju Opera Troupe and has been handed down to these days.

During the years of Tongzhi of the Qing Dynasty, Lu Feihong, a famous opera artist of Xialu troupe, taught and transmitted Yongju Opera to many people. And then he set up another troupe named "Saiqunying", which had more than 20 actors. Gutan Yongju Opera Troupe had a long run over various places including Long'an County, Pingguo, Daxin, Longzhou, Baise, Nanning, Qinzhou, Wuming, Fuhuan, Tuolu and even Vietnam. The opera troupes were welcomed and praised by audiences who live around the Zuojiang River and Youjiang River. In 1936, By improving the music, vocal tune and acting skills of Yongju Opera, Saiqunying was further enhanced by Chen Zhihua, the favorite pupil of Lu Feihong, and also the third generation of Zhangban Master (the drummer and the conductor of Yongju Opera band who keeps time).

Gutan Yongju Opera is a member of Pihuang tune system, and its aria and repertoire are similar to Guiju Opera. It is boasting of exquisite and mellow artistic skills, elegant stage manners, and quick-witted stage lines by assimilating art elements from Yueju Opera. It is mainly sung in official language of Southwest Guangxi with some Cantonese, and scattered common sayings, proverbs and allegorical sayings, all of which are based on the diatonic scale. The spoken parts with diverse forms are smooth and lively. When the opera is characterized by singing and acting, actors will pay more

古潭邕剧是广西邕剧的主流分支，流传于隆安县古潭乡。它伴随着古潭邕剧戏班的成立而盛极一时，并传承至今。

清同治年间，当时的“下路班”邕剧名艺人陆飞红到古潭街传艺授徒，组织邕剧戏班“赛群英”，戏班共拥有20多名演员。古潭邕剧戏班连续在各地演出，曾到隆安县城、平果、大新、龙州、百色、南宁、钦州、武鸣、扶绥、驮芦等地，并跨国境到越南去演出。所到之处，受到各地观众的赞赏与好评，红遍左右江沿岸地区。1936年，陆飞红的得意门生、邕剧掌板师傅三代传人、陈志华将“赛群英”发扬光大，他对邕剧的声乐、腔口、演技进行改进，使之精益求精，得到进一步的完善和发展。

古潭邕剧属于皮黄声腔系统，其唱腔和剧目与桂剧相近，也吸收了一些粤剧的艺术因素，具有精美圆熟的艺术技巧、优美典雅的舞台风格，以及机巧的戏剧语言。其唱腔以七声音阶作为调式的基础，语言以桂西南官话为主，兼有白话、民间俗语、谚语及歇后语等。邕剧的念白节奏明快、形式多样。其文戏注重表现人物的内心活动，以粗放的大动作结合面部表情加以夸张的表现；武打属南派，表演夸张、泼辣，以翻、腾、跳、铲、滚、挂、绞、甩等技艺来表现人物的激越感情，也有“变脸”“耍獠牙”“砸烂台”等特技。邕剧的舞美十分简朴，有“一桌两椅两台戏”的说法。古潭邕剧戏班的古装正本剧目主要有《金兰结义》《三气周瑜》《三战吕布》《穆桂英大战洪州》等。

古潭邕剧从第一代传承人陆飞红的传艺，到如今第七代传承人马双颖的接班，经七代历150年的坚韧传承。古潭邕剧曾因日寇入侵与“文革”影响，濒于灭绝，因此研究、抢救、传承、保护古潭邕剧的任务非常紧迫。鉴于此，隆安县政府加大了保护古潭邕剧的力度，扶持古潭邕剧戏班开展演出活动，并与教育部门协商，由第五代传承人闭加良到小学挑选学生演员，组建了少年邕剧班，邕剧出现了发展的新势头。2015年，古潭邕剧列入南宁市第六批非物质文化遗产名录。

attention to expression of the inner activities of the characters, usually they use exaggerated facial expression and movements to achieve the goal. As for acrobatic fighting scenes, the opera is famous for its bold and exciting skills that stem from southern martial art, such as somersault, prance, jump, kick, rolling, hanging, twisting, swinging, mask-changing, teeth-playing and smashing against tables. So simple and unembellished is the stage art that the opera is called "an art acts all kinds of joys and sorrows by two chairs and a table". The representative costume story plays includes *Sworn Sisters, Three Victories Against Zhou Yu, Three Heroes* and *Mu Guiying Saves Hongzhou*.

The opera has been passed down for 150 years from the first inheritor Lu Feihong to the seventh inheritor of Ma Shuangying, and it once suffered during the war of resistance against Japan and ten years of the Cultural Revolution. In this case, it is very urgent for us to study, rescue, inherit and protect Yongju Opera. The government of Long'an County has intensified efforts to protect the opera in the way of supporting the Gutan Yongju Opera Troupe to carry out performances. The government with local education departments helped the fifth inheritor of the opera Bi Jialiang to select pupils prepared for young troupe of Yongju Opera. All the efforts are paid off, and the development of Yongju Opera has shown a new momentum. In 2015, Gutan Yongju Opera was inscribed on the Sixth Nanning's Municipal List of Intangible Cultural Heritage.

传承人为小学员化装　摄影 李晶
The Inheritor Makes up for a Little Apprentice
Photo by Li Jing

丝弦戏

Sixian Opera

项目名称：丝弦戏

别称：宾州戏、司弦戏、思贤戏

分布范围：武鸣区、宾阳县、上林县、隆安县、马山县等

入选名录：2008年第二批自治区级非物质文化遗产名录
2007年第一批市级非物质文化遗产名录

保护单位：宾阳县文化馆

代表性传承人：陈光绍（已故）、熊兴亮

Element name：Sixian Opera

Alternative name：Binzhou Opera, Sixian Opera

Geographical location and range：Wuming District, Binyang County, Shanglin County, Long'an County, Mashan County and others

Element inscribed list：In 2008 on the Second Autonomous Region List of Intangible Cultural Heritage
In 2007 on the First Municipal List of Intangible Cultural Heritage

Competent body involved in safeguarding：Binyang County Cultural Centre

Representative inheritors：Chen Guangshao (Late), Xiong Xingliang

宾阳丝弦戏表演
Performance of Binyang Sixian Opera

丝弦戏又称“宾州戏”“司弦戏”“思贤戏”，是广西八大剧种之一，在桂中地区占有重要地位，是优秀的民间地方戏曲艺术。丝弦戏以宾阳县芦圩镇的新宾、新桥、邹圩为中心，广泛流传于武鸣区、上林县、隆安县、马山县等地区，颇受群众喜爱。

丝弦戏已有200多年的历史。据说，清乾隆年间，湖南一位姓白的师傅将丝弦戏传入宾阳，其落脚点起初在新桥尚武街，后来又移到新宾南街。第一个班主叫廖盛龄，后来新桥、太守、芦圩、新宾、邹圩等乡都有戏班。丝弦戏从传入到发展，曾出现一个鼎盛时期，直到20世纪60年代老艺人先后去世而冷落下来。

丝弦戏的行当、表演程式、唱腔板式、伴奏曲牌、管弦乐器等戏曲的主要成分，均比较完善齐全。丝弦戏的行当有生、旦、净、丑。生行有老生、文生、武生，旦行有老旦、正旦、花旦、摇旦、武旦，丑行有小丑、文丑，净行有大花脸、二花脸等。其中老生、老旦用本嗓，花脸用霸嗓，生、旦用小嗓演唱。因后期受广戏的影响，武打曾用过“五色真军器”（真刀真枪），属于南派武打。20世纪50年代之

Sixian Opera, also known as Binzhou Opera and Sixian Opera, is one of the major eight operas of Guangxi. It is of great significance in central Guangxi as it is a fine folk art much loved by people. Originating from Xinbin, Xinqiao and Zouxu in Luxu Town, Binyang County, it then widely spreads in Wuming District, Shanglin, Long'an, Mashan Counties and other areas.

Sixian Opera has a history for more than 200 years. It is said that the opera was brought to Binyang by an artist whose family name was Bai in the reign of Emperor Qianlong of the Qing Dynasty. It was firstly performed in Shangwu street of Xinqiao and then in Nan street of Xinbin. The head man of the first troupe of Sixian opera was Liao Shenglin, and similar troupes were set up in Xinqiao, Taishou, Luxu, Xinbin and Zouxu one by one. It once flourished during the whole history, but started its declination since many sophisticated artists passed away one after another in the 1960s.

The opera is fully equipped with unique types of roles, performing procedures, aria, accompanying tunes and orchestral instruments. The classification of roles includes male, female, face-painted, and clown roles. To be specifically, male roles are divided into elderly roles, Wen roles and Wu roles. Female roles are subdivided into elderly ones, demure ones, lively ones, Yao roles and Wu roles. The clown roles include xiaochou and wenchou roles. The face-painted roles consist of Dahualian roles and Erhualian roles. Among them, elderly male and female roles will perform by using their own voices, while other male and female roles sing in falsetto voice and face-painted roles sing in a Ba voice (a resonant and rugged voice). The martial plays, a branch of southern martial art, were once influenced by Guangxi Opera and used real weapons as props on the stage. All roles including female roles were all performed by male actors with simple makeup and costume before the 1950s. As for the music of the opera, it contains actors' aria, accompanying tunes and the sound of gongs and drums. Its aria mainly falls into two categories, that which we call southern aria and which we call northern aria. Another two named Chui and Za that belong to the clapper opera form of Pihuang system are also permitted to sing. The northern and southern arias are both sung in official language of Guiliu with reiterative lines. Actors lay more stress on singing words itself and sing arias according to it. It is inhabited to sing both two arias in the same repertoire or the same passage, but tunes both used in the north and the south could be performed in a play. Even for the same play, the opera could be performed different with diversified details. It is because all the operas are taught in oral way with no written records of arias and scores. There are about more than 200 traditional repertoires of Sixian opera, most of which are the same as those of Yongju Opera and Gui opera. The classic ones are *Taming of the Princess, Beat Drums and Scold Cao, Dingjunshan Mountain, Lion Pavilion, Family Fun, Yellow Crane Tower* and *Fengyi Pavilion.* The introductions drew in the 1960s are *The Red Lantern* and *Shajia Bang*. And there are a few adapted ones from some modern operas, such as *Two Bottles of Pesticide*.

Sixian opera now faces a predicament of few inheritors. To settle the problem, the authorities of Binyang County attach great importance to the protection work. They take the opera as a special culture project to improve, carry out in-depth census work, excavate and sort out the opera repertoires, and provide support to a number of amateur troupes of Sixian opera. Meanwhile, the opera was also brought to schools which offered platforms for it, so as to enhance its influence. In 2008, Sixian opera was included in the Second Autonomous Region List of Intangible Cultural Heritage, after the approval of the People's Government of Guangxi Zhuang Autonomous Region.

前，丝弦戏全部为男演员，旦角也是男扮女装，服饰化装简约朴素。宾阳丝弦戏的音乐，含唱腔、伴奏曲牌、锣鼓点三部分。唱腔以南、北路为主，兼有吹腔、杂腔小调，属皮黄系统板腔体结构。南、北路唱腔的句式为上下句复唱形式，用桂柳官话演唱，重语言本色、问字要腔。传统唱腔在使用上严格区分南、北两种板路；在同一剧目里最忌南、北路唱腔混用，同一唱段内也忌两路板式混用，故一出戏的唱腔仅用一路板式和南北路通用的小调杂曲。丝弦戏唱腔无曲谱文字流传，大都是由戏师口头传授，故各板路的板式又常因不同的传人而小有变异。丝弦戏有200多个传统剧目，大部分剧目与邕剧、桂剧相同，常演的有《打金枝》《打鼓骂曹》《定军山》《狮子楼》《全家福》《黄鹤楼》《凤仪亭》等。20世纪60年代后，曾移植了《红灯记》《沙家浜》，改编了现代戏《两瓶农药》等剧目。

目前，丝弦戏面临着传承人断层的情况，近年来，宾阳县委、县政府高度重视保护工作，把丝弦戏作为本县特色文化项目来保护，深入开展普查工作，组织力量挖掘整理丝弦戏传统剧目，重点扶持一批业余丝弦戏剧团；同时还开展“戏曲进校园”等活动，积极为丝弦戏搭建平台，不断扩大其影响力。2008年，丝弦戏经广西壮族自治区人民政府同意，列入第二批自治区级非物质文化遗产名录。

宾阳丝弦戏戏装
Costumes of Binyang Sixian Opera

马山丝弦戏

Mashan Sixian Opera

项目名称：马山丝弦戏

别称：司弦戏、思贤戏

分布范围：南宁市武鸣区、马山县、上林县、宾阳县，来宾市忻城县，河池市都安县等

入选名录：2016年第六批自治区级非物质文化遗产名录
　　　　　2015年第六批市级非物质文化遗产名录

保护单位：马山县文化馆

代表性传承人：廖玉兰

Element name：Mashan Sixian Opera

Alternative name：Sixian Opera

Geographical location and range：Wuming District, Mashan County, Shanglin County, Binyang County of Nanning City; Xincheng County of Laibin City, Du'an County of Hechi City and others

Element inscribed list：In 2016 on the Sixth Autonomons Region List of Intangible Cultural Heritage
In 2015 on the Sixth Municipal List of Intangible Cultural Heritage

Competent body involved in safeguarding：Mashan County Cultural Centre

Representative inheritors：Liao Yulan

重台别
Farewell

Mashan Sixian Opera, also known as Sixian opera, is a folk branch of Pihuang opera popular in Binyang, Shanglin, Laibin, Xincheng, Wuming, Du'an and Mashan regions. According to historical materials, The opera was brought to Mashan for more than 200 years by a Hunanese Wen Fucai in the late Qing Dynasty.

The opera is a folk art mainly composed of singing and supplemented by speaking, so that it can both display legends with characters and plots and sing concise episode. It has a similar performing form to Yongju Opera and each there are 6 opera singers who respectively act roles including male, female, and face-painted and clown roles. The music of the opera consists of three parts: aria, accompanying tunes, gongs and drums. Both southern and northern arias are regarded as the authentic ones, another two arias named Chui and Za that belong to the clapper opera form of Pihuang system are also permitted to sing. Even for the same play, the opera could be performed different with diversified details. It is because all the operas are taught in oral way with no written records of arias and scores. The northern and southern arias are both sung in official language of Guiliu with reiterative lines. Actors lay

马山丝弦戏属皮黄戏种，又称“司弦戏”“思贤戏”，是流行于马山、上林、宾阳、来宾、忻城、武鸣和都安等地一带的民间戏剧。据史料记载，丝弦戏清末由湖南人文福彩传入马山，迄今已有200多年的历史。

丝弦戏是一种民间说唱表演艺术，以唱为主，以说为辅，说唱穿插交替，容量较大，可以演唱有人物、有情节的大型故事，也可以演唱短小精悍的段子。演唱者一般为6人，分别扮演生、旦、净、丑等不同角色。表演形式与邕剧大同小异，音乐含唱腔、伴奏曲牌、锣鼓点三部分。唱腔以南、北路为主，兼有吹腔、杂腔小调，属皮黄系统板腔体。丝弦戏的唱腔无曲谱文字流传，大都是由戏师口头传授，故其各板路的板式又常因不同的传戏人而小有变异。南北路唱腔的句式为上下句复唱形式，用桂柳官话演唱，重语言本色，问字要腔。马山丝弦戏的音乐体现了我国古代音乐的一些曲牌，具有悠久的历史价值。其多样化的表演形式和个性化的演唱风格，使它具有独特的艺术价值。

丝弦戏分为两个流派，一是宾州流派，二是武鸣流派，而马山丝弦戏两派兼之，在表演、唱腔、道白方面有相同之处，也有不相同之处。历史上的班社有白山班、石塘班、定罗班、周鹿班、乔利班、古零戏、杨六班等。代表剧目有《快活林》《十五贯》《大战长坂坡》《包公斩世美》《梁山伯与祝英台》《打金枝》《拾玉镯》《姚刚南下》《四九问路》《武松打店》《秦香莲》《平贵回窑》《天女散花》《梅开二度》《鸿口岸》《梨花斩子》《重台别》等。

马山丝弦戏虽然盛极一时，但到1979年却只有白山业余剧团尚能演出。在县文化部门的鼓励下，他们恢复排演。由于停演时间太久，原来的骨干已经离世，很多的剧目、司鼓、曲牌已随之消失，如今所演的剧目和音乐曲调已经不太完整，失去了传统的味道。1982年，经过文化工作者的挖掘整理，曾一度失传的马山丝弦戏再次呈现在人们面前，县文化部门曾组织创作和排练两出独幕丝弦戏《生财之道》《一家人》。2008年，马山县通过开展非物质文化遗产普查，将马山丝弦戏的相关资料编印成册，2012年在白山镇建立了一个丝弦戏传承基地，由代表性传承人廖玉兰负责培训丝弦戏人才，已培养了20余名学员。马山丝弦戏有望重新焕发青春，重展昔日的璀璨风采。

more stress on singing words itself and sing arias according to it. The opera is of great historical and artistic value, not only for its music that reflects the ancient tunes, but also for its diversified forms and distinctive singing style.

Sixian opera mainly falls into two schools: one is Binzhou School, and the other is Wuming School. The opera in Mashan has both two, thus similarities and differences exist in Mashan's opera in the ways of performing, aria and Daobai (transitional words added by the actors according to the content of the around the libretto). The notable troupes in history included Baishan, Shitang, Dingluo, Zhoulu, Qiaoli, Guling and Yangliu. And representative repertoires are *The Delightful Forest, The Fifteen Strings of Coppers, The War on the Changbanpo, Baogong Slash Shimei, Liang Shanbo and Zhu Yingtai, Taming of the Princess, Picking Up a Jade Bracelet, Yaogang Goes South, Sijiu Ask the Way, Passing the Inn, Qin Xianglian, Pinggui Returns Home, The Heavenly Maids Scatter Blossoms, Plums Blossom Twice, Hongkou Bank, Lihua Beheads Her Son* and *The Separation on the Zhongtai.*

Although Mashan Sixian Opera was prosperous for years, no troupe was able to perform except Baishan Amateur Opera Troupe in 1979. Baishan resumed their rehearsal under the support of the Cultural Department of the Mashan County. However, the opera, with incomplete repertoires and music, has lost its traditional flavor, due to the long suspension of performance and the death of backbone actors. In 1982, the Sixian Opera, once even lost, was once again presented to people after efforts of digging and sorting by cultural workers. For example, the Cultural Department had organized to rehearsal two one-act operas, *The Way to Make Money* and *The Family*. In 2008, Mashan County compiled and printed the relevant materials of the Opera after conducting a general survey of intangible cultural heritage. In 2012, an inheritance base for Sixian Opera was established in Baishan Town, it is a place where representative inheriter Liao Yulan are responsible for training drama talents and more than 20 trainees had been trained. In such case, Mashan Sixian Opera is expected to rejuvenate its vigor and come back into fashion.

校椅临江壮歌剧

Xiaoyi Linjiang Opera of Zhuang Ethnic Group

项目名称：校椅临江壮歌剧

别称：临江戏

分布范围：横州市校椅镇及周边地区

入选名录：2020年第八批自治区级非物质文化遗产名录

2009年第二批市级非物质文化遗产名录

保护单位：横县文化馆

代表性传承人：李建伟（已故）

Element name：Xiaoyi Linjiang Opera of Zhuang Ethnic Group

Alternative name：Liangjiang Opera

Geographical location and range：Xiaoyi Town of Hengzhou City and the surrounding areas

Element inscribed list：In 2020 on the Eighth Autonomons Region List of Intangible Cultural Heritage

In 2009 on the Second Municipal List of Intangible Cultural Heritage

Competent body involved in safeguarding：Hengxian Cultural Centre

Representative inheritor：Li Jianwei (Late)

校椅临江壮歌剧演出
Performance of Xiaoyi Linjiang Opera of Zhuang Ethnic Group

校椅镇临江壮歌剧别称临江戏，是流行于横州市校椅镇及其周边地区的一个壮族曲艺品种。

作为临江壮歌剧团所在地区，校椅镇临江村及其周边广大区域是横州市壮族聚居的地区，这里壮族文化源远流长，盛行粤剧表演，成为临江壮歌剧得以孕育的土壤。临江壮歌剧团前身是临江粤剧团，以演古装戏为主。随着社会的发展，古装粤剧的演出不适合时代发展的要求，演出市场日趋冷落和沉寂。在这种情形下，该剧团年轻的艺人李建伟在出街入市（赶圩）收集民族民间传说、民间故事进行创编的同时，对粤剧团进行了改革，建立了壮歌剧团，在原来粤剧唱腔的基础上，对外来文化兼收并蓄，并不断丰富壮歌剧的音乐唱腔，经过不断的发展与完善，逐渐形成了特色鲜明的校椅临江壮歌剧并流传至今。

每逢节庆日或喜事，校椅镇临江村及其周边广大区域的壮民都以本地区特有的唱壮族山歌的形式来表达他们心中

Xiaoyi Linjiang Opera of Zhuang Ethnic Group, also called Linjiang Opera, is popular in Xiaoyi Town of Hengzhou City and neighboring regions.

The Troupe of Linjiang Opera was established in Linjiang village of Xiaoyi town where Zhuang people live. Linjiang Opera was spawned in the village, as Yueju Opera prevailed here and Zhuang culture has a long history. The troupe, formerly Linjiang Troupe of Yueju Opera, mainly plays costume operas. It seems that costume Yueju Opera was irreconcilable with modern life and hobbled with time goes by. In these circumstances, an young actor of the troupe Li Jianwei collected and rearranged folk tales on fairs, he also transformed the Yueju Opera troupe into a troupe singing opera of Zhuang. Linjiang Opera of Zhuang Ethnic Group, on the basis of aria of Yueju Opera, developed its distinctive features by assimilating extern culture and improving the music tunes.

Zhuang people live around the Linjiang Village like to sing folk songs to convey their inner joy, whenever there is a festival or happy event. What the opera troupe performs all come from the realities of Zhuang-inhabited villages, such as ethics, human nature and love, legal education, endowment insurance, health care, tax publicity and anti-corruption. The opera that sings in local Zhuang language is approachable, humorous, thought-provoking and easy to understand. Its performance forms include solo singing, duet singing and chorus, all of which sound melodious. Accompanying instruments are mainly gongs, drums, erhu, wooden fish and so on. Performing costumes are designed for the plot and adapt to reality. Most of the repertoires are compiled and arranged by directors of the troupe. Representative repertoires include *"Hard to Measure the Length of Yangtze River", "Dad-snatching", "Cold Plums Blossom among Spring Flowers", "Drunken and Senseless".*

Linjiang Opera was adapted by folk legends and stories circulating Zhuang-inhabited areas. It calls for less condition for time and space and flexible enough to play as the need of the audience, since its content stem from life and adapted by their own directors. It is much loved by people for its countryside flavor, local language, simple words, and humorous expression.

Linjiang Opera plays an important role in performing arts of Zhuang of Hengzhou City. In order to improve the development and inheritance of the opera, Hengxian Cultural Centre has established an inheritance base and provided support for amateur troupe that hold more performances. Besides, Linjiang Opera has been integrated into school education as a "local textbook", such campus popularization is expected to prepare more talents for the impartment of the opera.

的喜悦。校椅临江壮歌剧团创作及演出的内容多来源于壮族乡村的生活现实，主要内容涵盖伦理道德、人性爱情、法制教育、养老保险、保健防疫、税收宣传、反腐倡廉等。临江壮歌剧运用本地的壮语演唱，语言通俗易懂、亲切自然、诙谐幽默而能发人深省。其表演形式有一人独唱、二人对唱、众人合唱，唱腔悠扬。伴奏乐器主要有锣、鼓、二胡、木鱼等。演出服饰贴近剧情，贴近生活，贴近现实。临江壮歌剧曲目大多由校椅镇临江壮歌剧团的编导自行创编，代表剧目有《金尺难量长江水》《争父记》《寒梅斗春花》《酒醉不知天》等。

临江壮歌剧创作源自当地及周边壮族地区广为流传的民间传说、民间故事，它对演出的时间、空间要求不高，演出的机动性、灵活性大，可随时随地根据观众的需求开演，曲目内容源自生活，且为自创自编，服饰着装群众化，适合广大农村群众的口味，使用本地壮语方言演唱，语言通俗易懂，表达流畅诙谐，深受群众喜爱。

在横州市及其周边的壮族表演艺术中，校椅临江壮歌剧占有着重要的地位。为做好校椅临江壮歌剧的发展传承工作，横县文化馆在校椅镇建立了临江壮歌剧传承基地，并把临江壮歌剧作为“乡土教材”融入学校教育，利用校园进行普及，为校椅临江壮歌剧储备人才，同时，积极引导和扶持民间剧团，为演出提供平台。

打击乐伴奏
Percussion Accompaniment

横县壮族采茶戏

Hengxian Opera of Tea Collecting of Zhuang Ethnic Group

项目名称：横县壮族采茶戏

别称：茶歌、采茶歌、唱采茶

分布范围：横州市六景镇、峦城镇、南乡镇、百合镇等

入选名录：2010年第三批自治区级非物质文化遗产名录
2010年第三批市级非物质文化遗产名录

保护单位：横县文化馆

代表性传承人：甘美芬

Element name: Hengxian Opera of Tea Collecting of Zhuang Ethnic Group

Alternative name: Tea Song, Tea Collecting Song, Song of Picking

Geographical location and range: Liujing Town, Luancheng Town, Nanxiang Town, Baihe Town and others of Hengzhou City

Element inscribed list: In 2010 on the Third Autonomous Region List of Intangible Cultural Heritage
In 2010 on the Third Municipal List of Intangible Cultural Heritage

Competent body involved in safeguarding: Hengxian Cultural Centre

Representative inheritor: Gan Meifen

采茶戏表演
Opera of Tea Collecting Performance

Hengxian Opera of Tea Collecting of Zhuang Ethnic Group, also named Tea Song, Tea Collecting Song or Song of Picking, is a unique traditional drama developed from Zhuma singing. It has more than 10 forms of performances, such as Kaitai Tea (tribute tea), Nai Tea, Shisong Tea, Laozheng Tea and Yanghong Tea. The content of the performances, with countryside flavor, focuses on "Tea-Picking in December". The opera is a branch of tea-picking Opera of the Zhuang Ethnic Group in south Guangxi. It is popular in Liujing,

横县壮族采茶戏亦称"茶歌""采茶歌""唱采茶"，是由唱竹马发展为载歌载舞的一种独特的传统戏剧，有开台茶（恭茶）、乃茶、十送茶、老正茶、洋红茶等10多种表演形式，演唱的内容以"十二月采茶"为主，乡土气息浓厚。横县壮族采茶戏属桂南壮族采茶戏的一种，广泛流传于广西横州市的六景、峦城、南乡、百合以及相邻的宾阳、邕宁、灵山、钦州等广大地区。

明末清初，横县壮族采茶戏从江西赣南经粤北传入玉林市博白县，并很快传入横州市，距今约有300多年的历史。在清代，它逐渐形成自身独特的风格，到了民国期间，逐渐发展成熟。20世纪50年代中期至60年代初，横县壮族采茶戏已基本完成从地方小戏向舞台戏剧的过渡，那时，每个村都有采茶演出队，这里还进行过壮族采茶戏调演。但是1966—1976年间，壮族采茶戏被当作“四旧”中的“旧文化”被禁锢，采茶队遭到重创，壮族采茶戏停演。1978年后，虽然壮族采茶戏迎来了新的发展契机，但由于人才断层，很多采茶戏表演的中坚力量都无法再登台，采茶戏难以重现当年的辉煌。

横县壮族采茶戏的角色分为小生、小旦、小丑，也叫“三小戏”或“三角班”。其唱腔语言以壮话为主，也夹杂使用平话、客家话等，念白多为韵白，具有浓厚的地方特色。采茶曲牌，一是茶腔，即原套采茶曲调；二是茶插，即以“南昌小曲”“四季莲花”为基础，吸取各地民间小曲而成。它以锣、鼓、钹、木鱼等击乐和唢呐、笛子、二胡等器乐为伴奏，道具有彩带、钱鞭、花扇和手绢。表演载歌载舞，通常由一人扮作茶公，一人扮作茶婆，在歌舞中穿插一些情节。表演顺序大同小异，一般开端第一段为“开台茶”，表示恭贺戏主和观众，接唱“十二月采茶”，表现一年中开荒、点茶（即播种茶）、摘茶、炒茶、卖茶等劳动过程。通过这个过程，反映出劳动人民劳动的快乐和丰收的喜悦。横县壮族采茶戏原有传统剧目100多个，大部分已经失传，现存的传统剧目有《三姐下凡》《隔河看亲》《借亲配》《六个八》《九龙山摘茶》《上广东》《阿三打铁》《五岭之春》《花灯仙子》《吹鼓手招亲》等，这些剧目多为喜剧或闹剧，反映了广大劳动群众的日常生活，颇具地方特色和生活气息。

Luancheng, Nanxiang, Baihe and neighboring areas such as Binyang, Yongning, Lingshan and Qinzhou.

The opera was introduced from Gannan city of Jiangxi in the late Ming and early Qing Dynasties, firstly to Bobai County of Yulin City, and then soon to Hengzhou City 300 years ago. It formed its unique characteristics in the Qing Dynasty and developed further during the Republic of China. From the mid-1950s to the early 1960s, the opera has completely become a mature stage art, not a local drama any more. Every village then own opera troupes, and the operas were also performed in the city. However, from 1966 to 1976, the opera of the Zhuang Ethnic Group was regarded as the “old culture” of the“sijiu”(i. e. old ideas, old culture, old customs, and old habits, used esp. during the “Cultural Revolution”), and the opera troupes were so damaged that the opera was suspended at that time. After 1978, although the opera ushered in a new epoch for development, it is still difficult to resume the past glories due to the talent gap caused by the reduction of backbone actors.

The types of roles of the opera are divided into male, female and face-painted young-roles, which are together called “three-young team” or “triangle team”. It is mainly sung in Zhuang Language, and rarely in Pinghua Language or Kejia language. Most of the spoken parts of the opera rhyme lines with local flavor. There are two types of tunes for tea-collecting opera. One is Tea Tune (the original tune when people pick up tea), and the other is a mixed one based on folk tunes including “Nanchang tune” and “Tune of Four Seasons Lotus”. A few instruments are used to accompany the opera, such as gongs, drums, cymbals, wooden fishes, suona horns, flutes and erhu. The stage property includes ribbons, straps, drawn fans, and handkerchiefs. The opera is often performed by one person acting a tea man and another one acting a tea woman and interspersed with singing and dancing. The order of performances is very similar. The first part is usually “Kaitai Tea” that sends congratulations to the audience. And next part is “Tea Picking throughout Four Seasons”, which animates the scene of ploughing, wowing, picking, stir frying and selling tea and reflects the joy of the harvest. There are more than 100 traditional plays of the opera, most of which have been lost. The plays existing nowadays include *Sanjie Descend to The Earth*, *Matchmaking across the River*, *A Romantic Borrowing*, *Six Eight*, *Picking Tea at Jiulongshan Mountain*, *Journey to Guangdong*, *Blacksmith Ah San*, *Spring of Five Ridges*, *Festive Lantern Fairy* and *Trumpeter Looking for His Wife*. These plays are mostly comedy featured by local flavor, reflecting the daily life of the broad masses of working people.

Although the opera is familiar to folk people, it still faces many problems in its development nowadays, such as the gap and loss of talents in tea-picking opera, the loss of traditional plays, and the declining number of young audiences. However, it is an opera with rich flavor and social value has gradually been recognized by the society. Relevant departments of Hengzhou City have taken measures to protect the traditional ethnic culture. The authorities of the city have taken all-out efforts to support more than 130 performing teams active on the rural stage, offer them regular counseling and organize professionals to sort out *The Collection of Traditional Tea-Collecting Operas of The Zhuang Ethnic Group in Hengxian County*. Besides, they also pay attention to personnel training, aegis to relevant troupes and establishment of inheritance bases.

横县采茶戏在民间虽然有一定的群众基础，但在当代的发展中依然面临诸多问题，如采茶戏表演人才的断层和流失、传统剧目失传、青年观众逐年减少等等。不过，横县壮族采茶戏的社会价值已逐渐被社会认可，它是独树一帜、特色浓厚的地方剧种，因此，横州市有关部门已经采取措施对横县壮族采茶戏这一重要的民族传统文化进行保护。横州市党委、政府对活跃在乡村舞台上的130多个民间采茶戏演出团队给予大力支持，对他们进行定期辅导，还组织专业人员整理了《横县壮族采茶戏传统曲牌集》；同时，注重人才培养，扶持横州市壮族采茶剧团，建立采茶戏教育传承基地，积极培训演员、演奏员等各专业人才。

采茶戏

Opera of Tea Collecting

项目名称：采茶戏

别称：无

分布范围：邕宁区那楼镇、中和镇、新江镇、百济镇等

入选名录：2010年第三批自治区级非物质文化遗产名录

　　　　　2010年第三批市级非物质文化遗产名录

保护单位：邕宁区文化馆

代表性传承人：滕思队

Element name: Opera of Tea Collecting

Alternative name: None

Geographical location and range: Nalou Town, Zhonghe Town, Xinjiang Town, Baiji Town and others of Yongning District

Element inscribed list: In 2010 on the Third Autonomous Region List of Intangible Cultural Heritage

In 2010 on the Third Municipal List of Intangible Cultural Heritage

Competent body involved in safeguarding: Yongning District Cultural Centre

Representative inheritor: Teng Sidui

采茶戏表演

Performance of Opera of Tea Collecting

那楼镇壮族采茶戏

Opera of Tea Collecting of Zhuang Ethnic Group in Nalou Town

Opera of Tea Collecting is a traditional folk art spread among Nalou, Zhonghe, Xinjiang and Baiji Townships of Yongning District. It is a product of cultural collision throughout productive practice life of local Zhuang and Han peoples. It is beloved by the people for its rich glamour of south Guangxi and flexible performing style.

It is said that Namengpo (in Naliang village of Nalou town), still an uncultivated land in the early Qing Dynasty, then attracted nationalities to migrate here because of its fertile land and warm climate. The Ning family, originally Han Ethnic Group, moved here from Guangdong thousands of miles away; the Teng family, originally Zhuang Ethnic Group from Wutang Town hundreds miles away. The two nationalities live and work here in harmony. Namengpo began to thrive due to their hard work from dawn to dusk. And the tea-collecting song was created by two cultures colliding and blending with each other. When people sing the tea-picking song, they rise to dance and, this is how tea-picking dance of unique charm comes into being. Both of the song and the dance are much loved by the people for their easy-approaching features and graceful simplicity. Yongning's Opera of Tea Collecting of Zhuang Ethnic Group was spawned by the constant blending of the songs and dances. However, the development of the opera can be concluded as twists and turns. The opera once prevailed in all corners of Yongning County after 1949. It was banned in the mid-1960s, however, only those people who love it still secretly perform on festivals.

采茶戏是流传于南宁市邕宁区那楼、中和、新江、百济等乡镇的一种民间传统剧种。该剧种是当地壮、汉群众在长期的生产生活中文化相互碰撞交融的产物，是独特的民间戏剧表演形式，具有浓厚的桂南壮族气息，其表演形式活泼，深受群众喜爱。

清朝初叶，当时尚属未垦之地的那楼镇那良村那蒙坡，以其土地肥沃、气候温润吸引一些民族迁徙于此。其中，宁姓者原为汉族，从千里之外的广东迁入；滕姓者为壮族，从百里之外的兴宁区五塘镇迁入。两民族在此劳作生活，和睦相处。他们日出而作，日落而息，造就了那良村那蒙坡。两个民族，两种文化，互相碰撞交融，产生了独特的民间采茶歌。当人们唱起采茶歌时，即兴起舞，衍生了具有独特韵味的采茶舞，采茶歌歌词通俗易懂，采茶舞动作简朴优美，深受群众喜爱，经过发展演变，歌舞相互配合，便形成了今天的邕宁壮族采茶戏。但是，采茶戏的发展可谓一波三折。1949年之后采茶戏曾一度盛行，邕宁区各乡镇、各村坡，大街小巷都有采茶戏上演。20世纪60年代中期，采茶戏遭到禁止，但每逢欢庆节日，一些热爱采茶戏的群众仍偷偷演出。

20世纪80年代初，采茶戏又逐渐复兴，但已不复当年之盛，年轻人纷纷外出打工，演出人员不断流失，采茶戏只有在春节期间偶尔上演。

采茶戏的角色分小生、小旦、小丑，也叫“三小戏”或“三角班”。其唱腔语言主要以桂柳话、南宁白话和当地壮语为主，念白多为韵白，近年来，采茶戏演唱中还插入了少量的普通话，使其充满现代气息。采茶戏的曲牌有卖茶腔、红花腔、男音、四平腔、仙腔、忧腔、哭腔等50多种，乃兼收并蓄各地民间小曲而成。采茶戏使用的乐器以打击乐为主，有板锣、战鼓、苏锣、大钹、小钹、木鱼等10余种，同时还兼配吹奏乐器，如唢呐、箫、笛等。受到北方音乐元素的影响，采茶戏中有些表演还加入了二胡、京胡等乐器，演出更加丰富多彩。采茶戏的道具则相对简单，只有彩带、钱鞭、花扇和手绢等，体现了民间艺术的朴素和原始意识。茶戏演出服装一般以古装官服、西湖装、宫装为主，也有穿壮族姑娘装“上阵”的，更似年轻美丽的壮家姑娘上山采摘茶叶。采茶戏的剧目多为传统剧目，且多为喜剧、闹剧，有《采茶》《卖茶》《父教子成双》《北海娶妻》《浪荡娶妻》《马冯换妻》等。多年来，壮族采茶戏已经形成了开台茶、花茶、观音坐莲、打钱鞭、买茶、梳妆、收台等流水式剧目。

采茶戏作为植根于民间的地方传统戏剧，对丰富群众文化生活起到重要作用。然而，目前邕宁采茶戏也面临着人才断层的问题，为此，传承人滕思队于2002年重新组织了一支拥有老中青三代共20余人的采茶表演队伍，并创作了不少新剧本，语言更为生动，贴近生活，广受群众欢迎，就连一些青年人也慢慢被这一传统戏剧文化所吸引。邕宁区政府也加大投入力度，积极扶持采茶戏演出队伍，培养新人，让采茶戏得以代代相传。与此同时，利用春节、端午节、中秋节等节庆日，积极组织邕宁壮族采茶戏表演，将壮族采茶戏这一民间文化精品发扬光大。

In the early 1980s, the opera gradually revived, but couldn't rival with its peak any more. The opera was only occasionally performed during the Spring Festival as more and more young people left home for work.

The types of roles of the opera are divided into male, female and face-painted young-roles, which are together called "three-young team" or "triangle team". It is mainly sung in Zhuang Language with rhyme lines. Mandarin was also added into the stage lines recent years, granting the opera flavor of modernism. The tunes of the opera, based on folk tunes in different places, are including more than 50 types, such as Selling Tune, Honghua Tune, Nan Tune, Siping Tune, Xian Tune, You Tune and Ku Tune. the music of the opera is mainly played by percussion instruments including ban gongs, su gongs, drums, big and small cymbals and wooden fishes, others are wind ones including suona horns and flutes. Some operas influenced by northern culture, also use Erhu and Jinghu that convey multi-layered culture. The stage property is relatively simple with ribbons, straps, drawn fans, and handkerchiefs, all of these are reflecting the simplicity and primitive consciousness of folk art. The costume includes ancient official robes, Western Lake dress, maid's dress in the imperial palace and the Zhuang costume. Most of the operas are traditional comedy, such as *Picking Tea*, *Selling Tea*, *Father and Son*, *Taking a Wife at Beihai*, *Wanderer Married a Wife* and *Mafeng Changed His Wife*. Over the years, the opera has formed such sequenced plays as Kaitai Tea, Hua Tea, Guanyin Sitting Lotus, Whipping, Buying Tea, Dressing and Finale.

The opera deeply rooted in the folk has played a key role to enrich people's cultural life. Unluckily, it faces a gloomy future of few inheritors. In 2002, the inheritor Teng Sidui reorganized a team of opera performing with three generations of old, middle-aged and young people, totaling more than 20 people. he also created a few new scripts that use more vivid languages and closer to life, and the operas adapted by the scripts are welcomed by the masses. Even some young people are attracted by the traditional opera. The government of Yongning District has called for all-out efforts to support the training of the team, ensuring the opera can be handed down from generation to generation. At the same time, they also hold opera performances in Spring Festival, Dragon Boat Festival, Mid-Autumn Festival and other festivals, hoping to carry forward the exquisite folk culture.

上林傩戏

Shanglin Nuo Opera

项目名称：上林傩戏

别称：白圩傩戏

分布范围：上林县白圩镇

入选名录：2018年第七批自治区级非物质文化遗产名录
　　　　　2012年第四批市级非物质文化遗产名录

保护单位：上林县文化馆

代表性传承人：陈铭忠（已故）、谭少玉

Element name：Shanglin Nuo Opera

Alternative name：Nuo Opera of Baixu Town

Geographical location and range：Baixu Town of Shanglin County

Element inscribed list：In 2018 on the Seventh Autonomous Region List of Intangible Cultural Heritage
In 2012 on the Fourth Municipal List of Intangible Cultural Heritage

Competent body involved in safeguarding：Shanglin County Cultural Centre

Representative inheritors：Chen Mingzhong (Late), Tan Shaoyu

上林傩戏面具
Shanglin Nuo Opera Masks

上林傩戏表演
Performance of Shanglin Nuo Opera

上林傩戏是流传于上林县白圩镇一带的传统戏剧，也叫白圩傩戏，是白圩及周边一带最重要的民俗活动，在每年庙会上，农村的“社坛”安龙、农民家丧事等都请傩戏堂去演戏。

上林傩戏历史悠久，明代时已有演出活动。它源自北方的古傩戏，由于历史上大量的北人南下，一部分人定居上林，将傩戏带到了上林白圩一带，并与当地的一些宗教祭祀等活动融合在一起，逐渐形成了今天的上林傩戏。上林傩戏的来源有两支，一支大约是来自北京北面山区的“录浪”，后迁到广东，经过柳州、来宾四栏、邹圩到白圩，另一支由邕宁、武鸣来到白圩。目前这两支均拜“三元”“拜表”“行孝”“下公曹”，都使用壮语唱戏。上林傩戏具有独特的形式与活动内容，有独特的堂号、独特的收徒制、独特的纪律约制、独特的表演面具、特殊的演出场地。

上林傩戏表演要严格遵守一整套行规，每次表演要举行祭仪，从“开光”（上漆）、“开箱”(表演前将面具从箱内取出）到“封箱”（表演完毕将面具放存箱内），要将

Shanglin Nuo Opera, also named Nuo Opera of Baixu Town, is a traditional opera popular in and around Baixu Town of Shanglin County. As a significant folk custom, it is performed in temple fairs, funerals and sacrificial rites that worships the Thunder God.

The opera has a long history and has been performed as early as the Ming Dynasty. It was initially an ancient Nuo opera brought to Baixu by northern people, later it merged with some local religious sacrifices and finally Shanglin Nuo Opera came into being. There are two sources of Shanglin Nuo Opera. One was Lulang from the mountainous area north of Beijing; firstly it migrated to Guangdong, and then settled in Baixu after passing through Liuzhou, Silan of Laibin and Zouxu. The other is from Yongning and Wuming. Both of them sing opera in Zhuang language and they share customs including Sanyuan festival, writing prayers, Xingxiao and Xiagongcao. Shanglin Nuo Opera has its distinctive features that reflect on with its unique title, apprenticeship, discipline, performance mask and venue.

When the opera performed, actors should strictly abide by a set of rules fit for sacrificial ceremony. The ceremony includes “unveiling light” (painting), “opening box”(taking out the mask from the box before the performance) and “sealed box” (putting the mask in the box after the performance). In this process, actors will cut the head of a cock for fresh blood, and the blood with wax, joss paper is used to offer sacrifices to the gods. After the performance, the ceremony

上林傩戏在万寿节中表演
Shanglin Nuo Opera Performed at the Longevity Festival

of "sweeping the place" should be held. Actors wear masks in simple cloth robes or skirts, flags on their backs, and weapons like knives, guns in their hands, will fight with each other in the accompaniment of gongs and drums. It is a stirring scene when flags swing with their every movement. Shanglin Nuo Opera is sung in Zhuang language, accompanied by gongs, drums, cymbals, erhu and flute. The venue is built calls for few conditions or tools. Actors usually planted several wooden stakes in the ground and link them with bamboo mats in three directions by tied ropes, then the performance could begin. The content of the opera performing is of great variety and close to the masses, rooting in historical stories and folklore. The repertoires often performed include *Shun'er*, *Dong Yong*, *The Story of Three Families*, *Tang Monk's Birth*, *Liang Shanbo and Zhu Yingtai*, *Search Husband for Thousands of Miles*, *Felicitations from Three Daughters*, *Three Winners in the Highest Imperial Examinations*, *Two Girls Fight for A Man*, *Shi Chong* and *Shuangyin Girl*.

Most of the scripts of the opera follow the ancient ones. For example, some plays perform the stories come from talking and singing literature in the Tang Dynasty, such as *Narrative of Filial Shunzi*, *Transformed Texts of Dong Yong* and *Prose of Han Peng*. The literature is of great artistic value help us to

雄鸡头割破，供上鸡血、香蜡纸钱等等，傩戏班子一干人拜神祈祷，表演结束后还要举行“扫收场”的仪式。演员头戴面具，背插靠旗，手执刀、枪等兵器，穿着简单的布袍或战裙，时而角逐开打，在铿锵的锣鼓伴奏中，靠旗摇动，雉尾摆动，异常热闹。上林傩戏使用壮语演唱，用锣、鼓、钹、二胡、笛子乐器伴奏。演出场地则“缚栏为戏”，栽上几根木桩子，系上绳子，三四张竹垫围三面，就可以演出。演出内容以历史故事、民间传说为主，灵活多样，生动活泼，贴近群众，贴近生活。常演的剧目有《舜儿》《董永》《三家福》《唐僧出世》《梁山伯与祝英台》《千里寻夫》《三女拜寿》《三进士》《二女争夫》《石崇》《双印女》等。

上林傩戏演出的唱本大多都是沿袭古唱本、唐朝“金韵文”的说唱底本，如《舜子至孝变文》《董永变文》《韩朋赋》等，具有深刻的文化内涵，对于研究地方戏曲的历史和发展有着极为重要的艺术价值。上林傩戏是古傩艺术的遗存，经过长期的传播和发展，已经成为人民群众喜闻乐见的艺术表现形式，其深厚的群众基础和特色鲜明的艺术特性，对推动广西壮族傩文化的研究、丰富群众的精神文化生活都起到积极的促进作用。上林傩戏是上林壮族具有特色的民间艺术表现形式之一，作为上林县历史和社会文化的缩影，对它的研究有助于加深对当地壮民族的信仰风俗文化的了解。

1949年以前，白圩镇上林傩戏有傩戏堂15个，到现在只剩下8个傩戏堂能够演出。傩戏演员大部分都超过了70岁，年龄最大的已有80多岁。很少有年轻人愿意学习傩戏，上林傩戏传承出现断层。随着老艺人的去世，上林傩戏旧唱本和舞台表演技巧也在不断地消失，绝技也不断地失传。为了传承和发展这一文化遗产，上林县组织力量对上林傩戏进行调查；搜集传统傩戏剧本、唱本，并将傩戏的表演做成录像、录音并存档；对上林傩戏的代表性传承人等进行登记，打破以往只有男性演傩戏的老传统，吸收女性参加演出傩戏；整理传统剧目的同时，积极创编新剧目，如根据民间故事创作《山猿婆》；也对演员服装、面具、道具、布景、灯光等进行改进。

study the development and local opera. Shanglin Nuo Opera is a relic of ancient Nuo art and has become a popular art after long-term dissemination and development. It plays an active role in promoting the study of Nuo culture and enriching the cultural life of the masses in view of distinctive characteristics and profound mass basis. As an epitome of Shanglin's history and social culture, it will deepen our understanding for customs of Zhuang Ethnic Group if we make a thorough inquiry for the opera.

There were 15 Nuo opera troupes in Baixu before 1949, and now only eight troupes left to perform. Worse still, most of the actors are over 70 years old, and the oldest is over 80. Few young people are willing to learn Nuo Opera. Shanglin Nuo Opera faces an alarming future of no inheritance. What's more, more old scripts and performing skills are fading with the death of sophisticated artists and actors. In order to better inherit and develop this cultural heritage, authorities of Shanglin County take all-out efforts to investigate and collect materials about traditional Nuo opera, and made videos, recordings and archives of the performance of Nuo opera. The representative inheritors of Shanglin Nuo Opera were registered. Female performers, once were excluded from conventional Shigong Dance, are also absorbed in performances to enrich what Nuo Dance conveys. New plays are created while the traditional ones are put in order. For instance, *Mother Mountain Ape*, a new play has been produced based on folk tales. Besides, improvement could also be found in many aspects including the costumes, masks, props, scenes and lighting of the actors.

宾阳师公戏

Binyang Shigong Opera

项目名称：宾阳师公戏

别称：唱古人、唱师

分布范围：钦州市、横州市、宾阳县等

入选名录：2010年第三批自治区级非物质文化遗产名录
　　　　　2009年第二批市级非物质文化遗产名录

保护单位：宾阳县文化馆

代表性传承人：莫旭先

Element name: Binyang Shigong Opera

Alternative name: Song for the Ancients, Song for Shigong

Geographical location and range: Qinzhou City, Hengzhou City, Binyang County and others

Element inscribed list: In 2010 on the Third Autonomous Region List of Intangible Cultural Heritage
In 2009 on the Second Municipal List of Intangible Cultural Heritage

Competent body involved in safeguarding: Binyang County Cultural Centre

Representative inheritor: Mo Xuxian

宾阳师公戏，是宾阳县广大人民群众喜闻乐见的地方戏曲艺术形式，广泛流传于宾阳县、横州市、钦州等地区。师公即巫师，戴木面具或纸画脸谱，穿红色长袍，唱歌跳舞以娱神，师公戏即是由跳神鬼的师公舞（唱师）演变而来的一种戏剧表演形式，俗称唱古人、唱师等。

宾阳师公戏历史悠久，距今已有400多年的历史。据明《宾州志》记载："本地乡民，弱于浮屠、病不医药，吉凶服色欠辩，乡落唱和成风。"明朝末年，师公在由其单独主事的"安龙兴宅""安立神像""撰兵社坛""增粮添寿"等仪式，或由佛、道单独主事的"超度亡灵"仪式，以及由佛、道、师联合主事的"七、九日灵保斋""十一日龙华圣斋"重大仪式上，专职负责"演乐"这个科目，本地俗称"唱古人"或"唱师"，也就是今天的师公戏。师公在传承古傩仪式的同时，增加了做、打、念、唱等艺术要素，并在跳神基础上逐渐发展成为民间小戏。

从明末至今，由师公上演的剧目内容是按其科目仪式而定，例如由佛、道主事的丧事仪式，师公绝不能上演喜庆团圆、升官中考、欢乐情节的剧目，只能演些孝敬父母、伦理道德亲情内容的节目。而由师公主事的吉祥福禄寿的仪式，绝对不许演生离死别、伤亡害劫内容的剧目。同时，宾阳师公戏广泛地吸收了宾阳县民间故事传说，以丰富演出内容，戏中有唱词、唱腔和舞蹈。起初，师公表演时穿红衣戴木质面具，后以纸画脸谱代替，作为神的形象为人间驱鬼逐疫。随着时代的变迁和演出剧目的增多，师公戏由娱神向娱人变化，面具逐渐为化装所代替，师公表演逐渐发展成为一个剧种。

宾阳师公戏拥有众多观众和广阔的市场。其演出无女性角色，人物则以面具、服饰化装来区分。师公以宾阳方言演唱，语言通俗易懂，形象生动，幽默风趣。目前已收集、整理有唱腔曲板近30种，如"师公调"，旋律低沉哀伤，伴

Binyang Shigong Opera is much loved by the people of Binyang and it is also popular in other areas including Hengzhou City and Qinzhou City. It is named Song for the Ancients and Song for Shigong as well, as it originates from a sacrificial dance called Shigong Dance in which Shigong (the wizard) sings and dances in a scarlet robe with wooden or paper masks on face to entertain gods.

The opera has a long history for more than 400 years. According to *Annals of Binzhou*,"few of the locals are Buddhists, and they take no medicine when they are in illness. Nobody is able to foretell good or ill luck while they all like to sing". In the late Ming Dynasty, Shigong was in charge of music performing when in their rituals of "worshipping the thunder god and may a prosperous family", "laying statue of gods", "altar preparing" and "praying for more food and long life" and when in rituals of "expiating the sins of the dead" by Buddhists or Taoists. And this is how the alternative names of Shigong Opera came. While inheriting ancient Nuo rituals, Shigong dance became a folk opera by adding artistic elements, such as martial arts, fighting movements, speaking and singing.

What Shigong performance has been decided by strict regulations from the late Ming Dynasty to the present. For example, happy contents like reunion and promotion must not be performed in funeral rituals held by Buddhists and Taoists. Only operas taking filial piety, ethics and kinship as topics could be accepted. Equally, auspicious rituals prefer happy contents rather than doleful ones. Binyang Shigong Opera enriches its performance by assimilating folk tales and advances its stage lines, aria and dances. Shigong initially acted as a god help people expel ghosts and diseases by wearing scarlet robes with wooden masks that replaced by paper ones later. And it has developed into an opera for recreation rather than sacrificial rite with masks substituted by makeup.

Binyang Shigong Opera has a large audience and a broad market. Roles in it are all males and distinguished by costumes and masks. It sings in Binyang dialect with negotiable languages, vivid details and humorous plots. Nearly 30 kinds of arias and tunes have been collected and sorted out. For instance, Shigong aria is low and harrowing with a gong and a drum accompanied. The aria combines the essence of religious culture, national culture and local music art, sharing cultural richness with external culture. The performances of Shigong Opera are as follows: first actors dance for "Sanyuan Zhenjun", then for "Sishi" and "Jiugong", followed by "King Moyi", "King Gan" and "Sanjie Gong", etc. In this process, dancers will step back and forth, holding instrument and magic implement in hands. The whole dancing team will lead a formation imitating dragon spiting beads or a twisted rope with shuttling movements dancers made. The opera is of a primitive style for its rich dance language, steady motions, and diversified leg movements. The opera calls for no regulated stage background, and it is generally performed in halls or temples whose host needs it. In this sense, the opera could begin when stage curtains, one table and two chairs are prepared readily.

The teams with the opera performers could be found all towns of Binyang. It is not only welcomed in festivals, but also in joyful circumstances including wedding ceremony, birthday celebrating, housewarming, promotion and ribbon-cutting ceremony. It has been an indispensable part of the life of nationalities for the lively atmosphere and dazzling performance it carries. The efforts to popularize and improve Binyang Shigong Opera will play a stimulating role in occupying urban and rural cultural positions, enriching and enlivening the cultural life and building a harmonious society. The opera art of local level and of Guangxi level is hoped to advance if more study for Binyang Shigong Opera promoted.

奏只用一锣一鼓，融汇着宗教文化、民族文化和本地民族音乐艺术的精华，具有外来文化和本土文化共存共荣的文化丰富性。师公戏的表演程式为先跳“三元真君”，再跳“四师”“九宫”，后跳本地神“莫一大王”“甘王”“三界公”等。他们手持乐器、法器，走龙摆尾、龙吐珠、绞麻花的队形，犹如穿针，踩着罡步穿插行进。舞蹈语汇丰富，风格古朴，动作沉稳，腿部动作多。宾阳师公戏演出一般没有舞台布景，只挂一块小幕布和小中幕，摆上一张桌子和两把椅子，演出地点多为事主家的厅堂或庙宇。

目前，以演师公戏为主的文艺队遍及宾阳城乡各地，每逢节庆，无处不上演师公戏。在欢庆寿诞、新宅落成、升学参军、工程开工剪彩等喜庆日子，多有人家或单位邀请师公戏演出，为其增光添彩。普及、完善、提高、发展宾阳师公戏，对占领城乡文化阵地、丰富活跃群众文化生活、构建和谐社会都将起到促进的作用，研究宾阳师公戏的发展史，对发展地方戏曲艺术，乃至广西民间戏曲史的发展和完善也将起到良好的推动作用。

参与祭祀活动
Performance in Sacrifice Activities

第五章 传统美术

Chapter Five Traditional Art

点米成画

Pasteup Picture with Rice

项目名称：点米成画

别称：无

分布范围：邕宁区蒲庙镇孟莲村那莲古圩

入选名录：2016年第六批自治区级非物质文化遗产名录
2015年第六批市级非物质文化遗产名录

保护单位：邕宁区文化馆

代表性传承人：曹文碧

Element name：Pasteup Picture with Rice

Alternate name：None

Geographical location and range：Nalian Ancient Market of Menglian Village of Pumiao Town in Yongning District

Element inscribed list：In 2016 on the Sixth Autonomous Region List of Intangible Cultural Heritage
In 2015 on the Sixth Municipal List of Intangible Cultural Heritage

Competent body involved in safeguarding：Yongning District Cultural Centre

Representative inheritor：Cao Wenbi

点米成画是一种传统工艺美术，以五谷种子蘸糨糊进行点画创作，为南宁市邕宁区蒲庙镇孟莲村那莲古圩所独有，已有数百年历史。以五谷、六畜、牛郎织女等吉祥图案制成的工艺美术品，被视为吉祥的载体，挂于厅堂、马车、舟船上，用于祈求五谷丰登、六畜兴旺和吉祥平安。作画用的五谷为水稻、黍子、高粱、麦子和豆类，作画时先将画纸或画布覆盖在竹筛等圆形器物上晾干，用铅笔在上面勾勒出草图，再根据草图内容设计颜色，用手指撮取事先染上各种颜色的“五谷”，一粒一粒蘸糨糊将其粘在画纸或画布上，制作出五彩斑斓的美术作品。

点米成画的发源地邕宁区蒲庙镇孟莲村那莲古圩，地处广西邕江流域八尺江中段邕宁区南部。古代那莲古圩地理位置独特，陆路北达南宁，南通灵山、钦州；水路可上溯龙州、百色，下可达梧州出海。这里土地平坦肥沃，水利条件优越，物产丰饶，促进了各行业的繁荣发展。点米成画的产生与我国七夕节有关，也与那莲赛巧节联系密切。农历七月初七是传说中织女与牛郎鹊桥相会之日，那莲古圩的妇女在这天晚上摆出时令瓜果和精心制作的手工艺品祭天，乞求天上的仙女赋予她们聪慧的心灵与灵巧的双手。清乾隆五十八年（1793），那莲北帝庙竣工，又恰巧临近那莲赛巧节，在双喜庆典中，姑娘们精心制作的“巧品”——点米成画——成为赛巧的主要作品，深受民众喜爱。自此，点米成画数百年来长盛不衰。

作为妇女展示手艺的代表作品，点米成画多取材于民间生活，题材广泛，最为常见的有牛郎、织女形象，也有日常生活中各色事物，如山村风景、家禽家畜、喜鹊报春、各种花卉等，寓意虽不尽相同，但都表达了农村百姓对美好生活的祈愿。作画工艺看似简单，却需认真对待，各类经过精挑细选的谷粒被染色、风干，不同种类谷粒特有的自然色结合颜料，呈现出饱和度极高的不同色彩，作画者将其逐粒掇起，蘸取糨糊，按照事先勾勒好的图形小心翼翼地进行点

Pasteup Picture with Rice is a traditional craft art. The picture is made with five kinds of cereals and paste. It is unique in Nalian Ancient Market in Menglian Village, Pumiao Town, Yongning District, Nanning. With hundreds of years' history, this picture stands for good luck and fortune for five cereals, six domestic animals, cowboy and woman weaver and other symbols of luck are painted on the picture. People hang the pictures on the lobbies, carriages, boats and other places in order to pray for harvest, wealth, good luck and peace. The materials for painting are rice, millet, sorghum, wheat and beans. First people dry paper or cloth on bamboo sifter or other round equipment and draw draft with pencil. Then, people design the composition and choose the color of the picture. Use finger to pick up cereals painted with different colors and stick them to the paper or cloth with paste. In this way a colorful picture is made.

Pasteup Picture with Rice originated in Nalian Ancient Market, Menglian Village, Pumiao Town, Yongning District, Nanning, which is located in southern part of Yongning District. Yongning District lies in the middle of Bachi River of Yongjiang River basin in Guangxi. Nalian Ancient Market has unique geographic features. It is connected with Nanning by land in north and Lingshan and Qinzhou in south. By taking a boat, people can reach Longzhou and Baise upstream and Wuhai downstream. With abundant resources, this region has flat land and privileged water system, which promotes the prosperity of all social sectors. The birth of Pasteup Picture with Rice is closely related to Double Seventh Festival and Saiqiao Festival in Nalian County. It is said that Woman Weaver and Cowboy will meet each other on the bridge of magpies in the sky. Women in this region will fete the sky with fruits and delicate handicraft to pray for intelligent mind and ingenious hands. Nalian North God Temple was built in 1793 in Emperor Qianlong period of the Qing Dynasty. By that time Saiqiao Festival in Nalian County was also approaching so that people celebrated the festival and the construction of temple together. During the ceremony, women made delicate tributes to god—Pasteup Picture with Rice, which earned most favor from people in the ceremony. Since then, Pasteup Picture with Rice remained popular in the last hundreds of years.

As a representative for women to show their skills, Pasteup Picture with Rice usually finds inspiration from normal life and has diversified content. Cowboy and Woman Weaver are commonly seen and other elements from life including natural scenery, poultry and livestock, magpie singing for spring and different flowers are all content of

Pasteup Picture with Rice. Different designs have different connotations, but they all show rural people's wish for a better life. The process of Pasteup Picture with Rice is seemingly easy but requires carefully. Carefully selected cereals are dyed and dried. Combined with original color, the dyed cereals have saturated color with different spectrum. Painters pick the cereals one by one and stick them to the draft with paste carefully. An outstanding picture will have bright colors. The cereals are well ripened and arranged orderly. They also change the arrangement and allocation due to different shapes. Although pictures choose scenery in normal life as themes and have simple patterns, they require long time to make. The painters must be patient and carefully with excellent skills. This is also why Pasteup Picture with Rice becomes the representative of women to show their handicraft.

Pasteup Picture with Rice has profound charm of folklore. It is originated from Double Seventh Festival Nalian Saiqiao Festival and choose fairies who are good at weaving and weeding as idols. Labor women express their wishes for a better life in Pasteup Picture with Rice and the wishes for agreeable weather and harvest are commonly shared by labor people. Most Nalian Saiqiao Festivals are sponsored voluntarily by people so that Pasteup Picture with Rice which is attached to the festival have solid mass base. With unique form, the Pasteup Picture with Rice remains its authentic and original style and local characteristics. Protecting and inheriting this traditional handicraft is important and influential to promoting national culture and advancing the development of cultural tourism. With the development of tourism, Pasteup Picture with Rice received warm welcome from tourists and also aroused the attention from artists, painters, art teachers and students from painting organizations and art academy. It will be embraced by the grand hall of art.

Nowadays, Nalian Ancient Market has been marginalized in geography and the influence of Saiqiao Festival also decreased. Pasteup Picture with Rice has a narrowing platform and the inheritance of this handicraft is also interrupted. In 2009, the government of Yongning District invested in recovering the ancient building of Nalian Ancient Market and improve regional environment in order to solve this problem. 2010 witnessed the establishment of travel companies and opening of Pasteup Picture with Rice training courses. With the support of various parties, Pasteup Picture with Rice frequently occurs in the travel products or festival activities nowadays. It catches the eyes of foreign and Chinese tourists and show the charm of folk art.

画。优秀的点米画作品色泽鲜亮，谷粒饱满匀称，排列均匀，甚至根据不同图形变换排列走向，富有立体感，甚为美观。画作虽多为生活“边角之景”，用色和图案单纯简洁，却需作画者长时间点画，作画者需心态平和，心细且手巧，因此点米成画成为妇女们赛巧节展示手工技艺的代表。

点米成画具有浓郁的民间色彩，因其源于“七夕”和那莲赛巧节，以能耕善织的天仙织女、七仙女作为偶像，寄托了广大妇女追求美好生活的愿望。由于对风调雨顺、五谷丰登的祈愿是群众共有的，那莲赛巧节活动经费大多由群众自发筹集，依存于传统节日的点米成画具有广泛的群众基础。点米成画形式新颖独特，手工技艺奇巧罕见，地方特色浓郁，至今依然保留着原汁原味的古朴风格。保护和传承这一传统技艺，对弘扬民族优秀文化、推动文化旅游业的发展具有重要的价值和深远的影响。伴随着旅游业的兴起，点米成画广受游客欢迎，也被绘画机构和艺术学院的画家、师生注意，进入文化艺术的大雅之堂。

如今的那莲古圩地理位置逐渐被边缘化，赛巧节的影响力逐渐减弱，点米成画的展示平台也随之变窄，传承人出现断层现象。2009年，邕宁区政府针对此状况投入资金，维修那莲古圩古建筑，并整治周边环境。2010年，旅游开发有限公司成立，组织开展了点米成画培训活动。经多方支持，点米成画得以经常出现在旅游或节日活动中，吸引着国内外游客的目光，展示出民族艺术魅力。

传承人在工作
The Inheritor is Working

壮族刺绣

Embroidery of Zhuang Ethnic Group

项目名称：壮族刺绣

别称：绡花、订花

分布范围：马山县

入选名录：2016年第六批自治区级非物质文化遗产名录
2013年第五批市级非物质文化遗产名录

保护单位：马山县文化馆

代表性传承人：蓝淋

Element name: Embroidery of Zhuang Ethnic Group

Alternative name: Xiaohua, Dinghua

Geographical location and range: Mashan County

Element inscribed list: In 2016 on the Sixth Autonomous Region List of Intangible Cultural Heritage
In 2013 on the Fifth Municipal List of Intangible Cultural Heritage

Competent body involved in safeguarding: Mashan County Cultural Centre

Representative inheritors: Lan Lin

壮族刺绣
Embroidery of Zhuang Ethnic Group

传承人
The Inheritor

Embroidery of Zhuang Ethnic Group is also called "Xiaohua" or "Dinghua" and is a unique handicraft skill in folk. It is widely spread in the hometown of folk art— Mashan County and has more than 1000 years' history. Embroidery usually chooses "full moon and beautiful flowers", "pine and crane", "blooming flowers and spring", "mandarin ducks", "birds and flowers" and other traditional symbols for good luck as patterns. Embroidery is commonly seen on ethnic clothes of Zhuang Ethnic Group like shoes, belt, bags, hats and aprons, as well as normal housewares such as curtains, quilt covers, drapery and desk covers. Handkerchief, balls, bags and sachets, with appreciating value, are decorated with delicate embroidery of Zhuang Ethnic Group, which become representatives of handicraft of Zhuang Ethnic Group.

Embroidery of Zhuang Ethnic Group is mainly spread in habitats of Zhuang, Yao and Han nationalities of Mashan County. It has a history of more than 1800 years. Ancestors of Zhuang Ethnic Group lived in the centre of ancient Luoyue around Daming mountain regions and embroidery was the tribute for ancient monarchs. The culture of embroidery was deeply rooted in daily life of Zhuang people since ancient times. Young men will give needles and thread to their lovers and women will return with shoes, handkerchiefs and bags with embroidery. During the ceremonies of various festivals, women's decorated shoes will catch people's eyes. Bags and belts are necessities from grandmothers to grandchildren. Weaving, needlework and embroidery are necessary skills for

壮族刺绣，壮语称作“绡花”“订花”，是壮族独有的民间手工美术技艺，流传于中国民间文化艺术之乡马山县，至今已有1000多年的历史。壮族刺绣多绣“花好月圆”“松鹤延年”“百花迎春”“鸳鸯戏水”“鸟语花香”等各种经典吉祥图案，绣于布鞋、背带、腰带、围腰、花帽等壮族服饰，以及门帘、被面、帐帘、桌布等日常居家用品。锦帕、绣球、挎包、香包被精美的壮绣装饰起来，成为壮族特有的信物与民族手工艺品的代表，具有很好的观赏价值。

壮族刺绣主要流布于马山县广大壮族、汉族、瑶族地区，已有1800多年的历史。壮族先祖原居于环大明山区域的骆越古国中心，壮族刺绣即为当地百姓向土司上贡的贡品。自古以来，刺绣文化深深植根于壮族人民的日常生活当中，青年男女订婚有男方送女方针线，女方回赠以布鞋、绣花手帕、挎包等习俗。在壮族各个节庆集会上，妇女盛装下的绣花鞋夺人眼球，绣花背带则是壮族外婆送给外孙的必备礼物。织布、挑花、秀锦是壮族妇女必备的技能，农闲时节，她们就相聚在屋檐下切磋技艺，交流经验。

绣女
A Woman Who Does Embroidery

绣花绷子
Embroidery Frame

壮族刺绣以盘绣为主体，绣法密集，以大面积繁绣为特色，在讲究刺绣整体格局的同时，也于细微处“见文章”，针针见功底，线线出效果，精工耗时。民间刺绣多以红、黄、紫、黑、白“五彩”为基本色，五色任意搭配，精彩纷呈。“破”是壮绣特有的色彩技艺，刺绣艺人对色彩的选择往往以强烈对比或毫不相干的两种颜色相邻搭配，用色大胆热烈，显露出壮族人热情直爽的性格。刺绣纹样常见有二方连续、四方连续、阴阳、共形、对称等基本造型，以水波纹、太阳星芒纹、花草鸟兽居多，大致分为简洁规整的几何纹样、具象的自然纹样与具有象征意味的抽象纹样三类，近取诸身，远取诸物，在似与不似之间创造图案，是壮族民间生活以及壮族文化的鲜明印记。纹样的选取搭配看似漫无边际，实则别有寓意，如以背带纹样区分男女，男孩背带中间往往绣一果实，女孩背带往往绣花朵，周围花枝缠绕，富丽绝美。

壮族刺绣与壮民生活及文化习俗相互依存，是壮族民族文化艺术的代表，色彩鲜艳夺目，纹样生动且布局和谐，注重整体构图与色彩搭配，富有立体感，寓意深远。作为承

women in Zhuang Ethnic Group. In slack seasons, they will compete and communicate with each other under the roof.

Embroidery chooses Pan school as the body part and has dense stitches. It is famous for large-scale embroidery. It put emphasis on general pattern as well as detail design. Every stitch will show the excellent skills of makers and every thread will have brilliant appearance. Embroidery chooses red, yellow, purple, black and white as the basic colors. The five colors are spread randomly and give a colorful display. “Break” is a unique feature of Zhuang Embroidery. Makers will choose colors with strong contrast and put them together. The color selection is bold which shows the straightforward personality of Zhuang people.“Er’fang lianxu”, “Sifang lianxu”“Yinyang”“Gongxing” and symmetry are common patterns. Embroidery usually uses the shape of water wave, sun, star, birds and animals. It could be classified into simple geographic patterns, nature patterns with special meanings and abstract patterns. People get inspiration from normal life and natural scenery. Designs are created in similarities and dissimilarities. Embroidery is representatives of life and culture of Zhuang. Sometimes, the patterns are seemingly meaningless but are actually meaningful. For example, boys and girls have different straps design. Boys will have a fruit while girls have flowers which are beautiful and prosperous.

Embroidery is closely related with life of Zhuang people and their living habits. It is the representative of Zhuang culture and art and has bright colors, vivid patterns and harmonious layout. It focuses on general design, color matching and have three-dimensional feeling and connotative meanings. As the live fossil which bears the culture of Zhuang, it tells the history of Zhuang. Different shapes are in harmony for makers have ultimate freedom of color allocation. Delicate designs grant unique expressive force of embroidery. Manmade embroidery is better than embroidery made by machine. Manmade embroidery is rich in creativity and shows the excellence of skills.

With the advancement of time, the market has a decreasing demand of manmade embroidery. Compared with other modern handicraft, the production efficiency of embroidery is relatively low and new generation producers could no longer make a living on embroidery, which leads to fewer workers. Embroidery of Zhuang Ethnic Group is faced with difficulties in survival and development. In order to address this problem, cultural department of Mashan County starts a deep investigation and establishes an inheriting base named "Zhuangmeifang" for inheritor training in Baishan Town, in which embroidery is concentrated distributed. Since 2006, governments of county and village keep investing in promotion and popularizing in order to support its development. In 2016, embroidery was enlisted in the Sixth Autonomous Region List of Intangible Cultural Heritage. It has opportunities to join various exhibitions and has become a key brand with local characteristics in Mashan county.

载壮族文化记忆的“活化石”，它反映了壮族生息繁衍的历史。各种图案搭配和谐，凝聚了淳朴的壮族性格，具有独特的艺术审美价值。尤其值得一提的是，壮族刺绣由纯手工制作而成，完全由艺人掌握色彩的搭配。精工巧制赋予了壮族刺绣生动的表现力，手绣比机绣更精美、更富于创造力，体现出壮族手工艺人高超的艺术水准。

由于时代的发展，市场对手工刺绣需求减少，与其他现代工艺品相比，壮族刺绣效益低下，新一代艺人难以借此维持生计，刺绣从业者越来越少，壮族刺绣的生存状况每况愈下，发展举步维艰。针对壮族刺绣的濒危状况，马山县文化部门开展深入普查，在其集中分布区域白山镇建设了“壮美坊”传承基地，培养传承人。自2006年以来，县、乡财政在项目宣传展示方面不断投入资金，扶持其发展。2016年，壮族刺绣列入第六批自治区非物质文化遗产名录，有机会参加各类民族工艺品展览，成为马山县重点打造的地方特色文化品牌。

绣女
Women Who Do Embroidery

第六章 传统体育、游艺与杂技

Chapter Six Traditional Sports, Entertainment and Acrobatics

抢花炮

Grabbing Huapao

项目名称：抢花炮

别称：无

分布范围：邕宁区中和乡

入选名录：2021年第五批国家级非物质文化遗产名录
2007年第一批自治区级非物质文化遗产名录
2007年第一批市级非物质文化遗产名录

保护单位：邕宁区文化馆

代表性传承人：孙子奇

Element name：Grabbing Huapao

Alternative name：None

Geographical location and range：Zhonghe Town of Yongning District

Element inscribed list：In 2018 on the Fifth National List of Intangible Cultural Heritage
In 2007 on the First Autonomous Region List of Intangible Cultural Heritage
In 2007 on the First Municipal List of Intangible Cultural Heritage

Competent body involved in safeguarding：Yongning District Cultural Centre

Representative inheritor：Sun Ziqi

歌圩上的抢花炮比赛
摄影 尹宗浩
Grabbing Huapao Competition in the Song Fair Photo by Yin Zonghao

抢花炮是流传于广西壮族地区的一项传统民俗活动，距今已有600多年的历史，于每年的农历二月初二举行，以南宁市邕宁区中和乡最为驰名。壮族抢花炮是通过抢夺花炮圈来祝愿获胜的村屯年年五谷丰登，蕴含着积极意义和美好愿望。因其争抢的激烈程度可与西方的橄榄球赛比肩，从而被外国民间体育运动专家誉为“东方的橄榄球”。

农谚有“二月二，龙抬头，大仓满，小仓流”的说法，民间认为，龙系吉祥物，主管云雨，而“二月二”则是龙升天的日子。早在明朝，邕宁区中和乡一带的乡民将土灰从门外撒到宅厨中，旋绕水缸一周，称为“引龙回”，又恰因二月初二是“土地真君”的生辰，所以，娱人、娱神的壮乡抢花炮便悄然兴起。由于抢花炮活动既能祭祀龙神和土地神，又寄托着人们的美好愿望，还有很强的娱乐健身功能和观赏价值，因此极富生命力，历经600多年，不仅长盛不衰，还与时俱进，规模越来越大。据中和乡孙振俺和孙振刚两位古稀老人回忆，日寇入侵广西时村里就有抢花炮的活动。由此可见，在古老的邕宁大地上，抢花炮这项民间体育活动正如老人们所描述的那样：“每年既有二月二，每年就有抢花炮”。

在举行抢花炮活动的日子里，远近壮乡的男女老少，都会穿上节日的盛装，一大早就争先恐后地拥向草坪，他们有的是为了给自己认识的花炮选手加油助威，有的是去感受

Grabbing Huapao (a circle or a ring wound with colorful cloth) is a traditional custom that is popular in Guangxi Zhuang Autonomous Region, which has a history of over 600 years. It is held on the 2nd day of the 2nd lunar month every year and is most famous in Zhonghe Town of Yongning District of Nanning. The activity of Huapao grabbing bears the Zhuang people’s desire of bumper harvest and other positive and auspicious wishes. As it is as fierce as the western rugby contest, Huapao grabbing of Zhuang Ethnic Group has been praised as “Oriental Rugby” by foreign folk sports experts.

There is a proverb goes like that “lunar February 2nd, dragon rises head; big barns fill, small barns spill”. Dragon is regarded as an auspicious symbol among the folk. People believe that the dragon controls clouds and rain and the lunar February 2nd is the day for the dragon to ascend to heaven. As early as in the Ming Dynasty, the villagers in Zhonghe Town of Yongning District would scatter dust from the door to the kitchen and whirl around the water tank, which was called "bringing the dragon back". Just because the 2nd day of the 2nd lunar month was the birthday of the "Earth God", the activity of Huapao grabbing was quietly raised to entertain both people and gods. As Huapao grabbing activity not only offers sacrifices to the Dragon God and the Earth God, but also reflects people’s good wishes, it has a strong entertainment and fitness function and bears ornamental value, thus it is an activity full of vitality. After more than 600 years, it not only keeps its flag flying, but also can keep pace with the times and become larger and larger. As Zhonghe Town’s two seventy-two-year-old villagers Sun Zhen’an and Sun Zhengang remember, the Huapao grabbing activity still existed when the Japanese aggressors invaded Guangxi. Therefore, on the ancient land of Yongning, Huapao grabbing activity is just as what the old people described, so long as there is the Spring Dragon Festival (the 2nd day of the 2nd lunar month), there is the activity of Huapao grabbing.

On the day of Huapao grabbing competition, men, women and children from far and near will put on their festival clothes and rush to the lawn in the early morning. Some of them want to cheer for the players they know; some want to feel the lively and joyous atmosphere, and some girls want to find a good husband among the players. In the villages where the Huapao grabbing activity is to be held, a master with a high skill will be invited to knit three to five bowl-sized large circles (the so called Huapao) with bamboo strips or rattan. The circles will be wrapped with red cloth and tied with red and green silk threads. When the host announces the start of the Huapao grabbing activity, the circle will be held on the iron gun muzzle and then it will be ejected to the sky. When the circle is falling down, players from all villages will vie with each other to grab Huapao with thunderous applause from the audiences. Sometimes the circle falls to the ground and sometimes it may fall into the pond, the hillside, the roof or the branches… But no matter where it falls, everyone will rush to the fore to find it, and everyone will strive to be the first. In the game of Huapao grabbing, the competitors will strictly follow the traditional rules, not beating others or cheating in the game, and will win the game by their wisdom, strength and speed. After Huapao is grabbed, the holder must overcome all the difficulties in the way, thus the activity usually lasts for a long time. When the player sends the circle to the judging platform in the temple, gun salute will be fired with three voices to indicate the successful end of the first round. Then, the second and third round of grabbing will begin. After the Huapao is grabbed in the third round of competition, the sounds of drums, suona horn, hurrah and fire crackers will resound through the skies and the competition will be finally finished with three voice of gun salute. The prize for the winner in the first round is very considerable and the activity will be held in his village next year. However, the winner will have to prepare the same prize next year, which is called "returning Huapao". If Huapao can be captured by the same player in succession, it will symbolize good harvests in consecutive years in his village and ladies nearby will also be eager to marry men in this village.

The emergence and development of Huapao grabbing are accompanied by the development of other traditional festivals. It has formed a fixed and perfect mode during the long-term development of folk traditional festivals. Huapao grabbing activity has also absorbed good features from other places so that it has a multi-source characteristic. After approaching the modern times, Huapao grabbing activity has integrated with modern sports and cultural styles, which plays an important role in folk sports activities in Guangxi and has become an excellent representative item of folk sports of Zhuang Ethnic Group. In 1990, the government of Yongning District assisted Zhonghe Town to hold the largest and most successful folk sports event of Huapao grabbing. Since then, this activity is held on each lunar February 2nd in Zhonghe Town in Yongning District. Later, women's competition of grabbing Huapao also began to be held in Yongning. In 2021, with the approval of the People's Government of the Guangxi Zhuang Autonomous Region, Grabbing Huapao was inscribed on the Fifth National List of Intangible Cultural Heritage.

热闹欢腾的气氛，有些姑娘则是想在众多花炮选手中寻得一个称心的郎君。凡是要举行抢花炮的村屯，事先会请编织手艺高的师傅，用竹篾或藤条编织三至五个碗口大的圆圈，外面缠以红布，再以红绿丝线扎牢。当主持人宣布“抢花炮开始”时，就将花炮圈放在“地连”的铁炮筒口上，火药将花炮圈射上空中，落下时各个村屯的选手争先抢夺，顿时全场欢声雷动。花炮圈有时落地，有时也可能落到水塘里或是山坡上、屋顶上、树枝上……但无论落在哪里，大家都会争先恐后地寻找，个个奋勇，人人争先。抢花炮时，选手都严守传统规矩，不打踏人，不弄虚作假，全凭智慧、力量和速度取胜。抢到花炮圈之后，还必须在多人争抢中“过关斩将”，因此抢花炮一般都要争夺很长时间。当选手把花炮圈送到庙里的裁判台上后，鸣炮三响，表示“头炮”胜利结束。接着还要进行二炮、三炮的争抢。抢到三炮后钟鼓齐鸣，唢呐声、欢呼声、鞭炮声犹如山呼海啸，最后以三声炮响来宣告抢花炮活动的结束。凡是抢得“头炮”者，奖品都非常可观，来年的抢花炮活动便由其所在的村屯主办，不过，该获奖者第二年需要准备同样的奖品，称为“还炮”。倘若连续抢到花炮，人们就会认为该村屯连年五谷丰登，附近的姑娘也向往能嫁到那里去。

抢花炮是伴随着民间传统节日产生和发展的，在长期的民间传统节日活动中形成了比较固定和完善的模式，在其形成和发展过程中，不断吸收外地抢花炮的一些特点，因而具有多源性的特点，发展到现代又与现代体育和文化样式相互结合，在整个广西民间体育活动中占有重要地位，是广西壮族民间体育的优秀代表项目。1990年，邕宁区政府协助中和乡成功地举办了有史以来规模最大、最成功的邕宁壮族抢花炮民间体育盛会，自此以后，邕宁区中和乡每年农历二月初二都要举办抢花炮活动，后来在开展男子抢花炮民间体育活动比赛的同时，也进行女子抢花炮比赛。2021年，经广西壮族自治区人民政府同意，抢花炮列入第五批国家级非物质文化遗产名录。

壮族迪尺

Dichi Sport of Zhuang Ethnic Group

项目名称：壮族迪尺

别称：打鸡头、打勒则

分布范围：广西壮族自治区

入选名录：2014年第五批自治区级非物质文化遗产名录
　　　　　2013年第五批市级非物质文化遗产名录

保护单位：南宁市民族文化艺术研究院（南宁市非物质文化遗产保护中心）

代表性传承人：陆显通

Element name：Dichi Sport of Zhuang Ethnic Group

Alternative name：Hit the Chicken Head, Hit Leze

Geographical location and range：Guangxi Zhuang Autonomous Region

Element inscribed list：In 2014 on the Fifth Autonomous Region List of Intangible Cultural Heritage
In 2013 on the Fifth Municipal List of Intangible Cultural Heritage

Competent body involved in safeguarding：Nanning Ethnic Culture and Art Research Institute (Nanning Intangible Cultural Heritage Protection Centre)

Representative inheritor：Lu Xiantong

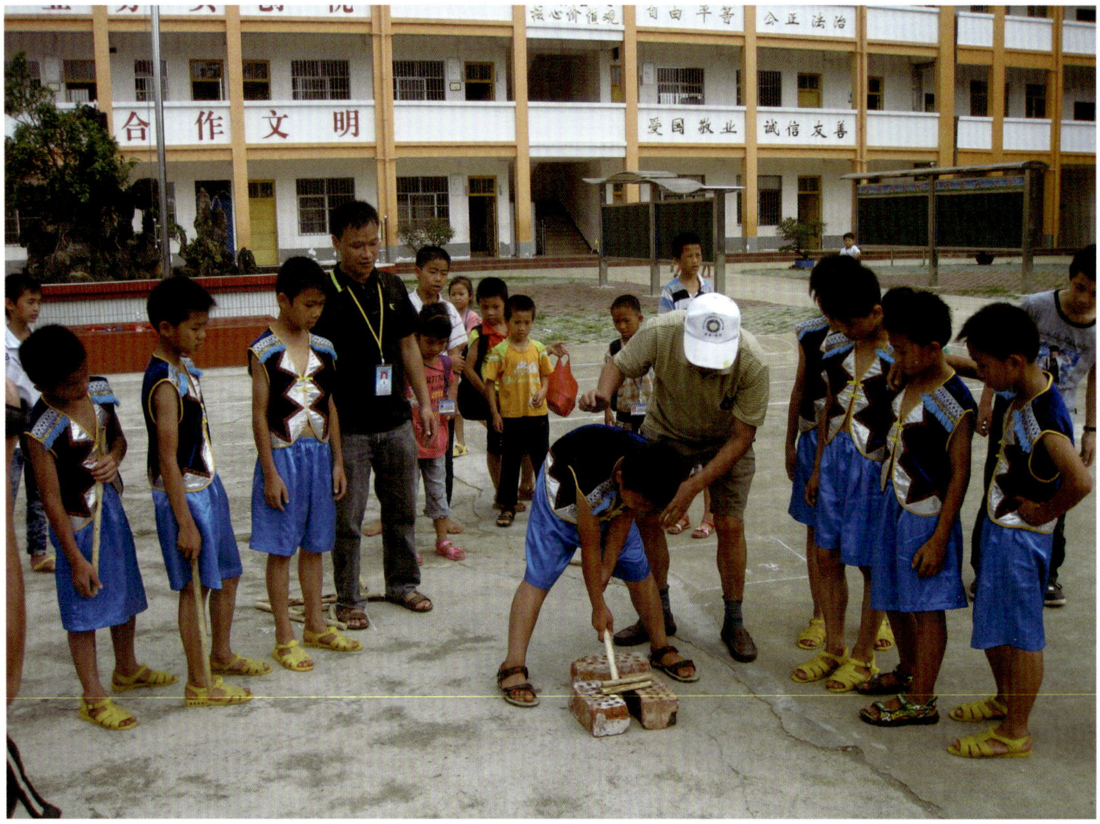

老师在指导
The Teacher is Guiding

Dichi Sport of Zhuang Ethnic Group is a unique sports activity for Zhuang people. It is mainly in Guangxi Zhuang Autonomous Region and Zhuang habitats in Guangdong and Yunnan. "Di" is the translation of "Hit" in ancient language of Zhuang and Dichi is also called "Hit the Chicken Head" or "Hit Leze". As an entertaining sports activity, Dichi has various and active performance forms. Audience could watch the sport in a long or short distance, which laid a solid foundation of Dichi among normal people.

Dichi originated from the hunting. In ancient times, people needed to use wood sticks which were easy to find as the major tools for hunting. People needed to have high accuracy when throwing the sticks. As a result, people started to learn how to throw sticks accurately. Later, the hunting tool has been improved and people could use arrows and slingshots. With no need to throw sticks, the practice of throwing sticks gradually became one sport activity.

The venue of Dichi is about 3-4 meters wide and 8-10 meters long and the ground is flat cement or grass. On one end of the venue is a pit which is 20 centimeters long and 3

壮族迪尺是壮族人独有的传统民间体育竞技活动，主要活跃于广西壮族自治区以及广东、云南的壮族聚居区域。“迪”为壮语“打”的译音，壮族迪尺又名“打鸡头”“打勒则”，作为一种极具娱乐性的竞技活动，其形式活泼多样，表演流动性强，观众远近观赏皆可，因此在民间具有广泛的群众基础。

壮族迪尺来源于壮族人的狩猎传统。在远古时代，由于狩猎的需要，人类使用随处可得的木棒作为主要狩猎工具，在投掷木棒时，要求极高的准确性，于是，人们就开始练习投掷木棒。后来，狩猎工具得到改进，有弹弓和弓箭，便不再依靠木棒掷击野兽，这种投掷木棒的练习就逐渐演变成一种体育竞技活动。

壮族迪尺的活动场地一般为宽3—4米、长8—10米的平坦水泥地或草地。场地的一头挖一个长约20厘米、深约3厘米、两头尖中间深的“尺坑”，此为迪尺的“阵地”。参赛人数一般为4人，分成两组。比赛道具是一条长约35厘米、直径4厘米的圆木棍，作为“迪尺”的“尺母”，“尺子”则是由一条长约15厘米、直径4厘米的圆木棍制成。一般而言，一场比赛的时间为30分钟（也有以一根香燃尽为止），比赛过程中，两个对手如此围着三个顺序打尺，时间一到，统计尺数，多者为赢家。

壮族迪尺具有极高的健身价值和娱乐价值，而迪尺活动的发生发展，与壮族地区的社会发展和历史文化密切关联，承载着厚重的文化价值，对研究我国体育史有重要的作用。近年来，南宁市非物质文化遗产保护中心组织专家深入壮族地区调查研究，收集整理相关资料，对壮族迪尺全力挖掘、整理和保护，采取切实可行的措施，加大壮族迪尺的宣传力度，在中小学校园中开展迪尺活动的展示和竞赛活动等。2014年，壮族迪尺经广西壮族自治区人民政府同意，列入第五批自治区级非物质文化遗产名录。

centimeters wide. The pit is narrow in the ends and deep in the middle. There are four people participating in the game and they are divided into two groups. The tool of game is a stick with round end which is 35 centimeters in length and 4 centimeters in diameter. This will be the object of Dichi. The subject of Dichi is a stick which is about 15 centimeters in length and 4 centimeters in diameter. The time of one game is 30 minutes and competitors throw the subject of Dichi to the object in a specific order. When time runs out, the one who hits the target most will be the winner.

Dichi of Zhuang Ethnic Group has value in exercise and entertainment. The birth and development of Dichi is closely related to the social development and historical culture in Zhuang habitats. Dichi contains profound culture and is of great significance to the research of sports history in China. In recent years, Nanning Intangible Cultural Heritage Protection Centre organized experts to investigate Dichi in Zhuang habitats and collected documents. They spared no efforts in exploring, categorizing and protecting Dichi. Practical measures are implemented in order to enhance the promotion of Dichi. In primary schools and middle schools, they start exhibitions and competitions of Dichi. In 2014, with the approval of the Government of Guangxi Zhuang Autonomous Region, Dichi was inscribed on the Fifth Autonomous Region List of Intangible Cultural Heritage.

比赛
Competition

壮族斗竹马

The Competition of Bamboo Horse of Zhuang Ethnic Group

项目名称：壮族斗竹马

别称：无

分布范围：青秀区长塘镇、邕宁区、良庆区及周边地区

入选名录：2010年第三批自治区级非物质文化遗产名录
　　　　　2009年第二批市级非物质文化遗产名录

保护单位：青秀区文化馆

代表性传承人：李青礼

Element name: The Competition of Bamboo Horse of Zhuang Ethnic Group

Alternative name: None

Geographical location and range: Changtang Town of Qingxiu District, Yongning District, Liangqing District and the surrounding areas

Element inscribed list: In 2010 on the Third Autonomous Region List of Intangible Cultural Heritage
In 2009 on the Second Municipal List of Intangible Cultural Heritage

Competent body involved in safeguarding: Qingxiu District Cultural Centre

Representative inheritor: Li Qingli

壮族斗竹马是一种群体性壮族民间体育竞技活动，主要流传于南宁市青秀区长塘镇及邕宁区、良庆区等周边地区，一般在每年农历四月初八和其他重大节日举行。斗竹马就是竞技者站在用竹子制成的“马”上，通过有技巧的碰撞使对方“下马”，从而获得胜利。一般来说，斗竹马是两队人的竞技，因此群众能够广泛参与其中，这不仅是平衡技巧的较量，更是智谋与勇气的较量。其比赛场面欢腾、热烈，具有极强的娱乐性、竞技性和观赏性。

斗竹马的产生最初与战争有关。相传明末清初年间，明军被李自成的义军打败之后，退到广西南宁市长塘镇，败军到处掳掠，人民不得安生。其时，天堂村村民李化龙组织民团训练，用竹木作武器，在长塘三皇岭一带起义对抗明军，最后寡不敌众，躲入三皇岭。深山之中无粮充饥，而此时恰逢农历六月，三皇岭上到处长满了豆稔果，李化龙带领村民吃豆稔果充饥，才渡过一劫。后人为了纪念李化龙，把三皇岭改称为逃军山，并把李化龙奉为李哑王，在村中立庙祭拜，并于每年农历四月初八李化龙生日时，模仿李化龙练兵时所用的竹木器制作竹马，通过斗竹马活动来纪念他。这种活动慢慢发展演变，成为当地及周边地区的一项民间体育竞技活动，逢农历四月初八或重大节日，男女老少广泛参与。

壮族斗竹马活动对场地的要求不高，草坪或者房前屋后的空旷地域均可，大小、长宽视场地的宽窄和参赛人数而定，但不管宽窄大小，都要求坚实平整，无障碍物，比赛时用线条画出界限（旧时常用麻绳作界线）。每场比赛不限参赛人数，人员分为红蓝两方，一方为“兵”队，另一方为“勇”队。比赛时双方所用的竹马制作较为讲究，竹竿要结实坚硬，而且要有自然的竹眼，以此作为支撑点，便于参赛者放脚，竹马的长度一般为3米左右，但没有严格的限制。比赛前，参赛者要先沐浴，并在双方各自领队的带领下，到村中李哑王庙祭拜。比赛开始后，由锣鼓助威，双方各执一面旗，队员踩在竹马上，先过场两次，第三次开始对冲，以

The Competition of Bamboo Horse of Zhuang Ethnic Group is an athletic group sports which is mainly popular in Yongning, Liangqing, Changtang town of Qingxiu District in Nanning and neighboring region. Every year it is held on lunar April eighth and other major festivals. Competitors will stand on the “horses” made of bamboo. By crashing others skillfully, competitor will win the match if other participants are crashed down from the bamboo horses. Generally speaking, participants will be divided into two teams which could invite mass people to join the game. This is not only the competition of balance skills but also courage and intelligence. People are enthusiastic and the game is rejoicing with entertainment, competitiveness and appreciation value.

Bamboo horses was born from wars. It is said that in the late Ming Dynasty and the early Qing Dynasty, Ming army was defeated by revolt army of Li Zicheng and retreated back to Changtang town in Nanning. The defeated army robbed and killed everywhere and brought sufferings to local people. At that time, villager Li Hualong organized and trained local people for defense. They used bamboo sticks as weapons and fought against defeated Ming army in Sanhuang Hill of Changtang. In the end, local army was hopelessly outnumbered and retreated back to Sanhuang Hill. With no food in the mountains, Li Hualong led villagers eat “Dounian”, a fruit commonly seen on Sanhuang Hill in lunar June. After surviving the disaster, people changed the name of mountain as “Defeated Army Hill” in memory of Li Hualong. People worshipped him as Liya King and built a temple for him in the village. On lunar April 8th, which is the birthday of Li Hualong, people will use bamboo weapons to make bamboo horse and will held bamboo horse competition. These activities gradually become a sport activity among people in local areas and neighboring regions. Every year on lunar April 8th or other festivals, men and women of all ages will participate in the activity.

This activity does not have a high requirement of venue. It could be hold on the grassland and the open space in front of or behind houses. The size of venue is depended on the number of participants. The venue must be flat, solid and clear of obstacles regardless of how large it is. People will draw the boundary of venue (people used hemp rope as boundary in ancient time). There is no limitation on the number of participants and players will be divided into two groups, red team and blue team, which are also called “Soldier” team and “Warrior” team. The bamboo horses used in competition are carefully made. The stick must be firm and have natural bamboo jointed on which competitor could put his or her foot. The length of bamboo horse is normally 3 meters long but there is no specific standard. Before the competition, competitors will have a shower and pay their tribute to Liya King in the temple led by their team leaders. When the match starts, gongs and drums will cheer them up. Every team will have one banner. Team members stank on the bamboo horses and walk pass the other team for twice. They will charge towards each other at the third time. The team which crashes all members of the other team down from the horses will be the winner. Winner needs to have the best of three. Winners will have a roasted pig used to honor the god. Old man with reputation will be the judge. During the competition, players could only jump and walk on the bamboo horse and crash others with their shoulders. Any brute acts will be punished. After the competition, the whole village will enjoy a dinner party in the evening. The winner team will lead all villagers to float river lanterns in Yongjiang river in memory of Li Hualong and pray for agreeable weather, a good harvest and peace for people.

As a unique traditional sports activity in Zhuang habitat with profound historical value and reference value for research in traditional sports of Zhuang. It will also promote national culture, enrich sports activity, strength people's body and advance and drive the development of tradition sport. In recent years, Qingxiu district attached great importance in protecting and inheriting Bamboo Horse of Zhuang Ethnic Group. It organized many bamboo horse activities and also established an organization in culture centre of Changtang Town, where training courses will be held by old players. On the 2nd day of the second lunar month, the eighth day of the fourth lunar month or other festivals, grand bamboo horse competition will be held in Changtang Town. These activities are beneficial to the heritage of bamboo horses. In 2010, with the approval of Guangxi Zhuang Autonomous Region, Bamboo Horses of Zhuang Ethnic Group was inscribed on the Third Autonomous Region List of Intangible Cultural Heritage.

一方队员将另一方队员全部撞倒为一局，三局两胜制，胜方赢得一头祭神用的烧猪。裁判一般由当地有威望的老人担任，比赛期间，队员只能踩在竹马上行走跳跃，并用双肩撞击对方，使用任何粗野动作都会被视为犯规而被罚出场。斗竹马比赛活动结束后，当天晚上全村举行聚餐，餐后比赛人员带上全村男女老幼到邕江边放河灯，以此纪念李化龙的功德，并祈求全村风调雨顺、五谷丰登、人民平安幸福。

作为壮族地区独具特色的传统体育竞技活动，斗竹马本身承载着厚重的历史价值，对研究壮族传统体育具有重要的参考价值，对丰富民族文化、发展民族体育活动、增强人民体质、带动和促进传统民族体育的发展和弘扬都将产生推动作用。近年来，青秀区高度重视壮族斗竹马的保护和传承，积极组织民间壮族斗竹马活动，在长塘镇文化站设立斗竹马活动辅导小组，组织老艺人进行斗竹马的培训，并于每年农历二月初二、四月初八等日子，在长塘镇举行规模盛大的斗竹马比赛，使斗竹马这一民间体育竞技活动得到传承。2010年，壮族斗竹马经广西壮族自治区人民政府同意，列入第三批自治区级非物质文化遗产名录。

斗竹马
The Competition of Bamboo Horse

壮族香火球

Xianghuo Ball of Zhuang Ethnic Group

项目名称：壮族香火球

别称：无

分布范围：良庆区南晓镇、大塘镇，钦北区小董镇、那蒙镇、大寺镇、长滩镇、新棠镇

入选名录：2008年第二批自治区级非物质文化遗产名录

保护单位：良庆区文化馆

代表性继承人：班继联

Element name：Xianghuo Ball of Zhuang Ethnic Group

Alternative name：None

Geographical location and range：Nanxiao Town, Datang Town of Liangqing District; Xiaodong Town, Nameng Town, Dasi Town, Changtan Town, Xintang Town of Qinbei District

Element inscribed list：In 2008 on the Second Autonomous Region List of Intangible Cultural Heritage

Competent body involved in safeguarding：Liangqing District Cultural Centre

Representative inheritor：Ban Jilian

香火球比赛

Match of Xianghuo Ball

Xianghuo Ball of Zhuang Ethnic Group is a traditional activity of Zhuang spread in Nanxiao Town of Liangqing District in Nanning, Datang Town and Xiaodong, Nameng, Dasi, Changtan and Xintang of Qinzhou. It originated in Guyuan village in Nanxiao county. With 300 years' history, it is said to have close relationship with agricultural production.

It is said that in the late Ming Dynasty a village named Xiaocun stood near Guyuan village. Villager Bantaigong had two sons. Their mother died when they were thirteen or fourteen years old. Three years later, Bantaigong married another woman and had another son. His love to the youngest son made the two older brothers jealous. Brothers regarded the small son as a rival and made difficulties to him. Old Bantaigong wished that three sons could live in harmony but disappointedly he failed. One day, an old man with dirt and scars on his body visited the village. He fell to the ground due to weakness and tiredness. The youngest son came into him coincidently and brought him back for treatment until he recovered. The old man found the son honest and kind-hearted and told him that he found a place of treasure in Gulian named "Duck Paddling Water". He would be prosperous and rich if he moved to this place. Bantaigong passed away before long and the son remembered the old man. He moved with his mother to Guyuan village. He worked

壮族香火球，是一项流传于南宁市良庆区南晓镇、大塘镇及钦州市的小董、那蒙、大寺、长滩、新棠一带的壮族传统体育竞技活动。它起源于南宁市良庆区南晓镇古元村，传说与农事密切相关，距今已有300多年的历史。

相传在明朝末年，距离古元村不远处有一个晓村，村里有个班太公，生有两子，两子十三四岁时，他们的母亲病逝。三年后，班太公再娶，又生了一个儿子。他甚为喜爱小儿子，两个哥哥心生妒忌，把弟弟视为外人，对他百般刁难。年迈的班太公希望三兄弟能和睦相处，但并未如愿。一天，村里突然来了一位老者，满身污泥和伤痕，因体力不支晕倒在地。班太公的小儿子恰巧遇见，立即把老者背回家中救治，悉心照料，直至他痊愈。老者觉得这孩子忠厚老实，便对他说：“我在二里外的古楝那边觅得一风水宝地，名为‘宝鸭戏水’，住之可兴家旺业，你不妨迁往另立新家。”不久班太公辞世，小儿子想起老者的话，便与母亲一起来到了古元村，勤奋耕耘，不久，新垦的几亩田地栽上了稻菽蔬果，且收成不错，他们的生活很快有了转机。遗憾的是，垦荒种植的庄稼被周边林中的鸟兽肆意蹂躏，丰收在望的庄稼转眼颗粒无收。聪明的小弟想到了一个好办法，他将三支鸡毛插在竹笋壳上，挂在田地旁，就像一只捕食鸟鼠的老鹰，威风凛凛地护卫着田地。果然，鸟兽再不敢来，庄稼获得丰收。因为竹笋壳太轻，容易被风吹走，后来的人又在底座上加了两枚铜钱，然后插上鸡毛，这样不但经久耐用，神态也更逼真了。后来大家纷纷效仿，人们在用它保护庄稼的同时，经常用于茶余饭后的娱乐项目，最初是两人对拍，后来双打或多人拍打。

壮族香火球的形状类似现代的羽毛球，开展活动的场地一般长约十步、宽五步，中线两端各竖一根竹竿作支架，高度为1.6米左右，中间横一根细长平直的竹竿作为“网”，场地的四角各钉一根高约两寸的竹钉，并各插三根香，以麻绳缚住竹钉圈起场地。因古时活动多在夜间进行，所以在场地四周常用竹筒灌火油或香油点燃照明，参与人数以场内不拥挤为宜。比赛以麻绳为边线，球出线外属违例，手或球击中中线、竹竿或脚逾中线、踩线亦视为违例。一般以五局为一场，每局打15个球，以胜三局为胜方，可进行单打、双打、混合双打等比赛，裁判员一人或两人，男女均可。

壮族香火球与其他民间文化表现形式一样，是在传统文化背景下产生的，它是壮族人民在漫长的历史长河中不断创造并遗留下来的宝贵财富，是壮民族精神与情感的重要载体，具有浓郁的民族风格和地方特色。作为一项民间传统竞技活动，壮族香火球是壮族稻作经济的产物，反映着鲜明的稻作文化特征，可以说它在岭南地区民族民间传统体育中一枝独秀，在整个广西壮族地区的民族民间体育中独占一席，是古老壮族地区体育竞技的一支，是传统体育运动大家庭中不可或缺的一个特色项目。2008年，壮族香火球经广西壮族自治区人民政府同意，列入第二批自治区级非物质文化遗产名录。

hard and planted vegetables and fruits on the land. Good harvest was about to light their life up. Unfortunately, their plants were destroyed by animals and birds from regional forests and the crops in the hope of a good harvest were in vain in a blink of an eye. Intelligent man had an idea. He stuck three chicken feathers on the shell of bamboo shot and hung it near his farm. It seems that a fierce eagle is guarding the farm. The animals and birds never appeared since then and he had a harvest. However, the shell of bamboo shot was too light and was easy to be blown away. People put two coins at the bottom and made it firm and vivid. It was learned by many people. On one hand, it could protect the crops. On the other hand, it was also an entertainment. At first only two people played in the game and gradually doubles or more people could play one game simultaneously.

The shape of Xianghuo ball is like badminton ball. The venue is usually 10 steps long and five steps wide with two poles standing on the ends of middle line. The poles are about 1.6 meters long and a long thin stick is hanged in the middle as "net". Four two-cun-long (about 0.66 decimeters) bamboo nails stand on four corners of the venue and the venue is circled by hemp rope. Three incenses will be lighted during the match. In ancient times, the match usually took place in the evening so that people would light the venue with bamboo filled with oil. Playground should not be too crowded. Hemp rope functions as the border of the game. Players violate the rules when ball falls out of the venue, hands or ball touch the middle line, bamboo stick or feet cross the border, or steps on the border lines. There will be five matches in one competition and 15 strikes in every match. Winners need to have best three of five. Singles, doubles and mixed doubles are all accepted. It is all acceptable whether one or two judges appear on the venue. Judges can be male or female.

The form of Xianghuo Ball of Zhuang Ethnic Group is similar to other folk activities and is born in the background of traditional culture. It is valuable treasure created and inherited in the long history of Zhuang Ethnic Group. As a symbol of spirit and feelings of Zhuang, it has unique ethnic style and is rich in local characteristics. As a competition activity, Xianghuo Ball of Zhuang Ethnic Group is the product of rice agricultural economy with prominent features of rice culture. It plays an important role in folk sports in habitats of Zhuang due to its unique features. As an integrated and irreplaceable part of traditional sports, it was inscribed on the Second Autonomous Region List of Intangible Cultural Heritage in 2008 with the approval of the People's Government of the Autonomous Region.

壮族功夫

Kung-fu of Zhuang Ethnic Group

项目名称：壮族功夫

别称：南蛮拳、军拳

分布范围：南宁市、崇左市、百色市、北海市、钦州市等

入选名录：2015年第六批市级非物质文化遗产名录

保护单位：南宁市民族文化艺术研究院（南宁市非物质文化遗产保护中心）

代表性传承人：无

Element name：Kung-fu of Zhuang Ethnic Group

Alternative name：Nanman Boxing, Military Boxing

Geographical location and range：Nanning City, Chongzuo City, Baise City, Beihai City, Qinzhou City and others

Element inscribed list：In 2015 on the Sixth Municipal List of Intangible Cultural Heritage

Competent body involved in safeguarding：Nanning Ethnic Culture and Art Research Institute (Nanning Intangible Cultural Heritage Protection Centre)

Representative inheritors：None

壮族功夫，在壮语中被称作“昂拳”，也叫作“军拳”，是壮族所特有的拳种，主要分布于广西壮族自治区的南宁、崇左、百色、北海、钦州等地。壮族功夫有着“南拳始祖”之美誉，对江苏、浙江、福建、广东沿海一带的南拳影响深远。

壮族功夫历史悠久，源远流长。宋仁宗庆历年间（1041—1048），壮拳又被称作“南蛮拳”，壮族义军首领侬智高十分精通南蛮拳，将其用于训练官兵来增强自己的军事力量。王安石曾称道：“粤右良兵，天下称最”，由此可见其兵将之勇猛、拳术之精湛。南宋周去非的《岭外代答》中记载：“邕州溪峒之民，无不习战，刀弩枪牌、用之颇精。”又载：“建炎初，诸峒丁壮，常团结训练。”由此不仅可以看出当地学习壮族功夫的人数众多，而且习拳之人大都精通拳术和器械，常常相互切磋，具备丰富的实践经验。明孝宗弘治十年（1497），壮族女英雄瓦氏夫人将古老的壮拳与北长拳的功架相糅合，使后来的壮族功夫兼备大架子，并用此架势功夫来训练狼兵（也叫“俍兵”，壮族土司组建的地方武装），六千狼兵在抗倭战争中大显身手，屡建战功，保护了一方平安。明朝民族英雄戚继光、俞大猷在训练自己的队伍时，也曾吸取壮拳技艺来加强部队的作战能力。

作为一种适用于实战的拳种，壮族功夫主要是根据壮族人的身体特点、壮族地区的地理形势以及大量的实战经验创造出来的。因此，壮族功夫的动作彪悍粗犷、灵活多变，功架清晰准确，整体沉实稳健，在动作上拳刚、势烈，多短打，擅标掌，少跳跃，并在出手时借声气发力，使全身力量集中，动作迅猛。在训练时，壮族功夫采用“站桩”“打沙袋”“打树桩”“走梅花桩”“七步铁线基本桩功”等方法，讲究技巧的同时更重视基础的牢固与否，力主做到无论是拳还是械，都架实劲猛、灵敏迅速，非常适合在广西山区练习和实战。目前，壮族功夫的拳术套路主要有35种，现存的器械有14种，现存对练套路有2种，都可以称得上是壮族

Kung-fu of Zhuang Ethnic Group is also called “Ang Boxing” and “Military Boxing” in Zhuang dialect and is unique for Zhuang Ethnic Group. It is mainly spread in Nanning, Chongzuo, Baise, Beihai, Qinzhou and other areas. Kung-fu of Zhuang enjoys the reputation as the ancestor of southern China boxing. Its influence reached southern boxing in Jiangsu, Zhejiang, Fujian and coastal areas in Guangdong.

Kung-fu of Zhuang has a long history. In Emperor Qingli period of the Song Dynasty (1041-1048), leader of local military force Nong Zhigao was good at Nanman boxing, which was the ancient name of Kung-fu of Zhuang. He used it to train his soldiers and strengthened his military power. Wang Anshi, a poet and politician, once praised that “Soldiers from Guangxi region is the best in the world”, which vividly shows how strong and brave the soldiers were and how skillful their Kung-fu was. Zhou Qufei who lived in the Song Dynasty wrote in his *Ling Wai Dai Da* that “people lived in Xidong of Yongzhou were all good at fighting and were excellent in knife, crossbow, sword, shield and other weapons”. He also wrote that “teen warriors usually trained together”. This shows that a large number of people learned Kung-fu of Zhuang and they were good at boxing and using weapons. People fought with each other and had rich experience. In 1497 in the Ming Dynasty, heroine Ms. Washi combined ancient Zhuang kung-fu with Northern Long boxing. Zhuang Kung-fu had the defense techniques since then. She used this to train “Wolf Soldiers” to protect peace and security and won glories during the wars. Hero Qi Jiguang and Yu Dayou in the Ming Dynasty also learned from Zhuang Kung-fu to strengthen their army.

As a martial art used for real combat, Zhuang Kung-fu was created based on body features of Zhuang people, geographical features of Zhuang habitats and abundant combat experience. The movements are usually fierce and changeable. People who practice Zhuang Kung-fu will attack their enemies accurately and the defense is stable. The attack is brute and quick. It emphasizes bunt and reduces jumping. In an attack, attackers will concentrate all his or her power to the fist and hit his rival quickly. During the training, “Standing Piles”, “Hitting Sand Bag”, “Jumping on Meihua Piles”, “Seven Steps Iron Line Pile” and other courses will be used. The training courses focus on solid foundation. Players must be fierce and quick regardless of using fists or weapons. Zhuang Kung-fu is an ideal martial art in mountain areas of Guangxi for exercise and real combat. Currently, there are 35 kinds of fist skills and 14 weapon skills. Two training courses also exist. They are the essence of Zhuang Kung-fu.

Zhuang Kung-fu is closely related to military events and

combats. It is important for ancient people to defend their homeland and their national dignity. Nowadays, it still plays an active role in regional areas. People exercise with Zhuang Kung-fu. They will not only have a strong body but also spiritual pleasure, which makes it a popular sports event. With the advancement of protection, various documents about Zhuang Kung-fu were published, including *China Traditional Sport—Guangxi Volume, Record of Martial Art in Guangxi* and *Traditional Sport of Minorities in Guangxi*. In recent years, heritage of Zhuang Kung-fu was carried out orderly. Nanning Ethnic Culture and Art Research Institute organized experts to investigate in rural areas and collected documents about Zhuang Kung-fu. The institute also cooperated with middle schools and primary schools in Nanning and included Zhuang Kung-fu into physical exercise courses, which enables teenagers to exercise and learn about Zhuang Kung-fu. This lays a solid foundation for its heritage and development. Additionally, learners of Zhuang Kung-fu also participated in regional and national martial art competition and Zhuang Kung-fu fully shows its charm on sports arenas. In 2015, with approval of the municipal government of Nanning, Zhuang Kung-fu was inscribed on the Sixth Municipal List of Intangible Cultural Heritage.

功夫之精华。

壮族功夫在古代与军事斗争紧密相连，对古代人民捍卫自己家园、维护民族尊严有着重要意义。如今，壮族功夫仍活跃于壮族地区，人们以此来锻炼身体，既可以舒筋活骨、强身健体，又可以获得精神上的愉悦，俨然成为一项广受欢迎的体育活动。随着壮族功夫挖掘整理工作的开展，《中国传统体育志广西篇初稿》《广西拳械录》《广西少数民族传统体育》等书籍相继问世，记载了壮族功夫及其套路的相关内容。近年来，南宁市壮族功夫的传承活动也得到有序开展，南宁市民族文化艺术研究院组织专家下乡调研，收集整理壮族功夫资料，并与南宁市各高校及中、小学合作开展壮族功夫传承活动，将其列入体育课程教学当中，让新一代的青年人有机会接触壮族功夫、了解壮族功夫，为其传承与发展打下坚实的基础。另外，壮族功夫的学习者还参加了区级、国家级武术赛事，并荣获多个奖项，使壮族功夫在当今体育竞技舞台上大放异彩。2015年，壮族功夫经南宁市人民政府同意，列入第六批市级非物质文化遗产名录。

壮族功夫传承人黄受程在示范壮族功夫套路“霸王拳”
Huang Shoucheng, the Inheritor, is Demonstrating Skills of "Overlord Boxing"

壮族功夫传承人在示范壮拳套路“春秋大刀”
The Inheritor is Demonstrating the "Chunqiu Broad Sword"

宾阳露圩传统武术

Luxu Traditional Kung-fu in Binyang

项目名称：宾阳露圩传统武术

别称：露圩功夫

分布范围：露圩镇浪利村欧村、百合村平睦村等

入选名录：2018年第七批自治区级非物质文化遗产名录
2017年第七批市级非物质文化遗产名录

保护单位：露圩镇文化体育和广播影视站

代表性传承人：无

Element name：Luxu Traditional Kung-fu in Bingang

Alternative Name：Luxu Kung-fu

Geographical location and range：Oucun of Langli Village in Luxu Town, Pingmu of Baihe Village and others

Element inscribed list：In 2018 on the Seventh Autonomous Region List of Intangible Cultural Heritage
In 2017 on the Seventh Municipal List of Intangible Cultural Heritage

Competent body involved in safeguarding：Culture, Sports, Broadcasting and TV Station of Luxu Town

Representative inheritors：None

宾阳露圩传统武术表演
Performance of Luxu Traditional Kung-fu in Binyang

宾阳露圩传统武术训练
Practice of Luxu Traditional Kung-fu in Binyang

Luxu Traditional Kung-fu in Binyang is also called Luxu Kung-fu, it is a traditional martial art spread in Oucun of Langli Village in Luxu Town, Pingmu of Baihe Village and other 46 natural villages. From martial art used for defense country and homeland to an important belt connected blood and feelings, Luxu Kung-fu never stopped in inheriting.

According to old people in Luxu town, Luxu Kung-fu was introduced in the Song Dynasty. At that time people lived in isolated mountains and the economy is backward, so that it was difficult to find written document. However, as people in Luxu, exercising martial art is their daily necessity for martial art will protect homeland from foreign attack. Martial art is not only for defense but also for a strong body. As a result, worship for martial art is succeeded in Luxu Town.

Luxu Kung-fu is mainly succeeded in families, which protects its essence. Being similar to other traditional martial arts, only man could practice Luxu Kung-fu. Different families have different skills and techniques. Few of them exchange their own kung-fu with others and they are very conservative. In slack seasons (mainly during Spring Festival), the elderly in families will select descendants who are good at martial art and teach them Kung-fu as well as virtue of Kung-fu.

Luxu Kung-fu is included in southern kung-fu and is a practical close combat technique. People will use palm to parry fist, crash rivals with shoulder, hit with elbow and seldomly

宾阳露圩传统武术又名露圩功夫，是一项分布在露圩镇浪利村委欧村、百合村委平睦村及全镇46个自然村的传统武术技艺。从最初保家卫国、看家护院的功夫，到如今维系血脉和情感的重要纽带，露圩传统武术从未停下传承的脚步。

据露圩镇老辈人说，露圩功夫于宋朝传入，由于当地人民多居住在僻远山区，经济相对落后，因此露圩功夫很难找到相关的具体文字记载。但作为露圩的居民，练武是他们的日常功课，这主要因为功夫在动荡时可以维护家族领地不受外族侵犯，生活中不仅能够以此防身，又可以强身健体，所以，好武习武之风在露圩镇便得以代代相传。

露圩壮族武术主要是以家族传承为主，家族代代相传的形式使其精华得以保留，而且和许多祖传武术一样——传男不传女。各家族都有不同的表现形式。各个村不同的家族之间，在武功方面交流较少，都非常保守，对于自己的独门绝技一般不外传。传授的方式是在平时农闲时（主要是在春节期间），家族长者中的功夫好手负责传授武术、操练以及讲授武德。

露圩功夫为南派武功，是一种实用的近身战术，以硬桥硬马、拳打掌推、肩推撞、肘击为主，极少起脚。因为当地多山，道路不平，加上气候温和多雨，路边杂草繁茂，如在交手时起脚极容易摔倒，所以壮族前辈结合本地实际创造了适合当地环境的本土功夫，扬长避短、极富特色。露圩功夫的器械有棍、叉刀、耙等，各种日常生产生活用具都可当作武器，如：板凳、椅子、头巾、手巾、锄头等等。

如今的露圩功夫已从封闭逐渐走向了开放，在周边乡镇名声远扬，作为族人间维系血脉和情感的重要纽带，露圩功夫已成为露圩壮族圩逢节活动的一项重头戏。随着时代的发展，露圩功夫的意义不断丰富，成为促进民族融合、增进民族感情与交流的重要文化符号。

在露圩镇党委、政府、镇商会的大力支持下，2012年，露圩传统武术依托露圩镇商会成立了露圩镇功夫协会，这一协会的成立，使露圩功夫的影响力大大提高，同时，武术技艺也得到了很好的传承和发展。特别是从2014年起，镇党委、政府、镇商会提出创建蓝衣壮文化品牌以来，参与人群的增加、交流活动的开展，都使得露圩功夫在形式和内容上都有了质的飞跃。2017年，宾阳露圩传统武术经南宁市人民政府同意，列入第七批市级非物质文化遗产名录，2018年列入第七批自治区级非物质文化遗产名录。

move their feet. There are many mountains in local areas and the land is not flat. The weather is humid and grass thrived on the road sides. Jumping or moving feet will make people slip. Ancestors of Zhuang created local kung-fu based on local environment. With unique characteristics, this kung-fu makes best use of the advantages and bypasses the disadvantages. Stick, knife, rake and other daily used tools could be weapons of Luxu Kung-fu, including chair, bench, towel, handkerchief, hoe, etc.

Nowadays, Luxu Kung-fu gradually steps from exclusiveness to opening with high reputation in neighboring regions. As an important belt connected families and breed, Luxu Kung-fu has become a performance in festivals. With the development of society, connotation of Luxu Kung-fu is enriching. It is a cultural symbol to promote the integration of ethnic groups and enhance the relationship between different ethnic groups.

With the support of the party committee, local government and chamber of Luxu, in 2012, Luxu Kung-fu Association was established with the assistance from Luxu chamber. The establishment of association increased in influence of Luxu Kung-fu and the martial art is developed and inherited. After 2014, the party committee, local government and chamber of Luxu started to establish Lanyi Zhuang Cultural Brand. The increasement of participants and the operation of exchange lead to leap in quality and content of Luxu Kung-fu. In 2017, with the approval of the municipal government of Nanning, Luxu Traditional Kung-fu in Binyang was inscribed on the Seventh Municipal List of Intangible Cultural Heritage and inscribed on the seventh Autonomous Region List of Intangible Cultural Heritage in 2018.

马山加方上刀山下火海

Mashan Jiafang Climbing Sword Mountain and Stepping on a Sea of Fire

项目名称：马山加方上刀山下火海

别称：无

分布范围：马山县加方乡、古寨乡、里当乡、白山镇、百龙滩镇等各村及山里弄场；上林县镇圩瑶族乡、塘红乡、乔贤乡；忻城县遂意乡，北更乡；都安县龙湾乡、菁盛乡、百旺乡等

入选名录：2018年第七批自治区级非物质文化遗产名录

保护单位：马山县文化馆

代表性传承人：蒋智杰

Element name: Mashan Jiafang Climbing Sword Mountain and Stepping on a Sea of Fire

Alternative name: None

Geographical location and range: Jiafang Town, Guzhai Town, Lidang Town, Baishan Town, Bailongtan Town and other villages and mountain farms of Mashan County; Zhenxu Town of Yao Ethnic Group, Tanghong Town and Qiaoxian Town of Shanglin County; Suiyi Town, Beigeng Town of Xincheng County; Longwan Town, Jingsheng Town and Baiwang Town of Du'an County and others

Element inscribed list: In 2018 on the Seventh Autonomous Region List of Intangible Cultural Heritage

Competent body involved in safeguarding: Mashan County Cultural Centre

Representative inheritors: Jiang Zhijie

下火海
Stepping on a Sea of Fire

上刀山
Climbing Sword Mountain

马山加方乡地处马山县东部大石山区，大明山北麓，东连忻城遂意乡，本县古寨乡，西邻白山镇，南靠古零镇，北连里当乡，都安县龙湾乡。距县城40千米，全乡行政区域面积213平方千米，辖17个行政村，总人口30497人，聚居着壮、汉、瑶等民族。

马山加方上刀山下火海是古代腊月举行的一种驱邪避灾的仪式，是古时在绝境中引进来的，于明代弘治年间由姓蒋一户人家从湖南迁徙到加方乡加让村后传播，周边邻近县各乡镇尚无发现，是个鲜为人知的古老文化遗存，长期以来始终保持原汁原味，传承不息的原生态，相传至今已有五百多年历史。

Mashan Jiafang Township is located in Dashi mountain area in the east of Mashan County, north foot of Daming Mountain.It connects Suiyi Town of Xincheng and Guzhai Town of the County in the east, as well as BaishanTown in the west, Guling Town in the south, Lidang Township and Longwan Township of Du'an County in the north. It is 40 kilometers away from the county centre and has an administrative area of 213 square kilometers. It governs 17 administrative villages with a total population of 30497, and is inhabited by Zhuang, Han, Yao and other ethnic groups.

Mashan Jiafang's climbing sword mountain and stepping on a sea of fire is a ritual of exorcising evil spirits and avoiding disasters held during the last month of a lunar year in ancient times. It was introduced from the desperate situation in ancient times. During the reign of Hongzhi in the Ming Dynasty, a family with the name Jiang moved from Hunan to Jiarang village in Jiafang Township and started to introduce the ritual. It has not been found in neighboring counties and towns. It is a little-known ancient cultural existence. It has always kept its original flavor and passed on its original ecology for a long time. It is said that it has a history of more than 500 years.

According to historical records, the Nuo Opera cannot be complete without the ritual of climbing sword mountain and stepping on a sea of fire. Nuo opera is a kind of ritual of exorcising evil spirits and chasing epidemic diseases held in the ancient times in the last month of a lunar year. The situation of expulsion is expressed by singing and dancing acrobatics. The Nuo dance may be performed by a number of protagonists. The performers wear masks and crowns, four golden eyes, bear skin, and dagger-ax and shield. The performance will also make "Nuo" sounds through their mouths. Another kind of performance can be performed by 12 people with red hair, while wearing painted clothes, holding several feet long hemp whips in their hands, and swinging the whips to make sounds, as well as shouting the names of all

据史料记载，上刀山下火海来自傩戏。何谓傩戏？傩戏是古代在腊月举行的一种驱邪逐疫的仪式，驱逐的状况通过歌舞杂技之类动作来表现，傩舞或由主角若干人表演，表演者头戴面具和冠，金色四目，身穿熊皮，手执戈盾，口中发出“傩傩”之声。另外一种表演是由十二人，朱发画衣，手执数尺长麻鞭，甩动作响，并高呼各种专吃恶鬼，猛兽之神名，称十二神舞。后演变为“傩戏”。至今浙江、湖广等地流行傩戏表演。而加方乡加让村何家屯上刀山下火海是从傩戏中的一部分衍生出来的。

上刀山是在木梯上安装锋利的刀子作为梯级，赤足踏在利刃上蹬上蹬下，脚底的肌肤竟丝毫无损，并有大鼓、锣、钹、铙等相关器具助兴，表演非常惊险，扣人心弦。下火海则是在地上堆积燃烧的木炭，长近十余米，再由表演人依次

上刀山表演
The Perform of Climbing Sword Mountain

赤脚从红通通的炭上走过。

上刀山下火海作为地域文化的一种独特表现形式，历经百余年的传承流变而至今不衰，表现了这一民间文化的生命力，而且对加强文化认同，具有不可替代的重要作用。它的丰富内容和基本特征及其传承历史，在我国古文化中实属罕见，对它的抢救、传承和保护有着很高的价值。

kinds of evil spirits and demons. This performance is called the 12 Gods dance. Later, it evolved into "Nuo opera". Up to now, Nuo opera performances are popular in Zhejiang, Huguang and other places. However, the ritual of climbing sword mountain and stepping on a sea of fire in Hejiatun of Jiarang village of Jiafang township is derived from part of Nuo opera.

Climbing Sword Mountain: sharp knives are installed on a wooden ladder as steps, the performer will step on barefoot on the sharp edges, however his feet will not be hurt at all, and there are drums, gongs, cymbals, cymbals and other related instruments to boost the fun. The performance is very thrilling and exciting. Stepping on a Sea of Fire: the burning charcoal is piled up on the ground, nearly ten meters long, and then the performers walk barefoot on the red charcoal one by one.

As a unique form of regional culture, climbing sword mountain and stepping on a sea of fire have gone through more than 100 years' inheritance and changes, which shows the vitality of this folk culture and plays an irreplaceable role in strengthening cultural identity. Its rich content, basic characteristics and heritage history are rare in ancient Chinese culture, which have high value for its rescue, inheritance and protection.

法师为下火海者擦拭符水净脚
Mage Wipes Magic Water and Cleans Feet for Those Who Descend the Fire

第七章　传统技艺

Chapter Seven　Traditional Craft Skills

壮族服饰制作技艺

Dress Making Skills of Zhuang Ethnic Group

项目名称：壮族服饰制作技艺

别称：无

分布范围：广西壮族自治区及周边省份

入选名录：2014年第五批自治区级非物质文化遗产名录
2013年第五批市级非物质文化遗产名录

保护单位：南宁市民族文化艺术研究院（南宁市非物质文化遗产保护中心）

代表性传承人：蓝轲

Element name：Dress Making Skills of Zhuang Ethnic Group

Alternative name：None

Geographical location and range：Guangxi Zhuang Autonomous Region and the surrounding provinces

Element inscribed list：In 2014 on the Fifth Autonomous Region List of Intangible Cultural Heritage
In 2013 on the Fifth Municipal List of Intangible Cultural Heritage

Competent body involved in safeguarding：Nanning Ethnic Culture and Art Research Institute (Nanning Intangible Cultural Heritage Protection Centre)

Representative inheritor：Lan Ke

壮族服饰制作技艺是壮族独有的服装与配饰制作手工艺，是壮族传统文化的结晶，其制作成品中服装部分包括首服、身服、足服，身服包括上衣、下裳，足服包括鞋、袜等。配饰包括头饰、耳饰、颈饰、肩饰、胸饰、腰饰以及首饰等各种可穿戴的装饰物。纺纱、织布、染布是壮族最为常见的家庭手工技艺，壮族妇女擅用棉纱织布，染成黑色、蓝色或棕色并制成服装。壮族男子、女子服饰各有特色，体现出壮民族特有的审美观念。

自古以来，壮族人生活在中国西南边陲地区的广西及周边省份，如云南文山、贵州从江和广东连山等地，壮族服饰制作技艺也随之分布广泛。壮族人自古以来就以稻作农业为生，这不仅为壮族服饰的选材提供了丰厚的物质条件，还催生出壮族服饰独特的制作技艺与审美风尚。壮族先民在原始社会末期即掌握了纺织技术，汉代已人工种植麻，到了清代，棉织业进入繁荣时期。壮族服饰随着时代的变化不断变化：从清朝末年壮族女性穿大襟蓝干衣、长褶裙或宽裤，脚穿圆口绣花鞋，男性头包黑巾，着黑布对襟衣、黑布宽裤，穿土布鞋或龙凤鞋，到民国时期的女子穿唐装衣裤、半边围裙，男子穿对襟唐装衣、宽裤子、土布鞋以及黑布巾，壮族服饰虽少有变化，却始终保持着样式与色彩的民族审美特色。如今，壮族服饰形成了一套独特的形制，包括首服、身服、足服，以及与之配套的一套完整的制作技艺，包括纺织、印染、刺绣、佩饰工艺。

壮族服饰制作技艺一般分为纺织、印染、刺绣等手工艺。首先，将产于岭南的葛、麻、棉、蕉、竹、木等原料纺纱成线，织成布匹作为服饰面料。再将布匹染色，染色分为平染、蜡染、扎染、糯米染。通过刺绣工艺用各色丝线将动植物、花卉等吉祥图案绣于衣襟、袖口、裤脚、鞋面等处，图案纹样纷繁复杂，千姿百态。壮族各类配饰也由手工制成。

Dress making skills of Zhuang Ethnic Group is a unique handicraft to make dress and accessories, which is the crystallization of the traditional culture of Zhuang. The finished products include dress such as head clothing, body clothing and footgear, among which body clothing consists of upper clothing as well as bottom clothing and footgear consists of shoes and socks. Accessories include wearable accessories like headwear, earrings, necklaces, shoulder knots, brooches, waist decorations and hand ornaments. Spinning, weaving and dyeing are the most common household skills of the Zhuang people. Women of Zhuang Ethnic Group are good at weaving with cotton yarn and then dyeing the cloth into black, blue or brown to make clothing. The costume and dress of men and women of Zhuang have their own features respectively, which reflects the unique aesthetic concepts of Zhuang Ethnic Group.

Since ancient times, people of Zhuang began to live in the southwest Guangxi and its neighboring provinces of China, such as Wenshan Autonomous Prefecture of Yunnan Province, Congjiang County of Guizhou Province and Lianshan Autonomous County of Guangdong Province, from which the dress and accessory making skills of Zhuang Ethnic Group began to spread over other places. People of Zhuang Ethnic Group have been living on rice farming since a long time ago, which not only has provided colorful resources for the dress material selection, but also has promoted the development of the unique dress making skills and aesthetic fashion of Zhuang costumes. The ancestors of Zhuang mastered textile technology at the end of the primitive society. In the Han Dynasty, people began to plant flax artificially and the cotton industry began to flourish after entering the Qing Dynasty. The dress of Zhuang also changed with the times. For example, in the late Qing Dynasty, women of Zhuang often wore blouses, long pleated skirts or trousers, and embroidered shoes with round necks, but began to wear Tang suits and trousers as well as half apron after entering the period of the Republic of China. Similarly, the costumes of men of Zhuang also changed from black kerchiefs, beahraangcnac (a kind of Chinese-style jacket with buttons down the front), black cloth pants, cloth shoes or dragon and phoenix shoes to the Tang suits with buttons down the front, wide trousers, cloth shoes and black kerchiefs. Although the Zhuang costume has few changes, it has always maintained the ethnic aesthetic characteristics in style and color. Nowadays, the dress of Zhuang has formed a special set of clothing system including head clothing, body clothing and footgear, and a complete set of production techniques such as spinning, printing and dyeing, embroidery and accessory making.

The dress making skills of Zhuang Ethnic Group can be divided into spinning, printing and dyeing, embroidery and other handicrafts. First, raw materials produced in Lingnan areas such as kudzu vine, flax, cotton, broadleaf plants, bamboo and wood will be spun into yarn and woven into cloth so as to make dress. Then, the cloth will be dyed through techniques like plain dyeing, batik, bandhnu or dyeing with sticky rice. In addition, through the embroidery process, various kinds of silk threads are used to embroider plants, animals, flowers or other auspicious patterns on the front of the clothing, cuffs, bottom of trouser legs, vamps or other places. These patterns are often complicated and varied. By the way, accessories of Zhuang Ethnic Group are also made by hand.

The dress making of Zhuang Ethnic Group involves the coordination of various traditional handicrafts, such as dyeing and spinning, embroidery, silver carving and so on, which is an integration of handicrafts with distinctive characteristics of Zhuang Ethnic Group. The materials reflect the living environment and production mode of Zhuang Ethnic Group since ancient times. The simplicity and exquisiteness in style and color imply the special ideas and beliefs of Zhuang Ethnic Group, which contains profound ethnic cultural meanings. In terms of manufacturing skills, dyeing and cutting represent a sense of simplicity while embroidery and silver carving are exquisite and meticulous. Such special skill bears a strong ornamental value. The dress making skills of Zhuang Ethnic Group once was influenced by the making skills of Han costumes. Its development has represented the process of exchanges and integration of dress making skills between Zhuang and Han nationalities. Even today, people living in the settlement of Zhuang Ethnic Group still maintain the custom of making dress by hands. These skills have an important reference value for the study of traditional culture of Zhuang Ethnic Group.

At present, modern clothing fabrics are becoming increasingly diversified and traditional costumes has been more like formal dress rather than daily clothing. The inheritance of dress making skills of Zhuang Ethnic Group has suffered head wind and had few successors. In 2012, Nanning Ethnic Culture and Art Research Institute established a group to particularly protect the dress making skills of Zhuang Ethnic Group. The group members have made an in-depth exploration of these skills and raised funds every year to support the skills' inheritance and development. In 2014, with the approval of the People's Government of the Guangxi Zhuang Autonomous Region, the dress making skills of Zhuang Ethnic Group was inscribed on the Fifth Autonomous Region List of Intangible Cultural Heritage.

壮族服饰制作需由各类传统手工艺配合完成，如染织工艺、刺绣工艺、银器雕花制作等，是壮族特色手工艺之集成，其材质反映了壮族人民自古以来的生活环境以及生产方式，其样式以及用色于朴拙中见精美，寓意壮民族特殊的观念和信仰，蕴含着深厚的民族文化内涵。在制作技艺方面，染织与剪裁秀美朴拙，刺绣及银饰雕花精巧细致，工艺独特，具有极高的观赏价值。壮族服饰制作技艺受到汉服的影响，其发展历史体现了壮、汉民族之间服装制作技艺交流、融合的过程。直至今日，壮民族聚居地仍保持手工制作服饰的习惯，壮族服饰制作技艺对于研究壮族传统文化有重要参考价值。

目前，现代服饰面料日趋多元化，传统服饰具有礼服化的趋势，壮族服饰制作技艺虽有传承，却日渐式微，后继乏人。2012年，南宁市民族文化艺术研究院组织成立了壮族服饰制作技艺保护小组，对其进行调查挖掘，并每年筹集经费用于保护其传承与发展。2014年，经广西壮族自治区人民政府同意，壮族服饰制作技艺列入第五批自治区级非物质文化遗产名录。

为服饰刺绣
Embroidery for Clothing

壮族五色糯米饭制作技艺

Five-color Glutinous Rice Production Skill of Zhuang Ethnic Group

项目名称：壮族五色糯米饭制作技艺

别称：无

分布范围：广西壮族自治区

入选名录：2010年第三批自治区级非物质文化遗产名录
2007年第一批市级非物质文化遗产名录

保护单位：武鸣区文化馆

代表性传承人：黄硕英

Element name：Five-color Glutinous Rice Production Skill of Zhuang Ethnic Group

Alternative name：None

Geographical location and range：Guangxi Zhuang Autonomous Region

Element inscribed list：In 2010 on the Third Autonomous Region List of Intangible Cultural Heritage
In 2007 on the First Municipal List of Intangible Cultural Heritage

Competent body involved in safeguarding：Wuming District Cultural Centre

Representative inheritor：Huang Shuoying

用于上色的植物
Plants Used for Dyeing

Five-color glutinous rice is a traditional snack made of high-quality glutinous rice that dyed with various colored plants and cooked into steamed rice. Its name is originated from the five colors of the glutinous rice, including black, red, yellow, purple and white. This snack is regarded as a symbol of grain harvest and good luck by people of Zhuang Ethnic Group. Five-color glutinous rice is often used to worship ancestors or entertain relatives and friends on Tomb-Sweeping Day, the third day of the third lunar month or other traditional festivals every year.

Five-color glutinous rice production skill is widely spread in the settlements of Zhuang Ethnic Group. However, the legends of five-color glutinous rice are different in places. One of the legends said that the ancient people of Zhuang Ethnic Group highly praised concepts of "five directions", "five colors" and "five elements". In the legend of Zhuang Ethnic Group, there were five "Gods of Thunder" in charge of wind and rain who could control good weather and bumper harvest of the world in the east, west, south, north and the centre in the heaven respectively. The "five colors" referred red, green, black, white and yellow, which were in correspondence with

壮族五色糯米饭，是用多种植物将优质糯米染成彩色，并蒸煮成饭的一道传统风味小吃，因糯米呈黑、红、黄、紫、白五种颜色而得名。它被壮族百姓看作五谷丰登、吉祥如意的象征，在每年清明节和农历三月三等传统节日中，用来祭祖或招待亲友。

壮族五色糯米饭制作技艺流传于广西壮民族聚居地，其来历在广西各地有不同的传说。一说来自古代壮族人对“五方”“五色”“五行”观念的推崇。壮族传说中上天有五位“雷神”掌管风雨，分别在东、南、西、北、中五个方位，五神能保人间风调雨顺，五谷丰登。“五色”，即红、青、黑、白、黄，分别和“五行”中的金、木、水、火、土相对应，“五方”“五行”“五色”共同构成了神秘的信仰体系，五色成为天德或天意的象征，五色糯米饭之五色即源于此。除此之外，另有传说壮族五色糯米饭源于农历三月三祭祀青年英雄韦特桂，他曾运用聪明才智为百姓解除疾苦，最终被土皇帝杀害于枫树下。另有为纪念不畏强权、服毒抱枫树而死的一对男女青年而创五色糯米饭的说法，还有壮族青年特侬为了防止猴子抢夺母亲的糯米饭，便用枫叶将饭染成黑色的传说故事。目前可以确定的是，五色糯米饭的起源与壮族三月三有关，据地方志《民俗编》、清代顾禄的《五缘县图经》记载，农历三月初一至初十，五色香糯米饭便作为定情后的精致食品，被青年男女相互赠送品尝。《壮族通史》则记载五色糯米饭用于清明祭扫祖坟。

五色糯米饭主料为优质糯米，另有四种植物原料用于染色：红色用红兰草或大红叶、什锦叶，紫色用紫兰藤，黑色用嫩枫树叶，黄色用黄姜或黄花。制作方法十分讲究，每年农历三月初一和初二天未亮，人们需到田间野外采摘各种原料。制作时先把各色植物清洗干净，分别用石臼捣碎，加水煮沸成汁，将其过滤后装进容器，待染汁凉下来，将糯米分别浸泡于染汁染色，另留一部分用清水浸泡。经过4个小时以上的浸泡，糯米完全变软并充分着色，沥干水分，以黑、白、黄、红、紫的顺序分层放入木笼的竹篾网中，盖上蒸笼并锁上插销，放入蒸锅，烧柴蒸煮3个小时即成。

壮族五色糯米饭广泛流传于壮族民间，是古代壮族人生活智慧的结晶，反映了壮族对“五方”“五色”“五行”的崇拜与信仰，体现出壮族深厚的文化积淀，五色糯米饭制作技艺对研究壮族历史文化具有重要参考价值。五色糯米饭虽色泽鲜艳，却不添加任何化学制剂，由纯天然植物原料制成，至今，其制作技艺一直严格遵循传统。糯米饭的选材还具有一定的药用价值，其中红兰草具有补血作用，黄花或栀子花能够清热凉血，黑色的枫叶“止泄益睡，强筋益气力，久服轻身长年”，充分体现了壮族自古以来天人合一的哲学观念和善于摄取自然物质强身健体的智慧。民间有吃了“三月三的五色糯米饭，能消灾除疫、交好运”的说法。

the “five elements” of metal, wood, water, fire and earth. The “five directions”, “five elements” and “five colors” jointly built a mysterious belief system, in which the “five colors” symbolized the virtue or the will of the heaven. This is the first legend about the origin of the five-color glutinous rice’s name. In addition, there was another legend that the five-color glutinous rice was originated from the ritual activity to commemorate the young hero Wei Tegui on the third day of the third lunar month. He used his wisdom and intelligence to remove the sufferings of common people but was finally killed by the emperor under the maple tree. There are some other legends such as that the five-color glutinous rice were created to commemorate a young couple who did not fear of power and suicided by taking poison under the maple tree, and that Te Nong, a young man of Zhuang Ethnic Group, dyed the rice into black with maple leaves so as to prevent monkeys from robbing his mother’s glutinous rice. Although there are many different legends, what is confirmed is that the origin of the five-color glutinous rice is closely related to the festival on the third day of the third lunar month of Zhuang Ethnic Group. According to the local chronicle *Folk Custom Compilation* and the *Maps and Records of Wuyuan* written by Gu Lu in the Qing Dynasty, from the first day to the tenth day of the third lunar month, five-color glutinous rice would be used as a delicate food after young men and women pledging their love. However, *General History of the Zhuang* records that five-color glutinous rice was used for tomb-sweeping for ancestors.

Five-color glutinous rice is mainly made of high-quality glutinous rice. There are also four kinds of plants used for dyeing: peristrophe roxburghiana, ludwigia glandulosa, and assorted leaves are used for red color; Chinese wisteria is used for purple color; soft maple leaf is used for black color and yellow ginger or yellow flower are used for yellow color. The production methods of five-color glutinous rice are very particular. Before the dawn of the first and second days of the third lunar month, people need to go to the field to collect a variety of raw materials. During the making process, the plants of various colors need to be washed first and mashed with stone mortar. Then, people have to add some water into the thick liquid and boil it into juice. Next, people need to filter the juice and put it into a container. At the same time, a part of the glutinous rice will be dyed in different colored juice and another part will be soaked in clean water. After being soaked for over 4 hours, the glutinous rice will be completely soft and fully colored. Then, people need to drain the water and put the glutinous rice on the bamboo layers in the wooden cage in the order of black, white, yellow, red and purple. Finally, people only need to cover the steamer, lock the bolt and steamed the glutinous for three hours.

The five-color glutinous rice is widely spread among people of Zhuang Ethnic Group, which was the crystallization of the living wisdom of the ancient Zhuang Ethnic Group. It has reflected Zhuang people's worship and belief of "five directions", "five colors" and "five elements" as well as profound cultural accumulation, which bears important reference value for studying the history and culture of the Zhuang Ethnic Group. Although the colors of five-color glutinous rice are bright, they are made of pure natural plants rather than chemical additions. The production skill of this glutinous rice has been strictly following the tradition until today. The plants used for dyeing are seriously selected in accordance with their certain medicinal values. For example, peristrophe roxburghiana can nourish blood; yellow flower or gardenia can clear away the heat and cool blood; black maple leaf can "prevent diarrhea, improve sleep quality, strengthen muscle and vital energy and even can prolong life-span by taking for a long time", which fully represent Zhuang people's philosophical view on "harmony between man and nature" as well as their wisdom to strengthen health by taking natural substances. By the way, people also believe that eating five-color glutinous rice on the third day of the third lunar month can eliminate plagues and turn up trumps.

Currently, due to the change of the natural environment, the number of wild plants used for dyeing has been gradually decreasing. Coupled with the impact of the foreign cooking culture, the five-color glutinous rice production skill has been endangered and the successors are too little. Under such condition, the government of Wuming District has funded this skill by producing five-color glutinous rice for thousands of jins (a unit of weight, equivalent to 1/2 kilogram) to entertain distinguished guests and friends during the Song Fair on the third day of the third lunar month, and has explored and protected the planting of raw materials and related production tools. The five-color glutinous rice has become a unique snack in today's Zhuang ethnic areas. The protection and inheritance of its production skills is not only beneficial for the transmission of Zhuang ethnic culture, but also conducive to promote cultural exchanges and national unity between Zhuang and Han nationalities.

目前，自然环境的变化使野生染料植物逐渐减少，加之外来饮食文化的冲击，壮族五色糯米饭制作技艺逐渐濒危，后继无人。对此，每年壮族三月三歌圩期间，武鸣区政府投资制作上千斤五色糯米饭招待嘉宾友人，并对植物原料的种植和制作器具进行挖掘保护。五色糯米饭作为当今壮族地区独特的风味小吃，对其制作技艺的保护与传承，不仅有利于壮民族文化的传续，还有利于促进壮、汉民族经济文化交流与民族团结。

五色糯米饭
Five-color Glutinous Rice Production

南宁铁鸟酱料制作技艺

Nanning Tieniao Sauce Production Skill

项目名称：南宁铁鸟酱料制作技艺

别称：无

分布范围：兴宁区

入选名录：2012年第四批自治区级非物质文化遗产名录

保护单位：兴宁区文化馆

代表性传承人：杜瑜玲

Element name：Nanning Tieniao Sauce Production Skill

Alternative name：None

Geographical location and range：Xingning District

Element inscribed list：In 2012 on the Fourth Autonomous Region List of Intangible Cultural Heritage

Competent body involved in safeguarding：Xingning District Cultural Centre

Representative inheritor：Du Yuling

发酵
Fermenting

Nanning Tieniao sauce is originated from Xingning District of Nanning. It is an epitome of the cooking culture of Nanning and the surrounding areas. Sauce is an indispensable seasoning for Nanning people in daily cooking and banquets. The sauce of Tieniao brand is the most famous one in Nanning, whose products include soy sauce, Chinese wampee sauce, hoisin sauce, plum sauce and black vinegar. These products are all made by high-quality raw materials and exquisite production methods. With pure and good taste, these sauces are deeply loved by local people. Nowadays, the sauces have been sold in municipal cities in Guangxi, Guangzhou, Shanghai, northeastern China and even the southeastern Asia.

Xinging District is in the centre of Nanning. As the oldest district as well as the commercial and trade centre of Nanning, it is advanced in commerce, trade and service sectors. According to *The Records of Nanning Prefecture*, during the reign of the Emperor Xianfeng, Dashengxiang Sauce Store, the earliest sauce store of Nanning, was established jointly by two people of Guangdong Province Li Yiwan and Liang Dichen on Shajie Street (Jiefang Road today). Its most well-known product was soy sauce, which also brought a booming business of the store. In the first year of the reign of Emperor Tongzhi (A.D. 1862), workers of Dashengxiang Sauce Store Deng

南宁铁鸟酱料源于南宁市兴宁区，其制作技艺是南宁及其周边地区饮食文化发展的缩影。酱料是南宁人日常煮菜、酒宴不可或缺的佐料，“铁鸟”牌系列酱料在南宁最负盛名，主要产品有豉油、黄皮酱、海鲜酱、酸梅酱、黑米醋等，选料上乘，制作讲究，味道纯正，长期以来深受本地民众喜爱，还销往广西其他地市以及广州、上海、东北等地区，甚至远销东南亚。

兴宁区位于南宁市中心，作为南宁市最老的城区和商贸中心区，商贸服务业发达。据《南宁市志》记载，清咸丰年间，南宁最早的酱料铺——大盛祥酱园由广东人李亿万、梁迪臣合资开设于沙街（今解放路），产品以酱油最为有名，生意颇为兴旺。清同治元年（1862），大盛祥酱园的工人邓廷光、邓炬光在沙街开设万利酱园，并自设工场制作酱料。清光绪二十六年（1900），南宁酱料的生产进入鼎盛时期。“大盛祥”在民生路、水街、渡船口、中山路等路段，一连开了6家分店，酱油年产量达35万—40万公斤，酱料类产品达5万—8万公斤。当时南宁除大盛祥酱园和万利酱园外，还有义利、民生、陆裕德等几十家酱园，各地商贩往来不绝。常常一家酱园的酱料就多达几百大缸，酱料出售生意兴隆，或水运或马拉，场面壮观。1949年，在南宁仅剩大盛祥、广兴等7家店铺。1949年以后，“大盛祥”与其他酱园一起被合并为南宁市酱料厂，工厂地址即为南伦街原“大盛祥”加工厂厂址，年产200多吨酱料。到了20世纪80年代，南宁传统酱料产量已发展到年产500多吨。后来，南宁市酱料厂所生产的酱料产品注册“铁鸟”牌商标。

南宁铁鸟酱料的制作原料有黄豆、小麦粉、菌种、黄皮果、梅子、辣椒、蒜、精盐、生姜、葱、白糖。制作流程为：将优质黄豆、野生山黄皮果、上好的酸梅洗净，除去杂质，选上等小麦粉加水搅拌，高压蒸煮、制曲、发酵（分为保温发酵和天然发酵两种，为了保证酱脂香味醇厚，天然发酵需日晒夜露）、熬制、磨成酱料，再灌装，经灭菌后即为成品。

南宁铁鸟酱料味道鲜美纯正，入口回味无穷。它包含一系列不同的酱料，种类丰富，享誉周边县市，主打产品黄皮酱和老友酱，酸、甜、嫩、辣，迎合南宁人嗜酸、辣、甜的口味，且因食材不同而具有不同的功效。黄皮酱酸甜可口，提神开胃，解暑清热；老友酱辛辣醇厚，帮助消化并能防治感冒。铁鸟酱料制作考究，选材严格，要选用优质本地黄豆、龙州的野生山黄皮、野生鲜竹笋等。黄皮酱使用的配方，由大盛祥酱园的师傅传下来，至今保留着独特又固定的制作工艺。南宁铁鸟酱料制作技艺对研究南宁社会生活和历史文化、饮食习俗具有重要的参考价值。酱料独具南宁地方风味，形成了南宁特色饮食文化品牌。

近年由于饮食市场竞争激烈，在现代化批量生产制作的竞争下，传统饮食加工业效益低下，铁鸟酱料制作技艺日趋

Tingguang and Deng Juguang set up Wanli Sauce Store on Shajie Street and built workshop to make sauces. In the 26th year of the reign of Emperor Guangxu in the Qing Dynasty (A.D. 1900), the development of sauces in Nanning entered a period of great prosperity. Then, Dashengxiang established 6 branches on streets and roads such as Minsheng Road, Shuijie Street, the ferry of Nanning and Zhongshan Road. The annual output of its soy sauces reached 350,000 to 400,000 kilograms and the output of sauce-related products reached 50,000 to 80,000 kilograms each year. In addition to Dashengxiang and Wanli, there were also tens of sauce stores like Yili, Minsheng and Luyude with merchants ceaselessly coming and going. Each sauce store usually had hundreds of jars for sauce making and their business was flourishing. Traders from other places often used ships or horses to transport sauces, which created a splendid scene. By the year of 1949, there were only 7 sauce stores in Nanning such as Dashengxiang, Guangxing and some others. After 1949, Dashengxiang Sauce Store and other sauce stores were merged into Nanning Sauce Factory at the location of the original workshop of Dashengxiang, with an annual output of over 200 tons. Until the 1980s, the annual output of traditional sauce in Nanning exceeded 500 tons. Later, Nanning Sauce Factory registered the brand “Tieniao” for its products.

The raw materials of Tieniao sauces include soybean, wheat meal, zymophyte, Chinese wampee fruit, plum, chili, garlic, refined salt, ginger, Chinese onion and sugar. In production process, workers need to wash out the high-quality soybeans, wild Chinese wampee fruits and good plums to remove the impurities. Then, high-quality wheat meal and water will be added to the raw materials and stirred well with them. Through steaming or boiling by pressure cooker, koji-making, fermenting (Fermenting can be divided into insulation fermenting and natural fermenting. To maintain the mellow flavor of the sauce, sauce made by natural fermenting method need to experience weather exposure.), the semi-finished sauce will be decocted, grinded, canned and sterilized. Finally, the production process of sauce is finished.

With delicious and pure flavor, Tieniao sauces will leave a mellow aftertaste in people’s mouth. Tieniao sauces include a series of products of various kinds, which have gained a good reputation in the neighboring areas. The featured products of Tieniao are Chinese wampee sauce and Laoyou sauce, which are sour, sweet, fresh and spicy in taste, catering to Nanning people’s preference of sour, spicy and sweet flavor. Due to the different kinds of raw materials, these sauces have different effects to people’s health. The Chinese wampee sauce is delicious with slight sweetness and sour, which can refresh appetizer and beat summer's heat. The Laoyou sauce is mellow and spicy in taste, which can aid digestion and prevent people from getting cold. The Tieniao sauce is exquisite in production skill and fastidious in raw material selection. For example, it only chooses high-quality local soybeans, wild Chinese wampee fruit from Longzhou County and fresh wild bamboo shoots. The recipe of Chinese wampee sauce is passed on by the sauce makers of Dashengxiang and is still maintaining the fixed yet unique production skills until today. The production skill of Nanning Tieniao sauce bears an important reference value for studying Nanning's social life, history and culture as well as cooking skills. With the local characteristics in flavor, the Tieniao sauce has become a kind of cooking culture with distinctive Nanning features.

In recent years, due to the fierce competition of food market and the impact of modern volume production mode, the traditional food processing industry seems to be insufficient and the production skill of Tieniao sauce has been marginalized. To create more development space for Tieniao sauce, the company has increased its investment, open new markets and upgraded technologies. The government of Xingning District has brought the production skill of Tieniao sauce into the range of intangible cultural heritages that need to be safeguarded. In 2012, with the approval of the People's Government of the Guangxi Zhuang Autonomous Region, Nanning Tieniao sauce making skill was inscribed in the Fourth Autonomous Region List of Intangible Cultural Heritage.

边缘化。为了使其有更大的发展空间，企业加大投资，开发市场并改造技术。兴宁区政府将南宁铁鸟酱料制作技艺纳入城区非物质文化遗产保护范畴。2012年，经广西壮族自治区人民政府同意，南宁铁鸟酱料制作技艺列入第四批自治区级非物质文化遗产名录。

生产车间
Production Workshop

南宁老友粉

Nanning's Laoyou Rice Noodle

项目名称：南宁老友粉

别称：无

分布范围：南宁市及周边地区

入选名录：2008年第二批自治区级非物质文化遗产名录

2007年第一批市级非物质文化遗产名录

保护单位：南宁市民族文化艺术研究院（南宁市非物质文化遗产保护中心）

代表性传承人：无

Element name: Nanning's Laoyou Rice Noodle

Alternative name: None

Geographical location and range: Nanning City and the surrounding areas

Element inscribed list: In 2008 on the Second Autonomous Region List of Intangible Cultural Heritage

In 2007 on the First Municipal List of Intangible Cultural Heritage

Competent body involved in safeguarding: Nanning Ethnic Culture and Art Research Institute (Nanning Intangible Cultural Heritage Protection Centre)

Representative inheritor: None

酸笋
Sour Bamboo Shoots

老友粉配料
Laoyou Rice Noodle Ingredients

Nanning Laoyou Rice Noodle is a popular local delicacy in Nanning and the surrounding areas, which is a gold-lettered signboard of Nanning's traditional local snack. It once gained laurels such as "The Top Traditional Chinese Snack" and "The Most Popular Local Snack of Guangxi". It contains abundant materials and is exquisite in production. This rice noodle is well-known for its "sour and fresh, spicy and salt" flavor and its functions to refresh appetite, drive away coldness, and awaken mind, which has long been praised as "the breakfast for Nanning people".

Eating sour food is conducive to refresh appetite, beat the summer heat and quench thirst. In most of times, the climate in Nanning is usually hot, humid and rainy, thus Nanning people extremely prefer sour food. It was said that at the beginning of the 1900s, a group of good friends often came to a tea house for gatherings in the city. One day, one of the friends was bedridden due to the bad cold, thus other friends gathered together to discuss how to relieve the disease for this friend. At this time, the owner of the tea house suggested that he would be willing to cook a bowl of special noodles to cure the friend's disease. Therefore, he made a bowl of hot refined noodles with seasonings such as minced garlic, fermented soya beans, chili and sour bamboo shoots and then sent it to the friend. Surprisingly, on smelling the sour flavor, he suddenly got a great appetite and ate the noodles out. Then he began to sweat profusely and recovered from the illness. To express his appreciation, he made a plaque with four characters "Lao You Chang Lai (old friends often coming here)" to the owner of the tea house. As Nanning people

南宁老友粉是南宁及周边地区备受欢迎的风味小吃，是南宁传统小吃的金字招牌，曾荣获“中华名小吃”和“广西大众化优良风味小吃”等称号。其原料十分丰富，制作技艺考究，以“酸酸鲜，辣辣咸”的独特风味和开胃解腻、祛风散寒、通窍醒脑的功效深受百姓欢迎，一直以来被誉为“南宁人的早餐”。

食酸有利于开胃健体，解暑消渴，南宁气候湿热多雨，南宁人自古以来极喜酸味食物。据传20世纪初，邕城中心有一群好朋友经常到一茶馆聚会饮茶。某日，其中一人因患重感冒卧床不起，大家便讨论如何为朋友解除病痛。此时茶馆老板献计，特制一碗面条给他治病。以精致面条佐以蒜末、豆豉、辣椒、酸笋等，制成热汤面，送往朋友床边，朋友闻到酸香，胃口大开，吃完大汗淋漓，病痛即除。为表感谢，赠“老友常来”牌匾与茶馆老板。又因南宁人喜食米粉，茶馆老板便尝试用此烹面方法烹制米粉，备受食客热捧，老友粉因此得名。从20世纪初期诞生，南宁老友粉经历了近百年发展，曾遍布南宁的大街小巷，一度在南宁风味小吃史上占据霸主地位。

豆豉、蒜末
Soya Beans and Minced Garlic

南宁老友粉最初以爆香的蒜末、豆豉、辣椒、酸笋、牛肉末、胡椒粉、碎猪肉为佐料，酸辣鲜香。今天，纯正的南宁老友粉原料及调味料多达十几种：以猪骨熬制的鲜汤、新鲜切粉、纯正的猪油和浓香花生油、用传统方法腌制的酸笋和豆豉（以湿豆豉为佳）、腌制的酸辣椒、多种调料腌制的新鲜猪肉片、生抽、料酒、用料酒腌制的粉肠、猪肝、泡好的炸猪皮、牛杂料、香菜、葱花等。其烹制方法为：用大火将锅烧热，投入酸笋将其炒干，放入豆豉、蒜末、酸辣椒、足量的猪油爆炒，将辅料炒香以后放入猪肉、猪肝、猪皮翻炒，再加入料酒、酱油和米醋翻炒几下，倒入煮沸的汤水，放入肠粉，待汤水沸腾放切粉，盛入碗内，加几滴花生油，撒少许葱花、香菜即成。

南宁老友粉代表了岭南地区别具一格的饮食传统，它的选材以及制作工艺均与广西自然风物以及环境气候息息相关。经历了近百年的发展演变，南宁老友粉制作技艺不断积累经验，为能达到酸辣且鲜香的独特口味，选材考究，烹制讲究火候，佐料虽多样却需严格按照顺序放料，成为南宁饮食文化中最经典也最为成熟的工艺之一。南宁老友粉不仅价格实惠，而且酸香诱人，提神醒脑，祛风散寒，开胃解暑，

preferred eating rice noodles, the tea house owner also tried to cook rice noodles by using this method, which was widely praised by people who ate it. Then, such rice noodles got the name “Laoyou Rice Noodle”. From its creation in the early 1900s, Nanning Laoyou rice noodle has developed for over one hundred years, which once was at the dominating position in the history of Nanning local snacks.

At the very beginning, Nanning Laoyou rice noodle only had limited kinds of ingredients such as stir-fried minced garlic, fermented soya beans, chili, sour bamboo shoots, minced beef, pepper powder and minced pork, which enabled the rice noodle to be fresh in flavor yet sour and spicy in taste. Nowadays, the authentic Nanning Laoyou rice noodle has over ten kinds of raw materials and ingredients, including pork bone soup, fresh rice noodles, pure pork oil, mellow peanut oil, sour bamboo shoots and fermented soya beans (wet soy beans are better) made by traditional method, sour chili, pork slices pickled by several seasonings, light soy sauce, rice wine, sausages stuffed mainly with bean starch paste, pork liver, fried pork rind, beef offal, coriander and chopped green onion.

The production methods of Laoyou rice noodle are as follows:

(1) Dry the wok by the fire and then put the sour bamboo shoots in the wok to dry out.

(2) Add fermented soya beans, minced garlic, sour chili and enough pork oil into the wok and stir-fry them.

(3) After the ingredients are aromatic, add pork, pork liver and pork rind to the wok and continue to stir-fry them.

(4) After adding seasonings like rice wine, light soy sauce and rice vinegar to blend with other ingredients, the boiling pork bone soup can be poured into the wok.

(5) Put bean starch sausages first and the fresh rice noodles next after the soup boiling again.

(6) Put the rice noodles and other ingredients into a bowl and season them with several drops of peanut oil and a little chopped green onion. A bowl of Nanning Laoyou rice noodle is finished.

Nanning Laoyou rice noodle represents the unique cooking tradition of Lingnan areas. Its material selection and production skill are closely related to the environment and climate of Guangxi. Having experienced nearly a hundred years' development, the production skill of Laoyou rice noodles has been increasingly mature. To maintain the unique sour, spicy and fresh flavor, the making of Laoyou rice noodles is fastidious in material selection and strict in heat control. Although it consists of various ingredients, it still closely follows the cooking order. The production skill of Nanning Laoyou rice noodle has become one of the most mature and classic production skills in Nanning cooking culture. Laoyou rice noodle is not only affordable and attractive to people, but also has functions such as refreshing mind, driving away coldness, stimulating appetite and relieving summer heat, which has gained a solid mass base and attracted more and more foreign guests with a good reputation. To explore and protect Nanning Laoyou rice noodle has an important reference value for studying the history and culture of Nanning and is beneficial to promote the development of Nanning cooking culture.

Nowadays, the stores selling Laoyou rice noodles, once dotted the streets, have gradually out of the market. Driven by the profit, some rice noodle makers have simplified the production process and the flavor. The authentic production skill of Laoyou rice noodle is suffering a failure of passing down from past generations and facing a lack of successors. Under the high attention of the government, measures about revitalizing Nanning Laoyou rice noodle have been implemented. Various production skill competition, exchange activities as well as food festivals have been held to inject new impetus to the revitalization of Nanning Laoyou rice noodle.

因此具有深厚的群众基础，以良好的口碑吸引着海内外食客。发掘、保护南宁老友粉对研究南宁历史文化具有重要的参考价值，利于推动南宁饮食文化的发展。

目前，曾遍布大街小巷的老友粉店，受饮食多元化的冲击纷纷退出市场，某些老友粉制作商受利益驱动，使制作工艺简单化，正宗制作技艺逐渐失传，老友粉难再保持咸鲜酸香的正宗口味。正宗老友粉制作技艺濒临失传，人才断档。受政府部门的重视，南宁老友粉振兴措施开始进行，技能比赛与技艺交流、美食节等活动的举办使老友粉制作工艺重新振作。

把锅烧热
Drying the Wok by the Fire

翻炒配料
Stir-frying Ingredients

南宁生榨米粉制作技艺

Skill of Making Nanning's Raw Pressing Rice Noodle

项目名称：南宁生榨米粉制作技艺
别称：无
分布范围：南宁市各区县
入选名录：2016年第六批自治区级非物质文化遗产名录
　　　　　2015年第六批市级非物质文化遗产名录
保护单位：西乡塘区文化馆
代表性传承人：黄天玲

Element name: Skill of Making Nanning's Raw Pressing Rice Noodle
Alternative name: None
Geographical location and range: Counties and Districts of Nanning City
Element inscribed list: In 2016 on the Sixth Autonomous Region List of Intangible Cultural Heritage
　　In 2015 on the Sixth Municipal List of Intangible Cultural Heritage
Competent body involved in safeguarding: Xixiangtang District Cultural Centre
Representative inheritor: Huang Tianling

Raw pressing rice noodle is a traditional food for people of Guangdong and Guangxi to celebrate harvest as well as an indispensable food for people of Zhuang Ethnic Group during the season of harvest. It is fastidious in material selection and exquisite in production. Through various processes such as rolling, boiling, pounding, blending and kneading, the dough will be made into a ball shape, which can be pressed into noodles and cooked with other ingredients when it is needed.

Raw pressing rice noodle was originated from the most famous food street in Nanning, that is, Shuijie Street. As a representative of traditional food, the production skill of Shuijie raw pressing rice noodle has developed for over a hundred years. The raw pressing rice noodle was created by people of the ancient Luoyue state and derived from areas near Zuojiang River and Youjiang River as well as the southwest of Guizhou Province. The diligent and unsullied people of Zhuang Ethnic Group lived and farmed here for generations, gradually forming a culture of rice planting. A large area of rice planting enabled rice to be the staple food of Zhuang people and rice noodles became the most common food on Zhuang people's dining table. Most of the living areas of Zhuang people were humid and mountainous, thus eating sour food not only can drive away the coldness and humidity, but also is helpful for digestion. This is the reason why people of Zhuang Ethnic Group preferred to eat sour food since the ancient times. The raw pressing rice noodle, which is famous for its "slightly sour" and "slightly aromatic" flavor, has been introduced from rural areas to Shuijie Street for hundreds of years. During its development, the production of raw pressing rice noodle has constantly hewed to the traditional recipe and handmade making skills, which has been able to maintain the unique characteristics of not being rotten after long-time boiling, slippery mouthfeel and delicious taste. It is good to refresh appetite and suitable for both the old and the young, thus the raw pressing rice noodle has been welcomed by the locals and people from other places for decades.

The basic raw materials of Nanning raw pressing rice noodle are selected in proportion, including high-quality rice (1.5 kilograms), fresh pork (750 grams), green onion (500 grams), lettuce (500 grams), pickled Chinese cabbage (500 grams), purple perilla (500 grams), condensed soy (250 grams), raw oil (250 grams), ajinomoto (5 qians, a Chinese weight unit), salt (100 grams) and starchy flour (500 grams).

The production methods of raw pressing rice noodle are as follows:

(1) Soak the rice in water for one day and then drain the rice off.

(2) Dry the rice for one day and wash the rice out.

生榨米粉是两广农家为庆祝丰收制作的传统美食，是壮族民众在收获季节中必不可少的美味佳肴。它选料精细，制作考究，通过捏团、水煮、捣拌、手揉等多道工序将米粉制成粉团，随吃随榨，辅以配料制作而成。

生榨米粉来自南宁最为有名的美食街——水街，作为传统美食的代表，它的制作技艺自诞生至今已有100多年的历史。生榨米粉由古骆越人创制，起源于左右江流域和贵州西南部。勤劳淳朴的壮族人世代耕作于此，形成了独具民族特色的稻作文化。大面积的水稻种植使稻米成为壮族人的主食，米粉则成为广西人餐桌上最为常见的美食。壮族人生活在潮湿多山的地区，食酸不仅能够驱寒散湿，还能促进消化，维持身体健康，因此自古以来壮族喜食酸。而起源于壮乡的生榨米粉则以“微酸”和“微香”闻名，从农村传入南宁水街已有上百年的历史，在其发展过程中，恪守传统配方，坚持手工制作，继承了传统米粉久煮不烂、爽滑鲜香的独特风味，开胃健体，老少皆宜，深受本地及外地食客欢迎。

南宁生榨米粉的基本原料需按照比例选取：优质大米三斤、新鲜猪肉一斤半、生葱一斤、生菜一斤、酸菜一斤、紫苏半斤、酱油膏半斤、生油半斤、味精五钱、盐一两、生粉一斤。米粉制法为：先将大米浸泡一天，沥干，再存放一天，洗净、磨浆、压干，用手团成柚子状；而后入锅煮20分钟，待皮熟如柚子皮取出，存放发酵；待其散发出酸香味，放入生浆拌匀至不粘手，再放入榨筒，榨入开水锅至熟透捞起，加以配料即可食用。配料制作方法为：将猪肉、酸菜、紫苏、生菜爆炒后加入高汤、盐、味精、生粉，勾芡即成。

水街生榨米粉是岭南稻作文化的代表，制作技艺朴素简洁，食材较常见，以酸、辣、咸、香、鲜兼备的独特风味深受当地百姓喜爱，目前已形成独特而固定的制作方法。除此之外，有益于帮助生活在湿热地区的广西人开胃解腻、祛风散寒。研究水街生榨米粉技艺对了解近代南宁社会生活具有重要的参考价值，保护和传承水街生榨米粉制作技艺对于保护广西传统饮食文化、带动和促进南宁传统饮食文化精神建设、打造南宁特色饮食文化品牌十分重要。

随着现代社会生活节奏的不断加快，生榨米粉店日渐减少，生榨米粉传承技艺难以维持。为保护这一传统文化遗产，西乡塘区政府成立南宁生榨米粉保护工作领导小组，负责挖掘、保护和传承工作，并建设了广西第一座生榨米粉生产配送中央厨房，大力开展招商引资，统一配送经营，以“天天生榨米粉”为招牌进行品牌经营推广，为生榨米粉争取了市场效益，扩大了影响力。

加上调料，米粉做成
Add Some Ingredients, A Bowl of Raw Pressing Rice Noodle is Finished

(3) Grind out the thick liquid of rice and press to dry the rice again.

(4) Roll the rice dough into a pomelo shape.

(5) Boil the pomelo-shape dough for 20 minutes until the dough skin is similar as the pomelo skin.

(6) Take the dough out and store it to ferment.

(7) When the dough evolves a nice sour smell, the thick liquid of starchy flour can be put into the dough. Blend them well until the dough is no longer sticky to hand.

(8) Put the dough into presser to press the dough into noodles. Boil the noodles in the boiling water.

(9) When the noodles are thoroughly boiled, take them out and put them into the bowl. Add some ingredients. A bowl of raw pressing rice noodle is finished.

The ingredients making methods are as follows:

(1) Stir-fry the pork, pickled Chinese cabbage, purple perilla and lettuce in the wok.

(2) Thicken the ingredients with soup-stock, salt, ajonomoto and starchy flour.

Shuijie raw pressing rice noodle is a representative of rice planting culture in Lingnan areas with simple production skill and common ingredients. Its sour, spicy, salt and fresh flavor is deeply loved by local people, and it has formed a fixed yet unique production skill. In addition, it is helpful for Guangxi people who live in damp and hot areas to refresh appetite and drive away coldness. To study skill of making Nanning's raw pressing rice noodle bears a great reference value to understand modern social life of Nanning. To protect and inherit the making skill of Shuijie raw pressing rice noodle is significant for promoting the spiritual construction of traditional Guangxi cooking culture and establishing a special cooking culture brand for Nanning.

With the increasingly fast speed of social life, the number of stores selling raw pressing rice noodles is gradually decreasing and the inheritance of raw pressing rice noodles is suffering head wind. In order to protect this traditional cultural heritage, the government of Xixiangtang District has established a leading group for the exploration, protection and inheritance of Nanning's raw pressing rice noodle. The government has also built the first central kitchen for production and delivery of raw pressing rice noodle, which has begun to greatly invite investment, unify delivery and operation and popularize the brand with the slogan "Eating Raw Pressing Rice Noodles Every Day" to expand market efficiency and its influence.

扬美沙糕制作技艺

Skill of Making Yangmei's Sticky Rice Cake

项目名称：扬美沙糕制作技艺

别称：无

分布范围：江南区江西镇扬美村

入选名录：2012年第四批自治区级非物质文化遗产名录

保护单位：江南区文化馆

代表性传承人：杨文凯

Element name：Skill of Making Yangmei's Sticky Rice Cake

Alternative name：None

Geographical location and range：Yangmei Village of Jiangxi Town in Jiangnan District

Element inscribed list：In 2012 on the Fourth Autonomous Region List of Intangible Cultural Heritage

Competent body involved in safeguarding：Jiangnan District Cultural Centre

Representative inheritor：Yang Wenkai

扬美沙糕是广西南宁扬美古镇的著名小吃，松软香甜，被称为“扬美三宝”之一。始建于宋朝，在明清时代作为商贸集散地的扬美村，经济文化一度繁荣，伴随着扬美古镇的出名，扬美沙糕销路甚广。作为人们十分喜爱的小吃以及赠送亲朋好友的佳品，扬美沙糕远销至两广地区及东南亚，沙糕制作技艺传承至今，薪火不断。

江南区江西镇扬美村位于广西壮族自治区南宁市西部，始建于宋代，交通便利，江水清幽，景色宜人，徐霞客曾评价它“自南宁来，过右江口，岸山始露石，至扬美江，石始奇……余渭阳朔山峭濒江，建溪水激多石，无此岸之石，无此石之奇”。这里气候温和，雨量充沛，农作物生长以香蕉、水稻、玉米等为主。由于独占水路优势，扬美村迅猛发展，至明、清时期成为南宁市周边的主要商品集散地，并因此带动建筑业和手工业不断发展壮大，至今留有清代一条街、魁星楼、黄氏庄园、明代古屋、五叠堂等古代建筑。扬美沙糕起源于明、清时期，当时即为扬美特色食品之一，其制作技艺流传至20世纪四五十年代，出现了很多作坊。

扬美沙糕的主料为糯米和白糖，根据口味可添加绿豆粉、芝麻、花生等。制作扬美沙糕，首先将白糖加入水中，加热搅拌熬制成糖浆。选取优质糯米，用铁锅炒熟炒香，再磨成粉状，放置一段时间自然吸潮，制成沙糕粉。将芝麻、花生等馅料入锅焙香，再晾凉磨粉。按2：1的比例将糕粉和糖浆、芝麻、花生等馅料拌均匀，用木筒碾压至湿润后装模压实，等模中糕粉凝结至手碰不散再取出，按规格切成块状，加上精美的外包装即成。

扬美沙糕品种多样，绿色天然，有芝麻馅、花生馅、莲蓉馅、枣蓉馅、水晶馅、八宝馅等，香甜可口。经百年流传，扬美沙糕制作至今已形成独特而固定的工艺，从食材选择到制作方式各有讲究，不仅味道软糯香甜，还具有清热解暑、明目清肝、养胃健脾的功效，深受当地民众喜爱，成为

Yangmei sticky rice cake is a famous snack of the Yangmei Ancient Town of Nanning in Guangxi. It is soft and sweet and is known as one of the “Three Treasures of Yangmei”. Founded in the Song Dynasty and as a commercial centre in the Ming and Qing Dynasties, Yangmei Village once was flourished in economy and culture. With the fame of Yangmei Ancient Town, Yangmei sticky rice cake enjoys a large market. As a snack loved by people and a good gift for family and friends, Yangmei sticky rice cake has been sold to Guangdong, Guangxi and the southeast Asia. The making skill of this sticky rice cake has been passed down from generation to generation.

Initially founded in the Song Dynasty, Yangmei Village of Jiangxi Town of Jiangnan District is located in the west of Nanning of Guangxi with convenient transportation, clear river and beautiful scenery. Xu Xiake, a geographer of the Ming Dynasty, once commented Yangmei Village like this: “Starting from Nanning and passing through the Youjiang River, rocks begin to appear in the mountains. After arriving at Yangmei River, the shapes of rocks become rare and strange... Sushan Mountain in Weiyang is cliffy near the river and Chien River is torrential and stony, but the stones of these two places are not as same and rare as stones in Yangmei”. With mild climate and abundant rainfall, the major crops here are banana, rice and corn. Due to the special advantage of waterway, Yangmei village developed rapidly. During the Ming and Qing Dynasties, it became a major distribution center of commodities around Nanning City and promoted the development of construction industry and handicraft industry. Until today, Yangmei Village still retains ancient buildings such as street of the Qing Dynasty, Kuixing Pavilion, Huang’s Manor, ancient houses of the Ming Dynasty and Wudie Hall. Yangmei sticky rice cake was originated in the Ming and Qing Dynasties. It has been one of the special snacks of Yangmei from that time. Until the production skill passed down to the 1940s and 1950s, many workshops making Yangmei sticky rice cake appeared. The sticky rice cakes made by these workshops found a good sale in other cities of Guangxi, Guangdong and southeast Asia.

Yangmei sticky rice cake is mainly made of glutinous rice and white sugar, with mung bean flour, sesame and peanuts added to taste.

The production steps of Yangmei sticky rice cake are as follows:

(1) Add sugar to the water. Heat and stir the sugar to make syrup.

(2) Put high-quality glutinous rice into iron pot. Stir-fry the glutinous rice until it evolves a nice smell.

(3) Grind the glutinous rice into powder. Leave for a period of time to absorb moisture naturally so as to make it into sticky rice cake flour.

(4) Bake sesame, peanuts and other fillings in a wok, then cool them down and grind them into powder.

(5) Blend the rice cake flour and fillings like syrup, sesame and peanuts together in the ratio of 2:1. Roll the mixture to a wet condition by wooden cylinder.

(6) Compact the mixture into the model. Take it out until the mixture is solid and not loose when touching by the hand.

(7) Cut it into pieces in accordance with the size. Decorate them with outer packing. The production of Yangmei sticky rice cake is finished.

Yangmei sticky rice cake is numerous in variety, including rice cakes with sesame filling, peanut filling, lotus filling, date jam filling, crystal-like filling and mixed filling. Over the past hundred years, Yangmei sticky rice cake has formed a fixed yet unique production skill with exquisite material selection and production method. It not only has soft mouth feel and sweet taste, but also has the functions of beating the summer heat, brightening eyes, clearing liver and nourishing stomach. It has been deeply loved by local people and became one of the highlights of Nanning traditional cuisine. Protecting and inheriting the production skill of Yangmei sticky rice cake plays an important role in protecting and studying traditional cooking culture of Nanning as well as in expanding its influence.

Currently, due to the impact of foreign food culture and the development of diversified modern food, some traditional food has gradually faded out of people's life. As the number of workshops making Yangmei sticky rice cake has decreased, the inheritance of the making skill of the sticky rice cake has suffered a head wind. In order to protect this cultural heritage, the government of Jiangnan District has organized a team of intangible cultural heritage to investigate Yangmei ancient town for many times and further established protection measures. With the development of tourism in Yangmei ancient town, new varieties of Yangmei sticky rice cake have been introduced into market and its popularity has been improved.

南宁传统美食中的一大亮点。保护和传承扬美沙糕制作技艺对保护南宁传统饮食文化，研究南宁饮食习俗，扩大南宁饮食文化的影响力具有重要作用。

目前，由于外来饮食文化的冲击以及现代饮食多元化的发展，不少传统饮食逐渐淡出百姓生活，扬美沙糕专业作坊减少，沙糕制作技艺难以为继。为了保护这一文化遗产，江南区政府组织非物质文化遗产小组多次到扬美古镇实地考察，并进一步建立保护措施。随着扬美古镇旅游业的发展，扬美沙糕不断推出新品种，知名度一再提升。

制成的杨美沙糕
Completion of Yangmei's Sticky Rice Cake

扬美豆豉制作技艺

Skill of Making Yangmei's Fermented Soya Bean

项目名称：扬美豆豉制作技艺

别称：无

分布范围：江南区江西镇扬美村

入选名录：2010年第三批自治区级非物质文化遗产名录

2010年第三批市级非物质文化遗产名录

保护单位：江南区文化馆

代表性传承人：杜学芬

Element name: Skill of Making Yangmei's Fermented Soya Bean

Alternative name: None

Geographical location and range: Yangmei Village of Jiangxi Town in Jiangnan District

Element inscribed list: In 2010 on the Third Autonomous Region List of Intangible Cultural Heritage

In 2010 on the Third Municipal List of Intangible Cultural Heritage

Competent body involved in safeguarding: Jiangnan District Cultural Centre

Representative inheritor: Du Xuefen

将发酵的豆子放在竹簸箕中
Placing the Fermented Black Soybeans in the Indoor Wooden Bamboo Basket

放置15天
To Ferment Naturally for Two times Through 15 Days

Yangmei fermented soya bean is a special seasoning of fermented soybean products of Yangmei ancient town, which is also known as the "Three Treasures of Yangmei" together with Yangmei mustard and Yangmei sticky rice cake. Fermented soya bean was named "You Shu" or "Shi" in ancient times, which was seasoned by five different flavors. Its unique flavor is very attractive for people no matter as a food or condiment. Yangmei fermented soya bean is strict in material selection. The soybean has to be plump in size, bright in color and mellow in flavor. From the Qing Dynasty to today, Yangmei fermented soya bean has been famous for its "natural, handmade, non-additive" characteristic and "good handfeel, good mouthfeel and good quality".

Yangmei fermented soya bean was originated from Yangmei ancient town on the bank of Zuojiang River. The ancient town was founded in Song Dynasty along the river. It is a good place with beautiful scenery and outstanding people. In the Qing Dynasty, the ancient town was quite flourishing. Nowadays, there are still old streets, clear water, golden beach, rare stones, strange trees, and other unique landscapes as well as 25 sites of ancient buildings of Ming and Qing Dynasties, that are one of the ten famous landscapes of Nanning. Yangmei ancient town was an important commercial port with eight wharves in its heyday. There is a poem goes that "the sterns of big boats connect with the prows of small ones; people from all directions speak endlessly with different dialects; thousands of ship lights are on at night, twinkling like stars on river surface". Commodities within the circumstance of a hundred of li (a Chinese length unit) would be distributed

扬美豆豉是来自扬美古镇的特色发酵豆制品调味料，与扬美梅菜、扬美沙糕并称为“扬美三宝”。豆豉古称“幽菽”，也叫“嗜”，“五味调和，需之而成”，无论作为食物抑或调料，其独特风味都十分诱人。扬美豆豉选料严格，豆豉颗粒饱满，色泽透亮，香味浓郁，自清代流传至今，因“纯天然，纯手工，纯绿色”和“手感好，口感好，质感好”名扬广西。

扬美豆豉源于左江之畔的扬美古镇，古镇自宋代沿江而建，山水秀丽，人杰地灵，明清时期颇为繁荣，现留有老街、碧水、金滩、奇石、怪树等独特景观，明、清古建筑25处，是南宁市十大景观之一。古镇在兴盛时期是重要商埠，有八座码头，“大船尾接小船头，南腔北调语不休；入夜帆灯千万点，满江钰闪似星浮”，方圆百里商品集散于此，贸易活动频繁，壮、汉民族交融使这里传统文化积淀颇深，其中民间手工艺尤被人称道，扬美豆豉制作技艺即为其中一种。扬美古镇最有名的豆豉制作坊“杜家坊”始建于清光绪年间，由此可以推断，扬美豆豉制作技艺最迟始于光绪年间，距今至少有百余年的历史。历史上扬美豆豉老字号作坊有“广成号”“建华号”“杜家坊”等，鼎盛期时每年产量

扬美豆豉
Yangmei's Fermented Soya Bean

可达七八万斤，远销至福建、上海等地。今天，豆豉作坊仅剩“杜家坊”一家，其豆豉制作技艺经四代传承，依然飘香扬美。

扬美豆豉的原料为黑豆、食盐和水。制作流程为筛选黑豆、洗涤、浸泡、沥干、蒸煮、冷却、制曲、洗豉、浸焖、拌盐、发酵、晾干、成品。首先筛选出成熟且颗粒饱满、肉多皮薄的新鲜黑大豆，用水反复清洗，洗去杂质，然后用40摄氏度的温水将其浸泡约150分钟，再蒸煮15分钟。将煮熟的黑豆冷却至35摄氏度左右，接种沪酿进行制曲，一般时间为34个小时。制曲后需洗去附着在豆曲表面的孢子和菌丝，沥干水放于簸箕，再置于室内木盆或竹围里自然发酵，发酵需经过两次，用时约15天。最后将经过二次发酵的黑豆取出，拌上食盐晒干为成品。

扬美豆豉含有丰富的氨基酸和大量的维生素B1、蛋白质、脂肪、钙、磷、铁等营养物质，具有良好的保健功效，不加盐的豆豉可治疗痰多、胸闷、消化不良等症状，解表清

here and the trade activities were quite frequent in this place. The integration of Zhuang and Han nationalities promoted the accumulation of traditional cultures, among which the folk handicraft was particularly praised. The making skill of Yangmei fermented soya bean was one of them. Du's Workshop, the most famous fermented soya bean making workshop in Yangmei ancient town, was found in the reign of the Emperor Guangxu in the Qing Dynasty. Therefore, it can be inferred that the production skill of Yangmei fermented soya bean started in the Guangxu years at latest, with a history of at least 100 years. Actually, there were “Guangchen Brand”, “Jianhua Brand”, “Du's Workshop” and some other time-honored workshops of fermented soya been in the history. During the peak time, the annual output of fermented soya bean could reach 35,000 or 40,000 kilograms, which found a good sale in Fujian, Shanghai and other places. Today, Du's Workshop is the only left workshop producing fermented soya bean, whose making skill has been passed down for four generations and is still well-known by people.

The raw materials of Yangmei fermented soya bean are black soya bean, salt and water. Its production procedures include black soya bean selection, washing, soaking, draining, steaming, cooling, making koji, washing, simmering, blending with salt, fermenting and drying.

The detailed production methods of Yangmei fermented soya bean are as follows:

(1) Select the mature and full soybeans with thin coat. Wash the soybeans repeatedly until removing all impurities.

(2) Soak the beans for about 40 minutes in water of 40 Celsius degree and then steam them for 15 minutes.

(3) Cool the steamed black soybeans to 35 Celsius degree and then make koji with Huniang Aspergillus oryzae for about 34 hours generally.

(4) Wash off the spores and mycelium attached to the surface of koji and drain the water on a dustpan.

(5) Place the fermented black soybeans in the indoor wooden basin or bamboo basket to ferment naturally for two times through 15 days.

(6) Take out the black soybeans after secondary fermentations. Mix them with salt and dry them again. The production of fermented soya beans is finished.

Yangmei fermented soya bean is rich in amino acids and a large number of Vitamin B1, protein, fat, Ca (calcium), P (phosphorus), Fe (iron) and other nutrients, which has a good healthcare effect. The fermented soya bean without salt can cure the symptoms of expectoration, chest distress, dyspepsia, etc., and can also clear away heat and toxic materials in the body. In addition, Yangmei fermented soya bean, which is strictly processed by traditional techniques, has a strong flavor of soy sauce and a slightly pungent taste. No matter as a seasoning, side dish or main dish, it is deeply loved by the common people and occupies a place in the traditional diet of Nanning. Being different from ordinary fermented soya beans, the black beans selected by Yangmei fermented soya beans have thin coat and full size. Thanks to the environmental advantages of Yangmei's clean soil and fresh products, Yangmei fermented soya bean has better taste and higher nutritional content. Being once regarded as the most important material in cooking by the imperial chef of the Qing Dynasty, Yangmei fermented soya bean has become one of the most common ingredients on people's dining table today. The exploration, saving and protection of the making skill of Yangmei fermented soya bean play an important role in the study of traditional food culture in Nanning and surrounding areas.

Affected by the rapid economic development and diversified diet, Yangmei fermented soya bean, which once flourished in the surrounding areas of Nanning, is now facing a survival crisis. The number of Yangmei fermented soya bean workshops is gradually decreasing, and the inheritance of production skill of Yangmei fermented soya bean has suffered a head wind. In recent years, the government of Jiangnan District of Nanning has taken a series of protection measures, including holding training activities, cultivating successors, and introducing a series of dishes related to fermented soya beans by taking advantage of the tourism in Yangmei region, and intensified efforts to promote the inheritance of fermented soya bean production skill.

热，透疹解毒。除此之外，经传统技艺严格加工的扬美豆豉具有浓郁的酱香味，口感稍辛涩，作为佐料或配菜、主菜都深受百姓喜爱，在南宁市传统饮食中占有一席之地。与一般豆豉不同的是，扬美豆豉制作所选黑豆皮薄肉多，得益于扬美水土洁净、物产新鲜的环境优势，因此其口感更佳，营养含量更高。自清代御厨作为首选材料到如今进入千家万户的普通菜肴，扬美豆豉成为餐桌上最为常见的食材之一，发掘、抢救、保护扬美豆豉制作技艺对研究南宁及周边的传统饮食文化具有非常重要的作用。

如今受经济快速发展以及饮食多元化的影响，曾经在南宁周边盛极一时的扬美豆豉也面临着生存危机，扬美豆豉作坊逐渐减少，扬美豆豉制作技艺难以为继。近年，南宁市江南区政府采取一系列保护措施，举办培训活动，培养接班人，利用扬美地区的旅游优势推出一系列与豆豉相关的菜肴，加大力度推动扬美豆豉制作技艺的传承。

豆豉制成
The Production of Fermented Soya Beans is Finished

宾阳邹圩陶器制作技艺

Skill of Making Binyang's Zouxu Pottery

项目名称：宾阳邹圩陶器制作技艺

别称：无

分布范围：宾阳县邹圩镇下窑村、新窑村、江口窑村

入选名录：2016年第六批自治区级非物质文化遗产名录

2015年第六批市级非物质文化遗产名录

保护单位：宾阳县文化馆

代表性传承人：颜长希

Element name：Skill of Making Binyang's Zouxu Pottery

Alternative name：None

Geographical location and range：Xiayao Village, Xinyao Village and Jiangkouyao Village of Zouxu Town in Binyang County

Element inscribed list：In 2016 on the Sixth Autonomous Region List of Intangible Cultural Heritage

In 2015 on the Sixth Municipal List of Intangible Cultural Heritage

Competent body involved in safeguarding：Binyang County Cultural Centre

Representative inheritor：Yan Changxi

Binyang's Zouxu Pottery is made from Zouxu Town's speical red clay, which needs to be repeatedly refined and fired. This kind of pottery is simple and elegant in shape and it is a kind of indispensable utensil for people living in rural areas. Zouxu pottery has various types of products, such as porcelain, bowl, basin, pot and kettle. Different vessel shapes can be used to hold water, wine, oil and various acid products, etc. It has the irreplaceable advantages of no pollution, no seepage of water, oil and other materials. The making skill of Binyang's Zouxu pottery has inherited the pottery making skills of China from thousands of years ago. It was introduced to Zouxu Town in Binyang County from other places in the Qing Dynasty. After generations of craftsmanship inheritance, the making skill of Zouxu pottery has formed a complex and exquisite feature.

Zouxu Town is located in the northeast of Binyang County with convenient transportation. It is a settlement for Zhuang, Han and Yao nationalities, among which residents of Han Ethnic Group is the most. According to historical records, merchants coming to do business here made Zouxu Town a very busy rural market in Binyang County. Therefore, the ancestors of Jiangkouyao Village, Xiayao Village and Xinyao Village took this place as a geographically treasured place and settled here, passing on the pottery making skills from generation to generation. At the end of Emperor Qianlong period of the Qing Dynasty, Zouxu pottery making skills were brought back by several ancestors with surnames Yan, Su, Feng, Liang and Yuan from other places. Until the 1950s, villagers in these three villages still made living by making and selling pottery. After the year of 1949, Zouxu pottery gained great attention from the government and began to develop rapidly. However, after the 1990s, affected by the similar products in the market, the production and sales of Zouxu pottery has gradually entered a low ebb.

Binyang's Zouxu pottery is made by hand with complicated and exquisite skills. The production procedures of Zouxu pottery include mud washing, mud drying, mud filtering, pugging, blanking, blank drying, enamel frit making, glazing, secondary drying, loading of kiln, firing and drawing, among which blanking and enamel frit making are the most important procedures. The masters of blanking need to go through strict training so that they can use their fingers to quickly make the clay on the turntable into products with different sizes and shapes.

Binyang's Zouxu pottery is made by natural mud and fired at high temperature. It includes various types of products used for containing food, cooking oil and pickled products,

陶窑
Pottery Kiln

宾阳邹圩陶器是用宾阳县邹圩镇特有的红泥，反复炼制后烧制而成的陶制器皿，器形古朴精美，是乡间百姓居家不可或缺的生活器具。邹圩陶器有瓷、钵、盆、罐、壶等种类，不同器形可用于盛水、酒、油以及各种酸制品等，具有不污染、不渗水、不渗油等其他材质的器皿不可替代的优点。宾阳邹圩陶器制作技艺传承了我国几千年的制陶工艺，于清代乾隆末年从外地传入宾阳县邹圩镇，经世代匠心传承，工艺复杂且考究。

邹圩镇位于宾阳县城东北面，交通便利，是壮族、汉族、瑶族杂居之地，且汉族居民居多。据史料记载，商人前来经商，使邹圩镇成为宾阳县极为热闹的乡间集市，因此江口窑、下窑和新窑村的先祖们将此作为风水宝地并落脚于此，世代传承陶器制作技艺。清乾隆末年，邹圩陶器制作技艺由颜、苏、冯、梁、袁等姓氏的几位先祖从外地拜师学艺带回。直至20世纪50年代，这三个村的村民均以制作、贩卖陶器为生。1949年以后，邹圩陶业受政府部门的重视，发展迅速，陶器生产、销售进入鼎盛时期。20世纪90年代以后，受到市场同类产品的冲击，邹圩陶器制作与销售逐渐步入低谷。

宾阳邹圩陶器均为手工制作，技艺复杂考究，其工序大约有洗泥、晒泥、滤泥、练泥、制坯、晾晒坯、制釉、过釉、再晾坯、装窑、烧窑、出窑等10多道，其中以制坯、制釉尤为关键。制坯师傅需经过严格训练，靠指尖功夫迅速将抟车上的泥团抟制出不同规格、形状的产品。

宾阳邹圩陶器以天然泥料制作，经由高温烧制而成，盛装各类食物、食用油以及腌制品，不易变质，无污染无公害，卫生环保。其器形、花色可根据市场的需求灵活创造，但从选泥、制泥、制坯、过釉到烧制成品均以家庭隐秘性传承的方式延续，规模较小，十分珍贵。邹圩陶器制作技艺虽由外地传入，但在传承过程中可根据当地泥土以及气温等特殊状况不断改进完善，它既传承了中华民族五千年的制陶技艺，又具有民族特色，保护、传承邹圩陶器制作技艺对于保护、研究民族传统文化具有重要意义。由于邹圩陶器具有不同于其他器皿的特殊贮存功能，是乡间民众生活中的必需品，并且以此获得销售市场，因此保护与传承其制作技艺并开发新的陶制品，也具有满足人民群众对生活用品的需求和促进社会经济发展的实用价值。

由于社会经济的发展，目前江口窑许多制陶艺人已迁移他村，陶器生产难以为继，电饭锅、电茶壶等现代产品的出现使传统陶器的需求量大大减少，青年人也多为经济利益外出另谋职业，陶器制作传承人出现青黄不接的濒危状况。为保护邹圩陶器制作技艺，宾阳县文化主管部门和县文化馆将其资料搜集整理，有效开展各项保护工作，县政府划拨经费，开展项目普查，筹措五年保护计划。

which are not easy to deteriorate the food and are pollution-free, sanitary, and environmentally-friendly. Its shapes and colors can be flexibly created according to the market demand. But the selection of mud, mud making, blanking, glazing and the firing of finished products are in the way of small-scaled family inheritance, thus this kind of pottery is very precious. Although the making skill of Zouxu pottery was introduced from other places, it has been constantly improved in accordance with the local soil and air temperature. It not only inherits China's five-thousand-year traditional pottery making skill, but also bears ethnic characteristics. The protection and inheritance of Zouxu pottery production skills are of great significance for protecting and researching traditional ethnic cultures. Because Zouxu pottery has the special storage function which is different from other vessels, it is a necessity in the life of the rural people, and can find a good market. Therefore, protecting and inheriting its production skill and developing new pottery products also have a practical value of meeting people's demand for daily necessities and promoting social and economic development.

Nowadays, due to the social and economic development, many pottery makers in Jiangkouyao Village have moved to other villages, thus the production of pottery is hard to sustain. The emergence of modern products such as electric cookers and teapots has greatly reduced the demand for traditional pottery, and more and more young people begin to seek other jobs for economic benefits, thus the number of people who are willing to make Zouxu pottery is confronting with a temporary shortage. In order to protect Zouxu pottery making skill, the cultural department and culture centre of Binyang County have collected and sorted out the materials and effectively implemented various protection work. The government of the county has also allocated funds, carried out the project surveys, and made the five-year protection plan.

成型
Finishing

宾阳油纸伞制作技艺

Skill of Making Binyang's Oil Paper Umbrella

项目名称：宾阳油纸伞制作技艺

别称：无

分布范围：宾阳县陆村、潘村

入选名录：2014年第五批自治区级非物质文化遗产名录
　　　　　2013年第五批市级非物质文化遗产名录

保护单位：宾阳县文化馆

代表性传承人：陆玉贷（已故）

Element name: Skill of Making Binyang's Oil Paper Umbrella

Alternative name: None

Geographical location and range: Lu Village and Pan Village of Binyang County

Element inscribed list: In 2014 on the Fifth Autonomous Region List of Intangible Cultural Heritage
In 2013 on the Fifth Municipal List of Intangible Cultural Heritage

Competent body involved in safeguarding: Binyang County Cultural Centre

Representative inheritor: Lu Yudai (Late)

制伞工具
Umbrella Making Tools

覆盖油纸
Overlay Oil Paper

宾阳油纸伞制作技艺是宾阳县民间传统手工制伞工艺，以竹子和油纸为原料，按照制伞规格制成美观且实用的油纸伞，至今已有300多年的历史。宾阳纸伞伞面坚韧透明，可遮阳挡雨，美观耐用，在20世纪六七十年代，是家家户户必备的生活用具。

由于地理位置优越，交通便利，宾州镇自明、清时期便成为广西远近闻名的商埠。这里手工业种类多，全镇有10个专业市场，是较为传统的商品集散地。宾阳油纸伞制作技艺自明末清初由潘村、陆村的先人从桂林习得并引进，与蒙村、宋村的竹编雨帽技术竞相发展，成为两项闻名遐迩的传统手工技艺。20世纪50年代，陆村成立一家雨伞厂，专门生产制作油纸伞，生意火爆，产品远销国内外。后来，雨伞厂虽因种种原因倒闭，但直至20世纪80年代，陆村油纸伞依然很受欢迎。

宾阳油纸伞制作技艺十分繁杂，大致分为选料、制料、合成、过油、绘画、成品等，从选料到制作成品大概需要120多道工序。油纸伞以竹子、砂纸、桐油为基本材料，先

Skill of Making Binyang's Oil Paper Umbrella is a traditional handicraft in Binyang. It takes bamboo and oil paper as raw materials and makes beautiful and practical paper umbrella based on procedure of standard umbrella. Its history is more than 300 years long. Paper umbrellas are durable, and the surface is transparent. The umbrella could be used in sunny days and rainy days. In 1960s and 1970s, oil paper umbrellas are necessities for every family.

Due to its superior geographical features and transportation, Binzhou has been well-known business in Guangxi since the Ming and Qing Dynasties. A variety of handicrafts could be found here in 10 markets. Binzhou is traditional distribution centre for commodities. The manufacturing process of paper umbrella was introduced by forefathers of Lu village and Pan village in the late Ming Dynasty and the early Qing Dynasty. Developing and competing with umbrella manufacturers in Meng village and Song village, paper umbrella became a famous traditional handicraft in this region. In the 1950s, an umbrella factory was built in Lu village. Its business was thriving and sold umbrellas to foreign countries. Although the factory went bankruptcy for some reasons, umbrellas from Lu village remains popular until the 1980s.

Manufacturing process is complex for it includes selecting, raw material processing, mixing, varnishing and painting. There are about 120 procedures. Paper umbrella chooses bamboo, abrasive paper and wood oil as basic materials. First make framework, cover head, handle and umbrella line with bamboo. Then use fan-shaped paper to make umbrella paper. Fold one to four layers. Next make umbrella oil with local wood oil and apply the oil to the surface of the umbrella. Finally assemble them together and a nice-looking and useful paper umbrella is born. Paper umbrella has large, middle and small sizes. It could also be customized due to personal need of customers.

Binyang oil paper umbrella is durable and light. The surface is beautiful and transparent. It could be used under the sun or in the rain for it is waterproof and heat-removing. The umbrella has received warm welcome from local people. The raw materials, which are natural local materials in Binyang, are cautiously sorted. Framework of umbrella are made by 3 or 4 years old "steel" bamboo. Cover head of bamboo must be made by wild Yajiao Wood. Umbrella paper must be elastic and flexible. Paper from Hunan is mainly used. The manufacturing process is unique and tactfully. Every bamboo is sharpened by hand. Makers carefully drill holes on the bamboo and connect bamboo with umbrella surface. Oil making requires exact control of fire. In this way can a durable and elegant paper umbrella be made. Paper umbrella is not only used as household facility but also used to pray for luck in marriage. Additionally, umbrella also appears in performance to show ethnic charm of Guangxi and is sold as souvenir for local tourism. With various decorative and practical functions, paper umbrella should have broad prospect of development.

After the 1980s, however, nylon umbrellas, cloth umbrellas and plastic umbrellas attacked the market of paper umbrella. Handmade paper umbrella has low profits and complicate procedure. It is hard to inherit and seldom people pay attention to it nowadays. To solve the problem, Binyang County Cultural Centre answers the call of government and invites inheritors to hold training courses in primary schools.

将竹子按照制伞规格制成伞骨架、伞头、伞柄和伞线，组合成型。用扇形砂纸反复叠裱1至4层作为伞纸，再以本地的桐油熬煮成伞油，反复涂于伞纸，制成伞面，最后贴于伞骨，制成既实用又美观的纸伞。宾阳油纸伞一般分为大、中、小三种规格，也可根据客户所需规格而特制。

宾阳油纸伞坚韧耐用，伞骨简洁轻便，扇面美观透明，且晴雨两用，可散热，不渗水，在当地一直广受欢迎。其选料讲究，均为宾阳地方特有的自然材料，需要选取生长三四年左右的钢竹作为伞骨，坚韧无比，伞头的制作也必须用野生鸭脚木，砂纸需有较好的柔韧性与伸缩性，以湖南砂纸为主。制作技艺精巧独特，每根伞骨都由手工削平，组合伞棍与伞面需小心翼翼在竹面上打槽钻洞。熬制桐油要讲究火候，这样制作成的油纸伞才能收放有度，美观耐用。除了作为居家用品，宾阳油纸伞又是婚嫁所必需的吉祥物，且经常作为表演团体展现广西民族风情的独特道具，成为地方旅游纪念品，发挥着实用、装饰等多种功能，其制作技艺应有广阔的空间和发展前景。

20世纪80年代以后，各种尼龙伞、布伞以及塑料伞的出现，严重冲击了油纸伞的销售市场，手工艺制作不仅利润不高，且工序烦琐，难以传承，如今几乎到了无人问津的境地。针对此种情况，宾阳县文化馆响应政府号召，聘请传承人在小学开展制伞技艺的兴趣培训课。

大罗毛笔制作技艺

Skill of Making Daluo Brush Pen

项目名称：大罗毛笔制作技艺

别称：无

分布范围：宾阳县宾州镇大罗村

入选名录：2014年第四批自治区级非物质文化遗产名录
2012年第四批市级非物质文化遗产名录

保护单位：宾阳县文化馆

代表性传承人：罗儒供

Element name：Skill of Making Daluo Brush Pen

Alternative name：None

Geographical location and range：Daluo Village of Binzhou Town in Binyang County

Element inscribed list：In 2014 on the Fourth Autonomous Region List of Intangible Cultural Heritage
In 2012 on the Fourth Municipal List of Intangible Cultural Heritage

Competent body involved in safeguarding：Binyang County Cultural Centre

Representative inheritors：Luo Rugong

修整笔头
Dressing Brush

Daluo Village in Binyang is a famous brush pen specialized manufacturing village in southern China. Daluo Brush Pen is famous in Guangxi. Manufacturers carefully select the raw materials and the durable brush pens have neat brush and excellent water absorbing capability, which won customers' favor in a long time. Daluo Brush Pen has more than 300 different kinds, including Dou Pen, Changfeng Writing and Painting Pen, Supreme Weasel's Hair Pen, Sheep Pen, Rabbit's Hair Pen, Inch Script Pen, Large, Middle and Small Script Pen. It also has Hengxin, Hengchang, Hebi and other outstanding subsidiary brands.

Daluo Village, which is under administration of Guming village in Binzhou of Binyang county, is located in southern part of Binyang county. It is also called "Dawei" or "Xiaowei". About 2500 villagers live here and all of them are Han people. They make their living by making brush and brush pen. Daluo Village enjoys advantageous transportation which is beneficial to sales of brush pens. The business remains prosperous since ancient times. Daluo Village enjoys the reputation as "prosperous and civilized" village in Binyang. In 1648 in the Qing Dynasty, ancestors of Luo family moved from Fujian to Daluo village. In 1720, Wanquangong of Luo family learned the techniques of making brush pens in Shanlian in Zhejiang province and introduced it to his descendants. After 280

宾阳县大罗村是中国南方地区有名的毛笔生产专业村，以宾阳大罗毛笔闻名广西。大罗毛笔选料精细考究，笔毛整齐且不易脱毛，吸水性能好，长期以来深受客户的青睐。大罗毛笔有斗笔，长锋书画笔，极品狼、羊、兔毫笔，寸楷，大、中、小楷，排笔等300多种规格品种，并有“恒信”“恒昌”“鹤笔”等优秀品牌。

宾阳县宾州镇顾明村委的大罗村位于宾阳县城之南隅，又称“大维”“小维”村，全村2500多人，均为汉族，以手工制作毛笔与毛刷为生。大罗村交通便捷，利于毛笔的生产和销售，自古至今毛笔生意兴隆，成为宾阳县毛笔生产专业村和“小康文明村”。清朝顺治年间（约1648），罗氏先人自福建迁移至大罗村定居。康熙年间（约1720），罗氏三世祖万全公于浙江省善琏镇习得毛笔制作技艺，带回大罗村传授给子孙。大罗毛笔制作技艺历经280多年的发展与改革，形成了独特的制笔工艺和风格。20世纪50年代以前，大罗村以家庭为单位生产毛笔，60年代，“大罗毛笔厂”成立，生产规模进一步扩大，制作毛笔种类增加至300多种，远销岭南各地以及香港地区和日本等国。

大罗毛笔选料精良，以狼毛、兔毛、羊毛、鸡毛、狸毛为主，经过100多道的工序深加工制成，质料精细，成品质量上乘。大罗毛笔的特点为笔毛牢固整齐，吸水、吸墨性强，书写流利，经久耐用，规格齐全，品种多样，极受广大客商和客户的信赖和欢迎。毛笔作为中华民族文房四宝之一，自古以来是华夏民族写作、绘画的主要工具，大罗毛笔制作技艺为传统民间手工艺不可或缺的一部分，保护大罗毛笔制作技艺，对弘扬民族传统文化有着重要的历史研究价值和实用价值。

随着数字信息化时代的迅猛发展，大罗毛笔原料进价又较高，制作工序烦琐，毛笔销售市场逐渐萎缩，招收年轻人学习制笔技艺成为一大难题。针对此种情况，宾州镇成立了大罗毛笔保护领导小组，在各中、小学推广使用毛笔写作。镇政府和社会筹集资金召集老艺人于宾州镇开办大罗毛笔厂。

刻字
Carving Characters

打磨
Polishing

years' improvement and evolution, Daluo brush pen has its unique style and craft. "Hengchang", "Hengxin", "Hebi" and other well-known brands came into being. Before the 1950s, people in Daluo made brush pens in family unit. From 1960s to 1980s, Daluo Brush Pen Factory was established and kept expanding its production. More than 300 kinds of brush pens were sold in various regions in south of five ridges and Hong Kong, as well as foreign counties like Japan.

Daluo brush pen carefully selects its raw materials. The brushes are mainly made by hair of weasel, rabbit, sheep, chicken and fox. With more than 100 working procedures, the brush pens have high quality and refined design. The prominent feature of Daluo brush pen is its firm and neat brush with strong capability of absorbing water and ink. It is fluent in writing and is endurable. Daluo brush pen could satisfy diversified writing demand for it has many kinds of pens for different purposes. As "Chinese four treasures of study", brush pen has been an important device for people to write and paint with. Daluo brush pen is also irreplaceable in traditional national handicraft. Protection of Daluo brush pen promotes traditional culture and has its value in historical research and practical use.

Against the rapid development of digital economy, the market of Daluo brush pen gradually shrinks due to its high cost of raw materials and complicate manufacturing process. Recruiting young people to learn the techniques is also a difficulty. To address the problem, Binzhou establishes Daluo Brush Pen Protection Working Group. It promotes writing with brush pen in primary schools and middle schools. County government and the society also raise funds to attract old manufacturers and establish Daluo Brush Pen factory in Binzhou.

宾阳酸粉制作技艺

Skill of Making Binyang's Sour Noodle

项目名称：宾阳酸粉制作技艺

别称：无

分布范围：宾阳县宾州镇三联街、南街、仁爱街，新桥镇等

入选名录：2010年第三批自治区级非物质文化遗产名录

2010年第三批市级非物质文化遗产名录

保护单位：宾阳县文化馆

代表性传承人：无

Element name: Skill of Making Binyang's Sour Noodle

Alternative name: None

Geographical location and range: Sanlian Street, Nan Street, Ren'ai Street of Binzhou Town; Xinqiao Town and others in Binyang County

Element inscribed list: In 2010 on the Third Autonomous Region List of Intangible Cultural Heritage

In 2010 on the Third Municipal List of Intangible Cultural Heritage

Competent body involved in safeguarding: Binyang County Cultural Centre

Representative inheritors: None

宾阳酸粉是在宾阳米粉制作基础上加以改革创新而成的传统凉拌粉，是暑天解渴消暑、去火去热的美味佳肴，有滑而不粘、柔而不烂、韧而不坚、酸而不冲、辣而不呛、香而不火、脆而不燥等特点。宾阳酸粉名扬于世，是深受广大民众喜爱的传统风味小吃。

据制作酸粉的民间技艺传承人口述，宾阳酸粉制作技艺由宾阳米粉的制作衍变而来，宾阳米粉制作技艺迄今有900多年的历史。北宋皇祐年末（1049—1054），狄青率军南下征剿侬智高驻兵宾州城时，一位聪明的火头军见北方士兵吃不惯南方大米，便把大米磨成米浆，模仿面条的制作方法蒸粉切条制成“米条”，配以卤水肉片等佐料，将士们食之神清气爽，体力猛增，一举拿下昆仑关。此后宾州人将之改称为“米粉”。至明朝，宾州城内一位黄姓妇女因婆婆长期卧病不起，不思茶饭，便在米粉中加入糖、醋等佐料，婆婆吃后胃口大开，不久病患痊愈。此事被传为宾州佳话，不少人效仿米粉制法制作酸粉，不断改进工艺，制成了如今的宾阳酸粉。

Binyang Sour Noodle is a new cold noodle with sauce created based on traditional rice vermicelli. As an ideal dish to cool down in summer, Binyang sour noodle is smooth but not sticky, soft but not too over-boiled, chewy but not hard to eat, sour and spicy but not pungent, delicious but not oily, crispy but not dry. Binyang sour noodle enjoys high reputation and wins favor from people.

Based on oral record from inheritors, sour noodles originated from rice vermicelli in Binyang. Sour noodles have more than 9 hundred years' history. It is said from 1049 to 1053 in the Song Dynasty, General Di Qing led his army to eliminate Nong Zhigao in Binyang. A smart cook in the army grinded rice into rice paste for northern soldiers could not eat southern rice. He made rice noodles in the process of making flour noodles and cooked it with sliced salty meat. Soldiers felt refreshing and energized after eating the food and fought bravely in the victory of Kunlun Pass. Since then, people in Binyang adapted it into "rice vermicelli". In the Ming Dynasty, an old woman fell ill and could eat nothing. Her daughter-in-law Ms. Huang put sugar, vinegar and other ingredients in the rice vermicelli, which met her mother-in-law's appetite and cured the disease. This story was widely spread in Binyang and many people came to learn how to adapt rice vermicelli. The process was kept improving and finally Binyang sour noodles was born.

The materials of Binyang sour noodles include high-quality rice, fired peanuts, fried soybeans, pork, beef, sausages,

切米皮
Roll the Sheet up and Cut it into Slices

放调料
Add Ingredients

pickled carrot, pickled cucumber and mung bean sprout. The seasonings are rice vinegar, sugar and peppers. First, people will wash the rice and soak it into water for four to five hours. After the rice fully absorb water, people will add some rice. Then grind them to paste with stone mill. Put paste into cotton bag with small holes, tighten the bag and squeeze water out. After agglomeration to wet starch, people will put the wet starch to steamer and make starch sheet. Roll the sheet up and cut it into slices which are 2 or 3 centimeters long. Finally, add fired peanuts, fried soybeans, pork, beef, sausages, pickled carrot, pickled cucumber and mung bean sprout into the noodles and mix them with rice vinegar, sugar, peppers and other seasonings.

The process of Binyang sour noodles was complicate and should be strictly followed. There is high from selecting rice to make ingredients. Without boiling, sour noodles could be eaten in cold dish. The noodle is white and delicate while the flavor is sour and sweet. People feel refreshing and cooling down. The raw materials are rice, peanut, soybean and pickled cucumber. The making process is improved by generations of Binyang people. As a spot in Binyang, sour noodles remain as the tribute to ancestors in Tomb Sweeping Day and Double Ninth Day. It is also an important dish in people's daily and banquet for guests. People find raw materials local areas and take full advantage of the ingredients. Binyang sour noodles is the crystallization of wisdom of local people. Heritage of sour noodles promotes the studies of traditional food culture in Binyang and enrich local snacks. Sour noodles play an important role in developing local economy.

In recently years, most of handmade snacks are made by machine. Lured by profits, some people use poor raw materials and manufacturing techniques. They even manufacture low-quality products and even make fake sour noodles, which bring harm to the sales of authentic sour noodles. In order to ensure the health development of traditional food, government of Binyang listed sour noodles as the traditional dish served for guests during Paolong Festival. This increases the reputation of Binyang sour noodles and emphasizes the cultivation of inheritors. More room for development will be expanded in the future for Binyang sour noodles.

宾阳酸粉的主料有优质大米、油炸花生、油炸黄豆、猪肉、牛肉、香肠、酸萝卜、酸黄瓜、绿豆芽，佐料有米醋、糖、辣椒等。制作流程为：先将大米淘洗干净，浸泡4—5个小时，待米粒吸收水分软化，再添入适量米饭，用石磨磨成米浆。准备好有细孔的棉布袋，将米浆放入，扎紧袋口，施加压力挤出水分，直至米浆变成块状的湿淀粉，再将压干的湿淀粉放入蒸笼蒸制成粉皮。将粉皮卷成筒状，切成2—3厘米长的米粉条。最后用油炸花生、油炸黄豆、猪肉、牛肉、香肠、酸萝卜、酸黄瓜、绿豆芽制成配菜，拌上配菜以及米醋、糖、辣椒等佐料即可食用。

宾阳酸粉制作流程繁杂，工艺要求严格，从选米到配制佐料都十分讲究。宾阳酸粉冷盘即食，粉质雪白幼嫩，口味酸甜爽滑，食之消暑提神。酸粉制作食材虽为百姓常见的稻米、花生、黄豆、酸黄瓜等，其工艺却经勤劳智慧的宾阳人不断完善，成为宾阳一绝，使得宾阳酸粉由古至今传承不断，数百年来不仅作为清明、重阳节祭拜祖先的祭礼之一，还成为宾阳民众日常生活和招待宾客的重要食品。宾阳酸粉制作技艺凝聚了宾阳百姓就地取材、因地制宜地发挥食材功效的生活智慧，推动其传承发展对研究宾阳传统饮食文化、丰富广西特色小吃种类、促进宾阳经济发展具有十分重要的作用。

近年来，大部分手工制作技艺被机器生产代替，一些人受利益驱动在工艺制作和原料添加方面弄虚作假、以次充好，冲击正宗酸粉的销售市场。为了保证传统饮食业的健康发展，宾阳县政府将酸粉列为炮龙节接待贵宾的特色传统美食，提升正宗酸粉制作技艺的知名度，并着重培养传承人，努力为宾阳酸粉的制作技艺开拓发展空间。

横县南山白毛茶制作技艺

Hengxian Nanshan Baimao Green Tea Making Skill

项目名称：横县南山白毛茶制作技艺

别称：圣种白毛茶

分布范围：横州市那阳镇

入选名录：2012年第四批自治区级非物质文化遗产名录

　　　　　2012年第四批市级非物质文化遗产名录

保护单位：横县文化馆

代表性传承人：陈雄

Element name：Hengxian Nanshan Baimao Green Tea Making Skill

Alternative name：Shengzhong Baimao Tea

Geographical location and range：Nayang Town of Hengzhou City

Element inscribed list：In 2012 on the Fourth Autonomous Region List of Intangible Cultural Heritage

In 2012 on the Fourth Municipal List of Intangible Cultural Heritage

Competent body involved in safeguarding：Hengxian Cultural Centre

Representative inheritors：Chen Xiong

Hengxian Nanshan Baimao Green Tea Making Skill is also called "Shengzhong Baimao Tea". It is planted in Nanshan Mountain of Hengzhou City in Guangxi. The tea has white fluff on its leaf so that it was called "Baimao" tea. Baimao tea is a kind of green tea and is made by hand traditionally. With reputation in Lingnan regions and even in the whole country, Baimao tea is also honored as "Peculiar", "Better than Wuyi Tea", "Superior to Longjing in Flavor and Taste". It also won award in international exhibitions.

Hengxian Nanshan Baimao tea has a long history. According to *Book of Tea*, Emperor Jianwen in the Ming Dynasty grew 7 plants Baimao Tea in Yingtian Temple of Hengzhou City Nanshan when he escaped war to lower basin of the Yangtze River. This is why Baimao tea was called "Shengzhong". Yingtian Temple was built in the Tang Dynasty and there are still 6 or 7 strong tea trees standing beside the temple nowadays. Eventually, people in Hengzhou still believe their Baimao tea was brought by an emperor. In 1822 in the Qing Dynasty, Baimao tea attended Panama International Agricultural Product Exhibition and was awarded a silver medal. In 1915, in the World's Fair in Panama, Baimao tea won silver medal again. In 1933, Guangxi government honored Baimao tea as "Better than Wuyi Tea".

At present time, Baimao tea is mainly grown in regional areas of Nanshan Temple and main peak of Nanshan mountain whose altitude is about 800 to 1000 meters and average temperature is only 20 degree Celsius. According to *Book of Guangxi*, "Nanshan tea has white fluff on its leaf, should be picked in sprout. Its leaf is slim and soft and has the shape of silver needle. It is better than Longjing tea in flavor and taste. Drinking Baimao tea is refreshing. With natural fragrance of lotus flower, Baimao tea is peculiar." Tea trees grow straightforward and are above 3 meters high. The tea leaf is of middle size. The sprout is thriving, and fluff is dense, that is an ideal raw material for making Baimao tea. The leaf is slim and soft. As for Baimao black tea, the leaf is golden, and the tea is bright and red with strong flavor which is enduring. As for Baimao green tea, it has more white fluff and the fragrance is clear. The tea will be green. People will taste bitter and then sweet. Baimao tea is green. Tea soup is bright green with outstanding aroma. Appreciating the tea, people will enjoy the lasting aroma of lotus flower and milk.

Baimao tea needs to be carefully made. First-class tea only selects sprout and other classes will pick the sprout and one leaf. Generally, 500 grams of Baimao tea requires 45 thousand leaves. The process includes picking leaves, drying leaves under sun, water removing, rolling, shape settling,

横县南山白毛茶又名“圣种白毛茶”，产于广西壮族自治区横州市的南山，因其茶叶背面披着茂密的白色茸毛而得名。白毛茶属于绿茶，采用传统手工制作，驰名岭南地区乃至全国，曾在国际博览会上获奖，有茶中“异品”“品胜武夷”“味色胜龙井”之美誉。

横县南山白毛茶历史悠久，据《中国茶经》记载，明朝建文帝下江南避难时，携白毛茶七株种于横州市南山应天寺，是为“圣种”。应天寺始建于唐朝，寺庙旁边至今仍存有六七株粗壮的大茶树，因此，数百年来，横州市人一直相信“圣种白毛茶”是由建文帝带来的。清道光二年（1822），南山白毛茶就参加了巴拿马国际农产品展览会，并获得银质奖章。1915年，在巴拿马举办的万国博览会上，南山白毛茶再次荣获银质奖章。1933年，广西壮族自治区政府给南山白毛茶题匾“品胜武夷”。

目前，白毛茶茶园主要分布在横州市那阳镇的南山寺及南山主峰一带，那里海拔高约800—1000米，年平均温度20摄氏度左右，非常适宜茶树生长。《广西通鉴》中记载：“南山茶，叶背白茸如雪，萌芽即采，细嫩类银针，色味胜龙井，饮之清芬沁齿，天然有荷花香气，真异品也。”南山茶树树姿直立，高3米以上，茶叶品种为中叶，芽壮毫密，叶薄而柔嫩，是制白毛茶的理想原料。制红茶，则毫色金黄，汤色红亮，滋味强烈，香高，叶底黄铜色；制绿茶，则白毫特多，香气清，汤色浓绿，外形紧结，味带微苦而后苦醇。白毛茶色泽翠绿，条索紧结弯曲，叶底嫩绿匀整。茶汤清绿明亮，滋味浓厚，回甘滑喉，有荷花香和蛋奶香，香色纯正持久。

白毛茶焙制方法精细，上品茶只采一叶初展的芽头，其他品类则只采一芽一叶。通常，制500克特级白毛茶约需采4.5万个芽叶，加工程序包括鲜叶、摊青（即摊晾3小时以上）、杀青、揉捻、定型、足干、提香，每一个过程都极其讲究。杀青至提香五道程序中，炒制过程特重（保持不脱白毛），加工过程系用铁锅翻炒杀青，扇风摊晾，双手轻揉，炒揉结合，反复三次。最后在烧炭烘笼上以文火烘干，制作500克的茶叶需要控制在36个小时内。白毛茶成品茶色泽翠绿，冲泡时，既可以采用传统热泡，也可以冷泡，冷泡滋味更加清淡甘甜。

2006年，广西南山白毛茶茶业有限公司成立，南山白毛茶的系列产品得到开发，品质得到提升。不过，由于上等南山白毛茶需要传统手工制作，而且各项技能水平及要求极为苛刻，目前真正能够纯手工制作南山白毛茶的人寥寥无几。传统手工制作南山白毛茶的加工工具及其制作技艺也近消失。2009年以后，在各级文化部门的共同努力下，南山白毛茶传统制作工艺得到重视，对促进横州市茶文化的发展、弘扬民间优秀茶文化遗产，以及丰富地方旅游资源，都将产生推动作用。

drying and adding fragrance and every step should be done cautiously. In the five steps from water removing to adding fragrance, the weight of tea must be maintained which means that white fluff should not be destroyed. Iron pan is used for stirring and frying. Then spread the tea and blow wind to it. Roll with hand. Combine frying and rolling together and repeat for three times. Then bake the tea on steamers with light fire. Manufacturing time for 500 grams tea should be strictly controlled within 36 hours. And the finished product is green. When making tea, drinkers can either follow traditional method and make tea with hot water or make tea with cold water which will make the tea sweeter.

In 2006, Guangxi Nanshan Baimao Tea Co., Ltd was established and Baimao tea was developed and improved. However, due to its handmade process and high standard of skills, few people could make Baimao tea purely with their hands. And the manufacturing facilities and techniques are also dying. In 2009, with the mutual effort of cultural department at all levels, people start to attach importance to Baimao tea, which will drive forward the development of tea culture in Hengzhou City, promotion of cultural heritage and enriching local tourism resources.

炒茶
Stir-frying Tea

横县茉莉花茶制作技艺

Hengxian Jasmine Tea Making Skill

项目名称：横县茉莉花茶制作技艺

别称：无

分布范围：横州市

入选名录：2012年第四批自治区级非物质文化遗产名录

保护单位：横县文化馆

代表性传承人：谢大高、徐炳奇

Element name：Hengxian Jasmine Tea Making Skill

Alternative name：None

Geographical location and range：Hengzhou City

Element inscribed list：In 2012 on the Fourth Autonomous Region List of Intangible Cultural Heritage

Competent body involved in safeguarding：Hengxian Cultural Centre

Representative inheritors：Xie Dagao, Xu Bingqi

采摘茉莉花
Picking Jasmine

茉莉花茶是用含苞欲放的茉莉鲜花加入绿茶中窨制而成的茶叶品种，属于绿茶再加工茶。广西壮族自治区横州市是全国最大的茉莉花生产和花茶加工基地，享有“中国茉莉之乡”的美誉。茉莉花茶集茶叶与茉莉花香于一体，茶引花香，花增茶性，相得益彰，既保持了浓郁爽口的茶味，又有鲜灵芬芳的茉莉花香。

横州市的茉莉花种植历史悠久，早在明代就已经广泛种植。茉莉花喜阳，横州市的气候条件温暖，适合茉莉花生长。明朝王济的《君子堂日询手镜》中，就有关于横州市茉莉花种植的记载。目前，全市茉莉花种植面积近7000公顷，茉莉花年上市8万吨，茉莉花茶产量和加工量占全国茉莉花茶总产量的70%以上，占世界的60%以上，茉莉花销售收入5亿元。全县8个茉莉花交易市场中，横州市西南茶城是全国最大的茉莉花茶专业市场。全市拥有茉莉花加工企业180多家。

横州市茉莉花茶的传统制作工艺独特而复杂，制作原料有新鲜茉莉花、玉兰花、新鲜茶叶，一般要经过茶胚、窨花、堆窨、通花、收堆、起花、烘焙、冷却、转窨、提花、

Jasmine tea is made from sprouting jasmine flower and green tea. People process flowers and tea together and eventually create processed green tea. Hengzhou City in Guangxi Zhuang Autonomous Region is the largest jasmine tea manufacturing and processing base. It enjoys the reputation as “homeland for jasmine”. Jasmine tea combines the flavor of tea and the fragrance of jasmine. Tea gives out the fragrance of flower and flower enhances the flavor of tea. It has the strong taste of tea and the sweet fragrance of jasmine.

Cultivation of jasmine flowers has a long history in Hengzhou City which could be traced back to the Ming Dynasty. Jasmine flowers love sun shines. The climate in Hengzhou City is agreeable and suitable for jasmine. In *Daily Inquiry to Mirror in Junzitang* written by Wang Ji in the Ming Dynasty can people find the record about jasmine planting. At present, about 7000 hectares of jasmine are growing in Hengzhou City. Every year more than 80 thousand tons of jasmine are sold in market. The amount of jasmine growing and processing accounts for more than 70% of total amount in China and 60% of the amount in the whole world. Jasmine creates 500 million RMB revenue every year. Among the 8 trade markets of jasmine in China, Hengzhou City Southwest Tea Fair is the largest specialized market in China. There are more than 180 processing enterprises in Hengxian.

The traditional technique of Hengzhou City Jasmine Tea is unique and complex. Jasmine flowers, magnolia and fresh tea leaves are all raw materials. The procedures of making jasmine tea includes selecting tea leaves, mixing, baking, heat releasing, filtering, frying, cooling, lifting, piling and packaging. Among these procedures, mixing flowers with tea leaves is the key. Take one fifth or one third of tea leaves and spread them on the ground. The thickness should be 10 to 15 centimeters. Based on the proportion of tea and flower, take out one fifth to one third flowers and spread them evenly on tea leaves. One layer is tea and another layer are flowers. Repeat three or five times. Cut it through with iron rake and stir with rake. Then mix the flowers following the methods of box scenting, storage scenting and block scenting. The standard is high. Every step has strict requirement on temperature, humidity and time.

After these complex procedures, high quality jasmine tea remains the refreshment of green tea and also introduces the aroma of jasmine flowers. Jasmines contain tea polyphenol, theanine, vitamin and mineral elements. It also has the fragrance of jasmine flower. Hengzhou City jasmine tea has more than 20 kinds of chemicals including aromatic oil, geraniol, nerolidol and eugenol formation. It may help people release pressure, smooth breath, calm down, disperse blood stasis, cure migraine as supportive treatment, and so on. Jasmine tea is honored as top beverage in spring with the function of "disperse coldness and release depression". It received welcome from customers and has become one of the best natural healthy beverages in China and the whole world.

Currently, most of the manufacturers of jasmine tea adopt handmade methods or semi-machine method for frying, baking, selecting and other procedures. The efficiency is relatively low. First-class jasmine tea requires pure traditional handmade methods and outstanding skills. As a result, few people could truly obtain the making techniques of jasmine tea. The handicraft is at the edge of extinction. In order to inherit and develop making techniques of jasmine tea, Hengzhou City constructed a 2000 mu (about 1.3 square kilometers) jasmine garden for exhibition and tourism. The government aims to inherit and develop this handicraft in continuous exploration. In 2012, with approval of the government of Guangxi Zhuang Autonomous Region, Hengxian Jasmine Tea Making Skill was inscribed on the Fourth Autonomous Region List of Intangible Cultural Heritage.

匀堆、装箱等工序。其中，窨制花茶是制作的关键环节。其操作方法为，先把茶胚总量的三分之一至五分之一，平摊在干净窨花场地上，堆砌厚度为10—15cm，然后根据茶、花配比鲜花的用量，同样分出三分之一至五分之一，均匀地散铺在茶胚面上，这样一层茶、一层花，相间三至五层，再用铁耙从横断面由上至下扒开拌和。茶胚和鲜花边拌边按箱窨、屯窨、块窨方法进行“窨花”。茉莉花茶的制作技术要求很高，每一个工序对温度、湿度以及时间都非常讲究。

经过复杂工艺制作出来的优质茉莉花茶，不仅保持了绿茶浓郁爽口的天然特性，又饱含着茉莉花的鲜香味。茉莉花茶不仅保留了茶叶中的茶多酚、茶氨酸、维生素、矿质元素等大量有益成分，又吸收了茉莉花的香气，使横州市茉莉花茶含有大量芳香油、香叶醇、橙花椒醇、丁香酯等20多种化合物，具有理气、开郁、安神、和中、化瘀和辅助治疗偏头痛、疏肝解郁等保健功效，被世人称为“去寒邪、助理郁”的春季茶饮上品，深受广大消费者的欢迎，成为现代我国乃至全世界的最佳天然保健饮品。

目前，大部分茉莉花茶作坊还是纯手工或半机械制茶，包括炒茶、窨茶、拣茶等，生产力比较低下，由于上等茉莉花茶需要传统手工制作，而且各项技术水平要求极高，因此目前真正掌握茉莉花茶纯手工制作技艺的人不多，手工茉莉花茶的加工工具及其制作技艺面临失传。为传承和发展横县茉莉花茶制作技艺，横州市建成了2000亩的中华茉莉花园，开展茉莉花标准化栽培示范，茉莉花科研及新品种、新技术展示，茉莉花文化展示与旅游观光等，力求在不断的探索中传承和发展茉莉花传统制作技艺。2012年，经广西壮族自治区人民政府同意，横县茉莉花茶制作技艺列入第四批自治区级非物质文化遗产名录。

横县鱼生制作技艺

Hengxian Sashimi Making Skill

项目名称：横县鱼生制作技艺

别称：横县鱼宴

分布范围：横州市

入选名录：2010年第三批自治区级非物质文化遗产

保护单位：横县文化馆

代表性传承人：余富

Element name：Hengxian Sashimi Making Skill

Alternative name：Hengxian Fish Banquet

Geographical location and range：Hengzhou City

Element inscribed list：In 2010 on the Third Autonomous Region List of Intangible Cultural Heritage

Competent body involved in safeguarding：Hengxian Cultural Centre

Representative inheritor：Yu Fu

Hengxian Sashimi Making Skill is a special traditional handicraft and is known as "Peculiar to Hengzhou". Hengxian Sashimi Making Skill represents the highest level of cooking skills and food culture in Hengxian. It is also the best banquet for guests.

Hengxian Sashimi has a long history. It is said that ancestors Danren started to eat sashimi thousands of years ago. According to *Book of Hengxian* written in the Qing Dynasty, celebrity Dong Jing encounters immortal in the Jin Dynasty. The immortal made sashimi for him. Based on research from folk experts, when fishermen go fishing on the sea, they lacked ingredients of cooking. They had no choice but to eat raw fish. People in Hengzhou combined making techniques with the legend and cultivated an endurable food culture. This story shows the profound cultural connotation of sashimi.

Hengxian sashimi is famous due to its special techniques and delicate materials. "Three delicacy" which means delicate in knife work, decoration and raw materials, are the distinguished features of Hengxian sashimi. Cook will follow the general order: cut out fish gill and tail, deplete blood, clear the fish, dry the bold, slit the spine and cut off flesh from side bones. Then cook will remove the skin. Wrap the fish with special paper or towel to absorb remaining water and blood. Slice the fish to fillet which is as thin as cicadas' wings with sharp knife. The fish slices are connected but seemingly cut off. In the end, the sliced fish is like butterfly. Shinny slices

"横县鱼生制作技艺"是横州市颇具特色的一项传统手工技艺，堪称"横州一绝"，闻名遐迩。横县鱼生制作技艺代表着横州市的烹饪技术和饮食文化的最高水准，也是横州人招待宾客的最高礼遇。

横县鱼生制作技艺历史悠久，古已有之。据说，横州的先民蜑人早在几千年之前就开始食用鱼生。据清代乾隆年间《横县志》记载，相传晋元帝年间，隐居横州的逸士董京偶遇仙人，仙人为其制食鱼生。据相关的民俗专家考证，横县鱼生的产生，是由于古代渔民在郁江上靠打鱼为生，在缺少烹调原料的情况下，只得生食。而横州人将鱼生制作技艺与鱼生品尝的传说逸闻结合起来，成了一种长盛不衰的饮食文化。可见，横县鱼生这个传统手工技艺文化底蕴之深厚、内涵之丰富。

横县鱼生之所以著名，与其做法工艺之独特、选料配料之精细有着密切的关系。横县鱼生制作的独特之处在于"三精"，即刀工精细、摆设精致、选料精品。一般工序为：活鱼除腮斩尾、放血、净身、滴干血迹，从鱼脊下刀、

切鱼片
Slicing a Fish

摆盘
Dressing of the Plate

沿鱼侧骨轻轻剔下两侧鱼肉。然后去皮，用专业鱼生纸或毛巾包裹，以吸干鱼肉水分和残留血迹，用利刀轻而快速落刀将鱼肉切成薄如蝉翼的一片，在将断与未断之间连刀切下第二片，切断两片相邻鱼肉连成一块，一打开，鱼肉状如蝴蝶，展翅欲飞，两片鱼肉厚薄均匀，光彩照人，俗称“鸳鸯蝴蝶片”。鱼生制作的配料也十分讲究，品种多样，加工精细，有鱼腥草、鱼生草、紫苏叶、酸藠头、柠檬、大蒜、生姜、萝卜、香菜等20多种，这些配料经洗净、晾干后，切成细丝，要求大小均匀、细如发丝。五颜六色的配料放置在盘中，用上等的花生油、生抽、胡椒粉等佐料搭配。鱼生的食法为：鱼片夹放佐料小碗浸泡片刻，夹起放入自用的小碗里，将少许配料放入小碗鱼片上，加上炒香的花生一起食用。制作鱼生剩下的鱼头、鱼骨、鱼腩等配以香菜、葱、姜、芋头等，可以做成鱼汤。横县鱼生手工艺制作的鱼片，不仅形状美、肉色鲜嫩、晶莹剔透，而且加上五颜六色的配料，宛如一件艺术珍品。食用鱼生，有清热解毒、去湿除燥、养颜的功效，长期食用可以祛病强身、延年益寿。

长期以来，横县鱼生制作技艺虽然得到了发展，但依然存在不少问题。一是鱼生的制作方法在新时代多有变化，传统手工制作技艺被机械取代，鱼生制作技艺受到一定影响。二是随着环境污染加剧，鱼肉的品质没有保障，影响了鱼生市场的发展。针对这些状况，横州市政府加大资金投入，扶持横县鱼生技艺争霸赛等活动。2010年，经广西壮族自治区人民政府同意，横县鱼生制作技艺列入第三批自治区级非物质文化遗产名录。

are evenly thick and are called “mandarin duck butterfly slice”. Various ingredients of sashimi are also carefully chosen, including houttuynia cordata, fish grass, basil leaves, sour taro, lemon, garlic, ginger, radish, coriander and other 20 kinds. Being washed and dried, the ingredients are cut into slices which are of same size and are as thin as hair. Put colorful ingredients into plate and add peanut oil, soy sauce and pepper. Customers may put fish slices into seasonings for a while and then put it into his own bowl. Add some ingredients to the slices and eat with fried peanuts. Fish head, fish bones, fish rod and other remaining could be used to cook soup with coriander, onion, ginger and taro. Handmade sashimi is beautiful in shape and fresh in fish meet. Accompanied with colorful ingredients, Hengxian Sashimi is like an art work. Eating sashimi will cool people down, remove toxic elements and beautify the skin. Eating sashimi for a long time will prevent diseases, strengthen body and even prolong people’s life.

Although the techniques developed in the long history, there are still some problems occurs. First, the making techniques change in the new era and traditional handmade method is replaced by machine, which brings impact to manufacturing. The second problem is the pollution decreased the quality of fish and impeded the sales in the market. To address the problem, the government of Hengzhou City increased the investment and supported sashimi competition. In 2010, with the approval of Guangxi Zhuang Autonomous Region Government, Hengxian Sashimi Making Skill was inscribed on the Third Autonomous Region List of Intangible Cultural Heritage.

装盘
Putting Slices of Fish in the Plate

横县大粽制作技艺

Hengxian Big Zongzi Making Skill

项目名称：横县大粽制作技艺

别称：无

分布范围：横州市

入选名录：2010年第三批自治区级非物质文化遗产名录

保护单位：横县文化馆

代表性继承人：彭金妹

Element name：Hengxian Big Zongzi Making Skill

Alternative name：None

Geographical location and range：Hengzhou City

Element inscribed list：In 2010 on the Third Autonomous Region List of Intangible Cultural Heritage

Competent body involved in safeguarding：Hengxian Cultural Centre

Representative inheritor：Peng Jinmei

粽子是中国各地常见的传统美食。在广西壮族自治区的横州市，大粽是人们欢度新春佳节的主要食品之一，横州民间有着“无粽不成年”的说法，大粽便象征着美好、吉祥与节日的欢乐。

横县大粽色泽光亮，口味浓厚滋润，软糯鲜美。大粽的由来，以远古先民的年粽文化理念而论，其名称、形状、材料都起源于生殖崇拜。首先，“包粽子”的壮语为“独逢”，与“包襁褓”的壮语“独朋”语音极为相近。其次，粽子形状是平底、上拱、中部丰满隆起的长条形，为孕妇腹部的象征。包粽子所用材料是山上带香的粽叶和红绳索，寓意着吉祥。而内部材料的糯米象征胎胞，肉条象征脐带，绿豆则是供胎儿摄取的养分。据传，古时横州人因贫困而创造性地包制大粽，以辞旧迎新，更有春节期间人们互赠双数的粽子之“好事成双”、新婚夫妇第一次回娘家要担“茶粽”、娘家赠予粽子与发糕以表示庆贺、有白事的人家一年内不包制粽子等种种习俗，充分印证了大粽在横州的渊源历史及丰富的人文内涵。

横县大粽
Hengxian Big Zongzi

Zongzi is a famous traditional food in China. In Hengzhou City of Guangxi Zhuang Autonomous Region, big zongzi is one of the major foods for people to celebrate the Spring Festival. There is a saying goes in Hengzhou that the Spring Festival without zongzi cannot be called the Spring Festival. Therefore, big zongzi is a symbol of happiness, auspiciousness and festive joy.

Hengxian big zongzi is bright in color, mellow in taste and soft in mouthfeel. The name, shape and materials of the zongzi, in the view of the ancestors' culture of Spring Festival zongzi, was originated from the reproduction worship. First of all, in the Zhuang language, the pronunciation of "make zongzi" is "Du Feng", which is very similar to the pronunciation of "swaddle baby", that is, "Du Peng". In addition, Hengxian big zongzi has a flat bottom, an arching top and a rising middle part in the shape of long strip, which is a symbol of the pregnant woman's abdomen. Zongzi is often made with fragrant reed leaves and red ropes, which means good luck. The glutinous rice symbolizes fetus, the meat strip stands for umbilical cord and mung beans are the symbol of nutrition for the fetus. It is said that in ancient times, people in Hengzhou City made big zongzi creatively to bid farewell to the old year and usher in the new one because of poverty. Moreover, there are many customs related to big zongzi. For example, during the Spring Festival, people give even number of zongzi to each other because "good things should be in pairs"; newly married couples will give "tea zongzi" to the bride's parents when they go back the bride's home for the first time after their marriage and the bride's family will give zongzi and steamed sponge cakes back to express congratulations; families with funeral affairs within a year cannot make zongzi and so on, which fully confirms the historical origin and profound cultural connotation of big zongzi.

Hengxian big zongzi is fastidious in material selection and exquisite in production. The main materials are glutinous rice, mung beans, pork, rice wine, sugar, salt, ginger, green onion, aginomoto, five spice powder and pepper powder. People can also add other ingredients such as chestnut, dried shrimp, preserved meat and black rice according to different flavors.

The production methods of traditional Hengxian big zongzi are as follows:

(1) Prepare all kinds of main and auxiliary materials. Pickle the pork pieces that have been cut into oblong shape according to a certain proportion in advance with appropriate

amount of rice wine, ginger, onion, salt and aginomoto for one to two days.

(2) Tear the edges of the mung beans and soak them to peel the coats.

(3) Soak glutinous rice. Wash them out to remove impurities and dry the glutinous rice off. Add salt into the rice and blend well.

(4) Boil the reed leaves to clean them. Flat the leaf. Put glutinous rice and pork pieces on the leaf and cover with mung beans and other ingredients. Wrap the materials into ladder shape, and use rope to tie it up for several circles.

(5) Put zongzi into boiling water and wait for water to boil again with big fire. After the water boiling again, turn the big fire into the small one and add some water. After 3 to 4 hours, change the upper zongzi into the bottom of the pot so as to be evenly heated. (Big zongzi need 7 to 8 hours to cook.)

(6) When the zongzi is cooked thoroughly, it is better to take them out of the pot for fear that zongzi may lose the original taste after long-time soaking.

Steamed zongzi can be eaten directly. People can untie the rope, open the reed leaf and cut the zongzi into two parts. Then, people need to evenly spread out the glutinous rice and mung beans and crush the pork pieces to oil the rice. When the zongzi getting cool, they can be heated again or be cut into thick slices and fry to soft.

As a traditional food with Hengzhou City and Lingnan characteristics, Hengxian big zongzi once was in full flourish. It won gold medal in International Tourism and Food Festival of Southeastern Asia in China-ASEAN International Food Gala. Today, the mode of making big zongzi in Hengxian has been transformed from a single-family system to one run by qualified workshops, factories and companies. Hengzhou City has formed a standardized production base for big zongzi with large output, numerous varieties and high specification. The varieties include original flavor green bean pork zongzi, pig's feet rib zongzi, sweet chestnut zongzi, healthy black rice zongzi and so on, with different weight of 1.5 kilograms, 1.25 kilograms or 0.75 kilogram. The government of Hengzhou City strongly supports the inheritance of zongzi making skills. It has built a publicity platform to constantly promote Hengxian big zongzi to be popular in China and even in the world.

横县大粽选料精细，制作考究，其主要原料有糯米、绿豆、猪肉、米酒、糖、盐、姜、葱、味精、五香粉、胡椒粉等，也可以根据不同风味添加板栗、虾米、腊味、黑米等辅料。横县大粽传统的制作方法是：首先备好各种主料和辅料。接着腌制猪肉，猪肉事先按一定比例切成长方形，再用适量米酒、姜葱末、盐、味精等拌匀，腌渍一到两天。同时，将绿豆破边、浸泡去皮，糯米浸泡、淘沙沥干后，加盐拌匀。粽叶水煮清洗干净然后包制粽子，把粽叶叠好放平，铺上糯米和猪肉，再盖上相应的绿豆等材料，然后用粽叶将其包裹成长方梯形，再用绳索环绕粽身一圈圈地捆扎。粽子包好后，烧开水，粽子要沸水下锅，大火煮开，待水开后再用小火煮，适当加水，3—4小时后翻粽，把锅底、锅面的粽子分别互调位置。大粽子需7—8个小时才能煮熟。粽子煮熟后，最好抓紧时间捞出，以免在锅中被水浸泡时间过长而失去味道。蒸煮熟软的粽子即可直接食用，解开粽绳，揭开粽叶，用筷子把粽子从顶上分成两半，均匀摊开糯米、绿豆等，将粽心肉压碎，将油浸入粽子后食用。冷却后的粽子可回锅煮软后食用，也可切成厚片煎软后食用。

作为横州市及岭南地区颇具地方特色的传统美食，横县大粽曾盛极一时，在中国-东盟博览会的美食节活动中，获得过东南亚国际旅游美食节金奖。如今，横县大粽的制作形式已经从家庭单一制，逐渐转变为由资质达标的作坊、工厂及公司制作经营。横州市已经形成了产量大、品种多、规格高、标准化的大粽制作基地，其品种有原味绿豆猪肉粽、猪脚排骨粽、香甜板栗粽、养生黑米粽等，规格有3斤、2.5斤、2斤和1.5斤等。横州市政府大力支持大粽制作技艺的传承，搭建宣传平台，不断推介横县大粽，让世界认识横县大粽这一美食。

隆安构树造纸技艺

Long'an Paper Making Skill of Goushu

项目名称：隆安构树造纸技艺

别称：无

分布范围：隆安县南圩镇联造村及周边地区

入选名录：2014年第五批自治区级非物质文化遗产名录

保护单位：隆安县文化馆

代表性传承人：黄国佳

Element name：Long'an Paper Making Skill of Goushu

Alternative name：None

Geographical location and range：Lianzao Village of Nanxu Town in Long'an County and the surrounding regions

Element inscribed list：In 2014 on the Fifth Autonomous Region List of Intangible Cultural Heritage

Competent body involved in safeguarding：Long'an County Cultural Centre

Representative inheritor：Huang Guojia

Long'an Paper Making Techniques of Goushu is a traditional handicraft popular in Lianzao Village in Long'an County and neighboring regions. It has been handed down within families for nearly 200 years. Lianzao Village was once known as a papermaking hometown where paper was made by hand and sold in and around Guangxi and even to other countries including Vietnam.

Papermaking Techniques of Goushu is a folk handicraft making the best use of local conditions. Its main raw materials are bark of Goushu tree (a kind of mulberry) and Mihao (the name in Zhuang language of a wild plant with natural viscos). The paper produced is called "abrasive paper" by the locals. The process of the papermaking is complicated with 18 major stages and 72 small procedures, such as selecting, drying, soaking, dyeing, grinding, steaming, stamping, washing, bleaching, lashing, cooking, re-steaming, re-washing, re-soaking, filtering, fishing out, pressing, air-drying, baking, pinching out and uncovering. The locals have taken simple shacks as factory buildings, digging pools around that fill up with water. The paper is finally made by barks of trees under handy operation of family-scale workshop. Such paper made by natural raw materials has the advantages of toughness, cleanness, softness, smoothness, durability, anti-corrosion and moth-proof.

Lianzao Village lies close to Buquan and Dujie townships and adjoins Dashishan Mountain where Goushu trees grow abundant and papermaking materials are of rich

隆安构树造纸技艺是一种传统手工造纸技艺，流传于隆安县南圩镇联造村及周边一带，以家族传承的方式延续，迄今已有近200年的历史。联造村曾被誉为“造纸村”，手工构树造纸的产品远销广西各地市及云南等地，最远曾经销往越南等国。

构树造纸，是民间的一种因地制宜的土法造纸技术。其主要原料是构树皮和米呺（“米呺”为当地土壮话，是一种具有粘胶的野生植物），生产出来的纸被当地人称为“砂纸”。构树皮造纸工艺流程十分复杂，分为采料、晒干、泡料、染料、磕料、蒸料、踩料、洗料、漂料、打料、煮料、再蒸料、洗料、泡料、滤料、舀纸、压纸、晾纸、炕纸、钳纸、揭纸等18道大工序和72道小工序。该技艺自诞生以来，当地人以简易窝棚为厂房，挖地为池，引用沟水，就地取材，采用家庭作坊式纯手工制作。构树手工造纸技艺所用原材料和工具都是就地取材，纯植物原料生产出来的砂纸具有坚韧洁净、柔软光滑、久存不坏、力撕不破、防腐防蛀等优点。

联造村地处布泉、都结乡，毗邻大石山区。山区适宜构

抄纸
Dipping Paper

脱纸
Taking the Paper off the Curtain

树灌木的生长，有丰富的砂纸制造资源。100多年来，联造村古法造纸技艺靠前辈们口传心授，一代代传承下来。古老的造砂纸业在联造村曾经盛极一时。过去，如果走进联造村的任何一个屯，都可听到家家户户里传出有节奏的木槌捶打纱皮"贴贴，贴都贴的贴"的响声。由于现代造纸技术的飞速发展，"砂纸"逐渐被质优价廉的各类纸张取代，构树皮手工造纸工艺也逐渐淡出了人们的视野。

目前，由于现代化机械生产出来的各种纸张已经能够满足人们的各种需求，土造的砂纸应用范围不广，销路差；生产效率低、工序繁杂等问题已成为手工造纸的难题，很多会造纸的工匠嫌收入不高，都不造了。当地造纸人越来越少，造纸工艺濒危失传。目前联造村古斗屯，唯有黄国佳一家在传承构树造纸技艺。保护这项濒危的技艺迫在眉睫。2010年，隆安县政府拨出专项资金，负责构树手工造纸技艺的挖掘和保护，同时，大力发展构树种植，鼓励年轻人学习造纸术等，对构树皮造纸工艺进行保护。2014年，经广西壮族自治区人民政府同意，隆安构树造纸技艺列入第五批自治区级非物质文化遗产名录。

verity. Papermaking techniques, once flourishing for a period, have been passed down here in an oral form for more than 100 years. If you went into the village in the past, you could hear the sound of rhythmic beating by wooden hammer "stick, stick…stick" from every household. But now the papermaking handicraft has been replaced by paper with high quality and low price and has faded out of people's vision, due to rapid development of modern paper-making technology.

At present, a few papermaking artisans stops their work viewing that the paper has an increasingly narrow market, time-consuming process and low efficiency, while paper produced by modern machinery has been able to meet people's various needs. The number of papermakers in local is declining, only Huang Guojia's family inherits the paper-making skills in Gudoutun of the village. The papermaking techniques faces a gloomy future and conservation is urgently needed. In 2010, the government of Long'an County allocated special funds for the excavation and protection of hand-made paper-making techniques. Meanwhile, they also developed the cultivation of Goushu trees and encouraged young people to learn papermaking, and took actions to protect the papermaking techniques. In 2014, papermaking techniques of Goushu in Long'an was inscribed on the Fifth Autonomous Region List of Intangible Cultural Heritage , after the approval of People's Government of Guangxi Zhuang Autonomous Region.

晾干
Dry by Airing

完工
Finishing

红良打铁技艺

Puddling Skill in Hongliang

项目名称：红良打铁技艺

别称：无

分布范围：隆安县雁江镇红良村

入选名录：2010年第三批自治区级非物质文化遗产名录
　　　　　2009年第二批市级非物质文化遗产名录

保护单位：隆安县文化馆

代表性传承人：林乔万、林仁超

Element name：Puddling Skill in Hongliang

Alternative name：None

Geographical location and range：Hongliang Village of Yanjiang Town in Long'an County

Element inscribed list：In 2010 on the Third Autonomous Region List of Intangible Cultural Heritage
In 2009 on the Second Municipal List of Intangible Cultural Heritage

Competent body involved in safeguarding：Long'an County Cultural Centre

Representative inheritors：Lin Qiaowan, Lin Renchao

红良打铁技艺是壮族家族式民间手工技艺，流传于隆安县雁江镇红良村那瓜屯、汪莫屯、汪苏屯、伏塘屯一带。主要制作剪刀、锥、铁钉、锅铲、菜刀等家庭用具以及锄头、斧头、镰刀、耙子等各式小农具。

红良打铁技艺历史悠久，迄今已有近200年的传承历史。相传清道光年间，有一年轻力壮的外乡人，名叫林宽瑞，他逃难落脚到红良村那瓜屯。为了维持生计，他自制煽火木风箱、火炉，靠捡回零星破碎的废铁，开炉炼铁制作铁钳、铁锤、铁砧等简陋工具，用土法操起手工打铁业，开始制作剪刀、锥、铁钉、活页、锅铲、菜刀之类的家庭用具，拿到圩市摆卖，不但换回了粮食，还换回了更多的废铁器。林宽瑞起早贪黑、辛勤劳作，从制作小件家庭生活用具，发展到制造锄头、斧头、镰刀、耙子之类的生产用具，渐渐地，他除了能维持生计，还有了积蓄。他建起了房子，娶妻生子。儿子长大后又子从父业，祖祖辈辈从事手工打铁，代代相传。民国初年，村里人在林宽瑞家族的影响和传授下，也学会了手工打铁工艺，从此，屯里的村民兴起了手工打铁业。林家目前已经有第七代传人在继承祖辈流传下来的打铁

Puddling techniques in Hongliang is a family-scale handicraft of Zhuang Ethnic Group, which spreads in and around Naguatun, Wangmotun, Wangsutun and Futangtun of Hongliang Village, Yanjiang Town, Long'an County. The puddling tools include scissors, cones, nails, pot shovels, kitchen knives and other household appliances as well as hoes, axes, sickles, rakes and other small agricultural tools.

Puddling in Hongliang has a long history for nearly 200 years. It is said that during the reign of Emperor Daoguang of the Qing Dynasty, there was a young and strong stranger named Lin Kuanrui who fled to Naguatun. In order to make a living, he became a blacksmith after making wooden bellows and stoves himself and forged irons he picked up into tongs, hammers, anvils and other simple tools. Then he began to make household appliances by hand including scissors, cones, nails, pot shovels, kitchen knives, all of which are sent to fairs and exchanged for food and more iron scrap. Lin worked hard from dawn till the dark and gradually he was asked to make tools of production including hoes, axes, sickles and rakes. He got richer and had a family then. His son continued Lin's work and their posterity have been engaging in the iron-forging work. The villagers learned from the Lin family and mastered iron-forging techniques in the early years of the Republic of China. Since then, iron-making industry has sprung up in Naguatun. It is the seventh generation of descendants of the Lin family who inherit the iron-making skills handed down from their ancestors.

The production process of puddling techniques in

打磨
Polishing

锻打
Forging

Hongliang is as follows: first is forging and drawing. According to the needs of customers, select steels or iron pieces and put it into the furnace to make red. Forge it after fishing out it. And cut the steels by cutting machine according to sample draft drawn on an iron plate. Then burn it red in the furnace to take out, forged it evenly with air hammer or iron hammer. In particular, the cutting tools and knife edges should be flat and thin. After hammering the samples, they should be modified and shaped with the grinding wheel or punch so the whole product can be turned smooth, but some products only need such grinding on areas two or three cun off the cutting edge. Next, cold treatment should be carried out. The grinded product should be placed in fires burned by coke or charcoal with the fire-provoking bellows. Then take out the product and insert it into the water if the product burn red. If the edge of it is too white, it means that the surface of the product is too hard and easy to crack. If it is too blue, it means that it is too soft and easy to roll up. Puddling techniques in Hongliang has experienced much difficult but has never stopped. At present, 25 of the 38 households in the village have furnaces to make iron, and a few family iron-making workshops have emerged and developed into different types, such as cooperation of "husband and wife", "father and son" and of "brothers". Three villagers even have set up small factories, each employing 10-30 workers.

With time going by and the development the economy, the Hongliang villagers who have become wealthy by the traditional iron-making industry are not satisfied with the previous handicraft. Many of them have purchased modern mechanical tools such as air hammer, blower, welding machine, cutting machine, sand wheel, punch and drilling machine, as well as batches of raw materials such as steel and coke. The production has been increased and updated on the basis of the traditional workshops. Apart from iron farm implements and hardware such as hoe with round handle, hoe with square handle, hoe with twisted teeth , cross hoe, tent hoe, peanut hoe, sugarcane hoe, fish tail hoe, axe, flat knife, large brick knife, straight wood knife, matching knife, wood knife with small hook, grass sickle, fish fork, vegetable knife, they also produce relevant agricultural machine. For example, self-developed multi-functional thresher, is made for rice and corn crops threshing. A variety of models of cranes and fittings like iron wheels of tractors, rollers, iron plough head are also available. The products, forged compact with fine cold treatment appropriate, are hard and durable with tough and sharp edge. They are so popular that they are appointed by many foreign businessmen and sold to Nanning, Baise, Yunnan and even Vietnam.

技艺。

红良打铁技艺的制作工序为，首先要锻打、画样，根据产品需要，先把钢材或铁件放入火炉炼红，拿出锻打后，在铁板上画出样图，用切割机割出样品，再投入火炉烧红后取出，用空气锤或铁锤锻打，捶打要均匀，特别是刀具，刀口既要平又要薄，把样品捶打好后，再修改成型，随后上砂轮或冲床，把整个产品车光滑，有的产品只车刀口两三寸左右，要车平薄、锋利。接着要进行冷处理，用煽火风箱将炉膛里的焦炭或木炭烧红，将车好的产品插入火中，待烧红到一定程度，把刀口放入水里，观察刀口，如果太白则说明处理得太硬，容易崩裂，如果太蓝，则说明太软，用起来容易卷口。红良打铁技艺几经风雨，从未间断。目前，全村38户中就有25户开炉打铁，涌现出"夫妻炉""父子炉""兄弟炉"等打铁家庭，其中有三人办起了小型工厂，每家雇有10—30名工人。

随着时代的发展和经济的进步，靠传统的打铁业逐渐富裕起来的红良村村民不满足于现状，他们中有不少人购买了空气锤、鼓风机、电焊机、切割机、砂轮、冲床、钻床等现代机械工具，购进成批的钢铁、焦炭等原材料，在传统作坊的基础上，不断扩大更新产品，他们除生产圆柄沙锄、方形沙锄头、回齿锄、十字锄、帐篷锄、花生锄、甘蔗锄、鱼尾锄、斧头、扁刀、大砖刀、直柴刀、勾柴刀、小勾柴刀、草镰刀、鱼叉、菜刀等各种铁制农具和小五金外，还从事相关农机具制造，自行研制了多功能脱粒机，用于稻谷、玉米农作物的脱粒，还生产了多种型号的吊车、拖拉机铁轮、滚轮、铁犁头架等配件，这些产品锻打密实，冷处理得当，铁器坚硬耐用，刀口坚韧锋利，质量上乘，产品十分畅销，有不少外地客商上门订货，产品远销至南宁、百色、云南，甚至越南等地。

南宁壮族干栏建筑营造技艺

Construction Skill of Zhuang's Ganlan Architecture in Nanning

项目名称：南宁壮族干栏建筑营造技艺

别称：无

分布范围：南宁市及周边壮族聚居区

入选名录：2015年第六批市级非物质文化遗产名录

保护单位：南宁市民族文化艺术研究院（南宁市非物质文化遗产保护中心）

代表性传承人：无

Element name：Construction Skill of Zhuang's Ganlan Architecture in Nanning

Alternative name：None

Geographical location and range：Nanning City and the surrounding Zhuang-Inhabited Areas

Element inscribed list：In 2015 on the Sixth Municipal List of Intangible Cultural Heritage

Competent body involved in safeguarding：Nanning Ethnic Culture and Art Research Institute (Nanning Intangible Cultural Heritage Protection Centre)

Representative inheritor：None

Pile-dwelling structure is a kind of wooden architecture with high feet where people live above and livestock like cattle, sheep, dogs and pigs kept below. It was invented by the ancestors of Zhuang and Miao ethnic groups to prevent snakes, insects and beasts that spring up in mountain areas and southern climate, and it has developed distinctive characteristics of the two ethnic groups.

It has been a long history for the pile-dwelling structure. According to the archaeological discovery in Dingshi Mountain site, the ancient Zhuang along the Yijiang River were able to build such architecture long before 10000 years ago. Such building has been commonly built among the south China and ethnic group areas from ancient times to the present. *Book of Wei and Record for Qiu Officials records*, "the southern barbarians can be divided to many kinds, so they like to live scattered in valleys and build their house by piling up logs against giant trees. They will live on the second floor of the building called Ganlan (pile-dwelling structure)." The Zhuang people are one of the earliest creators of such building that experienced three times of improvement. They first built it by piling blocks against trees, and later they began to use wooden pillars buried in the ground and covered their house by leaves. At last, mortise and tenon joint and tenon through were used in the house strutting that covered by tiles.

Pile-dwelling structure is mostly constructed by local material, such as wood, stones, clay and tiles. It is generally built for two-story ones and divided into upper, middle and lower layers. The lower layer is built for keeping livestock, firewood and grain with no walls around but dozens of wooden columns supporting the weight of the whole building. Even walls are set up for the lower, they are made of bamboo strips tied together with gaps lied among them that conducive to the leaking of floods. The middle layer is mainly utilized for living with halls, living rooms, storage rooms and a fire pond in it. As for the upper layer, it is suitable for both living and storing. Both of the front and rear eaves will use bamboo and wood to set up a platform for drying grain. There are varies procedures before a pile- dwelling structure constructed, such as site selection, geomantic observing, leveling foundation, materials preparation, cutting materials, pushing materials, stabilization, fan arrangement, beam and timber construction, vertical building, upper beam placement, eaves design and roofing building.

There are three main features existing in the designing techniques of pile-dwelling structure. First, the types of the building cover a wide range including lake dwelling, turn turrets, octagonal building and other buildings with various

所谓“干栏”，是“人栖其上，牛羊犬豕畜其下”的木结构高脚楼建筑，一般为住宅之用。它是壮族、苗族先民根据自然地理环境和气候特点，为了预防蛇虫猛兽之害，创造性地发明出来的，具有独特的民族风格。

干栏式建筑建造技艺有着悠久的历史，顶蛳山遗址考古发现，在一万年前的邕江边，壮族先民就会建造干栏建筑。“干栏”从远古时代一直传承至今，广泛分布于我国南方和西南诸少数民族聚居地区。《魏书·毬僚传》记载：“盖南蛮之别种，种类其多，散居山谷依树积木，以居其上，名曰干栏。”壮民族是最早发明和建造干栏式建筑的民族之一，干栏建筑经历了三个发展阶段，分别为依树积木木构成巢、埋柱绑扎盖叶、榫卯与穿斗构架铺瓦。

干栏建筑建造多为就地取材，主要采用木材、石头、泥土、瓦片等材料建造，一般分为上、中、下三层，底部架空，用数十根木柱支撑楼上的重量，四周不设墙，主要用来蓄养家禽家畜，堆放柴火、谷物等，如果设墙也是由多空隙的竹篾围起，以利于洪水的通过。中层由木柱支撑在空中，主要用于居住，分设有厅堂、居室、储藏室、火塘等功能空间。上层为阁楼，用来存放粮食和杂物，也可以居住，前檐或后檐会用竹木架起可晒晾谷物的平台。干栏建筑建造工序繁多，主要有选屋场、看风水、平整地基、备料、裁料、推料、安磉磴、排扇、做梁木、立屋、上梁、搭檐断水、装屋以及其他附属工程。

南宁壮族干栏建筑建造技艺的主要特征有三：一是干栏形式多样。干栏建筑有吊脚楼、走马转角楼、八角楼和“凹”字形等多种干栏形式。二是具有适应性。干栏建筑建造技艺适应了南方地区高温多雨、气候潮湿的环境特点，满足了人们预防蛇虫猛兽之害的需要，广泛分布于南宁各县区的少数民族聚居地。三是具有实用性。榫卯发明以后，特别是带梢钉孔榫应用以后，加强了干栏建筑梁柱的连接，凌空而建的干栏式建筑更加牢固且具有实用性。

干栏式建筑建造技艺对深入了解壮族居住的地理位置、气候环境，研究壮民族生活习性、壮族传统民俗文化的丰富内涵具有重要意义。干栏建筑建造技艺是壮族先民留下的宝贵财富，保存它可以传承干栏文化，让更多的人了解骆越文明，有利于发展旅游经济，增加收入。干栏建筑建造技艺是壮族地区为了适应南方地区炎热多雨、地面潮湿、瘴气弥漫和猛兽横行的自然环境而发明建造的一种住居形式，满足了人们的生理和心理需要。

干栏建筑建造技艺及浓郁的民俗均具有重要的历史价值及社会价值。它的历史原貌和人文价值，是岭南人民宝贵的文化遗产，体现了壮族历史的多姿多彩的“干栏”建筑文化。但随着经济的快速发展和多民族文化融合，干栏建筑逐渐淡出人们的视野，干栏建筑建造技艺难以传承。作为维系民族感情、增强民族自豪感、推动民族团结稳定的重要精神纽带，干栏建筑建造技艺必须加以保护。

shapes. Second, it is built for respecting the local conditions. It not only suits for the south where there is rainy and humid with high temperature, but also meets people's needs of preventing snakes, insects and beasts. The last feature is that it is practical. The pillars can be better connected after the application of tenon with pin holes and tenons, and the building is more solid and durable than those built before.

Designing techniques of pile-dwelling structure is of great significance to understand the geographical location, climate and environment of the Zhuang inhabitants, to study the living habits and the rich connotation of the traditional folk culture of the Zhuang Ethnic Group. As a valuable culture left by the ancient Zhuang, more protection and promotion of it can spread Luoyue civilization, develop tourism-oriented economic and help increase revenue. Totally speaking, such architecture is invented to adapt to the hot and rainy climate, the wet ground, the diffuse lameness and the natural environment where beasts run rampant, which meets both of the people's physiological and psychological needs.

Designing techniques of pile-dwelling structure and relevant folk customs have great value in both historical and social terms. What it looks like and what it implicates are all cultural heritages of the Lingnan people, displaying the colorful culture of pile-dwelling structure. However, it has been gradually away from people's attention and trapped by increasingly difficult inheritance with the rapid development of economy and the integration of multi-ethnic cultures. The techniques must be well protected because it is a spiritual tie that shares ethnics' feelings, encourages national spirit and keeps ethnic unity and the stability.

干栏建筑内部结构
Internal Structure of Ganlan Architecture

南宁制陶技艺

Nanning Pottery Making Skill

项目名称：南宁制陶技艺

别称：无

分布范围：良庆区、横州市、宾阳县

入选名录：2015年第六批市级非物质文化遗产名录

保护单位：南宁市民族文化艺术研究院（南宁市非物质文化遗产保护中心）

代表性传承人：覃永宣、胡可可

Element name：Nanning Pottery Making Skill

Alternative name：None

Geographical location and range：Liangqing District, Hengzhou City and Binyang County

Element inscribed list：In 2015 on the Sixth Municipal List of Intangible Cultural Heritage

Competent body involved in safeguarding：Nanning Ethnic Culture and Art Research Institute (Nanning Intangible Cultural Heritage Protection Centre)

Representative inheritor：Qin Yongxuan, Hu Keke

拉坯
Shaping the Clay

晾干
Dry by Airing

南宁制陶技艺是南宁传统的手工技艺之一，是壮族地区壮、汉等民族勤劳和智慧的结晶。制陶技艺历史悠久，相传至今。目前，南宁市良庆区及横州市、宾阳县等地，均较好地保留着传统的手工制陶技艺。

南宁制陶技艺是新石器时期的产物。早在一万年前的新石器时期，南宁先民就已掌握了磨制石器、骨器的技术和制陶技术，并在此基础上创造了大石铲文化、顶蛳山文化和干栏文化。先秦以后，制陶技艺和手工纺织已达相当高的水平，又相继出现了陶纺轮和麻布。南宁制陶技艺的高度发达，得益于郁江流域提供的土壤。这里是古人类文明的摇篮，沿河地带水上交通便利，有丰富的优质石灰、石矿资源和大量的优质红黏土资源，为制陶技艺的发展提供了优越的地理环境和物质基础。同时，便利的交通条件、发达的商贸活动，又进一步推动、加速了制陶手工业的市场化进程。承载着历史印记的制陶技艺，对于研究南宁乃至广西传统手工制陶史，均有着极大的价值。

南宁制陶技艺包含多道工序，主要有选料、洗料、晾

Nanning Pottery Making Skill is one of the traditional handicrafts which is the crystallization of the industriousness and wisdom of the Zhuang and Han nationalities. It has a long history and has been handed down in areas of Liangqing District, Hengzhou City and Binyang County.

Making techniques of earthenware in Nanning is originated in Neolithic Age. As early as 10000 years ago, the people in Nanning had mastered the techniques of grinding stone tools, bone tools and pottery making. The culture of stone shovel, Dingshi Mountain Culture and Ganlan architecture culture were born in such cases. Pottery technology and hand-made textiles have reached a fairly high level after the Pre-Qin Dynasty, and ceramic spinning wheels and linen have appeared one after another afterwards. Nanning pottery making skill is highly developed due to the soil provided by Yujiang River. It is supposedly a cradle of ancient civilization convenient water transportation, abundant high-quality lime, stone mineral resources and a large quantity of red clay resources, providing a superior geographical environment and material basis for the development of pottery technology. Meanwhile, the marketization of pottery handcrafting was accelerated thanks to the convenient traffic conditions and developed commercial activities. Nanning pottery making witnessing the history is of great value in studying the history of traditional pottery handcrafting of Nanning and even that of Guangxi.

Several procedures are asked to follow to make

earthenware, such as material selecting, material washing, drying, rubbing, base making, glazing, kiln loading and firing. The earthenware is mainly made for daily utensils including crocks, jars, altars, pots, plates, bowls, pots, kettles and tiles. Ceramic products could be applied in a wide range of areas, as they are beautiful and bright, cheap and durable, and not easy to conduct heat. The earthenware produced in Nanning is more than 200 types, many of that are also rated as famous trademarks in Guangxi and sold well in Yunnan, Guizhou, Hunan, Hong Kong and Macao.

Although some people in Nanning still make pottery handcrafting these days, pottery handcrafting still faced a gloomy future of no inheritor, because of the decrease of people's demand for pottery and the reluctance of young people to concentrate on learning this ancient craft. In order to better inherit and develop making techniques of earthenware, Nanning Ethnic Culture and Art Research Institute has organized a group for studying and protecting pottery making techniques, which has gone deep into the investigation and excavation work of Nanning's pottery technology many times, and it also raised funds for the protection and inheritance of the techniques. Meanwhile, Nanning Intangible Cultural Heritage Protection Centre has formulated a "five-year protection plan" to protect the techniques, including publicity, training and promotion of relevant books and video materials; cultivation of pottery making masters; and cooperation with enterprises to establish an earthenware museum. Making techniques of earthenware got better protected and inherited under feasible action of relevant protection authorities.

干、搓泥、做坯、上釉、装窑、烧制等。所制陶器主要为缸、罐、坛、煲、盘、碗、壶、瓦等日用品。陶制品造型美观、釉质明亮、晶莹润泽、不易传热、价廉耐用，具有较为广泛的实用价值。南宁出产的陶制品种类繁多，数量可达200多种，有很多还被评为广西著名商标，畅销区内外的同时，远销云南、贵州、湖南及香港、澳门等地。

目前，南宁市虽有一些市县仍有以传统手工技艺制作陶器的习惯，但随着人们对陶器需求量的减少，也因年轻人不愿再潜心学习这门古老的手艺，南宁制陶技艺已面临失传的境况。为传承和发展南宁传统制陶技艺，南宁市民族文化艺术研究院组织成立了南宁制陶技艺保护和研究工作小组，多次深入南宁市各地区进行制陶技艺的调查、挖掘工作，并筹集经费用于南宁制陶技艺的保护和传承。与此同时，南宁市非物质文化遗保护中心制订了“五年保护计划”，对制陶技艺进行专项保护，内容包括编写相关的书籍及视频资料进行宣传、培训、推广，培养制陶工艺大师，与企业合作建立陶器博物馆。在相关保护单位切实可行的保护计划之下，制陶技艺得以更好地保护和传承。

化皮猪脚制作技艺

Huapi Pig's Feet Making Skill

项目名称：化皮猪脚制作技艺

别称：无

分布范围：西乡塘区水街

入选名录：2015年第六批市级非物质文化遗产名录

保护单位：西乡塘区文化馆

代表性传承人：神华生

Element name：Huapi Pig's Feet Making Skill

Alternative name：None

Geographical location and range：Shui Street of Xixiangtang District

Element inscribed list：In 2015 on the Sixth Municipal List of Intangible Cultural Heritage

Competent body involved in safeguarding：Xixiangtang District Cultural Centre

Representative inheritor：Shen Huasheng

Huapi Pig Foot, originally a folk traditional food spreads in Guangdong and Guangxi, has gradually evolved into a snack of Nanning and became one of the typical representatives of the specialties of Shui Street. Pig foot, also called pig hoofs, can be divided into types of fore and hind ones. The fore hoofs are straight with few bones while the hind ones are slightly curved with more bones. The snack is made by hand under the instruction of a traditional formula. The fore feet will be chosen to wash and dry drip, and then it will be pickled, deep-fried until golden brown. The cooked feet should be added with thirteen ingredients for three hours until the skin is soft, such as star anise, amomum tsao-ko and self-made spices. The snack is popular for its distinctive flavor and it has been awarded the titles of "Ten Gourmet Snacks in Nanning", "Golden Snacks in Guangxi" and "Famous Snacks in Guangxi", as it gets full marks for the color, fragrance, taste and shape.

Huapi Pig Foot was spawned by Yongjiang River culture and wharfs culture and has a long history for more than 100 years. Huang Tiyuan, a Zhuang poet in the late Qing Dynasty, wrote in his poem *Ode to Yongjiang River*, "faint singing announces the sun rising, the boatman calls for Yongcheng mooring. The river was all over the cargo shipping, and towering masts are out of counting. Walnut shells lying followed big ships, the dialect of north and the south never stops. The night is lit by thousands of lights, making the river twinkling bright. The boat shuttles back and forth, moon in rivers now in view, now hidden. Just bought fish porridge on the bow, the tail comes the pig foot vermicelli again." The poem not only depicts the prosperity of sailing and commerce along the Yongjiang River in Nanning, but also depicts the lively scene of Nanning night market in the Qing Dynasty. It fully shows that fish porridge and pig feet in Huapi have become popular in Nanning at that time.

Huapi Pig Foot snack is popular among people and became a tasty dish for its irreplaceable flavor and affordable price. It has higher nutritional composition and therapeutic value. Traditional Chinese medicine holds that pig foot is neutral in nature and tastes sweet and salty. *The Food Spectrum of Suixiju* (a famous book about diet therapy wrote in the Qing Dynasty) recorded that pig foot "is good for kidney, helping improve waist and feet; nourishing gastric juice to smooth the skin. It can contribute to muscles growth, ulcers healing, blood circulating and lactation". Pig hooves are rich in collagen protein and have lower fat content than fat. Collagen protein in pig hooves can be converted into gelatin during cooking, and the latter improves the physiological function of the body and the water storage function of skin

化皮猪脚，原本是两广地区的民间传统美食，如今已经逐渐演变成南宁的传统美食，是南宁水街传统美食的典型代表之一。猪脚又称猪蹄、猪手，分前后两种，猪前蹄肉多骨头较少，呈直形，猪后蹄肉少骨头稍多，呈弯形。化皮猪脚采用传统配方，手工制作，选用南宁本地土猪前脚下节，将其洗净，过水，过油腌制，入锅，炸熟，配以八角、草果、自制十三香等辅料卤制三个小时，骨化、皮软成型即成。化皮猪脚的色、香、味、形俱佳，风味独特，深受欢迎，先后荣获“南宁十大美食小吃”“广西金牌小吃”“广西名小吃”等称号。

化皮猪脚是伴随着邕江江河文化和码头而产生的，流传至今已有100多年的历史。清朝末年，壮族诗人黄体元的诗歌《邕江杂咏》道：“隐隐歌声报晓晴，篙公报到抵邕城。货船江面排鳞似，万杆桅樯数不清。大船结尾小船头，北调南腔话不休。照水夜来灯万点，满江红作乱星浮。小艇如梭去复回，满江如是月明开。船头刚买鱼生粥，船尾猪蹄粉又来。”诗中不仅描绘了南宁邕江沿岸帆桨如织、商贸繁荣的景象，同时也将清代南宁夜市的热闹景象描绘了出来，说明清朝末年鱼生粥、化皮猪脚等已经成为南宁地区大受欢迎的美食。

化皮猪脚具有深厚的群众基础，其独特的风味和实惠的价格深受老百姓的喜欢，是南宁人民的佐餐佳肴。猪脚有较高的营养成分和食疗价值。中医认为猪蹄性平，味甘咸，《随息居饮食谱》记载猪蹄“填肾精而健腰脚，滋胃液以滑皮肤。长肌肉可愈漏疡；助血脉能充乳汁，交肉尤补”。猪蹄含有丰富的胶原蛋白质，脂肪含量也比肥肉低，猪蹄中的胶原蛋白质在烹调过程中可转化成明胶，从而改善机体生理功能和皮肤组织细胞的储水功能，能防止皮肤干瘪起皱，增强皮肤弹性和韧性，具有延缓皮肤衰老、美容养颜、促进儿童生长发育等功效。

化皮猪脚
Huapi Pig's Feet

化皮猪脚粉
Huapi Pig's Feet Rice Noodle

在南宁传统饮食文化中，化皮猪脚曾兴盛一时，但随着社会经济的不断发展，饮食文化日渐多元，化皮猪脚的制作正面临发展困境，经营门店日渐减少，老一辈制作者年事已高，传统手工制作又对年轻人没有太多的吸引力，化皮猪脚的发展处于青黄不接的状态。为传承和发展这一非物质文化遗产，南宁市西乡塘区政府在南宁市古源香天天餐饮管理有限责任公司成立由业务部牵头、领导挂帅、门店主负责的南宁化皮猪脚保护工作领导小组，负责对化皮猪脚进行挖掘、保护和传承，并将其作为主打产品。目前已建成广西第一座化皮猪脚生产配送中央厨房，实行统一经营、统一配送的模式，各门店要挂上化皮猪脚专有门牌方可进行营业。在政府的努力下，化皮猪脚被不断推向市场。

tissue cells. It can also prevent and help cure dry and wrinkled skin, enhancing skin elasticity and toughness, delay skin aging, and promote the physical growth of children.

Pig foot snack has flourished for a while among Nanning's traditional dietary, but now it faces a dilemma of development with the continuous development of social economy and the diversification of dietary culture. The number of stores selling pig foot is decreasing, the sophisticated producers are in their declining years, and the traditional handicraft production has little attraction for young people. All of these have caused no enough trained younger ones ready to take over from older experts. In order to better inherit and develop this intangible cultural heritage, the government of Xixiangtang District established a leading group of pig foot protection work in Nanning's Guyuanxiang Daily Catering Management of Limited Liability., which was led by the business department, taken command in official leaders and taken in charge of by the shop owner. The group is set for excavating and protecting pig foot making and commercializing it as their main product. The first central kitchen for production and distribution the snack in Guangxi has been built successfully, which is equipped with unified operation and distribution. Only when the stores have the exclusive license of pig-feet making can they have normal business running. Huapi Pig Foot has been available in the market step by step thanks to the unremitting efforts of the government.

武鸣壮族刘氏“药仙翁”药茶制作技艺

Wuming Liu’s “Medicine Immortal” Pharmaceutical Tea Making Skill of Zhuang Ethnic Group

项目名称：武鸣壮族刘氏“药仙翁”药茶制作技艺

别称：无

分布范围：武鸣区太平镇朱董村

入选名录：2020年第八批自治区级非物质文化遗产名录

2015年第六批市级非物质文化遗产名录

保护单位：武鸣区文化馆

代表性传承人：刘力瑞

Element name：Wuming Liu’s “Medicine Immortal” Pharmaceutical Tea Making Skill of Zhuang Ethnic Group

Alternative Name：None

Geographical location and range：Zhudong Village of Taiping Town in Wuming District

Element inscribed list：In 2020 on the Eighth Autonomous Region List of Intangible Cultural Heritage

In 2015 on the Sixth Municipal List of Intangible Cultural Heritage

Competent body involved in safeguarding：Wuming District Cultural Centre

Representative inheritor：Liu Lirui

武鸣壮族刘氏“药仙翁”药茶，采用武鸣区太平镇朱董村刘氏家族家传秘方，根据传统壮医药学食疗食补原理加工配制而成。武鸣壮族刘氏“药仙翁”药茶种类繁多，药材配伍不同，功效各异。配方中的多种药材均采自武鸣区境内的大明山，主要成分有百合、决明子、罗汉果、麦冬、枸杞、灵芝、山楂、桂圆、桑叶、荷叶、玉竹、桑葚、甜茶、余甘子、菊花、薏苡仁、合欢花、玫瑰茄、茯苓、葛根、乌梅、薄荷、益母草、鸡爪果、菊花、金银花、夜交藤等。其分为外治和内治两大类，有利尿通便、清热解毒、降脂减肥，安神助眠、护肝解酒、祛痘治痔、化痰止咳、解郁舒心、益气舒精、消渴降糖、补肾强腰等功效，现已入选“广西旅游首选品牌”。

南宁市武鸣区太平镇朱董村，前接天井岭，背靠高峰岭和崇桑岭山脉。壮族刘氏家族世代聚居于此，以打猎采药为生，在长期与恶劣的环境和疾病抗争的过程中，积累了丰富的壮医药物及配方。相传，武鸣壮族刘氏“药仙翁”药茶起源于元朝至顺元年（1330），至今已有近700年的历史。刘氏先祖刘禄时任邕州通判，还乡途中遇黄氏独子饮酒导致昏厥，危在旦夕，他用自配自用的药茶救活黄氏的独子，而后配方一直沿用至今。据刘氏宗谱记载，刘氏第15世祖刘祥宗遗训，规定刘氏“药仙翁”所有药方均由族人相传。乾隆十五年（1750），规定药方传男不传女，该规矩一直承袭300多年，20世纪60年代初开始男女均传，沿承至今已历22代。

武鸣壮族刘氏“药仙翁”药茶制作技艺保留了家传配方和汤药熬制工艺，具有壮医药学基本特点。刘氏“药仙翁”药茶讲究药食同源，注重食疗食补。其所选用的药材多来源于武鸣境内的大明山，它是一座天然的中药材宝库。武鸣先民充分利用这份来自大自然的馈赠，改造生存环境，追求美好生活，刘氏“药仙翁”药茶制作技艺的出现、发展和成熟正是这种追求美好生活的体现。刘氏“药仙翁”药茶制作技

Medicine Tea of Liu Family from Zhuang Ethnic Group in Wuming is made by the secret recipe from Liu's family, which entails principles of diet therapy of traditional Zhuang Medicine. The tea differs in kinds made from various medicine materials of varied efficiencies, most of which are growing in the Daming Mountain, such as greenish lily seed, cassia seed, Momordica grosvenori, dwarf lilyturf, Chinese wolfberry, Ganoderma lucidum, hawthorn, longan, folium mori, lotus leaf, Polygonatum odoratum, mulberry, rubus suavissimus, Chinese olive, chrysanthemum, semen coicis, mimosa-tree flower, roselle, Poria cocos, the root of kudzu vine, smoked plum, mint, motherwort, honey tree, honeysuckle and tuber fleeceflower stem. The medicine materials heal the body by applying externally or taking internally in every aspect including promoting diuresis, clearing away heat, reducing weight, sleeping inducing, alleviating a hangover, treating acne and haemorrhoids, reducing phlegm, dispelling melancholy, tonifying qi, quenching thirst and tonifying kidneys. The tea has been rated as "the preferred brand of Guangxi tourism".

Zhudong Village, Taiping Town, Wuming District of Nanning City is situated behind Tianjingling Mountain and backed by Gaofengling Mountain and Dongsangling Mountains. The Liu family of the Zhuang Ethnic Group has lived here for generations, hunting and collecting medicines for a living, and has saved abundant medicines and wrote prescriptions in the long-term struggle against harsh environment and diseases. It is said that the medicine tea was originated from the Zhishun years of the Yuan Dynasty and has been existing for nearly 700 years. Liu Lu, an ancestor of Liu family in the Yuan Dynasty, was the commanding officer of Yongzhou on his way back to hometown. When he met Huang's only son who was in unconsciousness for drinking too much, he revived the boy with his medicinal tea made by himself, which has been used from generation to generation ever since. According to Liu's genealogy, Liu Xiangzong of the 15th generation of Liu's family left his last words which stipulated that no prescriptions of Liu's medicinal herbs permitted to be open, but only can be handed down within the family. In the fifteenth year of Emperor Qianlong reign (1750), prescriptions were only passed down among males of the family. And it wasn't inherited to females until the 1960s. It has gone through for 22 generations so far.

The medicine tea shares basic features with Zhuang medicine by retaining ancestral formula and decocting techniques. As the tea holds that "curing by eating", most of the medicine materials of the tea come from Daming Mountain that is supposedly a treasure-house of Chinese medicine materials granted by nature. The ancient people in Wuming pursued a better life by making full use of this gift and improving their living conditions. And the tea is a vivid demonstration of the efforts. As a crystallization of the wisdom of Wuming ancestors, the medicine tea boasts a profound civilization of Zhuang medicine and has been closely related to local life and breed. It is of great practical value to excavate, protect and inherit the medical cultural heritage of the Zhuang Ethnic Group. It also plays an important role in the academic exchange and the further development of Zhuang medicine.

The traditional Zhuang medicine has faded out of people's life with the development of modern science and medicine. And no enough trained younger ones are ready to take over the making techniques of the tea from aged experts for many reasons, such as decreasingly opportunities for relevant activities, the successive death of sophisticated Zhuang doctors, young man's fainting attention to the tea.

In order to better protect this cultural heritage, the Government of Wuming District set up a leading group aiming for special project protection in 2012, so as to excavate, protect and inherit the related content of making techniques of Liu's medicine tea. They also help push on the industrialization, commercialization and market-oriented development of the tea on the basis of Liu's ancestral formula and modern scientific processing technology. Their efforts have been paid off, the health tea has developed 11 products that have participated in the small and medium-sized enterprises expositions in Yulin for many times, and it was selected as the designated products during the Third China Guilin International Tourism Exposition. Making techniques of the tea has been well inherited and developed due to the efforts of the government and more promotion from the market.

艺是武鸣先民智慧的结晶，与当地的生产生活和繁衍生息相依托共存，具有深厚的壮医药文化底蕴。它不仅对于挖掘、保护和传承壮民族医药文化遗产有着重要的实用价值，同时对于医药学术交流和壮医药长足发展也有着重要作用。

随着现代科学和医药学的发展，人们对传统壮医药的认识日益淡薄，能够给传承活动提供的平台日益减少，老壮医相继谢世，刘氏“药仙翁”药茶制作工艺的传承出现断层，年轻人无法认识到刘氏“药仙翁”药茶的重要性，使得这项制作技艺的传承青黄不接。

为保护好这一文化遗产，武鸣区政府于2012年成立专门的项目保护工作领导小组，对刘氏“药仙翁”药茶制作技艺的相关内容进行挖掘、保护和传承。在刘氏家传配方药理的基础上，结合现代科学加工技术研制刘氏“药仙翁”保健药茶产品，实行产业化、商品化、市场化发展。目前，刘氏“药仙翁”保健药茶已开发出11个品种，产品多次参加玉林中小企业商机博览会，在第三届中国桂林国际旅游博览会期间被选为大会指定用品。在政府的努力和市场的推动下，刘氏“药仙翁”药茶制作技艺得到了较好的传承和发展。

武鸣壮酒制作技艺

Wuming Wine Making Skill of Zhuang Ethnic Group

项目名称：武鸣壮酒制作技艺

别称：骆越壮酒制作技艺

分布范围：武鸣区

入选名录：2015年第六批市级非物质文化遗产名录

保护单位：武鸣区文化馆

代表性传承人：阮朝鑫

Element name：Wuming Wine Making Skill of Zhuang Ethnic Group

Alternative name：Luoyue Wine Making Skill of Zhuang Ethnic Group

Geographical location and range：Wuming District

Element inscribed list：In 2015 on the Sixth Municipal List of Intangible Cultural Heritage

Competent body involved in safeguarding：Wuming District Cultural Centre

Representative inheritor：Ruan Chaoxin

The wine of Zhuang Ethnic Group in Wuming is also called the wine of Zhuang Ethnic Group in Luoyue, meaning health wine held by Zhuang people. It has the names because Wuming was the centre and the earliest city of the ancient Luoyue state. As one part of Luoyue culture, it has been handed down mainly through oral teaching. As a hand making wine, it is made after intricate procedures that examined for thousands of times. The main raw materials consist of brewed rice wine and selected traditional Chinese medicinal materials. The wine cannot be accomplished unless the materials are mixed in right ratio before vinification. The wine shared distinct characteristics with Zhuang medicine, for instance, the medicine materials include longan, ginseng, colla corii asini, pilose antler, hemp seed, mulberry, perotis indica, honeysuckle, the root of dahurian angelica, fennel seed, bitter cardamon, date, matrimony vine, citron, fingered citron and solomon's seal. The materials are said to help cure deficiency and reach a yin-yang harmony within the human body.

Wuming, the centre of the ancient Luoyue civilization, has a long brewing history. It has been discovered by Yuanlongpo archaeological works that health culture includes techniques of wine and herbs brewing has existed as early as the Shang Dynasty.It is said that the skills are enlightened by trachypithecus francoisi (called Wuyuan in Chinese), a kind of monkey is able to save fruits in stone caves. According to *Records and Maps of Wuyuan County,* long before the Song Dynasty, Zhuang people has known how to brew Chinese medicine and built folk workshops making health wine, such as Gula wine and Wuyuan wine. Unluckily, skills to make these health wines failed to remain for lost and ecological reasons. Wuming Wine Making Skill of Zhuang Ethnic Group could be traced back to the Song Dynasty. In 1053, Ruan Fenyuan, the ancestor of Ruan family, settled in Wuming after Diqing (a Han general of the Song Dynasty) defeated Nong Zhigao (a Zhuang general of an uprising army) in Kunlun Mountain. Ruan Zan, the descendant of Ruan Fenyuan, built Xianshan Yard in Yilingyan Mountain where he, on the one hand, collected and rearranged the health preservation recipes handed down from the ancient Luoyue according to Central China culture, and made pills of immortality and making health wine on the other hand. Later, Ruan Daoming, the tenth generation of Ruan, stepped further than his ancestors on the way to make a better health wine formula. In 1259, Ruan Daoming, a medical practitioner then, escaped from flames of the war incited by Mongolian army in Hengshan Village, and returned to Yilingyan Mountain to make elixir and wine of Zhuang Ethnic Group which has been handed down for 37 generations and more than 750 years.

武鸣壮酒，又称“骆越壮酒”，意为“壮家人的养生酒”。武鸣地区是骆越文化的中心，同时也是骆越古国最早的都城，武鸣壮酒以悠久灿烂的骆越文化为依托，通过口传心授的方式传承至今。武鸣壮酒采用传统手工制作，方法考究，过程繁复。其主要原材料需使用特酿小熬米酒，配以精选的药材，经过精细配比、传统调制、泡制和封存等工序加工而成。武鸣壮酒具有鲜明的壮医药学特点，其配方中含有桂圆、人参、阿胶、鹿茸、火麻仁、桑葚、茅根、金银花、白芷、小茴子、益智仁、大枣、枸杞子、香橼、佛手、黄精等20多种中药材，有补虚调气、阴阳调和的功效。

武鸣是骆越文化的中心，具有悠久的制酒历史，元龙坡考古发现证明，武鸣地区在商代已形成了包含制酒技术和中草药泡制工艺在内的养生文化。据说这种本领是受到乌猿的启发而创制的，乌猿会在石洞中储存浆果发酵成香糟。据清代《武缘县图经》记载，早在宋朝以前壮家人便掌握了中草药酿浸工艺，并开设了酿酒的民间作坊，已有了类似武鸣壮酒的养生酒，如古辣酒、乌猿酒等，而这些类似的养生酒或者失传或者因生态问题无法制作，都没有很好地留存下来。武鸣壮酒制作技艺可追溯到两宋时期。1053年，阮氏先祖阮芬元追随狄青在昆仑山打败侬智高后，定居于武鸣，其后代阮赞于伊岭岩创立仙山院，以中原文化为依托，对骆越古国流传下来的养生秘方进行整理，结庐炼丹，炮制药酒。而后阮氏第十代传人阮道明进一步收集药方，采办药材，使壮酒配方趋于完善。1259年，蒙古铁骑火烧横山寨，在此处行医的阮道明死里逃生后返回伊岭岩，结庐炼丹，酿造壮酒，传承至今已历37代，传承750余年。

武鸣壮酒制作技艺承载着骆越先民的勤劳和智慧，与壮医药一脉相承，与当地人民的生产生活以及社会发展密切相关。武鸣壮酒讲求药食同源、食疗食补，保健性强，具有春养肝、夏养心、秋养肺、冬养肾，四季壮骨强身的功效，老少皆宜。武鸣壮酒传承稳固，谱系清楚，以阮氏家传配方和手工制作工艺为基础，是壮族文化体系和传统壮医药配伍中的重要组成部分，是骆越先民智慧的结晶和延续，对挖掘保护和传承壮族医药文化遗产有着重要的实用价值。在现代医学和科学日新月异的今天，武鸣壮酒潜藏着巨大的商业价值，有待挖掘。

现代科学和西方医学的不断发展和兴盛，使得壮族传统医药养生学的生存空间不断被挤压，且武鸣壮酒制作技艺传承方式是口传心授，掌握技艺的老艺人相继谢世，新一代的人才培养跟不上，后继乏人，使其陷入了濒危的处境当中。基于这种情况，武鸣区政府采取两步走的方式，一方面对武鸣壮酒加强保护，合理利用，整体开发，对传统制作工序、相关器具、制品等进行保护和传承，另一方面将武鸣壮酒推向市场，为非物质文化遗产传承人阮朝鑫注册“骆越壮酒”商标、成立公司，并与广西中医药大学建立长期的科研合作伙伴关系。与此同时，武鸣区政府还不断组织义诊活动以及一系列与保护、传承有关的宣传活动，让人民群众能够对武鸣壮酒制作技艺有更全面的认识。

Wuming Wine Making Skill of Zhuang Ethnic Group is the eternal imprints of the industrious and intelligent people of the ancient Luoyue. As one part of Zhuang medicine, it is closely connected with productive practices and social development. The wine embraces the ideas that curing by eating and aiming at health protection. It is suitable for people acrossing all ages as it is good for liver, heart, lungs and kidney, and then good for your whole body. The wine boasts a stable and clear heritage process. It has assimilated Zhuang culture and Zhuang medicine on the basis of Ruan's formula and handmade techniques. It is useful to excavate and protect Zhuang medicine heritage, because it can be rated as crystallization and continuation of the wisdom of Luoyue ancestors. There remains great commercial value of the wine waiting us to exploit in these days as modern medicine and science fast change.

However, traditional culture of Zhuang health care hobbled when facing the flourishing of modern science and western medicine. Worse still, it was trapped by inefficient oral teaching and successive death of sophisticated artists. To address the challenge, the government of Wuming district takes two steps to achieve. On the one hand, they strengthen the protection of the wine by rational use of it and developing it as a whole, and help impart the traditional production process, related instruments and finished products. On the other hand, they support to introduce the wine to the market and help Ruan Chaoxin, the inheritor of the wine, to register the trademark of "Luoyue Liquor of Zhuang" and establish a wine-making company that established a long-term scientific cooperation partnership with Guangxi University of Traditional Chinese Medicine. Meanwhile, propagation activities and free clinics are held to promote the health wine, bringing people a more comprehensive understanding of Wuming Wine Making Skill of Zhuang Ethnic Group.

武鸣壮酒酿制
Wuming Wine Brewing of Zhuang Ethnic Group

武鸣生榨米粉制作技艺

Wuming Pressing Rice Noodle Skill

项目名称：武鸣生榨米粉制作技艺

别称：无

分布范围：武鸣区城厢镇、双桥镇、甘圩镇、宁武镇、太平镇、罗波镇、陆斡镇、马头镇、两江镇、府城镇、仙湖镇、锣圩镇、灵马镇，辐射南宁市、柳州市、百色市等

入选名录：2018年第七批自治区级非物质文化遗产名录
2017年第七批市级非物质文化遗产名录

保护单位：武鸣区文化馆

代表性传承人：张美玲

Element name：Wuming Pressing Rice Noodle Skill

Alternative name：None

Geographical location and range：Chengxiang Town, Shuangqiao Town, Ganxu Town, Ningwu Town, Taiping Town, Luobo Town, Luwo Town, Matou Town, Liangjiang Town, Fucheng Town, Xianhu Town, Luoxu Town, Lingma Town of Wuming District, influencing Nanning City, Liuzhou City, Baise City and others

Element inscribed list：In 2018 on the Seventh Autonomous Region List of Intangible Cultural Heritage
In 2017 on the Seventh Municipal List of Intangible Cultural Heritage

Competent body involved in safeguarding：Wuming District Cultural Centre

Representative inheritor：Zhang Meiling

生榨米粉
Raw Pressing Rice Noodle

武鸣生榨米粉是武鸣地区的传统小吃之一。武鸣生榨米粉采用自然发酵成酸，周期长，工序讲究，不添加任何酸醋、酸精等化学成分，是民间纯手工健康美食，有助消化、降压降脂，可做主食或辅食。武鸣生榨米粉的制作过程包括选米、泡米、发酵、磨粉、滚粉团、打粉团、揉粉浆、榨粉等八道工序。武鸣生榨米粉所选原料一般以早稻糙米最佳。泡米的操作方法随时令的变化而变化，夏天需用凉水，冬天则用温水，泡米时长控制在4个小时左右。武鸣生榨米粉在榨粉时使用樟木加工而成的工具，壮语称为“舟”，这样可以让生榨米粉不易被虫蛀，且自然留香。“舟”身呈圆柱形或正方形，由盛筒、压塞、粉筛、把柄等部件构成。用生铁锅把水烧开，把粉浆装入“舟”压、榨到锅里，榨粉浮出沸水面即熟，可直接装碗食用。粉较酸且粉汤稠，也可用开水冲淡，再根据个人口味加入佐料和调味料食用。

武鸣人农历四月初八、五月初五都有做榨粉吃榨粉的习俗，以府城、陆斡、锣圩、灵马最为出名。武鸣生榨米粉制作技艺的核心区域是南宁市武鸣区城厢、双桥、甘圩、宁武、太平、罗波、陆斡、马头、两江、府城、仙湖、锣圩、

Wuming Pressing Rice Noodle is one of the traditional snacks in Wuming. It was made through natural acidic fermentation, with long periods and selective processes, free from artificial chemicals. It is homemade, organic and healthy, a great choice of staple food and appetizers while having remedial effect on digestion, high blood pressure and fat. Wuming Pressing Noodle's production process includes 8 steps: rice selecting, rice dipping, fermentation, rice grinding, rice ball making, throwing rice dough, rice paste making, and rice pressing. Upon selecting, the best rice would be from the early season's unprocessed rice. The methodology of rice dipping depends on the seasons: cold water during the summer, and warm water in the wintertime for a duration of about 4 hours. A special tool made from camphorwood, which gives it a natural mild sweet smell, named “Zhou” in Zhuang language is utilized during the production process to keep the pests away. Zhou usually comes with the shape of a cylinder or square prism that consists a small container, a presser, a griddle and a hand for holding. The production begins with boiling water, usually in a big iron pot, and continues by putting the liquid rice paste into Zhou and pressing it to make rice noodles through the griddle. When the noodle floats on the surface, then it is ready to serve. Pressing noodle usually comes with a rather sour taste and the soup is quite sticky, thus it is common to add water into it to neutralize. People usually add spices according to their taste.

Locals in Wuming, especially people from Fucheng,

Luwo, Luoyu, Lingma, like to make pressing rice noodles on April 8th and May 5th in the lunar calendar. Wuming Pressing Noodle is mainly made and developed in Chengxiang, Shuangqiao, Ganxu, Ningwu, Taiping, Luobo, Luwo, Matou, Liangjiang, Fucheng, Xianhu, Luoxu, Lingma and other towns of Wuming District of Nanning City, influencing Nanning, Liuzhou, Baise and other cities. There is a long history behind Wuming Pressing Rice Noodle skill, but the original date of derivation is untraceable now. There is an ancient tale in Wuming "On April 8th, Big Flood Comes". The tales tells that once upon a time, there is a monster named Hanba in Wuming that brings many disasters upon the locals. Especially in the spring and autumn time, Hanba would bring huge droughts that cause the ground to shatter. People are struggling for their lives. In order to fight Hanba, people come to their farmland on April 8th in the lunar calendar, the same day when Thunder God and Dragon Mother patrols the world. They pray to the Thunder God and Dragon Mother for punishing Hanba and rainfall for the crops. Finally, Hanba was punished, and since that day, the locals begin making pressing rice noodles as a commemoration of Leigonglongmu, for a peaceful and bountiful year. This custom is practiced and preserved until this day. According to the Annals of Wuming County, Wuming was originally resided by the *Zhuang Ethnic Group*, and they have developed the skill of growing rice since the Tang Dynasty. We could assume that locals in Wuming have mastered the skill of pressing rice noodle since that time.

Wuming pressing noodle is made from half fermented rice balls, and it has become a defining local characteristic

灵马等13个镇，辐射南宁、柳州、百色等市区。武鸣生榨米粉制作技艺有着悠久的历史，其具体起源时间已不可考。武鸣有“四月八，大水发”的民谣。传说很久以前，武鸣有个叫旱魃的怪物危害人间，尤其在每年的春季和秋季，专门引发旱灾四处为孽，大地干裂，百姓遭殃。为了与旱魃做斗争，人们在农历四月初八雷公龙母出巡这天，来到地垄田头，祭拜雷公龙母，祈求雷公龙母能够主持公道，惩治旱魃，降下雨水。最终旱魃受到了应有的惩罚，为此，人们就以榨粉来供奉雷公龙母，祈求一年的风调雨顺、五谷丰登，武鸣农历四月初八做榨粉的习俗延续至今。据《武鸣县志》记载，武鸣是壮民族聚居地，唐宋时期就已经培育并大量种植了籼稻、细米、粳米。我们可以推测，当时的武鸣先民已经掌握了生榨米粉的技艺。

武鸣生榨米粉采用发酵半熟粉团压榨而成，这是武鸣生榨米粉的显著特征，彰显了武鸣生榨米粉浓郁的地域色彩。发酵是武鸣生榨米粉制作的关键环节之一。武鸣生榨米粉需要发酵多达5次，发酵后的米色如果色泽与泡米时的颜色相似，则发酵程度不够，制作出来的粉易断易碎且味寡不酸；而发酵后的米色如墨或者偏红、闻起来有一股腐臭味的

泡米发酵
Fermentation after Soaking Rice

和好的面团
Prepared Dough

话，则属于发酵过头，这样制作出来的粉味道偏酸；一般米色嫩黄且闻着有一股清香，则是发酵的最佳程度。这种对制作工序的严格要求和精确把控，无不彰显着壮族人民的辛勤与智慧。此外，武鸣生榨米粉起源的神话色彩和传奇性，无疑又增加了这项传统技艺的独特魅力。武鸣是壮族的发源地之一，被誉为“中国壮乡”，这里的生榨米粉承载着壮族先民对于美好生活的追求，彰显了壮族节庆习俗及壮族文化特色，对丰富群众饮食和传承民族饮食文化都有一定的意义。

随着时代的发展和科技的进步，传统手工艺制作在面对机械化生产时，处于一种非常不利的处境。再加上武鸣生榨米粉制作工序烦琐，能够熟练掌握技艺的人仍是少数，传承人普遍老龄化，亟待加大传承保护力度。为了继承和发展这一传统技艺，武鸣区政府和文化管理部门专门成立了武鸣生榨米粉的项目工作领导机构，全面深入调查、整理相关资料，利用武鸣三月三歌圩等传统民俗节庆活动，为武鸣生榨米粉的传承和发展注入新活力，提供新平台。

压榨米粉
Pressing Rice Noodle

of it. The fermentation of the rice noodle is one of the most significant process. It would take as many as 5 times in order to get the extent of fermentation just right: if the color does not change much after fermenting, then the rice noodle would lack its natural sour flavor and would be quite easy to break, thus more fermentation is necessary; On the contrary, if the noodle has a red greenish color, then it is over-fermented and would have a sticky smell. When the fermentation is just right, the rice noodle would have a light yellowish color with a mild sweetish smell to it. It is a rather tedious yet complex production, and how the locals have mastered that it is a grand materialization of Zhuang Ethnic Group's wisdom and diligence. The ancient legend of Wuming Pressing Rice Noodle also brings about a mythical vibe, adding it to its already unique glamour. Wuming is one of the natural habitat of Zhuang Ethnic Group, with the name "Chinese Zhuang Village". Wuming Pressing Rice Noodle is not only a local specialty, but a vehicle of Zhuang spirit and their pursuit of a wonderful life. It represents the Zhuang culture and custom—a great and meaningful contribution to Chinese diverse food and ethnic culture.

With the development of technology and advancement of the world, industrial manufacture has put traditional craftsmanship in peril. In addition, due to Wuming Pressing Rice Noodle's complex production procedure, less and less people are willing to inherit and develop this skill. The masters, as time goes, are getting older and older, thus culture protection of this skill is needed. In order to preserve this cultural legacy, Wuming's municipal government's culture management department has decided to commercialize Wuming Pressing Rice Noodle along with researches and assortment of information. With the incorporation of Wuming's March 3rd Folk Song Festival, aid the spreading of Wuming Pressing Rice Noodle and its future development.

宾阳织锦技艺

Binyang Brocade Making Skill

项目名称：宾阳织锦技艺

别称：忻城壮族织锦技艺、宾阳壮锦技艺

分布范围：宾阳县

入选名录：2010年第三批自治区级非物质文化遗产名录

保护单位：宾阳县文化馆

代表性传承人：谭湘光

Element name：Binyang Brocade Making Skill

Alternative name：Xincheng Brocade Making Skill of Zhuang Ethnic Group, Binyang Zhuang Brocade Making Skill

Geographical location and range：Binyang County

Element inscribed list：In 2010 on the Third Autonomous Region List of Intangible Cultural Heritage

Competent body involved in safeguarding：Binyang County Cultural Centre

Representative inheritor：Tan Xiangguang

宾阳壮族织锦
Binyang Brocade of Zhuang Ethnic Group

壮锦曾与蜀锦、云锦、宋锦并称为中国“四大名锦”，是其中唯一的少数民族织锦。壮锦一般用麻线或棉线染上各种色彩，以原色线为经，染色的线为纬，用本地木制土织机——“竹笼机”手工精编而成。宾阳壮锦可分为生活用品、艺术品和旅游纪念品，共20多个品种。生活用品主要以壮锦被面为主，艺术品以壮锦壁挂系列为主，旅游纪念品则有壮锦挂包等产品。壮锦的花纹图案有50多种，主要有框边回字形饰纹、莲花、牡丹、蝴蝶纹、葫芦纹、水纹、双喜、玫瑰、熊猫翠竹和民族花边等，具有鲜明的地域风格和较高的使用价值、观赏价值。

宾阳壮族织锦技艺起源于汉代，于唐宋时期逐渐成熟，距今已有2000多年的历史。据《后汉书·南蛮传》记载，汉代时期壮族先民就已经会织五彩“斑布”了，也就是我们现在所说的“壮锦”的雏形。广西罗泊湾汉墓出土的橘红色回纹锦残片，也恰好印证了史料。明清时期，壮锦极为兴盛，明朝时壮锦还被列为朝廷贡品。清末至民国初期，逐渐衰退。20世纪40年代，壮族织锦技艺杰出代表梁树英拜师深造，使宾阳壮族织锦有了质的飞跃。1956年，宾阳县响应国

Zhuang Brocade shares the name “Most Famous Four Brocade in China” together with Shu Brocade, Yun Brocade, and Song Brocade, being the only one made by minority nationalities. The threading of Zhuang Brocade is usually made from colored linen and cotton. Uncolored threads are used for “altitude” and colored ones are used for “latitude”, and all of these are hand-performed on a wooden local sewing machine named “Zhulong”. Binyang Brocade can be divided into more than 20 categories: everyday-uses, artworks, souvenirs, and so on. Daily-uses mainly focus on Zhuang Brocade quilt covers, while artworks and souvenirs are usually wall arts and belt bags. There are more than 50 patterns in Zhuang Brocade, and it mainly consists of “hui” character pattern, lotus, peony, butterfly, gourd, water, Chinese double-happiness pattern, rose, bamboo, and other local patterns. It is highly appraised for its beautiful patterns and its practical uses along with its unique regional styles.

Binyang Brocade of Zhuang Ethnic Group was originated 2000 years ago, in the Han Dynasty, and became widely used in the Tang and Song Dynasty. According to *Post Han Annals, Nanman Chapter*, Zhuang’s colorful brocades has been made by ancestors of Zhuang Ethnic Group since the Han Dynasty, and it is believed to be the predecessor of Zhuang Brocade. It is later proven with the excavation of an orange brocade with “hui” pattern on it in Luobo gulf, Guangxi. During the Ming and Qing Dynasty, Zhuang Brocade is highly appraised and has been served as tributes for the Emperor. The frenzy fades when the Qing Dynasty was replaced by the Republic of China. During the 1940s, a Zhuang Brocade master named Liang Shuying did arduous research and brought modern Zhuang Brocade to a new level, establishing factories making Binyang the largest Zhuang Brocade production site in China. Since 1970s, Zhuang Brocade has been exported into many countries and areas.

Binyang Brocade of Zhuang Ethnic Group strictly inherits the old production process and weaving techniques. It is a truly priceless cultural legacy. It manipulates multiple colors, mainly based on red, yellow, blue and green as foundation while adding different color layers on top. One great piece of Zhuang Brocade could use multiple even dozens of colors in mixture. Due to its complex use of colors, Zhuang Brocade is enabled to be grandiose while practical, luxurious but easy-to-use. It is the fruit of Zhuang Ethnic Group and their long history of lifestyle and wisdom. Patterns featured in Zhuang Brocade usually takes inspiration from common daily things, or traditional blessing patterns, symbolizing Zhuang people's good wish of a peaceful life. Vibrant colors and interchanging patterns reflect not only a progress of time and art, but a deeper understanding of Chinese embroidery as a whole.

As technology further develops, the living space for traditional embroidery industry has been eaten up by machinery and mass manufacturing business. Unanimous quality, high efficiency and less cost of machine brocade production makes traditional brocading less competitive. In addition, Those who are the primary workforce in brocading are women who have been unmarried and fasted for a life, and it is declining year after year as society progresses. In order to change the situation of Binyang Brocade of Zhuang Ethnic Group, Binyang county government has subsidized for schools specifically dedicated to Zhuang Brocade and media companies that focus on the spreading of Zhuang Brocade, developing and sending skilled workers to the industry and completing the business model with media coverage and publicity in biannual business and trade conferences. Binyang Zhuang Brocade is now expanding and developing.

家发掘民间工艺品的号召，成立壮族织锦工厂，使宾阳一跃成为全国最大的壮锦生产基地。自20世纪六七十年代以来，宾阳壮锦成品远销海内外多个国家和地区。

宾阳壮族织锦严格地传承了传统壮锦古老的织造机械、编织工艺、编织材料和图案风格，是壮族民族民间文化的珍品。运用宾阳壮锦技艺所织的壮锦多用重彩，以红、黄、蓝、绿为基本色，其他颜色作为补色，一幅壮锦，常常由几种颜色甚至十几种颜色混搭配置组成。巧妙的色彩搭配，使得壮锦斑斓绚丽、华而不俗，可谓纯朴中见丰富，素雅中见多彩，对比鲜明强烈，浑然天成。它是宾阳古代壮民在长期的生活和生产实践中创造的民间技艺，承载了宾阳先民的智慧结晶。壮锦的许多图案都选取于生活中的常见之物或象征吉祥幸福的花纹，表达着宾阳先民对于美好生活的向往。织锦色彩和图案的变化，印证着不同时代的审美风尚，为理解和研究中国的纺织史和少数民族纺织技艺提供了生动的材料。

随着科技的不断发展，机械生产正在逐渐挤占传统纺织行业的生存空间。在质量上，机械化生产的纺织品跟手工纺织品难分伯仲，且机械生产的效率更高，成本更低。而且在旧社会，壮族织锦的从业人员多为终身不嫁或吃斋的女性，社会制度变革后，人们的思想也随之改变，从业人员骤减。宾阳壮族织锦的传承与发展举步维艰。为了改变这一现状，宾阳县政府和有关部门高度重视，定期举办编织技艺培训班，持续往工厂输送人才，宾阳县壮锦厂的人员配置得到了落实；同时，建立壮锦编织技艺传承基地，创办宾阳织锦工艺业余学校和宾阳织锦文化发展传播公司，形成人才培养、人才输送、文化传播、市场销售的产业链，并利用两年一度的经贸会进行推介，从而促进宾阳壮族织锦的传承、传播与发展。

宾阳竹编技艺

Binyang Bamboo Knitting Skill

项目名称：宾阳竹编技艺

别称：无

分布范围：宾阳县新桥镇、芦圩镇、思陇镇、新宾镇、河田乡、太守乡等

入选名录：2018年第七批自治区级非物质文化遗产名录
　　　　　2015年第六批市级非物质文化遗产名录

保护单位：宾阳县文化馆

代表性传承人：张贵贤

Element name: Binyang Bamboo Knitting Skill

Alternative name: None

Geographical location and range: Xinqiao Town, Luxu Town, Silong Town and Xinbin Town, Hetian Town, Taishou Town and others of Binyang County

Element inscribed list: In 2018 on the Seventh Autonomous Region List of Intangible Cultural Heritage
In 2015 on the Sixth Municipal List of Intangible Cultural Heritage

Competent body involved in safeguarding: Binyang County Cultural Centre

Representative inheritor: Zhang Guixian

Binyang has been rated as the "home of bamboo" knitting where there is abundant Niutong bamboo, the main material of the bamboo knitting. A fine bamboo knitting could not be accomplished without selecting, knitting, dyeing, varnishing, painting and drying procedures. Hand makers of bamboo knitting spread in a wide area, especially in Xinqiao, Luxu, Hetian, Taishou, Silong and Xinbin of Binyang County. It is highly versatile with a variety of types and exquisite profiling, such as cereal basket, cereal basin, dustpan, round basket, fish base, hexagonal cap, seat, peach fan and all kinds of products specially for foreign trade including flower basket, basin, junket, hexagonal dustpan, bamboo duck and bamboo rabbit. Some products are painted red inward and golden outward, and printed with decorative patterns of peacock feathers. Some are even inserted with a picture of colored glaze, which is usually used in temples or memorial ceremony. Knitting bamboo products in Binyang win the trust of a great vast of customers for its novelty, fine quality, particularity and beauty. It has been sold to countries and areas including the United States, Japan, Canada, Australia, Singapore and Hong Kong.

The bamboo knitting has a long history for more than 1000 years in Binyang, where there are basins and hills and subtropical monsoon climate suitable for the growth of bamboo, vines and other plants. According to historical materials, bamboo knitting products in Binyang have been listed as a tribute as early as the Tang Dynasty. Summer sleeping mats made by bamboo has been famous in the Song Dynasty. And the bamboo knitting products made in Luban village of Xinqiao Town were once shopping-rushing goods during the time from the Qing Dynasty to the Republic of China. After 1949, both of the techniques and types of bamboo knitting have been advanced the great importance attached by the government. After the 21st century, Binyang's bamboo knitting has made great progress. The county's knitting products have developed from single bamboo knitting to more than 30 product series with thousands of colors including rattan knitting, straw knitting, rope knitting, Du (a plant) knitting, Dicranopteris dichotoma knitting and blended knitting.

Bingyang's bamboo knitting has distinct local flavor and ethnical imprint. The wisdom and aesthetic taste of Binyang people could be found in meticulous and complicated techniques, exquisite products and environmental friendly raw materials. It not only has special cultural value and commercial value, but also steps with the times. The knitting products change with the needs of the times, offering a way for us to understand the social style of different times. Although bamboo knitted crafts as living goods gradually fade out of people's vision these days, but it appears again in people's life as delicate and elegant ornaments and art works. Exploring and

宾阳县素有“竹编之乡”的美誉，宾阳竹编技艺以本土盛产的牛筒竹为主要材料，包括选料、破料、编织、着色、过油、过漆、晾干等多道工序。掌握宾阳竹编技艺的手工艺者分布非常广泛，尤以新桥、芦圩、河田、太守、思陇、新宾等地为主。其产品涵盖生产生活的多个领域，造型雅致、品种繁多，有谷箩、谷撮、泥箕、掺箕、圆篮、鱼曲、六角帽、座椅、桃子扇以及专供外贸出口的各种花篮、盆、篓、六角簸箕、竹鸭、竹兔等350余种。上好的竹编工艺品，有的通体髹漆，内饰红外漆金并压印出孔雀羽的纹饰，有的还镶嵌五彩琉璃图，专供佛寺祭扫之用。宾阳竹编工艺品以其“新、奇、优、特、美”的特点赢得了广大客户的青睐，远销美国、日本、加拿大、澳大利亚、新加坡等国家和中国香港地区。

宾阳竹编历史悠久，至今已有1000多年的历史。宾阳地形以盆地和丘陵为主，属亚热带季风气候，适宜竹子、蔓藤等植物生长。据史料记载，早在唐朝，宾阳竹制品就被作为贡品。宋朝时，宾阳所编织的凉席就已经闻名遐迩。清代至民国时期，新桥镇鲁班村的竹编产品一度成为抢手货。1949年后，在政府的重视下，竹编工艺技术有了进一步的提高，产品种类不断增加。21世纪之后，宾阳竹编又有了长足发展，全县编织产品由原来单一的竹编发展到藤编、草编、绳编、芏编、芒编、混编等30多个产品系列，有1000多个花色品种。

宾阳竹编具有鲜明的地域特色和民族特色，细致繁杂的工艺，精美绝伦的产品，天然环保的原材料，无不彰显着宾阳人民的智慧和审美情趣。宾阳竹编不仅拥有特殊的文化价值和商业价值，而且具有一定的时代性。随着时代需求的不同，宾阳竹编所生产的工艺品也存在差异，而这些差异恰好为我们了解不同时代的社会风貌提供了一个窗口。当今社会，虽然竹编工艺品作为生活用品逐渐淡出人们的视野，但精巧别致、典雅大方的竹编工艺品逐渐作为一种装饰品、艺

宾阳竹编
Binyang Bamboo Knitting

当地妇女在竹编
Local Wowen are Knitting

术品出现在大众的生活当中。发掘和保护宾阳竹编技艺，对传承和发展传统民间技艺、改善人民物质生活和精神生活都具有推动作用。

随着现代工业的迅猛发展，传统手工制造的竹编产业受到非常大的冲击。工业工艺品因其造价低廉、制作周期短等优势逐渐成为市场的主流，致使竹编工艺品在日常生活中的用途逐渐减少，需求量锐减，竹编技艺面临困境，竹编产业人才处于青黄不接的状况，行业前景渺茫。

面对这种情况，宾阳县政府贯彻和落实国家非物质文化遗产保护的相关政策，对竹编技艺进行传承和保护。宾阳县文化主管部门和县文化馆组织非物质文化遗产普查小组，深入全县各地，对宾阳竹编做全面普查，将普查资料做了整理归档，并且由县、镇、村多单位组成非物质文化遗产领导小组，以竹编老艺人为组长，进行一系列的项目保护工作。与此同时，宾阳县政府划拨一定数额的保护经费作为该项目前期保护工作的运作经费，并做好了五年保护工作计划及保护经费的预算与筹措。

protecting the bamboo knitting skills in Binyang can promote the inheritance and development of traditional folk skills and the improvement of people's material and spiritual life.

The traditional industry of bamboo knitting has been greatly impacted with the rapid development of modern industry. As a result, industrial handicraft has gradually become the mainstream of the market for of its low cost and short production cycling, while the use of bamboo knitted handicraft in daily life gradually reduced and the demand sharply reduced. Knitting techniques faces a gloomy future due to the shortage of the talent of bamboo knitting industry.

To address the challenge, Binyang County carries out and implements the relevant policies for the protection of the intangible cultural heritage of the state to inherit to better protect the bamboo knitting techniques. Cultural Authority and the Cultural Centre of Bingyang organized a team that went deep into all parts of the county and conducted a comprehensive census of the bamboo knitting and filed the census data. The leading group of intangible cultural heritage is composed of officials of counties, towns and villages levels, with the old bamboo knitting artists as the group leader, so as to carry out a series of protection work. Meanwhile, the County Government allocated a certain amount of funds for the operation of the early protection work, and completed the five-year protection work plan and the budget work for protection funds.

宾阳草席制作技艺

Binyang Grass Mat Weaving Skill

项目名称：宾阳草席制作技艺

别称：无

分布范围：宾阳县孟村

入选名录：2018年第七批自治区级非物质文化遗产名录
2017年第七批市级非物质文化遗产名录

保护单位：宾阳县文化馆

代表性传承人：黄荣金

Element name: Binyang Grass Mat Weaving Skill

Alternative name: None

Geographical location and range: Meng Village of Binyang County

Element inscribed list: In 2018 on the Seventh Autonomous Region List of Intangible Cultural Heritage
In 2017 on the Seventh Municipal List of Intangible Cultural Heritage

Competent body involved in safeguarding: Binyang County Cultural Centre

Representative inheritor: Huang Rongjin

宾阳草席是以莞草为材料制作的编织品。宾阳县孟村是宾阳草席制作的重镇。宾阳草席制作需经过备料和编织两个主要流程。材料备料需要经过种草、收草、分莞、晒草、储藏等工序；编织草席则需要经过布纲、送草、压机等10多道工序。宾阳草席成品规格多样，有2m × 1m、2m × 1.2m、2m × 1.5m、2m × 1.8m等形制。宾阳草席是纯天然的绿色环保产品，具有质地柔软、渗透性强、冬暖夏凉、舒适健康、造型美观、价廉物美、经久耐用等特点，是宾阳当地青年结婚时必备的床上用品，也是寻常百姓家居首选的床上用品之一。

宾阳草席制作技艺的历史较为悠久，传承至今大约已近400年。宾阳草席制作技艺的发源地孟村是古城村下属的一个自然村。古城村委曾为汉元鼎六年（前111）建制的领方县城旧址，是当时宾阳的政治、经济、文化中心。孟村在古县城的城墙脚下，系孟、钟二姓人家所造。明朝中叶，孟、钟二姓氏迁离孟村，广东黄氏、梁氏、卓氏人家先后移居，但村名未变，仍称孟村，一直沿用至今。宾阳草席的民间传统手工技艺便是当时的黄氏先民从广东带来的。20世纪80年代，宾阳草席制作空前繁荣，孟村的黄姓、梁姓、卓姓人家均都种草编席，宾阳草席深受广大人民群众的喜爱，多售往宾阳上林、武鸣、马山、来宾、横州、贵港、南宁、柳州等地，产品供不应求。20世纪80年代后，由于受到钢丝床、竹席等同类产品的冲击，从事草席制作的人员急剧减少，如今仅剩下几户黄姓人家在坚持制作，产品现主销售于宾阳县及南宁、贵港等地。

宾阳草席制作技艺体现了宾阳先民利用自然、改善自身生活条件的毅力，寄托了宾阳先民对美好生活的渴望以及对优质生活的不断追求。从简单而实用的生活必需品，到新婚青年结婚的必备之物，它随着民间习俗的演变发展而变化，对民间习俗具有依存性，对于挖掘和研究民间习俗的变革具有重大意义。宾阳草席制作技艺虽源于广东，却随着人口的

Binyang Grass Mat Weaving Skill uses material that is a knitted fabric made of Guan grass. Meng village in Binyang County is an important town for making Guan (grass) mats in Binyang. Binyang grass mat production has two main procedures: material preparation and weaving. Material preparation needs to go through grass planting, grass harvesting, dividing, straw drying, storage and other processes; while weaving straw mat needs to go through more than ten procedures such as laying foundation, grass feeding, pressing and so on. Binyang grass mat comes with various specifications, such as 2m×1m, 2m×1.2m, 2m×1.5m and 2m×1.8m. Binyang grass mat is a pure natural green product, with soft texture, strong permeability, suitable for all seasons, comfortable and healthy, with beautiful appearance, low cost, high endurance and good quality. It is a must-have bedding for the local youth in Binyang when they get married, and it is also one of the most popular beddings for the mass.

Binyang grass mat's production has a long technological history for about 400 years. Meng village, the birthplace of the production technique of Binyang grassmat, is a natural village under Gucheng Village. Gucheng Village Committee was the old site of the Lingfang County that is built in the sixth year of Yuanding reign (111BC) of the Han Dynasty. It was the political, economic and cultural centre of Binyang at that time. At the foot of the city wall of the ancient town, Meng village was built by the families of Meng and Zhong. In the mid-Ming Dynasty, the families of Meng and Zhong moved out of Meng village, and the families of Huang, Liang and Zhuo in Guangdong moved in succession. But the name of the village remains unchanged, still known as Meng village, and has been in use until now. The traditional folk handicraft of grass mat in Binyang was brought from Guangdong by Huang's ancestors at that time. In the 1980s, the production of grass mats in Binyang flourished unprecedentedly. Meng village's Huang, Liang and Zhuo families all grow Guan grass and weave mats. Binyang Grass mats are popular with the masses. They are sold to Shanglin, Wuming, Mashan, Laibin, Hengzhou, Guigang, Nanning, Liuzhou and other places. The products are in short supply. After the 1980s, due to the impact of similar products such as wire beds and bamboo mats, the number of people engaged in making grass mats decreased dramatically. Now only a few families with surname Huang are insisting on making them. The products are mainly sold in Binyang County, Nanning, Guigang and other places.

Binyang Grass mat production technology reflects the Binyang ancestors' perseverance to draw inspiration from nature to improve their living conditions. It symbolizes

Binyang's ancestors' desire for peace and their constant pursuit of a better life. From the simple and practical necessities to marriage for newlywed, it develops along with the culture, embedded deep in folk customs, and has great significance for researching and studying the evolution of folk customs. Although the production technology of Binyang grass mats originated from Guangdong, it took root and sprouted on the land of Binyang with the migration of people. Its products have strong regional characteristics. At the same time, it has built a bridge for the study of population migration in a specific period of history, and its own economic value and practical value cannot be ignored. As a traditional knitting technique, inheriting and protecting the knitting technique of Binyang grass mat plays an active role in inheriting and carrying forward the traditional national culture.

With the development of society and the acceleration of industrialization, mechanized production gradually shrinks the market space for traditional manual production. Due to the impact of similar products in the market and similar production process: from grass planting, weaving to sales in all aspects, sales are at a low ebb. The slump in market sales has made many families and craftsmen go out business. Only a few families in the village still inherit this skill. With the use of press weaving, it takes one to two years of training to be handy, which wears down the patience of many people. These circumstances undoubtedly put its inheritance and development into a precarious state. In order to inherit this traditional skill, Binyang County established Meng Village Grass Mat Weaving Technology Protection Committee, Binyang Grass Mat Weaving Technology Group and Binyang Grass Mat Inheritance Group. In-depth research and comprehensive study of Binyang grass mat production techniques are undergoing upon relevant contents, and a "five-year plan" is also assembled for continuous tracking and protection of it. Efforts are made to create platforms and promote products. At present, Binyang Grass Mat has become an exhibition product of ASEAN Expo.

迁移而在宾阳这块土地上扎根发芽，其产品具有很强的地域性特色。同时它又为研究历史上特定时期的人口迁移架起了一座桥梁，其自身的经济价值和实用价值也不可忽视。作为一项传统编织技艺，传承和保护宾阳草席编织技艺对继承和弘扬我国传统民族文化起到积极的作用。

随着社会的发展和工业化进程的不断加速，机械化生产逐渐挤压传统手工制作的生存空间。由于受市场同类产品的冲击，宾阳草席亦与其他地方的莞草席一样，从种草、编织到销售的各个环节都处于低谷。市场销售不景气，使许多编席的家庭和匠人都已改弦更张，村里仅有少数的人家仍在传承这项技艺，再加上使用压织机编织，需培训1—2年才能得心应手，消磨了很多人的耐心。这些情况无疑都使其传承和发展陷入一种岌岌可危的状态。为了传承这一传统技艺，宾阳县建立孟村草席编织技艺保护领导小组，并成立宾阳草席编织技艺普查工作队和传承领导小组。为深度挖掘、全面整理宾阳草席制作技艺的有关内容，宾阳县还制定了“五年计划”进行持续跟踪和保护，努力创造平台，推销产品。目前，宾阳草席已成为东盟博览会展销产品。

编织
Weaving

草席材料
Materials for Grass Mat

横县芝麻饼制作技艺

Hengxian Sesame Cake Making Skill

项目名称：横县芝麻饼制作技艺

别称：桂香饼

分布范围：横州市

入选名录：2012年第四批市级非物质文化遗产名录

保护单位：横县文化馆

代表性传承人：袁广武

Element name: Hengxian Sesame Cake Making Skill

Alternative name: Osmanthus Cake

Geographical location and range: Hengzhou City

Element inscribed list: In 2012 on the Fourth Municipal List of Intangible Cultural Heritage

Competent body involved in safeguarding: Hengxian Cultural Centre

Representative inheritor: Yuan Guangwu

Hengxian Sesame Cake which is named because the cake surface is covered with sesames, also known as Osmanthus Cake, is a famous special cake with a strong local flavor in Hengzhou City and it is one of the main offerings for the festival sacrifice. Hengxian Sesame Cake mainly has four kinds of fillings such as sweet potato, peanut, fat and roast pork. Among them, sesame cake with sweet potato fillings is the best seller with the largest output. The cake crust is made of high-quality glutinous rice and rice, and is accompanied by sesame, sugar, peanut oil, sweet potato, murraya euchrestifolia, and sweet-scented osmanthus sugar. With straw or pine needles as fuel, a special pan is used for frying. The finished product features color, fragrance, taste and shape, thin in skin and thick in fillings, sweet and delicious, which is ready to eat or can be stored for a long time. Hengxian Sesame Cake is famous for its delicious and crisp taste and is a good choice for visiting relatives and friends and long-distance travel.

Hengxian Sesame Cake making enjoys a long history. It is said that since the Emperor Taizong of the Tang Dynasty, Hengzhou, Baihe, Nayang and other places have had the custom of making Sesame Cake around the winter solstice and the Spring Festival, and it becomes more common in the Ming and Qing Dynasties. Hengxian Sesame Cake may have been used as a tribute in the beginning. During the Tang Dynasty, Buddhism flourished and people burn incense and worship Buddha on holidays to pray for peace. In Chinese culture, people advocate a round shape and believe that the round shape symbolizes reunion, perfection and beauty, so the ancestors of Hengzhou make round cake with glutinous rice flour and put sugar fillings in the cake when considering it as sacrificial supplies to represent happiness and sweetness of life. In order to enhance the aroma and beauty of the cakes, people sprinkle sesame seeds on the cake surface, which symbolizes "rise successively". At that time, some poor people who could not afford ingredients such as glutinous rice and sugar would sacrifice with Sesame Cake made of cassava or rice bran powder to pray for completeness and happiness. Full of the good expectations of the ancestors of Hengzhou, Hengxian Sesame Cake is a must-have cake for local residents to celebrate the holidays and it has a profound mass base and historical origins. The unique craftsmanship of Hengxian Sesame Cake requires complex and sophisticated procedure from the selection of ingredients to the production. The ingredients selected are all green food and no additives or preservatives are used in the production process. The sesame contains various minerals such as vitamin E, vitamin b1, calcium, phosphorus and iron and kinds of nutrients, which can not only improve eyesight and tonify weakness, but also alleviate diseases such

横县芝麻饼又名桂香饼，是横州市著名的具有浓厚地方风味的特色糕点，本为节日祭祀的主要供品之一，因其饼面遍撒芝麻，故而得名。横县芝麻饼主要有红薯馅、花生馅、肥肉馅、叉烧馅等四种馅料，其中红薯馅产量最多，最受大众欢迎。饼皮以优质的糯米、大米为主料，并佐以芝麻、白糖、花生油、红薯、山黄皮、桂花糖等辅料。用稻草或松针作为燃料，煎制时需使用特制的平底锅。成品讲究色、香、味、形，且皮薄馅厚，香甜可口，可即食也可长期储藏。横县芝麻饼以其鲜香酥脆的口感享誉八桂，是探亲访友、长途旅行常备佳品。

横县芝麻饼制作的历史悠久，相传自唐太宗时，横州、百合、那阳等地就有在冬至和春节前后制作芝麻饼的习俗，及至明清便更为普遍。横县芝麻饼最早可能是被作为祭祀供品而存在的。唐朝时期佛教兴盛，人们逢年过节都要烧香拜佛，祈求平安。中国文化崇尚圆形，认为圆象征着团圆、圆满、美好，所以在考虑祭祀用品的时候，横州先民用糯米粉制作了圆形的煎饼，并在煎饼里放入糖馅，代表生活幸福美满、甜甜蜜蜜。为了提升煎饼的香味和美观度，人们便在饼面上撒上芝麻，寓意着节节高升。当时一些买不起糯米和糖等原料的穷苦百姓，则会使用木薯或米糠粉制作的芝麻饼进行祭祀，以祈求圆满幸福，横县芝麻饼饱含了横州先民对生活的美好期望，是当地居民逢年过节必做的节日糕点，有着深厚的群众基础和历史渊源。横县芝麻饼拥有独特的制作工艺，从食材的选择到制作都非常复杂、考究。所选食材均是绿色食品，在制作过程中不使用任何添加剂和防腐剂，芝麻中含有维生素e、维生素b1、钙、磷、铁等矿物质和各种丰富的营养成分，既能明目、补虚，也可缓解贫血、高血压病、老年哮喘等疾病，符合绿色、健康、养生的生活观念。横县芝麻饼大小均匀，圆润饱满，色泽柔和，香甜可口，风味独特，老少皆宜，食后口齿留香，回味无穷，对丰富南宁传统饮食文化、带动和促进整个南宁饮食文化的发展、打造具有南宁特色的饮食文化品牌、推动地方经济的发展发挥着重要的作用。

随着经济的不断发展以及全球化进程的不断推进，横县芝麻饼的制作受到外来饮食文化的影响和冲击。再加上芝麻饼制作流程烦琐复杂，使得当下制作芝麻饼的人逐渐减少，一些老师傅年事已高，无法再从事这个行业，年轻人又不屑学习芝麻饼的制作，横县芝麻饼往日的繁盛已不复存在。为了传承这一非物质文化遗产，横州市政府采取两步走的办法，一方面借助每年举办“中华茉莉花艺术节”和“全国茉莉花茶展销会”的契机举办美食节，积极地在各种商贸洽谈会、商品交易会和食品展销会等活动中向国内外宾客推介横县芝麻饼，不断拓宽其市场领域，提高品牌影响力，另一方面稳抓横县芝麻饼的生产工作，横州市党委、政府于2010至2011年拨出专项资金，由横州市文化广播影视局和横州市体育局成立“横县芝麻饼制作技艺保护小组”，负责对横县芝麻饼制作技艺项目进行深入普查、挖掘，并在横州市百合镇的同生芝麻饼厂建立传承基地，大力支持和鼓励制作芝麻饼的老师傅开展传承授艺活动。

擀成面饼
Roll into Pancakes

as anemia, hypertension, and asthma in elderly, in line with the concept of green, healthy and nourishing life. Hengxian Sesame Cake is uniform in size, round and full, soft in color, sweet and delicious, with unique flavors for both young and old, and leaving a mouthful aroma and a long-last aftertaste after eating it. It plays an important role in enriching the traditional Nanning food culture, promoting and facilitating the development of the entire Nanning food culture, building a Nanning-style food culture brand, and driving the development of the local economy.

With the continuous development of the economy and the continuous advancement of globalization, the production of Hengxian Sesame Cake has been influenced and impacted by the foreign food culture. Coupled with the cumbersome and complicated production process of Sesame Cake, the number of people who make Sesame Cake is gradually reduced. Some of the masters are too old to work in this industry, while young people disdain to learn the production of Sesame Cake which results in that the prosperity of Hengxian Sesame Cake has gone with the wind. In order to inherit this intangible cultural heritage, the Hengzhou City government took a two-step approach. On the one hand, it takes advantage of the “China Jasmine Festival” and the “National Jasmine Tea Trade Fair” to hold the food festival and actively promotes and markets Hengxian Sesame Cake to domestic and foreign guests in events such as Trade Negotiation Fair, Commodity Fair and Food Exhibition to broaden its market segments and increase brand influence. On the other hand, in order to stabilize the production of Hengzhou Sesame Cake, the Hengxian City Party Committee and the government allocate special funds from year 2010 to 2011 and the “Hengxian Sesame Cake Making Skill Protection Group” is established by the Hengzhou Bureau of Culture, Radio and Television and the Hengzhou Bureau of Sports to make in-depth survey and exploitation to the Hengxian Sesame Cake Making Skill project. What’s more, a heritage base is established in the Tongsheng Sesame Cake Factory in Baihe Town, Hengzhou City to support and encourage the masters of Sesame Cake making to carry out the inheritance activities.

横县萡僧簸箕粉制作技艺

Shallow Basket Rice Pancake Making Skill in Tanseng, Hengxian

项目名称：横县萡僧簸箕粉制作技艺

别称：无

分布范围：横州市校椅镇青桐村、平马镇，马山县，宾阳县等周边地区

入选名录：2018年第七批自治区级非物质文化遗产名录

2017年第七批市级非物质文化遗产名录

保护单位：横县文化馆

代表性传承人：张洪

Element name：Shallow Basket Rice Pancake Making Skill in Tanseng, Hengxian

Alternative name：None

Geographical location and range：Qingtong Village of Xiaoyi Town, Pingma Town in Hengzhou City; Mashan County; Binyang County and the surrounding areas

Element inscribed list：In 2018 on the Seventh Autonomous Region List of Intangible Cultural Heritage

In 2017 on the Seventh Municipal List of Intangible Cultural Heritage

Competent body involved in safeguarding：Hengxian Cultural Centre

Representative inheritor：Zhang Hong

畨僧簸箕粉是横州市畨僧村壮民制作的一道传统小吃，因采用竹编的簸箕进行蒸煮而得名，本地人又称其为“炊（即蒸的意思）粉”“剪粉”。畨僧簸箕粉类似广州等地的肠粉，但做法又与肠粉不同。畨僧簸箕粉制作从选材到制作完成，每个程序都相当考究与细致。其主要原材料选用春桂米，经水浸泡6—8个小时，再加入少量煮熟的米饭拌匀，用手工石磨磨成米浆，磨米的人必须是有力气的男士，把适量米浆倒入抹有花生油的竹编簸箕内摊匀，放入盛有沸水的大锅内，盖上锅盖蒸片刻即可取出，然后用瓷羹沿簸箕周围刮一圈，趁热用手轻轻把粉剥下，晾在支起的竹竿上，最后配上酸辣柠檬酱、香菜、大料、紫苏、薄荷、猪头肉等，簸箕粉制作才算完成。

畨僧簸箕粉制作技艺主要分布于校椅镇的青桐村、平马镇以及周边的马山县、宾阳县等周边县乡镇地区，历史悠久，具体形成时间已不可考。据村史记载，畨僧簸箕粉制作技艺的传承都是由婆婆传给媳妇，如此一代一代传承。横州市畨僧现有簸箕粉制作加工生产个体8家，其销售范围从横州市逐步扩展到南宁市及周边县市。

畨僧簸箕粉制作技艺承载着当地壮族人民的厚重历史。畨僧簸箕粉讲究色、香、味、型俱佳，口感温软、有韧性，且带着淡淡的竹香和花生油的清香，简单而纯朴，是壮族人民饮食文化的代表之一。逢年过节或遇喜事，人们都会制作簸箕粉给亲朋好友品尝，庆祝喜庆丰收，具有深厚的群众基础。畨僧簸箕粉制作技艺在岭南地区特别是珠江-西江沿江流域，仅集中存在于横州市校椅及其邻近一带乡镇，但其作为一种手工艺传统文化却广泛影响着岭南地区。当然，在岭南地区，对稻作素食类传统手工艺及其文化表象的推崇与弘扬、研究与记载比比皆是，而对于稻作素食类传统手工艺及其文化形式的研究、记录则相对较少。畨僧簸箕粉制作技艺作为岭南地区稻作素食类制作技艺的一种特有形式，具有重要的学术研究价值。发掘、抢救和保护好手工簸箕粉制作技

Shallow Basket Rice Pancake, simple and delicious, is a traditional snack made by the people of Zhuang Ethnic Group in Tanseng, and it is named after being steamed and boiled in shallow basket weaved by bamboo, also called Chui (namely, steaming) fen- “Cooking Rice Pancake” or Jianfen-“Cutting Rice Pancake” by the locals. Shallow Basket Rice Pancake is similar to the Rice Roll in Guangzhou and other places, but the practice is different. The making of Shallow Basket Rice Pancake requires complex and sophisticated procedure from the selection of ingredients to the production. The main ingredient is spring glutinous rice, soaked in water for 6 to 8 hours, then mixed with a small amount of cooked rice, ground into rice pulp by hand millstone, which should be done by strong men. Then pour the right amount of rice pulp into the shallow basket smeared with peanut oil and spread evenly, put it into a large pot filled with boiling water, cover the lid and steam for a while and then take it out. In the following, scrape around the shallow basket with a porcelain spoon and gently peel the rice pancake off, air it on the bamboo poles, and then add the hot and sour lemon sauce, coriander, aniseed, purple perilla, mint, bath chap and other meat dishes. By then, the making of shallow basket rice pancake is done.

Shallow Basket Rice Pancake Making Skills, distributed mainly in Qingtong Village in Xiaoyi Town, Pingma Town, and surrounding counties and townships such as Mashan County and Binyang County, has a long history, but the specific formation time is not available. According to the history of the village, the inheritance of Shallow Basket Rice Pancake Making Skill is passed on from a mother-in-law to a daughter-in-law, and passed down from generation to generation. There are 8 individual businesses making shallow basket rice pancake in Tanseng, Hengzhou City, whose sales range has gradually expanded from Hengzhou City to Nanning and surrounding counties and cities.

Shallow Basket Rice Pancake Making Skill carries the heavy history of the local people of Zhuang Ethnic Group. Shallow Basket Rice Pancake featuring color, aroma, taste and appearance is a representative of the food culture of the people of Zhuang Ethnic Group, with its soft, mellow taste and toughness. It has light bamboo fragrance and aroma of peanut oil, simple and plain. People will make rice pancakes for family and friends to celebrate the festive harvest or joyous ceremonies, which has a deep mass base. Shallow Basket Rice Pancake Making Skill is distributed mainly in Xiaoyi town, Hengzhou City and its surrounding townships along Pearl River-Xijiang River in the south of Five Ridges, but it has wide influence on the south of Five Ridges area as a traditional handicraft culture. Advocation, development, study and record of traditional rice vegetarian handicraft and its cultural representations are abundant while the study and record of traditional rice vegetarian handicraft and its cultural form is relatively less. As a unique form of rice vegetarian Making Skill, Shallow Basket Rice Pancake Making Skill in Tanseng, Hengzhou City has developed a style of its own and it is of important academic research value. Excavating, rescuing and protecting handmade shallow basket rice pancake Making Skills will promote the richness and improvement of the entire traditional Nanning craftsmanship and food culture.

Although Hengxian Shallow Basket Rice Pancake Making Skill has considerable cultural and historical value, many young people are reluctant to learn because of the cumbersome making process, so that there is no inheritor of skills to carry the torch. Coupled with limited economic benefits, it is difficult to form a large workshop which also limits its development. Driven by economic interests, mechanized processing is flooding the market, making the Shallow Basket Rice Pancake Making Skill unsustainable and facing a crisis. In order to inherit this traditional skill, the local government has allocated special funds every year and a special investigation team is also set up by the county and town cultural management departments to carry out comprehensive and in-depth investigations to learn about and master the relevant content, circulation mode, scope of influence, historical origin and cultural values of the Making Skill. At the same time, the related materials and documents are sorted and archived to continuously excavate its cultural connotation. The county and town governments and their cultural functional departments have been supporting and carrying out the Shallow Basket Rice Pancake Making Skills activities for many years and organized multi-time inheritance training courses on the Making Skills. The Making Skill has been further popularized.

艺，对整个南宁市传统手工技艺和美食文化的丰富和完善都将产生一定的推动作用。

尽管横县稖僧簸箕粉制作技艺有着相当厚重的文化价值和历史价值，但是由于其制作过程极为烦琐，很多年轻人不愿学习，以致技艺传承后继乏人。加之经济效益限制，簸箕粉手工制作难以形成大作坊，也从另一方面限制了它的发展。由于经济利益的驱使，机械化的加工大量充斥市场，使得簸箕粉制作技艺难以为继，面临危机。为了传承这一传统技艺，当地政府每年拨专项经费支持，县、镇文化管理部门也成立了专门的调查小组，进行全面深入调查，了解和掌握制作技艺相关内容、流传方式、影响范围、历史渊源、文化价值等。同时将材料整理、归档，不断挖掘簸箕粉的文化内涵。县镇两级政府及其文化职能部门多年来坚持扶持、开展簸箕粉制作技艺活动，成立簸箕粉制作技艺多期传承培训班，簸箕粉制作技艺得到进一步普及。

蒸米皮
Steamed Rice Husk

横县红枣马蹄糕制作技艺

Hengxian Red Date Chestnut Cake Making Skill

项目名称：横县红枣马蹄糕制作技艺

别称：无

分布范围：横州市各乡镇及周边地区

入选名录：2017年第七批市级非物质文化遗产名录

保护单位：横县文化馆

代表性传承人：吴丹

Element name: Hengxian Red Date Chestnut Cake Making Skill

Alternative name: None

Geographical location and range: All towns of Hengzhou City and the surrounding areas

Element inscribed list: In 2017 on the Seventh Municipal List of Intangible Cultural Heritage

Competent body involved in safeguarding: Hengxian Cultural Centre

Representative inheritor: Wu Dan

Mati, whose scientific name is water chestnut. It is a perennation herbaceous plant that belongs to a member of monocotyledonous Cyperaceae. Hengxian Red Date Chestnut Cake is a traditional snack made from Horseshoe and red dates. It is very famous in Hengzhou City, and it is one of the representatives of simple dietary culture of Zhuang people. The material selection and making of Hengxian Red Date Chestnut Cake are very exquisite. The local heart-shaped red dates are used and it should be washed, cut in half and cored before use. The water chestnut should choose a kind of starchy chestnut with short pointed and protruding bottom that is on the market in spring. After peeling and washing, it is crushed by manual stone mill and packed in sacks. Then, it is pressed with big bluestone to squeeze the water out. One day later, spread the chestnut fiber with only a little water in a dustpan and expose it to the sun. After the water evaporated completely, mash it into chestnut powder. Infuse the chestnut powder with cold water in a certain proportion, then stir it evenly with hot water. The ratio of cold water to hot water is 1:2, then add a proper amount of white sugar. When making the cake, apply a thin layer of peanut oil on the inner wall of the steaming plate. After the water in the cauldron is boiled, stir the chestnut powder pulp again, put it in the steaming plate to steam it and spread red dates on it. When the surface turns reddish brown, the steaming plate can be taken out and it can be sliced and eaten after being dried in the shade for half an hour.

China is rich in chestnut. The cultivation of chestnut was first recorded in the Western Han Dynasty. The making of Hengxian Red Date Chestnut Cake has a long history. According to Wu's genealogy in Baziqiang village in Hengzhou City, Red Date Chestnut Cake Making Skill has a history of five or six hundred years. People make Red Date Chestnut Cake to entertain relatives and friends at the Chinese New Year or other festivities. With the continuous migration of people, Red Date Chestnut Cake is gradually distributed to various areas of Hengzhou City and spreads to Nanning and its surrounding areas. Today, Tanseng village, a natural village under the jurisdiction of the Qingtong village of Xiaoyi town, Hengzhou City is the core area of Hengxian Red Date Chestnut Cake Making Skill.

Hengxian Red Date Chestnut Cake is the embodiment of the dietary culture of the Zhuang people in Guangxi. Hengxian Red Date Chestnut Cake pays attention to color, aroma, taste and shape. The finished product is crystal clear, fragrance overflowing and clearly layered. Chestnut is sweet and rich in protein, vitamin C and other nutrients. It has the

红枣马蹄糕
Red Date Chestnut Cake

马蹄学名荸荠，属单子叶莎草科，为多年生宿根性草本植物。横县红枣马蹄糕是以马蹄和红枣为主要原材料制作而成的一道传统风味小吃，在横州市当地非常出名，是壮族人民简单而纯朴的饮食文化的代表之一。横县红枣马蹄糕的选材和制作都非常考究。红枣需选用本地所产的鸡心枣，将其洗净、切半、去核方能使用。马蹄则需选用本地春季上市的一种尖部短、底部凸出的粉蹄，削皮洗净后用手工石磨打碎装入麻袋中，再用大青石压在麻袋上将水分挤出。一天后，将只剩下少许水的马蹄纤维平铺在簸箕里，置于阳光下暴晒，待水分完全蒸发后，捣碎成马蹄粉。按一定比例将马蹄粉用冷水冲开，随后用热水搅拌均匀，冷水和热水的比例为1:2，再加入适量白糖。制作时将蒸盘内壁涂抹一层薄薄的花生油，待大锅内水烧开后，将马蹄粉浆再次搅拌均匀后舀进蒸盘里蒸，并撒上红枣，待其表面变成红褐色的时候便可出锅，在阴凉处晾半小时即可切块食用。

我国盛产马蹄，最早在西汉时期就已经有了关于种植马蹄的记载。横县红枣马蹄糕制作历史较为悠久。横州市八字墙村吴氏家谱记载，红枣马蹄糕制作技艺已有五六百年的历史，每逢过年过节，人们都会制作红枣马蹄糕招待亲朋好友。随着人员的不断迁徙，红枣马蹄糕逐渐分布到横州市各个区域，并辐射到南宁及周边地区。如今，横州市校椅镇青桐村下辖的自然村堷僧村，是横县红枣马蹄糕制作技艺的核心区域。

横县红枣马蹄糕是广西壮族人民饮食文化的体现，讲究色、香、味、形俱佳，成品晶莹剔透，清香四溢，层次分明。马蹄性甘，富含蛋白质、维生素C等营养元素，具有清热润肺、舒肝明目等功效，而红枣又能补虚益气、养血安神，具有很高的营养价值。红枣的香甜与马蹄糕的爽滑完美结合，双重美味在舌尖绽放，让人回味无穷。此外，横县红枣马蹄糕采用纯手工制作，无任何工业机械进行辅助。在蒸制时，由于马蹄粉会沉淀，因此在制作时不能一次性全部蒸完，而是要根据蒸盘的大小而定。每次蒸1—1.5cm，猛火蒸3—5分钟，再逐层添加马蹄粉浆蒸煮，直至总容量占蒸盘的八成时停止。红枣马蹄糕看似简单，实则饱含着横州先民对于饮食的细致追求。发掘、抢救和保护好横县红枣马蹄糕制作技艺，对整个南宁传统手工技艺和美食文化的丰富和完善都将产生一定的推动作用。在一些传统节日中，当地壮族人民都有制作红枣马蹄糕招待宾客好友的习俗，这不仅说明它有着深厚的群众基础，而且对促进文化交流、增进民族团结发挥着积极的作用。

横县红枣马蹄糕是横州地区招待亲朋好友的美食，并没有形成成熟的商业机制，使得其传播范围和经济效益均受到了限制，再加上学习制作红枣马蹄糕不仅要熟悉其制作流

effect of clearing away heat and moistening the lung, as well as soothing liver and improving eyesight. While red date can tonify deficiency and supplement the vital energy, as well as nourishing blood and tranquilizing mind, which is of high nutritional value. The perfect combination of the sweet of red dates and smoothness of chestnut making the double delicacies blossom on the tip of the tongue, leading people to endless aftertastes. In addition, Hengxian Red Date Chestnut Cake is made by hand without any assistance of industrial machinery. When steaming, chestnut powder will precipitate, so it cannot be steamed completely at one time, but depends on the size of the steaming plate. Steam 1-1.5cm each time, and steam for 3-5 minutes on big fire, then add chestnut pulp layer by layer to steam until the total capacity accounts for 80% of the steaming plate, stop it. Red Date Chestnut Cake seems simple, but it is full of Hengzhou ancestors' delicate pursuit of food. To excavate, rescue and protect Hengxian Red Date Chestnut Cake Making Skill will play a certain role in promoting the enrichment and perfection of the traditional handicraft and gourmet culture in whole Nanning. In some traditional festivals, the local Zhuang people have the custom of making Hengxian Red Date Chestnut Cake to entertain guests and friends, which not only shows that it has a deep mass base, but also plays a positive role in promoting cultural exchanges and national unity.

Hengxian Red Date Chestnut Cake is a delicacy for entertaining relatives and friends in Hengzhou area. It has not formed a mature commercial mechanism, which limits its scope of dissemination and economic benefits. Besides, when learning to make Red Date Chestnut Cake, we should not only be familiar with its making process, but also should control the proportion of materials accurately, which undoubtedly brings new difficulties to the inheritance of Hengxian Red Date Chestnut Cake. In order to protect and inherit this traditional skill, the Hengzhou City government and cultural administration have made in-depth investigations and consulted relevant documents, understood and mastered the relevant content, mode of spread, scope of influence, historical origins, cultural values, etc. of the Making Skill. They have made a comprehensive arrangement of investigation materials, filed them, and continuously excavated the cultural connotation of Hengxian Red Date Chestnut Cake. The government allocates special funds every year to support Hengxian Red Date Chestnut Cake Making Skill activities and actively promotes them in major folk festivals and activities. Hengxian Red Date Chestnut Cake Making Skill inheritance training courses were held many times to make the Making

程，还要精确把控材料的比例，无疑又给横县红枣马蹄糕的传承带来了新的困难。为了保护和传承这项传统技艺，横州市政府和文化管理部门深入调查、查阅有关文献资料，了解和掌握制作技艺相关内容、流传方式、影响范围、历史渊源、文化价值等，全面整理调查材料，进行归档，不断挖掘横县红枣马蹄糕的文化内涵。政府每年拨出专项经费，大力扶持横县红枣马蹄糕制作技艺活动，在重大民俗节庆习俗活动中积极推广；多次开办横县红枣马蹄制作技艺传承培训班，使制作技艺得到进一步普及；以横县红枣马蹄糕文化生态村为载体，开展横县红枣马蹄糕保护区；在保护、弘扬横县红枣马蹄糕的基础上，积极实施品牌创建计划，将其更好地推向市场。

Skill become more popular. They take Hengxian Red Date Chestnut Cake Cultural and Ecological Village as the carrier to develop Hengxian Red Date Chestnut Cake protection zone. On the basis of protecting and promoting Hengxian Red Date Chestnut Cake, they actively implement the brand creation plan to better promote it to the market.

磨马蹄粉
Grinding Chestnut Powder

横县青桐壮族织锦技艺

Brocade Making Skill of Zhuang Ethnic Group in Qingtong, Hengxian

项目名称：横县青桐壮族织锦技艺

别称：无

分布范围：横州市、宾阳县等地为主要分布区域，辐射上林县、马山县、云南省、广东省、海南省等壮族聚居区

入选名录：2017年第七批市级非物质文化遗产名录

保护单位：横县文化馆

代表性传承人：何美香

Element name: Brocade Making Skill of Zhuang Ethnic Group in Qingtong, Hengxian

Alternative name: None

Geographical location and range: Hengzhou City, Binyang County and other places are the main distribution areas, radiate to the Zhuang-inhabited areas of Shanglin County, Mashan County, Yunnan Province, Guangdong Province, Hainan Province and others

Element inscribed list: In 2017 on the Seventh Municipal List of Intangible Cultural Heritage

Competent body involved in safeguarding: Hengxian Cultural Centre

Representative inheritor: He Meixiang

织锦
Brocade Weaving

传统织机
Conventional Looms

Zhuang Brocade was once known as "China's four famous brocades" together with Shu Brocade, Yun Brocade and Song Brocade. The patterns of Brocade Making of Zhuang Ethnic Group in Qingtong, Hengxian mainly include frame hollow square style decoration, lotus, peony, butterfly pattern, gourd pattern, water pattern, double happiness, rose, panda and green bamboos and national lace. Fabrics are mainly daily necessities, supplemented by art works. The daily necessities mainly involve quilt cover, sheets, tablecloths, cushions, headscarves, shawls, straps, pillow towels, handkerchiefs and other items. Art works include large wall hanging, small wall hanging and other Zhuang brocade wall hanging series, which has a great variety of types. Brocade Making of Zhuang Ethnic Group in Qingtong, Hengxian is unique in design, exquisite in pattern and durable. It can not only meet people's daily household textiles and clothing needs, but also be used as a work of art and widely decorated in various clothing and bedding. It has strong practicability and ornamentation. Brocade Making of Zhuang Ethnic Group in Qingtong, Hengxian inherits and develops the ancient weaving equipment, knitting technology, knitting materials and pattern style of the traditional Zhuang Brocade. It is a treasure of folk craft culture of the Zhuang Ethnic Group.

Brocade Making Skill of Zhuang Ethnic Group in Qingtong, Hengxian is mainly distributed in Hengzhou City, Binyang County, etc., and spreads to the Zhuang inhabited

壮锦曾与蜀锦、云锦、宋锦并称“中国四大名锦”。横县青桐壮族织锦的花纹图案主要有框边回字形饰纹、莲花、牡丹、蝴蝶纹、葫芦纹、水纹、双喜、玫瑰、熊猫翠竹和民族花边等。织品主要以生活日用品为主，以艺术品类为辅。生活日用品类主要涉及被面、床单、台布、坐垫、头巾、披巾、背带、枕巾、手帕等物品。艺术品类有大壁挂、小壁挂等壮锦壁挂系列，种类繁多。横县青桐壮族织锦图案别致，花纹精美，结实耐用，能满足百姓日常家纺、衣饰需求，也可作为艺术品，广泛地装饰于各种服装、床上用品，具有较强的实用性与观赏性。横县青铜壮族织锦继承和发展了传统壮锦古老的织造器械、编织工艺、编织材料和图案风格，是壮民族民间工艺文化的珍品。

横县青桐壮族织锦技艺以横州市、宾阳县等地为主要分布区域，辐射至上林县、马山县、云南省、广东省、海南省等壮族居住地区。尤其是在横州市畲僧村还保存着较为完整的蓝靛色壮族服饰。壮锦具有悠久的历史，在距离青桐村约100千米的罗泊湾汉墓中就曾出土过数块橘红色回纹锦残片，这说明了早在汉代，广西就已经出现了织锦技术。南宋周去非《岭外代答》记载："邕州左右江峒蛮，有织白，白质方纹，广幅大缕，似中都之纹罗，而佳丽厚重，诚南方之上服也。"其中"白"即为壮锦。可见，壮族织锦的起源可追溯至汉代，至唐宋时代已发展成熟，至今已有1000多年的历史。横州青桐村现存100年以上的织锦机有10多台，其中一台已有300多年的历史。壮族织锦在明朝时被列为朝廷名贵贡品，清末至民国初年渐趋衰落。

横县青桐壮族织锦技艺是横州古代壮族人民在长期的生活和生产实践中创造出来的民族技艺。横县青桐壮族织锦技艺是壮锦文化中的一个分支，带有横州独特的地域性色彩。它是我国四大名锦之一，也是四大名锦中唯一的少数民族织锦。在线料和技法上，一般是将麻线或棉线染上各种色彩，

织锦
Brocade Weaving

areas of Shanglin county, Mashan county, Yunnan province, Guangdong province, Hainan province and so on. Especially in Tanseng village, Hengzhou City, there are still relatively complete indigo Zhuang costumes preserved. Zhuang Brocade has a long history. Several pieces of orange brocade fragments were unearthed in the Han Dynasty tomb in Luobowan, about 100 kilometers away from Qingtong village. This shows that brocade making technology had appeared in Guangxi as early as the Han Dynasty. In the Song Dynasty, Zhou Qufei's *Ling Wai Dai Da* recorded, "There are white fabrics at the left and right river of Yongzhou. It is white texture with square pattern. It has wide width and large wisp and like the pattern of central capital. It is beautiful and decorous, and really the superior clothes in south." In this record, "white" refers to Zhuang brocade. It can be seen that the origin of Brocade Making of Zhuang Ethnic Group can be traced back to the Han Dynasty, and it has developed mature to the Tang and Song Dynasties. So far, it has a history of more than 1000 years. There are more than ten brocade making machines in Qingtong village, Hengxian with a history of more than 100 years, one of which has a history of more than 300 years. Brocade Making of Zhuang Ethnic Group was listed as a valuable tribute in the Ming Dynasty, and declined gradually from the end of Qing Dynasty to the beginning of the Republic of China.

Brocade Making Skill of Zhuang Ethnic Group in Qingtong, Hengxian is a national skill created by the ancient Zhuang people in their long-term life and production practice. Brocade Making Skill of Zhuang Ethnic Group in Qingtong, Hengxian is a branch of Zhuang brocade culture, which has the unique regional color of Hengzhou. It is one of the four famous brocades in China and the only brocade making of minority among the four famous brocades. In terms of thread materials and techniques, linen or cotton yarn is usually dyed in various colors, with original linen or cotton yarn as warp, dyed linen or dyed cotton yarn as weft and hand-knitted on a local wooden loom. The looms used in Zhuang brocade are extremely of national characteristics and are commonly called "bamboo cage loom". During the long-term development of Brocade Making Skill of Zhuang Ethnic Group in Qingtong, Hengxian, in order to meet the needs of family production, it simplified the "bamboo cage loom" used in the traditional brocade making, but it did not affect the elegance of brocade. In addition, Brocade Making Skill of Zhuang Ethnic Group in Qingtong, Hengxian carries textile skills, folk customs, aesthetic concepts, etc. of Zhuang people in Qingtong village, Hengxian, which has important academic and social values for the study of traditional culture of the Zhuang Ethnic Group.

In the prosperous period, Brocade Making of Zhuang Ethnic Group in Qingtong, Hengxian is circulated and traded in the markets of surrounding cities and counties, bringing considerable economic income to the local people. With the rapid development of modern textile industry, various kinds of high-quality textile varieties and patterns emerge in endlessly, resulting in the use of Zhuang brocade in daily life gradually reduced, and the demand decreased sharply. At present, only a few dozen people in Qingtong village mastered the brocade making skills. With more young people choosing to go out to work and live, fewer and fewer people study the Brocade Making Skill of Zhuang Ethnic Group, and the inheritance of the Brocade Making of the Zhuang Ethnic Group falls into a difficult situation. In order to inherit this traditional skill, the Hengzhou City government allocates special funds every year to set up relevant investigation teams with the cultural management departments of counties and towns to conduct a comprehensive and in-depth investigation and access to relevant literature, to understand and master the related content, spread mode, influence scope, historical origin and cultural value of the Making Skill, and to carry out teaching and inheritance activities for Brocade Making Skill of Zhuang Ethnic Group in Qingtong, Hengxian, and held a number of inheritance training courses. With the joint efforts of the government and the people, Brocade Making of Zhuang Ethnic Group in Qingtong can be better inherited and developed.

以原色麻线或棉线为经，以染色麻线或染色棉线为纬，用本地木质的土织机手工精编而成。壮锦所使用的织机具有民族特色，一般被称为“竹笼机”。在长期的发展中，横县青桐壮族织锦技艺为适应家庭制作的需要，简化了传统织锦所用的“竹笼机”，但不影响织锦的精美高雅。此外，横县青桐壮族织锦技艺承载了横县青桐壮族人民的纺织技艺、民俗风情、审美观念等，对研究壮民族传统文化具有重要的学术价值和社会价值。

在兴盛时期，横县青桐壮族织锦在周边市县的市场上流通交易，为当地百姓带来了可观的经济收入。随着现代纺织工业的迅猛发展，各种优质纺织品的品种和花样层出不穷，致使壮锦在日常生活中的用途逐渐缩小，需求量锐减。目前，青桐村掌握织锦技艺的仅有几十人，随着更多的年轻人选择外出工作生活，学习壮族织锦的人越来越少，壮族织锦的传承陷入艰难境地。为了传承这一传统技艺，横州市政府每年拨出专项经费，与县镇文化管理部门建立相关调查小组全面深入调查、查阅有关文献资料，了解和掌握制作技艺相关内容、流传方式、影响范围、历史渊源、文化价值，开展横县青桐壮族织锦技艺教学传承活动，举办多期传承培训班。在政府与民众的共同努力下，青桐壮族织锦得以更好地传承和发展。

织锦
Brocade Weaving

雁江粉利制作技艺

Yanjiang Steamed Rice Noodle Making Skill

项目名称：雁江粉利制作技艺

别称：无

分布范围：隆安县

入选名录：2013年第五批市级非物质文化遗产名录

保护单位：隆安县文化馆

代表性传承人：潘云鹏

Element name：Yanjiang Steamed Rice Noodle Making Skill

Alternative name：None

Geographical location and range：Long'an County

Element inscribed list：In 2013 on the Fifth Municipal List of Intangible Cultural Heritage

Competent body involved in safeguarding：Long'an County Cultural Centre

Representative inheritor：Pan Yunpeng

成型
Shaping

盖上图案
Stamping with Decorative Pattern

Yanjiang Steamed Rice Noodle, originated in Yanjiang town of Long'an County, which is known as "little Hong Kong", is a famous snack in this region. Yanjiang Steamed Rice Noodle is made from rice, which is delicious in color and fragrant.

Yanjiang Steamed Rice Noodle has a long history, dating back to when Yanjiang was still a small village. Legend has it that Zhuge Liang created Yanjiang Noodle by way of his southern expedition during the Three Kingdoms period. Yanjiang is located on the bank of Youjiang River. It was founded in the 12th year of Emperor Jiajing (1533). Before Yanjiang town came into being, rice noodle had already appeared on this land. Legend has it that more than 1800 years ago, during the Three Kingdoms period, the town of Yanjiang was plagued by diseases and polluted water. When Zhuge Liang conquered southern barbarians to pass by, he ordered soldiers to dig wells to fetch water and steam and grind rice for marching and fighting. Later people called these wells dug by Zhuge Liang's soldiers "Kongming Wells". Nowadays, many "Kongming Wells" in Yanjiang town are still in use, and people still use well water to make flour during festivals.

Yanjiang Steamed Rice Noodle mainly goes through soaking, grinding, boiling, shaping, steaming and drying. We can also print the red seal of each design on the powder as decoration. Cooked flour can be eaten immediately or stored for a long time. However, it should be noted that the rice noodle made after cooling, in order to prevent cracking, generally put into cold

雁江粉利发源于素有“小香港”之美誉的隆安县雁江镇，是该地区远近驰名的一种小吃。雁江粉利以大米为原料制作而成，色鲜味美，香滑爽口。

雁江粉利历史悠久，早在雁江还是一个小村落时就已经出现了，传说是三国时期诸葛亮南征途径雁江所创制的。雁江地处右江之畔，始建于嘉靖十二年（1533），在雁江镇形成之前，粉利就已经出现在了这片土地上。相传约1800多年前的三国时期，雁江镇瘴疠流行，江水污染，诸葛亮征讨南蛮经过这里，看到这里恶劣的环境便命军士挖井取水，将大米蒸熟磨浆便于行军作战时食用，这便是粉利的雏形。后世人们将诸葛亮命军士挖的这些井称为“孔明井”。如今雁江镇的很多“孔明井”还在继续使用，逢年过节，人们仍会汲井水制作粉利。

雁江粉利的制作大致要经过浸泡、磨浆、翻煮、塑形、蒸熟、晾干等流程。作为装饰，也可以在粉利上印上各种图案的红印。蒸煮好的粉利可以即食，也可以长期储藏，但是需要注意的是：为防止制作完成的粉利在冷却后开裂，一般要放入冷水中保存，并且需要不定时换水。换水时要保证水质干净，而且要将水全部换掉。在浸泡的过程中，粉利表面会产生黏滑物质，这样可以防止粉利发酵，延长保存时间。雁江粉利色鲜味美、香滑爽口，食用时可以切条或切片，再配上腊肉、芹菜或菜花、青蒜等烩炒，也可以切块后加冰糖煮糖水，抑或像煮面条一样，做成汤粉利。

粉利承载着雁江厚重的历史与文化，至今雁江粉利还保持着家庭作坊式的纯手工制作传统。雁江粉利是原生态的大米制品，不含有任何添加剂和防腐剂。在选材上需要选用隆安特有的“硬米”。这种独特的而古老的“硬米”，与隆安稻作文化紧密相关。雁江粉利的产生充满着奇幻色彩和人文气息，无论是诸葛亮南征还是“孔明井”的传说，都让雁江粉利散发着一种神秘感和传奇性。雁江粉利是广西人文和历史的一个延伸，挖掘、抢救和保护雁江粉利，对丰富和完善广西壮族民间技艺和文化有着重要作用。

随着商品经济的不断发展，外来饮食文化不断挤占着雁江粉利的生存空间，而且雁江粉利采用家庭作坊式的纯手工制作，严格要求原料筛选和制作方式，无疑让它的处境更为被动。曾经每逢秋后粮食入仓，雁江镇的居民家家户户做粉利的盛况已经不再了。如今的雁江镇只剩下10多家作坊在制作粉利。基于这种情况，隆安县委、县政府做了大量的保护性工作。早在1987年，隆安县民间就对雁江粉利等民俗民间文化进行了阶段性调查，并提出雁江粉利应该作为隆安县重点保护和宣传的传统民间小吃。2007年9月，南宁市非物质文化遗产普查调研全面开展，隆安县文化馆对包括雁江粉利在内的多种传统文化再次进行普查。2013年，经南宁市人民政府同意，雁江粉利制作技艺列入第五批市级非物质文化遗产名录。

water to preserve, and need to change water from time to time. Make sure that the water is clean and completely replaced. In the process of soaking, sticky material will be produced on the surface of flour, which can prevent the fermentation of flour and prolong the storage time. Yanjiang Steamed Rice Noodle is delicious in color and fragrant with smooth mouth. When eaten, rice noodle can be cut into strips or slices and serve with preserved pork, celery or cauliflower, leek and other stew fried. It can also be cut into pieces and boiled with sugar, or it can be made into soup rice noodle like noodles.

The rice noodles bear the heavy history and culture of Yanjiang River. So far, Yanjiang Steamed Rice Noodle still maintains the pure handicraft tradition of family workshop. Yanjiang Steamed Rice Noodle is a primitive rice product, which contains no additives or preservatives. Long'an's unique "hard rice" should be selected in the selection of materials. This unique and ancient "hard rice" is closely related to Long'an rice culture. Yanjiang Steamed Rice Noodle is full of fantasy colors and cultural atmosphere. No matter the legend of Zhuge Liang's southern pilgrimage or the legend of "Kongming Well", Yanjiang steamed rice noodle has a sense of mystery and legend. Yanjiang Steamed Rice Noodle is an extension of the culture and history of Guangxi. Digging, rescuing and protecting Yanjiang Steamed Rice Noodle plays an important role in enriching and perfecting the folk skills and culture of Zhuang Ethnic Group in Guangxi.

With the continuous development of commodity economy, foreign food culture keeps occupying the living space of Yanjiang Steamed Rice Noodle. Yanjiang Steamed Rice Noodle is made by hand in a home-cooked way with strict raw material selection and production method, which undoubtedly makes its position more passive. Every autumn after the grain warehouse, there is no grand occasion that Yanjiang residents do rice noodles. Today, there are only more than ten workshops in Yanjiang town making noodles. Based on this situation, Long'an County Party Committee and the county government have done a lot of protective work. As early as 1987, Yanjiang Steamed Rice Noodle and other folk cultures were investigated in Long'an, and Yanjiang Steamed Rice Noodle should be the key traditional folk snacks in Long'an. In September 2007, Nanning's general survey of intangible cultural heritage was carried out in an all-round way. Long'an County Cultural Centre conducted a re-survey of various traditional cultures, including Yanjiang Steamed Rice Noodle. In 2013, with the consent of Nanning People's Government, Yanjiang Steamed Rice Noodle Making Skill was selected as the Fifth Municipal List of Intangible Cultural Heritage.

宋家米酒酿造技艺

Song's Home-made Rice Wine Brewing Skill

项目名称：宋家米酒酿造技艺

别称：无

分布范围：江南区宋村

入选名录：2015年第六批市级非物质文化遗产名录

保护单位：江南区文化馆

代表性传承人：宋祥年

Element name: Song's Home-made Rice Wine Brewing Skill

Alternative name: None

Geographical location and range: Song village of Jiangnan District

Element inscribed list: In 2015 on the Sixth Municipal List of Intangible Cultural Heritage

Competent body involved in safeguarding: Jiangnan District Cultural Centre

Representative inheritor: Song Xiangnian

宋家米酒是南宁三江口宋村宋氏家族世代传承的一项传统技艺。宋家米酒的制作原料选用当地生产的优质大米、水和上等的酒饼，口味醇香，略带些苦辣。宋家米酒采用传统方法酿造，制作方法十分考究。制作流程大致需要经过选料、大锅煮米、降温、发酵、封存、酿酒等环节。对于时间和温度都有严格的要求和控制，发酵前的温度需控制在25到27摄氏度之间，配以一定比例的酒饼进行发酵，然后封存。封存两天后加一次水，再封存半个月便可以进行酿酒。酿酒的设备主要是两口锅，下层装发酵好的大米，上层装凉水进行冷却，点火酿酒时上层水温超过50摄氏度时就需要重新换水。两口锅中间是出酒层，各层之间的衔接处需要用米糠或玉米粉加水调黏后封住。点火酿酒时，酒精挥发遇上层冷水冷却流出出酒管即成米酒。

宋家米酒酿造技艺的起源已不可考，但三江口宋村开村于明朝初年，从开村时就有用宋家土法酿造技艺酿造的米酒。据传明朝弘治年间，南宁府的官员就用其大宴宾客，传承至今至少有600多年的历史。三江口宋村宋氏家族人丁兴旺，《徐霞客游记》记载，宋家“聚落颇盛”，清朝流传至今有“四房八支十六杈”。600多年来，宋氏子孙不断传承、交流和学习米酒土法酿造技术。民国期间，三江口宋村族人用祖传酿酒技艺到东南圩、大同圩和南宁城开办酒坊，使宋家米酒走向更广阔的天地。

南宁三江口是稻作文化的发源地，土法酿造米酒颇得骆越文化之三昧。宋家米酒制作技艺融汇了壮族和平话汉族的民间文化元素，发展成富有地方特色的传统技艺。宋家米酒的酿造纯天然、纯手工、纯绿色，口感好、质感佳，深受广大民众喜爱。米酒被称为“液体蛋糕”，它含有10多种氨基酸，其中有8种是人体不能合成而又必需的。此外，它还有促食欲、助消化、温寒补虚、提神解乏、解渴消暑、促进血液循环、润肤等功效。米酒中的营养成分易于人体吸收，是中老年人、孕产妇和身体虚弱者补气养血之佳品。宋家米酒

Song's Home-made Rice Wine is a traditional making skill handed down from generation to generation by Song family in Song Village, Sanjiangkou, Nanning. The raw materials of Song's Home-made Rice Wine are local high-quality rice, water and fine wine cakes. The taste is mellow and slightly bitter and spicy. Song's Home-made Rice Wine is brewed in the traditional way, which is very exquisite. The production process roughly needs to go through the selection of materials, cooking rice, cooling, fermentation, storage, wine and other links. There are strict requirements and controls on time and temperature. Before fermentation, the temperature should be controlled between 25 and 27 degrees Celsius, with a certain proportion of wine cake for fermentation, and then sealed. After two days of storage, water needs to be added, and after another half a month, wine can be prepared. Brewing equipment is mainly two pots, the lower layer is loaded with fermented rice, the upper layer is loaded with cold water for cooling. When the upper water temperature exceeds 50 degrees Celsius, the wine needs to be replaced. The middle of two pots is the wine layer, the connection between the layers needs to use rice bran or corn flour and add water to glue after sealing. When a fire is lit to make wine, the alcohol volatilizes under the cooling of the upper cold water and flows out of the wine pipe to become rice wine.

Skill's origin cannot be ascertained, but Song Village in Sanjiangkou was built in the early Ming Dynasty. Since the built of Song Village, rice wine has been brewed by Song family's indigenous method. According to legend, during the Hongzhi period of the Ming Dynasty, Nanning officials used rice wine to feast guests, which has a history of at least 600 years. The Song family in Song village of Sanjiangkou has a prosperous population. According to the *Travel Notes of Xu Xiake*, the Song family has a large number of people. From the Qing Dynasty, there was a saying that "four houses, eight branches and sixteen branches". Over the past 600 years, Song's descendants have continuously inherited, exchanged and learned the technology of rice wine and soil brewing. During the Republic of China, Song villagers in Sanjiangkou used their ancestral brewing skills to open wine shops in Dongnan Xu, Datong Xu and Nanning city, which made Song's Home-made Rice Wine go to a broader world.

Nanning Sanjiangkou is the birthplace of rice culture. The indigenous brewing of rice wine embodies the three samadhi of Luoyue culture. Song's Home-made Rice Wine Making Skill combines folk culture elements of the Pinghua's Dialect of the Zhuang Ethnic Group and the Han Ethnic Group, and develops into traditional skills with local characteristics. Rice Wine's brewing is pure natural, pure handmade, pure green, good taste, good texture, and is loved by the general public. Rice wine is called "liquid bread", which contains more than ten kinds of amino acids, eight of which are not synthesized but necessary for human body. In addition, there are also appetite, digestion, warming cold and tonifying deficiency, refreshing and relieving fatigue, thirst and heat, promoting blood ring, moisturizing and other effects. The nutrients in rice wine are easy to absorb by human body. It is a good product for middle-aged and old people, pregnant and lying-in women and the weak. Song's Home-made Rice Wine Brewing Skill has a long history and witnesses the continuous development of society. Nowadays, some people in the Song family still retain the traditional tools of wine-brewing, and inherit the techniques of rice wine-making and soil-making. It contains the unique living condition and thinking mode of Song's ancestors and the working people. It is a living cultural symbol and an indispensable part of Nanning's traditional folk culture. and it is of great significance to inherit and develop the excellent traditional national culture.

There is a proverb in Song village, Sanjiangkou, which says, "The first rich man is soaked in water; the second rich man is steamed and milled Tofu." Song's Home-made Rice Wine, once brilliant for a time, has brought great economic benefits to the Song clan. However, with the progress of the times and the development of economy, the dietary culture has gradually diversified, and the convenience and speed of industrial production have made the traditional rice wine-making techniques in dire danger. Older generations are too old to make Song's Home-made Rice Wine, and young people can hardly be interested in this traditional technique, which makes it difficult for them to inherit and develop rice wine indigenous brewing techniques. In order to improve this situation, the Jiangnan Cultural Centre inherits and protects Song's Home-made Rice Wine Making Skill. To organize and set up a intangible cultural heritage census team to thoroughly understand and conduct a comprehensive census. The census data were sorted out and filed, and the declaration was made step by step. With the joint efforts of the government and the people, Song's Home-made Rice Wine Brewing Skill can be better inherited and developed.

酿造技艺历史悠久，见证着社会的不断发展。如今宋氏家族中的一些人还保留有酿酒的传统工具，并传承着米酒土法酿造技艺，蕴含着宋氏先祖和广大劳动人民特有的生活状态和思维方式。宋家米酒是活态的文化符号，是南宁民间传统文化不可忽视的一部分，对于传承和发扬民族优秀传统文化有着十分重要的意义。

三江口宋村有句谚语：“第一富，水浸布；第二富，蒸酒磨豆腐。”曾经辉煌一时的宋家米酒给宋氏族人带来了丰厚的经济效益。但随着时代的进步和经济的发展，饮食文化逐渐多元化，工业生产的方便快捷使得传统米酒土法酿造技艺岌岌可危，老一辈传承人年事已高，无法再进行宋家米酒的酿造，年轻人又很难对这项传统技艺产生兴趣，使得米酒土法酿造技艺面临着继承与发展的困难。为了改善这一现状，江南区文化馆对宋家米酒制作技艺进行传承和保护，组织成立非物质文化遗产普查小组，深入了解，全面普查，将普查资料做了整理归档，进行逐级申报。在政府与民众的共同努力下，宋家米酒酿造技艺得以更好地传承和发展。

蒸馏装置
Distillation Unit

都结豆腐制作技艺

Dujie Tofu Making Skill

项目名称：都结豆腐制作技艺

别称：陇坦豆腐

分布范围：隆安县都结乡

入选名录：2015年第六批市级非物质文化遗产名录

保护单位：隆安县文化馆

代表性传承人：梁丽卿

Element name：Dujie Tofu Making Skill

Alternative Name：Longtan Tofu

Geographical location and range：Dujie Town of Long'an County

Element inscribed list：In 2015 on the Sixth Municipal List of Intangible Cultural Heritage

Competent body involved in safeguarding：Long'an County Cultural Centre

Representative inheritor：Liang Liqing

Dujie Tofu, formerly known as Longtan Tofu, is produced in Longtan Tun, Longge Village, Dujie Xu, Long'an county. It is made by traditional handicraft and ancient method. The local dried soybeans with full granules are selected as raw materials. The dried soybeans are soaked in mountain springs and then processed by grinding, filtering and boiling. Finally, the dried soybeans are made by using gypsum and halogen as coagulants. The refining process of Dujie Tofu is different from that of general Tofu production. The refining process needs to be carried out twice to increase the toughness of Tofu finished products. Compared with Tofu in other areas, the refining process is more tender, smooth and durable. Dujie Tofu is nutritious, boiling and frying resistant. It is well known in Long'an County and even Nanning. It has been exhibited and promoted as Nanning's traditional craftsmanship products in China-ASEAN Expo for many times.

Dujie Tofu Making Skill has a long history and has been handed down for more than 200 years. It is said that more than 200 years ago, a group of peasants fled to a remote mountain depression in Longcao village, Dujie, in order to avoid the high taxes and miscellaneous taxes imposed by the local chieftain, and settled here, which is now Longtantun. At that time, Longtan tun was surrounded by high mountains, no mineral resources, and very limited arable land. But these farmers found that some of the soybeans carried in the mountains sprouted on the ground and grew well. People reclaimed barren hills and planted soybeans. Not only did it solve the problem of food and clothing, but it also made the surplus beans into Tofu, which brought good economic benefits to this barren mountain village. The soybean produced in Longtantun has a high protein content, and Tofu made by indigenous method is fresh, tender and delicious, and can endure cooking and frying. Longtan Tofu is welcomed by the diners outside the mountains, and the demand is increasing. The workshop of making Longtan Tofu moved from the deep mountains to Dujie Xu, so Longtan Tofu is also called Dujie Tofu.

Dujie Tofu is closely related to the life of Longtantun villagers. It is engraved with the continuous efforts and yearning for a better life of the ancestors of Longtan village in a tough environment, and has a very profound cultural impression. Dujie Tofu not only solves the problem of food and clothing for local residents, but also continuously creates economic value, which makes local residents become rich. Nowadays, Dujie Tofu's production has joined the mechanical equipment, but it has not lost its most essential thing. Dujie Tofu only uses mechanical pulping to process, and uses the

都结豆腐，原名“陇坦豆腐”，产于隆安县都结乡陇割村陇坦屯。它采用传统手工技艺，古法制作，在用料上选用当地出产且颗粒饱满的干黄豆，将干黄豆用山泉浸泡后再经磨浆、滤浆、熬浆等工序，最后以石膏和盐卤作为凝固剂点制而成。都结豆腐的磨浆工序与一般豆腐制作有所不同，需要将磨浆工序进行两次，从而增加豆腐成品的韧性，与其他地区的豆腐相比更为嫩滑爽口，久煮不烂。都结豆腐营养丰富、耐煮耐煎，在隆安县乃至南宁市内都颇有名气，多次在广西东盟博览会上作为南宁市非物质文化遗产传统技艺产品进行展示和推介。

都结豆腐制作技艺的历史较为悠久，传承至今已有200多年的历史。据说，200多年前，一群农民为了躲避当地土司征收的苛捐杂税，逃进了都结乡陇割村一个偏僻的山坳避难并定居下来，即现在的陇坦屯。当时，陇坦屯四面高山耸峙，没有矿产资源，耕地面积又非常有限，但是这些逃难的农民发现，进山携带的一些黄豆在逃难途中散落在地上发了芽，长势良好，于是人们开垦荒山，种植黄豆，不仅解决了温饱问题，还将富余的豆子做成豆腐，为这个贫瘠的山村带来了不错的经济效益。陇坦屯出产的黄豆蛋白质含量高，土法制成的豆腐鲜嫩可口，耐煮耐煎。陇坦豆腐受到山外食客的追捧，需求量也不断增加，于是制作陇坦豆腐的作坊从深山搬到了都结圩上，因此陇坦豆腐也被称为都结豆腐。

都结豆腐与陇坦屯村民的生活息息相关，铭刻着陇坦村先民在艰苦环境下的不断努力和对于美好生活的向往，具有非常深厚的文化印记。都结豆腐不仅解决了当地居民的温饱问题，而且还在源源不断地创造着经济价值，使当地居民走向致富之路。现如今都结豆腐的制作虽然也加入了机械设备，但是并没有丢掉其最为本质的东西。都结豆腐只在磨浆时使用机械，利用科技的便利使从业人员摆脱了一定的繁重劳动，但是为了保证其口感，增强其韧性，仍旧需要用石磨进行二次磨浆，并没有脱离传统手工制作的范畴。都结豆腐一直坚持使用山泉水和"盐卤凝结法"，更加深了其自身的民族特色和乡土气息。

都结豆腐一直是当地餐桌上备受青睐的日常美食，但是由于其制作工序较为特殊，工序更为繁杂，而"盐卤凝结法"的生产成本又比新型的化学凝固剂更高，生产效率更比不上机械化生产，导致利润空间逐渐缩小。加之一些熟悉都结豆腐制作流程的老师傅相继谢世，年轻人对这种繁复枯燥的工作不感兴趣，凡此种种都给都结豆腐带来了传承危机。为了更好地将这一项传统手工艺继承和发展下去，2013年5月，隆安县政府召开会议，决定加大宣传力度和经费投入，并结合旅游开发，着力将都结豆腐树立为隆安县传统技艺品牌。建立都结豆腐传统技艺名录领导小组，核定每年都结豆腐传承经费最低不少于2万元。现已建成政府资金补助与社会赞助机制，确保都结豆腐的传承后继有人。通过以上举措，都结豆腐制作技艺已渐渐走出困境，进入到稳步发展阶段。

convenience of science and technology to make employees get rid of some heavy labor. But in order to ensure its taste and enhance its toughness, it is still necessary to use stone mill for secondary pulping, which is not divorced from the traditional manual production category. In addition, Dujie Tofu has always insisted on the use of mountain springs and "salt brine condensation method", which has deepened its own national characteristics and local flavor.

Dujie Tofu has always been a popular daily delicacy on the local dining table. However, due to its special production process and more complicated process, the production cost of "salt-brine condensation method" is higher than that of new chemical coagulants, and the production efficiency is less than that of mechanized production, which leads to a shrinking profit margin. With the passing of some teachers who are familiar with the Dujie Tofu production process, young people are not interested in this tedious work, all of which has brought a crisis of inheritance to Dujie Tofu. In order to inherit and develop this traditional handicraft well, the Long'an County Government held a meeting in May 2013. It decided to increase publicity efforts and investment in funds. In combination with tourism development, Dujie Tofu should be established as a traditional handicraft brand in Long'an County. To set up a leading group being in charge of Dujie Tofu Traditional Skills Inheritance, and approve the minimum annual inheritance fund of Dujie Tofu not less than 20,000 yuan. A government subsidy and social sponsorship mechanism has been established to ensure the succession of Dujie Tofu. Through the above measures, Dujie Tofu Making Skill has gradually stepped out of the dilemma and entered a steady development stage.

煮豆浆
Cooking Soybean Milk

永州米酒制作技艺

Yongzhou Rice Wine Brewing Skill

项目名称：永州米酒制作技艺

别称：无

分布范围：以永州镇永固街、定罗街为中心，辐射马山县各村镇及南宁市、平果市等周边地区

入选名录：2017年第七批市级非物质文化遗产名录

保护单位：马山县文化馆

代表性传承人：韦明铭

Element name：Yongzhou Rice Wine Brewing Skill

Alternative Name：None

Geographical location and range：Centreing on Yonggu Street and Dingluo Street of Yongzhou Town, spreading to other villages and towns of Mashan County, as well as Nanning City, Pingguo County-Level City and the surrounding areas

Element inscribed list：In 2017 on the Seventh Municipal List of Intangible Cultural Heritage

Competent body involved in safeguarding：Mashan County Cultural Centre

Representative inheritor：Wei Mingming

按比例将捻成粉的酒饼撒在米饭上并均匀地搅拌
Sprinkle the Crushed Wine Cake on the Rice in Proportion and Stir Evenly

用米糠把蒸锅上下四周密封好，防止酒气外跑
Seal the Upper and Lower Sides of the Steamer with Rice Bran to Prevent the Wine from Escaping

永州米酒是马山县声名远扬的美食品牌，与永州鱼片、永州豆腐并称“马山永州美食三宝”。永州米酒采用传统工艺酿造，选料精细，制作考究，工序繁复。其制作需经过备料、酒饼制作、蒸煮、发酵、酿制等工序。永州米酒的酒饼需选用百根草等数种中草药，按一定比例与米粉搭配发酵。制作米酒所使用的原材料主要选用当地出产的优质大米，大米蒸熟后将米饭铲出倒入洗净的案板，晾至不烫手的温度，按比例将捻成粉的酒饼撒在米饭上并均匀地搅拌，然后放瓦缸密封发酵15天左右，冬天时间略长，夏天时间略短，待到整个房间弥漫酒香的时候，方可进行蒸酒。蒸酒时往大铁锅内倒入酒糟，使用陶瓷蒸笼盖严装好，蒸笼上放上一口锅，锅里注入冷水，水热了要及时换上冷水，通过锅里的冷水冷却蒸汽，凝结成酒。优质的永州米酒不酸不涩，入喉甘甜，无烧锅水汽味道。

永州米酒酿造技艺流布范围较广，以永州镇永固街、定罗街为中心，辐射到马山县各村镇以及南宁市、平果市等周边区域。永州米酒酿制技艺历史悠久，起源于唐朝，迄今已有1000多年的历史。明清时期极为兴盛，清朝同治年间《陈楼诗钞》载有诗人杨朝合“安得永州同宿醉，不枉人间来一

Yongzhou Rice Wine is a famous food brand in Mashan County, which is reputed as “Three Yongzhou Food Treasures of Mashan” along with Yongzhou Fish Fillet and Yongzhou Tofu. Yongzhou Rice Wine is brewed through traditional techniques, with refined materials, exquisite production and complicated procedures. Its production includes procedures, such as material preparation, yeast production, stewing, fermentation and brewery. The yeast of Yongzhou Rice Wine needs to select several Chinese herbal medicines, such as one-hundred-root grass. It is then fermented with rice flour of a certain proportion. The raw material for producing the rice wine mainly selects the local quality rice. After the rice is stewed, it is poured on the clean chopping board and dried to the proper temperature. Then the yeast ground into the powder is sprinkled on the rice and stirred averagely, and then put into the cylinder and fermented by seal for around 15 days. It is slightly longer in winter and shorter in summer. When the wine fragrance permeates the entire room, wine can be stewed. When the wine is stewed, distillers’ grains are poured into the big iron pan, which should be covered tightly with ceramics steamer. Cover a pot on the steamer and pour cold water into the pot. Timely change the cold water when the water is hot. Then the cold water in the pot cools down the steam and it is condensed into wine. The high-quality Yongzhou Rice Wine is not sour nor bitter; instead, it is sweet, without the flavor of the moisture within the enamelware pot.

The brewing technique of Mashan Yongzhou Rice Wine is widely spread. With Yonggu Street and Dingluo Street in Yongzhou as the centre, it spreads some villages of

Mashan County and surrounding areas such as Nanning and Pingguo. The brewing technique of Yongzhou Rice Wine has a long history. Originating from the Tang Dynasty, it has had the history of over 1000 years up to now. It was extremely prosperous in the Ming and the Qing Dynasties. *In Poem Collections of Chen Lou* during Emperor Tongzhi's reign in the Qing Dynasty, the poet Yang Chaohe wrote such a beautiful poem: "If I can get drunk in Yongzhou, it's worthwhile coming to the world", which shows the reputation and consumption group of Yongzhou Rice Wine. Meanwhile, Yongzhou Rice Wine also served as the tribute for praying for the divine and sacrificing. *Si'en Ritual Classics* recorded that Yongzhou people "put wine in the field to pay tribute to the heaven and the earth" on February 2, who specially sacrificed the heaven and the earth with rice wine and prayed for good weather for the crops.

Yongzhou Rice Wine is an embodiment of rice cultivating culture in Lingnan, which is filled with Yongzhou ancestors' wisdom and pursuit of the beautiful life. The rice floor takes the pure natural and harmless quality rice as the raw material, which contains multiple traditional Chinese medicines, and embodies the characteristics of medicine and food tonics of the Chinese dieting culture and wine culture. Rice wine is reputed as the "liquid cake", the nutrients of which are easily absorbed by human body. It is the good item for the middle-aged and the elderly, the pregnant and the weak to replenish qi and nourish flood. It has the functions, such as stimulating appetite, helping digestion, warming and tonifying deficiency, refreshing and recovering from fatigue, quenching thirst and relieving summer heat, promoting blood circulation and moistening skin; it is of great regimen value. Through a long evolution, the brewing of Yongzhou Rice Wine has formed the unique technique including processes, such as material selection, yeast production and brewing skill, and the wine culture with distinctive regional characteristics.

Out of the changes in social life, imbalance appears in the natural ecological environment and traditional human and ecological environment. At present, although Yongzhou Rice Wine Brewing Skill is inherited by the folk, yet it is declining out of the low profit. The number of rice wine workshops on Yongzhou Town is decreased from over 30 several years ago to less than 10 at present. Its unique making skill lacks inheritors. At present, the Yongzhou Rice Wine Brewing Skill enters the decline period, which requires the all-round system to protect and inherit it. In recent years, the government of Mashan County has organized the specific investigation team to systematically explore and sort out the national traditional

在蒸笼上架上锅，然后在上面的锅里加水
Put the Pot on the Top of the Steamer, and then Add Water to the Pot

回”的诗句，很好地体现了永州米酒的口碑和消费群体。与此同时，永州米酒也作为求神祭祀所用的供品。《思恩礼经》记载永州人民在“二月二，龙抬头”之日，“置酒田头，乃敬天地”，专门以米酒祭祀天地，祈求风调雨顺。

永州米酒是岭南稻作文化的一种体现，饱含着永州先民的智慧和对美好生活的追求。米酒以纯天然、无公害的优质大米为原材料，又加入多种中草药，也体现了中国饮食文化和酒文化中医食同补的特点。米酒被誉为“液体蛋糕”，其中的营养成分非常易于人体吸收，是中老年人、孕产妇和身体虚弱者补气养血之佳品，有促进食欲、帮助消化、温寒补虚、提神解乏、解渴消暑、促进血液循环、润肤等功效，具有很强的养生价值。经过漫长的演变，永州米酒酿造技艺形成了包括选料、酒饼制作、酿制工艺等工序在内的独特工艺以及地域特色鲜明的酒文化。

由于社会生活发生变化，自然生态环境、传统人文生态环境出现失衡现象，如今，永州米酒制作技艺在民间虽有传承，但因为利润较低而逐渐式微。永州镇上的米酒作坊由几年前的30多家缩减到现在的不足10家，其独有的制作技艺后继乏人。目前永州米酒制作技艺进入了衰退期，需要全面系统地予以保护传承。近年来，马山县政府组织专门的调研队伍对辖区内永州米酒制作技艺等民族传统技艺进行了系统挖掘整理，建立了数据档案，并编写《马山县非物质文化遗产普查资料汇编》，邀请专家开展研讨活动，研究永州米酒制作技艺的文化内涵和传承工作，探讨永州米酒制作技艺的发展路径。永州镇人民政府把打造永州米酒制作技艺文化品牌列为文化工作的一项重要内容，把保护传承永州米酒制作技艺纳入全镇文化建设发展的总体规划，还组织永州米酒制作技艺艺人到学校开展传承教学活动，以培养更多的传承人，挽救和保护原生态永州米酒制作技艺。

skills, such as Yongzhou Rice Wine Brewing Skill within the area under administration, set up the data file, compile Compilation of Census Data of Intangible Cultural Heritage of Mashan County, invite experts to carry out the seminar activities, study the cultural connotation and inheritance work of Yongzhou Rice Wine Brewing Skill, and discuss about the development path of Yongzhou Rice Wine Brewing Skill. Yongzhou Town People's Government lists the creation of the cultural brand of Yongzhou Rice Wine Brewing Skill as an important content of the cultural work, includes the protection and inheritance of Yongzhou Rice Wine Brewing Skill into the overall planning of cultural construction and development of the town. Meanwhile, it also organizes entertainers of Yongzhou Rice Wine Brewing Skill to carry out the inheritance teaching activities, cultivate more inheritors, save and protect the original Yongzhou Rice Wine Brewing Skill.

制作米酒材料
Materials for Making Rice Wine

永州鱼片制作技艺

Yongzhou Fish Fillet Making Skill

项目名称：永州鱼片制作技艺

别称：无

分布范围：以马山县永州镇永固街、定罗街为核心，辐射南宁市大多数地区

入选名录：2017年第七批市级非物质文化遗产名录

保护单位：马山县文化馆

代表性传承人：黄汉春

Element name：Yongzhou Fish Fillet Making Skill

Alternative name：None

Geographical location and range：Centreing on Yonggu Street and Dingluo Street of Yongzhou Town in Mashan County, and spreading to the majority places of Nanning City

Element inscribed list：In 2017 on the Seventh Municipal List of Intangible Cultural Heritage

Competent body involved in safeguarding：Mashan County Cultural Centre

Representative inheritor：Huang Hanchun

鱼生成品
Fillet Dish

永州鱼片是马山县声名远扬的美食品牌，是“永州美食三宝”之一。永州鱼片采用传统手工艺制作而成，工序复杂，制作考究。以当地永州暗河出产的河鱼作为主要食材，配以花生仁、白芝麻、香菜、生姜、精盐、花生油等，武火烹制而成。永州鱼片所使用的河鱼以2至2.5公斤重为佳，鱼片厚度要求在2至2.5毫米左右。烹制时要采用干净的生铁锅，用武火烧热，放入花生油，用锅铲将花生油沿锅四周不断浇淋，直至锅内冒出白烟时，将铁锅移离火灶，继续将锅内花生油沿锅四周浇淋，感觉油温稍降便可将切好的鱼片和配料一起倒入锅内拌匀，利用铁锅的余温将鱼片烹成稍卷状即出锅装盘。制作好的永州鱼片外观晶莹剔透，口感脆爽、鲜香甘甜，因具备鲜明的地方特色、独特的风味和口感而独具魅力。

永州镇地处亚热带海洋季风气候区，光热充足，夏长冬短，雨量充沛，适宜各类亚热带作物生长，草木经冬而不枯，植物种类繁多，生态环境十分优越。永州镇全境以石灰岩群峰与丘陵、岗地、平原相间交错，平原面积占多数。永

Yongzhou Fish Fillet is a famous food brand in Mashan County, which is reputed as one of the “Three Yongzhou Food Treasures of Mashan”. Yongzhou Fish Fillet is produced with the traditional handicraft, with complicated procedure and exquisite production. It takes the river fish produced in the local underground river of Yongzhou as the main food material, which is supplemented by peanut kernel, white sesame seed, coriander, ginger, refined salt and peanut oil; it is cooked by high heat. The river fish used by Yongzhou Fish Fillet generally has the weight of 2 to 2.5kg and the thickness of the fillet requires being from 2 to 2.5mm. In cooking, the clean cast iron pan is used. Warm it up with high heat, pour the peanut oil along the pot with the slice until white smoke rises from within the pot. Then put the iron pot away from the fire stove and continue to pour the peanut oil along the pot with the slice. When the oil temperature is slightly reduced, pour the well-cut fillets and ingredient into the pot and stir them averagely. Cook the fillets with the remaining heat of the iron pot into the slightly curly shape and then get them out of the pot and into the dish. The well-cooked Yongzhou Fish Fillet has the crystal appearance, crisp taste, mellow and sweet flavor. It is very charming out of its vivid local characteristics, unique flavor and taste.

Yongzhou Town is located at the subtropical marine monsoon climate area, with sufficient sunshine and heat, a long summer and a short winter, and sufficient rainfall. It is suitable for the growth of various subtropical crops. The grass and trees there do not get sere after winter. It boasts multiple plant types and an excellent ecological environment. Yongzhou Town has the interlaced limestone peaks, hills, down lands and plateaus, most of which are plateaus. The river fishes used by Yongzhou Fish Fillet all come from the underground river of Yongzhou, which is also named Yongzhou River, anciently known as Dingle River or Dingluo River. It is the river with the biggest water discharge except for Hongshui River in Mashan County. It has the advantaged natural growing environment.

Yongzhou Fish Fillet Making Skill has a wide circulation scope. With Yonggu Street and Dingluo Street in Yongzhou Town as the centre, it spreads to Nanning District and most districts and towns of Nanning. The making skill of Yongzhou fish in Mashan has a long history. According to the legend, it originated from the Qingyuan reign (around 1200 A.D.) of the Song Dynasty, with a history of over 800 years up to now. It is said that there was a dutiful son named Nong Yuan in Yongzhou at that time. Her mother loved eating fish a lot, so he harvested a big grass carp in Yongzhou River. Nong Yuan was afraid that his mother's throat would be blocked by the fishbone, so he cut the fish into slices for cooking. After the boil turned hot, the fillets were just put into the pot. However, a cat knocked over the water pot on the hearth and the fire was damped down by water, so the fillets became half-ripe. However, to their surprise, the fillets had crisp and unique flavors. Since then, the unique cooking method has been inherited by generations through thousands of years, and it becomes an exclusive local delicacy. According to the record of *A Brief History of Si'en* in the Qing Dynasty, "On July 13th, all the households eat fillets and use them for sacrificing and counteracting evil force." Its grand occasion can be thus seen.

Yongzhou Fish Fillet Making Skill originated from the traditional farming society of the local residents. Depending on the local geographical and hydrologic conditions in the local Yongzhou, it is of vivid regional characteristics and is one of the traditional local symbols of cooking culture. It is the product obtained by Yongzhou ancestors by making use of the nature and transforming the nature, so it is of profound cultural connotations. Yongzhou Fish Fillet is characterized by refined texture, crisp taste, and sweet flavor, so it is very popular with local residents and has a profound mass foundation. Its technique inherits the tradition and remains refined and complete, so it is of irreplaceability. Yongzhou Fish Fillet has strict standards for the cutting and slicing skill. The cooks are required to cut the fillet as thin as

州鱼片所使用的河鱼均采自永州暗河，又名永州河，古代叫定乐江或定罗江，是马山县除红水河之外水流量最大的河流，拥有得天独厚的自然生长环境。

永州鱼片制作技艺的流布范围较为广泛，以永州镇永固街、定罗街为核心，辐射南宁市区和南宁大多数区镇。马山永州鱼片制作技艺历史悠久，相传起源于宋朝庆元年间（约1200），迄今已有800多年的历史。据传，当时永州有个名叫农元的孝子，其母酷爱吃鱼，他便到永州河里捕了一条大草鱼。农元怕母亲被鱼刺卡到喉咙，就把鱼肉切成薄片进行烹制。锅烧热后，鱼片刚刚下锅，一只猫碰翻灶台上的水罐，灶火被水浇灭，鱼片便成了一种半生不熟的状态。但令人意外的是，这样的鱼片口感清脆爽滑，别具风味。从此，这种独特的烹制之法就这样一代代传承下来，成为当地独有的美味佳肴。清《思恩史略》记载："七月十三，家家户户尽食鱼片，并以祭祀辟邪。"可见其盛况。

永州鱼片制作技艺源于传统农耕社会时期，依托于永州当地的地理和水文条件，具有鲜明的地域性特征，是当地传

去鱼皮鱼骨
Peeling off Fish Skinbone

切片
Flaking Fish

统饮食文化符号之一。它是永州先民利用自然、改造自然的产物，具有非常深厚的文化内涵。永州鱼片具有质地细嫩、爽脆可口、鲜香甜美的特点，深受当地居民的喜爱，具有深厚的群众基础。其技艺秉承传统，精细完整，具有不可替代性。永州鱼片对刀功有严格的标准，鱼片需切得薄如蝉翼，且切鱼片前需要将鱼去鳞剔骨洗净，鱼肉用砂纸包紧，让砂纸吸干鱼肉表面水分，方能进行切片。此外对火候把握之精准也彰显了永州鱼片制作技术的高难度。其对传播民族传统文化和扩大当地经济文化知名度具有一定的推动作用。

由于社会生活发生变化，自然生态环境、传统人文生态环境出现失衡现象，永州鱼片制作技艺正在面临失却其民俗文化传承土壤的窘境。如今，永州鱼片制作技艺在民间虽有传承，但由于经营利润较低而逐渐式微，其独有的制作技艺后继乏人。为了传承和发展这一传统技艺，当地政府对辖区内永州鱼片制作技艺进行了系统的挖掘整理，建立了数据档案，编写了《马山县非物质文化遗产普查资料汇编》，同时还邀请专家开展研讨活动，研究永州鱼片制作技艺的文化内涵和传承方案，探讨永州鱼片制作技艺的发展路径。目前，永州镇政府已把打造永州鱼片制作技艺文化品牌列为文化工作的一项重要内容，把保护传承永州鱼片制作技艺纳入全镇文化建设发展的总体规划，并组织永州鱼片制作技艺艺人到学校开展传承教学活动，培育更多的传承人，挽救和保留原生态永州鱼片制作技艺。

possible; before cutting the fillet, they have to scale off the fish, debone and clean it, tighten the fish with sandpaper, and make the sandpaper absorb the superficial water of the fish. In addition, the accurate mastery of heat control also shows the higher technical difficulty of Yongzhou Fish Fillet. It helps to publicize the national traditional culture and expand the local economic and cultural reputation.

Out of the changes in social life, imbalance appears in the natural ecological environment and traditional human and ecological environment. Yongzhou Fish Fillet Making Skill is facing the dilemma of losing the inheritance soil of folk culture. At present, although Yongzhou Rice Wine Brewing Skill is inherited by the folk, yet it is declining out of the low profit. Its unique making skill lacks inheritors. In order to inherit and develop the traditional skill, the local government systematically explores and sorts out the Yongzhou Fish Fillet Making Skill within the area under administration, sets up the data file and compiles *Compilation of Census Data of Intangible Cultural Heritage of Mashan County*. Meanwhile, it invites experts to carry out the seminar activities, study the cultural connotation and inheritance work of Yongzhou Fish Fillet Making Skill, and discuss about the development path of Yongzhou Fish Fillet Making Skill. Yongzhou Town People's Government lists the creation of the cultural brand of Yongzhou Fish Fillet Making Skill as an important content of the cultural work, includes the protection and inheritance of Yongzhou Fish Fillet Making Skill into the overall planning of cultural construction and development of the town. Meanwhile, it also organizes entertainers of Yongzhou Fish Fillet Making Skill to carry out the inheritance teaching activities, cultivate more inheritors, save and protect the original Yongzhou Fish Fillet Making Skill.

永州豆腐制作技艺

Yongzhou Tofu Making Skill

项目名称：永州豆腐制作技艺

别称：无

分布范围：以永州镇永固街、定罗街为中心，辐射马山县各村镇及南宁市、平果市等周边地区

入选名录：2017年第七批市级非物质文化遗产名录

保护单位：马山县文化馆

代表性传承人：徐宝青

Element name：Yongzhou Tofu Making Skill

Alternative name：None

Geographical location and range：Centreing on Yonggu Street and Dingluo Street of Yongzhou Town, spreading to others villages and towns of Mashan County, as wwll as Nanning City, Pingguo County-Level City and the surrounding areas

Element inscribed list：In 2017 on the Seventh Municipal List of Intangible Cultural Heritage

Competent body involved in safeguarding：Mashan County Cultural Centre

Representative inheritor：Xu Baoqing

永州豆腐是马山县声名远扬的美食品牌，是“永州美食三宝”之一。它发源于永州镇永固街、定罗街的一些民间豆腐作坊。永州豆腐采用传统手工艺制作而成，其工序繁杂，制作考究，因具备鲜明的地域特色、独特的风味和口感而独具魅力。其成品最初为家庭菜肴，后来也作为宴席菜品及祭祀供品。其制作需选用当地出产的优质无公害黄豆，以富含矿物质的永州暗河地下水等作为原材料，经过备料、浸泡、磨浆、滤浆、烧煮、点浆、成形、油炸等工序，对时间、火候、品味等有着严格的要求。成形的豆腐以质地细嫩、色鲜味美、清润可口的特点，赢得了食客的追捧。而油炸豆腐外焦里嫩，口感软滑，自成风味，声名远扬。

永州豆腐的流布范围较广，以永州镇永固街、定罗街为核心，辐射到南宁市、马山县各个乡镇以及周边县区。其流布地区为广西多民族文化的腹地，拥有永州豆腐制作技艺赖以生存、发展的社会民俗文化土壤。马山永州豆腐制作技艺历史悠久，传承至今已有400多年的历史。据考证，明嘉靖四十一年（1562），戚继光从两广调兵抗倭，马山县永州籍将领黄至能随军赴闽粤作战，他发现日本豆腐外焦里嫩，味道、口感俱佳。回到永州后，他便参照其口感，经过多方研究和改进，独创了别具一格的豆腐制作工艺，也就是最早的永州豆腐。清朝时，永州豆腐曾被用作祭祀供品，而后持续走俏，直至民国时期还广泛流行于永州民间。1950年至今，永州豆腐一直广泛见于婚宴、丧葬、祭祀、日常食用以及商业流通。

豆腐营养极高，含铁、镁、钾、铜、钙、锌等元素，有“植物肉”之美称。豆腐为补益清热的养生食品，常食可补中益气、清热润燥、生津止渴、清洁肠胃。豆腐中的类固醇、豆固醇，均是抑癌的有效成分。永州豆腐制作技艺采用传统工艺制作，不添加任何化工原料，属于绿色食品，非常符合当下人民群众的饮食观念。永州豆腐制作技艺，源于当地居民传统的农耕生活，通过宗教祭祀、日常饮食、宴席、

Yongzhou Tofu is a well-known food brand in Mashan County and one of the “Three Treasures of Yongzhou Cuisine”. It originated from some folk Tofu workshops in Yonggu Street and Dingluo Street of Yongzhou Town. Yongzhou Tofu is made by traditional handicrafts with complicated procedures and exquisite workmanship. Because of distinctive regional characteristics, unique flavor and taste, it has its own charm. The finished product was originally a family dish, and later was also used as banquet dishes and sacrificial offerings. Its production needs to select high-quality, pollution-free soybeans produced locally, with mineral-rich underground water in Yongzhou as raw materials. Through preparation, soaking, grinding, filtering, cooking, pulping, shaping, frying and other processes, it could finally be completed, with strict requirements on time, temperature, taste and so on. Tofu, with its delicate texture, fresh color and delicious taste, has won the favor of diners. Fried Tofu is far more famous for its delicate outer coke, smooth taste and self-made flavor.

Mashan Yongzhou Tofu has a wide range of distribution, with Yongzhou Town Yonggu Street and Dingluo Street as the core, radiating to Nanning, various townships in Mashan County and surrounding counties and districts. Its spreading area is the hinterland of multi-ethnic culture in Guangxi. It is the soil of social folk culture which Yongzhou Tofu Making Skill depends for survival and development. Yongzhou Tofu Making Skill has a long history of more than 400 years. According to textual research, in the forty-first year of Emperor Jiajing in the Ming Dynasty (1562 A.D.), Qi Jiguang transferred troops from Guangzhou and Guangdong to fight Japan. Huang Zhineng, a Yongzhou general in Mashan County, accompanied the army to Fujian and Guangdong. He found that the Japanese Tofu had a good taste. After returning to Yongzhou, he created a unique Tofu manufacture process by referring to its taste after research and improvement, and it was also one of the earliest Yongzhou Tofu. During the Qing Dynasty, Mashan Yongzhou Tofu was once used as a sacrificial tribute. Later, Mashan Yongzhou Tofu continued to be popular among Yongzhou until the Republic of China. Since 1950, it has been widely seen in wedding banquets, funerals, sacrifices, daily food and commercial circulation.

Tofu is highly nutritious, containing iron, magnesium, potassium, copper, calcium, zinc and other elements, known as “botanical meat”. Tofu is a kind of health food for tonifying and clearing heat. Regular intake can help to strengthen vital energy, clear heat and moisten dryness, produce fluid and quench thirst, and clean intestines and stomach. Steroidal and soysterol in Tofu are effective components in inhibiting

选豆
Picking Beans

做豆浆
Making Soybean Milk

cancer. Yongzhou Tofu Making Skill is a kind of green food, which is made by traditional technology and does not add any chemical raw materials. It is very in line with the people's dietary concept. Yongzhou Tofu Making skills are derived from the traditional farming life of local residents. Unique food culture and social etiquette are formed and inherited through religious sacrifice, daily diet, banquet, business operation and other forms. The pulping process of Mashan Yongzhou Tofu uses traditional gypsum pulping to solidify. The finished product needs to be deep-fried until golden yellow. During the frying process, the temperature and heat of the wok should be accurately controlled. The Tofu should be neither too old nor too tender. It is difficult to operate and show its own technical and comprehensive characteristics. In addition, Yongzhou Tofu has had a far-reaching impact on the production and life of Yongzhou people for a long time, involving the traditional culture contents such as the living and production customs of local nationalities, food culture and social etiquette. It has a distinct regional color.

With the continuous development of economy and the continuous progress of industrialization, chemical food additives and preservatives have gradually become the materials used in the point production of Tofu, which not only improves the production efficiency but also reduces the production cost, making the traditional production of Tofu greatly hit. In addition, Mashan Yongzhou Tofu Making Skill, which operates at a low profit in the face of mechanical production, is unable to attract young people's attention in the current era of diversified industry choices, which

商业经营等形式形成独有的饮食文化和社交礼仪，并传承下来。永州豆腐的点浆工序采用传统石膏点浆凝固，成品需炸至金黄色后捞出，油炸过程中油锅的温度和火候要把握精准，炸出的豆腐既不可太老也不可太嫩，具有一定的操作难度，彰显出其自身的技术性、综合性等特征。此外，长期以来，永州豆腐在永州民众的生产、生活等方面都有着深远的影响，涉及当地民族生活生产习俗、饮食文化、社交礼仪等传统文化内容，具有鲜明的地域色彩。

随着经济的不断发展和工业化进程的不断推进，化学食品添加剂和防腐剂逐渐成为点制豆腐的用料，既提高了生产效率又降低了生产成本，使得传统制作豆腐的方式大受打击。此外，在机械生产面前，经营利润较低的永州豆腐制作技艺，在当下行业选择多样性的时代无法吸引年轻人的眼球，使得这项技艺面临濒危的困境。永州镇上的豆腐作坊在逐渐减少，形势颇为严峻。为了传承和发展这一传统技艺，马山县政府组织对辖区内永州豆腐制作技艺进行了系统的挖掘整理，建立了数据档案，并编写了《马山县非物质文化遗产普查资料汇编》。永州镇政府致力于打造永州豆腐制作技艺文化品牌，重点保护传承永州豆腐制作技艺。邀请专家开展研讨活动，研究永州豆腐制作技艺的文化内涵和传承工作，探讨永州豆腐制作技艺的保护及发展路径。如今在政府有关部门及传承人的共同努力下，永州豆腐已经逐渐走出困境，制作作坊逐渐增多，规模逐步扩大。

makes the technology facing an endangered dilemma. Tofu workshops in Yongzhou town are decreasing and the situation is quite serious. In order to inherit and develop this traditional skill, the Mashan County Government organized a systematic excavation and collation of Yongzhou Tofu Making Skill in the jurisdiction area, established data files, and formed the "*Compilation of the Intangible Cultural Heritage Survey Data in Mashan County*". Yongzhou Town Government is committed to building Yongzhou Tofu Making Skill a cultural brand, focusing on the protection and inheritance of Yongzhou Tofu Making Skill. Experts are invited to carry out seminars to study the cultural connotation and heritage of Yongzhou Tofu Making Skill and explore the protection and development path of Yongzhou Tofu Making Skill. Now Yongzhou Tofu has gradually come out of difficulties with the joint efforts of the relevant government departments and successors. The number of Yongzhou Tofu production workshops has gradually increased in numbers and the scale has gradually expanded.

销售
Selling

隆安布泉酸鱼制作技艺

Long’an Buquan Sour Fish Making Skill

项目名称：隆安布泉酸鱼制作技艺

别称：无

分布范围：隆安县布泉乡及周边地区

入选名录：2018年第七批自治区级非物质文化遗产名录

2017年第七批市级非物质文化遗产名录

保护单位：隆安县文化馆

代表性传承人：李天纯

Element name：Long’an Buquan Sour Fish Making Skill

Alternative name：None

Geographical location and range：Buquan Town of Long’an County and the surrounding areas

Element inscribed list：In 2018 on the Seventh Autonomous Region List of Intangible Cultural Heritage

In 2017 on the Seventh Municipal List of Intangible Cultural Heritage

Competent body involved in safeguarding：Long’an County Cultural Centre

Representative inheritor：Li Tianchun

布泉酸鱼制作技艺源于隆安县布泉乡布泉街一带。布泉酸鱼传承至今一直沿袭传统制作方法。其原材料需选取约1公斤重的野生鱼，把鱼头、鱼尾、鱼翅、鱼鳞、内脏除掉，洗净晾干。将鱼肉切成厚1.5厘米、长4厘米的小块，称重后按比例加入适量的精盐，将鱼肉和食盐搅拌均匀，再将熟透冷却后的碎玉米颗粒倒入鱼片中，加入一匙具有清热解毒、杀虫功能的葫芦茶浓汁拌匀，装入消毒过的瓷罐或玻璃瓶压实、密封，腌制两周即可食用。布泉酸鱼酸爽可口、营养丰富、味道独特、催人食欲，被奉为节庆、婚宴待客的特色美食，多次在广西东盟博览会产品展示会展销，并通过外地游客声名远播。

布泉酸鱼制作技艺以隆安县布泉乡布泉街为源头，以布泉街为中心，分布于全乡各个自然村。布泉酸鱼传统手工技艺已有200多年的历史。200多年前，紧傍布泉河依水而居的布泉街原住民“近山吃山，近水吃水”，常常在鱼类丰富的河中打鱼，将吃不完的鱼腌制储存，布泉酸鱼的发展逐步定型，经一代代传承，成为红白喜事餐桌上不可或缺的传统美食。虽然这一传统技艺也传至本县诸多地方，但其源于布泉街，因此始终以“布泉酸鱼”为名传续。改革开放后，布泉被开发为著名旅游区，来到布泉的游客都对布泉酸鱼情有独钟，布泉酸鱼的制作规模也随之扩大。

布泉酸鱼在当地有“酸品之王”的美誉，至今仍使用传统方法制作，即坚持以野生河鱼为原料，坚持传统手工制作，坚持葫芦茶汁绿色防腐。尤其是在原料选用上，一定要使用野生河鱼，因为它营养丰富，肉质好，符合环保要求，而饲养的塘鱼与网箱鱼的鱼肉水分含量高，韧性差且不耐储存。布泉酸鱼是壮族人民在生产生活中总结和创造的传统技艺，传承这一技艺对研究古代壮族人民的生产活动和生活方式大有裨益。在过去交通不便、经济欠宽裕的壮家山村，布泉酸鱼是很多家庭必备的菜肴，也曾是招待贵客时的佳品。布泉酸鱼历史悠久，在广西传统手工技艺中，其起源独特、

Buquan Sour Fish Making Skill originated in Buquan Street, Buquan Township, Long'an County. Buquan Sour Fish has inherited traditional production methods. The raw materials need to be selected from wild fish weighing about 1 kilogram, with fish head, tail, fin, scales, viscera removed, washed and dried. Cut the fish into small pieces with 1.5 cm in thickness and 4 cm in length. Weigh them. Add the right amount of refined salt according to the proportion. Mix fish meat and salt evenly, pour cooked and thoroughly cooled crushed corn particles into fish fillets, add a spoonful of gourd tea juice with heat-clearing, detoxification and insecticidal functions, mix them thoroughly and put it into sterilized pots or glass bottles. Compacted, sealed and marinated for two weeks. Buquan Sour Fish is sour, delicious, nutritious, unique and appetizing, and is regarded as a featured delicacy for festivals and wedding reception. It has been exhibited in the product exhibition of China-ASEAN Expo many times and has been well-known by foreign tourists.

Buquan Sour Fish Making Skill originates from Buquan Street, Buquan Township, Long'an County. It is located in Buquan Street and is distributed in various natural villages in the township. The traditional handicraft of Buquan Sour Fish has a history of more than 200 years. More than 200 years ago, the aborigines of Buquan street, close to the Buquan River, lived by the water. They used to fish in the rivers where there were plenty of fish and preserved the fish that could not be eaten. The making Skill is finalized. Throug passing down from generation to generation, it has become an indispensable traditional food on the banquets of weddings or funerals. Although this traditional technique has spread to many parts of the county, it originated in Buquan street and has been known as "Buquan Sour Fish". After the reform and opening up, Buquan has been developed into a famous tourist area. Tourists coming to Buquan are all fond of Buquan Sour Fish and thus the production scale of Buquan Sour Fish has been expanded.

Known as the "King of Sour Products" in the region, Buquan Sour Fish is still made by traditional methods, including wild river fish, traditional handmade cooking and green preservative of gourd tea juice. In particular, wild river fish must be used as raw materials since it is nutritious, meets environmental protection requirements, and has good meat quality. In contrast, fish raised in ponds and cages are high in water content, poor in toughness and not resistant to storage. Buquan Sour Fish is a traditional skill that the Zhuang Ethnic Group have summarized and created in their production and life. In the past, Buquan Sour Fish was a must-have dish for many families in Zhuang villages, where transportation and economic conditions were poor. It was also a convenient and affordable delicacy when entertaining distinguished guests. Buquan Sour Fish has a long history. Among the traditional handicraft techniques in Guangxi, Buquan Sour Fish has unique origins, production and flavor, strong ethnic characteristics and local flavor, and high market value. To excavate, rescue, protect and inherit the traditional handicraft of Buquan Sour Fish is of great value to enrich and perfect the traditional handicraft of Zhuang Ethnic Group in Guangxi.

Buquan Sour Fish has always followed the traditional method of making, adhered to manual production, and refused to use chemical preservatives, thus the production efficiency is low. With the advancement of mechanized production, the traditional handicraft of Buquan Sour Fish has been affected to a certain extent. In addition, since the number of wild river fish in Buquan River is decreasing year by year, the acquisition of raw materials is much more difficult. Moreover, with the death of many masters who are familiar with the traditional handicraft process of Buquan Sour Fish, young people are not interested in traditional handicraft. All these factors have contributed to the Buquan Sour Fish traditional handicraft inheritance crisis to a certain extent. In order to carry on and develop this traditional skill, the leading group of Buquan Sour Fish Making Skill was set up in Long'an county, which listed "Buquan Sour Fish Making Skill" as one of the major folk culture activities in Long'an County. The publicity efforts and funds were increased. The minimum annual budget for Buquan Sour Fish inheritance was approved to be no less than 20,000 yuan. Meanwhile, in combination with tourism development, Buquan Sour Fish Making Skill has been developed into a traditional skill brand in Long'an County. At present, a mechanism of government financial subsidies and social sponsorship has been established to ensure the succession of Buquan Sour Fish Making Skill. In recent years, Buquan Sour Fish's craftsmanship has come out of the dilemma and entered the normal inheritance.

配料　摄影 黄涛
Mixed Ingredients Photo by Huang Tao

制作独特、风味独特，拥有浓郁的民族特色与乡土气息，又有较高的市场价值。挖掘、抢救、保护和传承布泉酸鱼传统手工技艺，对于丰富和完善广西壮族民间传统手工技艺有重要价值。

布泉酸鱼始终沿袭传统制作方法，坚持手工制作，拒绝使用化学防腐剂，生产效率较低。随着机械化生产的推进，布泉酸鱼传统手工技艺受到一定的影响。此外，因布泉河野生河鱼的数量逐年减少，原料获取较为困难，加上不少熟悉布泉酸鱼传统手工制作技艺的师傅辞世，年轻人又对传统技艺不感兴趣等，在一定程度上造成了布泉酸鱼传统手工技艺的传承危机。为了继承发展好这项传统技艺，隆安县成立了布泉酸鱼制作技艺领导小组，把“布泉酸鱼制作技艺”列为隆安重大民俗文化活动，加大宣传力度和经费投入，核定每年布泉酸鱼传承经费最低投入不少于2万元；同时结合旅游开发，着力将布泉酸鱼制作技艺建设为隆安县传统技艺品牌。目前，已建立起了政府资金补助与社会赞助机制，确保布泉酸鱼制作技艺传承后继有人。近年来，布泉酸鱼制作技艺已走出困境，进入正常传承，产品销售市场不断扩大。

酸酱　摄影 黄涛
Sour Sauce Photo by Huang Tao

武鸣府城土制红糖

Wuming Fucheng Indigenous Brown Sugar

项目名称：武鸣府城土制红糖

别称：无

分布范围：武鸣区府城镇

入选名录：2018年第七批自治区级非物质文化遗产名录
　　　　　2017年第七批市级非物质文化遗产名录

保护单位：武鸣区文化馆

代表性传承人：曾树新

Element name：Wuming Fucheng Indigenous Brown Sugar

Alternative name：None

Geographical location and range：Fucheng Town of Wuming District

Element inscribed list：In 2018 on the Seventh Autonomous Region List of Intangible Cultural Heritage
In 2017 on the Seventh Municipal List of Intangible Cultural Heritage

Competent body involved in safeguarding：Wuming District Cultural Centre

Representative inheritor：Zeng Shuxin

Wuming Fucheng Indigenous Brown Sugar is one of the indigenous products produced only in the twelfth lunar month. It is made by hand in strict accordance with the production process of indigenous brown sugar recorded in *Exploitation of the Works of Nature.* In the production of Fucheng Indigenous Brown Sugar, sugar cane was first selected and then pressed. In the old days, sugar cane was pressed by ox roll and wood roll, but now mechanical press is often used. Other processes still follow the most traditional methods of sugar production. The boiling technique of Indigenous Brown Sugar is the technique of "straight-wind firewood stove" and "chain pot" which have been inherited for thousands of years. Sugar-smelting iron pans are arranged in series from large to small, which are used for boiling sugar juice layer by layer. In the process of boiling sugar, the whole continuous cooker stove with firewood does not stop burning and has been boiled for more than 20 minutes. When boiling to make thick sugar juice, pour it into a large iron pot and constantly turn the sugar juice to make the sugar juice condense as soon as possible. Finally, pour the molasses into a wooden mold. After it is completely set, it can be solidified and then demoulded, cut and stored.

Climate of Fucheng Town is a typical subtropical monsoon one. It is suitable for planting crops such as rice, sugar cane and fruits. Rich in sugar cane, it is the largest town in Nanning. Fucheng Indigenous Brown Sugar is widely distributed in the core area of Wuming District, Guangxi. It spreads outward to Mashan County, Shanglin County, Chongzuo City and even the whole area of Guangxi, as well as to Guangdong, Yunnan and Taiwan. Fucheng Indigenous Brown Sugar Making Skill has a relatively long history and has been handed down for more than 300 years. According to *Wuming County Records*, early in the period of Emperor Qianlong years of the Qing Dynasty, planting cane and boiling sugar have been quite common among Wuming people. Due to the complexity of making skill, this traditional handicraft gradually faded out of the public's vision. Today, only Dingfu village and Fuliang village in Wuming District make Indigenous Brown Sugar with traditional techniques. There are 18 brown sugar workshops in the village, and 120 related employees, with an annual output value of more than 1.2 million yuan.

Fucheng Indigenous Brown Sugar is a unique specialty produced by folk traditional techniques. It reflects the wisdom of working people, inherits and develops the dietary custom culture, and contains rich cultural connotations. Sugar cane is a gift from nature. The ancestors of Fucheng made use of

老式榨蔗木辊
Old Cane Roller

府城土制红糖是只在腊月制作的土特产之一，严格按照《天工开物》中记载的土法红糖的制作工艺，纯手工熬制而成。府城土制红糖制作时先甄选好做糖的甘蔗，然后进行榨蔗，旧时用牛拉石辊、木辊榨蔗，现在多使用机械压榨机进行。其他工序仍旧沿承着最传统的土法制糖工艺。土糖的熬煮采用的是传承了上千年的“直风柴灶”和“连环锅”技艺。炼糖铁锅由大到小依序连环排开，用于层层熬制糖汁。在熬糖的过程中，整个连环锅灶加柴不停火，一直熬制20多分钟。当熬制成浓浓的糖汁时，倒入大铁锅中不停地翻动糖汁，使糖汁尽快凝结。最后将翻好的糖浆倒入一个木质的模具中，完全凝固后便可脱模切割、存放。

府城镇属典型的亚热带季风气候，适宜种植水稻、甘蔗、水果等作物，盛产甘蔗，是南宁市甘蔗种植第一大镇。府城土制红糖流布范围较广，以南宁市武鸣区府城镇为核心，向外辐射到马山县、上林县、崇左乃至整个广西，以及广东、云南、台湾等地。府城土制红糖制作技艺有着较为悠久的历史，传承至今已有300多年。根据《武鸣县志》记载，早在清乾隆年间，武鸣民间种蔗熬糖已相当普遍。由于制作技艺的繁杂，这一传统手工技艺逐渐淡出群众视野。如今武鸣区内仅剩府城镇富良村定富屯在利用传统技艺制作土制红糖，该屯共有红糖作坊18家，相关从业人员120人，年产值达120多万元。

府城土制红糖是以民间传统技艺制作的独具地方特色的产品，它既是劳动人民智慧结晶的反映，又是饮食习俗文化的传承和发展，蕴含着丰富的文化内涵。甘蔗是大自然的馈赠，府城先民因地制宜，运用当地独特的自然资源丰富自己的饮食文化内容。府城土制红糖制作技艺承载着府城先民对美好生活的追求与企盼。府城土制红糖采用传统的十八道古法技艺，历经榨汁、打泡、赶水、过滤、摇漂、打沙、成型等工序，经过五榨取、三滤、二浮、一沉等工艺制成。火焰的熬煮成就了古法红糖的醇厚香甜。红糖性温、味甘、入脾，具有益气补血、健脾暖胃、缓中止痛、活血化瘀的作用，适合产后妇女和大病初愈的老人食用。府城土制红糖因采用土法红糖熬制，所以保留了人体必不可少的苹果酸、核黄素、胡萝卜素、烟酸及钙、铁、铬、锰等微量元素和营养成分，且纯天然，无添加剂，保留了蔗汁中的营养成分。

local unique natural resources to enrich their dietary culture. Fucheng Indigenous Brown Sugar Making Skill bears the pursuit and expectation of the ancestors of Fucheng for a better life. Fucheng Indigenous Brown Sugar adopts the traditional eighteen ancient techniques, such as juice pressing, foaming, water driving, filtering, shaking, sand beating, shaping and so on. It is made through the process of five extraction, three filtration, two floating, one sinking and etc. The boiling of flame made the traditional brown sugar mellow and sweet. The brown sugar is warm, sweet, and enters the spleen. It has the functions of strengthening vital energy and blood, invigorating spleen and warming stomach, relieving pain, activating blood circulation and removing stasis. It is suitable for postpartum women and the elderly who have recovered from serious illness. Fucheng Indigenous Brown Sugar boiled with brown sugar by indigenous method, thus retains essential trace elements and nutrients such as malic acid, riboflavin, carotene, nicotinic acid, calcium, iron, chromium, manganese, etc., which are indispensable to human body. Moreover, it is pure natural without any additives.

Fucheng Indigenous Brown Sugar has always adhered to the most traditional production method and does not use additives. It is packaged in cartons and adheres to the philosophy of health and environmental protection. But in the context of preservatives and all kinds of plastic packaging, it has brought a certain impact to Fucheng Indigenous Brown Sugar. In addition, the complex technology, time and

甘蔗汁水分蒸发，即将熬成糖浆
Sugarcane Juice Evaporates and is about to Boil into Syrup

土糖出锅，倒入模具凝结成型
Out of the Pot, Pour in the Mould and Form

labor consumption and high labor cost also influenced the development of Fucheng Indigenous Brown Sugar. However, in the hearts of Fucheng people, Indigenous Brown Sugar is not only a means to make money, but also a kind of regional culture, which has been passed on consciously. The overall survival condition of Fucheng Indigenous Brown Sugar Making skills was good. In order to make this traditional technique develop better, the Wuming District government and relevant departments set up the Fucheng Indigenous Brown Sugar Protection Working Group, issued the *Implementation Plan for the Wuming District to Establish the Intangible Cultural Heritage Fucheng Brown Sugar Inheritance Base* and invested special funds to organize personnel to carry out census, excavation, protection, inheritance and various activities related to Fucheng Indigenous Brown Sugar. Based on the preservation of the Indigenous Brown Sugar flavor, we have developed new brown sugar such as ginger, rose, and osmanthus. At the same time, the traditional offline business model is adjusted to online sales model, featuring green brands, vacuum bags, cans and bowls, and accompanied by text logo, further enhancing the market competitiveness of brown sugar.

府城土制红糖一直坚守着最传统的制作方式，不使用添加剂，以纸箱包装，坚持健康和环保的理念。但是防腐剂、各式塑料包装食品随处可见的环境，给府城土制红糖带来了一定的冲击，同时工艺复杂、耗时耗力、人工成本较高等因素也给府城土制红糖的发展带来了一定的影响。但是在府城人心中，土制红糖并非只是赚钱的手段，更是一种地域文化，一直有人在较为自觉地传承。目前，府城土制红糖制作技艺的整体生存状况良好，为了让这一传统技艺更好地发展下去，武鸣区政府和相关部门成立了府城土制红糖保护工作小组，印发了《武鸣区建立非物质文化遗产府城制红糖传承基地实施方案》，投入专项经费，组织人员对府城土制红糖进行普查、挖掘、保护、传承，并开展各种传习活动，在保留土制红糖原味的基础上研发出添加生姜、玫瑰花、桂花等的新型红糖。同时，将传统的线下经营模式调整为网上销售模式，主打绿色品牌，采用真空袋装、罐装、碗装，并配以文字标识，进一步增强土制红糖的市场竞争力。

土制红糖切割成块、包装存放
Local Brown Sugar is Cut into Pieces, Packed and Stored

武鸣柠檬鸭制作技艺

Wuming Lemon Duck Cooking Skill

项目名称：武鸣柠檬鸭制作技艺

别称：无

分布范围：武鸣区

入选名录：2018年第七批自治区级非物质文化遗产名录
2017年第七批市级非物质文化遗产名录

保护单位：武鸣区文化馆

代表性传承人：甘保辉

Element name：Wuming Lemon Duck Cooking Skill

Alternative name：None

Geographical location and range：Wuming District

Element inscribed list：In 2018 on the Seventh Autonomous Region List of Intangible Cultural Heritage
In 2017 on the Seventh Municipal List of Intangible Cultural Heritage

Competent body involved in safeguarding：Wuming District Cultural Centre

Representative inheritor：Gan Baohui

Wuming Lemon Duck, an authentic popular local dish in Nanning, is one of the top ten famous dishes in Guangxi. Inherited by the local Gan family, it has a history of more than 100 years. The material selection of Gan's Gaofeng Lemon Duck is very fastidious. In terms of duck, we need to choose free ranging Jiepai pond native duck in local mountains, whose meat is tender and sweet. In terms of lemon, we need to choose wild lemons picked outside the front door of the house, which have a "clear fragrance" after pickling. In terms of water, we need to use mountain spring water in Baisha'ao, Jiepai, which is "pure, refreshing and sweet". When cooking, we need to braise and bake the duck in a big iron pan with laurel wood to keep duck's "fresh and delicious taste". For ducks made in other places, we can choose native ducks fed with authentic bran coat, and we'd better choose lemons that have been pickled for 3 years or more. The main methods are as follows: cut the duck that has been slaughtered into nuggets, chop lemons that have been pickled for years into strips, prepare enough ingredients such as sour Chinese bulbous onion, sour pepper, garlic, fresh ginger, peanut oil, salt, white sugar, yellow rice wine and sauce, have a good control of heating's duration and degree, stir-fry duck nuggets and ingredients like lemons with peanut oil, simmer the duck with slow fire until it is completely ripe, then use strong heat to stir-fry the duck until the juice is changed into paste, and finally the dish can be put into a plate for eating.

The distribution area of Wuming Lemon Duck is centered on Wuming District, Nanning, and is radiated to all districts in Nanning and most of the country's provinces and cities. Wuming Lemon Duck originated in the third year of the Republic of China (1914). At that time, in order to glorify and illuminate his ancestors, Lu Rongting, governor of Guangdong and Guangxi, whose ancestral home was Wuming, decided to split Gaofeng mountain for carving out a way and built the first highway in Guangxi, namely, Yongwu highway. One day, Lu Rongting took a rest at the Jiepai pavilion of Jiefeng village, and saw that Zhuang brocade patterns used for decoration on the pavilion had been variegated, so he asked some people to repair it. Villagers were grateful, so farmers slaughtered local ducks to serve him, and cooked ducks with their own pickled lemon, sour pepper, garlic and ginger. The dish was sour and refreshing, fragrant but not greasy, and Lu Rongting greatly appreciated it. The story of "Lu Ronting eating ducks at Jiepai" spread like wildfire. Since the road was built at that time, a large number of migrant workers were concentrated there every day, and the Gan family set up a small restaurant on the side of the road. With the opening of the road, the number of vehicles and people going to Yunnan Province and Guizhou

柠檬鸭
Lemon Duck

武鸣柠檬鸭，是南宁本土原汁原味的大众菜肴，是广西十大名菜之一，由当地甘氏一脉传承，至今已有100多年的历史了。甘氏武鸣柠檬鸭选料极为讲究，选用本地山地放养的界牌水塘土鸭，肉质鲜嫩甜美；选用自家房前门外采摘的野生柠檬腌制，才有“清香味”；用界牌白沙坳山泉水，才能“甘洌清凉甜美”；烹煮时要用桂树柴大铁锅焖火焗，才“入味鲜香”。其他地方制作的鸭子可选正宗谷糠喂大的土鸭，柠檬最好是腌制3年以上的。主要做法为：将鸭宰杀好后切成块，将陈年腌制的柠檬去核切成条状，备足酸藠头、酸辣椒、蒜头、鲜姜、花生油、盐、白糖、黄酒、酱料等配料，掌握好火候，将鸭块及柠檬等配料用花生油爆炒，再用文火细焖到鸭肉熟透，接着改用强火翻炒至汁水成糊状便可装碟食用。

武鸣柠檬鸭的流布区域以南宁市武鸣区为中心，辐射到南宁各市区以及全国大部分省、市。武鸣柠檬鸭起源于民国三年（1914），当时祖籍武鸣的两广都督陆荣廷为了光宗耀祖，决定劈高峰山开路，修建广西第一条公路——邕武公路。一日，陆荣廷在界峰村的界牌亭小憩，见亭上所饰壮锦图案已斑驳陆离，随嘱修葺，村民感激，农户宰杀土鸭招待，用自家腌制的柠檬、酸辣椒、蒜头、生姜等烹饪，酸辣爽口，香而不腻，陆荣廷大加赞赏。“陆荣廷界牌吃鸭”的故事不胫而走。由于当时修建公路，每天有大批民工聚居，甘家人便在路边支起小店，随着道路开通，去往云贵两省的车辆和人流不断增多，20世纪80年代，甘家柠檬鸭第二代传人甘祥盛开了第一家甘家柠檬鸭店。1991年，甘祥盛和甘小忠一同制作的武鸣柠檬鸭荣获广西大众名优菜点一等奖、武鸣首届非物质文化遗产美食大赛一等奖。

武鸣柠檬鸭制作技艺流程复杂，每道工序的细腻程度之高，是其他美食难以比拟的，而且武鸣柠檬鸭有促进人体肠胃消化和抗凝血的作用，不失为一道延年益寿的养生食品。制作好的武鸣柠檬鸭，看其外观，冒着油汁，金黄诱人；闻其香，柠檬与鸭肉香飘扑鼻；品其味，柠檬酸香中透着梅子的甜味，微辣中藏着鸭肉的细腻。它是一道味酸辣适宜，清新爽口，香而不腻，极其开胃的美食，深受当地人民和广大游客的喜爱。

Province was on the rise. In the 1980s, Gan Xiangsheng, the second generation of Ganjia Lemon Duck, opened the first Ganjia Lemon Duck Restaurant. In 1991, Wuming Lemon Duck, made by Gan Xiangsheng and Gan Xiaozhong together, won the first prize of Guangxi Popular Famous and Excellent Dishes and the first prize of Wuming First Intangible Cultural Heritage Food Competition.

The process of Wuming Lemon Duck Cooking Skill is complex, and the fine degree of each process is so high that it is difficult for other food to compare with it. Moreover, Wuming Lemon Duck has the effect of promoting gastrointestinal digestion and anticoagulation, so it is also a health food that prolongs life. For Wuming Lemon Duck that has been cooked well, if you see its appearance, it's golden and attractive with flowing oil juice. If you smell the dish, the smell of lemon and duck is tangy. If you taste the dish, you will find lemon's sour fragrance containing plum's sweetness and duck's delicacy lies in slight pungency. It is a moderately sour, suitably hot, refreshing, fragrant, not greasy and extremely appetizing food, which is loved by the local people and the vast majority of tourists.

Due to the difficulty of Wuming Lemon Duck Cooking Skill, the long period of practice, and the laborious making processes such as stir-frying and heat control, some young people feel frustrated and powerless, but a quite number of

用大火炒
Stir Fry

配制好的鸭肉
Prepared Duck

young people think they can learn practical skills to increase their income, so the skill's inheritance is benign. Nowadays, green food is more and more favored by people, and local duck breeding industry that feeds ducks with bran coat is developing and expanding in rural areas. In addition, lemon's price in the market is not low, so the planting area is on the rise, and the raw material supply channel is smooth. All these factors play a positive role in the existence and development of Wuming Lemon Duck Cooking Skill. As Wuming Lemon Duck Restaurants, especially the century-old restaurants, set up branches all over the country, the number of chefs continues to increase, and the brand effect of Wuming Lemon Duck will become more visible. Both social and economic benefits are achieved gradually. Generally speaking, Wuming Lemon Duck is in a steady development trend. In order to make the traditional skill have a bigger development space, Wuming District Government has established Nanning Wuming District Wuming Lemon Duck Cooking Skill protection work leading group, responsible for the organization, coordination and implementing of Wuming Lemon Duck Cooking Skill's protection work. Nanning Wuming District Wuming Lemon Duck Food and Catering Association is established for the training of Wuming Lemon Duck Cooking Skill to develop chef group of Wuming Lemon Duck Cooking Skill. Wuming Lemon Duck Restaurant is opened with the government's support. Thus, social and economic benefits are continuously improved. Over the years, a total of more than 100,000 yuan has been invested, and personnel are organized, who are responsible for the excavation, general survey and protection work of Wuming Lemon Duck Cooking Skill. In Wuming District, the First Intangible Cultural Heritage Food Competition and Zhuang Ethnic Group Food Exhibition on 3rd, March that Wuming Lemon Duck all took part in were held.

由于武鸣柠檬鸭制作技艺有一定难度，习艺周期长，难以把握的熟炒、火候等，确实让一部分年轻人望洋兴叹。但也有不少年轻人认为可以学习实用技术，增加收入，因此传承情况较为良好。如今，绿色食品越来越受到人们的青睐，谷糠喂大的土鸭养殖业在农村不断发展壮大，加之柠檬市场价格不低，种植面积有所增加，原料供给渠道畅通，这些因素都对武鸣柠檬鸭制作技艺的存续状况发挥着一定的积极作用。随着武鸣柠檬鸭饭店特别是百年老字号店在全国各地开设分店，厨师队伍不断扩大，武鸣柠檬鸭的美食品牌效应将越发显现，逐步实现了社会效益和经济效益的双丰收。目前武鸣柠檬鸭正处于一种稳健发展的势态，为了让这一传统技艺有更大的发展空间，武鸣区政府成立了南宁市武鸣区武鸣柠檬鸭制作技艺保护工作领导小组，负责武鸣柠檬鸭制作技艺保护工作的组织、协调和实施；成立了南宁市武鸣区武鸣柠檬鸭餐饮协会，对武鸣柠檬鸭制作技艺进行培训，以发展壮大武鸣柠檬鸭制作技艺厨师队伍；扶持开办武鸣柠檬鸭饭店，不断提高社会效益和经济效益。多年来，共投入10多万元人民币，组织人员对武鸣柠檬鸭制作技艺进行挖掘、普查保护工作，举办有武鸣柠檬鸭参加的武鸣区首届非物质文化遗产美食大赛和壮族三月三美食展销活动。

武鸣灵马旱藕粉制作技艺

Wuming Lingma Dry Lotus Root Starch Making Skill

项目名称：武鸣灵马旱藕粉制作技艺

别称：无

分布范围：武鸣区灵马镇

入选名录：2018年第七批自治区级非物质文化遗产名录
2017年第七批市级非物质文化遗产名录

保护单位：武鸣区文化馆

代表性传承人：何春连

Element name：Wuming Lingma Dry Lotus Root Starch Making Skill

Alternative name：None

Geographical location and range：Lingma Town of Wuming District

Element inscribed list：In 2018 on the Seventh Autonomous Region List of Intangible Cultural Heritage
In 2017 on the Seventh Municipal List of Intangible Cultural Heritage

Competent body involved in safeguarding：Wuming District Cultural Centre

Representative inheritor：He Chunlian

采收回基地待加工的旱藕　摄影 张美基
Dry Lotus Root to be Processed in the Recovery Base Photo by Zhang Meiji

晾粉和干水工序　摄影 张美基
Sheet Jelly Drying and Dry Water Process Photo by Zhang Meiji

Dry lotus root, namely, achira, is called as "Jiang Fu" in local Lingma, and also known as Wangsun, Mumeng and Jiaoyu. Lingma Dry Lotus Root Starch Making Skill has a long history and the making process is unsophisticated, complex and exquisite. Four filtration processes and five precipitation processes are needed to remove impurities and get starch pulp. After five days of repeated stirring, precipitation, drainage and starch extraction, quality grades are determined according to color differences. Generally speaking, the top layer is yellowish in color, which belongs to the first class. The bottom layer may contain fine impurities, which belongs to the second class and can be used as high quality seasoning starch after drying. The rest layers are superior quality products, which are used for processing high quality dry lotus root starch. After that, part of materials that can be used for making dry lotus root starch are selected for steaming, and the steaming process needs at least three people to cooperate with each other. One person is responsible for adding wood, controlling fire, mixing pulp, putting it in the pallet and pouring it into pot. One is responsible for taking the starch out from the pot, delaminating and spreading starch. One is responsible for drawing and airing starch. After having aired dry lotus root starch, it is cut, put in bundles, dried and tied. In Wuming, "Lingma Dry Lotus Root Starch" is as famous as "Lingma Catfish", and it can be boiled as soup, dry-fried, dressed with

旱藕，即姜芋，灵马当地称之为"姜抚"，又名王孙、牡蒙、蕉芋。灵马旱藕粉制作技艺历史悠久，工序古朴、复杂、考究。首先，需经过四道过滤工序、五道沉淀工序，以达到去杂质、取粉浆的目的。其次，需经过为期五天的反复搅拌、沉淀、排水、取淀粉，并按照颜色的不同来确定质量等级的不同。一般而言，最上层颜色呈微黄色，属一等品；最底层可能会含有细微杂质，为二等品，烘干可做优质佐料淀粉；其余的为上等品，用于加工成优质旱藕粉。再次，选出可以制作旱藕粉的一部分进行蒸制，蒸制过程至少需要三个人一起配合完成，一个添柴管火、调浆、装托下锅；一个负责起锅、剔粉和摊粉；一个负责拉粉和晾粉。等旱藕粉晾晒结束后再进行切粉、装榻、晒粉、绑粉等工序。在武鸣，"灵马旱藕粉"与"灵马鲶鱼"齐名，可汤煮、干炒、凉拌或者做火锅配菜使用。

灵马旱藕粉制作技艺分布区域较广，以广西南宁市武鸣区灵马镇汉族区域为中心，辐射到府城镇和武鸣周边县，在广西西北部以及贵州省、云南省部分地区也均有分布。灵马旱藕粉制作技艺具体起源于何时已不可考，相传南明永历五年（1651）十二月，永历皇帝西逃途经灵马镇，当时何腾蛟驻永宁阻挡清军，就曾食用过姜芋粉，据此而证旱藕粉至少已有300多年的历史了。旱藕粉制作在20世纪50年代至70年代最为盛行。如今，旱藕粉已走出广西，走向全国，并于2007年被选入国宴食材之一，用以款待各国外宾。

灵马旱藕粉是采用民间传统纯手工制作的绿色食品，具有煮食方便、久煮不煳、质地细腻、弹韧透亮等特点。旱藕有助于人体进食消化、排泄人体多余脂肪，含有丰富的钙、磷、铁及17种氨基酸、维生素B、维生素C等，经常食用可以益血补髓、消热润肺、降脂减肥，是当地居民日常饮食生活中必不可少的佐餐佳品。灵马旱藕粉承载着武鸣地区厚重的历史，细致繁杂的制作工序也从侧面反映出灵马人民对细腻、精致的饮食文化之追求。几百年来，它一直伴随着灵马人民的生活，是一项活态的技艺，是灵马历史的见证人，对于了解和研究灵马地区的饮食文化变革具有深远的意义。发掘和保护灵马旱藕粉制作技艺，不仅对研究和传承民族传统美食具有重大意义，而且对饮食文化的对外交流有着深远影响。

灵马旱藕粉的主要原材料来源于本地生产的旱藕，传统种植的旱藕于3月种植，在11月收获，生长期较长，对种植环境要求较为苛刻，需要种植在未施过化学肥料的旱地和山坡地。此外，由于旱藕局限于季节性种植和加工制作，使得灵马旱藕粉的产量极低。再者，掌握旱藕粉制作技艺的老人相继谢世，年轻人对传统手工技艺没有兴趣，传承后继乏人。为了继承和发展这项传统技艺，武鸣区政府和区镇文化主管部门成立了武鸣区非物质文化遗产普查和保护工作领导小组，设立武鸣区壮文化保护传承中心、文化馆民族文化传承保护部（“非遗部”）和项目工作领导小组，专门负责非物质文化遗产保护具体工作，并将非物质文化遗产工作列入

cold sauce or used as side dish for hot pot.

The distribution area of Lingma Dry Lotus Root Starch Making Skill is very wide, which is centered on Han people area in Lingma Town, Wuming District, Nanning, Guangxi, and is radiated to Fucheng Town and peripheral counties of Wuming, and is also distributed in Guangxi’s northwest as well as some parts of Guizhou Province and Yunnan Province. When Lingma Dry Lotus Root Starch Making Skill originated remains unknown. Legend has it that in December of the fifth year of Emperor Yongli (1651) in the Southern Ming Dynasty, Emperor Yongli fled westerly and passed by Lingma Town, and at that time He Tengjiao was stationed in Yongning to resist the Qing army and he had eaten dry lotus root starch. According to this, dry lotus root starch at least has a history of more than 380 years. Dry lotus root starch making was most popular from the 1950s to the 1970s. Nowadays, dry lotus root starch has already gone out of Guangxi and gone to the whole country. In 2007, it was selected as one of the food materials for state banquet to serve foreign guests from various countries.

Lingma Dry Lotus Root Starch is a purely hand-made green food that adopts folk tradition. It is easy to cook, and not sticky after long time cooking. It is also delicate and fine, tough and translucent. Dry lotus root can help human body to eat, digest and excrete excess fat, which is rich in calcium, phosphorus, iron and 17 kinds of amino acids, vitamin B and vitamin C. Regular consumption of dry lotus root can enrich blood, supplement marrow, eliminate heat, moisturize lung, reduce fat and lose weight, which is an indispensable food in the daily diet of local residents. Lingma Dry Lotus Root Starch carries the heavy history of Wuming area, and its meticulous and complicated making process also reflects the delicate and exquisite food culture pursuit of Lingma people from one side. Lingma Dry Lotus Root Starch Making Skill has been with the lives of Lingma people for hundreds of years without interruption. It is a living skill and a witness to the history of Lingma, which is also of great significance to understand and study the change of food culture in Lingma area. It is not only of great significance to the study and inheritance of national traditional food, but also impactful for the food culture exchange with foreign countries to excavate and protect Lingma Dry Lotus Root Starch Making Skill.

The main raw material of Lingma Dry Lotus Root Starch comes from locally produced dry lotus root. The traditional dry lotus root is planted in March and is harvested in November. Its growing period is long, its planting environment is demanding, and it needs to be planted on dry land and mountain slope where chemical fertilizer has not been applied. In addition, because the dry lotus root is limited to seasonal planting and hand-made processing, the yield of Lingma Dry Lotus Root Starch is very low. Moreover, the elderly who master Dry Lotus Root Starch Making Skill have died one after another, but young people are not interested in traditional craftsmanship, so there are no successors. In order to inherit and develop this traditional skill, Wuming District Government and cultural authorities in District and Towns established Wuming District Intangible Cultural Heritage Survey and Protection Work Leading Group, and set up the Wuming District Zhuang Culture Protection and Inheritance Centre as well as Cultural Centre National Cultural Inheritance Protection Department (Intangible Culture Heritage Department) and Project work Leading Group, who are responsible for the specific work of intangible cultural heritage protection. The work on intangible cultural heritage has been included in the government's work agenda, and the funds for the protection and inheritance of intangible cultural heritage were included in the annual budget. The leading groups excavate the relevant data of Lingma Dry Lotus Root Starch in depth, sort and file it, and declare it step by step. With the support of the District Government, the inheritor of intangible cultural heritage registered and established Lingma Town Village Dry Lotus Root Cooperative in 2012 to build up the planting, inheritance and production bases for processing and producing Lingma Dry Lotus Root Starch as well as farm products related to Dry Lotus Root. At the same time, a sound marketing system has also been established. In addition, the enthusiasm of local village farmers has been aroused, resulting in the expansion of dry lotus root's planting area. At present, the planting area of dry lotus root in Lingma Town is more than 700 *mu*, nearly 200,000 kg of dry lotus root starch can be produced, and the output value is about 1.4 million yuan.

晾晒粉条　摄影 张美基
Drying Lotus Root Starch Noodles　Photo by Zhang Meiji

政府工作议程，将非物质文化遗产保护传承活动经费列入年度财政经费预算，深度挖掘灵马旱藕粉的相关资料并整理归档，进行逐级申报。在区政府的支持下，由非物质文化遗产传承人于2012年注册成立灵马镇乡村旱藕专业合作社，建立种植、传承和生产基地，用以加工和生产灵马旱藕粉和旱藕相关农产品，同时还建立起较为健全的营销体系。此外还调动当地村屯农民的积极性，扩大了旱藕种植面积。目前灵马镇旱藕种植面积达700多亩，可生产旱藕粉近20万公斤，实现产值140万元左右。

拉粉和收水工序　摄影 张美基
Sheet Jelly Making and Drying　Photo by Zhang Meiji

灵马鲶鱼制作技艺

Lingma Catfish Cooking Skill

项目名称：灵马鲶鱼制作技艺

别称：无

分布范围：武鸣区灵马镇邻近地区

入选名录：2013年第五批市级非物质文化遗产名录

保护单位：武鸣区文化馆

代表性传承人：朱宝书

Element name：Lingma Catfish Cooking Skill

Alternative name：None

Geographical location and range：Vicinity of Lingma Town in Wuming District

Element inscribed list：In 2013 on the Fifth Municipal List of Intangible Cultural Heritage

Competent body involved in safeguarding：Wuming District Cultural Centre

Representative inheritor：Zhu Baoshu

Lingma Catfish is a local delicacy in Lingma Town that is known as "West Gate" of Wuming, and is also a traditional and famous food brand in Wuming and even in the whole Guangxi catering industry. Legend has it that it originated in Emperor Tongzhi period of the Qing Dynasty and has a history of more than 150 years. The main materials of Lingma Catfish are wild catfish and locally made soft Tofu with seasonings such as soy sauce, monosodium glutamate and oyster sauce. The production process is not complicated, the dish focuses on original taste and flavor, and usually the pine wood is used as the firewood to burn the dish in a big iron pan. Lingma Catfish's bright color, together with its fat but not greasy and smooth but not incompact mouthfeel makes it gain popularity among masses.

Lingma Catfish, a family delicacy, is said to have been created by a poor family surnamed Zhu at the start of Lingmaxu during the Emperor Tongzhi period of the Qing Dynasty. This dish is not only a family delicacy, but also a must-eat food for guests. But what really made Lingma Catfish famous was the use of Lingma Catfish to save people by Zhu's young generation. It is rumored that in the period of the Republic of China, a driver from other province overturned on Nanning-Baise transit highway that had just been built. The Zhu family's young generation passed by, took the seriously injured driver home, and used their best materials to make catfish with braised Tofu for the injured. After being saved, the driver must visit his saviors every time when he passed by Lingma, and praised the righteousness of Lingma people and the delicacy of catfish to others. Lingma Catfish spread rapidly, and it became famous in Guangxi and then widely known with Nanning-Baise highway as the centre. In the 1980s, with the continuous progress of reform and opening up, Zhu's brothers opened the first special Lingma Catfish Restaurant on Nanning-Baise transit highway. They continued to innovate on the basis of the traditional wood firing to make catfish's taste achieve a new level, thus creating a series of Lingma farmhouse specialties.

Lingma Catfish is part of the food culture in Wuming District. Catfish has much meat and few fish bones, and it is fresh and tender. At the same time, Tofu becomes more delicious, fresh and sweet as it absorbs the taste of catfish. Lingma Catfish is simple in production, but it is recherche in dish's color, smell and taste. Catfish's refreshing taste should be preserved, and it must be fat but not greasy and smooth but not incompact. Only possessing above qualities, can the dish be excellent. The cooking of Lingma Catfish is the crystallization of Lingma ancestors' wisdom and the

灵马鲶鱼成品
Catfish Dish

灵马鲶鱼是素有武鸣“西大门”之称的灵马镇的一道本土佳肴，同时也是武鸣乃至整个广西饮食产业中的一个传统而又响亮的饮食品牌。相传它起源于清朝同治年间，距今约有150多年的历史了。灵马鲶鱼的主要食材是野生的河鲶鱼和当地制作的水豆腐，并佐以酱油、味精、蚝油等调味料。其制作工序并不复杂，讲求原汁原味，多用松木作柴火在大铁锅中烧制而成。灵马鲶鱼色泽鲜亮，肥而不腻，滑而不融的口感受到广大群众的喜爱。

灵马鲶鱼，相传是清朝同治年间灵马圩头一户朱姓的穷苦人家创制的。这道菜不仅是自家的家庭美食，同时还是宴请宾客的必备佳肴。而真正让灵马鲶鱼声名鹊起的是朱家子弟用灵马鲶鱼救人的故事。据传民国时期一个外省司机在刚修通的南宁至百色的过境公路上翻了车，路过的朱家子弟将身受重伤的司机带回家中，用自家最好食材给伤者制作鲶鱼焖豆腐。司机得救后，每次路过灵马必定要拜访救命恩人，还逢人就称赞灵马人的义气和鲶鱼的美味。一传十，十传百，灵马鲶鱼以南（宁）百（色）公路沿线为中心名扬八桂，声名远播。20世纪80年代，随着改革开放进程的不断推进，朱氏兄弟在南宁到百色的过境公路上开设了第一家灵马鲶鱼饭店，在传统火烧土制的基础上不断推陈出新，让鲶鱼的口味更上一层楼，创制出一系列的灵马农家特色菜。

灵马鲶鱼是武鸣区饮食文化的一环。鲶鱼肉多刺少，口感鲜嫩，豆腐因为吸收了鲶鱼的滋味变得更为可口、鲜甜。灵马鲶鱼在制作上朴实无华，但是对菜品的色、香、味都颇有讲究，要保留鲶鱼爽口的风味，而且在口感上要肥而不腻、滑而不融，方为上品。灵马鲶鱼的烹饪是灵马先民智慧的结晶和生活的写照，对于研究饮食文化有着一定的价值。鲶鱼有强精壮骨和延年益寿的作用，还有利于伤口的愈合，我国南方从古代就有用鲶鱼做药膳的习惯。灵马鲶鱼是名贵的营养佳品，史书中记载它是可以与燕窝、鱼翅相媲美的。鲶鱼性温、味甘，含有丰富的蛋白质和矿物质等元素，特别适合体弱虚损、营养不良等人群食用，还可以改善消化功能不佳以及女性产后乳汁不足的问题，有利尿和治疗水气浮肿的功效。

灵马鲶鱼依托南宁至百色的过境公路而崛起，据统计，

portrayal of their life, which is of certain value to the study of food culture. The catfish has the effects of consolidating essence, strengthening bone and prolonging life, and is also beneficial to wound's healing, so there has been the habit of using catfish as herbal cuisine in the south of our country in ancient times. Lingma Catfish is a valuable nutritious product, and history books have recorded that it can be on a par with bird's nest and shark's fin. Catfish is warm in nature and sweet in taste, which contains abundant protein and minerals, so it is especially suitable for people with weak body and malnutrition. It can improve problems such as poor digestive function and women's insufficient breast milk after delivery, and it has the effects of diuretic action and edema treatment.

Lingma Catfish rose rapidly relying on Nanning-Baise transit highway. According to statistics, in the most glorious days, nearly 60 restaurants gathered on both sides of the highway in Lingma Town, bringing more than 1 million-yuan tax revenue to Lingma Town every year. With the opening of Nanning-Pingguo secondary highway and nearby expressway, the vehicles passing through Lingma Town have gradually decreased since 2000, and the development of Lingma Catfish industry has met new challenges. When the local government was aware of this situation, a number of efforts and exploration were carried out in various way. At present, Wuming District People's Government has listed Lingma Catfish as the key protection project of intangible cultural heritage and has set up corresponding management and organizational structure to

烧豆腐
Braised Tofu

用柴火灶做菜
Cooking with a Firewood Stove

formulate relevant protection policies and measures in a timely manner. Local party and government also timely change ideas, guide restaurants that produce Lingma Catfish to "go out", and turn their direction to all parts in Guangxi, such as Nanning, Baise and Hechi, and even to some more distant provinces like Guizhou and Yunnan. In order to promote the industry's benign competition and regulate the industry's operation, since 2008, pushed by the local government and led by Zhu brothers, whose operation scale is relatively large, "Lingma Catfish Restaurant and Catering Association" has been set up to uniformly standardize Lingma Catfish cooking skill and collectively coordinate the management. In 2011, the county government invested more than 100,000 yuan to strengthen the management of Lingma Catfish Restaurant and Catering Association and to cultivate famous chefs and masters who can make Lingma Catfish for restaurants in Lingma. In 2012, the county government invested more than 150,000 yuan to produce promotion brochures and videos and held the First Wuming District Intangible Cultural Heritage Food Making Skill Competition. The popularity of Lingma Catfish has been enhanced through the promotion of media at all levels. In 2013, Lingma Catfish was inscribed on the Municipal List of Intangible Cultural Heritage , and in 2016, its heritage base was established in the Zhuang people gourmet restaurant. At present, the total number of Lingma Catfish restaurants opened by farmers in Lingma Town is nearly 500. Based on the average annual profit of 200,000 yuan, the farmers who run Lingma Catfish restaurants can obtain more than 100 million yuan a year.

在最辉煌的时候，灵马镇公路两旁汇聚了将近60家饭店，每年为灵马镇带来100多万元的税收。随着南宁至平果的二级公路和附近高速公路的开通，从2000年起过往灵马镇的车辆逐渐减少，灵马鲶鱼产业发展遇到了新的挑战。当地政府意识到这种情况后，便进行了多方努力和探索。目前，武鸣区人民政府已经将灵马鲶鱼列入非物质文化遗产重点保护项目，并成立相应的管理和组织机构，及时制定相关保护政策及措施。当地政府也及时转变思路，引导经营灵马鲶鱼的饭店“走出去”，将目光转向南宁、百色、河池等广西各地，甚至是更远些的贵州、云南等省。为了促进产业的良性竞争，规范产业经营，从2008年起，当地党委、政府搭桥牵线，以经营规模较大的朱氏兄弟牵头，成立了“灵马鲶鱼餐饮协会”，对灵马鲶鱼的制作工艺等进行统一规范，共同协调管理。2011年，县政府投入10万多元，加强对灵马鲶鱼餐饮协会的管理，培养各大灵马饭店制作灵马鲶鱼的名师、名厨。2012年，县政府投入15万多元，制作宣传手册和宣传片，并举办武鸣区首届非物质文化遗产美食烹饪大赛，通过各级各大媒体的大力宣传，提高了灵马鲶鱼的知名度。2013年，灵马鲶鱼列入市级非物质文化遗产名录，并于2016年在壮家人美食馆建立传承基地。如今灵马镇农民在区内外开的灵马鲶鱼店总数近500家，以每家年均20万元利润计，经营灵马鲶鱼店的农民一年创收可达1亿多元。

第八章 传统医药

Chapter Eight Traditional Medicine

壮族谭氏草药疗骨法

Treatment of Bone with Tan's Herbal Medicine of Zhuang Ethnic Group

项目名称：壮族谭氏草药疗骨法

别称：无

分布范围：隆安县南圩镇

入选名录：2014年第五批自治区级非物质文化遗产名录
2013年第五批市级非物质文化遗产名录

保护单位：隆安县文化馆

代表性传承人：谭润丹

Element name: Treatment of Bone with Tan's Herbal Medicine of Zhuang Ethnic Group

Alternative name: None

Geographical location and range: Nanxu Town of Long'an County

Element inscribed list: In 2014 on the Fifth Autonomous Region List of Intangible Cultural Heritage
In 2013 on the Fifth Municipal List of Intangible Cultural Heritage

Competent body involved in safeguarding: Long'an County Cultural Centre

Representative inheritor: Tan Rundan

传承人在制药
TheInheritor is Preparing Herbal Medicine

草药疗骨是用草药治疗骨伤，是广西壮族自治区富有特色的传统骨伤疗法。在广西，隆安县南圩镇的谭氏草药疗骨法最具代表性。

谭氏草药疗骨法始于1733年，传承至今，已历经五代约280余年。清代，南圩山高谷深，道路崎岖，交通闭塞，骨折骨伤患者只能靠自己摸索以草药自救。草药治骨伤经谭氏的先人研究，在多年行医的实践过程中不断总结，得以基本定型，并一代代传续。谭氏草药疗骨法的传承讲究传内不传外，传男不传女，每代仅传一人，严防秘方外泄。谭氏草药疗骨法历经五代，救死扶伤，传承至今。

谭氏草药疗骨法用羊蹄藤、穿破石、吹风藤、小榕叶、小榕根等10多种草本、木本植物，切碎捣烂入药。这来自山野原汁原味的草药，疗效显著，安全无副作用。其治疗的顺序是，先给患者正骨、复位，再用捣烂的草药搅米酒敷患处，每隔3个小时将药搅酒再敷，一日敷4次，连敷20至30

Treatment of bone with herbal medicine is a traditional way of healing in Guangxi Zhuang Ethnic Group Autonomous Region. Within Guangxi, treatment of bone with Tan's herbal medicine of Zhuang Ethnic Group in Nanxu Town of Long'an County is the most representative.

Tan's approach originated from 1733 with a long history of over 280 years. In the Qing Dynasty, Nanxu Town hasn't been developed yet: being in a mountainous region, roads are uneven making Nanxu nearly unreachable for large traffics. People who suffered from bone fractures could only use local herbal medicines for minimal remedial effects.

Ancestors of Tan had started research on herbal medicine and developed their own treatment approach through practical experiences which was passed on from generation to generation. Tan's treatment of bone would only pass onto one male familial member every generation to prevent leakage of medicinal prescription. Five generations have passed since the first; many are saved until this date.

Tan's treatment of bone uses more than 10 herbal medicines, including sagittaria amurensis, cochinchina cudrania root, wintersweet wine, ficus microcarpa root and leaves. These natural herbs are grinded into mushes during production. The effects are remarkable, and it is safe without side effects.

Practitioners would first set the bone into the right position, then applies mushed herbal medicine along with rice wine on the wound at a 3 hour interval, 4 times a day. Repeating this process for 20 – 30 days the fracture would heal completely. Then, medicinal potion is used for external wounds instead of herbs. The entire therapy would take 81 days for it to heal completely, and patients are restrained from eating beans, fishes, acidic food, eggs and glutinous rice in this period.

The most important characteristic of Tan's treatment of bone is surgery-free. It could relieve pain within 3 minutes with common natural herbs without any side effects. Because of its remarkable effects and its cheap cost, it is widely welcomed by the patients. Many patients come to Nanxu for Tan's Treatment of Bone every day from Nanning, Baise, Chongzuo, Pingguo, Daxin, Tiandeng and other surrounding cities.

Due to Tan's treatment of bone's unique nature of inheritance, Tan's treatment of bone is facing a development dilemma. As modern medical technology becomes more and more advanced, less and less market space is left for traditional medicines. Tan's treatment of bone managed to have its share of market due to its good reputation, cheap price and remarkable therapeutic results. In order to preserve this priceless cultural heritage, Long'an county government has subsidized considerate amount of money into Tan's treatment of bone study since 2010. Treatment of Bone with Tan's Herbal Medicine of Zhuang Ethnic Group has approved by Guangxi Zhuang Autonomous Regional Government to be on the Fifth Autonomous Region List of Intangible Cultural Heritage in 2014.

天，断骨即愈合。此时停用草药外敷，改用以草药浸泡的药酒外擦患处。整个疗程共81天，患者需要禁食豆类、鱼类、酸类、蛋类和糯米饭，断骨即完好如初。

壮族谭氏草药疗骨法的特点是不施手术，敷药3分钟即可解除痛苦，敷药、换药简单，药源足，易采、无副作用，标本兼治。因其疗效显著，无后遗症，且经济实惠，深受患者欢迎，声名远播，每天都有南宁市、百色市、崇左市、平果市、大新县、天等县等地的患者慕名前来求医。

由于壮族谭氏草药疗骨法的生存和发展环境发生了变化，壮族谭氏草药疗骨法的传承和发展也出现了不少问题。随着现代医学的进步与发展，医院拥有现代宣传工具，掌握现代医学科学前沿技术，对民间传统的草药疗骨强力挤压，壮族谭氏草药疗骨法仅凭可靠的疗效、信誉、价钱低廉等优势勉强占有一席之地，致使传承传统医药出现危机。为传承和发展这一宝贵的文化遗产，自2010年以来，隆安县政府投入财力，对壮族谭氏草药疗骨法进行调研，利用相关资料对其进行宣传。2014年，壮族谭氏草药疗骨法经广西壮族自治区人民政府同意，列入第五批自治区级非物质文化遗产名录。

问诊
Interrogation

壮医经筋疗法

Channels and Tendon Therapy of Zhuang Medicine

项目名称：壮医经筋疗法

别称：无

分布范围：南宁市及周边地区

入选名录：2016年第六批自治区级非物质文化遗产名录
2013年第五批市级非物质文化遗产名录

保护单位：南宁市民族文化艺术研究院（南宁市非物质文化遗产保护中心）

代表性传承人：韦英才

Element name：Channels and Tendon Therapy of Zhuang Medicine

Alternative name：None

Geographical location and range：Nanning City and the surrounding areas

Element inscribed list：In 2016 on the Sixth Autonomous Region List of Intangible Cultural Heritage
In 2013 on the Fifth Municipal List of Intangible Cultural Heritage

Competent body involved in safeguarding：Nanning Ethnic Culture and Art Research Institute (Nanning Intangible Cultural Heritage Protection Centre)

Representative inheritor：Wei Yingcai

In the long progression of history, the ancestors of the Zhuang Ethnic Group created a unique system of Zhuang medicine, among which Channels and Tendon Therapy is a typical representative. Under the guidance of the classical Twelve channels and tendons theory and combined with the traditional channels and tendons technique of the Zhuang, the channels and tendons therapy of Zhuang medicine is a new non-drug therapy, which is used to diagnose and treat diseases by "tendons knotting" and "channels disentangling".

It has a very long history for Chinese traditional medicine to use channels and tendon therapy to treat tendon ailments. In the 1980s, two shallow bronze needles were unearthed in the tomb of Ma Tou Town of Wuming District, Nanning City. The unearthed needles are believed having medical functionality, and their sharp edges are consistent with the "micro needle" described by the ancients. The history of microneedle therapy for ailments in the ancestors of the Zhuang Ethnic Group can probably be traced back to the Western Zhou Dynasty.

The channel-tendon therapy of Zhuang medicine is based on the mechanism of "muscle-tendon instability inflicting tendon pain" of channel-tendon syndrome and the therapeutic principles of "tendon release", "tendon disentanglement", "tendon relaxation", "tendon movement" and "tendon-body integrity". Combining with the folk relaxation method of kneading, clapping, pulling and twisting techniques of the Zhuang people, we can achieve the ideal effect of "loose-smooth-pain-dredging". The operation process of channel tendon therapy in Zhuang medicine is roughly as follows: first, the tendons are massaged, loosened, then the needling is performed with the acupuncture therapy, and finally the cupping is done upon channels and tendons to enhance therapeutic efficacy. The main operation methods are tendon disentanglement, acupuncture, cupping and auxiliary treatment. The principle of "knot is the acupoint" is implemented through the tendon massage. Doctors cooperate closely with both hands. Left hand helps to pinpoint the diagnostic site. Right hand inspects the channels and tendons according to the physiological shape of the site, the thickness and level of muscles and tendons, the tension between tissues, and the structural shape of the tissues, using the fingertips of the thumb, the pulp of the thumb and the combined force of the thumb and the four little fingers. The first step is the channels and tendons massage of Zhuang medicine. The doctor first rolls back and forth three to five times in the lesion area by hand rolling method, so that the local muscles and tendons are fully relaxed and giving off heat.

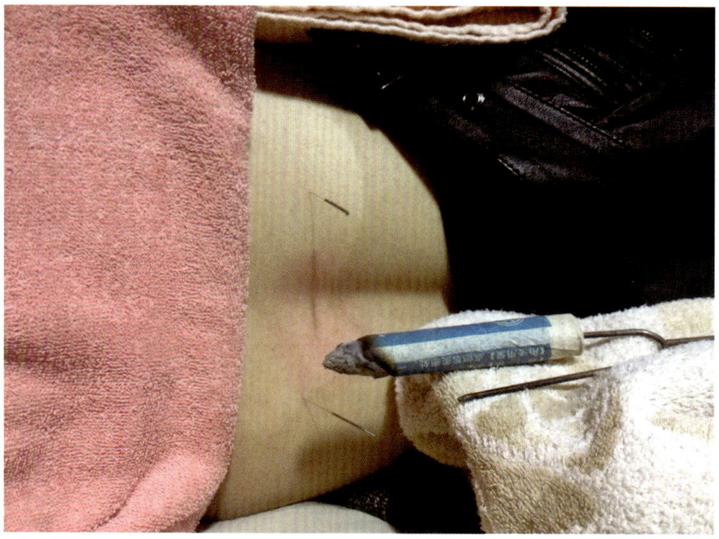

经筋疗法辅助治疗"艾灸"
Treatment of "Moxibustion" by Jingjin Therapy

在长期的历史发展中，壮族先民创造了独具特色的壮医药体系，壮医经筋疗法便是其中的典型代表。壮医经筋疗法是在古典十二经筋理论指导下，结合壮族民间传统经筋术总结出来的，以"经筋摸结"诊病和"经筋解结"治病的一种新型非药物疗法。

壮医运用经筋疗法治疗筋病的历史非常久远。20世纪80年代，南宁市武鸣区马头乡在西周末年的古墓中出土了两枚青铜浅刺针。经考证，出土的刺针为医疗用针，其锋微细，与古人描述的"微针"一致。壮族先民用微针治疗疾病的历史，大概可以追溯到西周时期。

壮医经筋疗法是根据经筋症候的"肌筋失稳，筋结致痛"机理以及"松筋解结""结解则松""筋松则顺""筋顺则动""筋动则通"的治疗原则，结合壮族民间捏筋、拍筋、拔筋、绞筋等手法，筋柔骨顺，疏通两路，达到"松—顺—痛—通"的理想功效。壮医经筋疗法的操作流程大致为，首先经筋摸结，接下来松筋解结，继而用针刺疗法进行

"针刺解结"，最后经筋拔罐，以增强功效。其操作方法主要有：理筋手法、针灸、拔罐以及辅助治疗。经筋摸结贯彻"以结为腧"的原则。医者两手密切配合，左手协助固定诊察部位，右手根据所检查部位的生理形态、肌筋的厚薄及层次、正常组织的张力、结构形状等情况，分别运用拇指的指尖、指腹及拇指与四小指的指合力，对经筋线进行检查。经筋解结分三步，第一步为壮医经筋手法，医者先用滚法在病变部位来回滚动3—5遍，使局部肌筋充分放松发热；然后采用肘关节配合拇指及四小指顺着病变部位的经筋线进行全线按、揉、点、推、弹拔、捏拿等分筋理筋手法。第二步为壮医经筋针法，以"固结行针"为原则。医者左手固定筋结，右手持2寸或3寸毫针，对准筋结快速进针，要求以"中结调气"为目的，可根据不同筋结选用"一孔多针、局部多针、透针穿刺、移行点刺、尽筋分刺、轻点刺络"等多种针法，使针刺部位出现酸、麻、胀或传电感为宜，不留针。如病候属寒性，可采用古老的"燔针劫刺"法，操作方法是：在选定的筋结部位上常规消毒，然后将针尖在酒精灯上烧红，迅速刺入治疗部位，得气后迅速出针；针刺的深度主要根据病

Then the elbow joint, thumb and four little fingers were used to press, knead, point, push, pull and pinch the whole line along the channel and tendon line of the lesion. The second step is the channel-tendon needling method of Zhuang medicine, which is based on the principle of "knot needling". Doctors would pinpoint tendon knots in their left hand and hold 2-inch or 3-inch microneedles in their right hand. Quick needling of alignment tendon knots requires "regulating Qi in the middle knot". According to different tendon knots, many needles can be selected, such as "one hole with multiple needles, local multiple needles, penetrating needle puncture, transitional point puncture, tendon division puncture, light collateral puncture" and so on, resulting soreness, numbness, distension and feelings of minor electric shock. If symptoms are defined as "cold", the old "burnt needle pinpointing" method can be used. The operation method is: routinely sterilize selected tendons, then burn the needle tip red on the alcohol lamp, quickly pinpoint and penetrate treatment site, and quickly release the needle after getting Qi; the depth of the needle is mainly based on the aliment severity, physical condition, age, muscle thickness and neuro and blood vessel distribution of the needle site. The third step is the method of tendon-cupping. The method of cupping by flashing fire can be used upon tendons knots or directly on the tendons for a duration of 8-10 minutes.

Through the research and reorganization of Guangxi

筋经疗法器具"火罐"
Tendons Therapy Appliance "Cupping Jars"

Academy of Ethnic Medicine, the channel-tendon therapy of Zhuang medicine has been further improved, continuously inherited and developed, with remarkable clinical efficacy and outstanding characteristics of Zhuang medicine, which has high clinical practical value and academic research value. The therapy has played an important role in promoting the health of the Zhuang people.

Due to the lack of written records, the inheritance is mainly imparted orally and personally. Many precious resources of Zhuang medicine have been lost, some of which are extinct already. In order to protect and inherit the channel and tendon therapy of the Zhuang Ethnic Group, the therapy has been included in the national "Twelfth Five-Year Plan" key construction projects for research and collation. Guangxi Zhuang Medical Hospital also carries on the inheritance by means of short-term training and long-term follow-up counseling in the form of further research and apprenticeship. It also carries out extensive academic exchanges at home and abroad to expand the influence of the channel and tendon therapy of the Zhuang Ethnic Group. Since 2010, relevant departments have continuously invested special funds to support scientific research, theoretical discovery and personnel training. After vigorous promotion, the channel and tendon therapy of the Zhuang Ethnic Group has had a significant impact at home and abroad, and has become the symbolic brand and famous treatment method of Zhuang medicine.

情、体质、年龄、针刺部位肌肉的厚薄及神经、血管的分布而定。第三步为经筋拔罐法，采用闪火拔罐法在针刺筋结部位或经筋线上拔罐8—10分钟即可。

壮医经筋疗法经过广西民族医药研究院的发掘整理，这一特色的壮医疗法得到了进一步提高，在不断传承与发展下，临床疗效显著，壮医特色突出，具有很高的临床实用价值及学术研究价值。该疗法为促进壮族人民的身体健康发挥了重要作用。

由于缺乏文字记载，传承主要靠口传心授，壮族地区许多具有重要壮医药价值的资源大量流失，有些甚至已经失传。为了保护和传承壮族经筋疗法，该疗法已经纳入国家“十二五”重点建设项目，进行研究和整理。广西壮医医院还通过进修、师带徒的形式，以短期培训、长期跟踪辅导的方式进行传承，并在国内外开展广泛的学术交流活动，扩大壮族经筋疗法的影响。从2010年开始，相关部门不断投入专项资金，支持科学研究、理论发掘和人才培养。经过大力推广，壮族经筋疗法已在国内外产生了较大的影响，成为壮医学的标志性品牌和著名的治疗方法。

壮医药物竹罐疗法

Bamboo Tube Therapy of Zhuang Ethnic Group

项目名称：壮医药物竹罐疗法

别称：无

分布范围：南宁市及周边地区

入选名录：2016年第六批自治区级非物质文化遗产名录

2013年第五批市级非物质文化遗产名录

保护单位：南宁市民族文化艺术研究院（南宁市非物质文化遗产保护中心）

代表性传承人：李凤珍

Element name：Bamboo Tube Therapy of Zhuang Ethnic Group

Alternative name：None

Geographical location and range：Nanning City and the surrounding areas

Element inscribed list：In 2016 on the Sixth Autonomous Region List of Intangible Cultural Heritage

In 2013 on the Fifth Municipal List of Intangible Cultural Heritage

Competent body involved in safeguarding：Nanning Ethnic Culture and Art Research Institute (Nanning Intangible Cultural Heritage Protection Centre)

Representative inheritor：Li Fengzhen

Guangxi's unique climate and soil conditions have bred a large number of high-quality medicinal herbs, known as the "natural Chinese medicine bank". In their production activities, the Zhuang people have made simple medical tools and gradually formed a unique system of Zhuang medicine. Bamboo tube therapy is a valuable heritage accumulated by the working people of the Zhuang Ethnic Group in their long-term struggle against diseases, and it is one of the traditional medical techniques with strong characteristics of the Zhuang Ethnic Group.

Bamboo tube therapy is widely spread in the areas inhabited by Zhuang people in Guangxi. It uses bamboo tubes made of phyllostachys sulphura from Baise in Guangxi and authentic high-quality Zhuang medicine in Guangxi. Bamboo cupping therapy is a kind of external treatment of Zhuang medicine, which integrates cupping, pricking blood and applying Zhuang medicine. It can treat rheumatism, arthralgia, shoulder and back pain, hemiplegia, fall injury and stasis after fracture through the functions of negative pressure, heat and medicine. It has made great contributions to the health of the people in Zhuang region. As the saying goes, "Prick a needle and pull a cup, half of the symptoms disappear." Bamboo Tube Therapy of Zhuang Ethnic Group has been praised and welcomed by the general public.

The implementation of Bamboo Tube Therapy of Zhuang Ethnic Group should follow standard processes: first, select the phyllostachys sulphura with upright roots to make bamboo tubes, and then mix according to prescriptions. Take appropriate amounts of Eucommia ulmoides, Sanqiansan, Five-clawed Wind, Sarcandra, Octagonal Wind, Tenebrio cramp, stinky peony, Acanthopanax senticosus, Chicken feces rattan, etc., and put them into a small bag, and soak it into a bamboo tube filled with water for 5- 10 minutes. Then choose the acupoint, select the acupoint in the most painful area and go about 1.5 inches at each cardinal direction with the acupoint as the centre in the shape of a plum blossom. The first cupping was performed after the selection of points. The prepared bamboo tubes were buckled on the selected parts and removed after about 5-10 minutes. Next, prick blood. After routinely disinfection at cupping site, use disposable needle to prick 1-3 times on the skin of the cupping site, with a small amount of local bleeding as the best. Then it comes the second round of cupping. Take the hot bamboo tubes at the needle point and quickly cupping again, about 5-10 minutes later take off the bamboo tubes. If there are a considerate amount of white bubbles on the bamboo tubes, then perform cupping 1-2 times more. Finally, it is the heat applying. Apply cupping

广西独特的气候和土壤条件，孕育出大量品质上乘的药材，素有“天然中药库”之称。在生产活动中，壮族人民制造了简单的医疗工具，逐步形成独具特色的壮医药体系。壮医药物竹罐疗法是壮族劳动人民在与疾病进行长期斗争的过程中积累起来的宝贵经验，是壮族特色传统医疗技法之一。

壮医药物竹罐疗法流传于广西壮族聚居的地区，使用的是产自广西百色的金竹制作的竹罐和广西地道的品质上乘的壮药。壮医药物竹罐疗法是集拔罐、刺血及壮药物热熨于一体的壮医外治疗法，通过负压、热力、药力的作用，治疗风湿痹痛、肩背酸痛、半身不遂、跌打损伤、骨折愈后瘀积等，对壮族地区人民的身体健康做出了巨大贡献。俗语常说，“扎针拔罐子，病好大半子”。壮医药物竹罐疗法，受到广大民众的赞誉和欢迎。

实施壮医药物竹罐疗法需遵循规范的操作步骤：首先，选取根部正直的金竹制作竹罐，然后配制药方，取杜仲藤、三钱三、五爪风、肿节风、八角风、抽筋草、臭牡丹、五加皮、鸡屎藤等适量，装入布袋，加清水适量煎成药液，浸煮竹罐5—10分钟。继而选穴，在疼痛最严重的部位取穴，以此穴为中心上下左右旁开约1.5寸各取一穴，呈梅花之形。选穴之后进行第一次拔罐，将备好的竹罐扣拔于选定的部位上，约5—10分钟后取下。接下来进行刺血，在拔罐部位常规消毒后，用一次性注射针头在罐印部位皮肤上浅刺1—3针，以局部少量渗血为度。然后进行第二次拔罐，取煮热的竹罐在针刺部位再次迅速拔罐，约5—10分钟后取下竹罐，若竹罐上出现白泡较多可多拔1—2次。最后进行热熨，用药巾热熨拔罐部位，待热度合适时热敷约5分钟。

壮医药物竹罐疗法具有较高的实用价值、学术研究价值和社会价值，广西壮医医院将其应用在临床实践中，并不断进行完善。广西民族医药研究所成立后对壮医药物竹罐疗法进行发掘整理和临床验证，取得良好的临床疗效。目前，在广西区内20多家县级中医民族医院临床使用，应用范围不断推广，深受群众的欢迎。

1985年，广西民族医药研究所成立，为传承和发展壮医药物竹罐疗法，挖掘、整理和研究壮医药物竹罐疗法工作不断展开。此后，壮医药物竹罐疗法被编入《壮族医学史》《中国壮医学》《简明壮医药学》等壮医著作。2006年，广西壮医医院壮医风湿病科建立壮医药物竹罐疗法治疗室，通过购买相关器具和设备，不断改善基础设施和治疗环境，提高服务能力。壮医药物竹罐疗法还被列入国家统一考试的壮医执业医师考试，其操作技术得到进一步规范。2016年，壮医药物竹罐疗法列入第六批自治区级非物质文化遗产名录。

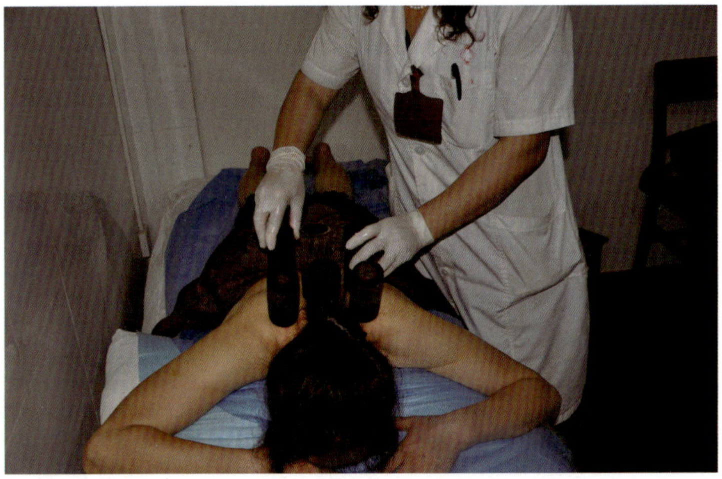

放罐
Put Bamboo Tubes

part with medicated towel and compress for about 5 minutes when the heat is appropriate.

Bamboo Tube Therapy of Zhuang Ethnic Group has high practical value, academic research value and social value. Guangxi Zhuang Medical Hospital has applied it in clinical practice while constantly improving it. After the establishment of Guangxi Institute of Ethnic Medicine, the Bamboo Tube Therapy of Zhuang Ethnic Group has been studied thoroughly, collated and clinically verified, and good clinical efficacy has been achieved. At present, more than 20 county-level hospitals of traditional Chinese medicine for all nationalities in Guangxi have been widely using Bamboo Tube Therapy in clinic, and it is welcomed by the masses.

In 1985, the Guangxi Institute of Ethnic Medicine was established. In order to inherit and develop Bamboo Tube Therapy of Zhuang Ethnic Group, the researching of it was carried out continuously. Since then, bamboo pot therapy has been compiled into the *Medical History of Zhuang Ethnic Group, Study of Chinese Zhuang Medicine, Concise Study of Zhuang Medicine* and other works of Zhuang medicine. In 2006, the Department of Rheumatology of Zhuang Medicine, Guangxi Zhuang Medical Hospital, established the treatment room of Bamboo Tube Therapy of Zhuang Ethnic Group. By purchasing related equipment and apparatus, the infrastructure and treatment environment were continuously improved, and the service capacity also increased. Bamboo Tube Therapy of Zhuang Ethnic Group has also been included in the National Doctor Examination for Practicing Zhuang Medicine, and its operation technology has been further standardized. In 2016, Bamboo Tube Therapy of Zhuang Ethnic Group was inscribed on the Sixth Autonomous Reigon List of Intangible Cultural Heritage.

竹罐
Bamboo Tubes

宾阳封氏烧伤创疡治疗术

Feng's Treatment of Burns, Wounds and Ulcers, Binyang

项目名称：宾阳封氏烧伤创疡治疗术

别称：无

分布范围：南宁市宾阳县、来宾市、贵港市、柳州市、玉林市、岑溪市、梧州市等

入选名录：2014年第五批自治区级非物质文化遗产名录

保护单位：宾阳县文化馆

代表性传承人：封香朝、封大为

Element name: Feng's Treatment of Burns, Wounds and Ulcers, Binyang

Alternative name: None

Geographical location and range: Binyang County of Nanning City, Laibin City, Guigang City, Liuzhou City, Yulin City, Cenxi City, Wuzhou City and others

Element inscribed list: In 2014 on the Fifth Autonomous Region List of Intangible Cultural Heritage

Competent body involved in safeguarding: Binyang County Cultural Centre

Representative inheritors: Feng Xiangchao, Feng Dawei

草药
Herbal Medicine

宾阳封氏烧伤创疡治疗术流传于南宁市宾阳县，影响辐射至南宁各县区及来宾、贵港、柳州、玉林、岑溪、梧州等地，甚至湖南、广东、云南等外省患者也慕名前来求医。

封氏烧伤创疡治疗术已有120多年的历史。清光绪年间，宾阳封氏烧伤创疡治疗术创始人封国持（1869—1955），师从广东吴氏伤医郎中学得跌打疗伤之术。因宾阳民间有生产爆竹传统，在行医中，封国持常遇被火药爆炸烧伤因无良药治疗而致破相伤残的患者，深感痛惜。宾阳中草药资源十分丰富，于是封国持便潜心研究本地中草药的药性功效，创制出专治水火烫伤的良药“烧烫灵”，其有“药到痛止、快速治愈”之功效，且愈后极少留下瘢痕。此方治愈患者无数，享誉宾阳及周边，奠定了封氏烧伤创疡治疗的基业。

封氏烧伤创疡治疗术以中医疮疡理论为指导，经不断实践完善，形成了独特的理论体系，即局部治疗与整体扶正相结合、安内攘外的治疗法则。封氏烧伤秘方“烧烫灵”由金

Feng's Treatment of Burns, Wounds and Ulcers is widely spread in Binyang County of Nanning City. Its influence radiates to all counties and districts of Nanning and to Laibin, Guigang, Liuzhou, Yulin, Cenxi, Wuzhou and other places. Even patients from Hunan, Guangdong, Yunnan and other provinces come for medical treatment.

Feng's Treatment of Burns, Wounds and Ulcers has a history of more than 120 years. During the reign of Emperor Guangxu in Qing Dynasty, Feng Guochi (1869-1955), the founder of Feng's Treatment of Burns, Wounds and Ulcers, learned from wound doctor Wu in Guangdong. Because of the tradition of producing firecrackers in Binyang, many patients there are suffering from disfigurement and disability caused by gunpowder explosion and burn due to maltreatments. Binyang has rich resources of Chinese herbal medicine. Therefore, Feng Guochi devoted himself to the study of the medicinal efficacy of local Chinese herbal medicine, and created a good medicine for scald, “Shao Tang Ling”, which has the effect of “pain relief and quick cure”, and rarely leaves scars after healing. This method cures numerous patients and is well-known in Binyang and surrounding places. It has laid the foundation for the treatment of Feng's Treatment of Burns, Wounds and Ulcers.

Under the guidance of traditional Chinese medicine theory of ulcers, Feng's Treatment of Burns, Wounds and Ulcers has formed a unique theoretical system through continuous practice and improvement, that is, the combination of local treatment and integral strengthening, and the treatment principle of internal and external treatment. Feng's secret recipe for scald "Shao Tang Ling" is made of honeysuckle, charcoal, mast, Radix Zanthoxyli, tassle blower, Boston ivy and Clerodendrum. It has good analgesic and anti-inflammatory effects, muscle astringent, assisting in healing and reducing chances of scars. After a hundred years of continuous summary and innovation, Fengshi Burn Ointment, Qufushengji Zhangpi Ointment and Fire Burn Yarn have been developed.

Feng's Treatment of Burns, Wounds and Ulcers has the advantages of easy material selection, simple manufacture, low cost and obvions curative effect. It is the crystallization of folk wisdom and has made important contributions to the health of the people. It has high medical value, academic research value and social value.

However, there are some serious problems in the inheritance of Feng's Treatment of Burns, Wounds and Ulcers. Firstly, it is a typical folk medicine methodology. Although the curative effect is good, it has not passed the strict clinical certification by the state, and is not widely recognized by the western medicine community. The drug has no production license, which seriously restricts the further development. Secondly, because large mountainous forests are now being opened up to grow fast-growing eucalyptus and other cash crops, the original environment for drug growth has been destroyed, and the collection of drug sources is becoming more and more difficult. At present, Binyang County has established the Fengshi Guangxi Ethnic Characteristic Burn Wound and Ulcer Therapy Research Association to improve Feng's Treatment of Burns, Wounds and Ulcers from the theoretical level. At the same time, a research base for burn wounds and ulcers with national characteristics in Fengshi Guangxi was established, and training courses were held to promote Feng's Treatment of Burns, Wounds and Ulcers. In 2014, Feng's Treatment of Burns, Wounds and Ulcers was approved by the People's Government of Guangxi Zhuang Autonomous Region and inscribed on the Fifth Autonomous Region List of Intangible Cultural Heritage.

银花、火炭母、栀子、两面针、一点红、爬山虎、路边青等配伍炼制而成，具有良好的镇痛消炎、收敛生肌、促进伤口愈合和减轻瘢痕的作用。封氏烧伤创疡治疗历经百年，经不断总结与革新，又研发出了封氏中药烧伤膏剂、祛腐生肌长皮膏、烧伤中药油纱等新产品新技术。

封氏烧伤创疡治疗术具有取材容易、制作简单、成本低廉、疗效明显等特点，是民间智慧的结晶，为人民群众的健康做出了重要贡献，具有较高的医疗价值、学术研究价值和社会价值。

但是，封氏烧伤创疡治疗术的传承也存在一些严峻的问题。首先，它是典型的民间医药技术，尽管疗效好，但是因为没有通过国家严格的临床验证，不被西医界广泛认可，药品无生产许可证，严重制约了它的进一步传承与发展。其次，由于现在大片山林被开荒种植速生桉等经济作物，原来的药物生长环境受到破坏，药源采集越来越困难。目前，宾阳县成立了封氏广西民族特色烧伤创疡治疗术研究会，从理论层面上提升封氏烧伤创疡治疗术水平，同时设立封氏广西民族特色烧伤创疡科研基地，开办培训班，推广封氏烧伤创疡治疗术。2014年，宾阳封氏烧伤创疡治疗术经广西壮族自治区人民政府同意，列入第五批自治区级非物质文化遗产名录。

龚氏痛症疗法

Gong's Pain Therapy

项目名称：龚氏痛症疗法

别称：无

分布范围：南宁市、玉林市及周边地区

入选名录：2013年第五批市级非物质文化遗产名录

保护单位：江南区文化馆

代表性传承人：龚俭仪

Element name：Gong's Pain Therapy

Alternative name：None

Geographical location and range：Nanning City, Yulin City and the surrounding areas

Element inscribed list：In 2013 on the Fifth Municipal List of Intangible Cultural Heritage

Competent body involved in safeguarding：Jiangnan District Cultural Centre

Representative inheritor：Gong Jianyi

药材
Herb

Gong's Pain Therapy is a kind of Pain Therapy which is handed down from generation to generation by Gong's family and made traditional medicine liquor and ointment with ancestral secret recipe. Through external application and massage, Gong's Pain Therapy mainly treats all kinds of bone injuries and lumbar vertebral, cervical and neuropathic pains.

Gong's Pain Therapy was founded in the fifteenth year of Emperor Jiaqing in the Qing Dynasty (1810), originally spread in Yulin area, and then gradually spread to Nanning and its surrounding areas. Over the past 200 years, in the process of inheritance, a unique traditional method of bone injury treatment has been formed through plaster external application. Gong's Pain Therapy has been developed in a continuous and in-depth way. Up to now, it has been handed down for seven generations by descendants. Nearly 20 Gong's family members are doctors. Many pharmacies and clinics of Gong's Pain Therapy have been set up in Nanning, Yulin and other places in Guangxi.

Gong's Pain Therapy uses natural medicinal herbs produced in southern Guizhou, mainly including Radix Zanthoxyli, Laohujiao (Maoerci), Caulis Spatholobus, Ardisia Quienquegona, Poria Cocos, Philipine Flemingia root, Kamuning, Rhizoma Drynariae and nearty 30 kinds. These herbs would go through sun-dry, air-dry, mashing, grinding, and other complex processes. External application of ointment and application of medicinal wine were the main treatment methods. It is suitable for all kinds of bone injuries, lumbar vertebrae, cervical vertebrae and neuropathic pain. Its treatment mechanism is to stimulate the pain area by external application, dredge the fire road Qi mechanism of Longlu Road, play the role of dispelling wind and pain, promoting blood circulation and removing blood stasis, eliminating swelling and resolving nodules, warming channels and dredging tendons, etc., generally 10 days as one cycle of treatment. Its operation process is relatively simple, with no knife, no hospital, no wound, trivial pain and so on along with no environmental pollution, effective relief, low cost, easy to learn and good reputation. It has been welcomed by the majority of patients, in Nanning, Yulin and other southern and southeastern areas of Guizhou. Gong's Pain Therapy definitely enjoys a good reputation and lots of acclaims.

The medication process of Gong's Pain Therapy is to first pick yam, then dry it in the sun or in the shade and grind it into powder. Then, according to different symptoms, a certain proportion of various powders will be prepared correspondingly. Then, liquor with about 50 degrees and various powders were soaked. Generally, liquor was soaked in

龚氏痛症疗法是龚氏家族世代相传的、以家传秘方自制传统药酒、药膏，通过外敷、辅之以按摩的一种痛症治疗法，主治各类骨伤以及腰椎类、颈椎类、神经类痛症。

龚氏痛症疗法始创于清嘉庆十五年（1810），原流传于玉林地区，后逐渐流传至南宁市及周边地区。200多年来，在传承过程中，形成了独特的传统骨伤治疗方法，在膏药外敷治疗骨伤疾病和痛症方面独树一帜。龚氏痛症疗法一脉相承，并不断深入发展，至今，靠嫡系相传了7代，龚氏家族从医者近20人，在广西南宁、玉林等地开办了多家龚氏痛症疗法药堂和门诊部。

龚氏痛症疗法采用桂南地区出产的天然植物药材，主要包括两面针、老虎脚（又名猫儿刺）、鸡血藤、大罗伞、松木茀茯苓、千斤拔、大小计、九里香、骨碎补等近30种，经过阳晒、阴干、捣碎、研磨、炮制等复杂过程制作而成，以药膏外敷、涂药酒为主要治疗方法，适用于各类骨伤以及腰椎类、颈椎类、神经类痛症。其治疗机理是通过对痛处进行外敷的刺激，疏通龙路、火路气机，起到祛风止痛、活血祛瘀、消肿散结、温经通络等作用，一般以10天为一个疗程。其操作过程较为简单，具有不开刀、不住院、无创口、痛苦小等特点，且无环境污染，疗效确切，费用低廉，易于学习与推广，一直深受广大患者的欢迎，在南宁、玉林等桂南及桂东南地区享有很好的口碑和声誉。

龚氏痛症疗法的制药过程为：首先要采山药，然后将药材晒干或者阴干，打成药粉。再根据不同的痛症，按一定的比例将各种药粉进行科学配制。继而根据不同的痛症，分别用50度左右的白酒与各种配置好的药粉进行浸泡，一般按20斤药材配100斤白酒的比例进行浸泡，15—25天之后便可制成药膏或药酒。龚氏痛症疗法的治疗过程为，首先在疼痛部位进行穴位按摩5—10分钟，以松散紧张的肌肉，促进药力的吸收，再将药膏或药酒均匀摊在药棉上，用保鲜膜盖住，敷在痛处30—40分钟，如果是骨头断折，则敷24小时换一次药。龚氏痛症疗法不但给腰椎类、颈椎类病患带来了福音，而且对探讨中医药骨科文化、丰富我国民间传统治疗方法、推动我国传统中医药事业的发展发挥积极的作用。

受到现代医学发展的影响，龚氏痛症疗法正逐步被西医排挤，发展举步维艰。另外，龚氏痛症疗法传到第七代传人只有2人，急需培养优秀的接班人，摆脱后继乏人的困境。加之龚氏痛症疗法所需要的各种原生药材，在现代社会越来越难挖掘到，各种原生中草药出现了匮乏的现象。2005年之后，龚氏家族每年在玉林、南宁市等地，不定期地以免费治疗等形式进行宣传。2012年，南宁市江南区文化馆组织非物质文化遗产工作小组深入了解龚氏痛症疗法，并进行了全方位的调查、资料收集等工作。

the proportion of 20 catties of medicinal materials with 100 catties of liquor. After about 15 to 25 days, it could be made into ointment or medicinal liquor. Gong's pain treatment process: first, massage acupoints on pain sites for 5 to 10 minutes to loosen tense muscles and promote the absorption of medicinal power, then spread ointment or wine evenly on cotton wool, cover with fresh film, apply to pain sites for 30 to 40 minutes, if the bone is broken, apply 24 hours for dressing change. Gong's Pain Therapy not only brings good news to lumbar and cervical spondylosis, but also plays an active role in exploring orthopedic culture of traditional Chinese medicine, enriching traditional folk treatment methodology and promoting the development of it.

Influenced by the development of modern medicine, Gong's Pain Therapy is gradually being excluded by Western medicine, which makes it difficult to spread. In addition, Gong's Pain Therapy has been passed down to the seventh generation with only 2 people. It is urgent to cultivate excellent successors in order to solve this predicament. In addition, it is more and more difficult to find all kinds of original medicinal herbs needed for the therapy in modern society, and there is a lack of all kinds of native Chinese herbal medicine. After 2005, Gong's family would give out free treatment every year in Yulin, Nanning and other places. In 2012, the Cultural Centre of Jiangnan District of Nanning organized a group on intangible cultural heritage to deeply understand Gong's Pain Therapy and conducted a comprehensive survey and data collection.

制药
Preparing Medicine

壮医目诊

Visual Diagnosis of Zhuang Medicine

项目名称：壮医目诊

别称：无

分布范围：广西壮族自治区壮族聚居区

入选名录：2013年第五批市级非物质文化遗产名录

保护单位：南宁市民族文化艺术研究院（南宁市非物质文化遗产保护中心）

代表性传承人：李珪

Element name: Visual Diagnosis of Zhuang Medicine

Alternative name: None

Geographical location and range: Zhuang Ethnic Group Inhabited Area of Guangxi Zhuang Autonomous Region

Element inscribed list: In 2013 on the Fifth Municipal List of Intangible Cultural Heritage

Competent body involved in safeguarding: Nanning Ethnic Culture and Art Research Institute (Nanning Intangible Cultural Heritage Protection Centre)

Representative inheritors: Li Gui

目诊
Visual Diagnosis

壮医目诊，属壮医望诊的范畴，流传于广西壮族聚居的地区，历史悠久。老一辈的壮医主要是通过肉眼观察患者眼睛上的神采色泽，眼睛的灵活度、干涩与否，眼睛上脉络的变化等来诊断疾病。后来通过不断的总结和提高，并受牛马等兽医目诊的启发，形成了如今使用的一套目诊诊断方法。现代壮医目诊专家在继承前人目诊经验的基础上，经多年的临床实践，总结出用放大镜进行目诊，实用性更强、准确率更高的一整套方法。

壮医目诊的基本内容首先是器械准备，准备一个5—50倍的放大镜和一个小型聚光手电筒，配合数字化裂隙灯眼前段分析系统。检查步骤为：首先，患者端坐放松，两眼自然平视，特殊患者可站立或仰卧、侧卧。检查者左手持放大镜，并用食指和拇指将患者上下眼睑撑开，将放大镜移动至理想观察位置，右手持手电筒依次照射患者眼睛，以诊者眼睛观察清晰为度，依次由上到下，由内而外观察球结膜，叮嘱患者眼球向下、向上、向外、向内移动，而后平视，诊者将虹膜由外向内进行观察，同时检查对侧眼睛。壮医总结目诊的变化规律可用壮族山歌表达：“着色深浅判新旧，弯曲

Visual diagnosis of Zhuang medicine, which belongs to the category of Zhuang looking diagnosis, has a long history and is widely spread in the areas inhabited by Zhuang Ethnic Group in Guangxi. The older generation of Zhuang doctors mainly diagnose diseases by observing the appearance and color of the eyes, eye flexibility, degree of dryness, and changes in the veins of the eyes. Later, through continuous summary and improvement, and inspired by veterinary ophthalmologists of horses and cows, a set of methods of ophthalmic diagnosis has been formed. Based upon many years of clinical practice and experience of predecessors, modern experts in Zhuang medicine have summed up a set of methods using magnifying glass for visual diagnosis, which is more practical and accurate.

The basic content of Zhuang medicine's visual diagnosis is equipment preparation, a magnifying glass zooming 5-50 times, and a small flashlight, together with digital slit lamp anterior segment analysis system. Examination procedures are as follows: first, patients sit up and relax, eyes naturally looking forward, special patients can stand, lie down on the side, or lie down facing up. The examiner holds the magnifying glass in his left hand and stretches the upper and lower eyelids of the patient with his forefinger and thumb. The magnifying glass is moved to the ideal observation position. The right-hand flashlight irradiates the patient's eyes in turn, depending on the clarity of the observation. From top to bottom, the conjunctiva was inspected from inside to outside. The patient was instructed to move the eyeball downward, upward, outward and inward, and then to look straight. The doctor observed the iris from outside to inward and examined the opposite eye at the same time. The rule of visual diagnosis summarized by Zhuang doctors can be expressed by Zhuang folk song, "The shade of coloring judges severity, the curving frequency tells the condition, the veins are turbid because of humidity, the veins are scattered because of wind, the veins near pupil because of fire, the veins on the side because of cold, black clots because of blue spot worms, Zhuang visual diagnosis just works." This catchy folk song summarizes the methods and significance of visual diagnosis of Zhuang medicine.

As one of the important diagnostic methodologies of Zhuang medicine, the visual diagnosis of Zhuang medicine has the characteristics of accurate, rapid diagnosis, simple operation, no side effects, cheap, safe, precise conjecture and profound insight. It is widely used in clinic environment. Visual diagnosis of Zhuang medicine is a precious cultural heritage of the Zhuang people and an important part of traditional Chinese medicine. It is still circulated in all parts of Zhuang inhabited region, and is a key means for Zhuang medicine to diagnose diseases and guide medication. Visual diagnosis of Zhuang doctors has made indelible contributions to the health and continuation of the Zhuang Ethnic Group throughout history.

At present, the research on the standardization of Zhuang medicine's visual diagnosis has been carried out. However, due to the lack of written records and mainly relying on oral tradition, there are difficulties in the inheritance of Zhuang medicine's visual diagnosis. For this reason, Guangxi Zhuang Medical Hospital has done a lot of work to inherit and develop the visual diagnosis of Zhuang medicine. It has applied for the establishment of special department of the State Administration of Traditional Chinese Medicine and the District Health Department, which both obtained approval. In the process of construction, it has carried out the standardization research of Zhuang Medical Visual Diagnosis. Today, the "Eleventh Five-Year Plan" National Science and Technology Support Project "*Research on Standardization of Techniques for Diagnosing Gastroduodenal Ulcer by Visual Diagnosis of Zhuang Medicine* "has been carried out, as well as the scientific and technological development project "*Research on Standardization of Techniques for Diagnosing Uterine Fibroids by Visual Diagnosis of Zhuang Medicine*" of the Science and Technology Department of the Autonomous Region in 2013.

频率别轻重，脉络混浊有湿气，脉络散乱多为风，脉络近瞳属于火，脉络靠边属于寒，黑斑瘀来蓝斑虫，临床目诊辨分明。”此山歌说明了壮族目诊的方法及意义。

壮医目诊作为壮医重要的诊断技法之一，具有诊断准确迅速、操作简便、无副作用、经济安全、司外揣内、见微知著的特点，在临床上应用广泛。壮医目诊是壮族人民宝贵的文化遗产，是中国传统医药的重要组成部分，至今仍在壮乡各地流传，是壮医诊断疾病、指导用药的重要手段。壮医目诊在长期的医疗实践中为壮族人民的健康、繁衍做出了不可磨灭的贡献。

目前，壮医目诊的规范化研究已经展开，然而，由于缺乏文字记载、主要依靠口耳相传，其传承仍然存在一定的困难。为此，广西壮医医院为传承和发展壮医目诊方法做了大量工作，申请成立国家中医药管理局和区卫生厅重点专科，并获得批准。目前已经开展“十一五”国家科技支撑计划项目《壮医目诊法诊断胃十二指肠溃疡技术规范化研究》和2013年自治区科技厅科技开发项目《壮医目诊诊断子宫肌瘤技术规范化研究》等。

瑶族壁和骨伤疗法

Bihe Bone Injury Therapy of Yao Ethnic Group

项目名称：瑶族壁和骨伤疗法

别称：无

分布范围：江南区及周边地区

入选名录：2017年第七批市级非物质文化遗产名录

保护单位：江南区文化馆

代表性传承人：李祈谦、李映浩

Element name：Bihe Bone Injury Therapy of Yao Ethnic Group

Alternative name：None

Geographical location and range：Jiangnan District and the surrounding areas

Element inscribed list：In 2017 on the Seventh Municipal List of Intangible Cultural Heritage

Competent body involved in safeguarding：Jiangnan District Cultural Centre

Representative inheritor：Li Qiqian, Li Yinghao

处理草药
Treating Herbs

Bihe Bone Injury Therapy of Yao Ethnic Group is passed down from generation to generation, a representative of the traditional bone injury therapy with the medical characteristics of the Yao Ethnic Group in Guangxi. Bihe Bone Injury Therapy of Yao Ethnic Group originated in Du'an County, Hechi City. At present, it is mainly prevalent in Jiangnan District of Nanning City and its surrounding areas.

Bihe Bone Injury Therapy of Yao Ethnic Group originated in Emperor Guangxu period of the Qing Dynasty. It has been handed down for four generations and has a history of about 110 years. Du'an, the birthplace of Bihe Bone Injury Therapy of Yao Ethnic Group, is located in the west of central Guangxi, 120 kilometers away from Nanning City. At present, Yao people account for about 22% of the county's population. The territory is densely populated with swamps, continuous rocky mountain, and is copious in animal and plant species. For thousands of years, the local Yao people live in the mountains making them easier to suffer from bone injuries. The only way to deal with limb injuries is to use

瑶族壁和骨伤疗法是世代相传的、富有广西瑶族医学特色的传统骨伤疗法。瑶族壁和骨伤疗法发源于河池市都安县，目前主要流行于南宁市江南区及周边地区。

瑶族壁和骨伤疗法起源于清光绪年间，传承至今已历四代传人，约有110多年的历史。壁和骨伤疗法的发源地都安位于桂中部偏西，距南宁市120千米，目前瑶族约占全县人口的22%，境内洼地密布，石山连绵，动植物种类丰富。千百年来，当地瑶人山居游耕，极易患跌打损伤，随手使用身边的动植物是处理肢体伤痛的唯一办法。瑶族先民慢慢摸索总结了与骨伤疾病做斗争的经验。瑶族历史上没有自己的文字，瑶医药的传承全靠口耳相传。壁和骨伤疗法创始人彭云彪从都安行医至南宁，定居于此，写下《彭云彪真传》一书，为疗法的传承和保护奠定了坚实的基础。

瑶族壁和骨伤疗法以瑶医“风打药物分类”理论为指导，治疗常见骨折。采摘鲜药后晾晒干，分别配伍使用。入山虎、毛老虎、黑九牛等10余味“打药”研磨成粉，调酒成膏；钻地风、九节风、青九牛等20余味“风药”和“打药”打粗末成洗剂，或直接泡酒备用。治疗方法为骨折固定后，药膏外敷接骨。骨折愈合后，改用熏洗及外搽药酒，同时要求配合循序渐进的功能训练。该疗法用药安全无创、病痛缓解快、疗程短、动静结合、筋骨并重、操作简单，病人花费较少。瑶族壁和骨伤疗法充分体现了“简、便、验、廉”的特点，受到患者的广泛好评。

瑶医是中华民族医药的瑰宝，富有深厚的哲学思想和人文底蕴，其独特的技法用药、显著的防治保健作用和相对低廉的诊疗费用，值得深入挖掘研究。过去瑶医因没有文字记载而缺少系统的医学典籍，而壁和骨伤疗法结合百年来的临床实践总结成文，对于推动瑶医药的研究具有重要意义。壁和骨伤疗法自彭云彪始，其第三、第四代传人继承先业，至今尚存有祖传药粘传捣药臼、家传秘方《彭云彪真传》手抄

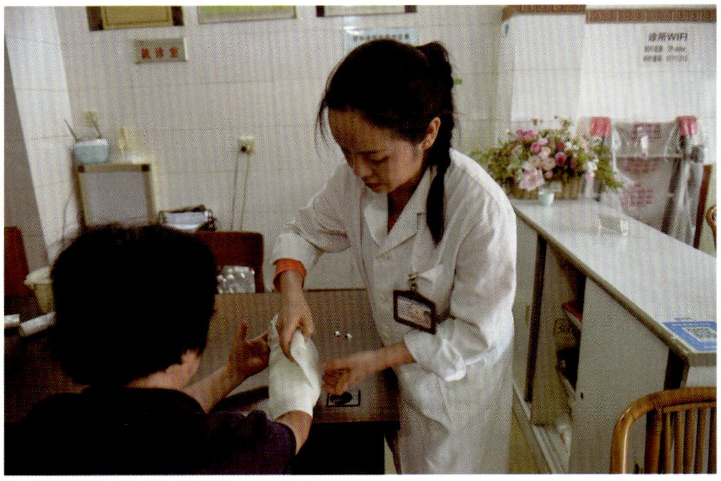

治疗
Treatment

the animals and plants around them freely. The ancestors of Yao Ethnic Group progressed slowly and summarized their experience in dealing with bone injuries. Yao Ethnic Group has no written language in its history, and the inheritance of Yao medicine depends on oral tradition. Peng Yunbiao, the founder of Bihe Bone Injury Therapy of Yao Ethnic Group, travelled and finally settled in Nanning. He wrote the book "*The True Biography of Peng Yunbiao*", which laid a solid foundation for the inheritance and protection of the therapy.

Bihe Bone Injury Therapy of Yao Ethnic Group is guided by Yao medicine "Wind Wound Drug Classification" theory to treat common fractures. After picking fresh herbs, they are dried in the air and used separately. More than 10 plants such as Mountain Tiger, Mao Tiger and Black Nine Bull are ground into powder and mixed with wine into paste; more than 20 herbs such as *Zuandifeng, Jiujiefeng and Qingjiuniu* are used as "wind medicine" and "wound medicine" to make raw powder into lotion, or directly soak wine for later use. After fracture fixation, the ointment was applied to the bone. After fracture healing, fumigation and medicinal wine should be used, and functional training should be carried out step by step. The characteristics of this therapy are safe and surgery-free, quick pain relief, short treatment period, combination of functional training and convalescence, equal emphasis on muscles and bones, simple operation, and low cost for patients. Bihe Bone Injury Therapy of Yao Ethnic Group fully embodies the characteristics of simplicity, convenience, efficacy and cost-efficiency and is widely praised by patients.

Yao medicine is a treasure of Chinese medicine. It has profound philosophical and humanistic connotations. Its unique techniques, medication, remarkable efficacy and relatively low cost of diagnosis and treatment are worth further study. In the past, Yao doctors lacked systematic medical classics because of lack of written records. Combining Bihe Bone Injury Therapy of Yao Ethnic Group with clinical practice over the past 100 years, it is of great significance to promote the research of it. Since the beginning of Peng Yunbiao, his third and fourth generations have inherited the techniques consequently. Up to now, there are still some ancestral medicinal mortar, hand-written copy of *Peng Yunbiao's Secret Recipe*, etc. At the same time, the therapy has been constantly improved and carried forward.

Bihe Bone Injury Therapy of Yao Ethnic Group has the characteristics of quick effect, safety, convenience, minimal side effects and simple operation. It has the advantages of quick relief, short recovery period and remarkable effect for patients with fracture before and after. Therefore, it is well known domestically and abroad, and there are more and more people who come to the Yao clinic for their medical treatment. However, because the therapy is inherited by the family and handed down from generation to generation, its influence is severely limited. It is urgent to train excellent successors to ensure that this skill can be carried forward. Moreover, at present, many dense primitive mountain forests have been cut down or replanted with other tree species. The number of Chinese herbal medicines is becoming scarcer and scarcer. It is more and more difficult to excavate the original medicinal materials in the ancient prescriptions of Bihe Bone Injury Therapy of Yao Ethnic Group. It needs to be protected in order to avoid the lack of available ancient prescriptions and medicines due to the lack of raw materials. In 2017, Guangxi will implement the revitalization plan of traditional Chinese medicine of Zhuang and Yao. This will provide a new opportunity for researching, sorting out and protecting the Bihe Bone Injury Therapy of Yao Ethnic Group, and will certainly enrich the traditional Chinese medicine culture, so that more people can benefit from this all around the world.

本等。同时，传人不断改进该疗法，将其发扬光大。

瑶族壁和骨伤疗法具有见效快、安全便捷、无毒副作用、操作简便的特点，对于骨折和骨折术后患者的治疗起效早、康复期短，效果显著，因此名扬海内外。慕名到壁和中医骨伤诊所求医者不断，但是由于该疗法为家族传承，代代单传，影响力严重受限，急需培养优秀接班人，确保这一绝技能够发扬光大。再者，目前许多茂密的原始山林被大量砍伐或被改种经济林木，中草药数量日渐稀少，壁和骨伤疗法古方中的原生药材越来越难挖掘，需要加以保护，以免空有古方却因原料匮乏而无法制药。2017年，广西实施中医药壮瑶医药振兴计划，为挖掘、整理、保护瑶族壁和骨伤疗法提供了新的契机，丰富了中华民族传统医药文化，让更多的人受益于此。

第九章　民俗

Chapter Nine　Folk Customs

壮族三月三

The Lunar March 3rd Festival of Zhuang Ethnic Group

项目名称：壮族三月三

别称：无

分布范围：武鸣区、隆安县、上林县、宾阳县、马山县等

入选名录：2014年第四批国家级非物质文化遗产扩展项目名录
2008年第二批自治区级非物质文化遗产名录
2007年第一批市级非物质文化遗产名录

保护单位：武鸣区文化馆

代表性传承人：李超元、黄存

Element name：The Lunar March 3rd Festival of Zhuang Ethnic Group

Alternative name：None

Geographical location and range：Wuming District, Long'an Town, Shanglin Town, Binyang Town, Mashan Town and others

Element inscribed list：In 2014 on the Fourth Extended National List of Intangible Cultural Heritage
In 2008 on the Second Autonomous Region List of Intangible Cultural Heritage
In 2007 on the First Municipal List of Intangible Cultural Heritage

Competent body involved in safeguarding：Wuming District Cultural Centre

Representitive inheritor：Li Chaoyuan, Huang Cun

"三月三"歌圩活动——横鼓舞 摄影 尹宗浩
The Lunar March 3rd Festival Activity: Horizontal Drum Dance Photo by Yin Zonghao

壮族三月三是广西武鸣壮乡的传统节日，于每年农历三月初三举行祭祖先、拜龙母、办歌圩等盛大民俗活动，唱歌为其活动的主要内容。武鸣地处广西壮族自治区首府南宁市北部，是壮族三月三的发祥地和主要流传地。

三月三原是古骆越人的祭祖节，祭祀骆越古国的祖母王"佬浦"和骆越大王"召骆"。传说骆越祖母王"佬浦"是珠江守护神"尾龙"的养母，南汉皇帝把骆越祖母王"佬浦"封为"龙母夫人"，使三月三祭祀骆越祖母王的习俗成为岭南重要的民间祭祖活动。汉代就有"三月三上巳节"的记载。明清时期，壮族受民间道教真武信仰影响，三月三祀真武迎神赛会逐渐形成具有壮族特色的祭祖先、祀玄天、拜龙母、会男女的盛大节庆。清代三月三歌圩已在民间形成传统，光绪《武缘县图经》中有"答歌之习，武缘仙湖、廖江二处有之，每三月初一至十日，沿江上下，数里之内，士女如云"的记载。

总体来说，壮族三月三的特色是五色糯米饭祭祖，娱神是三月三习俗的内涵，歌圩活动是其派生的表现形式。如今，壮族三月三的民俗活动主要有：在祖神庙里摆祭坛，供

The third day of the third lunar month is a traditional festival in Wuming, a Zhuang inhabited region in Guangxi. On that day, the Zhuang people hold grand galas with lots of activities including ancestor worship, Dragon Mother Worship and Folk Song Fair. Singing is the main content of the gala. Wuming is located in the northern part of Nanning, the capital of Guangxi Zhuang Autonomous Region. It is the birthplace of the Zhuang people, where they thrive until now.

The 3rd day of Lunar Third Month was originally the ancestor worship festival of the ancient Luoyue people, offering sacrifices to Laopu, the grandmother of the ancient Luoyue kingdom, and Zhaoluo, the king of Luoyue. It is said that Laopu, the grandmother king of Luoyue, was the adoptive mother of a dragon, the guardian God of the Pearl River. The emperor of the Southern Han Dynasty named Laopu, the grandmother king of Luoyue, as "Mrs. Dragon Mother", making it a custom to worship Luoyue every March 3rd in Lingnan. There has been a record of it since the Han Dynasty. During the Ming and Qing Dynasties, influenced by the Taoist belief in Zhenwu, this very festival has only gotten bigger, including ancestor worship, Xuan Tian worship, Dragon Mother Worship and the mingling of Zhuang men and women. During the Qing Dynasty, it has become an important tradition among the people. In Emperor Guangxu's *Records and Maps of Wuyuan County*, sentences are recorded "There are two places, Xianhu Lake and Liaojiang River in Wuyuan. From the first to the tenth of every March, along the river, within a few miles, scholars and women are like clouds".

Generally speaking, the specialty of the Lunar March 3rd Festival of the Zhuang Ethnic Group is five-color glutinous rice for ancestor worship, entertaining gods is the connotation of the festival, and Folk Song Fair is the materialization of it. Today, Zhuang Ethnic Group's folk activities in March are altar offerings in the ancestral temples, livestock (pig, cattle, and sheep) sacrifices, and five colors of glutinous rice. Abbots are invited to hold the event. They would lift their ancestral gods with colored sedan chairs, travel around to pray for peace and blessings. The commons would worship, in unit of a family, at home. The theatre troupe sings opera along with the abbot. Those who have particular wishes would invite them to perform, lift the sedan chair to the stage, meaning inviting the ancestral God to see the opera. The host would light fireworks, fire the red circle to the sky. When it falls, the contestants of each team compete for the first place. All activities would start then including singing in pairs, singing competition, singing appreciation, embroidery ball throwing, "fighting eggs" and so on.

The element is significant in order to inherit and carry forward the traditional culture of the Zhuang Ethnic Group, enhance community cohesion and promote national unity as well as having important historical and folklore research values. The Lunar March 3rd Festival of Zhuang Ethnic Group carries rich and colorful cultural and artistic forms, provides an important source of life for modern literary and artistic creation, and is of great significance to enhance the national characteristics of modern literature and art.

Due to the changes in social life, less and less people attended the Lunar March 3rd Festival of Zhuang Ethnic Group, and the folk artists were faced with a dilemma. Wuming District has set up a leading group of the Lunar March 3rd Festival Project of the Zhuang Ethnic Group, and set up the inheritance base of the Lunar March 3rd Festival of Wuming. Special funds were invested to support its inheritance and development and survey and research of folk activities are also conducted. Fortunately, the people of the Zhuang are very conscious of their cultural heritage, and the cultural advocate is rising day by day. At present, the inheritance of this festival is on the right path. Under the leadership of the local government, the festival will be held on schedule every lunar March 3. As of 2018, they have been held for 38 consecutive years. In 2014, The Lunar March 3rd Festival of Zhuang Ethnic Group was inscribed on the Fourth National List of Intangible Cultural Heritage expansion elements under the approval of the State Council.

抢花炮　摄影 尹宗浩
Grabbing Huapao Photo by Yin Zonghao

猪、牛、羊三牲和五色糯米饭，请师公和道公班主持祭祀祖神；用彩轿抬出祖神，师公跳舞开路，巡游各村寨，驱邪祈福；村民在家中祭祀祖先，需要还愿的主家请戏班唱戏，将祖神彩轿抬至戏台前安放，意为请祖神看戏；抢花炮，主持人点上火药放炮，将红炮圈射上高空，炮圈落下时各队的选手争先抢夺；对歌，包括对歌择偶、赛歌、赏歌等；抛绣球、“斗蛋”等活动。

该项目对于弘扬壮族优秀的传统文化、增强社区凝聚力、增进民族团结有着重大意义，亦有重要的历史学、民俗学价值。三月三民俗承载着丰富多彩的文化艺术形式，为现代文艺创作提供了重要的生活源泉，对增强现代文艺的民族特色有重要意义。

由于社会生活发生变化，壮族三月三的文化空间受到影响，民间艺人面临青黄不接的情况。武鸣成立壮族三月三活动项目工作领导小组，建立武鸣壮族三月三项目传承基地。投入专项经费扶持壮族三月三的传承和发展工作，组织人员对壮族三月三民俗活动进行普查、挖掘。可喜的是，壮族民众传承这一节庆民俗自觉性很高，保护的呼声日益高涨，目前传承状况良好。在当地政府的主导下，每年的武鸣壮族三月三民俗节日活动都会如期举行，截至2018年，已连续举办38年。2014年，经国务院批准，壮族三月三被列入第四批国家级非物质文化遗产扩展项目名录。

跳竹竿舞　摄影 尹宗浩
Bamboo Dance Photo by Yin Zonghao

壮族歌圩

Folk Song Fair of Zhuang Ethnic Group

项目名称：壮族歌圩

别称：无

分布范围：南宁市武鸣区、良庆区、邕宁区、横州市、马山县、上林县、隆安县及百色市、河池市、柳州市等

入选名录：2006年第一批国家级非物质文化遗产名录
2007年第一批自治区级非物质文化遗产名录
2007年第一批市级非物质文化遗产名录

保护单位：南宁市民族文化艺术研究院（南宁市非物质文化遗产保护中心）

代表性传承人：刘正成

Element name: Folk Song Fair of Zhuang Ethnic Group

Alternative name: None

Geographical location and range: Wuming District, Liangqing District, Yongning District, Hengzhou City, Mashan County, Shanglin County, Long'an County of Nanning City; Baise City, Hechi City, Liuzhou City and others

Element inscribed list: In 2006 on the First National List of Intangible Cultural Heritage
In 2007 on the First Autonomous Region List of Intangible Cultural Heritage
In 2007 on the First Municipal List of Intangible Cultural Heritage

Competent body involved in safeguarding: Nanning Ethnic Cluture and Art Research Institute (Nanning Intangible Cultural Heritage Protection Centre)

Representitive inheritor: Liu Zhengcheng

Folk Song Fair of Zhuang Ethnic Group is a Festival gathering and singing activity held by the masses of the Zhuang Ethnic Group at a specific time and place. The Zhuang language is called "xu huan", "xu feng", "long dong" and "wopo". It is not only a traditional cultural activity of the Zhuang people, but also a place for young men and women to socialize. The folk song fair is mainly spread in Wuming District, Liangqing District, Yongning District, Hengzhou City, Mashan County, Shanglin County, Long'an County, Baise City, Hechi City, Liuzhou City and other places in Guangxi Zhuang Autonomous Region. In Guangxi Zhuang Autonomous Region, folk song fair is held mainly in spring and autumn. In spring, fairs are held most frequently in March and April, and on the third day of the third month of the lunar calendar. In autumn, they are concentrated in August and September of the lunar calendar, especially in the Mid-Autumn Festival.

The Zhuang people have a habit of singing in ancient times. The folk song show of the Zhuang people could be traced way back. They were originated from the sacrificial activities in the era of clan tribes. With the development of history, sacrificial activities have gradually evolved into communication among the people. The primitive ritual song and dance has changed from "entertaining gods" to "entertaining people", from "dancing" to "singing". Over the time, the activities have formed into groups. According to the documents, the folk song fair was popular as early as the Song Dynasty. Zhou Qufei's *Ling Wai Dai Da* in the Southern Song Dynasty recorded that the Zhuang people "wrote their own songs repeatedly, with sad feelings, and refused to follow suit. During this period, there were excellent people." What I'm talking about here is the folk song show for young men and women's gatherings. By the Ming Dynasty, the folk song fair had undergone through new development and was held regularly in a fixed place. Folk song show has a strong symbolic and cohesive force, and it has a profound impact on every Zhuang people and family. Looking back at the development of folk song show, there are many legends, such as praying for a good harvest year, selecting a son-in-law by singing songs, singing fairy Liu Sanjie's biography and so on.

There are four main aspects in the activities of folk song fair. One is the sacrificial ceremony of the fair. Before the traditional large-scale shows were held, there were worship ceremonies, such as worship of Liu Sanjie, Buluotuo, Huapo and so on. The altar is generally located in the cave, and the large ones are usually held in caves, such as Ganzhuang Mountain Folk Song Fair in Tianyang County, Guangxi,

壮族歌圩是壮族群众在特定时间、地点举行的节日性聚会歌唱活动，壮语称为“圩欢”“圩逢”“笼峒”“窝坡”等。它是壮族民间的传统文化活动，也是男女青年进行社交的场所，歌圩主要流传于南宁市武鸣区、良庆区、邕宁区、横州市、马山县、上林县、隆安县以及百色市、河池市、柳州市等地。在广西壮族自治区境内，凡是壮族较大的聚居区都有歌圩，举办歌圩的时间主要在春季和秋季，春季歌圩以三四月间最为繁多，农历三月初三举办的次数最多；秋季歌圩集中于农历八九月份，尤以中秋节最为集中。

壮族人自古有爱好唱歌的习俗，壮族歌圩历史悠久，源远流长，起源于氏族部落时代的祭祀活动。随着历史发展，祭祀活动逐渐演变成以民众间的交流为主。原始仪式性的群体歌舞由“娱神”向“娱人”过渡，从“舞化”向“歌化”发展，久而久之，便形成了群体性的歌圩活动。据文献记载，歌圩早在宋代就已经流行。南宋周去非的《岭外代答》载，壮人“迭相歌和，含情凄婉，皆临机自撰，不肯蹈袭，其间乃有绝佳者”。这里所说的就是男女青年聚会的歌圩。到了明代，歌圩又有了新的发展，定期在固定地点举行。歌圩具有很强的象征性和凝聚力，壮族歌圩对每一个壮族人、每个壮族家庭来说，都有着深刻的影响。在长期发展中，壮族歌圩有着许多动人的传说，如祷祝丰年、赛歌择婿、歌仙刘三姐传歌等。

歌圩活动的内容主要有四个方面：一是歌圩祭祀仪式。传统的大型歌圩在举行之前有祭拜仪式，如祭拜刘三姐、布洛陀、花婆等。祭台一般设在岩洞中，规模较大的歌圩一般在有岩洞的地方举行，如广西田阳县敢壮山歌圩、田东县仰岩歌圩、来宾市麒麟歌圩等。二是歌场交情，即倚歌择配。一般要经过游歌、见面歌、求歌、和歌、盘歌、相交歌、信歌、思歌、离别歌和约歌等对唱阶段。三是赛歌赏歌，有盘歌、猜歌、对子歌、连故事和别具特色的抢歌、斗歌等。四是文体自娱歌圩，圩期伴有抛绣球、抢花炮、斗蛋活动等，甚至还有壮剧、师公戏、采茶戏等文艺演出。

凡壮族聚居地区均有歌圩活动，广西壮族自治区共有640多个歌圩举办点。歌圩是壮族民歌的自然载体，它已成为壮族传统文化娱乐活动的代表形式，造就了壮族特有的歌圩文化，对于壮族各类传统民歌的产生、传承与发展具有重要的作用。同时它又是壮族民间文学的宝库，对了解和研究壮族古代社会生活具有重要的价值。歌圩还为广大民众提供了学习山歌和展示才艺的场所，满足了他们崇尚山歌、展示自我的需求。

随着现代化步伐的加快，民族民间传统文化受到严重冲击，歌圩活动也逐渐减少，不少歌圩因为老歌手退出后没有中青年歌手接班而逐渐走向消亡。南宁市政府以保护为主，以传承为核心，建立了比较完备的保护制度，在全社会形成自觉保护传统的意识，对歌圩的歌词、曲调进行研究，并举办国际民歌艺术节等活动，推动歌圩文化的活态传承。2006年5月20日，经国务院批准，壮族歌圩列入第一批国家级非物质文化遗产名录。

壮族歌圩表演
Performance of Folk Song Fair of Zhuang Ethnic Group

Yangyan Folk Song Fair in Tiandong County, Qilin Folk Song Fair in Laibin City, etc. The second is the mingling happening during the fair, that is, choosing partners based on singing. Generally, it goes through the stages of recital, such as traveling song, meeting song, begging song, harmony song, pan song, intersection song, letter song, missing song, farewell song and date song. Thirdly, contest songs, including tray songs, guessing songs, song pairs, stories and unique qiang song, fighting songs and so on. Fourth, recreational singing fairs are accompanied by throwing embroidery balls, lighting fireworks, fighting eggs, and even Zhuang Opera, Shigong Opera, Tea Collecting Opera and other literary and artistic performances.

There are fairs in all areas inhabited by the Zhuang Ethnic Group. There are 640 fair sites in Guangxi Zhuang Autonomous Region. The song fair has become the vehicle for Zhuang folk songs. It has become the representative of traditional cultural and entertainment activities of the Zhuang people. It has created the unique folk song fair culture, and it plays an important role in the inspiration, inheritance and development of all kinds of traditional folk songs of the Zhuang. At the same time, it is also the treasure house of Zhuang folk literature, which has important value for understanding and studying the ancient social life of the people. Folk song fair also provides a place for people to learn folk songs and express their talents. On this stage, they are not only promoting the culture, but presenting the best of themselves.

With the progression of modernization, the traditional ethnic and folk culture has been seriously impacted, and the activities of folk song fairs have gradually decreased. Many pools are dying out because there are no young and middle-aged singers to take over after the old generation has quitted. Nanning Municipal Government has established a relatively complete protection system with "protection" as the main focus and inheritance as the core. It has created a self-consciousness of protecting the tradition in the whole society. It has studied the lyrics and tunes of the poems and held activities such as the International Folk Song Art Festival to promote the dynamic inheritance of the folk song culture. On May 20, 2006, the Folk Song Fair of the Zhuang Ethnic Group was approved by the State Council and inscribed on the First National List of Intangible Cultural Heritage.

宾阳炮龙节

Binyang Cracker Dragon Carnival

项目名称：宾阳炮龙节

别称：无

分布范围：宾阳县

入选名录：2008年第二批国家级非物质文化遗产名录

保护单位：宾阳县文化馆

代表性传承人：伍学规、邹玉特

Element name：Binyang Cracker Dragon Carnival

Alternative name：None

Geographical location and range：Binyang County

Element inscribed list：In 2008 on the Second National List of Intangible Cultural Heritage

Competent body involved in safeguarding：Binyang County Cultural Centre

Representitive inheritors：Wu Xuegui, Zou Yute

宾阳炮龙 摄影 冯革里
Binyang Cracker Dragon Photo by Feng Geli

炮龙节是一项综合性民间节庆系列活动，融合了汉、壮民族文化特色，流传于南宁市宾阳县，于每年农历正月十一举行。

宾阳炮龙节发端于宋元时代，在清末和民国初年趋于成熟，至今已有上千年的悠久历史。相传宋仁宗皇祐年间，狄青率大军赴广西征剿侬智高，在宾阳昆仑关屡攻不克。当时正值元宵节，狄青令兵士以稻草扎成龙形，放火烧竹，在竹子燃烧爆裂后发出的炮仗般响声中舞龙大闹元宵，以此麻痹敌方。侬智高果然放松了戒备，最终为狄青所克。当地人据此认定舞炮龙能带来吉祥好运，每年农历正月初十至十五都要舞龙，后来相沿成习，舞龙活动固定在正月十一进行，逐渐形成独特的炮龙节。

宾阳炮龙节活动主要由“游彩架”“灯会”“舞炮龙”三个部分组成，每部分各有特色。“游彩架”也叫“彩架游行”，游行队列由彩色台架、舞龙队、舞狮队等组成，长达半里甚至一里以上，中间彩架台上有数名孩童，分别坐立于特制的手指、伞、扇、剑、弓、刀之类的小道具上，装扮成

Binyang Cracker Dragon Carnival is a comprehensive series of folk festivals, which combines the cultural characteristics of Han and Zhuang nationalities. It is spread in Binyang County, Nanning City in Guangxi Zhuang Autonomous Region, and is held on the eleventh day of the first lunar month every year.

Binyang Cracker Dragon Carnival began in the Song and Yuan Dynasties and became well-developed in the late Qing Dynasty and the early Republic of China. It has a long history of thousands of years. According to legend, during the reign of Emperor Renzong in the Song Dynasty, Di Qing led a large army to Guangxi to fight against Nong Zhigao and failed to conquer the Kunlun Pass in Binyang. During the Lantern Festival, Di Qing ordered his soldiers to tie straws into dragons, then set them on fire, and perform dragon-dance in the sound of firecrackers after the bamboo burst in order to deceive the enemy. Nong Zhigao relaxed his guard and eventually defeated by Di Qing. According to this, the local people believe that dragon dancing can bring good luck. Every year, dragon dancing takes place from the tenth to fifteenth day of the first lunar month. Later, dragon dancing activities are fixed on the eleventh day of the first lunar month, gradually forming a unique carnival.

Binyang Cracker Dragon Carnival are mainly composed of three parts, namely “Game Rack Seeing”, “Lantern Festival” and “Cracker Dragon Dance”. Each part has its own characteristics. “Game rack” is also called “color rack parade”. The parade is composed of color rack, dragon dance team, lion dance team and so on. It lasts half a mile or more. In the middle of the rack, there are several children sitting on special props of finger, umbrella, fan, sword, bow, knife and other small things. They dress up according to specific situations. It’s quite an interesting scene. “Lantern Festival” is commonly known as “Lighting and Drinking Festival”, including rural drinking, lighting and other activities. Rural drinking is in unit of villages and alleys, and the parents of the last-year-born male act as “leaders” to raise money named “Ding Kuan”. Each family sends a male to the ancestral hall or village community to discuss the agricultural production problems of that year, listen to village regulations and folk conventions, and then have dinner. On the day of the Lantern Festival, the leader called “head man” led the parade to the “father-in-law holding flowers”—male parent of three men and two women and the "mother-in-law holding flowers" who were good at mountain songs. They set out from the village temples or ancestral halls together to send “lotus lanterns” to the people. “Lantern receiving” alludes to the blessing of a birth of a child.

Cracker Dragon Dance is the climax of the whole festival. At 7:00 p.m. on the 11th day of January, in temples or common areas, the head of the meeting would bite the rooster's crown and light the Cracker Dragon's eyes with its blood. Dragon dancers all went to battle barebacked, wearing hats like those of Qing officers and soldiers (all bamboo braided and smeared black), opening the way with dragon balls, dragon signs (dragon lanterns), gongs and drums, and performing Chinese opera, with lively cracker dragon dance. Lighting and dragon guard teams follow the dragon head and tail, where the dragon goes, each family greets each other, lights out the firecrackers prepared beforehand, and throws them to the dragon. There is a saying that "the sound of guns keeps on, and the dragon dances ceaselessly". After dancing to the designated place at the end of the village, the traditional dragon-sending ceremony was held under the leadership of the head of the meeting.

Binyang Cracker Dragon Carnival is an important part of the Chinese dragon culture. It can satisfy the psychological needs of people to pray for a good year and create a peaceful festival atmosphere. Therefore, it has become a great research object of folklore, culture and other disciplines and a useful reference for the construction of a harmonious society. With the acceleration of modernization, the impact of foreign culture on Chinese traditional culture is becoming more and more serious, and the Binyang Cracker Dragon Carnival is inevitably affected. In recent years, activities have been restored, and the number of "cracker dragon" has increased, with more and more participants, including tourists at home and abroad in the surrounding counties and cities of Binyang. Under this circumstance, Binyang Cracker Dragon Carnival is gradually developing into a festival celebrating the blending of multi-ethnic cultures. On June 7, 2008, Binyang Cracker Dragon Carnival was approved by the State Council and inscribed on the Second National List of Intangible Cultural Heritage.

特定情景下的形象造型，神气毕见，妙趣天成。“灯会”俗称“灯酒会”，包括乡饮、取灯等活动内容。乡饮以村屯和街巷为单位，由上一年生男丁的家长担任“头人”筹集“丁款”，每户派一男性到祠堂或村社商讨当年的农业生产问题，聆听村规民约，然后会餐。取灯有“求嗣取丁”之意，灯会当日，“头人”引领生有三男两女的“抱花岳父”和擅长山歌的“抱花岳母”同众人一道从村社庙宇或祠堂出发，为取灯人家送去“莲花灯”。舞炮龙是整个炮龙节的高潮，正月十一晚七时整，在庙宇或代表社稷之处，由会首或师人咬破公鸡之冠，以鸡冠之血点亮开光龙眼后，方可万炮齐鸣，龙亦方可腾跃而起。舞龙者均赤膊上阵，头戴如清朝官兵之帽（均为竹编并涂抹黑色），以龙珠、龙牌（龙灯）、锣鼓、文武场开路，举行热闹火爆的舞炮龙表演。照明及护龙队首尾随龙而进，炮龙所到之处，各家各户夹道相迎，将事先准备好的鞭炮拿出来燃放，抛向炮龙，有“炮声不停，龙舞不止”之说。舞到村头街尾的既定地点后，在会首带领下举行传统的送龙升天仪式。

宾阳炮龙节是中华龙文化的重要组成部分，它可以满足民众禳灾祈福的心理需求，营造祥和的节日气氛，因而成为民俗学、文化学等学科研究的对象及和谐社会建设运动的有益借鉴。随着现代化进程的加速，外来文化对中国传统文化的冲击日趋严重，宾阳炮龙节也不可避免地受到一定影响。近年来，炮龙节活动得到恢复，“炮龙”数目有所增加，参加者愈来愈多，其中包括宾阳周边县市及国内外的游客。在此形势下，宾阳炮龙节正逐渐发展成为一个多民族文化交融的节庆盛典。2008年6月7日，经国务院批准，宾阳炮龙节列入第二批国家级非物质文化遗产名录。

鸡血点龙眼
Adding the Finishing Touchon Dragon with Chicken Blood

壮族会鼓习俗

Hui Drum of Zhuang Ethnic Group Custom

项目名称：壮族会鼓习俗

别称：无

分布范围：马山县

入选名录：2021年第五批国家级非物质文化遗产名录
2008年第二批自治区级非物质文化遗产名录
2007年第一批市级非物质文化遗产名录

保护单位：马山县文化馆

代表性传承人：韦建廷

Element name: Hui Drum of Zhuang Ethnic Group Custom

Alternative name: None

Geographical location and range: Mashan County

Element inscribed list: In 2021 on the Fifth National List of Intangible Cultural Heritage
In 2008 on the Second Autonomous Region List of Intangible Cultural Heritage
In 2007 on the First Municipal List of Intangible Cultural Heritage

Competent body involved in safeguarding: Mashan County Cultural Centre

Representative inheritor: Wei Jianting

2007年12月，马山首届文化旅游美食节开幕式千人会鼓展演
In December 2007, at the Opening Ceremony of the First Mashan Culture, Tourism and Food Festival Hui Drum was Performed by Thousands of People

Hui drum custom is an exclusive recreation custom of Zhuang Ethnic Group in Mashan County and much loved by Zhuang people because of its stirring beats with great momentum. It originated from the Song Dynasty and prevailed in the Qing Dynasty. Initially, the main purpose of playing the drum was to exorcise ghosts and demons, to warn of attacks, and to pray for good luck.

According to some historical materials of the Song Dynasty, General Nong Zhigao, with his uprising troop of Zhuang, built bastions in Mashan to against the Song army led by Di Qing. The situation remained a stalemate in the day, but when night fell, "the Song army had no choice but to retreat, while the uprising troop could be inspired by drumbeats to attack". There still circulates a legend among the local people: Long time ago, a man would always be harassed by a ghost rest on his shoulders every time on his half way to the fair, and he could only hear what it had said but caught nothing of it with his eyes. At night when he arrived home, with the ghost following still, only to find that his children began to cry in fear and cats and dogs unsettled. To address the problem, he tried to ask the ghost what its killer was, and then he gradually got to know it feared thunder and lightning. At last the ghost

壮族会鼓习俗是广西壮族自治区马山县壮族人民独有的一种有关民间娱乐活动的习俗。马山县壮族会鼓始于宋末元初，盛行于清代，最初主要是为了驱鬼镇妖、警示外袭、祈求吉祥。因壮族会鼓敲起来气势磅礴、热血沸腾，后渐渐成了民间喜爱的一种娱乐活动。

马山县会鼓最早出现于宋朝，有资料记载：宋代时侬智高叛乱，狄青率军平乱，在马山当地筑城屯兵抵御，双方僵持不下，每天一到天黑，“宋军鸣金收兵，土民擂鼓而进”。至今在马山壮族民间，还流传着这样一个传说：古时有一人，每逢赶圩行至半路，都会有一个野鬼跃上其肩，只闻其言不见其行，到了晚上，家中孩童惊叫、鸡犬不宁。这人就试探性地问鬼怕什么，后来发现鬼不怕人，但怕电闪雷鸣。此后，人们就用牛皮制成鼓，以鼓声代替雷声，来驱鬼辟邪，使生活安定。

马山壮族会鼓所使用的鼓一般为牛皮鼓，这种鼓多是选用生长时间长，木质较坚硬，而且粗大的樟、榕、枫等原木，锯成长约1.5米的木段，挖成空心后做成鼓壳，两头盖上牛皮，用竹篾或铁丝从四周把两张牛皮拉紧后晒干而成。因为制作精良，所以敲击时声音洪亮、浑圆、厚重。最大的“鼓王”有450岁，重500多斤，用樟木和两张黄牛皮制成。

马山壮族会鼓表演，经过广大会鼓传承者的艺术加工，谱了会鼓曲，会鼓表演已经是一个精彩的文艺节目。人们表演会鼓时，除了主角鼓外，还有锣、镲等充当配角，这些配角以洪亮、清脆的声音来点缀鼓点，使整个演出鼓声洪亮有力，节奏整齐，点数变化多端，既震撼人心又悦耳动听。会鼓有很多种打法，有混鼓打（序曲）、狂欢鼓、舞龙鼓、扁担鼓、花灯鼓等，中间还有各式各样的插曲鼓。敲打时，多人协作，鼓声撼动四面八方。

在马山，会鼓表演场面往往群情激昂，每临重大庆典活动，或者庆祝丰收、村寨喜事，人们都会抬出会鼓，尽情演绎一段，释放出生命的热能，表达着一个民族无限的喜悦心情。每逢此时，整个壮山瑶寨就是一片欢腾热烈的海洋，一浪高过一浪。壮族会鼓让世界领略到壮乡独具特色的民族文化魅力，成为壮族传统文化的一张亮丽名片。2021年，壮族会鼓习俗列入第五批国家级非物质文化遗产名录。

was frightened away and the man resumed his quiet life by beating a cowhide-drum simulating rumbling thunders.

Hui drum is usually cowhide drums. The body of the drum is mostly made of hard logs of years, such as camphor, banyan and maple wood, which would be sawn to 1.5 meters long and hollowed out. And then two heads are covered with two pieces of cowhides that dried by the sun and stretched by bamboo splits or iron wires. Only after these sophisticated procedures can the sound of the drum be resonant and sonorous. The biggest Hui drum made by camphor wood, is already 450 years old and weighs more than 500 jin.

After several times of artist modification by countless inheritors, Hui drum performance composed with lovely music has finally been a wonderful literary and art program. In the whole process of the performing, other instruments like Gong and Chai (a percussion instrument) would act as supporting roles. Adorning the drums with clear and crisp sounds, they are good at helping make the drums sound powerful and changeable in regulated rhythm and provide an exciting and pleasing performance. Besides, Hui drum covers a wide range of types including Mixed Drum (prelude), Carnival Drum, Dragon-dance Drum, Carrying-pole Drum and Festive-lantern Drum. They are studded with varied interludes of drums and performed by collaboration to make it heard miles away.

That passionate feeling is often seen in Mashan's drum performance. Whenever there is a celebration for harvest or for wedding, playing drums will be their first choice, as it is an accustomed means for the locals to express their unquenchable joy and pour their passion for life. In such case the whole village will be the sea of great rejoicing with cheers rang out continuously. Actually, Hui drum, serving as the brand of the traditional culture of Zhuang Ethnic Group, displays the world the impressing unique charm of the land of Zhuang. In 2021, Hui Drum of Zhuang Ethnic Group Custom was inscribed on the Fifth National List of Intangible Culture Heritage.

壮族毬丝歌会

Qiusi Song Party of Zhuang Ethnic Group

项目名称：壮族毬丝歌会

别称：无

分布范围：良庆区

入选名录：2014年第五批自治区级非物质文化遗产名录

保护单位：良庆区文化馆

代表性传承人：苏文学

Element name：Qiusi Song Party of Zhuang Ethnic Group

Alternative name：None

Geographical location and range：Liangqing District

Element inscribed list：In 2014 on the Fifth Autonomous Region List of Intangible Cultural Heritage

Competent body involved in safeguarding：Liangqing District Cultural Centre

Representitive inheritor：Su Wenxue

唱本与道具
Libretto and Props

毬丝歌会流布于南宁市良庆区，辐射到邕宁、武鸣、马山等地，以壮族嘹啰山歌为表现形式，伴随嘹啰山歌的产生而形成。

壮族毬丝歌会迄今已有1000多年的历史。南宋周去非的《岭外代答》载："广西诸郡，人多能合乐，城郊村落，祭祀婚嫁喜葬，无不用乐，虽耕田亦必口乐相之。"自古以来，良庆区的壮民凡是节日、婚嫁、生日或庆典都是即兴而歌，对唱为乐。相传古代壮族村寨流行抛鸡选婿的风俗，待嫁女孩家把鸡当作定情信物抛向人群，抢到者即为如意郎君。待选的壮家后生为了吸引女方的关注，口中高呼"嘹啰"（壮语意为"看啰"），若有幸能接到鸡，也喊"嘹啰"（意为"笑啰"）。壮族人民就以"嘹啰"为歌头编唱了嘹啰山歌。后来，定情信物锦鸡被以鸡毛编织成的"毬"取代了，形成了以嘹啰山歌为主要形式的毬丝歌会。

壮族毬丝歌会分放毬、还毬两个阶段。放毬的方式有两种：放毬方或事先约定接毬方，送毬前往，或以放毬告示征

Qiusi Song Party of Zhuang Ethnic Group mainly spreads in Liangqing District of Nanning, radiating to Yongning, Wuming, Mashan and other places, taking the Liaoluo folk song of the Zhuang Ethnic Group as its manifestation along with the production of Liaoluo folk song.

Qiusi Song Party of Zhuang Ethnic Group is developed along with the production of the Liaoluo folk song, which has been formed for more than 1000 years. In the Song Dynasty, Zhou Qufei's *Ling Wai Dai Da* contains "There are many people in Guangxi counties who can enjoy music together. In suburban villages, music is used in sacrifice, marriage and funeral, even if they plow the fields, they will have the same pleasure." Since ancient times, the Zhuang people in Liangqing District have sung impromptu songs for festivals, weddings, birthdays or celebrations, and enjoyed singing in pairs. Legend has it that the custom of throwing chickens to choose a son-in-law prevailed in ancient Zhuang villages. Girls to be married threw chickens as a token of love to the crowd, and those who grabbed them were the wishful groom. In order to attract women's attention, Zhuang males who are to be selected would shout "Liao Luo" (meaning "look at me"). If they are lucky to receive chickens, they also shout "Liao Luo" (meaning "laugh"). The people of the Zhuang compiled and sang the folk song with the title of "Liaoluo". Later, the chicken—symbol of love was replaced by "Qiusi" woven with chicken and wool, forming a Qiusi Song Party in the main form of Liaoluo folk song.

Qiusi Song Party of Zhuang Ethnic Group can be divided into two stages, Qiusi bestowing and receiving. There are two ways of bestowing: both parties were usually agreed in advance, then Qiusi is either sent to or being asked for by the receiving party. The receiving party would choose a major festival in the following year to return it, which was the climax of the song party. The two sides sat around at a table more than ten meters apart, named "Eight Immortal Table". Two young male singers from the returning parties, carrying bags of inner garments and cakes, would go toward the other party while singing. After singing the last sentence, they handed the bags to the other party's female singers and sang the next sentence while going back to their original position. After taking the bags, the female singer puts them on the knee of those male singers. This is repeated until one side running out of songs. Off-site singers also sing in pairs freely, sometimes as many as one or twenty groups, singing one after another, forming a spectacular scene.

The two-part Liaoluo folk song of the Zhuang Ethnic Group starts with the word "Liaoluo" in its singing method. Its singing method is unique. It covers astronomy, geography, history, science and technology, philosophy, ethics, morality, religion, art and other fields. Its melody is really distinct, and its lyrics are mostly in the form of "four or three" with seven words and four sentences. The Qiusi song will take "Qiusi" as a symbol, with a strong and unique regional style. Most of the Zhuang people living in Yongning and Liangqing have participated in or paid attention to the Qiusi Folk Song Fair. Therefore, all along, it has rich cultural connotations and a broad population base.

In order to better protect and inherit the Qiusi Folk Song Fair, Liangqing District Cultural Centre of Nanning City has set up a leading group for the protection of the Qiusi Folk Song Fair. Protection funds are designated in the local financial budget, and money is raised every year to support the development of more than 30 Liaoluo folk song teams, actively build a platform for the Qiusi Folk Song Fair, promoting this cultural heritage. In 2014, with the consent of the People's Government of Guangxi Zhuang Autonomous Region, the Qiusi Folk Song Fair was selected to be in the Fifth Autonomous Region List of Intangible Cultural Heritage.

求接毬方。还毬方选择次年的某个重大节日还毬，此为歌圩的高潮。双方围坐在相距10多米的八仙桌旁，由还毬方的两名男青年歌手提着内装毬、糕饼的包袱，边唱边走向对方，唱完上句，将包袱交给对方女歌手，唱下句走回原位。放毬方接包袱后，由女歌手将包袱放在对方男歌手的膝上。如此反复进行，直到放毬方对歌输后接受毬丝。场外的歌者也自由组合对唱，有时多达一二十组，歌声此起彼落，形成壮观的歌海。

壮族二声部嘹啰山歌在唱法上均以“嘹啰”两字固定为开唱，唱法独特，内容涉及天文、地理、历史、科技、哲学、伦理道德、宗教、艺术等各个领域，曲调富有特色，歌词多为七言四句的“四三”格式。而毬丝歌会以“毬丝”作为信物，具有浓郁而独特的民族风格。生活在邕宁、良庆一带的壮族民众，大多都参加过或关注过毬丝歌会。因此，一直以来，毬丝歌会具有丰富的文化内涵和广泛的群众基础。

为了更好地保护、传承毬丝歌会，南宁市良庆区文化馆成立了毬丝歌会保护工作领导小组，将毬丝歌会的保护经费列入地方财政经费预算，每年筹集资金用于扶持三十多支嘹啰山歌队的发展，积极为毬丝歌会搭建平台，支持毬丝歌会的系列传承活动。2014年，经广西壮族自治区人民政府同意，壮族毬丝歌会列入第五批自治区级非物质文化遗产名录。

壮族罗波庙会

Luobo Temple Fair of Zhuang Ethnic Group

项目名称：壮族罗波庙会

别称：无

分布范围：武鸣区

入选名录：2014年第五批自治区级非物质文化遗产名录
　　　　　2013年第五批市级非物质文化遗产名录

保护单位：南宁市文化馆

代表性传承人：陆映春

Element name: Luobo Temple Fair of Zhuang Ethnic Group

Alternative name: None

Geographical location and range: Wuming District

Element inscribed list: In 2014 on the Fifth Autonomous Region List of Intangible Cultural Heritage
In 2013 on the Fifth Municipal List of Intangible Cultural Heritage

Competent body involved in safeguarding: Nanning Cultural Centre

Representitive inheritor: Lu Yingchun

Located in the south of Luobo Street, Luobo Town, Wuming District of Nanning in Guangxi, Luobo Temple is one of the most well-preserved Longmu Cultural Temple of the Zhuang Ethnic Group. Most of the myths and materials related to the Tejue in the temples around Daming Mountain are preserved in the temples of Luobo. The Zhuang language of Luobo Temple used to be called "temple man servant", which is translated into Chinese as Great Grandma Temple. Luobo Temple Fair is a grand folk custom activity of the Zhuang people, whose main content is offering sacrifices to "Laopu" (Dragon Mother) on the second day of March of the lunar calendar every year.

Luobo Temple is the main place for later generations to sacrifice "Laopu" (Dragon Mother), also known as Dragon Mother Temple. The Luobo Temple in Wuming is the ancestor temple of the ancient Luoyue people. The worship of Luoyue's grandmother king takes place on March 3rd of the lunar calendar every year. Dragon Mother Culture has a profound impact on the Pearl River Basin and Southeast Asia. The legend of "Pu" originated from "Luobo". Many towns in the Pearl River Basin have "Bo" or "Pu" derived from Longmu culture, such as "Linpu" in the ancient Daming Mountains, Pumiao in the ancient Yongning County, Ningpu in the ancient Hengzhou, Bushan in the ancient Guigang and Huangpu in the port of the Pearl River Estuary. The worship of dragon mother is the most influential folk belief in the Pearl River Basin and Southeast Asia. It is also an important folk custom of Luoyue descendants. The dragon mother has always been regarded as the embodiment of love and peace, and Dragon Mother Temple along the Pearl River is the most visited. Luobo Temple is located in Daming Mountain area of Guangxi, which is the earliest capital of the ancient country Luoyue and the centre of ancient Luoyue culture. In the late Ming and early Qing Dynasties, pilgrims gathered in the temple of Luobo, from which the temple fair and the polder of Luobo were formed.

The main contents of Luobo Temple Fair are: (1) Enlightenment. At daybreak, the abbot is asked to wish the statue of the ancestor to be enlightened. (2) Sacrificial ceremonies. Ten thousand people bowed to their ancestors on the stage, offered baskets of flowers, offered sacrifices, offered incense and worshipped them. (3) Worship. People went to the temple of Luobo to set up altars to worship pigs, wine and five-color glutinous rice, and then sacrificed their ancestors at home. (4) Tour. Raise the "Laopu" in a colorful sedan chair, and the master dresses up as "Luo Yi" (that is, the God of birds and snakes with Nuo Face) to dance and open the way.

庙会开幕式
Opening Ceremony of Temple Fair

罗波庙位于南宁市武鸣区罗波镇罗波街南面，是目前保存比较好的壮族龙母文化庙之一。广西壮族环大明山各地庙宇歌颂特掘的相关神话及材料，应以罗波庙保存的居多。罗波庙壮语旧称“庙佬仆”，汉译即高祖母庙。罗波庙会是壮族人每年农历三月初二以祭祀“佬浦”（龙母）为主要内容的盛大民俗活动。

罗波庙是后人祭祀“佬浦”（龙母）的主要场所，也叫龙母庙。武鸣罗波庙是古骆越民族的祖神庙，每年农历三月三骆越祖母王祭祀。龙母文化在珠江流域和东南亚影响深远。龙母姓“蒲”的传说就源于“罗波”，珠江流域的城镇多有“波”或“蒲”字的龙母文化基因，如古大明山地区叫“临浦”，古邕宁县城叫“蒲庙”，古横州叫“宁浦”，古贵港叫“布山”，珠江口的港口叫“黄埔”等。龙母崇拜是珠江流域和东南亚最有影响的民间信仰，也是珠江流域骆越后裔民族的重要民俗，龙母历来被当作慈爱和平安的化身，珠江沿江一带的龙母庙香火最盛。罗波庙所在的广西大明山地区，是骆越古国最早的都城所在地，也是古骆越文化的中心。明末清初，罗波庙香客云集，罗波庙会及罗波圩由此形成。

罗波庙会的主要内容有：1.开光。天亮时请庙祝对始祖王像进行法事开光。2.祭祀大典。万人在戏台对始祖鞠躬、敬献花篮、敬献祭品、上香、祭拜。3.祭拜。人们各自到罗波庙里摆祭坛，供猪头、酒水和五色糯米饭祭拜，随后在家祭祀祖先。4.巡游。用彩轿抬出“佬蒲”，师公扮“骆垌”（即戴傩面鸟神和蛇神）跳舞开路，巡游各村寨，驱邪祈福。5.演师公戏。请“佬蒲”及参与庙会的众人看师公戏。6.唱山歌。群众自发到罗波庙及罗波潭边唱山歌，包括对歌择偶、赛歌、赏歌等。7.抢花炮。主持人点上火药放炮，将红炮圈射上高空，炮圈落下时各队的选手争先抢夺，一般是抢三炮结束比赛。8.多锅宴。祭祀结束后，当地人邀请外地嘉宾、游客聚会品尝五色糯米饭等壮族传统美食。

为传承和发展这一文化遗产，武鸣区成立领导机构，划拨专项资金，组织人员对罗波庙会民俗活动进行普查、挖掘、保护、传承，组织开展各种扶持活动，多年来以“政府主导、民间主体、群众参与”的方式举办了罗波庙会祭祀民俗节日活动。2013年，南宁市政府公布，壮族罗波庙会列入第五批市级非物质文化遗产名录。2014年，经广西壮族自治区人民政府同意，壮族罗波庙会列入第五批自治区级非物质文化遗产名录。目前，罗波庙建筑保存完好，香客不断，庙会参与群众盛况空前，正从当代壮族人的心中走向前台，发挥着文化传承的历史责任和文化现实作用。

He tours villages to exorcise evil spirits and pray for good luck. (5) Shigong performances. Invite “Laopu” and people who attend the temple fair to watch Shigong Opera. (6) Singing folk songs. People spontaneously went to Luobo Temple and Luobo Lake to sing folk songs, including choosing spouses, singing competitions and appreciating songs. (7) Snatching fireworks. The host fires the gunpowder and shoots the red firework circle high into the air. When the circle falls, the players of each team compete for the first place. Generally, they finish the competition by three guns. (8) Multi-pot feast. After the sacrifice, the local people invited guests from other places and tourists to gather to taste the traditional Zhuang delicacies such as five-color glutinous rice.

In order to inherit and develop this cultural heritage, Wuming District set up a leading committee, allocated special funds, conducted surveys, researched, and advocated the protection and inheritance of the folk activities of the Luobo Temple Fair. Over the years, the annual Luobo Temple Festival has been held in the form of “government-led, civil subjects and mass participation”. In 2013, the Nanning Municipal Government announced that the Luobo Temple Fair was inscribed on the Fifth Municipal List of Intangible Cultural Heritage. In 2014, with the consent of the People’s Government of Guangxi Zhuang Autonomous Region, the Luobo Temple Fair of the Zhuang Ethnic Group was inscribed on the Fifth Autonomous Region List of Intangible Cultural Heritage. At present, the temple of Luobo is well preserved, pilgrims continue visiting, and the temple fair is high-participated. It is moving from the hearts of the contemporary Zhuang people to the front stage, giving full play to its historical responsibility as a cultural heritage and the role of cultural reality.

千人宴
Thousands of People Banquet

壮族伏波庙会

Fubo Temple Fair of Zhuang Ethnic Group

项目名称：壮族伏波庙会

别称：无

分布范围：横州市云表镇

入选名录：2007年第一批自治区级非物质文化遗产名录

保护单位：横县文化馆

代表性传承人：无

Element name：Fubo Temple Fair of Zhuang Ethnic Group

Alternative name：None

Geographical location and range：Yunbiao Town of Hengzhou City

Element inscribed list：In 2007 on the First Autonomous Region List of Intangible Cultural Heritage

Competent body involved in safeguarding：Hengxian Cultural Centre

Representative inheritor：None

庙会现场
Scene of Temple Fair

祭拜
Worship

壮族伏波庙会又称伏波诞庙会，是盛行于珠江流域的广东、广西一带的融民间信仰、世俗性、群众性、娱乐性为一体的综合性民间民俗文化活动，其中以横州郁江的壮族伏波庙会历史最久、规模最大、影响最为深远。伏波庙会是当地群众为纪念东汉伏波将军马援南征交趾定疆界、平乱安民、疏河通航的功绩而形成的，于每年农历四月十四伏波诞日时举行。

伏波庙始建于东汉建宁三年（170），是为纪念东汉伏波将军马援平乱靖边的功绩而建，宋庆历年间以及明洪武、嘉靖年间，伏波庙屡次重修，现庙位于横州市云表镇站圩村东南3000米的郁江之乌蛮滩北岸。关于伏波庙会源于何时，目前尚无确切说法，只能从历代重修伏波庙的相关记载中初步推断伏波庙会理应与朝廷修建庙宇的历史同步。据清光绪十七年《大滩伏波庙碑记》记载，光绪帝曾于当年正月二十七日御赐“铜柱勋留”匾额一方，悬挂于伏波庙中，并将马伏波列入春秋祀典。因此，清朝末年之前，伏波庙一直属官民同祀，民国时取消官祀，伏波庙的祭祀活动转变成民间的自发性行为。

Fubo Temple Fair of the Zhuang Ethnic Group, also known as Fubo Temple Fair, is a diverse folk cultural activity that combines folk beliefs, secularity, popularity and entertainment in Guangdong and Guangxi, which is prevalent in the Pearl River Basin. Among them, Fubo Temple Fair of the Zhuang Ethnic Group in Yujiang, Hengxian has a longest history, the largest scale and the most profound impact. The Fubo Temple Fair was held every year on the 14th day of April in the lunar calendar—the birthday of General Fubo in the Eastern Han Dynasty to commemorate his achievements of guarding his country, suppressing the revolution and dredging the river.

The Fubo Temple in Hengzhou City was first built in the third year of Jianning in the Eastern Han Dynasty (170 A.D.) to commemorate General Fubo's contribution to suppressing the revolution of the borders. During the Qingli period of Song Dynosty and the Hongwu and Jiajing periods in the Ming Dynasty, Fubo Temple was rebuilt several times. The Temple is now located on the Northern Bank of Wumantan, 3000 meters southeast of Zhanwei Village in Yunbiao. As to when the Fubo Temple Fair originated, there is no definite statement at present. It can only be inferred from the relevant records of the restoration of Fubo Temple in the past dynasties that the Fubo Temple Fair should be synchronized with the history of the construction of temples by the court. According to the *Chronicle of Datan Fubo Temple*, Emperor Guangxu of the Qing Dynasty has bestowed a Plaque inscribed “Bronze Pillar Commeration of War” to Fubo Temple, and the general was included in the Sacrificial Rites of Spring and Autumn Period. Therefore, before the end of the Qing Dynasty, the Fubo Temple had been worshipped by both officials and the people. The official worship was abolished in the Republic of China, and the sacrificial activities of the Fubo Temple changed into the spontaneous behavior of the people.

There are many kinds of folk activities in Fubo Temple Fair of Zhuang Ethnic Group, and there are abundant folk culture and art programs. In summary, there are mainly worship ceremonies, celebration performances, folk activities, boat sacrifices, Taoism and witchcraft. The worship of General Fubo is the main content of Fubo Temple Fair. Local people not only respect Ma Yuan as a generation of warriors of peace and stability, Who is well-educated and trained in military exercised, but also regard Ma Yuan as a “Fubo God” who punishes the evil and restores peace to the people. Every April 14th of the lunar calendar, local people, especially fishermen, go to Fubo Temple to worship. One is to commemorate

General Fubo's efforts to suppress the revolution and open up the river for transportation. The other is to pray for General Fubo to protect peace and pray for blessings. Dragon dance, lion dance, phoenix dance and Kirin dance are the traditional programs of Fubo Temple Fair. During the temple fair, more than a dozen dragon, lion, Phoenix and Kirin performance teams gathered from Hengzhou City at Xiaoyi Town, Lingzhu Town, Lingshan County, Guigang City and Binyang County, and the scene was very lively. During the temple fair, folk singers from Hengzhou, Binyang, Lingshan, Guigang and other cities and counties flocked to sing on the evening of the 13th lunar calendar. When singing, male and female singers form groups of three or five, singing and answering each other. Performers would perform the Shigong opera. The content of the performance is mostly 24 fragments of filial piety stories. During the Fubo Temple Fair, large groups of Shigong drama troupes from Mashan, Baihe, Yunbiao, Xiaoyi and other towns in Hengzhou and Guigang City all came to Fubo Temple to perform, and it is a lively atmosphere. Since the abolition of official sacrifices in the Republic of China, the sacrificial activities of Fubo Temple have become spontaneous folk behavior. Among the folk sacrifices, Taoists and witches, the highest god of Taoism, Sanqing and Guan Shiyin, make an interesting scenery in temple fairs. Taoism practitioners did all kinds of performances, such as crossing the three-day gate, standing on knifves and so on. On the day of the temple fair, there was a surge of people, along with firecrackers, gongs and drums, dragons and lions, singing and singing. It was a huge festival.

In recent years, Hengzhou City Government has done a lot of research, rescue, inheritance and promotion of Fubo Temple Fair. As a heritage with a long history and rich cultural value, Fubo Temple Fair of the Zhuang Ethnic Group has a profound impact. Therefore, strengthening the construction of Fubo Temple and standardizing the management of Fubo Temple Fair are of great significance to the inheritance of it. In 2007, with the approval of the People's Government of Guangxi Zhuang Autonomous Region, the Fubo Temple Fair of the Zhuang Ethnic Group was inscribed on the First Autonomous Region List of Intangible Cultural Heritage.

壮族伏波庙会民俗活动种类繁多，民间文化艺术节目丰富，归结起来主要有祭拜仪式、庆典演出、民间活动、船祭、道巫法事等内容。祭拜伏波将军，是伏波庙会最主要的内容。当地百姓不仅把马援尊崇为安邦定国、文德武功的一代战将，而且把他当作降妖除魔、惩凶保平安、镇守恶滩的“伏波大神”。每到农历四月十四日，当地老百姓特别是船家渔民都前往伏波庙祭拜，一为纪念伏波将军平乱安民、疏河通航之功，二是祈求伏波将军神灵保护平安、逢凶化吉。舞龙、舞狮、舞凤、舞麒麟是伏波庙会的传统节目。庙会期间，十几个龙、狮、凤、麒麟表演队从横州校椅镇、灵竹镇、灵山县、贵港市、宾阳县等地聚集而来，场面非常热闹；横州、宾阳、灵山、贵港等市县的民歌歌手纷至沓来，于农历十三日晚进行对歌，男女歌手各自三五结队，形成若干对唱群，相互唱和或问答；横州马山、百合、云表、校椅等乡镇以及贵港市一些大型的师公戏班组都纷纷来到伏波庙开场演出，内容多为二十四孝故事片断，场面热闹非凡。自从民国取消官祀以来，伏波庙的祭祀活动变为民间的自发性行为。在民间祭祀中，有民间道家最高神“三清”和观世音的道公和女巫成为庙会活动中一支活跃的队伍。道公做各种法事，如过三天门、过刀山火炼等。庙会当日，人潮如涌，香烟缭绕，爆竹阵阵，锣鼓喧天，龙狮翻腾，歌声四起，热闹非凡，参与者众。

近年来，横州市党委、政府对伏波庙会做了许多发掘、抢救、继承和弘扬等工作。壮族伏波庙会作为历史悠久、文化价值丰厚的遗产，具有深远的影响。因此，加强伏波庙建设，规范伏波庙会的管理，对伏波庙会的传承具有深远意义。2007年，经广西壮族自治区人民政府同意，壮族伏波庙会列入第一批自治区级非物质文化遗产名录。

壮族安龙歌会

Anlong Folk Song Fair of Zhuang Ethnic Group

项目名称：壮族安龙歌会

别称：无

分布范围：南宁市、来宾市、贺州市及周边地区

入选名录：2014年第五批自治区级非物质文化遗产名录

保护单位：西乡塘区文化馆

代表性传承人：卢洪良

Element name：Anlong Folk Song Fair of Zhuang Ethnic Group

Alternative name：None

Geographical location and range：Nanning City, Laibin City, Hezhou City and the surrounding areas

Element inscribed list：In 2014 on the Fifth Autonomous Region List of Intangible Cultural Heritage

Competent body involved in safeguarding：Xixiangtang District Cultural Centre

Representitive inheritor：Lu Hongliang

The Anlong Folk Song Fair of the Zhuang Ethnic Group is a folk custom spread in Nanning, Laibin, Hezhou and other surrounding areas. It is a folk song festival that holds the Anlong ceremony usually took place when building houses, temples and ancestral houses.

The Anlong Folk Song Fair of the Zhuang Ethnic Group has a deep historical relation with the local religious sacrificial activities. The ancestors of the Zhuang Ethnic Group believed in "all things are spiritual and polytheistic". They believed in the Taoist gods of Sanqing and Sanyuan. With the increasing exchanges of cultures among different nationalities, the ancestors of the Zhuang Ethnic Group gradually accepted the concept of dragon worship on the basis of snake worship, and worshipped the Dragon God very piously, so the ceremony of "offering sacrifices to dragons" came into being. In the Zhuang Ethnic Group area, folk songs mostly appear in the sacrificial activities of greeting gods and entertaining gods. Such folk festivals including sacrifice ancestors, folk celebrations, folk disaster relief prayers, especially in the construction of ancestral temples and large houses, all must hold a solemn Anlong foundation-laying ceremony, that is, to place the five dragon gods in the building base, to guard the temple foundation, to protect the good fortune and safety of the people. In addition to the ritual ceremony, it often integrated folk songs to entertain the gods. After 1979, with the development of society, the Anlong Folk Song Fair will gradually develop from the initial parade to a folk activity that entertains both gods and people.

The Anlong Folk Song Fair mainly includes the Anlong Foundation Laying Ceremony and other celebration activities. Anlong sacrificial ceremony mainly includes the procedures of inviting masters, summoning dragons, singing praises, lining dragons and grand summons. The Taoist Open Altar invites masters and gods from all sides to be in place and invites gods to dance meritorious deeds in order to amuse gods. After that, all Taoists sat in front of the altar to praise the gods and dragons. Then the Taoist head master sings thanks and praises to the five parties respectively, inviting the dragon gods of all parties to return to their positions, and putting the gift of birth and gold and silver treasures into the earth caves of the five sides, and putting the grains with the seal of Fa Yin behind the altar to worship the dragon god. Then all the Taoists joined in singing "*Jielongke*" and began to line up the dragon. Finally, Taoist master would sing "*Zhaolongke*", and threw eggs in eight directions, blocking the evil spirit of the dragon god, so that the dragon god can be stabilized here. The pitch of the Anlong Folk Song Fair is mainly composed of three

对歌
Singing in Antiphonal Style

壮族安龙歌会是流传于南宁市、来宾市、贺州市及其周边地区的一项壮族民俗项目，它是在建造房屋、庙宇、祖屋时举行安龙仪式并聚会贺歌的一种民间歌会活动。

壮族安龙歌会与地方宗教祭祀活动有着深厚的历史渊源关系。壮族先民信仰“万物有灵，多神崇拜”，信奉道教神灵三清、三元。随着各民族文化的日益交流，壮族先民在蛇崇拜的基础上，逐渐接受了龙崇拜的观念，并对龙神的崇拜十分虔诚，于是产生了“祭龙”仪式。在壮族地区，山歌多出现在民间迎神娱神的祭祀活动中，如民间节日祭祀祖先、民间庆典、民间消灾祈福，尤其是建造祖庙、大型房舍时，都必须举行隆重的安龙奠基仪式，即把上天的五方龙神安置于建筑基地，以镇守庙基，保一方民众吉祥平安，除祭祀仪式外，还往往融入山歌娱神活动。1979年之后，随着社会的发展，安龙歌会由最初的歌颂神灵逐渐发展成为一种既娱神又娱人的民俗活动。

壮族安龙歌会主要包括安龙奠基祭祀仪式和贺歌活动。安龙祭祀仪式主要有安坛请师、招龙、唱赞词、接龙、大招等程序。由道公开坛请师，盛请各方神主到位，由师公跳功曹乐舞娱神。之后众道公坐于神坛前颂表，把各方龙神招回。接着道首分别向五方唱安谢赞词，请各方龙神归位，并将牲礼及金银财宝放入五方土穴，将加盖法印的五谷置于神坛后敬献龙神。接着众道公齐唱《接龙科》开始接龙。最后道首唱《招龙科》，并将鸡蛋投掷于八个方位，封住侵扰龙神的邪气，让龙神安稳于此。壮族安龙歌会的腔调主要由高腔、平腔、快腔三种组成。曲调以五声音阶作为调式基础，音程跨越9度，歌词多用五言四句，押腰韵。这种独特的演唱方式，具有很强的娱乐性和观赏性。通过祭龙，把上天五方龙神安置于建筑基地，以求风调雨顺、吉祥平安。贺歌活动是为增添安龙祭祀仪式的喜庆热闹氛围而举行的聚会赛歌形式，安龙期间，邻近的山歌手自行相邀歌友，在歌师带领下，以吉祥平安、招财进宝、人丁兴旺、富贵长寿的歌词唱入主人家祝贺道喜；主人家组成山歌队在门前迎接和答谢。来者以歌贺喜，迎者也以歌答谢。主客两队歌手一唱一和，天南地北、古今趣事，无所不唱、无所不答，形成一片热闹喜庆的赛歌庆典场面。

壮族安龙歌会经过不断的发展演变，现已发展成为一种既娱神又娱人的民间习俗活动，其浓郁的地方特色和宗教色彩，既保留壮族先民对原始图腾崇拜的痕迹，又饱含了人们祈求平安、五谷丰登的美好愿望，其丰富多彩的山歌文化，充分体现了壮族人民团结的精神风貌，是壮族传统文化的重要组成部分。2008年，西乡塘区政府组织开展了壮族安龙歌会的收集、整理工作，其中安龙高腔已编纂收入《中国民歌集成》。此后几年，西乡塘区政府不断划拨专项资金，用于扶持安龙歌会的开展。2014年，经广西壮族自治区人民政府同意，壮族安龙歌会列入第五批自治区级非物质文化遗产名录。

kinds: high-pitched, flat-pitched and fast-pitched. The tune is based on the pentatonic scale. The interval of the tune is over 9 degrees. The lyrics are mostly composed of five words and four sentences. It rhymes middle words. This unique singing format has a strong entertainment and ornamental function. By offering sacrifices to dragons, the five gods of dragons in heaven are placed in the building base in order to make the weather smooth, auspicious and safe. The celebration is a form of party song contest to increase the festive and lively atmosphere of the ceremony. During the fair, the neighboring mountain singers invited their friends to join the host's house to congratulate the homeowner with the lyrics of auspicious peace, wealth, prosperity and longevity. The home-owner would welcome and thank them at the door, while visitors would congratulate and greet the owner with songs. Host and guest singers sing in harmony with each other and form a festive festival of singing competitions.

After continuous development and evolution, the Anlong Folk Song Fair has become a folk custom activity that entertains both gods and people. Its rich local characteristics and religious elements not only retain the traces of the ancestral worship of the original totem, but also full of people's good wishes for peace and plentiful harvest. Culture, which fully reflects the spirit of unity of the Zhuang people, is an important part of the traditional culture. In 2008, the government of Xixiangtang District organized the collection and collation of the Anlong Folk Song Fair. Among them, Anlong high-pithed has compiled into the *Collection of Chinese Folk Songs*. In the following years, the Xixiangtang District Government continued to allocate special funds to support the development of the Anlong Folk Song Fair. In 2014, with the approval of the People's Government of Guangxi Zhuang Autonomous Region, the Anlong Folk Song Fair was inscribed on the Fifth Autonomous Region List of Intangible Cultural Heritage.

壮族“四月四”

The Lunar April Fourth Festival of Zhuang Ethnic Group

项目名称：壮族“四月四”

别称：壮族祈丰节、拜秧节、“四月四”祈丰节

分布范围：武鸣区马头镇敬三村及周边地区

入选名录：2014年第五批自治区级非物质文化遗产名录

保护单位：武鸣区文化馆

代表性传承人：韦文义

Element name：The Lunar April Fourth Festival of Zhuang Ethnic Group

Alternative name：Praying for Harvest Festival of Zhuang Ethnic Group, Rice Shoot Worship Festival, Praying for Harvest Festival on the Lunar April Fourth of Zhuang Ethnic Group

Geographical location and range：Jingsan Village of Matou Town in Wuming District and the surrounding areas

Element inscribed list：In 2014 on the Fifth Autonomous Region List of Intangible Cultural Heritage

Competent body involved in safeguarding：Wuming District Cultural Centre

Representative inheritor：Wei Wenyi

千人宴
Thousands of People Banquet

壮族祈丰节，又名拜秧节、“四月四”祈丰节，在农历四月初四举行，以南宁市武鸣区马头镇敬三村为中心，主要分布于敬三村周边各村屯，罗波镇天马村、石梁村，陆斡镇旧陆斡，两江镇环大明山一带，以及武鸣区其他少数民族区域。

壮族“四月四”活动流传于民间，具体起源时间已不可考。大明山地区为骆越古国最早的政治、经济、文化中心，是壮族方国最早所在地。武缘县是骆越人故地的中心区域，民风淳厚，虽历千百年岁月，却依然保存着骆越人的文化习俗。这里自古就有“三月三，龙拜山”的传说，每年三月初三，龙神都会到大明山顶祭扫母亲的墓，所到之处必有大风大雨，利于春耕。民间隆重的祭祀龙母大典也由此而来，后来演变成每年盛大的壮族祈丰节。

壮族“四月四”的主要内容有：请师公娱神祈丰祈福；祭拜骆越中府大王仪式；抬龙母巡村保佑仪式；祭田祭社仪式；舞水龙求雨祈福；洗牛感恩仪式，感恩牛一年来辛苦的

Praying for Harvest Festival of Zhuang Ethnic Group, also known as Rice Shoot Worship Festival or Praying for Harvest Festival on the Lunar April Fourth of Zhuang Ethnic Group, is held on the 4th day of the 4th lunar month. With Jingsan Village of Matou Town of Wuming District in Nanning of the Autonomous Region of Zhuang Ethnic Group as the centre, this festival is widely spreading in its surrounding villages, such as Tianma Village and Shiliang Village of Luobo Town, Jiuluwo Village of Luwo Town, surrounding areas of Daming Mountain of Liangjiang Town, Wuming District and some other settlements for minorities.

The Lunar April Fourth Festival of Zhuang Ethnic Group is popular among the people of Zhuang, but its origin time is hard to be traced. As the earliest political, economic and cultural centre of the ancient Luoyue state, the area around Daming Mountain is the earliest location of the state of Zhuang Ethnic Group. Wuyuan County is the central area of Luoyue people's hometown, where people were simple and honest. Although thousands of years have passed already, the culture and customs of Luoyue people have been preserved from generation to generation. Since the ancient times, the legend of "the dragon visiting its mother's grave on the 3rd day of the 3rd lunar month" had begun to prevail in this place. It is said that the Dragon God would come to Daming Mountain to commemorate his mother at the grave. At this time, the storm would burst in all its fury with lightning flashes and thunder rumbles, which would be beneficial to spring ploughing. The grand folk ceremony to worship Dragon Mother was also originated from this legend, which later evolved into the grand annual Praying for Harvest Festival of Zhuang Ethnic Group, which also known as the Lunar April Fourth Festival.

The major activities of the Lunar April Fourth Festival include inviting Taoist priests to worship gods and praying for harvest and happiness; worshiping the King of Luoyue State; carrying the Dragon Mother to tour in the village for blessing; worshiping the field and the state; performing water dragon dance to pray for rain; showering the cattle to thank its labor in the past year; holding coming-of-age ceremony for the young people of Zhuang Ethnic Group, worshiping the ancient tree under the leading of the elderly with high prestige in the clan and chanting the clan scriptures by the Taoist priest; transmitting the torch ignited by flint to light the bonfire; holding jubilant traditional song fairs with people of Zhuang Ethnic Group dancing, middle and aged people singing for fun and the young singing to express affection; performing Luodong dance; demonstrating traditional skills such as weaving straw shoes and strings, making five-color glutinous rice and brewing sweet glutinous rice wine; holding "multi-pot" banquet with thousands of people to taste delicious food and drink traditional wine of the Zhuang Ethnic Group; singing folk songs of Zhuang Ethnic Group so as to jointly enjoy the special grand Lunar April Fourth Festival of Zhuang Ethnic Group.

Praying for Harvest Festival of Zhuang Ethnic Group was originated from the ancient folk worship activity that prayed for harvest. Since 2010, organized by the village committee of the Jingsan Village of Matou County, the festival was finally named as Praying for Harvest Festival on the Lunar April Fourth. Since 2012, the government of Matou County began to hold this festival in Matou Community and has gradually increased the input toward folk activities. Various special facilities, venues and art teams for promoting folk culture development have been built today such as Bronze Drum Stage and Square in Jingsan Village, Jingsan Village Cultural Stage, Matou Luoyue Cultural Square and Luoyue Cultural Exhibition Hall, Corridor and Stage. In 2014, with the approval of the People's Government of the Guangxi Zhuang Autonomous Region, the Lunar April Fourth Festival of Zhuang Ethnic Group was inscribed on the Fifth Autonomous Region List of Intangible Cultural Heritage.

劳作；壮家后生行成人礼仪式，成年青年由族老引领祭古树，师公颂经，宣读祖传训言等；传递火种仪式，壮族人民有对火的崇拜习俗，用打火石引燃火把为火种，相继传递点燃篝火；举行传统的篝火夜歌圩，大家围着篝火喝酒，齐跳壮民族同乐舞，中老年人以歌取乐，年轻后生以歌传情或以歌择偶，热闹非凡通宵达旦；展演壮族骆垌舞，现场演示传承编织草鞋、草绳，制作五色糯米饭、特酿壮家老黄酒糯米甜酒等传统耕织技艺；举办千人"多锅"宴，饱尝壮家美食，畅饮壮家老酒；唱壮家山歌，对壮家情歌，同享壮族祈丰节特色民俗盛会。

壮族祈丰节原自发于民间古老传统的祈丰祭祀活动，2010年起由马头敬三村村委组织举办，并定名为"四月四"祈丰节，2012年开始由马头镇政府主办，在马头社区举行，并逐渐加大投入力度。现建有敬三村铜鼓舞台和广场、敬三村文化舞台、马头骆越文化广场、骆越文化展馆、长廊和舞台等专用设施、场地及艺术队等。2014年，经广西壮族自治区人民政府同意，壮族"四月四"列入第五批自治区级非物质文化遗产名录。

篝火晚会
Campfire Party

求雨仪式
Rain Seeking Ceremony

壮族芒那节

Mangna Festival of Zhuang Ethnic Group

项目名称：壮族芒那节

别称：稻神祭

分布范围：以隆安县为中心，波及左右江三角洲地带

入选名录：2010年第三批自治区级非物质文化遗产名录

保护单位：隆安县文化馆

代表性传承人：无

Element name：Mangna Festival of Zhuang Ethnic Group

Alternative name：Ritual of Rice God

Geographical location and range：Long'an County as the centre, spreading over the delta of Zuojiang River and Youjiang River

Element inscribed list：In 2010 on the Third Autonomous Region List of Intangible Cultural Heritage

Competent body involved in safeguarding：Long'an County Cultural Centre

Representative inheritor：None

Mangna Festival of Zhuang Ethnic Group, a special cultural folk festival of Long'an County, is often held on the 6th day of the 6th lunar month. It originates from the Rice God worshiping activity of ancient Luoyue people of the Zhuang Ethnic Group, and it is an important part of sacrificial ceremony for Rice God.

Long'an Mangna Festival is a worship activity created by Zhuang people of southwest Guangxi in the long-time farming and rice planting activities, which represents strong local characteristics of god worship. It involves various fields such as history, religion, folk customs, art, commerce and some other cultural fields. There is a legend related to the origin of Mangna Festival in Long'an County. It is said that the Zhuang ancestors in ancient times lived on wild fruit and sometimes the fruit was insufficient for them to fill the belly. Then King Ya (a goddess of Zhuang Ethnic Group) brought about yellow-colored rice seeds and taught people how to plant and harvest. To express their gratitude toward King Ya, people of Zhuang Ethnic Group honored King Ya as the "Rice God" or the "Great King" in some places, and built temples for her. People of Zhuang Ethnic Group also regarded the birthday of King Ya, the 6th day of the 6th lunar month, as the birthday of rice so as to hold sacrificial ceremony on this day. In *the Records of Long'an County, the Records of Wuming County and the Records of Pingguo County*, there are relevant records of Mangna Festival of Zhuang Ethnic Group, which indicate that this festival has had a long history and spread over a very wide range.

On Mangna Festival, every family in the village will hold the activity to worship Rice God and pray for harvest. People will also invite friends to their families, which will create a jubilant scene. The major sites for sacrificial activities include Bolang Village, Ruhao Village and some others that were densely covered by the Dashichan sacrificial ruins. The worship activity toward Rice God is rooted in the Dashichan sacrificial activities with long history and profound cultural connotation, which is a precious intangible cultural heritage of the Autonomous Region of the Zhuang Ethnic Group. People in Bolang Village, the major sacrificial site, will hold the traditional worship activity for Rice God on Niaotian ruins. People will stick the thatched javelin in their own fields and invite Taoist priests to perform inviting Rice God, calling back the spirit of the Rice God and expelling the evil spirit of the field. With the characteristics of local original and ecological "Na" culture, the performance of the "Rice God worship activity" in Long'an County is a breathtaking experience for the visitors. Coupled with Luodong dance of Na culture,

田间祭祀
Sacrifice in the Field

农历六月初六，是隆安县独具文化特色的民间节庆“芒那节”。芒那节源于壮族先民古骆越人的稻神祭活动，是稻神祭中的一个重要组成部分。

隆安壮族芒那节是桂西南壮族人民在长期的农耕生活和稻作习俗中形成的以娱神为内容的带有浓郁地方特色的祭祀活动，含有历史、民俗、艺术、商贸等诸多文化内容。在隆安当地，流传着芒那节起源的传说：远古壮族先民以野果为生，常常食不果腹。娅王就给人们送来了黄澄澄的稻种，并教人们种植和收割水稻的技术。为了感谢娅王，人们把娅王尊为“稻神”，有些地方尊为“大王”，还为她立了大王庙，并将她的生日六月初六作为水稻的诞生日，每年在这一天进行祭祀。《隆安县志》《武鸣县志》《平果县志》中，都有关于壮族芒那节的记载，说明其不仅历史悠久，而且范围非常广泛。

壮族芒那节当天，各村的各家各户都要举行祭稻神祈丰收活动，并且广邀亲朋好友前来做客，活动场面既热闹又隆重。这一主祭祀活动在大石铲祭祀遗址密布的博浪、儒浩等村屯举办。稻神祭根植于大石铲祭祀，历史悠久，文化内涵深厚，是隆安县和广西壮族自治区珍贵的非物质文化遗产。作为“稻神祭”活动主祭区的博浪村群众在“鸟田”遗址举行传统的稻神祭仪式，由各家在自己的田里插上茅草标并举行祭稻神仪式，师公班师公则在大祭坛演示传统的请稻神、招稻魂、驱田鬼仪式，“稻神祭”活动以其当地原生态的“那”文化祭祀习俗遗存表演让现场游客叹为观止。在该县乔建镇博浪村博浪小学舞台上表演传统的“那”文化遗产壮族骆垌舞与“娅王赐福”舞，以及天琴、葫芦丝等骆越古乐器演奏及民歌演唱，则让慕名而来的游客领略到了原汁原味的古典“那”文化艺术。

除了求雨，壮族芒那节活动还包括“祭农具”、六月初六“招稻魂”“驱田鬼”“请娅王”、七月二十“祭姆王”等六大活动。整个祭祀活动以六月初六的“招稻魂”“驱田鬼”“请娅王”最为热烈、隆重，是整个壮族芒那节的核心。一系列稻作祭祀活动，从农历四月初八开始，至七月二十结束。近年来，壮族芒那节期间，除了举办传统的祭祀活动外，还增加了“百家宴”活动，六月初六，主要的祭祀仪式结束后，全村上下拖家带口来参加百家宴。酒足饭饱后，由村民集资请来的各种文艺团体开始表演，以粤剧、壮剧、舞狮和山歌对唱为主，还有猜谜语、打篮球等群众喜闻乐见的文体活动。

隆安壮族芒那节对于研究我国桂西南壮民族的历史、经济、文化等都具有重要的历史价值以及深远的民族学、民俗学价值。壮族芒那节中所表演的师公舞蹈和师公配乐以及服饰，具有完善而独特的艺术价值。2010年，经广西壮族自治区人民政府同意，壮族芒那节列入第三批自治区级非物质文化遗产名录。

the performance of “King Ya’s Blessing”, the traditional instrument performance of Tian zither (an instrument of Zhuang Ethnic Group) and cucurbit flute and folk song singing on the stage of Bolang Primary School in Bolang Village, the visitors who are attracted to come here can get an opportunity to have a taste of the original and classical “Na” culture and art.

In addition to praying for rain, the complete activities of Mangna Festival include three activities on the 6th day of the 6th lunar month, “offering agricultural tools”, “calling back the spirit of the Rice God” and “expelling the evil spirit of the field”, and one activity of “offering King Mu” on the 7th day of the 7th lunar month. Among the whole sacrificial activity, the three rituals, “offering agricultural tools”, “calling back the spirit of the Rice God” and “expelling the evil spirit of the field”, are the most boisterous and grand ones, which jointly form the core of Mangna Festival. A series of rice worshiping ceremonies often begin from the lunar April 8th and end by the lunar July 20th. Besides the traditional sacrificial activities, “Hundred-Family Banquet” has also been added to Mangna Festival in recent years. On the lunar June 6th, families in the village will attend the banquet after the sacrificial activities. After the banquet, various kinds of groups invited by the villagers will perform Cantonese opera, Zhuang opera, lion dance and folk song singing. Many activities loved by people such as guessing riddles and playing basketball will also be held.

Long’an Mangna Festival of Zhuang Ethnic Group has important historical value, and far-reaching ethnology and folklore value for studying the history, economy and culture of the Zhuang Ethnic Group in southwest Guangxi. The music and costumes of Shigong dance that performed on the festival also bear comprehensive and unique artistic value. In 2010, with the approval of the People’s Government of the Guangxi Zhuang Autonomous Region, Long’an Mangna Festival of Zhuang Ethnic Group was inscribed on the Third Autonomous Region List of Intangible Cultural Heritage.

壮族亥日

Hai Day of Zhuang Ethnic Group

项目名称：壮族亥日

别称：无

分布范围：隆安县南圩镇

入选名录：2010年第三批自治区级非物质文化遗产名录

保护单位：隆安县文化馆

代表性传承人：无

Element name：Hai Day of Zhuang Ethnic Group

Alternative name：None

Geographical location and range：Nanxu Town of Long'an County

Element inscribed list：In 2010 on the Third Autonomous Region List of Intangible Cultural Heritage

Competent body involved in safeguarding：Long'an County Cultural Centre

Representative inheritor：None

隆安县南圩镇壮族“亥日”是西南地区较大的牲畜交易圩场，它是在长期的农耕生活中形成的以猪、牛、马等牲畜交易为主的传统大圩日，是隆安县独特的地理环境造就的习俗活动。因其以天干地支计算而定，以12天为期，故俗称“亥日”，距今已有300多年的历史。每到“亥日”，除本县各乡镇群众赶集外，邻近县如平果、田东、田阳、那坡、靖西、德保、云南、大新、武鸣均有客商来赶集，批发、购买产品，远至广东、云南、贵州，甚至越南、泰国也常有人往来做生意。

隆安县南圩镇位于县城南面，故名南圩。据《隆安县志》记载，早在明清时，南圩镇就是当地的主要圩市之一，与其他圩市一样每三天为一圩日，后来形成了每隔12天为一大圩的“亥日”。亥日的商贸极为活跃，上市物品繁多，尤其是猪、马、牛、羊、农具、嫁妆等，各类禽畜物品交易划定区域，如生活用品在圩的中部，农具、嫁妆类位于圩的北部，禽畜交易在圩场的南部，逐步演变成为桂西南最大的禽畜专业交易市场之一。

每到壮族亥日，四面八方赶来的猪牛交易者集中在南圩镇。和一般的日常交易市场不同的是，“亥日”里牛的交易不用称，大家公开评估、按膘论价，买卖双方全凭眼力进行挑选和评估，判断牛的年龄、重量，皮多大，值多少钱，瘦肉多还是肥肉多，甚至还能判断出牛的脾气、性格、干活的力气等。随着交易量的增加，南圩镇慢慢发展成为隆安县及周边地区以牲畜交易为主的传统圩场，交易的商品也逐渐扩大，除了牲畜外，还包括水果、日用品、生产资料以及铁具、竹具、木具等农具产品。

壮族亥日期间，还举行相关的种牛比赛和斗羊、斗狗活动，以及唱戏等文体活动、技能比赛。种牛比赛，就是从各地选送的种牛通过斗牛决出冠军，对主人进行嘉奖。每届种牛比赛，武鸣、天等、平果、扶绥、大新、百色、南宁等

The “Hai Day” fair of Nanxu Town of Long’an County is a relatively large fair for livestock transaction in southwest China. The Hai Day is a traditional date for domestic animal transaction such as pig, cattle and horse which was created during people’s long-time farming life. It is also a custom formed by the unique geographical environment of Long’an County. Because it is calculated by Heavenly Stems and Earthly Branches (Chinese era), thus the fair is held every twelve days and gets the name of “Hai Day” (“Hai” is the twelfth as well as the last one of Earthly Branches). The Hai Day Fair has a long history of over 300 years. On Hai day, in addition to the villagers of Long’an County, people from neighboring counties, provinces and even countries such as Pingguo, Tiandong, Tianyang, Napo, Jingxi, Debao, Daxin, Wuming, Guangdong province, Yunnan province, Guizhou province and even Vietnam and Thailand will also come to the fair to wholesale and purchase goods.

Nanxu Town is located in the south of Long’an County, thus it is named as Nanxu, which means the fair in the south. According to the *Records of Long’an County*, Nanxu town had become one of the major fairs in Long’an County as early as in the Ming and Qing dynasties. At that time, it was same as other fairs that were held every three days. Later, it gradually developed into a big fair held every twelve days. The commercial and trade activities on Hai Day Fair are very active. The fair involves various kinds of goods, especially pig, horse, cattle, goat, agricultural tools and trousseau. Each kind of goods are sold in particular areas. For example, the articles of daily use are in the middle, the trousseau and agricultural tools are in the north and the transaction area of livestock is in the south of the fair. The Hai Day Fair has been gradually evolved into the largest special market of livestock transaction in southeast Guangxi.

On the Hai Day, the traders from all direction will come to Nanxu Town to sell their pigs and cattle. Different from the common fairs, the transaction of pigs and cattle on Hai day Fair need not to be weighed by scales. The price of pigs and cattle will just be determined by public evaluation and according to the fat. The sellers and the buyers will select and calculate the price by their eyes and experience. They need to figure out the age, weight, the size of the skin, the price and the proportion of the fat meat and lean meat of the pigs and cattle. They may even know the temper, character and strength of the pigs and cattle. With the increase of trading volume, Nanxu town has gradually developed into a traditional fair mainly dealing with livestock in Long’an County and surrounding areas. The kinds of commodities traded here have also been gradually enriched, including fruits, daily necessities, means of production, iron tools, bamboo tools, wooden tools and other agricultural tools.

During the Hai Day, various of cultural and sports activities and skill competitions will also be held, such as bullfight, goat fight, dog fight and traditional opera performances. In the bullfight, the bull kept for covering selected from neighboring areas will be sent to the competition and the champion bull will be determined through bullfight. The owner of the champion bull will also be awarded. The cattle traders from Wuming, Tiandeng, Pingguo, Fusui, Daxin, Baise, Nanning and other places will come to attend the competition with their cattle every year. In addition to bullfight, there are also goat fight competition and dog fight competition, which aim to heighten the atmosphere of "Hai Day", expand the trading volume and the fair's influence. Another aim of these activities is to praise excellent livestock and their breeders, so that people can better understand the livestock market and breeding methods. People will also jointly invite professional troupes from other counties or the local troupes to perform on "Hai Day". However, due to the expensive transportation fees, the trade volume of Hai Day Fair in Nanxu Town is declining compared with previous years.

The Hai Day Fair is a unique livestock fair of Long'an County, which plays an important role in promoting the local economic development. Therefore, it is necessary to explore and protect Hai Day Fair of Zhuang Ethnic Group. In recent years, the local government has taken a series of measures to protect this custom, including inviting folklore professionals to research this custom and make clear its history. At the same time, the government has also strengthened the safety maintenance work of the fair, issued subsidies to the farmers, provided livestock, expanded the scale of the fair and improved the turnover, etc. At present, the scale of Hai Day has been increasingly larger and the fair has made great contributions to the local economy. In 2010, with the approval of the People's Government of the Guangxi Zhuang Autonomous Region, the Hai Day of Zhuang Ethnic Group was inscribed on the Third Autonomous Region List of Intangible Cultural Heritage.

地的牛贩都会赶来参加。除了种牛比赛，还有斗羊、斗狗活动，活动的目的一是为了增加“亥日”的热闹气氛，扩大“亥日”的交易量、影响力，二是为了对优秀的牲畜及其饲养人进行褒奖，让人们更加了解牲畜的行情及饲养方法。在“亥日”里，大家还会自发组织起来，邀请外地的专业剧团前来演出，有时也请当地的戏班演出。南圩镇的壮族亥日贸易较之往年有所下滑，原因在于货源运输成本昂贵。

壮族亥日是隆安县的特色牲畜圩场，为促进当地经济的发展发挥了重要作用，挖掘和保护壮族亥日十分必要。近年来，当地政府采取了一系列措施，邀请民俗专家进行研究，摸清了壮族亥日的历史沿革；同时做好圩场的安全维护工作，为养殖户发放补贴，进一步扩大养殖业，扩大南圩亥日的规模和成交量等。目前，壮族亥日的规模越来越大，为当地经济的发展做出了重要贡献。2010年，经广西壮族自治区人民政府同意，壮族亥日列入第三批自治区级非物质文化遗产名录。

牲畜交易市场
Livestock Market

壮族添粮补寿习俗

Custom of Supplementing Food and Life of Zhuang Ethnic Group

项目名称：壮族添粮补寿习俗

别称：无

分布范围：兴宁区三塘镇那安村、马山县

入选名录：2016年第六批自治区级非物质文化遗产名录

2015年第六批市级非物质文化遗产名录

保护单位：兴宁区文化馆

代表性传承人：蒙德祺

Element name：Custom of Supplementing Food and Life of Zhuang Ethnic Group

Alternative name：None

Geographical location and range：Na'an Village of Santang Town in Xingning District, Mashan County

Element inscribed list：In 2016 on the Sixth Autonomous Region List of Intangible Cultural Heritage

In 2015 on the Sixth Municipal List of Intangible Cultural Heritage

Competent body involved in safeguarding：Xingning District Cultural Centre

Representative inheritor：Meng Deqi

南宁市三塘镇添粮补寿仪式相关制品
Products Related to the Ceremony of Adding Grain and Replenishing Life in Santang Town, Nanning

添粮补寿是南宁市具有民族特色和地方特色的壮族传统习俗，流传于南宁市兴宁区及马山县。凡年过六十花甲的老人，家中子孙便为其立一个寿粮缸。此缸置于老人床头，可装10多斤米。立缸时，子孙们每人都往缸中倒入上等好米，装满为止。缸中寿米平常不吃，只是老人遇身心不适时才煮些吃，但切忌将米吃完。每年重阳节，子孙们都要给老人补满粮缸。

壮族添粮补寿的习俗，是壮族原始宗教观念在生活中的反映。壮族先民认为人的生命与稻米密切相关，老人生病了就要举办添粮补寿仪式，用稻米的元气补充人的元气，人才能健康长寿。这一习俗是稻作起源地补寿习俗的“谪传”，保留了许多原生态的文化信息，并且融入了汉族戏剧程式化的元素，因此弥足珍贵。

壮族添粮祝寿仪式分为点炮、请寿星上座、持红、唱祝寿歌、添粮、拜寿、敬酒、送红包、唱十保歌等程序，其中添粮是中心环节。添粮时要在寿星面前摆出一个小米缸，要向一小米缸添加九斤九两米，以表示阳寿久久。十保歌的

Adding rice into rice jar to symbolize longevity of the elderly is a traditional custom of Zhuang Ethnic Group with distinctive local and ethnic characteristics in Nanning, which is popular in Xingning District and Mashan County. When a person is over sixty years old, his or her children will place a rice jar, which can contain over 5 kilograms rice, at the head of the old person's bed. When the jar is set up, each of his or her children will pour the best rice into the jar until it is full. The rice in the jar will only be eaten when the elderly is under the weather and it is a taboo to eat out all the rice in the jar because rice symbolizes the life of the elderly. On the Double Ninth Day every year, the elderly's children will add rice to the jar until it is full.

The custom of adding rice to symbolize longevity of the elderly reflects the impact of primitive religious idea in Zhuang people's daily life. The ancestor of Zhuang Ethnic Group believed that there is a close relation between rice and people's life. When a person is getting old or ill, the rite of adding rice to prolong life should be held for him or her, because people believe that rice can help the person regain strength and vitality so that he or she can have a long life. This custom has been passed down from generation to generation, which still maintains many original cultural information and also incorporates the stylized elements of the opera of Han Ethnic Group, thus it is very precious.

The process of the rite of adding rice to symbolize

内容是：一保种田多得谷，二保生意多赚钱，三保房中添贵子，四保四季得发财，五保五福临门口，六保六畜满笼边，七保七子团圆好，八保老人寿百年，九保全家平安好，十保十足十齐全。

给老人“补粮”，不仅是晚辈从物质上关心长辈，更重要的是给老人精神上的安慰，实质上起到了精神疗法的作用。“补粮”习俗是壮民族民俗文化与现代文明中多元而丰富的精神生活和谐相融的体现，这些原生态的民俗文化渗透到人们的生活当中，成为不可或缺的精神食粮。壮族添粮补寿习俗是壮族珍贵的非物质文化遗产，也是壮族民族风情中一道独特的长寿文化风景线。

在快速城镇化的影响下，壮族添粮补寿习俗也受到冲击，参与人数日趋减少。目前，南宁市兴宁区文化馆正积极启动切实可行的保护计划，全面开展文化普查和保护传承工作，同时也确定了习俗的传承人，以保障壮族添粮补寿习俗后继有人。2015年，壮族添粮补寿习俗列入第六批市级非物质文化遗产名录。

南宁市三塘镇添粮补寿仪式歌本
Song Script of the Ceremony of Replenishing Grain and Longevity in Santang Town, Nanning City

longevity include shooting off fireworks, inviting the old man, draping over red cloth on the elderly's shoulder, singing song of birthday congratulation, adding rice, offer birthday felicitations, toasting, offering red packet and singing Song of Ten Blessings, among which adding rice is the most important process. In the process of adding rice, a small rice jar will be held in front of the elderly and people need to add nine jin (a Chinese weight unit, which equals to 500 grams) and another nine liang (a Chinese weight unit, which equals to 50 grams) into the jar to symbolize a long life because the pronunciation of "nine" is same as the pronunciation of "long" in Chinese. The content of Song of Ten Blessings mainly includes ten kinds of blessings: the first is to bless bumper harvest; the second is to bless making money from business; the third is to bless a newborn in family; the fourth is to bless fortune for a year; the fifth is to bless good descending upon the house; the sixth is to bless thriving domestic animals; the seventh is to bless family reunion; the eighth is to bless longevity of the elder; the ninth is to bless safeness of the family and the tenth is to bless that all the wishes mentioned above can come true.

To add rice for the elderly is not only to care for the elderly materially, but also to give the elderly spiritual comfort, which in essence plays an important role in psychotherapy. The custom of adding rice to symbolize longevity is the embodiment of the harmonious integration of the folk culture of Zhuang Ethnic Group and the diversified and rich spiritual life in modern civilization. This original folk culture has permeated into people's life and became an indispensable part of people's spiritual nourishment. The custom of adding rice to symbolize longevity is not only a precious intangible cultural heritage, but also a unique part of longevity culture of Zhuang Ethnic Group.

With the impact of rapid urbanization, the custom of adding rice to symbolize longevity has also been affected and the number of people who conduct this custom is decreasing. At present, Xingning District Cultural Centre is actively launching feasible protection plans and implementing comprehensive cultural investigation, protection and inheritance work. At the same time, the inheritors of this cultural heritage have been determined to ensure the continuity of the custom. In 2015, the custom of adding rice to symbolize longevity was inscribed on the Sixth Municipal List of Intangible Cultural Heritage.

南宁元宵花灯节

Nanning Lantern Festival

项目名称：南宁元宵花灯节

别称：元宵闹花灯

分布范围：南宁市城区及周边地区

入选名录：2014年第五批自治区级非物质文化遗产名录

保护单位：江南区文化馆

代表性传承人：黎炳生

Element name：Nanning Lantern Festival

Alternative name：Lantern Performance on the Lantern Festival

Geographical location and range：Urban areas of Nanning City and the surrounding areas

Element inscribed list：In 2014 on the Fifth Autonomous Region List of Intangible Cultural Heritage

Competent body involved in safeguarding：Jiangnan District Cultural Centre

Representative inheritor：Li Bingsheng

赏花灯
Enjoy Lanterns

元宵节是中国乃至汉字文化圈地区和海外华人的传统节日之一，又称上元节、元夕或灯节，相传起源于2000多年前的汉文帝时期。南宁元宵花灯节原称元宵闹花灯，是南宁市在正月十五元宵节期间所举行的民俗活动。其内容非常丰富，主要包括制作花灯、展示花灯、猜灯谜、吃汤圆、舞龙舞狮、歌舞表演等。

南宁元宵花灯节广泛流行于南宁市城区及周边地区，以江南区菠萝岭、石柱子岭、五一路以及兴宁区的水街、解放路、人民路、中山路、新华路一带最为盛行。南宁元宵闹花灯习俗是传统元宵节习俗的衍生，其起源已不可考，据花灯制作传承人黎炳生介绍，南宁元宵闹花灯习俗在清朝中叶就已经盛行，至少有近200年的历史了。该习俗在20世纪60年代至70年代中期曾中止过一段时间，随后得以恢复，20世纪90年代正式更名为南宁元宵花灯节。

为迎接元宵花灯节，当地居民往往在春节前后就开始进行花灯的制作，一人一盏，同时还有多制作一盏寓意添丁的“余灯”，并于农历正月十五时将自家制作好的花灯挂到

The Lantern Festival is one of the traditional festivals of China and even among Chinese cultural circles and overseas Chinese. It is also known as Shangyuan Festival, Yuanxi or Festival of Lanterns. It is said that the Lantern Festival was originated from the reign of Emperor Wen of the Han Dynasty over 2000 years ago. Nanning Lantern Festival was originally named as Lantern Performance on the Lantern Festival, which was a traditional folk event held in Nanning on the 15th day of the 1st lunar month. This festival includes various activities, such as lantern making, lantern displaying, riddle guessing, eating sweet dumplings, dragon and lion dance performances and other singing and dancing performances.

Nanning Lantern Festival is widely spread over Nanning and its surrounding areas. It is particularly popular in Boluo Ridge Community, Shizhuzi Community and Wuyi Road of Jiangnan District and Shuijie Street, Jiefang Road, Renmin Road, Zhongshan Road and Xinhua Road of Xingning District. The custom of Lantern performance on the Lantern Festival was derived from the traditional Lantern Festival, whose origin is hard to be traced. According to the introduction of Li Bingsheng, the inheritor of lantern making, the custom of lantern performance on the Lantern Festival had already been prevailing in the middle period of the Qing Dynasty with a history of not less than 200 years. From the 1960s to the middle 1970s, this custom was once suspended for a time and then restored. In the 1990s, it was officially renamed as Nanning Lantern Festival.

In order to welcome the Lantern Festival, the locals often start to make lanterns since the Spring Festival. Each of the residents usually owns one lantern. Meanwhile, people will also make an “extra lantern” to symbolize having a baby born into the family. These lanterns will be hung at the doors and on the side of the roads. At about seven o’clock in the evening of the Lantern Festival, one of the elders with high prestige of the community or subdistrict will light on the lantern personally. In the past, pine oil was often used to light on lanterns while electricity has replaced it nowadays. The lanterns of Nanning Lantern Festival have a lot of varieties, including traditional lantern, lotus lantern, pomegranate lantern and string lantern. They also have various shapes such as twelve Chinese zodiac signs, cartoon image, birds and beasts. All of these kinds of lanterns are dazzling with diversified shapes, which bear strong interestingness and artistry.

With a long history, Nanning Lantern Festival bears profound cultural deposits. This festival was initially a folk custom praying for happiness and blessing for people, which carried Nanning people’s good wishes for happy life and grand-generativity. The Nanning Lantern Festival is dominated by lanterns and accompanied by a variety of cultural activities. Each of these activities has been endowed with different cultural connotations, which can satisfy various spiritual and cultural needs of people. The lanterns used for Nanning Lantern Festival are mostly made by bamboo skin with various shapes and colors. They are a kind of handicrafts integrating various skills such as painting, paper-cutting, pasting, weaving and shaping. With constant changes and innovations, the lantern of Nanning Lantern Festival has become an effective channel to understand and study the economy, politics and culture in different historical periods of Nanning. In addition, people, both old and young, will go out to view lanterns, guess riddles and watch performances on every Lantern Festival, which has greatly promoted the communication between people.

Since the resumption of Nanning Lantern Festival, the government of Nanning and the government of Jiangnan District have attached great importance to this traditional custom. Since 1991, the government of Jiangnan District has begun to give certain support to Nanning Lantern Festival each year and has gradually expanded the scale of the activities of the festival. Over the past 20 years, Nanning Lantern Festival has attracted over 80,000 to 100,000 visitors each year coming to view the lanterns, which has become an influential folk event in Nanning. At the same time, to actively respond to the implementation of the National Intangible Cultural Heritage Policy of China, the government has also organized the group for intangible cultural heritage exploration so as to make in-depth understanding, comprehensive investigation and clear file tidying, initially establishing the inheritance system. Jiangnan District Cultural Centre has supported the old artists to hold lantern-making class in Primary School of Boluo Ridge Community in Jiangnan District regularly so that the skill of lantern making can be passed down continuously.

家门口和路边。在元宵节傍晚七点左右，由社区或街道的一位长老亲自点灯，以前大多以松油为点灯的燃料，近些年主要用电来操作。南宁花灯种类繁多，一般有传统宫灯、莲花灯、石榴灯、串联灯，也有十二生肖、卡通形象、飞禽走兽等造型的花灯，各种造型流光溢彩，绚丽夺目，具有较强的趣味性和艺术性。

南宁元宵花灯节历史悠久，蕴含着深厚的文化底蕴。南宁花灯节最初是一项百姓祈福的民间习俗，承载着南宁市民对于美好生活的向往与对惬意人生、子孙满堂的美好愿望。南宁花灯节以花灯为主导，并伴有多种文艺活动，每项活动都被赋予了不同的文化内涵，能够满足人民大众多样的精神文化需求。南宁元宵花灯节所使用的花灯大多采用竹篾扎制，造型丰富，色彩艳丽，是集绘画、剪纸、裱糊、编织、造型等技艺于一体的综合性、纯手工工艺品。它不断变化创新，是了解和研究南宁市各个历史时期的经济、政治和文化的一种有效渠道。此外，每到元宵花灯节，人们扶老携幼，赏花灯、猜灯谜、看演出，增进了人与人之间的感情。

自南宁花灯节重新恢复之后，南宁市政府和江南区政府便对这一传统民俗活动非常重视。1991年起，江南区政府每年对元宵节花灯会给予一定的扶持，不断扩大元宵花灯会活动的规模。20多年来，每年吸引观灯群众达8—10万人次，使其成为南宁市较有影响力的传统民俗活动。与此同时，江南区政府积极响应国家非物质文化遗产政策，组织非物质文化遗产普查小组，深入了解、全面普查，将相关普查资料做了整理归档，初步建立了传承机制。江南区文化馆扶持老艺人定期到江南区菠萝岭小学举办花灯制作兴趣班，培养青少年对花灯制作的兴趣，传承花灯制作技艺。

马形灯
Horse-like Lantern

南宁土地诞

Nanning Land God Birthday Celebration

项目名称：南宁土地诞

别称：无

分布范围：南宁市各区县，辐射广西壮族自治区各地

入选名录：2014年第五批自治区级非物质文化遗产名录

保护单位：南宁市民族文化艺术研究院（南宁市非物质文化遗产保护中心）

代表性传承人：莫若珍

Element name：Nanning Land God Birthday Celebration

Alternative name：None

Geographical location and range：All districts and counties of Nanning City, spreading to other places of Guangxi Zhuang Autonomous Region

Element inscribed list：In 2014 on the Fifth Autonomous Region List of Intangible Cultural Heritage

Competent body involved in safeguarding：Nanning Ethnic Culture and Art Research Institute (Nanning Intangible Cultural Heritage Protection Centre)

Representative inheritor：Mo Ruozhen

Land God Birthday in Nanning, commonly known as "Land Festival" or "Dragon-head-up Festival", is a festival held every year on the second day of February in the lunar calendar, celebrating the birthday of Fude, the God of Land in Chinese folklore. It is said that Fude is a god helping guard people's home and keep evil spirits outside and bless people with a thriving business as well. Most of the celebrating activities for the festival are spontaneously organized by villagers. Traditionally, actors acting Daogong and Shigong would be invited by the head of the village for the activity, also the sacrifice (pigs, sheep and cows) would be prepared for worshipping the God of Land. Folklore activities, such as convening actors, sending invitations to Tangma, temple cleaning by temple attendant, bridging for saints and religious performance, would be carried out to express people's wishes for disaster repelling and happiness recruiting. In addition, other recreational activities are also popular in some places including basketball matches, singing and dancing parties, tea-picking operas, folk songs, music with eight pitches, dragon and lion dance.

As a folk custom with distinctive features, Land God Birthday has a profound cultural civilization throughout its long history. It mainly distributes in counties of Nanning, and it could also be found in other cities of Guangxi. There are a few circulating legend about the god of land though the actual original time of the custom remains unknown. One of the legends says that a long time ago there was an official named Zhang Fude who was responsible for tax revenue in the city. He was kind and honest, and loved the people in the city. If a villager failed to pay taxes due to poor turnover, he would be lenient with the former, and even for farmers who were unable to pay taxes, he would pay subsidies himself. Whenever the people encountered difficulties, he would try his best to help them with no hesitation. But after his death, a new tax officer, totally different from Fude, was very strict with the people and made them live in an abyss of misery. People had no choice but to erect ancestral halls to worship Fude and his wife, that was, the hall we called "Fude hall", and he was honored as "God Fude".

Nanning Land God Birthday Celebration is rooted in the local land worship, which is the reflection of rice-cultivating culture. The god of land was regarded as a patron saint of peace and wealthy life for Nanning ancestors. All good wish for a better life, such as a thriving business, flourishing livestock and bumper harvest, is expected to come true through worshipping the god of land. The god of land has a wide range of popularity and mystery that fully displayed in lore about it. People of all nationalities will go to the Land Temple

南宁土地诞，俗称“土地节”或“龙抬头”，是纪念土地公福德正神的节日，于每年农历二月初二举行。土地公的职责是驻守屋外，阻挡邪灵进入屋内，负责保护家宅平安。此外，他还可以招财进宝，因此也有“门口土地财神”之称。南宁传统土地诞多由村民自发组织集资筹办，由村里的会首统一安排相关人员，按照传统的习惯聘请当地的道公、师公数人，准备三牲祭拜，恭请土地公。随之进行安旗召集兵马、报唐马送请柬、庙祝扫楼、架桥请圣、过火炼以及表达消灾纳福之愿的满散等民俗活动。此外，有些地方也会举办一些文娱活动，如篮球赛、歌舞晚会、扮演采茶戏、山歌对唱、八音齐奏、舞龙舞狮等。

南宁土地诞作为南宁的特色民俗活动，承载着深厚的文化底蕴，在历史长河的不断淘洗中流传至今，主要流布于南宁各县区，并辐射到广西各县市。南宁土地诞具有悠久的历史，具体的起源时间已不可考。至于土地公公的由来，坊间亦有不少传说。其中一个传说为：很久以前有一位叫张福德的官员负责城内税收，他为人慈祥正直，爱护老百姓。如村民因周转不灵未能交足税款，他会宽容处理，甚至对于没有能力缴税的农民，亦会自己出钱补贴。每当百姓们遇上困难事，他都会尽力协助，为他们努力奔波也在所不辞。但当他离世后，新一任的税务官却与他截然不同，对老百姓十分严苛，令老百姓生活在水深火热之中。这时他们开始怀念张福德的情义，为他与夫人立祠，供人们敬拜，亦即我们常见到的“福德祠”，并尊称他为“福德正神”。

南宁土地诞民俗活动根植于当地的土地崇拜，是农耕文化的反映。土地神的形象在南宁先民的印象中是保佑平安、纳财进宝的象征，可以保佑生意兴隆、六畜兴旺、五谷丰登。南宁先民将对美好生活的向往与追求，都寄托在了土地神上，具有广泛的群众性和神秘性。关于土地神出现的各种传说，也在彰显着它自身的传奇性色彩。南宁土地诞民俗活动当天，各族人民都会前往土地庙祭拜。祭拜后欢聚一堂，

平话师公戏艺术团在表演平话师公戏
Pinghua Shigong Opera Troupe Performing Shigong Opera in Pinghua Language

烧纸马
Preparing to Burn Paper Horses

共进晚餐，主人家拿出自酿的米酒招待亲朋好友，庆祝土地公的诞辰，构建了一个交流感情、沟通消息的平台，搭造了一座融合民族文化、促进民族团结的桥梁。此外，丰富的节庆活动又给广大群众提供了一个可供娱乐的机会，其民俗性、娱乐性和商业性相互交织，对文化和经济的发展都具有重要意义。

随着文化交流的不断深入，越来越多的外国节日开始在年轻人中盛行，而且年轻人对于民俗文化的认识逐渐淡漠，使得南宁土地诞的参与群体出现了断层。一些了解和熟悉土地诞流程的老艺人，年事已高，逐渐退出土地诞活动，让这项历史悠久的民俗活动岌岌可危。为了传承和发展好这项民俗活动，南宁市非物质文化遗产保护中心于2013年5月多次召开了保护、传承和发展非物质文化遗产项目座谈会，制定相关政策措施。南宁土地诞系列民俗活动的举办，在会首组织，村民集资、捐款的传统做法外，增加了南宁市政府拨款资助的环节，组织一系列传承与普及活动，向广大群众介绍土地诞习俗，让青年人了解土地诞，传播土地诞所承载的民族文化内涵。

to worship on the day of the festival in Nanning. People will gather in someone's home after the worship, while the host takes out his own rice wine to entertain relatives and friends, celebrating the birthday of Fude. In such case, a platform for message exchanging and emotional communication has been constructed, and a bridge has been built to integrate ethnic culture and promote ethnics unity. Besides, the festival is of great significance for the development of culture and of economic, as it provides a recreational activity that embodies intertwined features of folklore, recreation and commerce.

With the deepening course of cultural exchanges, more and more foreign festivals prevail among young people, while less and less young people understand the folk culture. All of these worsen the inheritance of Land God Birthday Celebration in Nanning. Some sophisticated artists who know and are familiar with the process of the festivals are in their declining years, casting the custom in a gloomy future. In order to better inherit and develop this folk activity, Nanning Intangible Cultural Heritage Protection Centre held several symposiums with themes about the protection, inheritance and development of intangible cultural heritage projects in May 2013, and relevant policies and measures were formulated as well. And relevant activities for the festival are also granted by the government of Nanning, apart from the support from the heads of the villages and villagers' raising funds. In addition, a series of inheritance and popularization activities are held to introduce the customs to the masses. More young people are expected to understand Land God Birthday and disseminate the ethnical culture within it.

南宁花婆节

Nanning Huapo Festival

项目名称：南宁花婆节

别称：无

分布范围：南宁市各区县，辐射广西壮族自治区各地

入选名录：2014年第五批自治区级非物质文化遗产名录

保护单位：南宁市民族文化艺术研究院（南宁市非物质文化遗产保护中心）

代表性传承人：无

Element name: Nanning Huapo Festival

Alternative name: None

Geographical location and range: All districts and counties of Nanning City, spreading to other places of Guangxi Zhuang Autonomous Region

Element inscribed list: In 2014 on the Fifth Autonomous Region List of Intangible Cultural Heritage

Competent body involved in safeguarding: Nanning Ethnic Culture and Art Research Institute (Nanning Intangible Cultural Heritage Protection Centre)

Representative inheritor: None

南宁花婆节又称花王节、花王圣母节，是祭祀壮族生育女神花婆的节日。花婆节源于南宁地区的花婆信仰，是南宁先民“花”图腾崇拜的遗风。壮族地区多有修筑花王庙。南宁各地区举办花婆节的时间不尽相同，隆安县以农历二月二十九为花婆神的诞辰日，而南宁市郊的平话人聚居地则在农历三月初六举办花婆节。花婆节的主要内容是祭祀仪式、对歌会友、师公戏表演等。参与祭祀仪式的多为妇女，并备办鸡鸭等牲礼、香烛纸钱和鞭炮等到花婆庙供祭花婆神，然后成群结队到野外采花佩戴，祈求花婆神赐花送子或保佑小孩健康成长。花婆节当天，南宁民间请师公队在花婆庙前表演师公戏，主要剧目有《送鸡米》《八仙贺寿》《洛阳桥》《赞花王》等，一方面是为了主持祭祀仪式，另一方面也丰富了民众的文化生活。

Nanning Huapo Festival, also called Huawang Festival and the Festival of Female Deity Huawang, is celebrated for Huapo, the Birth Goddess of Zhuang Ethnic Group. The festival originated from the Huapo belief in Nanning, which is a relic of the totem of Hua (meaning flower in Chinese). Huawang Temples are mostly built in Zhuang-inhabited area. The time for holding Huapo Festival varies from region to region in Nanning. The people in Long'an County celebrate it on February 29th of the lunar calendar, while the people speak Ping language in suburban area of Nanning host the festival on March 6th of the lunar calendar. The main performances held for Huapo Festival are sacrificial rites, pairs singing and Shigong Opera, etc. Most of the participants in the ceremony were women, who prepared sacrifices such as chickens and ducks, incense candles, joss paper and firecrackers to sacrifice Huapo in temples. Then they gathered flowers in the wild and wore them in groups, praying for Huapo to give them a child or to protect their children's health. On Huapo Festival, troupe of Shigong opera will be invited to give various performances including *Handselling, Birthday Blessing from the Eight Immortals, Luoyang Bridge* and *Ode to Huawang.* The performance is held on the one hand for sacrificial ceremonies, and to enrich people's cultural life on the other hand.

花婆节流布于南宁各县区，辐射到广西各地市，其形成年代已不可考。传说，壮族中专司生育的创世的姆六甲——又称米洛甲、姆洛甲，被世人奉为花婆。清人李调元在描写广西风土人情的《南越笔记》中有“南越”居民向花王圣母求子的记载，表明至迟在清朝乾隆年间花婆祭祀的习俗就已经产生了，距今至少有近300年的历史。随后不断发展兴盛，民国初期刘锡蕃《岭表纪蛮》中记载当时的花婆节“搭彩楼，建斋醮”，可谓热闹非凡。

The custom of Huapo Festival distributes mainly in counties of Nanning and it could be found in other cities of Guangxi. Its original time could not be traced out. In the legend of Zhuang Ethnic Group there is a god in charge of reproductive affairs called Muliujia, or Miluojia and Muluojia, who is hailed as Huapo. According to *Nanyue Notes*, a book describes the local conditions and customs of Guangxi by Li Diaoyuan of the Qing Dynasty, the residents of Nanyue asked for their sons from the Huawang. It clearly shows that the custom had already come into being in the Qianlong years of the Qing Dynasty, at least 300 years ago, and it has prevailed for years. As it recorded in *Documentary of Barbarians in Lingbiao* (by Liu Xifan at the beginning of the Republic of China), people enjoy the uproar of the festival when they "erect Huawang tower and build a Zhaijiao(a place where rites are performed)".

南宁地区的花婆信仰经过发展演变传承至今，形成了具有鲜明地域特色的花婆节文化。它以花婆庙为依托，有着非常广泛的群众基础，是南宁先民在母系社会对生殖崇拜的一种体现。花婆赐花送子，白花为男、红花为女的传说带有神秘性和传奇性，体现了南宁先民对于人丁兴旺和家庭幸福、安康的美好希冀。曾经向花婆许愿求子的女性若日后怀孕，为保证孩子在出生后拥有灵魂，须请师公到野外念经求花，并在路边小沟做架桥仪式，把花从桥上接过来。孩子出生后，要在产妇床头摆放花婆神位，供奉花婆。这些习俗无不体现着南宁先民对于生命的原始探索，是其生活与精神面貌

The culture of Huapo Festival has developed its distinctive local features after the long-time evolution of the folk belief. It is so popular because it is fertility worship in matriarchal society that deeply rooted in religious activity held by Huapo Temple. The legend of Huapo is full of mysterious and marvelous color, saying that the white flower signifies a boy and the red flower indicates a woman. It reflects the good

群众争抢寓意为“儿子”的花
The Masses Scramble for the Flower which Means "Son"

祭祀人员准备散花
The Wicked Persons Prepare to Distribute So-called Flowers

hope of Nanning ancestors for a thriving family, happiness and good health. For example, if a pregnant woman who once wished her child had a soul after birth, she must invite Shigong to read sutras and seek flowers in the field, and make bridging ceremony in a roadside ditch to connect all flowers on the bridge. After the child was born, Huapo's Shrine should be placed at the head of the maternal bed to worship Huapo. Customs about Huapo reflect the original exploration of life by the ancestors of Nanning, and spiritual outlook of the ancestors that carries the ethnical spirit and gene of Zhuang Ethnic Group.

Huapo Festival culture hobbled with the social development. The festival is losing its space where it could be inherited as more and more Huapo temples are demolished all over Nanning. It seems facing a gloomy future since more people who were its advocator turn to other diversified culture. In order to address the challenge, the government of Nanning and Nanning Ethnic Culture and Art Research Institute work together and organized a census team that aims to inherit and protect the folk culture. Besides, an art troupe of Nuo culture has been built in Xixiangtang District where many young actors are attracted to learn Shigong opera. During Huapo Festival, performances are performed at Huapo Temple everywhere in Nanning to ensure that the sacrificial ceremony of Huapo Festival can go smoothly.

的体现，承载着壮族人民的民族精神和民族基因。

随着时代的发展和社会的进步，南宁花婆节的生存空间也一直被挤压。南宁各地的花婆庙不断被拆除，让花婆节失去了其传承发展的空间载体。文化的多元性让外来节日不断跟花婆节抢占受众，使花婆节的地位岌岌可危。面对这种情况，南宁市政府和南宁市民族文化艺术研究院联合，组织成立非物质文化遗产普查小组，深入了解、全面普查，将普查资料做了整理归档，对南宁花婆节这一重要民俗活动进行传承和保护。同时，在政府的支持下，南宁市西乡塘区陈东村成立傩文化艺术团，并积极吸收年轻人学习师公戏，在花婆节期间到南宁各处的花婆庙进行演出，以确保南宁花婆节的祭祀仪式得以顺利进行。

那莲赛巧节

Nalian Saiqiao Festival

项目名称：那莲赛巧节

别称：无

分布范围：邕宁区蒲庙镇孟莲村那莲圩

入选名录：2014年第五批自治区级非物质文化遗产名录

保护单位：邕宁区文化馆

代表性传承人：曹文碧

Element name: Nalian Saiqiao Festival

Alternative name: None

Geographical location and range: Nalian Xu of Menglian Village of Pumiao Town in Yongning District

Element inscribed list: In 2014 on the Fifth Autonomous Region List of Intangible Cultural Heritage

Competent body involved in safeguarding: Yongning District Cultural Centre

Representative inheritor: Cao Wenbi

用彩色纸折叠制作成的大龙虾
Lobster Made by Folding Colored Paper

用七彩线、绒刺绣各种图案及编织各种香包、动物等
Embroidering All Kinds of Patterns and Weaving All Kinds of Sachets and Animals with Colorful Thread and Velvet

Nalian Saiqiao Festival is a traditional celebration with unique local characteristics in Menglian Village, Pumiao Town, Yongning District, Nanning City. It is held on the seventh day of the seventh lunar month every year. It starts with legendary and romantic folk activities such as worship of "the Seventh Sister" and "Picking Qixian Water" held at the ancient pier along the Bachi River, and one of the most important parts of the festival is playing and ranking various exquisite articles. The exhibited articles are divided as handiwork mainly made of vegetables and fruits, embroidery work made by seven-color thread and silk, and painting work with rice. Seven beautiful girls who made the articles would be voted as Qiaonü (meaning girls who are quick-witted and nimble-fingered) by respected artists. Finally, a strand of hair of the selected Qiaonü was tied to the kite that later would be sent to the sky with incense curling upward.

The festival boasts distinctive historical features, although it shares the same cultural function with traditional double-seventh day. In the legend circulating among Nalian, seven fairies would go down to the earth to bathe in the Baishitan Lake beside the Bachi River in Guxu on the seventh day of July every year and select girls who are quick-witted and nimble-fingered. So on the night before July 7th, the local girls will set up a table at their doorstep with exquisite handicrafts they make, in order to meet the Cowherd, the Weaver Girl and the seven fairy girls. There is no essence a Saiqiao Festival. It is an activity through which girls display their nimble fingers and beg for a weaving skills without competitive match. Such

那莲赛巧节，是南宁市邕宁区蒲庙镇孟莲村那莲圩独具地方特色的传统节日庆典，于每年农历七月初七举行。它以在八尺江边古码头举办祭拜“七姐”“挑七仙水”等富有传奇和浪漫色彩的民俗活动为开端，以展示和评选各项巧品为重要环节。参与展示的“巧品”有以时蔬水果做成的工艺品，用七彩线、绒刺绣各种图案和编织各种香包，“点米成画”作品等三大类。由德高望重的民间老艺人组成评委会，评选出七位巧女，最后将所选出的“巧女”的一缕头发拴在风筝上，焚香放飞风筝，送“巧女”上天。

那莲赛巧节虽然带有乞巧节的文化功能，但是还有着不同于乞巧节的独特的历史渊源。在那莲当地传说中，每年七月初七都会有七仙女下凡，降在那莲古圩八尺江畔的白石潭沐浴，挑选心灵手巧的女子。因此当地的姑娘们都会在七月初七的前夜，在自家门口设案摆上制作精巧的手工艺品，迎接牛郎织女相会和七仙女下凡，施巧、乞巧，但并没有赛巧的实质性内容。那莲先民的赛巧活动最早出现在清乾隆五十八年（1793），当时那莲北帝庙建成竣工，适逢农历七月初七将近，于是庙宇竣工庆典和节庆一起举行，并首次通过比赛选出“巧女”，让那莲人民在七月初七所过的节日成为真正意义上的赛巧节。而赛巧技、选巧女便成了那莲赛巧节的传统活动，一直传承至今。

那莲赛巧节拥有着丰富的文化内涵和独特的韵味。无论是时蔬水果还是大米，都能成为那莲群众工艺品制作的原材料。这些构思巧妙、做工精美的工艺品，承载着那莲人民对于美好生活与精湛技艺的追求和向往，体现了那莲人民的智慧与勤劳。那莲赛巧节的一系列活动均由群众自发举办，经费多由群众自发捐献筹集，具有强大的吸引力和广泛的群众参与性。那莲赛巧节是当地人民群众祈福的重要存在，它与那莲北帝庙会、传统七夕“乞巧”等民俗活动有着紧密的联系，具有较强的仪式感。

曾经那莲古圩的地理位置也处于交通要道，陆路北通南宁，南达灵山、钦州；水路上溯龙州、百色，下至梧州。但随着交通运输的发展，那莲古圩逐渐失去了交通枢纽的地位，因而也降低了赛巧节的人气以及影响力。再加上文化和娱乐形式日渐多样，年轻人的注意力开始转向其他方面，能够熟练掌握点米成画等手工技艺的匠人大多年岁已高，技艺传承出现断层。为了传承这一重要文化遗产，邕宁区政府于2010年投入1.2万元，由区文化馆组织普查小组，对那莲赛巧节进行全方位挖掘，将其作为邕宁区文化品牌进行重点打造，使其重焕光彩。同年，在区政府的鼓励和支持下，由赛巧节传承人曹文碧成立那莲乡村民俗文化旅游开发有限公司，开发赛巧节文化旅游资源，现已初见成效。2011年到2013年，邕宁区政府连续三年划拨资金，邕宁区文化馆、那莲乡村民俗文化旅游开发公司以及当地群众联合举办那莲赛巧节，进一步提高赛巧节的知名度，有计划、有力度地推进赛巧节的保护工作，使其成为邕宁区乃至南宁市较有影响力的民俗节日。

activities appeared as early as in the fifty-eighth year in the region of Emperor Qianlong (1793). The celebration for Beidi Temple completion was held on the days close to the seventh day of the seventh month of the lunar month, so Saiqiao Festival was held together with the completion celebration and Qiaonü was selected for the first time through the competition at that time. Nalian Festival was given a brand-new activity since then and the custom of selecting Qiaonü has been handed down to these days.

Nalian Saiqiao Festival bears rich cultural connotation and unique charm, as handicraft articles could be completed by Nalian people whether the raw materials are vegetables, fruits or rice. And these exquisite workmanship crafts with ingenious ideas carries human aspire for a better life and amazing craftsmanship. It embodies the wisdom and diligence of Nalian people. Its strong appeal and popularity could be displayed when it is spontaneously held and supported by people in Nalian. The festival is an important part of the local people's belief. It has a strong sense of ritual and is closely tied with the Beidi Temple Fair and folk activities in traditional double-seventh day.

Guxu of Nalian was located in the main road of transportation. Thc land road extended northward to Nanning, southward to Lingshan, Qinzhou, and the water road stretched northward to Longzhou and Baise, and southward to Wuzhou. Nalian has been losing its position as a transportation hub and Saiqiao Festival has been losing its leverage with the more transportation route newly built. The skills in the festival face a gloomy future without inheritors, as sophisticated artists who are able to draw paintings with rice are in their declining years and many young people turn their attention to other diversified recreation. In order to better inherit this important cultural heritage, the government of Yongning District invested 12,000 yuan in 2010 to the protection and inheritance and organized a census team by the Cultural Centre to excavate the culture of the festival in an all-round way. They also try to make it glorious again by focusing on forging it as a cultural brand of Yongning District. In the same year, Cao Wenbi, the representative inheritor of Saiqiao Festival established Nalian Rural Folk Culture Tourism Co., Ltd with the support of the regional government which has achieved initial results. From 2011 to 2013, the Yongning Government allocated funds for the festival for three consecutive years. Yongning District Cultural Centre and the company mentioned above jointly organized activities for Saiqiao Festival to further enhance the popularity of the festival. And the festival has been promoted to a more influential folk in Yongning District and even Nanning City with planned and powerful actions for more protection.

斑山庙会

Banshan Temple Fair

项目名称：斑山庙会

别称：无

分布范围：青秀区刘圩镇、南阳镇及周边地区

入选名录：2014年第五批自治区级非物质文化遗产名录

保护单位：青秀区文化馆

代表性传承人：李松伦

Element name：Banshan Temple Fair

Alternative name：None

Geographical location and range：Liuxu Town, Nanyang Town of Qingxiu District and the surrounding areas

Element inscribed list：In 2014 on the Fifth Autonomous Region List of Intangible Cultural Heritage

Competent body involved in safeguarding：Qingxiu District Cultural Centre

Representative inheritor：Li Songlun

2013年农历四月十四斑山庙会盛况
Banshan Temple Fair on the 14th of the Fourth Month of the Lunar Calendar in 2013

正月初七民间的舞狮舞龙活动在土地庙前隆重上演
On the Seventh Day of the First Month, the Folk Lion Dance and Dragon Dance were Staged in front of the Temple of the God of Earth

斑山庙会是流传于南宁市青秀区刘圩镇、南阳镇及其周边地区的民间庙会。原本是一项求雨祈福活动，后逐步发展壮大，最终形成庙会。斑山庙会每年举行两次，即正月初七的春季庙会和四月十五的夏季庙会，两次庙会都在刘圩镇的斑山上举行，但内容和风格不同。春季庙会主要进行拜祭、舞龙舞狮、抢花炮等活动。抢花炮是庙会中的一项重头戏，是当地群众参与最多的一项民间体育竞技活动，主要是为了盼望来年风调雨顺、家庭和睦、多子多孙等。夏季庙会主要进行师公戏演唱、青年男女对唱、学业祈福、观测风水等，此外还会表演一些民间绝技，如口叼铁火犁头、手持火铁链、赤脚踩火碳等。

刘圩镇斑山庙会民俗活动历史悠久，起源于宋朝，传承至今已有七八百年的历史。相传盘古开天辟地之时的刘圩镇本是没有斑山的，一位名叫谏议的神仙路过刘圩镇时，看到此处土壤肥沃，却经常受旱失收，农民苦不堪言。于是谏议决心将青龙江口堵住，令河水改道，灌溉田地。虽然最后因为很多原因将江水堵截到了其他村庄，但刘圩人民仍然非常感谢他，遂在他“搬”来的斑山上为他建了一座“谏议王侯

Banshan Temple Fair is popular in Liuxu Town, Nanyang Town and its surrounding areas in Qingxiu District of Nanning City. It was originally a prayer ritual for rain and good blessing, and it developed into a temple fair eventually. It is held twice a year, namely the Spring Temple Fair on the seventh day of the first lunar month and the Summer Temple Fair on the fifteenth of April. Both fairs are held on Banshan in Liuxu Town, though their content and style are different. Spring temple fairs mainly carry out worship activities, dragon and lion dance, fireworks and so on. As an important part of spring temple fair, firecracker snatching attracts the most number of people because people believe it can help pray for a timely weather, harmonious and thriving family. As for summer temple fair, its mainly performances include Shigong Opera, pairs singing, praying for successful study and geomantic observation. And some folk aerobatic performance will be performed as well, such as swallowing iron plough, holding iron chains with bare hands and stepping on burning carbon barefoot.

The folklore activities of Banshan's Temple Fair have a long history, which originated in the Song Dynasty. It is said that there was no mountain in Liuxu Town at the beginning of time, it was an immortal named Jianyi who passed through the town that changed river source. He decided to block the blood by moving Banshan Mountain here and make fields get regular irrigation when he saw farmers here suffered a lot for the drought disasters. People of Liuxu thanked him very much although the river was finally blocked to other villages for reasons. They built a Temple of Jianyi Immortal for him on Banshan Mountain to commemorate his help and held a rain worship ceremony in front of the temple at 24 o'clock on April 15th of the lunar calendar every year. And praying activities began to prevail since Banfeng Academy was built at the foot of Banshan Mountain.

The temple fair in Liuxu Town, relying on sacrificial activities, shows the ancestors' reverence and worship of nature. And the legend about Jianyi is full of mysterious and marvelous color, carrying the pursuit of a better life of the ancestors. Banshan Temple Fair has gradually transformed from a simple praying for rain to a comprehensive folk activity. Its own sacrificial ritual color is weakening, while its secular and entertaining functions are gradually strengthened. The continuous transformation is actually the constant renewal and change of mass thinking. It is held twice a year, varying from annual holding before. It not only embodies the continuous transformation of people's pursuit of a better life, but also signifies a profound mass foundation. Generally speaking, Banshan's Temple Fair can not only satisfy the people's belief needs, but also meet people's spiritual and cultural needs. As it covers religious beliefs, culture and art, making religious activities and folk activities can be integrated organically. Besides, the different programs in Banshan's Temple Fair have also set up a platform for folk artists to improve their skills, which has played a positive role in many aspects of social life.

The temple culture has been impacted due to the changes in social life, and there are few inheritors prepare well to inherit the folk art. However, the current status of inheriting is fine seeing that it is deeply rooted in sacrificial activities. In order to better protect, inherit and develop this folk custom activity, in 2012, a leading group of Banshan Temple Fair Protection Leading Group was set up in Qingxiu District, which is responsible for excavating and protecting the Banshan Temple Fair and promoting it into one of the traditional activities with characteristics of Qingxiu District. Special funds are also allocated for the organization and preparation of the temple fair each year, so that more people can understand and appreciate the cultural value of Banshan's temple fair.

祠”以作纪念，并于每年农历四月十五日零时起在“谏议王侯祠”前举行求雨祭祀的拜祭活动。清代，斑山脚下又建了一座斑风书院，学业祈福也逐渐盛行起来。

刘圩镇斑山庙会依托祭祀活动，展现了刘圩镇先民对于自然的敬畏与崇拜。斑山庙会中的谏议传说非常神秘，具有一定的传奇色彩，承载着刘圩镇先民对美好生活的追求。斑山庙会从最初较为单一的求雨祈福活动，逐渐转化成综合性的民俗活动，其本身的祭祀色彩和仪式性基调在不断减弱，而世俗性、娱乐性等功能逐渐增强。这种功能的不断转化其实是群众思维的不断更新、变化。从最初的一年一次到一年举办两次斑山庙会，这其中不仅仅是人们追求美好生活的目标不断转化的体现，更体现了斑山庙会本身所具有的深厚的群众基础。总体而言，斑山庙会的活动内容涵盖了宗教信仰、文化艺术等领域，使宗教活动和民俗活动有机融合，既娱神又娱人，既能满足人民群众的信仰需要，又可以满足广大人民群众的精神文化需求。斑山庙会中不同类型的节目，不仅为民间艺人提高技艺搭建了平台，还对社会生活的很多方面都产生了积极作用。

由于社会生活发生了变化，斑山庙会的文化空间也受到了一定的影响，民间艺人面临青黄不接的窘境。但由于其本身植根于祭祀活动，传承的自觉性较高，目前传承状况良好。在此基础上，为了更好地保护、传承和发展这一民俗活动，2012年，青秀区成立斑山庙会保护工作领导小组，负责对斑山庙会进行挖掘和保护，将其定为青秀区特色传统文化活动之一，每年划拨专项资金，用于庙会的组织筹备工作，让更多人认识和感受斑山庙会的文化价值。

军山庙会

Junshan Temple Fair

项目名称：军山庙会

别称：逃军山庙会

分布范围：青秀区长塘镇

入选名录：2012年第四批自治区级非物质文化遗产名录

保护单位：青秀区文化馆

代表性继承人：李春仪

Element name: Junshan Temple Fair

Alternative name: Taojunshan Temple Fair

Geographical location and range: Changtang Town of Qingxiu District

Element inscribed list: In 2012 on the Fourth Autonomous Region List of Intangible Cultural Heritage

Competent body involved in safeguarding: Qingxiu District Cultural Centre

Representative inheritor: Li Chunyi

Junshan temple fair, also known as Taojunshan temple fair, is one of the oldest and largest folk temple fairs in Changtang Town and its surrounding areas in Qingxiu District of Nanning. It is held on the 8th day of the 4th lunar month every year and has a history of more than 300 years. Junshan temple fair mainly has six activities, including worshiping, dragon and lion dance, Shigong opera performance, singing folk songs in antiphonal style, costume opera performance and modern song and dance. Generally, some other cultural and entertainment activities such as the competition of bamboo horse, kylin dance, Bajiao spark dragon dance and floating river lanterns will also be held. The dragon and lion dance at Junshan temple fair are indispensable traditional performances with local characteristics. The temple fair brings together the dragon and lion performance teams from Qingxiu District, Yongning District and even some counties and towns in Qinzhou City. The costumes of dragon and lion dance are very exquisite in production and diverse in shapes. Accompanied by drums, suona horns and other wind and percussion instruments, the dragon ball will guide the dancing dragon and the images like the Buddha, Monkey King and Pigsy will lead the way of lion dance during performance, which is magnificent and exciting. The dragon and lion dances are usually performed from the 8th day to the 15th day of lunar April, which can heighten the atmosphere of the temple fair and also symbolize prosperity and auspiciousness.

The Junshan temple fair was originally a small-scale worship and blessing activity for local people, but it has gradually developed into one of the largest temple fairs in Qingxiu District. With Changtang Town of Qingxiu District as the centre, it is radiating to Nanning, Beihai, Qinzhou, Liuzhou, Guizhou and the surrounding areas. Junshan temple fair was originated from the worship of Li Ya, a leader of peasant uprising troop. It is said that Li Ya was a villager of Liuxu Town. In late Ming and early Qing dynasties, the farmlands were damaged by the flood from the Yongjiang River and not a single grain was reaped. People suffered from hunger and cold but the government still insisted to impose taxes on grain. Under such condition, Li Ya organized an uprising troop at the foot of Junshan Mountain, killing the local government officials to resist despotic rules and opening the barn to distribute grains. Li Ya helped the suffering people and won their support, then Li Ya was honored as the King Li Ya by the locals. Later, the government of the Qing Dynasty sent troops to encircle and suppress the uprising troop who was then besieged in the Taojunshan Mountain. Soon the food was running out and the uprising troop was in danger of annihilation. When finding the food in the mountain for the

军山庙会又称逃军山庙会，是南宁市青秀区长塘镇及其周边地区历史最悠久、规模最大的民间庙会之一，于每年农历四月初八举行，传承至今已有300多年的历史。军山庙会主要有祭拜、舞龙舞狮、唱师公戏、山歌对唱、古装戏和现代歌舞等六项内容，一般也会进行一些斗竹马比赛、舞麒麟、舞芭蕉香火龙、放河灯等文娱活动。军山庙会的舞龙舞狮活动极具地域特色，是庙会上不可或缺的传统节目。庙会汇集了青秀区、邕宁区，甚至钦州市一些县乡的龙狮表演队，龙狮制作精巧，形态多样。舞龙舞狮伴随着锣鼓唢呐等吹打乐器进行，舞龙以龙珠引路，舞狮以“大头佛”“孙悟空”“猪八戒”开道，舞姿雄壮威武，令人振奋。舞龙舞狮表演从农历四月初八一直持续到四月十五，增加了庙会的热烈气氛，寓意盛世丰年，象征吉祥美好。

军山庙会起初只是本地群众规模较小的祭祀祈福活动，而后逐步发展成青秀区最大的庙会之一。其流布区域以青秀区长塘镇为中心，辐射到南宁、北海、钦州、柳州、桂林乃至周边一些省份。军山庙会源于对明末清初一位农民起义军首领李哑的祭拜。据传，李哑系刘圩乡人，明末清初之际邕江洪水泛滥，农田被淹，颗粒无收，农民饥寒交迫，官府还征粮加税。李哑就在军山下组织了一支义军，杀官抗暴，开仓放粮，救济受苦受难的百姓，深得百姓的拥护，被尊为李哑王。后来清政府派兵围剿，起义军被围困在逃军山上，很快粮食就要吃完了，起义军面临着覆灭的危险。李哑在山中为起义军寻找食物，一不小心，手臂被荆棘划破流了很多血，血所滴过的地方都长出了豆捻树，并结满了果实。李哑撩开衣袖，拿起刀满山放血，山上到处长满了豆捻树，起义军借豆捻果实充饥，继续和清军战斗，最终因寡不敌众，李哑和起义军都壮烈牺牲。当地群众为纪念李哑的功德，为他在逃军山上修建庙宇，此后每年农历四月初八李哑生日时便举行盛大庙会。

军山庙会源于佛教寺院以及道教庙观的宗教活动，吸收众多本土和外来宗教文化中的优秀成分，糅合了巫、道等各派的内容，形成了独特的文化特色，并伴随着民间宗教活动而发展、流传。李哑血化豆捻的神话，以及血战军山的传说，具有浓厚的传奇色彩和地域特征。尤其是李哑从农民起义的英雄逐渐蜕变成无所不能的神祇，也彰显着军山先民思维的变化。现如今军山庙会既含有原本的祭祀祈福功能，又含有娱乐大众、丰富群众精神生活的功能，其作为一项综合性的民俗活动，具有不可估量的社会价值。

军山庙会作为当地人民的一种价值符号，其传承从未间断，虽然其生存的文化空间受到了外来文化和众多外来节日的影响，但并没有动摇其根基，传承状况良好。为了更好地保护、传承和发展这一传统民俗节日，2007年4月，青秀区政府召开军山庙会保护工作会议，明确提出军山庙会是青秀区特色传统文化活动之一，要全面挖掘、整理、保护和弘扬军山庙会文化。每年的军山庙会期间，着力做好安保工作，在军山李哑王庙建立军山庙会传承基地，扶持其开展祭祀活动，使其更好地传承和发展。

师公戏表演
Performance of Shigong Opera

uprising troop, Li Ya's arm was cut by thorns and bled a lot. To his surprise, wherever the blood trickled, the bean twigs grew and were full of fruit. On seeing this, Li Ya just lifted up his sleeve and decided to bleed on the mountain by using his sword. Then, the mountain was covered with bean twigs. Therefore, the uprising troop could eat the fruit on bean twigs to fill their bellies and continue to fight against the troop of the Qing Dynasty. Unfortunately, Li Ya and the uprising troop were outnumbered and finally died bravely in the fight. To commemorate Li's merits and virtues, the local people built a temple for him on the Taojun Mountain. Since then, every year on Li's birthday, that is, the 8th day of the lunar April, people would hold grand temple fair on Junshan Mountain.

The Junshan temple fair originated from the religious activities of Buddhist temples and Taoist temples, which has absorbed the excellent elements of many local and foreign religious cultures and integrated with various religious factions such as witchcraft and Taoism, forming a unique cultural feature and accompanying the development and dissemination of folk religious activities. The legend of Li Ya's blood growing into bean twigs and the legend of the bloody battle in Junshan Mountain, especially Li's transformation from a peasant uprising hero to an omnipotent god, bear strong legendary atmosphere and regional characteristics. Such a change also represents the change of thinking of ancestors in Junshan Mountain areas. Nowadays, Junshan temple fair not only has the original function of offering sacrifices and blessing, but also has the function of entertaining the public and enriching the spiritual life of the masses. As a folk activity with multi-functions, it bears an inestimable social value.

As a value symbol of local people, the inheritance of Junshan temple fair has never been interrupted. Although the cultural space for its survival has been influenced by foreign cultures and numerous foreign festivals, its foundation has not yet to be shaken and its inheritance is still in good condition. In order to better protect, inherit and develop this traditional folk festival, in April 2007, the government of Qingxiu District held a meeting on the protection of Junshan temple fair, which explicitly proposed that Junshan temple fair was one of the traditional cultural activities with characteristics in Qingxiu district, and the culture of Junshan temple fair should be comprehensively explored, organized, protected and promoted. During the annual Junshan temple fair, efforts have been made for a good security work. The government has also built an inheritance base at Temple of King Li Ya in Junshan Mountain to support the worship activity so that this temple fair can be better inherited and developed.

疍家婚礼

Dan Boat Dwellers Wedding

名称：疍家婚礼

别称：无

分布范围：南宁市邕江、郁江的沿江地带

入选名录：2008年第二批自治区级非物质文化遗产名录

保护单位：江南区文化馆

代表性传承人：张秀华

Element name：Dan Boat Dwellers Wedding

Alternative name：None

Geographical location and range：Areas along the Yongjiang River and Yujiang River of Nanning City

Element inscribed list：In 2008 on the Second Autonomous Region List of Intangible Cultural Heritage

Competent body involved in safeguarding：Jiangnan District Cultural Centre

Representative inheritor：Zhang Xiuhua

接亲仪式
Marriage Ceremony

疍家人是水上人家，以渔业为生。南宁疍家婚礼是一种古老的传统婚俗，主要分布在南宁市邕江、郁江的沿江地带。疍家婚礼历史悠久，具体起源时间已不可考。疍家人很早就在广西生活，南宋周去非的《岭外代答》中就已经出现了疍家人的相关记载。疍家婚俗表现在男女未订婚的船家，女方家需放置一盘花于船尾，男方家则置一盘草于船尾，以此招媒人撮合婚事。其婚礼隆重而又极富特色，传统婚礼一般举行两天，包括叹歌、放堂歌、绕台围、接亲等仪式。

疍家婚礼的整个过程都离不开“唱叹”，有“哭嫁歌”“十月怀胎歌”等，疍家人“以歌代哭”，其内容大多是怀念父母养育之恩、倾诉兄弟姐妹和婶嫂之情以及离别亲人之苦。每首歌只有两句，以七言为主，压同一韵脚，而且上句必须为仄声，下句为阳平声，固定不变。唱的时候问字取腔，句中可加入衬字和表示称谓的衬词，尾句有拉腔。不管衬字多少，节拍需与七言句等同。“唱叹”的类型有伴娘互叹、新娘独叹、母女互叹、姐妹互叹等。

The Dan people refer to the boat dwellers who live on fishery. The wedding for Dan people is an ancient wedding custom mainly spreading over the areas along the Yongjiang River and Yujiang River of Nanning. The Dan wedding has a long history, but its origin time is hard to be traced. The Dan people have lived in Guangxi for a long time, which has been recorded in the famous geographical book *Ling Wai Dai Da* written by Zhou Qufei during the South Song Dynasty. The customs of Dan wedding are that the family of the lady who has not been engaged will place flowers at the stern of the boat and the family of the man who has not been engaged will place grasses at the head of the boat so as to ask a matchmaker to make a match. The wedding is grand and has distinct characteristics. The traditional wedding is generally held for two days, including singing songs, playing music, walking around the platform and taking the bride home.

The whole wedding process can hardly do without chanting and singing, which include songs like Song of Crying for Marriage, Song of Ten Month's Pregnancy and so on. The Dan people replace crying by singing songs. The main content of the song includes the gratitude toward love and care from parents, expressing the deep affection between siblings and the anxiety of separation from the family. Each of the songs only has two lines of seven-word lyrics with the same rhyme. The first line must be oblique tone and the second line must be level tone, which cannot be changed randomly. When singing the songs, people can add words for balance or euphony or the words for titles with a long tune in the last lyric. No matter how many words are added to the lyric, the rhythm of the whole sentence should be the same as that of seven-word lyrics. The types of chanting and singing include duet of bridesmaid, solo of the bride, duet of mother and daughter, duet of sisters and so on.

The Dan wedding is a vivid textbook that represents the history and culture of the Dan people in the areas along the Yujiang River. The Dan people express their best wishes of happy life to the new couples through this unique wedding ceremony, which bears sincere hopes and affections of Dan people. The unique geographical environment and job have shaped unique personality, language, clothing, marriage customs and religious belief of Dan people. The customs formed during living on the boats have gradually integrated with the living elements of local Zhuang people, which has formed unique living habits different from that of Dan people living in other areas. The Dan people have lived in the Autonomous Region of Zhuang Ethnic Group for a long time, thus they have been deeply affected by the Zhuang culture.

Although the whole process of Dan wedding is accompanied by chanting and singing traditional songs, the offerings and food on the wedding ceremony are five-color glutinous rice, chicken, longan and other food with Zhuang characteristics, which has formed a kind of multi-culture. Furthermore, the Dan wedding is a cultural life epitome of the unique boat dweller groups, which is of great value in studying the history and culture of the boat dwellers in China.

With the change of times and the improvement of people's livelihood, the Dan families who once lived on the water gradually moved ashore in the mid-1960s, and their attitudes toward love and marriage have also changed. The young people have been free to fall in love and can marry land dwellers. The custom "replacing car by boat" has gradually changed into "replacing boat by car". The wedding ceremonies of the new generations of Dan people who have been affected by the foreign wedding customs have become more and more similar to that of the land dwellers. Nowadays, the Dan people have gradually shed the label of boat dwellers and integrated into the urban life, resulting in the fading away of the Dan wedding and the great challenge of its inheritance and development. In order to protect, inherit and carry forward this excellent folk culture, the Dan wedding custom was put on the screen by the Jiangnan Cultural Centre in the 1990s with a strategic and forward-looking view. Today, the government of Jiangnan District has been further investigating and protecting the custom and preserving complete written, audio and video materials. The Dan wedding performances are held on an irregular basis to provide a large amount of coverage on the Dan wedding performances, thus providing a chance for its continuous inheritance and development.

南宁疍家婚礼可以说是一部充分展现郁江流域疍家历史文化的生动教材。南宁疍家人通过这种独具特色的婚礼习俗来祝福新婚夫妇的婚姻生活能够美满、幸福，寄托了疍家人深切的愿望，饱含着疍家人真挚的情感。独特的地理环境和职业，使疍家人在性格、语言、服饰、婚俗和宗教信仰等方面均自成一体。一直承袭的水上生活习惯，又逐渐融入当地壮族人民的生活元素，形成了有别于其他地区疍家人的独特生活习俗。由于南宁地区的疍家人长期生活在壮族聚居区，深受壮族文化的影响。疍家婚礼全程在唱叹声中完成，而婚礼中的供品及食品却是壮族特色的五色糯米饭、大阉鸡、桂圆等，已经形成了一种多元文化类型。此外，南宁疍家婚礼是一个独特群体的文化生活缩影，对于研究我国水上人家的历史文化具有重要的价值。

随着时代的变革和生活水平的提高，20世纪60年代中期，长期生活在水上的疍家人逐渐开始迁居到岸上，婚恋观也随之变化，年轻人可以自由恋爱并和陆上居民通婚，曾经“以船代轿”的通行方式逐渐转变成“以车代轿”。新一代疍家渔民受到外来婚俗的影响，水上居民的结婚礼仪也逐渐向陆上居民靠拢。如今的疍家人逐渐摆脱了水上民族的标签，逐步融入城市生活。疍家婚礼习俗逐渐淡出人们的视野，其传承和发展遇到了极大的挑战。为了保护、传承和发扬这一优秀民俗文化，江南区文化馆曾于20世纪90年代将疍家婚礼习俗搬上荧幕，具有战略眼光和前瞻性。如今，江南区政府还在进一步展开对该习俗的调查和保护工作，保存完整的文字、录音和影像资料，不定期举行较大规模的疍家婚礼展演，使其得以不断传承和发展。

接亲仪式
Marriage Ceremony

南宁大王节

Nanning King Dawang Festival

项目名称：南宁大王节

别称：无

分布范围：南宁市及周边地区

入选名录：2016年第六批自治区级非物质文化遗产名录
2015年第六批市级非物质文化遗产名录

保护单位：西乡塘区文化馆

代表性传承人：无

Element name：Nanning King Dawang Festival

Alternative name：None

Geographical location and range：Nanning City and the surrounding areas

Element inscribed list：In 2016 on the Sixth Autonomous Region List of Intangible Cultural Heritage
In 2015 on the Sixth Municipal List of Intangible Cultural Heritage

Competent body involved in safeguarding：Xixiangtang District Cultural Centre

Representative inheritor：None

Nanning King Dawang Festival is a traditional festival for descendants of the Luoyue state to commemorate the universe creator Queen Ya in their ethnic group. According to the legend, Queen Ya was an incarnation of a bird. She died on the lunar July 18th and was buried on the moon by sparrows on the lunar July 20th. On the 21st day, the queen was brought back to life. Therefore, there is a proverb goes like that "the Queen got ill on 17th and died on 18th; a coffin was made on 19th and buried her on 20th". On the day of the resurrection of Queen Ya, the villagers would hold a blessing ceremony together to celebrate the reincarnation and resurrection of her, which could be called the Easter of Zhuang Ethnic Group in China. To commemorate the creators of the universe, the people built temples and held a series of sacrificial activities to express their reverence. At present, the most influential temples for Great King include Temple for Two Kings in Zhoucun Village of Wuxu Town, Great King Temple in Gusi Village of Nahong Town, Temple for Three Kings and Yonghe Great King Temple of Junshan Mountain in Changtang Town. Yonghe Great King Temple is the largest and the most famous one that is located at the bank of Yongjiang River of Xixiangtang District in Nanning. The Great King temple fair held on the 8th day of the 4th lunar month will also attract a lot of visitors.

The establishment time of Yonghe Great King Temple, the largest temple of the Great King with the longest history, is hard to be traced. The earliest existing inscription records that it was rebuilt during the reign of Emperor Yongzheng of the Qing Dynasty. The temple was originally located at the bank of the Carp Pool. The ancestors of Zhuang Ethnic Group lived on fishery, but the current at the Carp Pool was rapid, thus causing many accidents at this place. People believed that there was god in the pool named "Lang Ling" to control the safety of the boat. Therefore, they set up temple here to hold sacrificial rites and ensure the safety of fishermen. Later, because of the revamp of the dike of Yongjiang River, the temple was relocated to Jiangbei Avenue. Yonghe Great King Temple now includes Lang Ling Hall, Hua Wang Hall, Cui Official, Guanyin Hall and other buildings. In the past, the gods offered in this temple are Lang Ling (Guang Lang), Wu Mu (Du Mu) and three kings of Zhongfu while today the gods offered in the temple are the King Lang Ling and the Goddess Hua Wang. The worship toward king and goddess is actually a part of the worship of ancient Luoyue gods. In the ancient Zhuang language, "Lang" meant "King" and "Ling" referred to "deep pool", thus the meaning of "Lang Ling" is the god or the king in the deep pool.

给大王献花
Flowers for King Dawang

大王节是骆越民族后裔纪念创世祖先娅王的传统节日。娅王是一个鸟王转世的女王，她在七月十八日逝世，七月二十日麻雀把她抬到月亮上埋葬，七月二十一日又重新复活，因此有谚语说“十七大王病，十八大王死，十九造棺木，二十葬大王”。在娅王复活的这天，乡亲一起举办祈福活动，庆祝大王转世复活，可以称得上是中国壮乡的复活节。为了纪念创世祖先，人们修建庙宇，并举行一系列的祭祀活动，来表达自己心中的崇敬。现今南宁市范围内影响较大的大王庙有吴圩周村二王庙、那洪古思大王庙、长塘道军山三王庙、永和大王庙。其中永和大王庙是位于南宁市西乡塘区城区邕江边最大、最著名的大王庙，每年农历四月初八的大王诞庙会都会吸引多地的群众参与。

作为历史悠久、规模最大的大王庙，永和大王庙始建于何时已不可考，现存最早的碑文记载它于清雍正年间重新修建。永和大王庙原庙址在永和村邕江鲤鱼潭边，壮族先民多以航运和打鱼为业，而此地水流湍急、事故多发，人民认为潭中有一个神灵“郎灵”管理行船安全，因此设庙祭祀，以保平安。后来因南宁市修建邕江大堤，将此庙迁建至江北大道。永和大王庙内现有朗灵殿、花王殿、催官衙、观音殿等建筑。原来供奉的神祇是朗灵（广浪）、乌目（都木）、中府三位大王，现在庙内供奉的主神是郎灵大王和花王圣母。大王崇拜和祖母王崇拜是骆越的祖神崇拜，“郎”在古壮语中是“大王”的意思，“灵”是“深潭”的意思，即潭中的神灵。

南宁大王节每年有三次活动，分别于农历的二月十九、三月初六和四月初八举行，其中四月初八的大王诞最为隆重，参与人数最多时达数万人。大王节的主要活动有道公和师公的祭祀法事、群众性的祈福活动、民俗表演和百家宴等。近年来，南宁大王节的节庆活动除了常见的流程外，还会有民俗表演，如陈村师公队、秀灵村师公队、陈村道公队、水上人家的歌队、舞狮、舞龙、男女青年对歌等，以祭祀为契机，充分展示壮族的独特民俗文化，同时能够让当地和慕名前来的外地民众感受一场热闹非凡、意蕴深厚的文化盛宴。如今，随着时间的推移、社会的发展，南宁大王节已从过去的烧香祈福演变为有着庙会性质的文体娱乐活动，成为西乡塘区民俗文化节庆活动的代表性项目。

作为一个凝聚了古骆越祖神崇拜文化的节日，南宁大王节历史悠久、规模宏大、内容丰富，深刻反映了当地的经济、社会和历史文化发展演变状况，是永和村及其周边地区历史文化的缩影。近年，大王庙香火渐旺，成为南宁市又一个新的游览景点。目前，大王庙建筑保存较好，庙会盛况空前，给南宁大王节这一传统民俗文化的发展带来了极佳的氛围和契机。随着时间的推移，南宁大王节在保持其原生形态的同时，融入了更多的时代内容，娱神又娱人，使古骆越文化有了新的意义。2016年，经过南宁市人民政府同意，南宁大王节列入第六批自治区级非物质文化遗产名录。

Nanning King Dawang Festival in Nanning is often held on the lunar February 19th, the lunar March 6th, and the lunar April 8th respectively, among which the last one is the largest and the grandest one with participants nearly approaching tens of thousands. The major activities of Nanning King Dawang Festival include sacrificial rite made by Taoist priests, mass blessing activities, folk performances and Hundred-Family banquet. In recent years, in addition to the common process, many other folk performances have been added to the festival, such as Shigong dance performed by the troupes of Chencun Village and Xiuling Village, Daogong dance performed by the troupe from Chencun Village, the chorus of boat dwellers, lion and dragon dance, folk song singing between young men and women and so on. Taking sacrificial rite as an opportunity, these performances can fully display the unique folk culture of the Zhuang Ethnic Group. At the same time, both the locals and people from other places can enjoy a lively and profound cultural feast. With the passing of time and the development of society, Nanning King Dawang Festival has evolved from burning incense and praying for good luck in the past into a kind of recreational activities with the nature of temple fairs, which has become a representative item of folk culture festival activities in Xixiangtang District.

As a festival that embodies the ancestral god worship culture of ancient Luoyue, Nanning King Dawang Festival in Nanning has a long history, a large scale and rich content, which profoundly reflects the development and evolution of local economy, society and historical culture and is the epitome of the history and culture of Yonghe Village and its surrounding areas. In recent years, with the increasing popularity, the temple has now become a new scenic spot in Nanning. At present, the Temple of Great King is well preserved, and the scale of temple fair has become unprecedentedly large, which has brought an excellent atmosphere and opportunity for the development of the traditional folk culture of Nanning King Dawang Festival in Nanning. As time goes by, Nanning King Dawang Festival, while maintaining its original form, has integrated with more modern contents to entertain both gods and people, giving new significance to the ancient Luoyue Culture. In 2016, with the approval of the People's Government of Nanning, Nanning Great King Festival was inscribed on the Sixth Autonimous Reigon List of Intangible Cultural Heritage.

南宁下楞龙舟节

Nanning Xialeng Dragon Boat Festival

项目名称：南宁下楞龙舟节

别称：无

分布范围：以西乡塘区坛洛镇为中心，广泛流传于南宁市沿江地区

入选名录：2016年第六批自治区级非物质文化遗产名录
2015年第六批市级非物质文化遗产名录

保护单位：西乡塘区文化馆

代表性传承人：无

Element name: Nanning Xialeng Dragon Boat Festival

Alternative name: None

Geographical location and range: Tanluo Town of Xixiangtang District as the centre, spreading over the riverside areas of Nanning City

Element inscribed list: In 2016 on the Sixth Autonomous Region List of Intangible Cultural Heritage
In 2015 on the Sixth Municipal List of Intangible Cultural Heritage

Competent body involved in safeguarding: Xixiangtang District Cultural Centre

Representative inheritor: None

南宁下楞龙舟比赛
Xialeng Dragon Boat Race

比赛用的桨和锣
Oars and Gong for Competitions

南宁下楞龙舟节是在赛龙舟的基础上发展起来的、融祭祀和体育竞技于一体的传统水上习俗，其活动范围以南宁市西乡塘区坛洛镇为中心，波及南宁市的沿江地区。作为一项传统的民俗活动，南宁下楞龙舟节于每年农历五月初五端午节在下楞村举行，按照习俗，龙舟赛开始前要做一系列的仪式，有祭龙、点睛、摆头、翻身、下水等。这些仪式也各有各的讲究：祭龙是为了唤醒龙舟，让沉寂了一年的龙舟游动；点睛是让龙舟识方向，在波涛澎湃的江上不易被大浪掀翻。龙舟赛结束后，还有颁奖游街、拜祭祖先、百家宴、放河灯、跨福桥、供奉河神等活动，以此祈祷百姓安居乐业、社会安定和谐。

南宁下楞端午赛龙舟，起源于古骆越人的祭水神习俗。被祭祀的水神叫罗波，汉译为祖母王，也叫白母娘和白马娘娘。因为下楞是左江古水道上的重要码头，是壮族人聚居的古圩市，因此祭祀水神是为了使当地减少灾难、安定和睦。而下楞端午龙舟节习俗就是古骆越人祭水神习俗的一部分。在宁明花山岩画上有描绘古骆越人赛龙舟的场面，按照学术

Dragon Boat Festival in Xialeng of Nanning, based on dragon-boat racing, is a traditional custom integrating sacrifice activity and sports. It is especially popular in Tanluo Town of Xixiangtang District, and it could also be found in areas along the rivers in Nanning City. As a traditional folk activity, it is held in Xialeng Village on the 5th May of the lunar calendar every year. Traditionally, a series of ceremonies will be performed before the Dragon Boat Race starts, such as offering sacrifices to the dragon, lighting dragon's eyes, shaking dragon's head, turning over and launching the water. These rituals are done for sacrificial reasons, for example, the purpose of the Dragon sacrifice is to wake up the dragon boat and enliven the boat that kept silence for a year. Lighting dragon's eyes is performed to make sure the Dragon Boat can see its direction, so that it is not easy to be overturned by the big waves in the surging river. After the dragon boat race, activities such as prize-giving tours, ancestor worship, family banquets, floating river lanterns, crossing Fuqiao Bridge, worship river gods will be carried out to pray for a peaceful life and harmonious society.

The festival originated from the custom of sacrificing the God of Water by the people in ancient Luoyue State. The god, named Luobo in Luoyue language, is translated into Grandmother King in Chinese and also called Baimu and Goddess Baimu. Xialeng was an important wharf at that time, people living there believed that the disasters could be effectively reduced and life could be more peaceful by sacrificing the god. Dragon Boat Festival in Xialeng was a part of the sacrificing procedures. Academic circles concluded that the festival has a history for more than 2000 years according to rock paintings of in Ningming that depicts the scene of Dragon Boat Race of ancient Luoyue people. Besides, its long history could also be proved by unearthed relics used for dragon boating from riverside areas, such as bronze drums and buckets.

The dragon boat will be put in the river one month before the Dragon Boat Festival, and the race will not begin unless a series of sacrificial ceremonies carried out. The racing in Xialeng is special for its sailing against the water current while most of the dragon boat races in other areas are along the river. Such distinctive race is also a reflection of the spirit of the local people. As a well-preserved folk cultural activity in Nanning, it bears rich connotations and auspicious implications. It is of great significance in studying folk customs and history.

Nowadays, the festival has an increasingly extended scale and influence with water launching ceremony, dragon boat race and other recreational activities. Every year, more than 20 thousand people participate in the festival. Liang Xiuting, the representative inheritor of the custom, not only presides over the Dragon Boat Festival ceremony every year, but also teaches skills of dragon boating, so that more young people have the chance to take over the race and make more contribution for further protection and impartation. In May 2006, Bureau of Culture and Sports in Xixiangtang District launched a census to sort out data and expand publicity, which greatly enhanced the influence of the Dragon Boat Festival in Xialeng. In 2012, special funds were allocated to support the festival by the Government of Xixiangtang District. In 2016, Dragon Boat Festival in Xialeng of Nanning was inscribed on the Sixth Autonomous Reigon List of Intangible Cultural Heritage after the approval of People's Government of Nanning.

界认定的岩画的年代推论，下楞赛龙舟习俗应当起源于2000多年前。此外，沿江一带出土的文物中，有许多绘有古骆越人祭祀水神举行龙舟竞渡时所用的铜鼓、铜桶等，由此可见，赛龙舟习俗历史悠久。

在端午节前一个月，参赛者会把龙舟放到河里，端午节当天进行一系列的祭祀仪式后，热闹的赛龙舟就开始了，比较特别的是，其他地区的龙舟赛事大多是顺水竞龙舟，而南宁下楞龙舟节则一直保持着逆水竞龙舟的古老习俗，这种龙舟精神正是当地人民的精神写照。作为一项保存较好的南宁民俗文化活动，它内涵丰富，并且每一项仪式都蕴含吉祥、美好的寓意，是人们的情感寄托，对民俗、历史等方面的研究有着重要的价值。

如今，南宁下楞龙舟节的活动规模和影响越来越大，其内容包括下水仪式、龙舟竞赛及多项文娱活动等，每年参与群众多达2万多人。项目代表性传承人梁秀廷不仅年年主持龙舟节仪式，还积极传授技艺，让更多的年轻人接触到龙舟赛事，为南宁下楞龙舟节的传承和发展做出了重要贡献。2006年5月，西乡塘区文体局启动了南宁下楞龙舟节的普查工作，整理资料，扩大宣传，极大地提高了南宁下楞龙舟节的影响力。2012年，西乡塘区政府对南宁下楞龙舟节划拨专项资金予以扶持。2016年，经过南宁市人民政府同意，南宁下楞龙舟节列入第六批自治区级非物质文化遗产名录。

西乡塘歌圩

Xixiangtang Folk Song Fair

项目名称：西乡塘歌圩

别称：无

分布范围：西乡塘区、邕宁区、良庆区、武鸣区等

入选名录：2016年第六批自治区级非物质文化遗产名录
　　　　　2015年第六批市级非物质文化遗产名录

保护单位：西乡塘区文化馆

代表性传承人：无

Element name: Xixiangtang Folk Song Fair

Alternative name: None

Geographical location and range: Xixiangtang District, Yongning District, Liangqing District, Wuming District and others

Element inscribed list: In 2016 on the Sixth Autonomous Region List of Intangible Cultural Heritage
In 2015 on the Sixth Municipal List of Intangible Cultural Heritage

Competent body involved in safeguarding: Xixiangtang District Cultural Centre

Representative inheritor: None

Folk song fair in Xixiangtang, as a typical representative of song fairs in places where Zhuang and Han inhabit, is created by the folk and full of ethnical features. Every year on the 15th of August and the 9th of September in the lunar calendar, boys and girls in villages will go with their companions and gather together in order to find the right person in the lively and happy parth in Shibu, Anji, Xinxu, Fude, Qiaoban and other places where song fairs are held. Boys will sing to attract girls that the former fall in love with. The fair will be enlivened by folk songs sung in Ping language or in Zhuang language. The number of onlookers gathering around will be more than a thousand at least, sometimes it could be up to thousands of people. The fair usually lasts three days and three nights with songs floating around valleys.

Folk song fair in Xixiangtang develops throughout the course of the history of Zhuang Ethnic Group. Towns are the sacrificial centres for ancestors who built Sanjie Temple and Dawang Temple to worship, and the first town of Zhuang people in Xixiangtang District appeared as early as the time of Ancient Luoyue State. A conclusion can be drawn that folk song fair, as an activity closely connected with Luoyue temple fair, was popular at that time. Liu Xun of the Tang Dynasty wrote in *Ling Biao Lu Yi (Notes on the South of Five Ridges)*, "people in areas of the south of five ridges trade in Shixikou of Yongzhou, which is still called Liao Fair in these days". Liao Fair was the trading occasion where Liao people (the ancestor of Zhuang people) gathered together. The folk song fair among Liao people in Xixiangtang flourished in the Tang Dynasty. And it was still thriving during the Ming and Qing dynasties. In *Annals of Nanning Prefecture* written in the forty-third years of the Ming Dynasty (1564), we can see that Zhuang people "find their better half through pairs-singing when they have an outing in spring". Several places thus became important gathering sites to hold song fairs, such as Shibu, An'ji, Xinxu, Fude and Banqiao. Such song fairs, once held twice a year among counties of Nanning, has become a fixed activity held only in Xinxiu Park once a week.

Songs in the fair are mainly folk songs in Zhuang and Ping languages. As a monophonic music, folk Song in Ping language puts emphasis on rhyme. The songs follow the rules of ancient regulated poems to compose lyrics. In terms of songs' form, folk song in Ping language can be divided into Seven-Word Verse and Family Letter. The folk songs of Zhuang Ethnic Group are euphemistic and melodious and are mainly composed of five-word lines. Most of the lyrics are improvisations. Both kinds of folk songs are lively and expressive, using a lot of rhetoric devices. People who

西乡塘歌圩是民间自发形成的、具有民族特色的传统山歌集会活动，是壮、汉歌圩的一个典型代表。每年的农历八月十五和九月初九，西乡塘以及周边地区的男女青年，为了在热闹欢乐的聚会中寻找自己的意中人，就会和同伴们相携而行，一起聚集到石埠、安吉、心圩、富德、桥板等地赶赴歌圩。在集会上，如果一帮小伙子看中了一伙姑娘，就用山歌来逗引，或用平话山歌，或用壮族山歌，场面热闹非凡。此时，围观群众少则千余人，多则数千人，歌声山鸣谷应，十分壮观。歌圩活动一般要持续三天三夜。

西乡塘壮族歌圩的历史和壮族的历史密切相连。早在骆越古国时代，西乡塘区就出现了壮族历史上最早的城镇，即壮族先民的祭祀中心，再加上西乡塘区沿江多有三界庙、大王庙等骆越祖神的祭祀庙，由此分析得知，和骆越庙会活动密切相关的歌圩活动此时已十分兴盛。唐代刘恂《岭表录异》载："夷人通商于邕州石溪口，至今谓之獠市。""獠市"是壮族先民"獠人"的集市，以西乡塘区石埠为中心的壮族先民集市"獠市"的歌圩在唐代已相当繁华。在明清时期，西乡塘歌圩仍兴盛不衰，明嘉靖四十三年（1564）《南宁府志》记载土人"婚姻以答歌踏青为媒妁"，石埠、安吉、心圩、富德、桥板等地成为传统歌圩的重要场所。西乡塘歌圩活动延续至今，从分散到各个点赶歌圩发展到如今都集中在南宁新秀公园演唱，时间也从每年两次变为每周一次。

西乡塘歌圩主要是以壮族山歌和平话山歌为主。平话山歌属单声部民歌，是古律诗的一种，在形式上有七言家和家信（家书）两种。壮族山歌婉转悠扬，以五言为主，对唱时用壮语方言，歌词大多即兴而成。两种山歌都大量使用各种修辞，语言生动活泼，表现力十分丰富。每逢周末，热爱对歌传统的群众都会汇聚到西乡塘新秀公园对歌，歌手们会在人群中寻觅自己的对手，选定歌伴后开始对歌。对歌的主要内容由生产、生活逐渐深入个人理想、观念等，他们三五成群，慢悠悠地在公园里漫步对歌，悠闲自得而又充满趣味。

西乡塘歌圩的山歌，曲调婉转悠扬，易唱易记，充分体现了壮族地区的文化特色。同时，歌圩的音乐素材、旋法、结构、发声方法、演唱形式和作品，既保留了浓厚的民间色彩，又具有鲜明的时代特征，不仅对研究壮、汉民族文化习俗的产生、发展具有重要参考价值，而且对于中国少数民族音乐的研究也具有重大意义。

在现代社会中，节日民俗传统被淡化，西乡塘歌圩对青年人已经缺乏了原有的吸引力，因此会唱山歌的民众越来越少。为了保护、继承这一具有民族特色的传统文化，当地有关部门与社会各界共同努力。目前，西乡塘区已组建有一批优秀的歌圩演唱队伍，每个周末都自发到新秀公园开展歌圩活动，让西乡塘歌圩的优美旋律继续悠扬。2016年，经过南宁市人民政府同意，西乡塘歌圩列入第六批自治区级非物质文化遗产名录。

love traditional pairs-singing will gather in Xinxiu Park every weekend and find their partners in the crowd before antiphonal singing. What they sing for covers a wide range from productive practice and daily life to personal opinion and aspiration. They enjoy an unfettered time with fun when they sing along walking in the park.

The folk songs in the fair are melodious and easy to sing and record, which fully reflects the cultural characteristics of Zhuang-inhabited areas. Strong folk color and distinctive features are vividly displayed by music elements including musical material, melody models, structures, phonation and singing style. It has critical reference value for the study of the development of the customs of Zhuang and Han peoples, and the study of ethnical minority music will benefit a lot as well.

Traditional folklore has been fading away and a lot of people who are able to sing folk songs are declining, since the folk song fair attracts less and less young people in modern society in order to protect and inherit this traditional culture with ethnical characteristics. The local authorities make great efforts with people from all walks of life. A group of excellent singing teams have been set up in Xixiangtang District who bring beautiful melodies to Xinxiu Park. In 2016, Folk song fair in Xixiangtang was inscribed on the Sixth Autonomous Reigon List of Intangible Cultural Heritage after the approval of People's Government of Nanning.

西乡塘歌圩
Xixiangtang Folk Song Fair

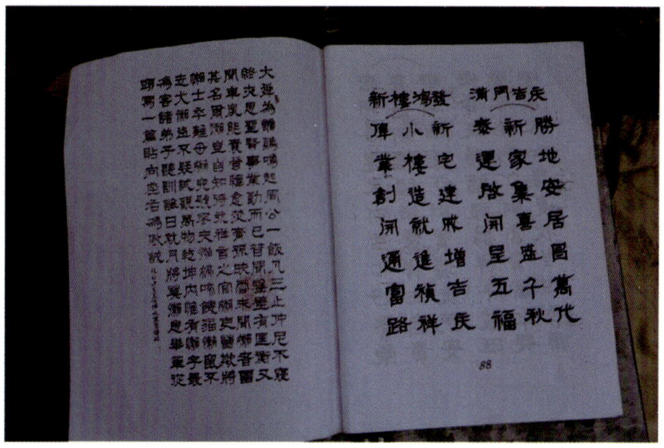

平话山歌歌本
Pinghua Folk Song Book

灵水壮族歌圩

Lingshui Folk Song Fair of Zhuang Ethnic Group

项目名称：灵水壮族歌圩

别称：无

分布范围：武鸣区

入选名录：2016年第六批自治区级非物质文化遗产名录

　　　　　2015年第六批市级非物质文化遗产名录

保护单位：武鸣区文化馆

代表性传承人：潘宝山

Element name: Lingshui Folk Song Fair of Zhuang Ethnic Group

Alternative name: None

Geographical location and range: Wuming District

Element inscribed list: In 2016 on the Sixth Autonomous Region List of Intangible Cultural Heritage

In 2015 on the Sixth Municipal List of Intangible Cultural Heritage

Competent body involved in safeguarding: Wuming District Cultural Centre

Representative inheritor: Pan Baoshan

灵水庙
Lingshui Temple

灵水壮族歌圩是武鸣壮族人民在农历三月三、八月十五举行的传统性歌圩活动。对于能歌善舞的壮族人民来说，唱山歌是其聚众娱乐的主要活动之一，因此歌圩也就成了节日盛会必不可少的项目。自从1982年政府倡导由民间组织在农历八月十五举办第一次灵水之秋歌圩以来，此后每年农历三月三、八月十五，壮族老少都会齐聚湖畔，搭台拉歌，欢声笑语，热闹非凡。如今，灵水歌圩已成为广西歌王大赛的固定举办地，所有受邀参加的歌手都会保持最好的状态，发挥最好的水平，向广大宾客展现灵水壮族山歌的魅力。

灵水位于武鸣区南部，又名灵犀水，传说曾经有两只灵犀鸟在此栖居，时常在水面上嬉戏翩跹，体态优美，色彩亮丽。灵水是一个天然的泉水湖，湖水来自九股从湖边岩石缝隙中不断涌出的清泉，泉水清澈甘润，有“九龙喷水”“龙津吐碧”的美称，并且四季恒温，冬暖夏凉，是温泉旅游胜地。在这样一个风景宜人的地方，当地人民以唱山歌的方式表达对生活的热爱、对未来的祝愿和对美好的向往。

Lingshui Folk Song Fair of Zhuang Ethnic Group is a traditional song fair held by Zhuang people in Wuming District on the lunar March 3rd and the lunar August 15th. For the Zhuang people who are good at singing and dancing, singing folk songs is one of the major activities for the gathering and entertainment. Therefore, the Folk Song Fair is also an indispensable activity in the festival. Since the government initiated the holding of the first Autumn Folk Song Fair of Lingshui on the lunar August 15th in 1982, the Zhuang people, old and young, will gather at the lakeside to sing on the stage with happy laughter and cheerful voices each year on and the lunar March 3rd and the lunar August 15th. Nowadays, Lingshui Folk Song Fair has become a fixed place for the holding of Guangxi Best Singer Competition. The singers being invited to the competition will show the charm of Lingshui folk songs to the guests in their best condition and at the highest level.

Lingshui, the venue of the Folk Song Fair, is located in the south of Wuming District, which is also known as Lingxishui. It is said that there once was two Lingxi birds that often played at the water surface with graceful postures and bright colors. Lingshui is a natural spring water lake, where the water is from nine streams of water emerged from the cracks in the rocks at the lakeside. The water there is clear and sweet, thus it gains reputations of “Water Streams from Nine Dragons” and “Clear Water Bestowed by Dragon”. It can maintain a constant temperature throughout the year, which makes it an attractive resort of hot spring that is warm in winter and cool in summer. In such a beautiful place, the locals often express their love for life and best wishes for a better future by singing folk songs.

As a traditional song party, the singing of folk songs is an indispensable part of Lingshui Folk Song Fair. Folk song singers will gather here to show their superb singing skills every time the Folk Song Fair is held. The traditional songs are humorous and closely related to daily life, which allows the audience to experience the vivid charm and interest of folk song singing of Zhuang Ethnic Group. In addition, Lingshui Folk Song Fair will invite excellent folk song singers both in and out of the Zhuang Autonomous Region to participate into the annual Guangxi Best Singer Competition. Those outstanding singers will comprehensively practice and prepare for the competition, and strive to show their voice on the stage and win the prize of “the Best Singer”. Just as the water streams of Lingshui lake flows day by day, Lingshui Folk Song Fair has also been held year by year without interruption. As time goes by, the lunar March 3rd and the lunar August 15th have become the fixed days for the holing of Lingshui Folk Song Fair every year. On these days, people will gather here and sing folk songs passed down from the ancestors so as to appreciate the long-time happy and harmonious life, which bears the traditional culture of Zhuang Ethnic Group for thousands of years.

Nowadays, the great changes in the society have also affected the cultural space of Lingshui Folk Song Fair to some extent. Fortunately, people of Zhuang Ethnic Group have a high awareness of the inheritance of this folk custom and a strong call for its protection. Therefore, the inheritance of Lingshui Folk Song Fair is in an optimistic condition. In 2013 and 2014, the government of the county allocated special funds for the custom investigation, and organized staff to carry out research and protection work on Lingshui Folk Song Fair. At the same time, various relevant activities have also been held. The activities such as Lingshui Best Singer Competition and Bird Fighting Competition held on the lunar March 3rd in 2014 and 2016 made the Folk Song Fair more colorful and interesting. In 2015, with the approval of the People's Government of Nanning, Lingshui Folk Song Fair of Zhuang Ethnic Group was inscribed on the Sixth Autonomous Reigon List of Intangible Cultural Heritage.

灵水壮族歌圩作为传统歌圩活动，必然少不了山歌的演唱。每逢灵水歌圩举办之时，前来参与的山歌手们都会聚集在此，展示自己高超卓越的歌技。传统的歌唱内容风趣幽默、贴近生活，观众们可以真切地体会到壮族山歌的趣味与魅力。此外，灵水壮族歌圩每年都会邀请自治区内外的山歌高手来灵水进行对歌比赛，一年一度的广西歌王大赛就在此地举行。每年比赛前，优秀的歌手们都会认真练习，积极备赛，争取在歌台上一展歌喉，拿下“歌王”桂冠。灵水日日流，歌圩年年有。久而久之，每年的壮族三月三和农历八月十五就成为灵水歌圩固定举办的日子，人们在此欢聚一堂，唱着祖祖辈辈流传下来的民歌，怀念着一直以来的幸福和谐的日子，表达着对未来生活的美好向往，传承着千百年来的壮族传统文化。

如今，社会的巨大变化也使灵水歌圩的文化空间受到了一定的影响，但所幸壮族民众对于传承这一节庆民俗的自觉性比较高，保护的呼声也相对比较强烈，因此灵水壮族歌圩的传承状况比较乐观。2013年、2014年，县政府划拨普查专项经费，组织人员对灵水歌圩进行调研和保护，并开展各种传习活动。2014和2015年农历三月三期间，还举办了广西歌王大赛“灵水歌圩”歌王对抗赛、斗鸟等民俗活动，使歌圩活动更加丰富多彩。2016年，经过南宁市人民政府同意，灵水壮族歌圩列入第六批自治区级非物质文化遗产名录。

对歌
Singing in Antiphonal Style

扬美龙舟上水节

Yangmei Dragon Boat Sailing Festival

项目名称：扬美龙舟上水节

别称：龙船节、上水节

分布范围：以江南区扬美古镇为中心，广泛流传于南宁市沿江地区

入选名录：2014年第五批自治区级非物质文化遗产名录
2013年第五批市级非物质文化遗产名录

保护单位：江南区文化馆

代表性传承人：无

Element name：Yangmei Dragon Boat Sailing Festival

Alternative name：Dragon Boat Festival, Sailing Festival

Geographical location and range：Yangmei Ancient Town of Jiangnan District as the centre, spreading over the riverside areas of Nanning City

Element inscribed list：In 2014 on the Fifth Autonomous Region List of Intangible Cultural Heritage
In 2013 on the Fifth Municipal List of Intangible Cultural Heritage

Competent body involved in safeguarding：Jiangnan District Cultural Centre

Representative inheritor：None

扬美龙舟上水节祭祀仪式
Sacrificial Ceremony of Yangmei Dragon Boat Sailing Festival

With the Yangmei Ancient Town of Jiangnan District in Nanning as the centre, Yangmei Dragon Boat Sailing Festival is a traditional folk activity widely spreading over the areas along the river in Nanning City. This festival is often held at the Jinma wharf of the Yangmei section of Zuojiang River on the Dragon Boat Festival (the 5th of the 5th lunar month) every year, which is an important original and ecological custom on the Dragon Boat Festival of Yangmei.

Yangmei Dragon Boat Sailing Festival was originally named as Dragon Boat Festival or Sailing Festival, which is a unique sailing custom developed from the dragon boat race that integrates with both worshiping activities and sports competition. As a traditional folk activity, Yangmei Dragon Boat Sailing Festival once was a ceremony held by the dwellers living beside the river. Its real meaning was to put the dragon into the water, thus it can also be called "into-water ceremony". However, to pursue an auspicious and a positive meaning, the dwellers generally called such a ceremony as "above water ceremony" or "sailing ceremony", which was the origin of the name of this festival.

One month before the Dragon Boat Festival every year,

扬美龙舟上水节是以南宁市江南区扬美古镇为中心，广泛流传于南宁市沿江地区的一项传统民俗活动。每年农历五月初五端午节，龙舟上水节在扬美左江河段的金马码头举行，是当地重要的原生态端午习俗。

扬美龙舟上水节原本名为龙船节、上水节，是在赛龙舟的基础上，融入祭祀和体育竞技活动，进而丰富发展起来的一项独具民族特色的水上习俗。作为传统民俗活动，扬美龙舟上水节原是傍水而居的船家人举行的一种上水仪式，其真正寓意是将龙舟放下水面，因此也可以称为“下水仪式”，但船家人为图吉利，一般称之为“上水”，扬美龙舟上水节也由此得名。

每年端午节前一个月，当地人们会把龙船搬进河里泡水，在端午节前两天各家各户包粽子、准备祭祀用品，到了农历五月初五当天，把准备好的祭祀用品按要求摆放至仪式现场，由当地德高望重的长老和道公举行隆重的上水仪式，祈祷风调雨顺、人民幸福安康。整个仪式十分隆重，包括颂词祈福、请师、召龙、走龙、请神、祭河神、画龙点睛、龙舟上水等仪式，通过拜祭祖先、供奉河神、来寄托乡民们的美好祝愿。伴随着龙舟上水节的举行，金马码头还会有传统的歌舞表演、舞龙舞狮和民间杂耍等活动，热闹而喜庆的气氛弥漫在这盛大的节日中，每个人都手舞足蹈、喜笑颜开。经过复杂而隆重的上水仪式后，激动人心的龙舟竞赛就开始了。

作为扬美地区保存完好的民俗传统，扬美龙舟上水节既能满足民众拜祭祖先、供奉河神、求神祈福的心理需要，又能满足民众娱乐竞技的精神需求，是极具代表性的活态扬美民俗文化符号，它传承意义重大，发展前景良好，因此保护和支持扬美龙舟上水节是当地必不可少的一项工作。

1997年后，江南区政府对扬美龙舟上水节予以大力支持，活动规模和影响越来越大，其内容包括上水仪式、龙舟竞赛及文娱活动等，每年到场群众达2万多人。2011年6月，江南区政府将扬美龙舟上水节列入江南区级非物质文化遗产名录。2012年，江南区政府对扬美龙舟上水节划拨专项资金予以扶持。2014年，经广西壮族自治区人民政府同意，扬美龙舟上水节列入第五批自治区级非物质文化遗产名录。

people will put the dragon boats into the water. Two days before the festival, the local families will begin to prepare zongzi and other offerings. On the fifth day of the fifth lunar month, people will put the prepared offerings as required to the ceremony. The ceremony will be hosted by the local Taoist priests with high prestige, in which they will pray for good weather and happy life for people. The whole ceremony is very grand. It includes praying, inviting Taoist priests, calling for the dragon, touring the dragon, inviting the god, sacrificial rite for the River God, drawing the dragon and putting dragon boats above the water. Through worshiping ancestors and the River God, the festival represents people's good wish for the future. To accompany the holding of the Dragon Boat Sailing Festival, traditional dancing and singing performances, dragon and lion dances and folk sideshows will also be held at the Jinma wharf. The grand festival will be filled with lively and jubilant atmosphere and people all will light up with pleasure. After the complicated and solemn ceremony, the exciting dragon boat race will begin.

As a well-preserved folk tradition in Yangmei region, Yangmei Dragon Boat Sailing Festival can not only satisfy people's psychological need of worshiping ancestors, offering River God and praying for blessings, but also can meet people's spiritual demand of entertainment and sports competition, which is a representative cultural symbol of Yangmei folk customs. The inheritance of the festival bears great significance and has a good prospect, thus the protection and support of Yangmei Dragon Boat Sailing Festival is an indispensable to the local departments.

After 1997, the government of Jiangnan District began to give great support to Yangmei Dragon Boat Sailing Festival, and the scale and influence of the festival has become larger and larger. The major activities of the festival include above-water ceremony, dragon boat race and some other cultural and entertainment activities, with nearly 20,000 people coming to visit every year. In 2011, the government of Jiangnan District inscribed Yangmei Dragon Boat Sailing Festival on the Intangible Cultural Heritage List of Jiangnan District. In 2012, the government allocated special funds to support the development of the festival. In 2014, with the approval of the People's Government of the Guangxi Zhuang Autonomous Region, Yangmei Dragon Boat Sailing Festival was inscribed on the Fifth Autonomous Region List of Intangible Cultural Heritage.

宾阳“三娘乖”习俗

Binyang Sanniangguai Folkways

项目名称：宾阳“三娘乖”习俗

别称：无

分布范围：宾阳县

入选名录：2012年第四批自治区级非物质文化遗产名录

保护单位：宾阳县文化馆

代表性传承人：无

Element name：Binyang Sanniangguai Folkways

Alternative name：None

Geographical location and range：Binyang County

Element inscribed list：In 2012 on the Fourth Autonomous Region List of Intangible Cultural Heritage

Competent body involved in safeguarding：Binyang County Cultural Centre

Representative inheritor：None

宾阳"三娘乖"习俗是宾阳县的特色民俗活动，流传于宾阳县全境。"三娘乖"历史悠久，起源自唐贞观五年（631）。相传，三娘是天上的仙女，投胎做了凡人。她心灵手巧，禀性聪慧，据说如今宾阳乡间妇女所做的纺纱织布、绣花绘画、磨谷碓米、播种插秧等手艺，都是由她传授而流传下来的。当时宾阳有一个县官的儿子叫赵昂，长相丑陋，横行乡里，见三娘长得既漂亮又有手艺，便想娶她为妻。他多次差媒求亲无果后，便使诡计向三娘逼婚，三娘不从投粪坑而死。从此，每年正月初四晚上开始，得到三娘生前传艺的姐妹们，都来到粪坑祭拜她。

宾阳"三娘乖"的参拜者均为农村未婚少女，年龄在12—15岁之间，该活动从正月初四开始进行，视参加的人数而决定活动的持续时间，有多少人就需要持续多少天，而且每晚都要参加祭拜三娘活动。每个晚上祭拜"三批香"的时间，每批燃三根香。在祭拜活动之前，众姐妹要将三娘偶像扎好。众姐妹聚于一处后，将三娘偶像及供品等装进加盖的箩筐，然后每人手持一根点燃的香紧随，一同前往村外某个已停止使用的旱粪坑处请三娘。请回三娘后需将其抬到早已选定的某参拜者家中，不能置于夫妻居住过的房屋，以示少女的贞洁。祭拜活动为音乐演唱兼念诵形式，有《请娘歌》《引娘歌》《十姐妹》《赞娘歌》《传艺歌》《四季思歌》《诉苦歌》《散了思歌》等约400行。其中《散了思歌》又称《送神歌》，为祭祀活动的收尾作品。该歌唱完之后，便将"三娘"焚化以示送别升天，而后比赛吹烤葱和穿花针。"葱"与"聪"谐音，吹响烤葱，寓意在三娘的佑护下会越来越聪慧；穿花针的比赛仅仅以一支香作照明工具，最先将丝线穿过针孔的孩子获胜。没有获胜的人只能等明年再参与比赛。比赛活动之后，众人回家会餐吃素菜米粉，整个活动宣告结束。

宾阳"三娘乖"习俗，承载着宾阳先民特别是宾阳女性对于美好生活的向往。"三娘乖"仪式饱含了长辈对少女

Binyang Sanniangguai folkway is a folk activity popular in Binyang County. It has a long history originated in the fifth year of Zhenguan of the Tang Dynasty (631 A.D.). It is said that Sanniang was once a fairy who was reborn as a mortal. She was clever in mind and skillful in hand. It is said that many skills, such as spinning and weaving, embroidery and painting, rice milling and planting, are handed down by women of generations from the fairy. A legend says that the son of the county magistrate was named Zhou'ang, who was ugly and domineering. When he saw Sanniang, who is either beautiful or skilful, the girl enchanting him very much, he wanted to marry her at once. After several courtship failed, he forced her to marry by wicked tricks. Sanniang had no choice but to commit suicide by jumping into dung pits. Since then, girls who had learned skills from Sanniang came to the dung pit to worship her on the fourth night of the first lunar month every year.

Worshippers are all rural virgins whose age were between 12 and 15. The activity started on the fourth day of the first lunar month, and the end time depends on the number of participants. Every night sacrificial activity will be held for three batches of incense with three incenses each batch. Thc figure of Sanniang should be prepared before sacrifice, which will be placed with offerings into the covered baskets. Then each of the girls held burning incense and went to an abandoned dung pit outside the village to invite Sanniang. They would carry her to the home of a worshipper that had been selected for a long time. Sanniang could not be carried to the house where the couple lived, so as to show the virginity of the girls. The worship activities are composed of singing and chanting. There are about 400 lines, such as *Song to Invite Sanniang, Song to Guide Sanniang, Ten Sisters, Hymn to Sanniang, Art Song, Yearning for Four Seasons* and *Relieving Melancholy*. Among them, the last is also known as "*Farewell to the God*", which is the end of sacrificial activities. After the song was finished, Sanniang is burned to show farewell to heaven, and then the game of blowing grilled scallions and threading needles will begin. Scallions in Chinese are homophonic to Cong (meaning clever in Chinese), so blowing grilled scallions implies that girls will become more and more intelligent under the blessing of Sanniang. When in the competition of threading needles, only incense could be used as a lighting tool, and the winner is the girl who first makes the thread through the pinhole. Those who lose have to wait next competition until next year. The activities will not be over unless people go home to enjoy vegetarian noodles for dinner after the competition.

The custom bears ancestors' (especially women) yearning for a better life. The ceremony of "Sanniangguai" is full of elders' expectations for a bright future of their girls. They hope that girls could be as clever as Sanniang after marriage, be a person who has handicraft and knows agricultural production, and be a daughter-in-law of a respected family, so that they can relish their happy marriage life. Traditionally, only girls of a certain age can participate in the custom, and males could not participate in the activities. Moreover, this kind of worship by singing and reciting is also one of the few recreations for rural women to learn culture and art. It is not only of great cultural value, but also of great significance in forming a positive system of values of young girls. Girls at a very young age learn that productive labor is benificial and a satisfying life should be created by their own strength, when they absorb know-how of handicraft making, agricultural cultivation and livestock feeding.

The educational opportunities have been expanded to rural areas with the development of economic and culture. Sanniangguai folkway has been impacted a lot and few inheritors are prepared for impartment and further development, as it is a traditional folk custom based on former rural environment. In order to protect, inherit and develop this custom, Binyang County has set up a special leadership group to conduct a detailed and comprehensive census for it. Teaching groups of "Sanniangguai" project were set up in primary and secondary schools as well as compiling group of singing and recitation. A special competition on singing and reciting of "Sanniangguai" will be held every two years, and some customs has gradually restored in several areas. More people are expected to join the custom practicing as era characteristics are added to brighten the folkways.

们生活的企盼，希望她们在嫁人后能够向三娘一样心灵手巧，做一个既有手工技艺又懂得农业生产的人，做个好人家的媳妇，婚姻生活幸福美满。传统“三娘乖”习俗只有特定年龄的少女才能参加，男性是不能参加活动的。这种以演唱和念诵的方式进行的祭拜活动，也是农村女性学习文化艺术的渠道和为数不多的娱乐活动之一，有着深厚的文化价值。此外，在向少女们传播一些手工艺和农业种植、饲养知识的时候，也是在逐步培养她们从小热爱生产劳动，用自己双手去创造幸福的意识，这对孩子形成正确的价值观有着重要的作用。

随着经济的发展和文化的繁荣，农村教育不断普及，立足于农村环境的“三娘乖”习俗的影响力逐渐减小，其传承和发展陷入尴尬的局面。为了保护、传承和发展这一传统习俗，宾阳县建立专门的保护传承领导小组，进行细致而全面的普查工作；在各中小学设立“三娘乖”项目教学工作组，并设立中小学演唱、诵念编写组；每两年举办一届“三娘乖”演唱和念诵专题比赛，逐步将某些地区的“三娘乖”习俗恢复起来；在该习俗中加入时代特色，让更多人参与进来，以扩大其受众范围。

“三娘乖”习俗现场
Sanniangguai Folkways

游彩架

Caijia Parade

项目名称：游彩架

别称：游色架

分布范围：宾阳县

入选名录：2008年第二批自治区级非物质文化遗产名录

保护单位：宾阳县文化馆

代表性传承人：覃凤梧、周宏年、何丹健

Element name：Caijia Parade

Alternative name：Sejia Parade

Geographical location and range：Binyang County

Element inscribed list：In 2008 on the Second Autonomous Region List of Intangible Cultural Heritage

Competent body involved in safeguarding：Binyang County Cultural Centre

Representative inheritors：Qin Fengwu, Zhou Hongnian, He Danjian

游彩架
Caijia Parade

安装彩架
Installation of Caijia

Caijia Parade, also named "Sejia Parade" or "Caijia" for short, is often held during the Spring Festival, which is a folk custom loved by the locals of Binyang County.

Caijia Parade boasts a long history of more than 100 years. According to historical data, it was introduced here by a Cantonese Li Ruozhu in the thirteenth year of Emperor Tongzhi in the Qing Dynasty (1874). He taught the local artists to make Caijia by using a Caijia set he had brought from his hometown. In such case, Binyang Caijia came into shape with exquisite decoration and breathtaking performing, such as Picking up Jade Bracelet, Making A Living by Martial Arts in Pairs, Mirror with Image of Sika and Xiangjiang River Convention. It is an art form which combines skills and fine sculpts, with wooden or iron board tables as its carrier. A group of 5-6-year-old children, after clever dressing up, are fixed on the upper, middle, lower, left and right positions of a square table, and the plot of the legends will be conveyed to audience through modeling, makeup and some text tips. Binyang Caijia Parade actually could be divided into procedures of figure design and parade performing. The former is including pre-design, square table devising, fork making, welding fame and frame fixing. The fame, also called strips, cannot be welded more than 3.5 meters, and the design hanging over should

游彩架又叫“游色架”，简称“彩架”，一般于春节期间举行，是宾阳县群众喜闻乐见的民俗项目。

游彩架民俗活动历史悠久，据史料载，宾阳游彩架于清代同治十三年（1874）由广东佛山武举人李若珠传到此处，至今已有100多年的历史。李若珠自老家带回一套彩架道具，指导民间艺人按中国古典文学中的人物形象进行造型，制作成“拾玉镯”“双卖武”“梅鹿镜”“湘江大会”等彩架，以精美的装饰和惊险的表演引人注目，这便是宾阳彩架的开始。游彩架以木质或铁质板桌为载体，是一种技巧与造型相结合的艺术形式。将一组5—6岁的孩童巧妙装扮后，固定在方桌板的上、中、下，左、右等不同位置上，通过造型、化妆以及一些文字提示，为人们展演一组古今故事。其主要流程分为艺术造型的制作和游行表演。艺术造型的制作又分为前期设计、方桌设计、护叉制作、焊台架、装架等工序。焊台架又称“焊发条”，发条最高点为3.5米，高空造型的宽度不能超过台阁桌面，发条中心要均衡。游行表演时要有四人抬桌或者推行，并有两人持叉随行，时刻注意保护演员安全。游行时伴以舞龙、八音等。

彩架经过几十代艺人的更新改造，一直兴盛不衰。1991年秋，宾阳彩架曾参加全国第四届少数民族运动会开幕式表演，一时间轰动南宁，令观演群众叹为观止。

游彩架在新春之际进行，它依附于重大节日庆典，带给观众美轮美奂的视觉冲击，让节日气氛更为浓郁。宾阳游彩架具有较高的艺术性和观赏性，每台游彩架都在传达一个故事，都是以人物艺术形象为主体，造型各有千秋，艺术风格迥异，堪称空中的“活雕塑”。宾阳游彩架的制作与呈现集雕塑、绘画、化妆、服装、数学、力学、美学等多学科知识与技艺为一体，是一项综合表演形式，对丰富节日庆典和人民群众的文化生活有着重要作用。

游彩架制作技艺高超，声名远播，进入20世纪90年代后，得到宾阳县委、县政府以及社区群众的大力支持和广泛参与。游彩架活动是当地节日庆典中必不可少的项目，经常应邀组团到外地进行表演，传承队伍不断扩大，影响力不断增强。2006年，宾阳县政府组织游彩架表演队参加全国彩架表演比赛，获全国十佳入围奖；同年，宾阳县游彩架表演队又受邀参加了八桂旅游狂欢节、南宁国际民歌艺术节等活动，受到当地观众的热烈欢迎和广泛好评。这些活动使游彩架这一民俗活动得到了较好的传承和发展。

游彩架
Caijia Parade

not be taller than the height of the table with a balanced holding strip. When a parade is carried out, there should be four people to raise or push the table forward, and two people holding forks to accompany, so as to ensure the safety of actors. The whole process will be accompanied by dragon dance and music with eight pitches.

After being upgraded by generations of artists, Binyang Caijia Parade has gone through a long history and still remains popular today. In the autumn of 1991, Binyang Caijia parade participated into the opening performance of the Fourth National Sports Event for Minorities, on which the performance made a great flutter and amazed all the audiences.

Caijia Parade is often held during the Spring Festival. It relies on major festivals and ceremonies and can bring people with exciting visual shock, which is good to heighten the festive atmosphere. Each of the Caijia has its own ancient or modern background and story, thus the parade bears high artistry and ornamental value. The images of the Caijia are often artistic figures with different materials, postures and styles, which bestows Caijia with more charm. Therefore, Caijia can be called the “live sculpture in the sky”. The production and presentation of Caijia has integrated with sculpture, painting, makeup, costume, mathematics, mechanics, aesthetics and other multidisciplinary knowledge and skills, thus the Caijia parade can be regarded as a comprehensive form of performance.

With exquisite making skill, Caijia Parade has been renowned nowadays. After entering the 1990s. with the strong support and wide participation of the party committee and the government of Binyang County and the local people, Binyang Caijia Parade has become an indispensable part of the local festival celebration. In addition, the Caijia parade is often invited to perform in other places, thus the scale and influence of the inheritance team has been gradually enlarged. In 2006, the government of Binyang County organized Binyang Caijia Parade performance team to participate in the National Caijia Parade Performance Competition and won the “Award of Top Ten”. In the same year, the parade team of Caijia was invited to participate in Bagui Tourism Carnival, Nanning International Folk Song Art Festival and other activities. Wherever the parade arrives, it will be warmly welcomed and well received by the local audience. All these activities have provided good opportunities for a better inheritance and development of Binyang Caijia Parade.

横县壮族三相圩逢

Hengxian Sanxiang County Fair of Zhuang Ethnic Group

项目名称：横县壮族三相圩逢

别称：无

分布范围：横州市石塘镇、灵竹镇，宾阳县甘棠镇、露圩镇

入选名录：2014年第五批自治区级非物质文化遗产名录

保护单位：横县文化馆

代表性传承人：梁肇儒

Element name：Hengxian Sanxiang County Fair of Zhuang Ethnic Group

Alternative name：None

Geographical location and range：Shitang Town and Lingzhu Town of Hengzhou City, Gantang Town and Luxu Town of Binyang County

Element inscribed list：In 2014 on the Fifth Autonomous Region List of Intangible Cultural Heritage

Competent body involved in safeguarding：Hengxian Cultural Centre

Representative inheritors：Liang Zhaoru

表演麒麟舞
Performing Kirin Dance at the Country Fair

“圩逢”在壮语中意为“歌圩”“庙会”，横县壮族三相圩逢是群众自发举行的民俗活动盛会，于每年三相庙庙诞——农历六月十四至十七举行。三相庙位于横州石塘镇沙江村凤凰岭中，奉祀刘备、关羽、张飞。圩逢持续三天四夜，内容丰富，节目繁多，主要有山歌对唱、民俗文化、祭祀酬神、三国文化传承、革命传统教育等活动。与其他地区的圩逢活动相比，横县三相圩逢持续时间更长，受到广大人民群众的喜爱。

横县三相圩逢历史悠久，形成于明朝永乐年间，传承至今已经有600多年。三相圩逢是横州先民以纪念刘备、关羽、张飞为依托而形成的一项民俗活动。相传三国时期，华南战乱，民不聊生，刘备携义弟关羽、张飞率兵为民除害。世人感其恩德，便在凤凰岭上为其树碑石祭祀，以作纪念。据载，古时人们对“三相”的信仰活动开始于南北朝时期，流行于唐朝，明朝时更为繁盛，明朝永乐元年（1403），当地民众集资在凤凰岭修盖庙宇，奉祀刘备、关羽、张飞三人，故称“三相庙”。而以纪念“三相”功德的圩逢也就应运而生，并沿袭至今。

Xufeng means song fair or temple fair in Zhuang language. Sanxiang Xufeng in Hengxian is a grand event of folklore held by people spontaneously. It will be held on the anniversary of Sanxiang Temple which is from lunar June 14th to lunar June 17th. Sanxiang Temple stands in Phoenix Hill, Shajiang Village, Shitang Town, Hengzhou City. Liu Bei, Guan Yu and Zhang Fei are enshrined and worshipped in the temple. Xufeng will last for three days and four nights. It has various contents and diversified activities including dialogue singing, folklore activities, worship to gods, heritage of culture in the Three Kingdoms, education of revolution and liberation, etc. Sanxiang Xufeng in Hengxian lasts longer compared with other Xufeng activities, which earned it the favor of people.

Born in Emperor Yongle period of the Ming Dynasty, Sanxiang Xufeng has a 600 hundred years' history. In memory of three heroes in the Three Kingdoms Liu Bei, Guan Yu and Zhang Fei, ancestors created this folklore event. It is said that in the Three Kingdoms, wars wreaked havoc in southern China and people struggled to survive. Liu Bei and his two brothers Guan Yu and Zhang Fei eliminate evil for people. Being gratitude to their kindness, local people establish monument for them on Phoenix Hill. According to classics, the worship to "three heroes" started from the Northern and Southern Dynasty, prospers in the Tang Dynasty and reached its peak in the Ming Dynasty. In 1403, the Ming Dynasty, local people raised funds and constructed a temple on Phoenix

Hill to worship the three heroes. And Sanxiang Xufeng which also aimed to commemorate the three heroes was also born. This event lasts till present time.

According to textual research, song fair of Zhuang Ethnic Group originated from the ancient scared activity, whose history can be traced back to clan tribe era. At first, people would worship ancestors or tribe leaders or other "legendary" characters. Time passed by and the song fair became less of religious mysterious rite but more of a platform for people to people exchange and a stage for singing. Sanxiang Xufeng is a distinguished representative of the song fair of Zhuang Ethnic Group. It still keeps the tradition of a night song fair. When night falls, people will gather and sing songs with touch light. The activity will last for the whole night and people will not leave until daybreak. Sanxiang Xufeng is a comprehensive event which covers the areas of religion, culture and art. With large scale and rich content, the song fair enables various cultures and art forms to integrate with each other. It is an epitome for local culture, as well as the reflection of Zhuang people's belief in the art and life. What's more, Sanxiang Song Fair originated from three heroes. It also reflects the culture exchange between Han Ethnic Group and Zhuang Ethnic Group. It is of great value in studying the spreading and influence of Han culture in minority habitats.

With the great support of leaders at all level, activities about Sanxiang Xufeng are smoothly operating. However, risks still remain in some places. For example, old masters of songs and Shigong Opera may gradually leave the stage due to poor health and economic factors. Teenagers do not have the sense of protection or heritage due to personal interests or economic factors. The future of this comprehensive event is worrying. In order to inherit and develop Sanxiang Xufeng, Centre for the protection of intangible cultural heritage in Hengzhou City had a comprehensive survey about Sanxiang Xufeng and sorted out the document of Xufeng. Meanwhile, the centre also trains a new generation of inheritors. The clothes and tools used in Xufeng are carefully recorded and preserved. With the help of tourism resources, localities also hold travel festival with local ethnic style themed by Sanxiang Xufeng, which will attract more people's eyes. Under the premise of maintaining the culture essence, performers will also have more income and will be more active in participating in the folklore activities.

据考证，壮族歌圩源于氏族部落时代的祭祀性歌舞活动，主要祭祀壮族先民始祖、部落首领等具有神话色彩的人物。后来，这种祭祀性活动逐渐演变成以民间交流为主，着重于歌唱活动而淡化其原始宗教的神秘形式。三相圩逢是壮族歌圩的典型代表，至今还保留着夜歌圩的传统。夜幕降临，歌手们打着手电筒聚在一起唱歌，通宵达旦，一直唱到早晨才各自离去。横县壮族三相圩逢是一项综合性的民俗活动，涉及宗教信仰和文化艺术领域。其规模宏大、内容丰富，各种文化和艺术样式互相交融，是岭南壮族民俗文化的缩影，是壮族人民宗教信仰的文化层面和生活层面的反映。此外，横县壮族三相圩逢也反映了汉族文化与壮族文化的交流与融合，对研究汉族文化在少数民族地区的传播和影响有着非常重要的价值。

横县壮族三相圩逢在各级领导的大力支持下，各种活动的开展都较为顺利，但是许多地方仍旧存在着一些隐患。比如山歌师傅和演出师公戏的师傅，因为身体、经济等原因逐步退出舞台，年轻人因为个人兴趣和经济等因素也没有形成保护和传承意识，致使这项综合性的民俗活动前途堪忧。为了传承和发展三相圩逢这一文化遗产，横州市非物质文化遗产保护中心对三相圩逢进行全面普查，将普查资料整理归档，同时培养了一批代表性传承人，并将三相圩逢活动中所使用的服装、道具进行统计和保存，依托旅游资源举办以三相圩逢为主题的民俗风情文化旅游节，以增加其知名度。在保留其文化底蕴的前提下，为三相圩逢的演职人员创收增收提供机会，以提高他们参与传统民俗活动的积极性。

露圩壮族圩逢

Luxu County Fair of Zhuang Ethnic Group

项目名称：露圩壮族圩逢

别称：无

分布范围：宾阳县露圩镇

入选名录：2014年第五批自治区级非物质文化遗产名录

保护单位：宾阳县文化馆

代表性传承人：黄桂梅

Element name：Luxu County Fair of Zhuang Ethnic Group

Alternative name：None

Geographical location and range：Luxu Town of Binyang County

Element inscribed list：In 2014 on the Fifth Autonomous Region List of Intangible Cultural Heritage

Competent body involved in safeguarding：Binyang County Cultural Centre

Representative inheritor：Huang Guimei

仙马巡游
Fairy Horse Parade

民俗游行
Folk Parade

In Luxu of Binyang, Niudan (Cattle Birthday) Festival will be held every year on lunar April 8th for the god of thunder. Grand song and art performance will also be held. In Zhuang language, people call it Xufeng, which means country fair. Xu means fair while "Feng" means carnival. Luxu is the habitat for Lanyi (Blue Clothes) Zhuang people. Xufeng is a folk festival based on the integration of local Zhuang culture and cultures of other ethnic groups. The festival shows that Zhuang people are good at literature and martial arts. They are hardworking and are skillful in singing and dancing. The festival shows people's uprising spirit and is peculiar in Binyang and the whole province.

According to inscription on bell of Luxu Temple which was rebuilt in Emperor Jiaqing period of the Qing Dynasty, Xufeng started from the end of the Ming Dynasty and prospered in the Qing Dynasty. It has more than 380 years' history. The birth of Luxu was said to be related to divine cattle. Long time ago, a god passed Luxu with cattle. People here are talented and the natural resources are abundant. One of the cattle was obsessed to the beautiful natural scenery. It stayed here hence and helped people with ploughing and weeding. Thanks to the cattle, local people got rid of harsh life and started a happy and flourishing life. The god found the missing cattle later and changed the cattle into a mountain. The cattle appeared on lunar April 8th and people took this day as the birth of cattle. Ancestors also built Leilu Temple

在宾阳县的露圩镇，每年农历四月初八均会举行祭祀雷神、纪念“牛诞日”的活动，并伴以盛大的山歌对唱及文艺表演，壮语将其称为圩逢。圩是集市，逢意为狂欢。露圩镇是蓝衣壮族人民聚居的地方，此地的圩逢便是在蓝衣壮民族文化的基础上，充分吸收其他民族的优秀文化得以形成确立的民俗节庆活动。通过盛大的圩逢，充分展现了壮乡儿女崇文尚武、勤劳勇敢、能歌善舞、昂扬向上的精神风貌，成为宾阳县乃至广西壮族自治区民俗文化之林中的一朵奇葩。

据清朝嘉庆年重修露圩大庙的钟鼓铭文记载，露圩圩逢始自明末崇祯年间，清朝年间尤盛，距今已有380多年的历史。露圩圩逢的成圩相传与神牛有关。很久以前，有位天神赶众神牛途经露圩，有头神牛见露圩山清水秀，田畴壮美，人杰地灵，十分留恋，遂停留此地帮助人们耕地耙田，结束了先民刀耕火种的艰苦劳动，人们因此过上了五谷丰登、幸福美满的生活。不久，天神寻找到丢失的神牛，将其点化为神牛岭。因神牛出现之日为农历四月初八，为感恩神牛，先民便将农历四月初八规定为“牛诞日”，并于神牛岭修建雷露庙供奉三帝。庙宇每年均会举行盛大的庙会活动，吸引了四方香客信众前来祈祷敬拜，可视作圩逢的雏形。承载了祭祀、感恩活动的圩逢，成为蓝衣壮人最独特的民族象征。

露圩圩逢活动开始于农历四月初八子时，三帝庙众僧侣道人及民间会首响鼓诵经，做法祭拜。晨起，僧侣为四方来客举行开光、请愿、还愿等法事活动。因感神牛之恩，各户还会于此日暂停牛耕，以枫叶水为牛擦身，喂牛以枫叶水煮成的糯米饭及甜酒饭，并为其披红挂彩。与此同时，各村屯的马娘队、舞牛队、舞彩凤队、舞麒麟队等民间艺术队也会陆续前来庙宇参拜三帝。祭礼过后，热闹的游行表演活动便正式开始了，其中包括唱山歌、文艺表演、武术表演等。将活动推向高潮的是山歌对唱环节，参与者均身着蓝衣，男男女女于流水竹林间以五言壮欢即兴对唱，抒发大家在生产、生活中的真知灼见，将壮族人民以歌言志、以歌会友、以歌传情的优良传统展现得淋漓尽致。圩逢节既满足了人们一年一度期盼风调雨顺、五谷丰登、丁财两旺的心理诉求，又给了民众沟通情感、休闲娱乐的契机。

如今，受到流行文化的冲击，类似壮欢这样古老的民间艺术在年轻人眼里显得“土气”和“过时”，舞马、舞凤、舞麒麟及扎马、扎凤、扎麒麟等技艺更是鲜少有年轻一辈愿意学习，露圩四月八圩逢节面临濒危的困境。针对这些现状，露圩镇政府做了一系列挖掘、抢救和传承的工作，如在镇中心小学成立蓝衣壮山歌兴趣班，招收上百名小学生，由乡镇比较有名气的山歌传承人在课堂上传授山歌。在当地政府的大力支持下，传统圩逢节得到了较好的传承。

on the mountain to worship gods. Every year the temple will have great ceremonies and temple fairs which attract many followers. This is the original form of Xufeng. Xufeng which bears tribute to gods and gratitude to ancestors has become the most distinctive feature for Lanyi Zhuang people.

Xufeng starts at one o'clock on lunar April 8th. Monks in Sandi Temple and leaders of local people will ring the bell and chant sutra. After the start of the ceremony, monks will hold blessing ceremony, present petition to gods and redeem the petition to gods. In memory of the mercy from the cattle, every family will stop ploughing and bathe their cattle with maple leaf water. People will feed the cattle with sticky rice and sweet alcohol rice. The cattle will also be dressed in red clothes. At the same time, horse team, cattle dance team, phoenix dance team, Kylin dance team and other artists will visit the temple and pay their tribute to the gods successively. After the ceremony, cruise activity will formally start. The activities include singing, art performance and martial art performance. Singing is the key part which will drive the whole event to its peak. Participants will wear blue clothes and sing five-character Zhuang folk songs intrusively towards each other in forests and near rivers. People could express their feelings and exchange inspiration from daily life. Zhuang people have the tradition to express thoughts and feelings in songs and make friends by songs. And this tradition is well showed in Xufeng. Xufeng satisfies people's need in praying for mild weather, harvest, richness and healthy. It also offers an opportunity for people to communicate and entertain.

Nowadays, under the shock of changeable fashion culture, young people think these old arts are outdated and rustic. Few young people would like to learn Horse Dance, Phoenix Dance, Kylin Dance, Making Horse, Making Phoenix, Making Kylin and other techniques. Xufeng in Luxu is faced with the risk of extinction. In order to address these problems, local government initiates a series of work in order to investigate, rescue and inherit Luxu. For example, local government promotes training courses about Lanyi Zhuang songs in central primary school and recruit hundreds of primary school pupils. Inheritors with fame will also teach on the classes. With the huge support from local government, traditional Luxu is well preserved and inherited.

横县笔山人生礼仪

Hengxian Bishan Life Etiquette

项目名称：横县笔山人生礼仪

别称：无

分布范围：横州市平朗乡笔山村及周边地区

入选名录：2014年第五批自治区级非物质文化遗产名录

保护单位：横县文化馆

代表性传承人：无

Element name：Hengxian Bishan Life Etiquette

Alternative name：None

Geographical location and range：Bishan Village of Pinglang Town in Hengzhou City and the surrounding areas

Element inscribed list：In 2014 on the Fifth Autonomous Region List of Intangible Cultural Heritage

Competent body involved in safeguarding：Hengxian Cultural Centre

Representative inheritor：None

新生儿满月男方家到"新丁会"庆贺
Celebration of a Baby's First Month of Life

在横州市平朗乡笔山村及其周边地区，流传着一系列独特的、极具地域文化色彩的传统民间习俗——笔山人生礼仪，据传已有500多年的历史。在笔山，每逢生育、成年、寿诞等人生重要环节，当地人均会举行特定的仪式。有着丰富内涵的人生礼仪，既体现了生育、家庭、宗教等社会制度对个人地位的规定和角色的认可，也体现着特定的文化规范对个体的人格塑造，是将个体生命加以社会化的程序和阶段性标志。根据不同历史时期的社会发展状况，笔山人生礼仪有着不同的表现形式，对我们研究当地民间习俗的发展演变有着较高的学术价值。

笔山，原名诗屋山，多丘陵、土山。笔山村位于平朗乡中部，是横州市笔山行政村下辖的一个自然村，全村总面积约3平方千米，总人口约为1350人。笔山村文化底蕴深厚，流传至今的人生礼仪习俗可追溯到明朝宣德成化年间。当年，邕宁天堂村人迁入笔山，成人礼仪随之进入此地。一

In Bishan Village of Pinglang, Hengzhou City and neighboring areas, one set of unique traditional folklore—Bishan Life Etiquette is widely spread. It is said to have 500 years of history. In Bishan village, on birthday, puberty rite or other important occasions, local people will hold special ceremonies with rich content. These ceremonies show family, religion and other social structures' recognition to people and their stipulation to people's social status. The ceremonies also represent the modeling of people character from the culture. They are the periodical symbols of the socialization of individual persons. Life etiquette has different forms in different historical periods and different societies. It is of high academic value for us to study the evolution of folklore.

Bishan used to be called Shiwushan. It has many hills and the landscape is earth hill. Bishan village is located in the centre part of Pinglang. It is a natural village under the administration of Hengzhou City. Bishan covers an area of 3 square kilometers and the population is 1350. Bishan has profound culture. The life etiquette which lasts to today can be traced back to Xuande and Chenghua periods of the Ming Dynasty. At that time, people from Yongning Tiantang village migrated to Bishan and brought the puberty rite to Bishan. Generations of Bishan people pass the tradition to present time by personal examples and verbal instructions. It has five centuries' history. During the War of Resistance Against Japan, War of Liberation and Cultural Revolution, the etiquette was once stopped but recovered in the 1970s and 1980s by a new generation of people in Bishan.

Life etiquette consists of pregnancy rite, birth rite for newborns, adult rite, marriage rite, birth rite for old people and funeral rite. They will be carried out by every families themselves. When a woman is pregnant, the family will hold rite in order to pray blessings from god and ensure the health of mother and child. After the birth, father will report the good news to parents-in-law. The mother of pregnant woman will then spread the good news to her relatives by marriage. On the very day of birth, three days after birth, one month after birth, one hundred days after birth and one year after birth, people will hold celebration and rite for blessings for the child. In the past, the newly married couple who have child will also join "newborn society" in local village. People will hold various ceremonies to pray for the children. When boys are 20 years old, men will hold "Hat Rite" and girls will change their hair style when they are 15 years old, which are symbols of adulthood. The marriage and pregnancy rite have two parts. Marriage rite includes Nacai, Qingqi, Yingqin and other three steps. Pregnancy rite is different for different genders. It has Nongzhang and Nongwa ceremonies. Parents will also entrust their children to another couple. Old people will hold a formal birthday banquet after 60 years old which includes Rulian, Chubin, Xiaoqi and other 8 steps. Life etiquettes in Bishan connect individual families with the society and enrich the spiritual life of local people.

With the advancement of technology and science and the implementation of basic national public health programs, people do not attach as much emphasis to Life Etiquette and Bishan Life Etiquette faces the threat of extinction. In order to inherit and develop the excellent cultural heritage, local government invests and starts multi-channel protection. It establishes a working group and designs the protection plan and measures. In 2014, it was inscribed on the Fifth Autonomous Region List of Intangible Cultural Heritage. With rescuing exploration, investigation, collection and sorting, the precious Life Etiquette could be inherited and promoted.

代代笔山人靠口传身授将礼仪传统延续，抗日战争、解放战争、“文革”时期曾中断，20世纪七八十年代后又重新恢复，被新一代笔山人所传承。

笔山人生礼仪包含怀孕礼、出生礼、成年礼、婚育礼、寿诞礼、丧葬礼六部分内容，由各家独自进行。逢女子怀孕，会施礼祈神，保母子平安。孩子出生后，一般由孩子的父亲先去岳父母家报喜，再由外婆到女儿家向亲家送喜，之后分别在出生当日、三朝、满月、百日、周岁这五个特定日期举行庆贺、祈福仪式。过去，新婚后生子的家庭，还会加入当地的“新丁”会，举行各种仪式为孩子祈福。男子长至20岁，会举行冠礼；女子长至15岁，则改变发式，做加笄，视作成年。婚育礼包含婚礼与育礼两部分，婚礼包括纳采、请期、亲迎等六礼，育礼则依据生男生女的不同，分别有“弄璋”“弄瓦”仪式和认寄父母仪式。自60周岁始，每整十年举办一次较为正式的寿宴，视作寿诞礼。生命终结时，则会举行丧葬礼，包含孝终、洗礼入殓、出殡、孝期等8个礼仪。笔山人生礼仪不仅沟通和连接了个人与群体的关系，也丰富了当地人的精神文化生活。

随着科学技术的进步和国家基本公共卫生服务项目的实施，人们对传统人生礼仪的重视度开始下降，笔山人生礼仪面临濒危的困境。为传承和发展这一优秀的民间文化遗产，当地政府拨款并着力开展了多渠道的保护工作。各级相关部门也成立了专项保护工作组，制定保护方案及措施。2014年列入第五批自治区级非物质文化遗产名录。通过抢救性地挖掘、收集、整理，这份珍贵的文化遗产得以传承和弘扬。

横县云表壮族歌圩

Yunbiao Gexu Festival of Zhuang Ethnic Group in Hengxian

项目名称：横县云表壮族歌圩

别称：威德宫歌圩

分布范围：横州市云表镇及周边地区

入选名录及批次：2012年第四批自治区级非物质文化遗产名录

保护单位：横县文化馆

代表传承人：蒙一文、李秀莲

Element name：Yunbiao Gexu Festival of Zhuang Ethnic Group in Hengxian

Alternative name：Weide Palace Gexu

Geographical location and range：Yunbiao Town of Hengzhou City and the surrounding areas

Element inscribed list：In 2012 on the Fourth Autonomous Region List of Intangible Cultural Heritage

Competent body involved in safeguarding：Hengxian Cultural Centre

Representative inheritors：Meng Yiwen, Li Xiulian

山上对歌的村民
Villagers Cross-singing in the Mountains

Yunbiao Gexu is the original Zhuang Ethnic Group song fair which is best preserved. It is held on lunar September 19th every year during the ceremony of Weide Palace Temple. It is also called Weide Palace Gexu. People in regional areas will gather in Rhino Hill near Weide Palace to sing songs. Meanwhile people will also hold dragon dance, Lion dance, gamecock, basketball match, art performance and other diversified activities. The event will last for several days and songs never cease in Rhino Hill. People in neighboring counties who love songs will come here to make friends through songs and express their feelings through music. Grand Gexu event is the representative of local folklore.

Yunbiao is located in northwestern Hengzhou. Zhenlong Mountain is on north of the county. 1400 people live here. Dengxu is one of the natural villages in Yunbiao. The weather is warm and water resource is abundant. The land is fertile and free from flood or drought. The talents of people complement the glory of land. Due to its long history and lack of written document, it is difficult to trace back when Gexu was born. However, a legend about Weide Palace is popular in localities. In ancient times, Luo Fuying, an artist from Shunde in Guangdong travelled to Dengxu. Touched by its beautiful natural scenery and friendly people, Luo Fuying settled here

云表歌圩是目前保留完好的原生态壮族歌圩之一，于每年农历九月十九威德宫庙宇贺诞日举行，故当地又称威德宫歌圩。每逢圩日，当地及周边县市的群众自发或有组织地云集威德宫犀牛岭附近进行山歌对唱活动，同时还组织舞狮、舞龙、斗鸡、篮球、文艺演出等丰富多彩的文体活动。一连数日人潮涌动，犀牛岭一带歌声阵阵，通宵达旦，热闹非凡。邻近县乡的歌迷、歌友也身着盛装从四面八方赶来汇集此地，以歌会友，以歌传情，交流情感，倾诉情谊。盛大的歌圩活动是壮乡风土民情的缩影。

云表镇地处横州西北区，北靠镇龙大山，现有人口1400多。邓圩是云表镇的自然村落之一，气候温暖，水源充足，田肥地茂，终年无水旱之灾，物华年丰，人杰地灵。流行于此地的歌圩何时成圩，因历史久远且无确凿文字记载已无从考证，不过，在当地流行着一个有关于威德宫歌圩的传说。相传，广东顺德艺人罗扶应携妻儿历游到邓圩，发现邓圩山清水秀、人杰地灵，便安居此地。闲时他与民众操练武术、编唱民歌、表演戏曲，丰富了当地人的娱乐生活。罗扶应一生行善、引悟众生和造福民众的功德深得邓圩人爱戴，故而，在他百年后，后人在犀牛岭旁为他修建庙宇，取名威德宫，每年举行盛大的歌圩活动。传说的真伪虽不可辨，但与庙宇祭祀相伴而生的云表歌圩，因其悠久的历史、深厚的文化内涵，已成为横州最具代表性的节日聚会歌唱活动，在横州西北部及其周边壮族地区一枝独秀，影响广泛而深远。

云表歌圩以对唱山歌为主，表现形式独特，唱法讲究。歌圩一般为男女对唱，双方自发表演，一人以歌发问，另一人回歌，二者一唱一和，形成对唱。山歌对唱的种类丰富多样，较为多见的有五言歌、七言歌、八言歌三种，此外还有以乡镇命名的山歌，如陶圩山歌等。各类型的山歌均用客话、壮语演唱，必须押韵，无韵不唱。若一人演唱时已使用过的韵脚，还歌者便不能再重复使用。歌手们在唱歌时会依据环境、场面、对象等的不同随机变换内容和形式，如贺酒堂歌、情歌、赞歌等。所唱山歌既能谈生产、谈生活，也能倾诉情谊、言情表意。歌圩对歌的灵活性和临场性对演唱者提出了极高的要求，既要能够掌握多种山歌体制，又要发挥临场应变能力，在每一次的对唱大都会对旧有的山歌有所创新突破。

为了更好地延续“歌圩”这种古朴的民间文化遗产，当地政府采用保护为主、传承为核心的方针，建立起了比较完备的保护制度。在现有基础上，县镇文化部门长期开展文化辅导扶持、普查调研工作，逐年加大普查力度并开展多样性保护传承活动。为了更好地开展动态的保护措施，当地政府拨款对歌圩活动的主干道及周边道路进行了维护、维修，加大了通电、通水及水泥路铺设等基础设施的建设力度，大大改善了群众参加歌圩活动的条件，也为歌手及游客提供了良好的道路环境。目前，横县云表歌圩已成为当地的民俗盛会，是县域内外旅游、休闲娱乐的理想之所，吸引了众多的游客。

with his family. In his spare time, he guided people to exercise martial art and make up songs and operas, which enrich the life of local people. His kindness and virtue won the respect of local people so that people built a temple named Weide near Rhino Hill. Every year people will hold grand event in memory of Luo Fuying. Although it is difficult to distinguish the authenticity of legend, one thing is clear that Gexu is born with the fete of temple. Its long history and profound culture make it one of the most representative gatherings in Hengzhou. As a unique event in northwestern Hengzhou and regional Zhuang habitats, Gexu has a huge influence in localities.

With special form and strict singing style, Yunbiao Gexu chooses dialogue songs as its major form. Young men and women sing to each other with improvised performance. One asks question with songs while the other responds with songs too. Two singers echo with each other. The content of songs is diversified. Five-character songs, seven-character songs and Batuan songs are frequently seen. There are still songs named by towns like Taoxu song. All kinds of songs shall be sung by Ke language or Zhuang language. Songs must have rhyme. One rhyme could only be used once. Singers will also change words or form according to different venues, environments or the objects. Toast songs, love songs and praise songs may all be included. People could sing about production, life, friendship or love affairs. The flexibility of Gexu has high requirements to singers. On one hand, singers must be capable of all genres of songs. On the other hand, singers should be able to adjust in accordance to the circumstances. Singers should have new breakthroughs every time in dialogue songs.

In order to better develop Gexu which is a cultural heritage from ancient time, the local government adopts the principles which takes protection as the key and heritage as the core. It establishes a complete protection system. County and town governments start a long-term cultural guidance and survey to support the protection based on current achievement. It gradually increases the efforts in survey and carries out various heritage activities. In order to operate dynamic protection, local governments invest in the maintenance of roads near Gexu venues and enhance the infrastructure construction like grid, water facility and cement road. Governments all provide sound conditions for the development of singers. Currently, Yunbiao Gexu in Hengxian has become a grand event of folklore. As an ideal place for entertainment and tourism, Gexu attracts many visitors.

横县炮会

Hengxian Fireworks Festival

项目名称：横县炮会

别称：炮期、葛麻十六炮会

分布范围：横州市马山乡、校椅镇、百合镇及周边地区

入选名录：2010年第三批自治区级非物质文化遗产名录

保护单位：横县文化馆

代表性传承人：黄道敬、邓享朝

Element name：Hengxian Fireworks Festival

Alternative name：Firework Event, Gema Sixteen Firework Festival

Geographical location and range：Mashan Town, Xiaoyi Town, Baihe Town of Hengxian and the surrounding areas

Element inscribed list：In 2010 on the Third Autonomous Region List of Intangible Cultural Heritage

Competent body involved in safeguarding：Hengxian Cultural Centre

Representative inheritors：Huang Daojing, Deng Xiangchao

每年的农历正月十六，南宁市横州市百合镇葛麻村都会举行炮会活动，迎接新春、送福入户。横县炮会，旧时称炮期、葛麻十六炮会，是当地群众自发举行的一项大型群众性民俗活动。横县炮会发源自葛麻村、武留村，广泛流行于马山、校椅等周边乡镇。炮会之日，村里龙腾狮跃，锣鼓喧天，爆竹齐鸣，人们欢天喜地、载歌载舞地庆祝开春，场面十分热闹，观者可达数万人。

横县炮会始于明朝中期，距今已有500多年的历史，相传与当地一个极具神奇色彩的民间神话有关。相传盘古开天时，曾有山龙诞生于此，当地人视龙之躯为神灵，视这块龙之地为宝地，山龙与村同在，人与山龙共存。某日，此地忽有妖怪作乱，危害人畜，惊扰了龙脉，砍伤了龙颈，龙血流满村前炮马场。适逢元宵佳节次日，观音下凡此地时见此景，便施法术战胜妖魔，治愈了山龙，同时告喻村人妖怪最怕爆竹声，居住龙头地的村人要常放爆竹，驱妖降邪，以保平安。故而，便有了每年农历正月十六祭祀驱邪、点炮迎接龙福的炮会习俗，一直保留至今。炮会活动在“文革”期间稍有停滞，20世纪70年代又重新恢复，并渐达至高峰，成为当地最具特色的开春仪式。

横县炮会分为走龙和不走龙两种形式，二者程序有所不同。走龙炮会每3—5年开展一次，炮会队伍由约200人的龙狮队、炮仗队、锣鼓队、喇叭队及道教队组成。待完成接龙福、拜祭社公、祠堂仪式之后，方可开始燃炮、聚餐。在接龙福仪式未完成前，外村人不得入村。不走龙炮会是为了纪念观音灭妖护龙而举行，每年一次，因在村中广场等空旷处燃放爆竹，故又称广场炮会。放炮活动从正月初一持续到正月十六，活动包括巡游全村、祭拜社庙、放炮等仪式以及龙狮闹场、文艺演出、武术表演等文体活动。

燃炮是炮会活动最为热闹的一环，“地冲炮”是其中最具地域特色的花炮类型，体型巨大，故得“炮王”之名。

Every year on lunar January 16th, firework festival will be held in Gema village, Baihe, Hengzhou City to welcome new spring and bring happiness to every household. Hengxian Fireworks Festival used to be called Firework Event or Gema Sixteen Firework Festival. This is a large-scale folk activity held by local people spontaneously. The event originated from Gema and Wuliu villages widely spreads over Mashan, Xiaoyi and neighboring villages and towns. On the festival, people will perform dragon and lion dance in villages and play drums and gongs. People light fireworks and celebrate the coming of spring with songs and dances. The festival is heated and will attract tens of thousands of participants.

Hengxian Fireworks Festival started from the middle Ming Dynasty and has more than 500 years' history. It is said that the event originated from a local legend. A dragon was born in this place after Pan Gu, an ancient god of China, who created the whole world. People regarded the dragon as divine and reckoned this was a place of treasure. The village relies on the dragon and would die with the death of dragon. One day, however, monsters came to harm people and their livestock. The monsters bothered the dragon and hurt the neck of dragon. Dragon blood flooded the firework factory in front of the village. Fortunately, Avalokitesvara visited the place during Lantern Festival coincidently. She used her power to defeat the monsters and cure the dragon. She also told local people that the monsters were afraid of the sound of fireworks so that people should frequently set fireworks in order to disperse viciousness and safeguard the peace. In this way, the firework festival came into being. People will set off fireworks and pray for the blessing from dragon on lunar January 16th. This tradition reserved to present time but was once stopped during the Cultural Revolution. After the restart of festival in the 1970s, firework festival gradually develops to its prime time and becomes one of the most distinctive local ceremony.

Firework Festival has two kinds "Walking Dragon" and "Non-Walking Dragon" which have different procedures. Walking Dragon is held every 3 to 5 years. 200 participants will join dragon and lion dance team, firework team, gong and drum team, trumpet team and Taoist team. Walking Dragon is composed by the teams. After receiving dragon's blessing, paying tribute to local god and ancestors, people will set off fireworks and have some food. People from other villages are forbidden to enter the village before the end of the ceremony. Non-Walking Dragon is to commemorate Avalokitesvara who killed the monsters. It will be held annually. It is also called "Square Firework Festival" for people will set fireworks on squares or other open places in the village. The festival lasts from lunar January 1st to January 16th. Activities in the festival include cruise in village, worship to temple and setting off fireworks. People will also play dragon and lion dance, artistic performance, martial art performance and other cultural and sports events.

Lighting fireworks is the most heated part of the festival. "Land Firework" is the most popular one with local characteristics. It enjoyes the name as "King of the Firework" due to its large size. Land firework is tribble-cracked-firework. The first crack is aimed to subdue monsters and bring agreeable weather. The second crack is for the land which will grant people harvest and abundant grain. The third crack is for the merciful goodness who will bring peace and prosperity. Local people call this "Three Launches and Three Cracks". 16 land fireworks will be launched during the festival. By that time the sound is tremendous. Dragon dance and lion dance team will chase after the fireworks and people will applaud for them. The fireworks bear people's wish for a better life.

In its 500-year-history, the development of Firework Festival went through twists and turns but keeps itself to current time, which shows its strong vitality. It was inscribed on the Municipal List of Intangible Cultural Heritage of Nanning in 2007. In 2010 it was inscribed on the List of Intangible Cultural Heritage of Autonomous Region. Local government attaches importance to the event with local features. The government provides material and manpower support to ensure that every year the activity will be held smoothly. Meanwhile, the government initiates public survey and investigation. It also holds tourism, culture and art festival every year in the name of Gema Firework Festival. With the mutual effort from government and people, Hengxian Firework Festival is well inherited and developed.

一般为三响炮：一放降妖，寓意风调雨顺；二放拜地，寓意五谷丰登；三放拜观音，寓意平安吉祥、丁财两旺。当地人称此为“三放三响”。炮会日共燃16枚“地冲炮”，燃炮之时，霎时间响声震天，龙狮欢腾争炮，喝彩声不断。炮声隆隆，寄托了人们对美好生活的向往。

在500多年的传承发展中，横县炮会虽历经波折，却依旧顽强地延续至今，展现了强大的生命力，于2007年被列入南宁市非物质文化遗产名录，又于2010年被列入广西壮族自治区非物质文化遗产名录。当地政府对这一极具地方特色的传统民俗活动十分重视，不仅投入人力物力加以扶持，以确保每年炮会活动能够顺利进行，还深入开展普查和挖掘工作，并组织筹办一年一度的葛麻炮会暨旅游观光文化艺术节。在政府和民众的共同努力下，横县炮会得以良好地传承和发展。

横县炮会
Hengxian Fireworks Party

节日上的舞狮活动
Lion Dance on the Festival

那桐农具节

Natong Farm Tools Festival

项目名称：那桐农具节

别称：浴佛节

分布范围：隆安县那桐镇

入选目录：2010年第三批自治区级非物质文化遗产名录

保护单位：隆安县文化馆

代表性传承人：无

Element name：Natong Farm Tools Festival

Alternative name：Yufo Festival (Festival of the “Bathing” of Buddha)

Geographical location and range：Natong Town of Long’an County

Element inscribed list：In 2010 on the Third Autonomous Region List of Intangible Cultural Heritage

Competent body involved in safeguarding：Long’an County Cultural Centre

Representative inheritor：None

农具节供品
Offering of Farm Tools Festival

农具交易
Farm Implements Trade

Natong Farm Tools Festival is a traditional folk one in Long'an county which will be held once a year. It has more than 400 years' history. The festival will be held every year on lunar April 8th and lasts for 2-3 days. Farm Tools Festival is also called Yufo Festival which was originally a sacrificial event praying for rain. With hundreds of years' development, Natong Farm Tools Festival has become a multi-faceted festival which integrated folklore and commercial activities. It is closely connected with people's daily life. Farm Tools Festival represents rice culture. It also symbolized creation of local people. On the festival, ancient and mysterious religion activities, diversified and various farm merchandises and brilliant cultural and sports events will attract tens of thousands of people to visit and participate in the festival.

The festival was first held in Wanli or Tianqi period of the Ming Dynasty. It is said that drought struck Natong at that time and farmers harvested nothing. In addition to raging insect pests and savage robbers and thieves, people had no way but endured the sufferings or fled to other places. In order to stop the disasters and pray for rain, local people raised money and held a ceremony in Sanjie Temple on lunar April 8th, which is said to be the birthday of Buddha. The very moment ceremony ends, wind started to blow and rains began to pour down. Rain filled every river and ponds and relieved the drought. Since then climate in Natong became agreeable. People were gratitude to the mercy of Buddha and they

一年一度的那桐农具节是隆安县传统的民间节庆活动，距今已有400多年的历史。活动于每年农历四月初八举行，一般持续2—3天。农具节又名浴佛节，起初是向神明祈雨的祭祀活动，历经数百年的发展演变，如今的那桐农具节已成为集民俗文化和商贸活动于一体的多元化的节庆活动，与人们的生产生活息息相关。农具节是稻作文化的重要表现，更是当地人民创造力的象征。每逢节庆，古老神秘的宗教仪式、琳琅满目的农具商品和精彩纷呈的文娱活动总能吸引来自区内外数以万计的群众到此赶集、聚会、观赏演出。

那桐农具节形成于明万历、天启年间。相传当时那桐一带遭连年大旱，农民颗粒无收，民不聊生，加之虫害肆虐，盗贼横行，百姓流离失所，苦不堪言。为抵御天灾人祸，祈求天降雨露，当地群众自发筹集资金，于农历四月初八释迦牟尼佛诞日在三界庙设坛打醮，礼拜佛祖，祈求庇护，为民消弭灾祸。为期三天的打醮仪式刚一结束，只见狂风大作，乌云翻滚，电闪雷鸣，大雨倾盆而下，一时间，塘溢溪满，水泛田埂，旱情因而得到缓解。自此之后那桐地区风调雨顺，五谷丰登。人们为报佛恩，每年农历四月初八于三界庙设案焚香，摆放供品，祭神求雨。清初至康熙中期，随着商品经济的发展，宗教祭祀活动开始转变为世俗性庙会活动，前来祭拜神灵的村民会带上自家制作的农具、家具出售，购销两旺，逐渐形成了农具集市的雏形。至康熙中晚期，浴佛节演变为颇具规模的农具交易市场，1965年正式更名为农具节。

那桐农具节由祭神、文娱活动及农具展销三个部分组成。祭神活动基本延续了过去求雨仪式的规制。活动于三界庙举行，由道公主持，包括开光仪式、求雨仪式以及神像巡游三个步骤。善男信女们在神像前虔诚叩拜，祈求佛祖、神仙保佑来年风调雨顺。随后由道公开路，人们抬如来佛祖像、玉皇大帝像、观音大士像、地藏王菩萨像出巡，八音队、锣鼓队、舞龙舞狮队随行。队伍所到之处，家家户户顶礼膜拜，迎福消灾。尔后，热闹的文娱活动便开始了，戏曲表演、山歌对唱、现代歌舞表演异彩纷呈，还有抢花炮、体育比赛等，场面热闹非凡。

农具展销是节庆活动的重头戏。每逢农具节，人们从各地赶来，圩市上到处摆满了犁、耙、锄、镰、铲、刀等传统农具，斗笠、箩筐、畚箕、竹篮、竹椅、簸箕等大量竹制品也陈列成行，整条那桐街成了农具的海洋。当地人认为，在举行感恩祈福的节日里添置农具，会给来年的生产带来好运气，故而大家争相选购，处处呈现着繁荣祥和的景象。

为更好地传承和发展农具节，当地政府不断加大宣传力度，投入经费打造独具特色的那桐农具节旅游纪念品。同时，为确保农具节活动后继有人，当地政府还积极培养农具制作传承人，鼓励和扶持壮族农具手工制作师傅，开展“传、帮、带”的收徒活动。目前，那桐农具节已成为当地重点打造的“文化旅游”品牌。

continued to pay tribute to Buddha on lunar April 8th. From the early Qing Dynasty to middle Kangxi period, with the development of commodity economy, the ceremony gradually became a temple fair. People who came to worship gods would bring their homemade farm tools and furniture for sale. In this way the farm tools market came into being. Until the late Kangxi period, Yufo Festival became a market for farm tool trade with a considerable scale. In 1965, its name was changed to Farm Tools Festival.

Natong Farm Tools Festival is composed of three parts, paying tribute to god, cultural and sports event and farm tools fair. Tribute to god follows the practice in ancient times. It took place in Sanjie Temple and was hosted by an old Taoist priest. Consecration ceremony, rain-seeking ritual and cruise of god statues. Followers will kowtow and pray in front of the god and wish Buddha and gods grant them agreeable weather and good harvest. Taoist priest will lead the way and people will carry the statue of Buddha, Jade Emperor, Avalokitesvara and Ksitigarbha for a cruise. Music teams, gong and drum team, dragon and lion dance team will follow the cruise. People will pay their tribute to the statue for inviting good luck and dispersing misfortune. After the cruise, cultural and sports events will start. Operas, folk songs, modern dance will be on performance. Sparkler grabbing and sport activities will also make the event become a lively scene.

Sales of farm tools are also a key part of festival. People from neighboring areas will come to the festival. Traditional farm tools like ploughs, rakes, hoes, sickles and knives are for selling at the market. People could also buy bamboo hats, bamboo baskets, dustpans, bamboo chairs and other bamboo wares. The street will become an ocean of farm tools in Natong. Local people believe that buying farm tools in festival praying for good harvest, buying farm tools will invite good luck to agricultural production in the next year. Thus farmers rush to purchase the tools. The festival has a sense of prosperity and peace.

In order to better inherit and develop Farm Tools Festival, the local government continues to strengthen the promotion and publication. It invests in creating unique souvenir of festival. Meanwhile, in order to ensure the heritage of festival, the local government endeavors to train successors of tools manufacturing. It encourages and supports old makers to pass their knowledge to trainees and guide trainees in manufacturing. Currently, this festival has become a key brand of “cultural tourism” in local region.

更望湖壮族歌圩

Gengwang Lake Gexu Festival of Zhuang Ethnic Group

项目名称：更望湖壮族歌圩

别称：无

分布范围：隆安县更望湖地区及周边地区

入选名录：2014年第五批自治区级非物质文化遗产名录

保护单位：隆安县文化馆

代表性传承人：黄权海

Element name：Gengwang Lake Gexu Festival of Zhuang Ethnic Group

Alternative name：None

Geographical location and range：Gengwang Lake Region of Long'an County and the surrounding areas

Element inscribed list：In 2014 on the Fifth Autonomous Region List of Intangible Cultural Heritage

Competent body involved in safeguarding：Long'an County Cultural Centre

Representative inheritor：Huang Quanhai

更望湖歌圩对歌现场
The Scene of Cross Singing at Gengwang Lake Gexu Festival

村民在对歌
Villagers Cross-singing

清人李调元写有"粤俗好歌，凡有吉庆，必唱歌以为欢乐"。作为隆安县内历史悠久、规模宏大的山歌集会，更望湖原生态歌圩将壮乡以山歌欢庆节日的民风民俗完好地传续至今。每年的农历三月初四是更望湖最热闹的日子，这一天，来自隆安县、大新县、天等县等地各村屯的上千群众纷至沓来，到此地共享节庆的喜悦。三月的更望湖麦花环绕，人们以草坪为台，以青山作景，身着艳丽壮族盛装的男女歌者在此倾情放歌，尽显壮族排歌和山歌的魅力。

更望湖歌圩的成圩时间已无从稽考，南宋周去非所著《岭外代答》、明代邝露所著《赤雅》、明末清初屈大均所著《广东新语》及民国二十三年《隆安县志》，均记载有壮人于三月三，男女各为行列，于山坡歌唱为乐、以歌会友的习俗，足见隆安山歌历史之悠久、民众基础之广泛。歌圩活动虽在"文革"时期被叫停，但随着"文革"的结束，歌圩活动在20世纪80年代后重新恢复，展现出了壮、瑶文化强大的生命力。

更望湖歌圩位于南圩多林村、四联村、邦宁村，布泉龙礼村，屏山文化村五村交界处，集中对歌的草坪被称为"歌

Poet Li Diaoyuan (1734-1803) in the Qing Dynasty once wrote that "The people of Yue like singing, in festivals people will sing for happiness." As one of largest gatherings with longest history in Long'an County, Gengwang Lake traditional Gexu(Song Fair) Festival maintains the folklore of songs in Zhuang habitats to present time. Lunar March 4th is the most heated day every year. Thousands of people from Long'an, Daxin and Tiandeng counties will gather here and share the happiness of festival. In March, flowers prosper around the lake. People sit on the lawn and appreciate beautiful mountains. Men and women in luxuriant traditional clothes will release themselves and sing in the festival, which will also show the charm of Paige (group song) and Shange (folk song) of Zhuang Ethnic Group.

It is hard to find when Gexu was born. According to old singers, Gexu has at least one-thousand-year history. In *Ling Wai Dai Da* written by Zhou Qufei in the Song Dynasty, *Chiya* written by Kuang Lu in the Ming Dynasty, *New Stories in Guangdong* by Qu Dajun in the early Qing Dynasty and *Long'an Record* in the Public of China, people can find the record that "on lunar March 3rd , men and women will gather in Gexu to sing songs and make friends by songs. This shows the long history of Long'an Gexu and solid foundation in people. Although Gexu was once stopped in the past, it recovered in the 1980s, which illustrated the strong power of culture of Zhuang and Yao ethnic grougs.

Gexu takes place in the "crossroad" of Duolin, Silian, Bangning, Buquanlongli and Pingshanwenhua villages. The lawn used for singing is called "Song Venue". The reed around the lawn is lush and the forests are flourishing. The venue is suitable for teenagers to sing. Meanwhile, the venue is isolated so that the songs will not be bothered by external influence. In that case, Gexu remains authentic and original.

Singing to each other is the high light of Gexu. The content of songs is diversified. People use songs for expressing their emotions, talking about their life and sharing knowledge. Teenagers usually come to Gexu for their lovers. Love is an important part of songs. Two singers will start from knowledge about life and production as tests. Then they will sing for individual experience, family, talents and gradually love. Teenagers never limit themselves in their own villages when they are looking for lovers. Language used in songs are western Zhuang language. There are five characters in one sentence and four sentences in one chapter. The lyrics are melodious and easy to remember. Lyrics can have rhyme, assonance or alliteration. People will write lyrics based on real situation. Metaphor, similarity, comparison and other rhetorical devices will be used. Fixed melodies combine with improvisational lyrics which integrated knowledge about space, geography, folklore and normal life. Anything can be sung. As a result, the songs have strong sense of performance. The scene is spectacular. Gexu will not end until sunset.

Besides singing in antiphonal style, Gexu also has excellent art performance like Zhuang Drum, Show of Zhuang Fashion, Zhugang Dance of Zhuang and so on. Competitions including board shoes speeding, ball throwing, sharing leg speeding of two people, basketball match, tug of war and so on. These activities invite more people to participate so that the size of Gexu keeps expanding.

In order to better inherit and protect Gexu of Zhuang Ethnic Group, the local government establishes protection group in order to investigate and edit a textbook of Gexu. Many teenagers have interests in listening and singing traditional songs. Ancient Gexu has new vigor. Currently, Gexu has successfully been inscribed on the Municipal List of Intangible Cultural Heritage. Every year on lunar March 4th, people will hold Gengwang Lake Gexu Festival of Zhuang Ethnic Group. By folk activities, Gexu in Gengwang Lake will be inherited.

央”，附近河流两岸苇丛密布、树林深深，很适合青年人对歌。同时，因歌圩地理环境较为锁闭，所传唱的山歌几乎未受外来因素影响，故一直保持着古朴厚重的原生态样貌。

山歌对唱是更望湖歌圩活动的重头戏。山歌内容包罗万象，既可交流情感，也可品谈生活、分享知识。赶歌圩的青年大都是为择意中人而来，爱情是对歌的重要内容。对歌双方通常以生产、生活相关的知识试探、考察对手，用山歌谈个人、谈家庭、论才能，逐渐切入爱情主题。青年们在寻觅对手时不限于本村范围内，也会邀别村异性进行对唱。所吟唱的山歌均属广西西部壮话山歌，五字成句，每四句为一节，曲调婉转悠扬，易唱易记。歌词押韵自由，可押韵尾，也可押韵头、韵腹，依据现场情况脱口而成。歌词大量使用比兴、比喻、对比等修辞手法，固定的曲调配以即兴的歌词，一问一答间将天文地理、民风民俗等融进歌词中，开口即歌，无所不能唱，表现力十分丰富。圩日歌声飞扬，山鸣谷应，场面蔚为壮观，直到黄昏时分活动才正式结束。

除对歌外，亦有精彩纷呈的文艺表演，如壮鼓表演、壮族服饰走秀、壮族竹杠舞等，此外还会举行板鞋竞速、抛绣球、两人绑腿竞跑、篮球比赛、拔河比赛等趣味项目比赛活动，使得人们的参与度进一步提高，歌圩的规模也得以不断扩大。

为了更好地传承和发展壮族歌圩山歌，当地政府成立了保护工作领导小组，对山歌进行普查并编写了更望湖壮族歌圩教材，很多年轻人开始有了听歌和问歌的兴趣，古老的歌圩重现生机。目前，更望湖歌圩已成功列入市级非物质文化遗产名录，并于每年农历三月初四在更望湖举办“更望湖壮族歌圩山歌比赛”活动。通过民俗活动，更望湖壮族山歌得以活态传承。

隆安稻草龙

Long'an Straw-bound Dragon

项目名称：隆安稻草龙

别称：无

分布范围：隆安县城厢镇

入选名录：2016年第六批自治区级非物质文化遗产名录
2015年第六批市级非物质文化遗产名录

保护单位：隆安县文化馆

代表性传承人：陆礼兴

Element name：Long'an Straw-bound Dragon

Alternative name：None

Geographical location and range：Chengxiang Town of Long'an County

Element inscribed list：In 2016 on the Sixth Autonomous Region List of Intangible Cultural Heritage
In 2015 on the Sixth Municipal List of Intangible Cultural Heritage

Competent body involved in safeguarding：Long'an County Cultural Centre

Representative inheritor：Lu Lixing

Straw-bound Dragon, a folk activity in Long'an, came into being in productive labor along with the "Na culture" and "dragon worship" of Zhuang Ethnic Group. So far, it has a history of nearly 200 years after six generations of inheritance. Based on folk activities, the dragon-dance activity is generally held during the temple fair on the 13th day of the fifth lunar month, the "Straw-God Offering" on the 6th of the sixth lunar month, the Spring Festival and the Lantern Festival. In the festival celebration, the dragon-dance team dances through the streets and lanes, from door to door. Everyone races forward to pluck the dragon's whiskers that are then tied on the chicken coops, pig sties, cattle pens and barns to pray for thriving domestic animals, a bumper grain harvest as well as good luck and peace.

Founded in the Ming Dynasty, Long'an County, as the birthplace of the straw-bound dragon, has a history of 480 years. Located in the alluvial plains of the Youjiang river valley, Long'an County is conducive to farming thanks to its flat and fertile soil. Its unique geographical environment enables people of Zhuang Ethnic Group living here plant rice in surrounding areas and gradually form the "Na culture". "Na", an ancient word of Zhuang Ethnic Group, refers to the rice field and "Na culture" is a unique rice culture created by ancestors of Zhuang Ethnic Group. In the past, production was low and people were often caught in overwhelming droughts, or vulnerable to wild animals that came for food. Sometimes the harvest could have been expected, but it turned out to be a crop failure due to sudden natural disasters. Therefore, people bound the shape of a dragon with straw and waved it in the fields to pray for blessings. The dancing "divine dragon" could not only drive away pests and "field ghosts", but also pray to heaven for favorable weather for the crops. Gradually, Straw-bound Dragon and the dragon-dance activity have become a unique local culture phenomenon and have been passed down, which are of significant academic value to the study of the manifestation of the ancient "Na culture" in modern society.

The craftsmanship of Straw-bound Dragon is complicated and altogether four processes are involved, namely selecting straw, weaving dragon scales, binding together the dragon body and making the dragon head. In terms of the traditional craftsmanship, the whole dragon is made of straw from the inside out and the head, body and tail of the dragon are decorated with colourful paintings. After the dragon making is completed, an auspicious day is chosen to burn incense to the god and the highly respected patriarch or the inheritor of Straw-bound Dragon dips in vermilion with brush to stipple the eyes of the dragon to make the finishing point.

隆安县江滨大王庙前的稻草龙　摄影 何宏生
Straw Dragon in front of Dawang Temple, Long'an County Photo by He Hongsheng

隆安稻草龙民俗活动伴随壮族“那文化”与龙崇拜在生产劳动中产生，历经六代传承人，传承至今已有近200年的历史。舞龙活动依托民俗活动而存在，一般于每年农历五月十三日庙会、六月初六“稻神”祭、春节及元宵节期间举行。在节日庆典上，舞龙队舞祥龙穿街入巷，穿门入户，人们争先上前抢拔龙须，将其扎于鸡笼、猪圈、牛栏和谷仓，以求六畜兴旺、五谷丰登、吉祥平安。

稻草龙的发源地隆安县于明代立县，距今已有近500年的历史。隆安县位于右江河谷的冲积平原上，这里土地平坦肥沃，利于农耕。因有着得天独厚的地理环境，居于此地的壮族人民先于周边许多地区栽种了水稻，并逐渐形成了“那文化”。“那”是古壮语，意为水稻田，“那文化”是壮族先民创造的独特的稻作文化。过去生产力低下，人们时常遭遇难以抗拒的旱灾，或是遇到出没的野兽抢食，有时眼看丰收在望，却因突如其来的天灾而颗粒无收。于是人们用稻草扎成龙的形状，在田间地头舞动祈福。舞动的“神龙”既可以驱走虫害和“田鬼”，也可以向上天祈求风调雨顺。渐渐地，扎稻草龙和舞龙活动便成为当地独特的文化现象并被传承至今，对于研究古老的“那文化”在现代社会的表现有着重要的学术价值。

稻草龙的制作工艺烦琐，历经选稻草、编龙鳞、串龙身、做龙头四道工序才可完成。整条龙从内到外均由稻草制作，于龙头、龙身、龙尾等处点缀色彩斑斓的彩绘。制成之后，择吉日焚香祭神，由德高望重的族长或稻草龙传承人用毛笔蘸朱砂点睛开光即成。因稻草制的龙头容易损坏，故制作者在龙头处做了改进：选用竹篾条扎成架子，使得龙嘴能够张开到理想角度，用白色泡沫来刻制龙牙、红色的塑料制成舌头、编织好的钢丝制成龙须。最能传神的龙眼则用专用材料，在晚上还可以通电使其发出光芒，真正起到了“点睛”的效果。

稻草龙成对制作，规格各为25米和18米。舞龙队分为男、女两队，男队着红黄色衣服，女队着青蓝色衣服，每队10人，其中9人掌龙、1人掌龙珠。舞龙队配合有锣鼓队、兵将等，可达35人之多。舞动的稻草龙栩栩如生，仿佛能够随时盘旋腾起，飞舞于九天之上，行云布雨。

随着科技和社会的不断进步，隆安稻草龙面临后继乏人的濒危状态，舞龙民俗活动日渐式微。针对这种状况，隆安县政府加大保护力度，结合隆安“那文化”，打造隆安“稻草龙之乡”品牌，大力扶持国泰社区舞龙队并协助传承人组建青年舞龙队。与此同时，稻草龙兴趣班也即将在当地各中、小学开展。在政府与民众的共同努力下，隆安稻草龙获得了区内外的广泛关注，它独特的魅力已经成为传承“那文化”的主力军。

Because the straw-bound dragon head is prone to damage, the maker improves the dragon head by using bamboo strips to make the skeleton so that the dragon mouth can be opened at an ideal angle. What’s more, white foam is used to carve the dragon teeth, red plastic is used to make the dragon tongue and woven steel wire is used to make the dragon whiskers. The most expressive dragon eyes are made of special materials, which can be electrified at night to give off light, really achieving the effect of “finishing touch”.

Straw-bound dragons are made in pairs, measuring 25 meters and 18 meters respectively. The dragon-dance team is divided into two teams of men and women, and men dancers are dressed in red and yellow while women dancers in cyan and blue. There are ten people in each team, nine of whom are in charge of the dragon and one is charge of the dragon ball. The whole dragon-dance team can reach as many as 35 people with the addition of a gong and drum team as well as troops. The dancing straw-bound dragon is so lifelike as if it could hover at any time, fly up to the sky and dance above the clouds.

With the continuous advance of technology and society, Long’an Straw-bound Dragon is faced with the endangered state of lack of successors and folk activities of dragon dance are declining gradually. In view of this situation, the Long’an county government enhances efforts in protection and creates the Long’an brand of “Hometown of Straw-bound Dragon” by integrating the “Na culture” of Long’an, strongly supports the dragon dance team of the Guotai community and assists the inheritor to set up the youth dragon dance team. Meanwhile, interest classes of Straw-bound Dragon will also be developed in the local primary and secondary schools. With the joint efforts of the government and the public, Long’an Straw-bound Dragon has attracted wide attention from inside and outside the district, and its unique charm enables it to be the main force to inherit the “Na culture”.

上林壮族万寿节

Shanglin Longevity Festival of Zhuang Ethnic Group

项目名称：上林壮族万寿节

别称：智城万寿节庙会

分布范围：以上林县为核心，辐射来宾市、宾阳县、马山县、忻城县等

入选名录：2012年第四批自治区级非物质文化遗产名录

保护单位：上林县文化馆

代表性传承人：何茂权

Element name: Shanglin Longevity Festival of Zhuang Ethnic Group

Alternative name: Zhicheng Longevity Festival Temple Fair

Geographical location and range: Shanglin County as the core area and spreading to Laibin City, Binyang County, Mashan County, Xincheng County and others

Element inscribed list: In 2012 on the Fourth Autonomous Region List of Intangible Cultural Heritage

Competent body involved in safeguarding: Shanglin County Cultural Centre

Representative inheritor: He Maoquan

万寿节迎公王仪式
The Ceremony of Greeting King Gongwang on Longevity Day

上林壮族万寿节又称为智城万寿节庙会，于每年的农历二月十一日举行，是上林县的壮族同胞为纪念寿公王韦厥的功德，于韦厥诞辰之日在智城举行的立庙奉祀仪式。上林壮族万寿节内容丰富多彩，形式多样，包括祭祀、抬神出游、师公戏演出、山歌对唱、文武场八音演奏等主要项目，同时还有舞龙舞狮、会餐等内容。

上林壮族万寿节流布区域广泛，以上林地区为核心，辐射到宾阳、来宾、马山、忻城等地。上林壮族万寿节历史悠久，其具体形成时期已不可考。相传唐高祖武德七年（624），韦厥被封为澄州刺史（今上林一带），奉命开拓这片蛮荒之地，于此励精图治，造福于民，深得百姓爱戴，受到皇帝嘉奖，后被封为万寿公王。当地人民为了纪念韦厥的功德，自发性地为其立庙奉祀，并于每年农历二月十一日韦厥诞辰之日举行万寿节活动。两宋时期，该民俗活动的规模逐步扩大，明清时期参与活动的人数可达万余人。2006年，随着智城遗址确立为全国重点文物保护单位，以及万寿

Shanglin Longevity Festival of Zhuang Ethnic Group, also known as Zhicheng Longevity Festival Temple Fair, is held on the 21st day of the second lunar month. It is a ceremony of Zhuang Ethnic Group in Shanglin county which is held in Zhicheng by setting up a temple to honor the merits and virtues of Weijue, Longevity Gongwang, on the anniversary of his birthday. With rich contents and various forms, Shanglin Longevity Festival of Zhuang Ethnic Group involves offering sacrifices, carrying god on a tour, Shigong opera performance, folk song duet and wenwu eight-tone performance, in addition to dragon dance, lion dance and a dinner party.

Shanglin Longevity Festival of Zhuang Ethnic Group is spread over a wide area, taking Shanglin as the core area and gradually radiating to Binyang, Laibin, Mashan, Xincheng and other areas. Although Shanglin Longevity Festival of Zhuang Ethnic Group has a long history, its specific formation period remains unknown. According to the legend, at the seventh year of Wude during the period of Emperor Gaozu in the Tang Dynasty (624), Weijue was appointed as the prefectural governor of Chengzhou (today's Shanglin area) to open up wild places. He aroused all his efforts here to benefit the local people, thereby winning the love of the people and being awarded and made Longevity Gongwang by the emperor. In order to commemorate the merits and virtues of Weijue, the local people spontaneously set up a temple to offer sacrifices to him. Thus, the longevity festival activity is held on the 21st day of the second lunar month on the anniversary of Weijue's birthday. Duirng the Song Dynasty, the scale of the folk activity gradually expanded, and by the Ming and Qing dynasties, the number of participants could reach up to ten thousands. As the Zhicheng site was designated as a protection unit of national key cultural relics and as the scale and number of participants of the longevity festival activity increased, the previously so-called Zhicheng Longevity Festival Temple Fair was renamed as Shanglin Longevity Festival of Zhuang Ethnic Group in 2006.

Shanglin Longevity Festival of Zhuang Ethnic Group originates from the worship of Weijue, the Longevity Gongwang, who holds a significant place in the hearts of the local people as a symbol of good life, peace and well-being. Shanglin county is known as "Hometown of Longevity" in China. With the continuous progress of science and technology, the reputation of "Hometown of Longevity" can also be explained by science. However, the belief of the local people in the Longevity Gongwang reveals its own mystery and legend in every aspect. With broad mass participation, the ritual ceremony of the longevity festival activity is in a solemn and awe-inspiring atmosphere and all worship personnel are dressed up and attend the activity in awe. After the professional Zhuang master of ceremonies delivers the sacrificial text, the on-site worship personnel perform the special worship of the Zhuang Ethnic Group to the Temple of Longevity Gongwang under the guidance of the slogan of the master of ceremonies, to pray for good weather, happiness and well-being as well as family harmony in future. In the final stage of the activity, all residents regardless of nationalities, men and women, old and young, gather at a table of ten and drink to celebrate the festival and share the dishes brought from their own homes such as five-coloured sticky rick, rice dumplings and rice cakes. With various forms, rich contents and unique religious and regional cultural characteristics, Shanglin Longevity Festival of Zhuang Ethnic Group, as an indispensable part of the Shanlin cultural system of Zhuang Ethnic Group, plays a significant role in promoting outstanding traditional culture and enriching the spiritual and cultural needs of the people.

With the continuous development of economy and the increasing impact of multiculture, the living space of Shanglin Longevity Festival of Zhuang Ethnic Group has been occupied. What's more, some old people who could perform sacrificial rites previously become too old to continue the activity, while young people's employment and value orientation lies elsewhere. Consequently, the inheritance of this folk activity has also been greatly affected. However, the Shanglin people's worship of Longevity Gongwang does not die out and the vision of health and longevity still continues. Therefore, the tradition of Shanglin Longevity Festival of Zhuang Ethnic Group has been continued as well, and the overall situation is still optimistic. In order to better protect, inherit and develop this traditional folk activity, under the leadership of Shanglin county government, county and town cultural authorities set up a special protection team of intangible cultural heritage, formulate a five-year plan and sort out and file sacrificial objects and folklore related to Shanglin Longevity Festival of Zhuang Ethnic Group. Moreover, the market of Shanglin Longevity Festival of Zhuang Ethnic Group is expanded based on the tourism resources of Zhicheng, such as gradually adding new elements to the festival, combining with car shows and food shows, so as to breathe new life into the festival.

节活动的规模和参与的人数愈来愈多，智城万寿节庙会更名为上林壮族万寿节。

上林壮族万寿节源于对万寿公王韦厥的崇拜，万寿公王在当地人民心中有着重要的地位，是美好生活与和平安康的象征。上林县是我国有名的“长寿之乡”，虽然随着科学技术的不断发展，对于“长寿之乡”的美誉也可以用科学去解释，但是当地人民对于万寿公王的信仰，无不彰显着其本身的神秘性、传奇性。万寿节活动的祭祀大典庄严肃穆，各敬拜人员衣冠整齐、心存敬畏。在专业壮族祭祀司仪诵读完祭文之后，现场参加敬拜的人员在祭祀司仪的口号引导下，向万寿公王圣殿施壮族所特有的敬拜礼，祈愿未来的日子里风调雨顺、幸福安康、家庭和美。在活动进入尾声阶段时，各村居民不论民族、不分男女老少，十人一席，举杯痛饮，分享大家从自家带来的五色糯米饭、粽子、糍粑、各色菜肴等，欢度节日。上林壮族万寿节具有多样的表现形式、丰富的活动内容以及独特的宗教和地域文化特色，对弘扬优秀传统文化、丰富人民精神文化需求都有着非常重要的作用，是上林壮族文化系统中不可缺失的一部分。

随着经济的不断发展以及多元文化的不断冲击，上林壮族万寿节的生存空间受到了一定的挤占，一些原先能够主持祭祀仪式的老人逐渐上了年纪，无法继续进行这项活动，而年轻人的就业重心和价值选择的兴趣点又不在此，使得该民俗活动的传承受到了很大的冲击。但是上林人民对于万寿公王的崇拜仍旧没有湮灭，对健康长寿的愿景仍旧持续，所以上林壮族万寿节的传统也一直在延续，整体情况较为乐观。为了更好地保护、传承和发展这一传统民俗活动，在上林县政府的领导下，县、镇文化主管部门成立了专门的非物质文化遗产保护小组，制订了五年计划，并对与上林壮族万寿节相关的祭祀器物、民间传说等进行整理归档，依托智城的旅游资源开拓上林壮族万寿节的市场，在节日中逐渐加入新的元素，与车展、美食展相结合，为其注入新的活力。

上林壮族灯酒节

Shanglin Lantern and Wine Festival of Zhuang Ethnic Group

项目名称：上林壮族灯酒节

别称：无

分布范围：以上林县巷贤镇为核心区域的大明山一带

入选名录：2010年第三批自治区级非物质文化遗产名录

保护单位：上林县文化馆

代表性传承人：石冠美、石二海

Element name: Shanglin Lantern and Wine Festival of Zhuang Ethnic Group

Alternative name: None

Geographical location and range: The area of Daming Mountain with Xiangxian Town as the core region of Shanglin County

Element inscribed list: In 2010 on the Third Autonomous Region List of Intangible Cultural Heritage

Competent body involved in safeguarding: Shanglin County Cultural Centre

Representative inheritor: Shi Guanmei, Shi Erhai

Shanglin Lantern and Wine Festival of Zhuang Ethnic Group is a traditional folk festival being popular in the area of Xiangxian Town, Shanglin County, which is held on the 11th day of the first month of the lunar year. In the Zhuang language of Shanglin, "Deng" and "Ding" are homonyms. "Lantern and Wine Festival" refers to the festival of able-bodied men. It is a festival formed in celebration of the birth of the newborn. On the day of the festival, for children born last year, the parents of the firstborn should devote one ram or one pig's head, and two-jin pork, one bottle of sweet wine, rice flower and cake. The parents of the second born or the firstborn girl should devote one chick or one pig's head. Households in the village also need to raise materials to the community, sing the congratulations of "three tributes" and conduct a series of sacrifice activities. After sacrifice is completed, the crowd have a dinner together and eat the "one-hundred-household banquet". Subsequently, the host organizes consolation, beats drums and shows congratulations to the new babies. The host will also give bonuses to the newborns, send the newborn register to the households for consecration. Then the ceremony is over.

Shanglin Lantern and Wine Festival of Zhuang Ethnic Group has a long history. According to the record, Shanglin Lantern and Wine Festival of Zhuang Ethnic Group appeared early in the pre-Qin Dynasty, and it was widely spread in the Tang Dynasty. It has been inherited till today for over one thousand years. It is mainly distributed in the area of Daming Mountain with Xiangxian Town as the core region. It kept declining since the mid of the 20th Century and even was suspended. It was recovered in 1980. Since then, its activity size has kept expanding and the number of participants has kept increasing.

Shanglin Lantern and Wine Festival of Zhuang Ethnic Group reflects the reproduction worship of ancestors of Zhuang Ethnic Group in Shanglin, and meanwhile is the product of agriculture civilization. Although Lantern and Wine Festival is called the festival of the able-bodied men, yet it is not merely to prefer to boys or girls, and show discrimination to females. Instead, it is a festival culture formed in order to adapt to the demands of the social productivity development at that time. It is a special product of male chauvinism in the patriarchal clan, with the

灯酒节中舞狮表演
Dancing Lions on Lantern and Wine Festival

上林壮族灯酒节是流行于上林县巷贤镇一带的民间传统节日，于每年农历正月十一日举行。在上林壮语中，“灯”与“丁”同音，“灯酒节”即男丁的节日，是为了庆祝新生儿降生而形成的节日。节日这天，去年出生的孩子，头胎为男孩的家长献上一只公羊或一个猪头，并献出猪肉两斤、甜酒一罐以及米花、糕饼等食物；第二胎或者头胎为女孩的家长需献上一只鸡或者一个猪头。村中的各家各户也需筹集物资至社坛唱“三献礼”祝词，并进行一系列祭祀活动。祭祀完毕后，众人集体进餐，吃“百家宴”。随后由主持人组织慰问，敲锣打鼓，恭贺添丁，并给新丁发红包，将新丁簿送到掌簿人家中上香供奉，仪式结束。

上林壮族灯酒节有着悠久的历史，据记载，早在先秦时期上林壮族灯酒节就已经出现，唐朝时广为流传，传承至今已逾千年。其主要分布在以巷贤镇为核心区域的大明山一带。20世纪中叶之后不断衰微，甚至中断，于1980年重新恢复，其活动规模不断扩大，参与人员不断增多。

上林壮族灯酒节是上林壮族先民生殖崇拜的一种侧面反映，同时也是农耕文明的产物。灯酒节虽然被称为男丁的节日，但并非是单纯的重男轻女、歧视女性，而是为了适应当时社会生产力发展的需要所形成的一种节日文化。它是父系氏族中男权主义的特殊产物，并带有男权特征。随着时代和文化的不断发展，上林壮族灯酒节也在不断焕发出新的时代特色。男权逐渐淡化，女权随之融合进来，越来越多的女性在壮族灯酒节中担当起越来越重要的角色。特别是中华人民共和国成立之后，部分地区也允许妇女参加节日祭祀和聚餐活动。实行“计划生育”政策后，一些村庄也将新生女婴吸收为“女丁”，跟男丁一同加入新丁名册。上林壮族灯酒节承载着当地民族最为浓厚的民族文化，是维系民族和谐发展的重要精神支柱，饱含着对新生命的渴求以及人丁兴旺的朴实愿望。上林壮族灯酒节在聚餐活动中将村民召集到一起，体现了这个节日所代表的团体性、群众性和协调性，是一项具有广泛参与性的节日盛会。

随着经济的不断发展、文化观念的不断更新和改变，上林壮族灯酒节的生存空间也在不断受到钳制。熟知灯酒节祭祀流程的老艺人逐渐减少，年轻人忙着为生计奔波，对于流程严格和考究的灯酒节提不起太高的兴致，致使上林壮族灯酒节的传承和发展陷入尴尬的境地。为了解决这一问题，使上林壮族灯酒节能够得到传承和发展，上林县政府和相关部门成立了专门的非物质文化遗产保护小组，对上林壮族灯酒节的相关资料进行挖掘、收集、整理和归档；建立了长期的保护机制，加大对上林壮族灯酒节的资金投入和补贴，合理利用当地的旅游资源，建立良好的旅游文化生态圈。

patriarchal characteristics. With the constant development of the times and culture, Shanglin Lantern and Wine Festival of Zhuang Ethnic Group also shows new characteristics of the times. Patriarchy is gradually fading and feminism is thus integrated. More and more females play an increasingly role in Lantern and Wine Festival. Especially after the founding of the People's Republic of China, some regions also allow females to participate in festival sacrifice and dinner activity. After the “family planning” policy was carried out, some villages also absorbed newborn female babies as the “able-bodied women”, who were added to the newborn register along with able-bodied men. Shanglin Lantern and Wine Festival of Zhuang Ethnic Group carries the most profound national culture of the local nation and remains the important spiritual pillar of maintaining the harmonious development of the nation. It is filled with the longing for a new life and the simple wish of flourishing population. In the dinner party, Lantern and Wine Festival of Shanglin Zhuang Ethnic Group collects all the villagers, which embodies the team, mass and coordination characteristics represented by the festival. It is not confined to the single family or organization; instead, it is a widely participating festival gala.

With the constant development of economy, constant update and change of cultural idea, the survival space of Shanglin Lantern and Wine Festival of Zhuang Ethnic Group also keeps being restrained. On the one hand, the number of old entertainers familiar with the sacrifice process of Lantern and Wine Festival is gradually decreased; the young are busy for life, so they have little interest in the Lantern and Wine Festival with strict and particular processes, thus leading the inheritance and development of Shanglin Lantern and Wine Festival of Zhuang Ethnic Group into embarrassment. In order to solve the problem, and ensure the inheritance and development of Shanglin Lantern and Wine Festival of Zhuang Ethnic Group, Shanglin County Government and related departments specially set up an exclusive protection group of intangible cultural heritage, which explores, collects, arranges and puts related data of Shanglin Lantern and Wine Festival of Zhuang Ethnic Group into file. They set up a long-term protection mechanism, enlarge capital input and subsidy of Shanglin Lantern and Wine Festival of Zhuang Ethnic Group, make reasonable use of local tourism resources, and establish the good ecosystem of tourism culture.

上林县渡河公

Shanglin Duhegong Festival

项目名称：上林县渡河公

别称：渡老头公

分布范围：以上林县三里镇为中心，辐射澄泰乡、黄楚村、黄境村、双良村、双罗村等周边地区

入选名录：2008年第二批自治区级非物质文化遗产名录

保护单位：上林县文化馆

代表性传承人：黄福莲

Element name: Shanglin Duhegong Festival

Alternative name: Dulaotougong

Geographical location and range: Centreing on Sanli Town of Shanglin County, spreading to Chengtai Town, Huangchu Village, Huangjing Village, Shuangliang Village, Shuangluo Village and the surrounding areas

Element inscribed list: In 2008 on the Second Autonomous Region List of Intangible Cultural Heritage

Competent body involved in safeguarding: Shanglin County Cultural Centre

Representative inheritor: Huang Fulian

上林县渡河公有着广义和狭义的区别。广义上，渡河公又叫渡老头公，是以上林三里镇为核心的壮族同胞于每年的农历五月初五举行的一项民俗活动，主要有祭祀祈福、放河灯、对山歌等活动。狭义上，渡河公是一种棉布缝制的手工香囊，呈人形，明朝装束。布人的怀中抱着一个金黄色的南瓜，其中有风干过的艾草、白芷、苍术等中草药，是该民俗活动中不可或缺的物品。五月初五傍晚时分，村里的男女老少一边吟唱祝词，一边把用渡河公制作成的河灯放到河里。河灯多采用一艘以竹片、芦苇或是铁皮制成的小巧船，点上红蜡烛，放到水里，任其漂流，夜间也会有人沿着河岸或者在树荫下对唱山歌。渡河公的场面极为热闹，人数最多时可达两万多人。

上林县渡河公的流布较为集中，主要以上林县三里镇为中心，并辐射到澄泰、黄楚、黄境、双良、双罗等周边乡村。该习俗历史悠久，始于明朝中叶，于清朝兴盛，距今已有400多年的历史。它的起源根植于上林先民的生殖崇拜和先祖祭祀，传说在远古时期，天河决堤，天河之水淹没了大地，整个世界成了一片汪洋，仅有一对金童玉女幸运地抱住了一只大南瓜浮在水面上，历经千辛万苦于五月初五漂到了上林县三里镇汇水河畔的船山上，人类因此而免受灭顶之灾。水灾过去之后，二人结为夫妻，养育后代，被当地人奉

渡河公
Duhegong Doll

Shanglin Duhegong Festival has the broad and narrow sense. Broadly speaking, Duhegong Festival is also named Dulaotougong. It is a folk custom activity held on the 5th of May in the lunar year in Zhuang Ethnic Group area centered on Shanglin Sanli Town. It has the activity processes, including sacrifice for blessing, floating river lanterns and singing the folk songs. Narrowly speaking, Duhegong Festival is a man-shaped manual sachet tailored by the cotton cloth, with the dress of the Ming Dynasty. The cloth person embraces a golden yellow pumpkin, which contains the traditional Chinese herbs, such as the dried wormwood, Angelica dahurica and rhizoma atractylodis, which are indispensable objects of the folk-custom activity. At dusk on the 5th of May in the lunar calendar, the men and women, the old and the young in the village sing the congratulations while putting the river lamp made by Duhegong Festival into the river. The river lamp generally adopts the small ship made by bamboos, weed or the iron sheet, where the red candle lights. It is then put into the water and drifts along. At night, some people will also sing the folk song along the river bank or under the shade. The scene of Duhegong Festival is very bustling. The biggest number of participants may reach over 20,000.

Shanglin Duhegong Festival is spread in a concentrated way. It mainly centres on Sanli Town, Shanglin County, and spreads to the surrounding villages, including Chengtai, Huangchu, Huangjing, Shuangliang and Shuangluo. The custom has a long history for over 400 years, which started from the mid of the Ming Dynasty, and prospered in the Qing Dynasty. Its origin was rooted in the reproduction worship and ancestor sacrifice of Shanglin ancestors. According to the legend, in the ancient times, the Celestial River had a levee failure; the water of the Celestial River drowned the ground. The whole world became the boundless sea. Only a pair of girl and boy luckily embraced a big pumpkin and floated on the water river; finally, they drifted to Chuanshan Mountain by the bank of Huishui River, Sanli Town, Shanglin County on the day of the 5th of May in the lunar calendar, so the humankind was thus free from the catastrophe. After the water disaster was passed, the two became a couple and cultivated post-generations, which was reputed by the local as the ancestor of humankind. In order to commemorate them, the people in the later ages conduct a series of sacrifice and blessing activities on the 5th of May in the lunar calendar per year.

The folk custom activities of Shanglin Duhegong Festival express the longing of people of Shanglin Zhuang Ethnic Group for the beautiful life, and their memory and awe of the ancestor. On the morning of the 5th of May in the lunar calendar, residents of Sanli Town, Shanglin County needs to prepare for the tributes for sacrifice at home. After bathing with the herbs, they will visit the neighbors, or send the sachet of Duhegong Festival, or talk with one another happily, thus creating the strong festival atmosphere. The elderly will generally hang the sachet of Duhegong Festival around the neck of children with the red or the yellow velvet, which hangs to the navel. People from Sanli Town hold that the sachet plays the role of driving away the evil and getting over the shock, and praying children for peace, which embodies the simple concern shown by the elderly to the young. The manually made sachet of the Duhegong Festival is of extremely high artistry and ornamental value. The sachets have different specifications; the biggest may be one meter long; the smallest is only the size of a bean. It has over ten types, with abundant colors and lovely modelling. Th sachet of Duhegong Festival is a handicraft deriving from the folk custom activity. It has gradually become a necessary object in the folk-custom activity. It has formed a cultural symbol embedded into the life of local people, which becomes a part of life. It is of the vivid regional characteristics and mass character.

With the constant economic development and the diversified festival cultures, the folk-custom activities of Shanglin Duhegong Festival have been influenced to a certain degree. Some old entertainers who make the Duhegong Festival sachet are getting older, who can no longer participate in the technique inheritance and development. And the transformation of the young's employment idea and the change of interest make the traditional folk customs neglected. In order to improve the phenomenon, Shanglin County Government, and the cultural competent departments of the county and the town increase the mining, rescue and protection of folk-custom activities of Duhegong Festival, set up the viable and effective protection mechanisms, regard it as the special brand of folk art of Shanglin County, and carry out special appropriation. They positively promote Duhegong Festival through multiple channels, such as "Singing Platform of the Green City" in Nanning International Folk Art Festival, and develop the tourism souvenirs of Duhegong Festival by combining the local tourism resources of Shanglin; increase the capital support for folk entertainers, create a good inheritance environment, encourage them to teach apprentices and participate in various folk customs performance activities, and expand the publicity channels of Duhegong Festival, so as to promote its inheritance and development.

为人类的先祖。后世的人们为了纪念他们，便于每年的五月初五进行一系列的祭祀与祈福活动。

上林县渡河公民俗活动表达了上林壮族人民对美好生活的向往和对祖先的缅怀与敬畏之情。五月初五一早，上林县三里镇的居民就需要在家中准备好祭拜时所用的供品，用药草沐浴后便要走访邻里亲朋，或是互送渡河公香囊，或是谈天说地，节日氛围十分浓郁。老人一般会将渡河公香囊用红色或者黄色丝线挂在小孩子的脖子上，并垂到肚脐左右的位置。三里镇人民认为香囊具有驱邪、压惊的作用，可以保佑孩童安康，体现了长辈对晚辈的一种极为朴素的关怀。手工制作的渡河公香囊具有很高的艺术性和观赏性。制作而成的香囊规格不同，最大的可达一米左右，最小的仅有黄豆大小，其种类又可细分成十种，且色彩丰富，造型憨态可掬。渡河公香囊是依托于这项民俗活动而衍生出来的手工艺品，逐渐成为这项民俗活动中必不可少的物品，已经作为一种文化符号嵌入到当地人民的生活中，成为其生活的一部分，既有着鲜明的地域特色，又具有广泛的群众性。

随着经济的不断发展和节日文化日渐多元，上林县渡河公民俗活动也受到了一定的影响。一些制作渡河公香囊的老艺人逐渐上了年纪，没办法从事技艺的传承和发展，而且年轻人就业观念的转型和兴趣的改变，使传统民俗备受冷落。为了改善这一问题，上林县政府和县、镇文化主管部门加大对渡河公民俗活动的发掘、抢救和保护力度，建立起一系列切实有效的保护机制，将其作为上林县民间艺术的特色品牌，实行专项拨款；利用南宁国际民歌艺术节"绿城歌台"等多种渠道积极推广渡河公，并结合上林当地的旅游资源开发渡河公旅游纪念品；加大对民间制作艺人进行资金帮扶，创造良好的传承环境，鼓励其带徒授艺、参与各种民俗表演活动，拓宽渡河公的宣传渠道，促进其传承和发展。

上林壮族龙母节

Shanglin Dragon Mother's Day of Zhuang Ethnic Group

项目名称：上林壮族龙母节

别称：三月三龙母节

分布范围：上林县塘红乡石门村及周边地区

入选名录：2014年第五批自治区级非物质文化遗产名录

保护单位：上林县文化馆

代表性传承人：无

Element name: Shanglin Dragon Mother's Day of Zhuang Ethnic Group

Alternative name: Dragon Mother's Day on March 3rd of the Lunar Calendar

Geographical location and range: Shimen Village of Tanghong Town in Shanglin County and the surrounding areas

Element inscribed list: In 2014 on the Fifth Autonomous Region List of Intangible Cultural Heritage

Competent body involved in safeguarding: Shanglin County Cultural Centre

Representative inheritor: None

Shanglin Dragon Mother's Day of Zhuang Ethnic Group is also called Dragon Mother's Day on March 3rd of the lunar calendar. It is a festival for the people of Shanglin Zhuang Ethnic Group to commemorate the Luoyue Grandmother Queen Laopu, the foster mother of Tejue, the safeguarding holy dragon of the Pearl River. It is held on March 3 of the lunar year, which is namely the "Mother's Festival" for people of Shanglin Zhuang Ethnic Group. On the day, the local residents will spontaneously prepare for sacrifice articles to sacrifice Tejue and Dragon Mother on Shimen and invite master's masters to recite prayers. In addition, they will hold recreational activities, such as beating the top, competing for the folk songs, gamecock and climbing a mountain of swords or plunging into a sea of flame, and carry out some trade activities, such as subsidiary agricultural products, handicrafts and daily articles.

Shimen Village, Tanghong Town, Shanglin County is a local publicly recognized source place of Dragon Mother culture. The radiation scope of Shanglin Dragon Mother's Day of Zhuang Ethnic Group centres on Shimen Village, Tanghong Township and radiates to Shanglin County and the surrounding area. The story of Dragon Mother has had a long history in Shanglin area. According to the local myth, the holy dragon Tejue was the 9th son of the Dragon King. The Jade Emperor forecast the drought disaster for humankind, so he ordered Tejue to solve the problem. Tejue was turned into a snake and was raised by a diligent and kind widow in Shimen. Raised by the kind mother, he carried out the mysterious power to benefit the local. When plague approached, Tejue collected the amazing grass and flowers, asked his mom to make it into the colored rice for the masses, so that the masses escaped from the disaster. Since then, the masses deified Tejue and his mother. The foster mother of Tejue lived till the age of 199 and died of no disease on March 1 of the lunar calendar of the year. At the deep night of March 3 of the lunar calendar, Tejue led the dragons to send his mother's remains to Baxian. As the folk saying goes, "on March 3, the fierce wind blows and Tejue sweeps the tomb and returns home". Shanglin Dragon Mother's Day of Zhuang Ethnic Group was closely connected to the local legend, with a long history. Emperor Nanhan in the period of five dynasties and ten countries reputed Luoyue Grandmother Queen Laopu as "Ms. Dragon Mother" and sacrificed her on March 3rd , with a history of over 1000 years up to now.

Shanglin Dragon Mother's Day of Zhuang Ethnic Group is a folk festival by depending on the local's belief in Dragon Mother. It is an important remain of the ecological

龙母节九龙祭母仪式　摄影 蒙健
Nine Dragons Offer Sacrifices to Dragon Mother at the Festival Photo by Meng Jian

上林壮族龙母节又称三月三龙母节，是上林壮族人民为纪念骆越祖母王、珠江守护神龙特掘养母佬浦的节日，于每年农历三月初三举行，相当于上林壮族人民的“母亲节”。每到这一天，当地居民就会自发地准备祭祀用品到石门上“敢仙”祭拜特掘和龙母，并请来师公、道公诵经祈福。在这一天，当地人民也会举行打陀螺、赛山歌、斗鸡、上刀山、下火海等文体活动，并开展一些农副产品、手工艺品、日常用品等的商贸活动。

上林县塘红乡石门村是被当地所公认的龙母文化的发源地。上林壮族龙母节以塘红乡石门村为核心，逐渐辐射到上林县以及周边地区。上林地区关于龙母的故事由来已久。据当地神话传说所讲，神龙特掘是龙王第九子，因玉皇大帝预见人间有旱灾发生，遂命他前往人间消灾解难。特掘化作一条花蛇，被石门一位勤劳善良的寡妇所抚养。在慈母的养育下，他施展神功为民造福。当瘟疫来临时，特掘采来仙草仙花，让母亲蒸成五色糯米饭分给百姓食用，使百姓逃过一劫，自此民间百姓便把特掘母子奉若神明。特掘的养母活到199岁，于那年三月初一无疾而终。三月初三深夜，特掘率众龙兄呼风唤雨把母亲送去岜仙安葬。民间有“三月三，狂风刮，特掘扫墓回到家”的说法。上林壮族龙母节与当地传说紧密联系，历史悠久。五代十国时期的南汉皇帝把骆越祖母王佬浦封为“龙母夫人”，并于三月初三进行祭祀，传承至今已有1000多年的历史了。

上林壮族龙母节是以当地人民的龙母信仰为依托而形成的民俗节日，是壮族生态文化的重要遗存，具有鲜明的壮族文化基因和地域特色，对于壮民族的文化、信仰、妇女地位、社会风貌等诸多领域都产生了深刻的影响，是壮族历史文化的重要组成部分，对于研究我国西南壮族文化有着非常重要的价值。上林壮族龙母节所形成的龙母文化，反映的是一种“孝文化”，赞扬和歌颂了知恩图报、孝敬父母的文化理念。此外，作为人民群众祈福许愿的节日，它具有非常广泛的群众性，而祭祀本身除了宗教活动以外也有很多的娱乐活动，既娱神又娱人，在很大程度上丰富了广大群众的娱乐生活和精神生活。

随着经济的不断发展和多元文化的不断冲击，上林壮族龙母节虽然也受到了一定的干扰和困难，但是整体传承和发展态势良好。为了使这一传统民俗节日更好地传承和发展下去，上林县政府和县、镇文化管理部门在塘红乡建立了壮族龙母节传承基地，并投入100多万元对龙母庙、真武神龙圣殿等进行修缮，使龙母文化的传播空间得以保障；对其传承活动加大资金扶持，借助上林县当地的旅游资源开发与龙母文化相关的旅游经典，逐步建立较为健全的旅游文化产业；逐步赋予壮族龙母节以时代特色，以符合时代需求。从2018年起，每年的三月三，广西壮族自治区公民都能放假两天，为让更多的人参与上林壮族龙母节创造了新的机会。

culture of Zhuang Ethnic Group, with strong cultural gene and regional characteristics of Zhuang Ethnic Group. It has had profound influence on the culture, belief, female's status and social appearance of Zhuang Ethnic Group. It is an important component of the historic culture of Zhuang Ethnic Group and is of important value to studying the culture of the southwest Zhuang Ethnic Group in our country. The Dragon Mother Culture formed by Shanglin Dragon Mother's Day of Zhuang Ethnic Group reflects a "filial culture", which praises and eulogizes the cultural idea of being grateful and respecting parents. In addition, as a festival for the masses to pray, it has a wide mass foundation. Besides the religious activities, sacrifice itself has also many entertainment activities, which entertains both the god and people, thus greatly enriching the entertainment life and spiritual life of the masses.

With the constant economic development and shock of diversified cultures, Shanglin Dragon Mother's Day of Zhuang Ethnic Group has been disturbed to a certain degree, yet the overall tendency of inheritance and development remains good. In order to better inherit and develop the traditional folk festival, Shanglin County Government and the cultural management departments of the county and the town have set up the Zhuang Ethnic Group Dragon Mother's Day Inheritance Base in Tanghong Township, and invested over 1 million yuan in repairing Dragon Mother Temple and Zhenwu Holy Dragon Palace, thus ensuring the communication space of Dragon Mother Culture. They increase capital support for the inheritance activities, develop the tourism classics that are related to Dragon Mother Culture through local tourism resources of Shanglin County and gradually set up a complete tourism cultural industry. They also gradually endow Zhuang Ethnic Group Dragon Mother's Day with the times characteristics, thus making it in line with the demand of the times. Since 2018, citizens of Guangxi Zhuang Ethnic Group Autonomous Region may have two-day off on March 3rd per year. It creates more opportunities for more Guangxi citizens to participate in Shanglin Dragon Mother's Day of Zhuang Ethnic Group.

三里壮族歌圩

Sanli Gexu Festival of Zhuang Ethnic Group

项目名称：三里壮族歌圩

别称：无

分布范围：上林县三里镇

入选名录：2016年第六批自治区级非物质文化遗产名录

2015年第六批市级非物质文化遗产名录

保护单位：上林县文化馆

代表性传承人：韦家林

Element name: Sanli Gexu Festival of Zhuang Ethnic Group

Alternative name: None

Geographical location and range: Sanli Town of Shanglin County

Element inscribed list: In 2016 on the Sixth Autonomous Region List of Intangible Cultural Heritage

In 2015 on the Sixth Municipal List of Intangible Cultural Heritage

Competent body involved in safeguarding: Shanglin County Cultural Centre

Representative inheritor: Wei Jialin

山歌比赛　摄影 蒙健
Folk Song Competition Photo by Meng Jian

三里壮族歌圩是上林县壮族群众于佳节庆典举行的聚会歌唱活动，主要在正月初一至元宵节、二月赶庙会、三月三歌节、五月五渡河公节、八月中秋节、十月唱丰收等节日举行。歌圩习俗由来已久，对歌人数由几十人发展至成百上千人，自明代延续至今。

上林县是广西壮族自治区南宁市市辖县，位于南宁市东北部，壮、汉、瑶三个民族聚居且以壮族为主。上林壮族歌圩主要分布于三里、乔贤、塘红、覃排、西燕一带，尤以三里汇水桥著称。三里镇建于明万历年间，地处上林东北角，地形半平原半山区，古代为军事重镇。三里镇群众自古以来就有对山歌的风俗，据县志记载，歌圩传统可追溯至明朝崇祯年间。徐霞客在其游记中记载：“正月初五起十五日止，男、妇答歌曰‘打跛’，举国若狂……”可见，三里歌圩明代即风靡一时。20世纪80年代，三里镇民众在距城厢街100多米处的小巷中对歌，最初几十人参加，随着对歌队伍壮大，人数增至上百人，小巷已容纳不下，对歌地点转移至城厢街。1966至1976年间，对歌活动被迫中断。1984年，千

As a gathering and singing activity of the Zhuang people in Shanglin county, Sanli Gexu Festival of Zhuang Ethnic Group is usually held from the first day of the first lunar month to the Lantern Festival, on the temple fair in February, on the singing festival on the third day of the third lunar month, on the Duhegong Festival on the fifth day of the fifth lunar month, on the Mid-Autumn Festival in August and on the Harvest Singing Festival in October. The custom of the singing festival has a long history which can be traced back to the Ming Dynasty, and the number of people participating in the antiphonal singing has grown from dozens to hundreds.

Located in the northeast of Nanning city, Shanglin County is a municipal county in Nanning, Guangxi Zhuang Ethnic Group Autonomous Region. Three ethnic groups of Zhuang, Han and Yao live here and most of them are the Zhuang people. The Gexu areas of Zhuang Ethnic Group in Shanglin County are mainly distributed in Sanli, Qiaoxian, Tanghong, Tanpai and Xiyan, particularly famous for the Sanli Huishuiqiao. Built during the Wanli period of the Ming Dynasty and located in the northeast corner of Shanglin county, Sanli Town is characterized by its terrain of half plain and half mountain, thus being a vital military town in ancient times. The people of Sanli Town have been singing folk songs in antiphonal style since ancient times. According to the county record, the tradition of singing festival dates back to the Chongzhong period of the Ming Dynasty. Xu Xiake wrote in his travel notes, “From the first day to the fifteenth day of the first lunar month, the folk songs singing in antiphonal style, which is called “Daba”, leads to a national carnival…” It can be seen that the singing festival of Sanli was all the rage in the Ming Dynasty. In the 1980s, the people of Sanli Town sang folk songs in an alley 100 meters away from the Chengxiang street. Initially there were dozens of participants, but as the singing group grew, the number of participants swelled to hundreds. The alley could not accommodate so many people and the singing spot had to shifted to Chengxiang street. Between 1966 and 1976, the singing festival was interrupted. By 1984, thousands of Zhuang folk singers spontaneously gathered at the shore of Huishuijiao to sing folk songs, and thus the singing festival was revived. Nowadays, Sanli has established the folk song association and holds the Zhuang folk song contest every year. Every year, on festivals such as the Spring Festival, the Lantern Festival and the singing festival of the third day of the third lunar month, folk singers from Sanli Town as well as surrounding counties and cities come to sing, witnessing an extremely lively scene.

Sanli Gexu Festival of Zhuang Ethnic Group in

Shanglin takes vocal singing as its main form, and the folk songs, rich in content, are handed down from generation to generation. There are folk songs that express the emotional communication between people such as greeting songs, friend-making songs, meeting songs, blessing songs, amorous songs, love songs and souvenir songs. There are also folk songs about Zhuang ethnic customs, such as folk custom songs, historical songs, sings to praise the prosperous times, fashionable songs and quiz songs. From big events of historical stories and current affairs to trifle things of reciprocity and life games, everything can be expressed in the form of singing. Duets come in diverse forms and the contents vary from person to person. Most of the folk songs are oriented to greeting friends and expressing love. There are four types of folk songs: jun folk songs, shigong tone, five word-four sentence shuangluo tone and five word-four sentence tone. Representative works include *The Sun Rises in the East* and *Always Shines the World, Beauty of Sanli, Rule-of-law Chinese Dream* and other works. These works are all written by the inheritor Wei Jialin, among which many have won awards.

Sanli Gexu Festival of Zhuang Ethnic Group in Shanglin is organized spontaneously and sung freely by the people. There are various forms, such as single-part, two-part, three-part and multiple-part folk songs. Also, sentence patterns are diverse, for example, five words four sentences, five words five sentences, five words six sentences, seven words four sentences, seven words multiple sentences and multiple words multiple sentences. Among them, five word-five sentence Lejiao song is a classic. As the crystallization of Zhuang folk culture and collective wisdom, the colorful folk songs provide significant reference value for the study of the origin and development of Zhuang folk culture. The government sets up special funds for folk song activities, regularly holds folk song training courses and organizes contests by taking advantage of various ethnic festivals, with an aim to promote the inheritance and development of the folk songs of Zhuang Ethnic Group in Sanli.

名壮族山歌手自发聚集于汇水桥岸对歌，歌圩再度形成。如今，三里镇每年都举办壮族山歌比赛，并成立山歌协会。每年春节、元宵节、三月三歌节等节日，三里镇以及周边县、市山歌手纷纷前来一展歌喉，场面极为热闹。

上林三里壮族歌圩以口头传唱为主，代代相传，内容丰富，有表达人与人情感交流的问候歌、交友歌、相会歌、祝愿歌、风情歌、爱慕歌、留念歌，有介绍壮乡民族风情的风俗歌、历史典故歌、赞盛世歌、时兴歌、猜谜歌，大到历史故事、时事新闻，小至礼尚往来、生活游戏，无所不唱。对歌形式多样，内容因人而异，多以歌会友、以歌传情。山歌分军山歌、师公调、五四句双罗调和五四句式调四种，代表作品有《江伦很罢东，总照红下吞》（意为：太阳从东边升起，总照亮天下）、《三里美》、《贝侬固欢昂来咯》、《法制中国梦》等，均为传承人韦家林自编，其中多首曾获奖。

上林三里壮族歌圩由群众自发组织，随性而唱，形式有单声部、二声部、三声部、多声部，句式多样，有五言四句、五言五句、五言六句、七言四句、七言多句、多言多句等，其中五言五句勒脚歌为经典之作。丰富多彩的山歌是壮民族民间文化与集体智慧的结晶，对研究壮族文化起源与发展具有重要的参考价值。上林县政府设立专项资金作为山歌活动经费，定期举办山歌培训班，利用各大民族节日组织比赛活动，以促进三里壮族山歌的传承和发展。

蒲庙花婆诞

Pumiao Huapo Birthday Festival

项目名称：蒲庙花婆诞

别称：无

分布范围：邕宁区蒲庙镇

入选名录：2018年第七批自治区级非物质文化遗产名录

2017年第七批市级非物质文化遗产名录

保护单位：邕宁区文化馆

代表性传承人：张月珍

Element name：Pumiao Huapo Birthday Festival

Alternative name：None

Geographical location and range：Pumiao Town of Yongning District

Element inscribed list：In 2018 on the Seventh Autonomous Region List of Intangible Cultural Heritage

In 2017 on the Seventh Municipal List of Intangible Cultural Heritage

Competent body involved in safeguarding：Yongning District Cultural Centre

Representative inheritor：Zhang Yuezhen

Pumiao Huapo Birthday Festival is an indispensable and traditional custom of Pumiao's day of commemoration. The activity mainly sacrifices Huapo, which is mainly held in Pumiao Town, Yongning District, Nanning City. The day of March 12 of the lunar calendar per year is the day for Pumiao Town to commemorate embankment opening, and the birthday of Pumiao Huapo. At that time, the large-sized commemoration activity will be held in the town; Pumiao Huapo Birthday Festival, as the main part of the commemoration activity, is preserved and continued.

Pumiao Huapo Birthday Festival has a long inheritance history and its influence scope keeps being expanded, radiating Xinjiang, Baiji, Nalou, Zhonghe in Yongning District, and some towns, streets and villages in Liangqing District. Pumiao Town is the gathering place of the aboriginal Zhuang residents in Nanning. According to the *County Record of Yongning*, Pumiao sets up the embankment in the 9th year of Yongzheng's reign (the year of 1731) in the Qing Dynasty, with the history of 286 years. With the profound humanistic deposits, flat and fertile land, rich products and convenient traffic, it boosts the economic development and cultural prosperity of the town. According to the legend, Huapo is the ancestor of Pumiao. During the reign of Kangxi, Yongjiang River suffered from a flood and an old grandma was drifted there. She lived by the wharf of Pumiao and sold porridge; she often gave porridge to the passers-by. It is said that after drinking the porridge of the grandma, people would get luck, namely the "luck of porridge" (the same pronunciation with "wish" in Chinese). Later, in order to commemorate the kind grandma, the local set up Huapo Temple for her. In the local dialect, "Pomiao" and "Pumiao" had the same pronunciations, so the town became the current Pumiao Town. In history, Yongjiang often suffered from floods and Pumiao was often drowned. The legend of Huapo also shows the psychological wish of Pumiao ancestors of praying for good luck and peace. Pumiao Huapo Birthday Festival was thus created and developed.

Pumiao Huapo Birthday Festival includes four parts. First of all, the folk-custom activities. To give free porridge and pray for wish, carry out the people first idea that focuses on collection of the one-hundred-household rice and praying for one-hundred-household blessings, and the mutual help spirit of charity. Second, the sacrifice activity. To put Huapo water lamp and hold the traditional religious sacrifice activity. Third, the trade and commerce activity. The local merchants take the annual Pumiao Huapo Birthday Festival as a platform to conduct various folk customs exchanges and commodity

花婆送花
Huapo Sends Flowers

蒲庙花婆诞是蒲庙开圩纪念日不可或缺的传统民俗，活动以祭祀花婆为主，主要流行于南宁市邕宁区蒲庙镇。每年农历三月十二日，是蒲庙镇纪念开圩的日子，也是蒲庙花婆诞之日。届时该镇会举办大型纪念活动，蒲庙花婆诞成为纪念活动的主要部分被保存和延续下来。

蒲庙花婆诞传承历史悠久，影响范围不断扩大，波及邕宁区新江、百济、那楼、中和等乡镇以及良庆区一些乡镇、街圩、村屯。蒲庙镇是南宁原住壮民聚居地，据《邕宁县志》记载，蒲庙自清雍正九年（1731）建圩，至今已有近300年的历史，人文底蕴深厚，土地平坦肥沃，物产丰饶，加之交通便利，带动了该镇的经济发展与文化繁荣。传说花婆是蒲庙的始祖，康熙年间邕江发大水，漂来一位老婆婆，她定居在蒲庙江边码头，摆摊卖粥，经常将粥施舍给路人。据说喝了老婆婆的粥，会沾上福气，即人们常说的“粥福”（与“祝福”谐音）。后来，当地人为了纪念这位善良慈悲的老婆婆，为其建造花婆庙，在当地方言中，“婆庙”与

"蒲庙"谐音，这个圩镇便成了现在的蒲庙镇。历史上，邕江常年发大水，蒲庙常常被淹，花婆传说的出现，也是蒲庙先人消灾祈福、渴求平安的心理写照，蒲庙花婆诞随之产生并发展。

蒲庙花婆诞可分为四部分：一、民俗活动：施粥、祈福，发扬集百家米、祈百家福为核心的民本思想和乐善好施的互助精神。二、祭祀活动：放花婆水灯，举行传统宗教祭祀活动。三、商贸活动：当地商家纷纷以一年一度的蒲庙花婆诞为平台，进行各类民俗交流和商品推介，商贸活动频繁。四、娱乐活动：蒲庙花婆诞活动正值蒲庙开圩纪念日期间，八音、壮鼓、舞春牛、巡游等娱乐活动贯穿其中。

蒲庙花婆诞以乐善好施、慷慨慈悲的花婆形象为基本依托，以粥福为主线，传递出民众仁爱的传统道德观。花婆信仰同时与南宁先民崇拜花图腾的遗风有关，万物由花而来，长久以来，花被奉为生育神，因此花婆传说也有求子求福的寓意。蒲庙花婆诞具有深厚的民本思想和人文情怀。花婆诞在南宁世代传承、活态存续，地方特色鲜明，是壮民族文化特色的充分体现。花婆善良、慷慨、慈悲的形象符合中华传统美德，花婆精神源远流长，世代相传。蒲庙花婆诞在南宁文化长廊中一枝独秀，具有珍贵的历史价值和文化价值，如今已经成为邕宁区具有代表性的优秀民俗活动之一。2011年后，每年蒲庙花婆诞都邀请海外华侨归国参与，将花婆精神传扬至海外。

recommendation, with frequent trade and commerce activities. Fourth, the entertainment activity. The activity Pumiao Huapo Birthday Festival is during the commemoration day of Pumiao, with entertainment activities, such as singing, beating Zhuang drum, dancing spring cattle and tour trip.

Pumiao Huapo Birthday Festival depends on the image of the benevolent and generous Huapo, with porridge luck as the main line, and conveys the traditional kindheartedness morals of the public. Huapo belief is also related to the worship of Nanning ancestors about flower totem, who believed that all things derived from flower. For a long time, the flower has been reputed as the god of birth, so the legend of Huapo also has the meaning of praying for offspring and luck. Pumiao Huapo Birthday Festival is of profound people first idea and humanistic feelings. Huapo has been inherited in Nanning for generations with vivid local characteristics, which fully shows the cultural characteristics of Zhuang Ethnic Group. The kind, generous and merciful image of Huapo keeps in line with the traditional Chinese virtues; the spirit of Huapo has been long inherited. Pumiao Huapo Birthday Festival remains unique in the cultural corridor of Nanning, with precious historical and cultural value. At present, it has become one of the representative excellent folk custom activities in Yongning District. Since 2011, Pumiao Huapo Birthday Festival has invited overseas Chinese to participate in it every year, so as to carry forward the spirit of Huapo abroad.

花婆点燃七星水灯，放入邕江
Release Water Lamps on Yongjiang River

南宁观音诞习俗

Nanning Bodhisattva's Birthday Folklore

项目名称：南宁观音诞习俗

别称：无

分布范围：兴宁区三塘镇、四塘镇、五塘镇、昆仑镇，横州市校椅镇、百合镇，宾阳县，邕宁区，青秀区及周边地区

入选名录：2017年第七批市级非物质文化遗产名录

保护单位：兴宁区文化馆

代表性传承人：无

Element name: Nanning Bodhisattva's Birthday Folklore

Alternative name: None

Geographical location and range: Santang Town, Sitang Town, Wutang Town, Kunlun Town of Xingning District; Xiaoyi Town, Baihe Town of Hengzhou City, Binyang County, Yongning District, Qingxiu District and the surrounding areas

Element inscribed list: In 2017 on the Seventh Municipal List of Intangible Cultural Heritage

Competent body involved in safeguarding: Xingning District Cultural Centre

Representative inheritor: None

南宁观音诞习俗是一种祈福活动，在农历二月十九日观音生日时举办。活动流程严格有序，具有极其丰富的文化内涵。

南宁观音诞广泛分布于南宁市兴宁区的三塘镇、四塘镇、五塘镇、昆仑镇，横州市的校椅镇、百合镇，宾阳县，邕宁区，青秀区及周边地区，尤其以兴宁区的三塘镇、四塘镇、五塘镇最集中、最热闹、规模最大、最具代表性。兴宁区位于南宁市中心，是南宁市最古老的城区之一，也是城市的商贸中心区，辖区内商贾云集，商贸服务业繁荣，这里也是壮汉民族相互交融、文化相互渗透融合之地。观世音菩萨是佛教慈悲和智慧的象征，在佛教众多菩萨中最为民间熟知并信仰。我国对观音的完整认识，大约起于东晋鸠摩罗什译《妙法莲华经》。南宁观音诞习俗很少有文字记载，但根据青秀山观音禅寺的发展历史，推测其起源最早可追溯至北宋时期。当时即有出家人在青秀山筑庐修行，至明朝万历年间，万佛禅寺建成，历经沧桑，成为今日的青秀山观音禅寺。近代，关于南宁观音诞的相关记述逐渐增多，民国时期

南宁观音诞最重要的内容——游神仪式
The Most Important Content of Guanyin Bodhisattva's Festival in Nanning: Worship Ceremony

Nanning Bodhisattva's Birthday Folklore is a blessing activity held on Bodhisattva's Birthday on February 19 of the lunar calendar. The activity process is strict and orderly, and it is of huge universal value and extremely abundant cultural connotations.

Nanning Bodhisattva's Birthday Folklore is widely distributed in Santang Town, Sitang Town, Wutang Town, Kunlun Town in Xingning District, Xiaoyi Town in Hengzhou City, Baihe Town, Binyang County, Yongning District, Qingxiu District and the surrounding areas; that in Santang Town, Sitang Town and Wutang Town in Xingning District is the most concentrated, the busiest, the biggest and the most representative. Xingning District is located at the downtown of Nanning City; it is one of the most ancient districts of Nanning City and the central trade and commerce area of the city. Within the area, there are various merchants, so its trade and commerce service industry is prosperous. It is also the place where Zhuang and Han Nationalities integrate and their cultures are mutually influenced. Arya Avalokiteshvara is the symbol of mercy and wisdom in Buddhism, which is the best-known to the folk among multiple Bodhisattva of Buddhism. Our country's complete understanding of Avalokitesvara roughly originated from *Lotus Sutra* translated by Kumarajiva in the Eastern Jin Dynasty. Nanning Bodhisattva's Birthday Folklore has few literary records. However, according to the development history of Avalokitesvara Temple of Qingxiu Mountain, it could be speculated that Nanning Bodhisattva's Birthday could be dated back to the Northern Song Dynasty. At that time, some ascetics built a house and cultivated themselves in Qingxiu Mountain. Ten Thousand Buddha Monasteries were built during Wanli's reign in the Ming Dynasty. Through ups and downs, it becomes the Avalokitesvara Temple of Qingxiu Mountain. Related records of Nanning Bodhisattva's Birthday have gradually increased in modern times. *Overview of Guangxi, Record of Nanning City, Folk Memory: Written Record of Folk Customs in Nanning, Series Books of Historic Culture of Nanning* published in the Republic of China have related literal and picture records.

The blessing activities of Nanning Bodhisattva's Birthday are roughly divided into three types. The first type is the fiesta type: 1. The opening ceremony. The Taoist master conducts a series of ceremonies, including altar opening, deity inviting, and praying according to Taoist's ceremony. 2. Three-Dynasty ceremony. After the opening ceremony, the Taoist master recites the scriptures for disaster removal in three periods one day. 3. Deity inviting and sacrificing ceremony. To place the tribute desk and sacrificial offerings, with the boy and girl by both sides; the master conducts the consecration ceremony of the lucky rice, flower and lamp bowl, and flower. 4. Blessing ceremony. 14 representatives get the flower on the stage; the immortal sing songs and send the flowers, meaning "blessing". 5. The deity tour ceremony. To set the incense burner table, place the furnace, candle and vase, as well as sacrifices, such as pork, wine, fruit, rice and vegetable, with flags, horses, towers and sedans around. They have the tour show along the village lane, which is called Bodhisattva's tour. The second type is the recreational and sports activity, including the recreational and sports tourism activity, literature and art performance, folk song competition and basketball competition. It attracts citizens and tourists to participate in it and feel the rural customs. By depending on the tourism activities, including "Village World", it promotes the development of local tourism industry and increases farmers' income. The third type is the one-hundred-blessing feast, where villagers, clans and guests get together to have the reunion dinner, send wishes to one another, and increase exchanges.

In the belief of Avalokitesvara, people have a strong sense of recognition of the myths related to Avalokitesvara, and have basically the same ways of worshiping Avalokitesvara, which embodies the common psychology of the nation and contains the social historic value. Avalokitesvara has the equal and selfless cherished desires. The belief and worship of Avalokitesvara reflect the public's kindness and gratefulness, which become their spiritual support, as well as the psychological symbol and sign. Nanning Bodhisattva's Birthday Folklore has an enormous structure and abundant contents, as well as multiple cultural connotations. The worship for gods or ceremonies is influenced by local customs, which keeps deriving from the mutual integration and collision of the Zhuang and Han national cultures, and gradually forms the unique regional culture, with important cultural values. The increase of the folk culture and art activities makes the repaying of Avalokitesvara gradually enter the social life, further forms the common cultural symbols of Zhuang and Han peoples, and provides precious materials for the research of local folk customs. In order to keep pace with the times, the modern song and dance performance has been added to the Nanning Bodhisattva's Birthday Folklore. The traditional blessing ceremony becomes simple increasingly and the tradition of Nanning Bodhisattva's Birthday is endangered. In 2017, Nanning Bodhisattva's Birthday Folklore was inscribed on the Municipal List of Intangible Cultural Heritage.

出版的《广西一览》《南宁市志》《民间记忆：南宁民俗笔录》《南宁历史文化丛书》等有相关文字和图片记载。

南宁观音诞祈福活动大致分为三类。第一类是祭典：1.开坛仪式：道公根据道家“进表”科仪，进行启坛、请圣、拜表等一系列仪式。2.三朝仪式：开坛仪式之后，道公在一天中分三个时段念诵消灾经等经文。3.请神、祭神仪式：放供桌、摆祭品，童男童女立左右，师公对福米、花灯碗、花进行开光仪式。4.赐福仪式：14户代表挂红上台领花，仙家唱曲，为其送花，寓意“赐福”。5.游神仪式：设香案，摆香炉、蜡烛、花瓶以及香猪、酒、水果、米、蔬菜等祭品，旗、马、塔、轿等随行左右，沿村道巡游，俗称观音过堂。第二类为文体活动，即举行文体旅游活动、文艺汇演、山歌比赛、篮球比赛等，吸引市民游客参与体验，感受农村风土人情，依托“乡村大世界”旅游景点活动促进当地旅游业的发展，增加农民收入。第三类即百福宴，村民和宗亲、嘉宾们聚集吃团圆饭，相互道福，交流情感。

在观音信仰中，人们对种种观音显灵的神话传说持有强烈的认同感，对观音顶礼膜拜的方式也基本一致，体现了民族共同心理，且具有社会历史价值。观音菩萨具有平等无私的广大悲愿，对观音的信仰与崇拜反映了民众从善、感恩的心态，成为民众的精神依托，也成为一种心理象征和标志。南宁观音诞习俗结构庞大、内容丰富，具有多重文化内涵，无论神灵崇拜抑或典礼仪规均受地方风俗的影响，在壮、汉民族文化相互交融与碰撞中不断衍变，逐渐形成了独具特色的地域文化，具有重要的文化价值。民俗文艺活动的加入使观音诞酬神习俗逐渐走进世俗社会生活，并进一步形成了壮、汉民族的共同文化符号，为地方民俗研究提供了宝贵的材料。为了跟上时代的脚步，现代化歌舞表演被加入南宁观音诞活动，传统祈福仪式却日趋简单，南宁观音诞传统已面临濒危。2017年，南宁观音诞习俗列入市级非物质文化遗产名录。

南宁开年习俗

Nanning Starting Year Folkways

项目名称：南宁开年习俗

别称：无

分布范围：南宁市各区县

入选名录：2018年第七批自治区级非物质文化遗产名录
　　　　　2017年第七批市级非物质文化遗产名录

保护单位：兴宁区文化馆

代表性传承人：无

Element name：Nanning Starting Year Folkways

Alternative name：None

Geographical location and range：All districts and counties of Nanning City

Element inscribed list：In 2018 on the Seventh Autonomous Region List of Intangible Cultural Heritage
In 2017 on the Seventh Municipal List of Intangible Cultural Heritage

Competent body involved in safeguarding：Xingning District Cultural Centre

Representative inheritor：None

Nanning Starting Year Folkways is a traditional folk activity held by Nanning people to celebrate the Spring Festival, which integrates sacrifice, entertainment and social functions and is widely spread in five counties and seven urban areas of Nanning City. In order to stagger the time for neighboring villages to congratulate each other, Nanning Starting Year Folkways is arranged at different time in each village and it is a cultural heritage that is highly cherished by the local community.

With Santang Town, Xingning District, Nanning City as the core area, Nanning Starting Year Folkways is distributed in Xixiangtang District, Jiangnan District, Liangqing District, Yongning District, Qingxiu District, Wuming District, Hengzhou City, Binyang County, Mashan County, Shanglin County, Long'an County and other areas. Xingning District is located in the centre of Nanning and is also the city's business centre. It is one of the oldest urban areas in Nanning with ethnic groups Zhuang, Han and Yao mainly living there. Here is abundant in rainfall with mild climate and a number of national tourist attractions are located here. "Starting Year" means the "beginning of the year". Nanning Starting Year Folkways has been particularly popular since ancient times. Before the 1960s, the date of Starting Year every year was from the fifteenth day to the twentieth day of the first month of lunar calendar. With the change and development of the times, the date of Starting Year is now from the third day to the tenth day of the first month of lunar calendar.

Nanning Starting Year Folkways has four main parts. The first is to worship the God of Land. On the opening day of the Starting Year, each household prepares sacrifices such as chicken, duck, and fish and through a series of sacrifices to the God of Land in Land Temple, they reward the God of Land for his care in the past and pray for good weather for the crops in the new year. The second is to worship the ancestors. After worshipping the God of Land, each household will bring his sacrifices home, then worship the ancestors, and pray to his ancestors to bless the peace of the old and the young. The third is folklore activities. After the worship, the folk culture programs, such as singing folk songs, Cantonese opera, song and dance begin. The most distinctive programs are Welcoming Guests by Waist Drum and Welcoming Guests by Dragon and Lion Dance, followed by blessing programs of the Starting Year such as Opening Altar by Shigong Master, Consecration of Blessing Rice, Sanniang Watering Blessing Flower and the God of Fortune Sending Blessing. The fourth is to entertain friends and relatives. After watching the performance, the villagers banquet each other and congratulate each other on the beginning of the new year, praying for a

昆仑师公队“开年”祈福仪式
"New Year" Blessing Ceremony of Kunlun Shigong Opera Troupe

南宁开年习俗是南宁民众为庆祝新春举办的集祭祀、娱乐、社交功能于一体的民间活动，广泛流传于南宁市五县七城区。为了便于邻村相互祝贺，南宁开年习俗在每个村的时间不尽相同，是当地社区民众极为珍视的文化遗产。

南宁开年习俗以南宁市兴宁区三塘镇为核心区，分布于西乡塘区、江南区、良庆区、邕宁区、青秀区、武鸣区、横州市、宾阳县、马山县、上林县、隆安县等地。兴宁区位于南宁市中心，也是城市的商贸中心区、南宁最古老的城区之一，主要居住民族有壮族、汉族、瑶族。这里雨量充沛，气候温和，有多个国家级旅游景区。“开年”即一年的开始。南宁开年习俗从古至今都尤为盛行，20世纪60年代以前，每年的开年日期为正月十五至二十。随着时代的变迁和发展，如今开年习俗的日期为正月初三至初十。

南宁开年习俗主要有四部分内容。一是祭土地神：开年当天各家各户准备鸡鸭鱼肉等祭品，轮番到土地庙祭拜，酬谢土地神的关照，并祈愿在新的一年风调雨顺。二是祭祖宗：祭拜土地神后，把自家祭品端回家中，再祭拜祖先，祈求先祖保佑老幼平安。三是民俗活动：祭拜结束，民俗文化节目开始，有唱山歌、粤剧、歌舞等，最富特色的是腰鼓迎宾和龙狮迎宾，接着是师公开坛、纳福米开光、三娘浇福花和财神派福等开年祈福表演。四是宴请亲朋好友：观看完演出，村民们在各家大摆宴席，互相恭贺新年伊始，祈求美好开端。

南宁开年习俗通过祭拜土地神与祖先，形成了具有宗教性的独特民俗活动。在新春来临之际，家家户户相互恭贺，这不仅仅代表着祝福，还体现出家人、亲友、邻居之间和谐相处的融洽气氛。各种民俗表演（如唱山歌、粤剧、歌舞等）汇集上演，师公开坛、纳福米开光、三娘浇福花和财神派福等开年祈福相继进行，民众在祈愿中娱乐，在娱乐中祈福，表达人们庆祝过去一年劳动收成的喜悦和向往新一年美好生活的朴素心愿，大量民众集体参与体现了当地民众的精神凝聚力。南宁开年习俗是壮、汉民族最具特色的传统节日庆典，是典型的社会群体性活动，它不仅仅是一个重要的节日庆典，也是人们情感得以释放、心理诉求得以满足的重要载体，具有重要的文化价值和民俗研究价值。在南宁市兴宁区政府的大力支持下，各家各户积极参与开年活动，每年的正月初三至初十都热闹非凡，三塘镇开年庆典目前传承状况良好。

good start.

Nanning Starting Year Folkways forms a unique religious folk activity by worshipping the God of Land and ancestors. every family congratulates each other on the arrival of the New Year, which not only represents a blessing, but also reflects the harmonious atmosphere among family members, relatives, friends and neighbors. Various folk performances such as singing folk songs, Cantonese operas, songs and dances are staged, accompanied by blessing programs such as Opening Altar by Shigong Master, Consecration of Blessing Rice, Sanniang Watering Blessing Flowers and the God of Fortune Sending Blessing. The people entertain themselves in prayers and pray for blessing in entertainment to express the joy of celebrating the labor harvest of the past year and the simple wish of yearning for a better life in the new year and the collective participation of a large number of people reflects the spiritual cohesion of the local people. Nanning Starting Year Folkways is the most distinctive traditional festival celebration of the Zhuang and Han ethnic groups and is a typical social group activity. It is not only an important festival celebration, but also an important carrier for people to release their emotions and satisfy their psychological demands, which has key cultural values and folklore research values. With the strong support of the government of Xingning District of Nanning City, all households actively participate in the Starting Year activities, every year, the time from the third day to the tenth day of the first lunar month is quite bustling, and the celebration of Starting Year Folkways in Santang Town is well inherited.

正月初七，三塘那安新村开年，醒狮开场表演
On the Seventh Day of the First Month, the New Year of Na'an New Village in Santang Begins with a Performance of Lion Dance

大家欢聚一堂，共享百家宴
Have a Joyous Gathering and Share a Hundred Banquets

那马龙狮

Nama Dragon-Lion Festival

项目名称：那马龙狮

别称：无

分布范围：良庆区那马镇

入选名录：2007年第一批市级非物质文化遗产名录

保护单位：良庆区文化馆

代表性传承人：无

Element name：Nama Dragon-Lion Festival

Alternative name：None

Geographical location and range：Nama Town of Liangqing District

Element inscribed list：In 2007 on the First Municipal List of Intangible Cultural Heritage

Competent body involved in safeguarding：Liangqing District Cultural Centre

Representative inheritor：None

那马龙狮表演
Performance of Nama Dragon-Lion Dance

那马龙狮是一项融武术、体育、竞技、舞蹈、音乐为一体的传统民俗活动，距今已有300多年的历史。龙狮为舞龙和舞狮表演，龙和狮被中华各民族人民视为瑞兽，象征吉祥如意，龙狮共舞意为求吉纳福、消灾除害、风调雨顺、天下太平。活动于每年春节（那马街开圩纪念日）以及各种庆典之日举行。

那马圩于清康熙二十四年（1685）建立，起初建于那马村，清道光十八年（1838）迁至八尺江岸，该镇民间文化历史悠久。那马龙狮队组建于1685年，由那马镇民间艺人徐二荣创建。那马龙狮的诞生、发展和定型一方面起源于当地的龙母井传说，另一方面由广东佛山一带的民间传说而来。相传距今300多年前，一场特大暴雨过后，那马圩共和村小麻坡附近的田边出现了一个洞，洞内流水汩汩。一日，一牧羊人欲赶羊到洞中躲雨，发现洞口有一条母龙正在产仔，龙仔受惊，不幸夭亡。村民得知后便纷纷赶往龙洞安葬龙仔，

Nama Dragon-Lion Festival is a traditional folk activity that integrates martial arts, sports, competition, dance and music, which has a history of more than 300 years. Dragon-Lion means dragon and lion dance performance. Dragon and lion are regarded as auspicious animals by the people of all ethnic groups in China, symbolizing good luck. That dragon and lion dance together means to seek good luck and blessing, pray for disaster elimination, good weather for the crops and peace in the world. The event is held every year during the Spring Festival, the anniversary of party starts in Nama Street, as well as various celebrations.

Nama Party was established in the 24th year of Emperor Kangxi (1685) of the Qing Dynasty. It was originally built in Nama Village and moved to the bank of the Bachi River in the 18th year of Emperor Daoguang (1838) of the Qing Dynasty. This town has a long history of folk culture. The Nama Dragon-Lion Festival team was founded in 1685 by Xu Errong, a folk artist from Nama Town. The birth, development and stereotype of the Nama Dragon-Lion Festival originates from the local legend of Dragon Mother Well on the one hand and folk legend from Foshan area in Guangdong on the other hand. Legend has it that more than 300 years ago, after a torrential rainstorm, a cave appeared in the field near the Xiaomapo in Gongma village, Nama Party, in which running water gurgled. One day, a shepherd tried to drive the sheep to the cave to take shelter from the rain when he found that a mother dragon was giving birth at the mouth of the cave. The baby dragon was frightened and unfortunately died. After learning that, the villagers rushed to dragon cave to bury baby dragon, only to find that baby dragon had turned into a pile of dragon-shaped stones. Since then, people have named the cave "Dragon Mother Well", and every festive day, carry out dragon dance activities to express their respect for the dragon, hoping that the dragon will give blessing to mankind. The legend from Foshan says that in ancient times, strange beast appeared in Zhongyi Township, Foshan Town, Nanhai County, Guangdong Province and it destroyed rice during the Spring Festival, so the villagers called it "Beast Nian (meaning spring festival)". In order to destroy The beast Nian and avoid disaster, some people offered a plan. The shape of the beast was made of bamboo strips, paper, and cloth and colored and dozens of warriors ambushed the beast Nian in the place where the beast Nian must pass, and when the beast Nian appeared, they beat the appliances. The sound was thunderous. Sure enough, Beast Nian was appalled and fled. In order to celebrate the success of driving Beast Nian away, the villagers took beast Nian props out and danced every Spring Festival, called Lion Dance. Since the dragon and lion are auspicious things, the posterities combine the two, hence Nama Dragon-Lion Festival dance is born.

The Nama Dragon-Lion Festival is rich in content, which basically can be divided into two parts, lion dance and dragon dance. First, the southern boxing is performed by lion dancer, called "open the pile", and then two people dressed as a lion start dancing, another person dressed as a big head Buddha and holding a big palm-leaf fan lead the lion to the stage. The lion dances are mainly based on the horse stance of southern boxing. The lions have blinking, washing their beards, licking their body, shaking hairs and other movements. There are performance routines such as picking green, drinking water from the high platform, lions spitting balls, and stepping on the quincuncial piles. On the first day of each lunar new year, the lion will go to the street to pay a new year call to shops and grab the packets. Lion dancers manipulate props to express the lion's eight states of pleasure, anger, sorrow, joy, movement, silence, surprise, and suspicion through difficult movements such as jumping, moving, flashing, fluttering, swinging, and leaping on the ground or piles. In dragon dance, the dragon is 18 meters long and needs 10 people to wave it. One of them needs to hold up the Dragon Ball to lead the dragon and when dancing, it will be

却发现龙仔已经化作一堆龙形石头。自此，人们便将此洞取名为“龙母井”，每逢喜庆之日进行舞龙活动，表示对龙的敬仰，希望神龙造福人类。佛山起源说则讲远古时期，广东南海郡佛山镇忠义乡出现奇兽，每逢春节专门破坏稻谷，村民将之称为“年兽”。为消灭年兽，避免灾患，有人献计：用竹篾、纸和布制成奇兽的形状并涂色，集勇士数十人持可敲打出响声的器具埋伏于年兽必经之地，待年兽出现，便击打器具，声音如雷贯耳。果不其然，年兽闻之惊骇，落荒而逃。为庆祝驱赶年兽成功，每年春节村民便拿着年兽道具出来舞动，名为舞狮。龙、狮都是祥瑞之物，后人便将二者结合，那马龙狮舞因此诞生。

那马龙狮内容丰富，基本可分为舞狮、舞龙两部分。先由舞狮人打一阵南拳，称为“开桩”，再由两人扮一头狮子耍舞，另一人戴大头佛笑面，手执大葵扇引狮登场。舞狮人动作多以南拳马步为主，狮子有睁眼、洗须、舔身、抖毛等动作，有采青、高台饮水、狮子吐球、踩梅花桩等表演套路。每年大年初一，狮子就会到街上店铺门前拜年抢封包。舞狮人操纵道具通过在地面或桩阵上腾、挪、闪、扑、回旋、飞跃等高难度动作，表现狮子喜、怒、哀、乐、动、静、惊、疑八种状态。龙舞中龙长18米，需要10人舞动，其中一人需高举龙珠引龙，舞动时融入武术功架，形成九套十式，分别为入场式、彩龙戏球、首尾穿越、首尾潜跳、龙身半转、左右翻肚、单双翻肚、总体翻肚、退跳诱龙，刚劲雄健，场面令人眼花缭乱，十分壮观。

那马龙狮不仅蕴含着民间历史传说，还是武术、舞蹈、音乐、工艺美术等民间文化艺术之集成。它集农耕文化、娱乐、健身于一体，传承300多年，至今基本保持原生态。龙舞灵活自如，整个龙身舞动翻腾，酣畅活跃，舞龙人操纵龙身游刃有余。狮舞具有惊、险、奇、绝、美等艺术特征，狮子的眼、舌、尾活动自如，能口吐条幅，令人称奇。高台表演动作大起大落，动人心魄，令人惊叹。狮头眼大能动，额高而窄，面颊饱满，口阔带舌，以黄、红、黑三色为主，代表智、仁、勇，舞动起来华美异常。舞龙、舞狮都将武术招式融入其中，于刚劲中见柔媚，令人赞不绝口。相对于民间普通舞龙、舞狮，那马龙狮的步法套路、鼓点样式更多，且在不同场合中各不相同，复杂却有条不紊。

那马龙狮是民间欢庆丰收、祈求吉祥安康的活动，对其进行发掘、抢救和保护，对了解当地民间社会生活和历史文化具有重要意义。1998年，群众自发组建那马龙狮队，分男、女两队，接受民间龙狮舞艺人培训，龙狮队设备齐全，队员舞技高超。那马龙狮队多次受邀参加重大节庆表演活动，从2001年起已参与多项比赛，并屡次获奖。

integrated into the martial arts to form ten styles of nine sets that are the entrance dance, color dragons playing ball, head and tail passing through the belly, head and tail diving, dragon body half turning, turning belly to left and right, turning belly in odd and even number, turning belly as a whole, retreating and jumping to lure the dragon, powerful and vigorous. The scene is dazzling and spectacular.

The Nama Dragon-Lion Festival not only contains folk historical legends, but also is the integration of martial arts, dance, music, arts and crafts and other folk culture and art. It integrates farming culture, entertainment and fitness into one, has been inherited for more than 300 years and basically maintained its original state. The dragon dance is flexible and free, the whole dragon body is dancing and swinging, sound and active, and the dragon dancer can easily manipulate the dragon body. The lion dance has the artistic characteristics of being surprised, dangerous, strange, unique and beautiful. The lion's eyes, tongue and tail are free to move, and the mouth can spit banner, which is amazing. The performances on the high platform have ups and downs, which is breathtaking and amazing. The lion's head with big movable eyes, high and narrow forehead, full cheeks, wide mouth and belt like tongue is mainly painted in yellow, red and black, representing wisdom, benevolence and courage, and it looks magnificent when dancing. Both dragon dance and lion dance incorporate the martial arts moves, showing morbidezza in strength, which is full of praise. Nama Dragon-Lion Festival's footwork routines and drumbeats are more diversified than folk ordinary dragon dance and lion dance, and change according to occasions, complex but orderly.

The Nama Dragon-Lion Festival is a folk activity to celebrate the harvest and pray for good luck and well-being. To excavate, rescue and protect it is of great significance to understand the life of local civil society and history and culture. In 1998, the masses spontaneously formed the Nama Dragon-Lion Festival team, divided into male and female teams, and received the training from folk dragon and lion dancers. The dragon and lion teams were fully equipped and their dancing skills were superb. Nama Dragon-Lion Festival team has been invited to participate in major festival performances many times. Since 2001, it has participated in various competitions at all levels and won numerous awards.

大明山歌圩

Mount Daming Song Party

项目名称：大明山歌圩

别称：无

分布范围：武鸣区两江镇、府城镇及马山县古零镇，以两江镇为核心区域，辐射周边各乡镇及上林县、大化县、都安县、平果市等

入选名录：2018年第七批自治区级非物质文化遗产名录
2017年第七批市级非物质文化遗产名录

保护单位：广西大明山国家级自然保护区管理局
南宁大明山风景旅游区管理委员会

代表性传承人：韦玉英、吴正标

Element name：Mount Daming Song Party

Alternative name：None

Geographical location and range：Liangjiang Town, Fucheng Town in Wuming District and Guling Town in Mashan County, with Liangjiang Town as the core area, spreading to the surrounding towns and Shanglin County, Dahua County, Du'an County, Pingguo County-Level City and others

Element inscribed list：In 2018 on the Seventh Autonomous Region List of Intangible Cultural Heritage
In 2017 on the Seventh Municipal List of Intangible Cultural Heritage

Competent body involved in safeguarding：Guangxi Mount Daming National Nature Reserve Administration
Nanning Mount Daming Scenic Area Management Committee

Representative inheritors：Wei Yuying, Wu Zhengbiao

搭台唱山歌
Set up a Platform to Sing Folk Songs

大明山歌圩是大明山周边地区壮族群众自发参与的传统对歌活动，于每月1日举办，民众依山傍水而歌，每圩规模少则3000人，多则可达5000人。大明山歌圩以两江镇为核心区域，分布于武鸣、马山、上林、平果、大化、都安等县区。

歌圩地处大明山旅游区，景色优美，交通便利，游客众多，周边壮族村落环绕，人口密集，是歌圩文化交流和传承的理想场所。大明山壮语名“芭赤”，意为“祖宗山”，地处武鸣、上林、马山和宾阳四县交界处，是“壮欢”山歌的富矿区，历史上歌圩活动极为兴盛。廖江歌圩曾是广西规模最大的歌圩之一，《武缘县图经》有“每三月初一日至初十日，沿江上下，数里之内，士女如云”的记载。《粤西丛载》也记载：“宾州罗奉岭，去城七里，春秋二社日，士女毕集，男女未婚者，以歌诗相应和，自择配偶。”20世纪60年代以前，大明山南麓地区沿山脚一带山坡地或圩场，于每年三月初三、三月初九、五月初五、八月十五、十月十五日或圩日，均有大大小小的歌圩活动，其中雷杨江歌圩已有

Mount Daming Song Party is a traditional singing activity in which the Zhuang people in the area around Daming Mountain spontaneously participate in. It is held on the 1st of each month, and the people sing in the mountains and near waters, with a scale of about 3000 people per party, sometimes up to 5000 people. Mount Daming Song Party with Liangjiang Town as the core area, is distributed in Wuming County, Mashan County, Shanglin County, Pingguo County, Dahua County, Du'an County and other counties.

Song Party is located in the tourist area of Mount Daming, with beautiful scenery, convenient transportation, numerous tourists, surrounded by Zhuang villages with dense population and it is an ideal place for singing cultural exchange and inheritance. Mount Daming, called “Ba Chi” in Zhuang language, meaning “Ancestor Mountain”, is located at the junction of Wuming County, Shanglin County, Mashan County and Binyang County, is the rich mining area of “Zhuang Huan” folk songs, and the singing party activities are extremely prosperous in history. Liao Jiang Song Party was once one of the largest song parties in Guangxi. *Recorks and Maps of Wuyuan County* has a record of “From the first day to the tenth day in the third month of lunar calendar, along the river, within a few miles, were numerous men and women, like clouds. ” There are also relevant records in *Anecdotes of Guangxi*, “In Luofeng Mountain, seven miles away from the city, on Spring and Autumn Community Day, single boys and girls answer each other with songs and poems and choose their own spouse.” Before the 1960s, on the slope or party area in the southern foothills of Mount Daming, small-scale and large-scale song parties are held on the third day and ninth day of the third month of lunar calendar, the fifth day of the fifth month of lunar calendar, the fifteenth day of the eighth month of lunar calendar and the fifteenth day of the tenth month of lunar calendar, or the day of Party. Among them, Leiyangjiang Song Party has a history of hundreds of years and is held on the first and fifteenth day of the lunar month, with a scale of 200 to 300 people. The song party once died out after 1976 and revived again in the 1980s, expanding to 300 to 800 people. Since 2016, the masses spontaneously organized and moved the location of the song party from the Leijiang intersection to the current site and received the support of the scenic spot. The scale and influence have been continuously expanding, and the activities become more richer in contents.

Mount Daming Song Party is mainly composed of antiphonal singing of folk songs, as well as various folk entertainment activities and product sales activities. 1. Traditional antiphonal singing of folk songs. People form the towns and villages such as Guling Village and Baishan Village of Mashan County and Fucheng County and Liangjiang County of Wuming adopt "Zhuang Huan" as the main form and freely sing in the Gate Square. 2. Public folk songs competition. The local champion singer is invited to defend the championship and audiences are welcome to launch challenge to him/her. The results of the challenge are divided into "outstanding", "success" and "failure", and every participant can get prizes or souvenirs. 3. Folkway performances. Show the ethnic customs, traditional skills and traditional competitions of surrounding areas, such as Mashan Drum, Shoulder Pole Dance, Board Shoes Dance, Master Shigong Dance, Walking on Stilts, Playing Tops, Throwing Xiuqiu (A Ball Made of Strips of Silk), Dragon Dance, Cockfighting. 4. Song and dance performances. They are performed by the surrounding community groups on the centre stage or the gate area, with ethnic songs and dances as the mainstay. 5. Food and agricultural products exhibition. The surrounding villagers sell flavor snacks, local agricultural products, tourist souvenirs and so on.

With the local Zhuang culture of a long history as the background, Mount Daming Song Party is developed from Lei Yangjiang Song Party and is held on the 1st of each month in the Gate Square of Mount Daming Scenic Spot. It is one of the a few "Monthly Song Parties" in Nanning and even Guangxi and is of great value to the study of the history of Mount Daming. The activities have a broad mass base and great social influence. People enthusiastically participate in and as many as two to three thousand participants at old, middle and young age, as well as tourists from other places and even foreign countries come to each party, which has a good effect of cultural inheritance and dissemination. Activities in Xiaoxu are very active, including not only traditional antiphonal singing of folk songs but also modern song and dance shows and Zhuang, Han, Yao and many other ethnic folk song cultures collide with each other and are organically combined with tourism activities, which have strong cultural compatibility. Co-organization of antiphonal singing, singing competition and folk-art exhibition activities has important folklore research value. Song Party develops with the development of tourism in Mount Daming, and becomes an eye-catching cultural landscape with national character, openness and interest. The continuous development of Song Party activities has a certain role in promoting the protection and development of Mount Daming and has also played a positive role in the construction of material and spiritual civilization in the local and surrounding communities.

上百年的历史，逢农历初一、十五日举办，规模为200—300人。该歌圩在1976年后一度消亡，20世纪80年代再度复兴，规模扩大至300—800人。自2016年起，群众自发组织，将歌圩地点从雷江路口移至现址并得到景区扶持，规模和影响不断扩大，活动内容更为丰富。

大明山歌圩以山歌对唱为主，兼有各类民俗娱乐活动和产品展销活动。1.传统山歌对唱。来自武鸣的府城、两江及马山的古零、白山等乡镇群众以“壮欢”为主要形式，于大门广场自由对歌。2.公众山歌擂台赛。请当地歌王守擂，观众自由攻擂进行擂台赛，攻擂结果分“出彩”“成功”“失败”，参与者均可获得奖品或纪念品。3.民俗表演。展示周边地区民族风情、传统技艺、传统竞技，如马山会鼓、扁担舞、板鞋舞、师公舞、踩高跷、打陀螺、抛绣球、舞龙、斗鸡等。4.歌舞表演。由周边社区团体于中心舞台或大门区表演，以民族歌舞为主。5.美食及农土特产品展销。周边村民自发售卖风味小吃、农土特产品及旅游纪念品等。

大明山歌圩以当地历史悠久的壮族文化为背景，由雷杨江歌圩发展而来，每月1日在大明山景区大门广场举办，是南宁乃至广西为数不多的“月歌圩”，对研究大明山历史具有重要价值。活动拥有广泛的群众基础，社会影响力大，群众参与热情高，每圩均有两三千名歌手和听众自发前来，参与者有老年、中年、青年，还有来自外地甚至外国的游客，具有良好的文化传承与传播效应。小圩市活动十分活跃，既有传统民歌对唱，也有现代歌舞展演，壮、汉、瑶等多个民族民歌文化于此交流碰撞，并与旅游活动有机结合，文化兼容性极强。对歌和歌唱比赛与民间技艺展演活动共同举办，具有重要的民俗研究价值。歌圩伴随大明山旅游业的发展而发展，并以民族性、开放性、趣味性成为引人注目的人文景观。歌圩活动的持续开展，对大明山的保护开发有一定的促进作用，对当地以及周边社区的物质文明和精神文明建设也产生了一定的积极作用。

甘棠彩凤

Gantang Colour Phoenix Festival

项目名称：甘棠彩凤

别称：无

分布范围：宾阳县甘棠镇

入选名录：2009年第二批市级非物质文化遗产名录

保护单位：宾阳县文化馆

代表性传承人：无

Element name：Gantang Colour Phoenix Festival

Alternative name：None

Geographical location and range：Gantang Townof Binyang County

Element inscribed list：In 2009 on the Second Municipal List of Intangible Cultural Heritage

Competent body involved in safeguarding：Binyang County Cultural Centre

Representative inheritor：None

甘棠彩凤巡游
Parade of Gantang Colour Phoenix

甘棠彩凤表演
Performance of Gantang Colour Phoenix

With a history of more than 300 years, Gantang Colour Phoenix Festival is a folk phoenix-dance activity held by people of Gantang Town, Binyang County, Nanning City to pray for luck, peace, good weather, a bumper grain harvest as well as happiness and well-being. It is usually held on the first day of the first lunar month, on the Lantern Festival and Lord Guan Gong's Birthday Festival as well as other festivals.

Gantang Colour Phoenix Festival is held in Gantang town and Luxu Town of Binyang County, as well as in Hengzhou City and other places. According to the legend, the ancestors of Gantang migrated from the state of Wu during the Spring and Autumn Period. Around the Qing Dynasty, Gantang Colour Phoenix Festival was created by Yi Bagong, who migrated from the place which is now known as Xiangtan city, Hunan province. In those days, Yi Bagong was forced by life and followed a troupe to learn art. He came up with an idea and created the script *The Divine Phoenix Queen* which was well received. As a consequence, the troupe quickly became renowned for the play. Yi Bagong believed that it was a sign of "divine phoenix" which would definitely bring happiness and well-being to people. He went back to his village and went up the mountain to cut bamboo together with the villagers. Then they went to Gantang street to buy paper and paint. They made a colour phoenix figure by using bamboo to weave the skeleton and papering over and painting the shell. What's more, they composed the colour phoenix dance and visited every family with the phoenix dance on the first of the

甘棠彩凤是南宁市宾阳县甘棠镇一带民众为祈求吉祥平安、风调雨顺、五谷丰登、生活幸福而举办的民间舞凤活动，至今已有300多年的历史，多于农历正月初一、元宵节、关公诞节以及各种节日举行。

甘棠彩凤分布于宾阳县甘棠镇、露圩镇和横州市等地。甘棠镇位于宾阳县东南部，是宾阳三大古镇之一。相传甘棠先人春秋时期从吴国迁移而来。甘棠彩凤大约于清朝由湖南湘潭市迁居而来的易八公创编。当年易八公为生活所迫，跟随戏班学艺，突发奇想并创编剧本《齐天神凤》，备受欢迎，戏班也因该剧目迅速走红。易八公认为这是“神凤”显灵，它一定能给人们带来幸福安康。于是他回到村子里，和村民上山砍竹子，再到甘棠街买来纸张和颜料，以竹编织，以纸裱外壳并上色，制成鲜艳夺目的彩凤形象，并创编彩凤舞，每逢年初一到各户舞凤拜年，祈求风调雨顺。当年村子果然五谷丰登，人财两旺。从此，下逢村就有了每年舞凤的习俗，并流传至整个甘棠镇及周边地区。

每逢佳节，舞凤队穿戴彩凤道具，到各家各户舞凤送祝福，每到一户门前，人们便拿出糖、饼、红包等答谢。在大型庆典活动中，舞凤为必不可少的展演部分，表演者多操纵道具展示“八字飞舞”“比翼双飞”等动作，并有“甘棠山歌调”“凤凰调”“甘棠出彩调”等音乐伴奏。舞凤分雌雄两种，“雄凤”冠高且红，引领“雌凤”跟随，翩翩起舞，雌雄成双成对，寓意男女婚恋成功、幸福美满。制作彩凤需选取上好的竹料，用石灰水浸泡3至5日，晒干后编织成彩凤框架，再用砂纸作裱，上色。凤舞的主要伴奏乐器为锣鼓和唢呐，锣鼓包括大鼓、大钹和大锣，唢呐需两支或四支。

甘棠彩凤表演不仅有模拟动物动态的元素，还将舞蹈律动融进其中，舞者身着民族服装，与彩凤的精美造型交相辉映，舞动起来羽翼翩翩，喜气洋洋，场景十分美观，其音乐、造型工艺也是广西民间艺术的一部分。凤乃象征吉祥、平安之物，甘棠彩凤通过凤舞制造节日气氛，表达人们对幸福生活的美好祈愿。甘棠彩凤是研究广西民俗文化重要的一部分，也对研究地域民间舞蹈、音乐、美术具有重要的参考价值。自2006年制作彩凤的老艺人宁育才去世后，甘棠彩凤制作技艺传承中断。作为宾阳县主要的传统文化项目之一，甘棠彩凤被县政府重点扶植保护，2009年列入第二批市级非物质文化遗产名录。

甘棠彩凤表演
Performance of Gantang Colour Phoenix

Lunar New Year to pray for good weather. That year witnessed a bump grain harvest and thriving life of people in the village. The custom of phoenix dance has been going on ever since in Xiafeng village and gradually spreads throughout Gantang town and the surrounding area.

During the festival season, the phoenix dance team is dressed up wearing phoenix props to visit each family to send blessings with the phoenix dance. Every time the phoenix dance team comes to the door of a house, people take out candies, cakes and red envelopes in return. The phoenix dance is an indispensable part of the show in big celebrations. Performers usually manipulate props to show movements such as “v-shape flying dance” and “flying wing to wing”. There is also music accompaniment, such as Gantang folk song tones, “phoenix tone” and “Gantang chucai tone”. The dancing phoenixes are divided into male and female. “Male phoenix” has a big and red crest and guides the “female phoenix” to dance. The male and female phoenixes dance in pairs which implies the success of marriage and happiness of life. To make colour phoenix, superior bamboo is required and soaked in lime water for 3 to 5 days, which is dried and woven into the skeleton of the colour phoenix. Then it is papered over with sandpaper and then painted. The main instruments used to accompany the phoenix dance are the gongs and drums and the suona, among which the gongs and drums include bass drums, top cymbals and big gongs, and altogether two or four suonas are required.

The performance of Gantang Colour Phoenix Festival not only involves elements that simulate movements and shapes of animals, but also integrates dance rhythms. National costumes that dancers wear and the elaborate shape of the colour phoenix add radiance to each other, and the dancing wings create a beautiful scene of jubilation. The music and the shape process are also part of Guangxi folk art. Phoenix symbolizes good luck and peace and Gantang Colour Phoenix Festival creates a festival atmosphere through the phoenix dance, expressing people’s good wishes for a happy life. As a significant part of research on Guangxi folk culture, Gantang Colour Phoenix Festival provides reference value for the study of regional folk dances, music and fine arts. Since Ning Yucai, the old artist of handicrafted colour phoenix, passed away in 2006, the inheritance of colour phoenix craftsmanship has been interrupted. As one of the primary traditional cultural projects in Binyang county, Gantang Colour Phoenix Festival has been fostered and protected by the county government. In 2009, it was inscribed on the Second Municipal List of Intangible Cultural Heritage.

宾阳甘棠圩逢

Binyang Gantang Country Fair

项目名称：宾阳甘棠圩逢

别称：无

分布范围：宾阳县甘棠镇

入选名录：2015年第六批市级非物质文化遗产名录

保护单位：宾阳县文化馆

代表性传承人：无

Element name：Binyang Gantang Country Fair

Alternative name：None

Geographical location and range：Gantang Town of Binyang County

Element inscribed list：In 2015 on the Sixth Municipal List of Intangible Cultural Heritage

Competent body involved in safeguarding：Binyang County Cultural Centre

Representative inheritor：None

宾阳甘棠圩逢舞狮表演
Lion Dance at Binyang Gantang Country Fair

“圩逢”意为“祭祀圩日”，甘棠圩逢是于宾阳县邓村举办的一系列大规模群众性游艺活动，每年农历三月十六日举行。当日，除了每户大摆宴席款待亲朋，还举行祭祀、舞龙、舞狮、舞凤、山歌对唱等活动。甘棠圩逢自清康熙年间传承至今，已有200余年的历史。

甘棠镇位于宾阳县东南方，主要居民为壮族人，邓村位于甘棠圩西南部，由于清朝初期由邓姓人家先行造村，因此得名“邓村”，并沿用村名至今。邓村圩逢节大致起源于清朝康熙末年，传说当时邓村连续多年出现人口非正常死亡现象，有风水先生告知村民，这是由于该村东南角一处形似棺材的岭坡犯煞，要解除恶煞需每年农历三月十六日组织人上山踩踏“棺材岭”。邓村人照办，果然得以保住村民平安。从此此项活动每年举办，并逐渐发展成邓村圩逢节，即宾阳甘棠圩逢。

从古至今，宾阳甘棠圩逢不设筹委会和组委会，活动内容和方式沿袭传统，亦具有一定的可变性，于20世纪70年代形成了祭祀、踏岭、欢娱、餐饮、再踏岭的活动流程。时

“Country Fair” refers to “Day of Sacrifice”. Gantang Country Fair is a series of large-sized mass entertainment activity held in Dengcun Village, Binyang County, which is held on March 16 of the lunar year. On the day, besides feasting friends and relatives, various activities, such as sacrifice, dragon dance, lion dance, phoenix dance and singing of folk songs will also be held. Since being inherited from Kangxi’s reign in the Qing Dynasty, Gantang Country Fair has had a history of over 200 years.

Gantang Town is located at the southeast of Binyang County, where residents of Zhuang Ethnic Group live. Dengcun Village is located at the southwest of Gantang. At the beginning of the Qing Dynasty, the family of Deng took the initiative to build the village, so it is called “Dengcun Village”, which has been used till now. Country Fair Festival in Dengcun Village roughly originated from the final year of Kangxi’s reign in the Qing Dynasty. As the legend goes, abnormal death occurred in Dengcun Village for multiple years at that time. Mr. Fengshui (geomancer) told villages that it was caused by a coffin-like mountain at the southeast corner. In order to drive away the devils, they had to organize villagers to the mountain to tread on the “Coffin Mountain” on March 16 of the lunar year. Villagers from Dengcun Village followed it and finally ensured the safety. Since then, the activity has been held per year and gradually developed into Country Fair Festival of Dengcun Village, namely Binyang Gantang Country Fair.

Since the ancient times, Binyang Gantang Country Fair has set no committee and preparatory committee. The activity contents and modes inherit the traditions, which can also be changed. In 1970s, it formed the activity process, including sacrifice, treading, entertainment, catering and treading again. When the festival approaches, every household of the village kills ducks and chicken and holds feasts to entertain guests from all directions. Guests firstly follow villages to make sacrifice in “Tingluan Temple” and then tread on the “Coffin Mountain”. After this, they will have carnivals for celebration, including dragon dance, lion dance, phoenix dance, singing of folk songs and attending carnival, etc. After the guests have dined and wined to satiety and have enough power, they will tread the “Coffin Mountain” again. At the beginning of 1950s, 34 PLA soldiers were sacrificed in order to encircle and suppress the bandits who illegally occupied Dengcun Village and emancipate villagers of Dengcun Village. Villagers held that they could only gain peace and happiness through CPC and PLA, so since 1970s, a series of activities centered on treading “Coffin Mountain” has turned into the centre on sacrificing the "Monument of Revolutionary Martyr". Since then, the connotation of Country Fair has changed.

Although Binyang Gantang Country Fair was somewhat of feudalistic superstition, yet since 1970s, it has changed its connotation and become closer to the reality, which aims to remove ill fortune and undertakes the folk's expectation for a peaceful life. To tread on the "Coffin Mountain" embodies villagers' quality of striving hard and worshiping justice. To sacrifice the revolutionary martyr show the masses of Dengcun Village of advocating Chinese Communist Party and showing gratitude to the revolutionary martyr. The activity contents are close to realistic life of villages, which keep developing with the change of the times. Country Fair Festival has abundant activities, including praying for peace, folk art show, gathering of mountain songs, and friend party, which is of important value to the research of folk-custom activities of minorities. The activities are organized by villagers and guests will attend it at the opening ceremony. It becomes a good opportunity for surrounding villagers, relatives and friends to communicate and strengthen national unity. To protect, inherit and develop Gantang Country Fair culture may help promote the construction of a harmonious society.

At present, there are no fixed organizers and leaders, so various activities of Gantang Country Fair meet some problems, such as disorderly organization. In addition, all the young go out for work, so some projects lack inheritors. The competent culture department of the county organizes the census team of intangible cultural heritage to conduct field investigation of the project. In 2015, it was inscribed on the Sixth Municipal List of Intangible Cultural Heritage.

逢节日，全村每户宰杀鸡鸭，大办筵席，款待来自四面八方的宾朋。宾客先随村民去“亭卯庙”祭拜，再纷纷踩踏“棺材岭”，之后进行狂欢庆贺，包括舞龙、舞狮、舞凤、对唱山歌、参加狂欢宴等，待大家酒足饭饱且攒足力气，便前往“棺材岭”再次踩踏。20世纪50年代初，34位中国人民解放军因围剿盘踞在邓村的土匪、解放邓村村民而牺牲。村民们认为只有依靠共产党和解放军才能获得村子的平安幸福，20世纪70年代以后，一系列以踩踏“棺材岭”为中心的活动转变为以祭拜“革命烈士纪念碑”为中心，自此，圩逢的内涵有了转变。

宾阳甘棠圩逢起初虽带有封建迷信色彩，但20世纪70年代以后转变为更加贴近现实，自始至终旨在去祸消灾，承载着民间对安康生活的期望。踩踏“棺材岭”体现了村民勇于斗争和崇尚正义的美好品质。祭拜革命先烈则体现出邓村百姓拥护中国共产党、感恩革命先烈的军民之情，活动内容贴合村民现实生活，并随着时代的变化不断发展。圩逢节活动丰富多彩，包括祈求平安、民间艺术秀、山歌荟萃、友情聚会等，对研究少数民族的民俗活动具有重要价值。活动由村民约定俗成，宾客届时光临，成为周边村民和亲朋好友沟通情感、增进民族团结的良好契机。保护、传承和发展甘棠圩逢文化，对构建和谐社会有促进意义。

目前，由于没有固定的组织和领导者，甘棠圩逢各项活动举办出现组织散漫、时冷时热的情况，加之青年人均外出打工，一些项目后继无人。县文化主管部门组织非物质文化遗产普查小队对该项目进行实地普查，2015年列入第六批市级非物质文化遗产名录。

宾阳关公诞

Binyang Lord Guan Gong's Birthday Festival

项目名称：宾阳关公诞

别称：无

分布范围：宾阳县甘棠镇、昆仑关及周边地区

入选名录：2008年第二批市级非物质文化遗产名录

保护单位：宾阳县文体局

代表性传承人：无

Element name：Binyang Lord Guan Gong's Birthday Festival

Alternative name：None

Geographical location and range：Gantang Town, Kunlun Pass of Binyang County and the surrounding areas

Element inscribed list：In 2008 on the Second Municipal List of Intangible Cultural Heritage

Competent body involved in safeguarding：The Culture and Sports Bureau of Binyang County

Representative inheritor：None

Binyang Lord Guan Gong's Birthday Festival, also known as "Guan Gong Broadsword Grinding Festival", is a folk activity to commemorate Guan Gong, a general of Shu in the Three Kingdoms, and to pray that Guan Gong would descend demons and shelter the people. Binyang Lord Guan Gong's Birthday Festival is held at Guan Gong Temple in Kunlun Pass on the 13th day of the fifth lunar month every year. It is a grand festival celebration in Gantang minority area, attracting hundreds of thousands of people from surrounding areas to worship.

Binyang Lord Guan Gong's Birthday Festival was born in Gantang Town and distributed in Gantang Town, Kunlun Pass and surrounding districts and counties. Gantang Town is adjacent to Shitang Town in Hengzhou City in the southeast and Luwei Town and Guli Town in the northwest. It has convenient transportation. Since the Qing Dynasty, trade and commerce have flourished. It has become a salt port around the Republic of China. Now it is a town with relatively complete preservation of private enterprises and handicraft traditions. According to historical records, in the 20th year of Emperor Daoguang in the Qing Dynasty (1840), Gantang people in Binyang County built Guan Gong Temple at the bridge head of Shiai Bridge on the Bank of Banjiang River, praying for Guan Gong's blessing. The lunar calendar on May 13th happens to be the birthday of Guan Gong in the legend, so the Temple of Guan Gong was built and opened for worship. There was a rain on that day, and there was a rain in the temple fair held every year thereafter. It was rumored that Guan Gong was going to show his spirits and needed water to grind his broadsword so that he could kill the demons and monsters to protect the people. Therefore, Lord Guan Gong's Birthday Festival is also called "Guan Gong Broadsword Grinding Festival". Every year, the temple fair is crowded with people, so the local Zhuang people call it Country Fair Festival. Since 1840, Lord Guan Gong's Birthday Festival has been held every year without interruption. The Temple of Guan Gong was destroyed between 1966 and 1976, thus people in Gantang invited the Guan Gong to worship in the temple. Therefore, Lord Guan Gong's Birthday Festival is held in the Dahuang Temple every year, and Guan Gong's statue is invited to take a parade. In 1997, Lord Guan Gong's Birthday Festival was officially named Gantang Ethnic Culture and Art Festival.

Binyang Lord Guan Gong's Birthday Festival includes opening ceremony and outing activities. First, Tao masters conducted a religious ritual, and then Guan Gong was be honored according to the route planned by the head of the

宾阳关公诞巡游
Parade of Binyang Lord Guan Gong's Birthday Festival

宾阳关公诞，又称“关公磨刀节”，是为纪念三国蜀将关羽，并祈求关公镇魔降妖、庇护百姓安宁的一项民俗活动。宾阳关公诞于每年农历五月十三日在昆仑关关公庙举行，是甘棠少数民族地区盛大的节日庆典，吸引周边群众数十万人前来祭拜。

宾阳关公诞产生于甘棠镇，分布于甘棠镇、昆仑关及周边区县。甘棠镇东南与横州市石塘镇接壤，西北面毗邻露圩镇和古辣镇，交通便捷，自清代以来商贸繁荣，民国前后成为盐埠，如今是私营企业和手工业传统保存较为完整的乡镇。据史料记载，清道光二十年（1840），宾阳县甘棠人在班江河畔之遗爱桥桥头建造关帝庙，祈求关公保佑。当年农历五月十三日，恰好是传说中关公华诞之日，关帝庙建成，开光启拜，当日又逢降雨，且在此后每年举办的庙会祭拜中均有降雨，人们便传言关帝显灵，需用水磨其大刀，方可斩妖除怪，庇护百姓，因此关公诞节又称“关公磨刀节”。每年庙会当天人山人海，热闹非凡，故当地壮族百姓称之为圩逢节。自1840年至今，关公诞年年举行，从未间断。关帝庙在1966至1976年间曾遭损毁，甘棠人便将关圣帝君请至大皇庙内祭拜，因此，每年关公诞节亦于大皇庙开光，请出关公坐像出游。受甘棠镇人民政府重视，1997年，关公诞正式被命名为甘棠民族文化艺术节。

宾阳关公诞包括开光、出游等活动，先由道公、师公开光做法事，再请关公坐像出游，按照会首拟定的路线进行。出游队形排列讲究，"关"字大旗、"关公诞节"横幅在先，彩旗、香炉和关公神像随后，紧接着有仙女扇、罗伞和两匹手工制作的高头大马。龙、狮、凤队以及各种方队随后。出游时锣鼓喧天，鞭炮齐鸣，沿线各街各户以街道为单位设坛迎祭关公，队伍至各街道，均有道公、师公诵唱吉祥如意之词，出游长达两天时间，结束时道公、师公再做法事，敬送关公神像重归庙内端坐。除作为主要活动的神像出游之外，当日还有舞龙、舞狮、舞凤以及各种体育比赛、山歌对唱、杂耍等文艺表演。甘棠各户杀鸡宰鸭，做糍粑、包米粽款待前来赶庙会的亲朋。

宾阳关公诞活动内容丰富多彩，涵盖多种宾阳地区独特的民族艺术形式，同时也是汉文化与壮族文化相互交融的佐证。甘棠人在关公磨刀节中既引进和传承了汉文化，又在活动中展现了壮族文化和风俗，使二者交融、相互渗透。祈求关公显灵保佑苍生、免除灾难，活动规模之大，热闹非凡，体现了宾阳人对关公刚直不阿、武艺超群等品质的肯定，以及对关公英雄形象的崇拜，且具有群体性特征。节日活动旨在满足民众消灾祈福的心理需求。研究、保护宾阳关公诞节日，对研究当地历史文化具有参考价值，对培养优良的道德品质具有积极的社会意义。甘棠镇政府把其列为甘棠镇重点特色文化项目，扶植团队开展文艺展演，将关公诞民俗文化节发展成为当地的知名文化品牌。

association. The formations of the tours were well arranged, with the banners of "Guan" and "Lord Guan Gong's Birthday Festival" in the first place, followed by the colorful flags, incense burners and statues of Guan Gong, then followed by fairy fans, parachutes and two tall horses made by hand. In the end, dragons, lions, phoenixes and various diamond teams followed. When traveling, gongs, drums and firecrackers roared in unison. Altars were set up to greet Guan Gong in the street units along the road. From the procession to the streets, Tao masters chanted auspicious words. They traveled for two days. At the end of the trip, Tao masters conducted the religious ritual again, and respectfully returned the statue of Guan Gong to the temple.

Activities in Binyang Lord Guan Gong's Birthday Festival are rich and colorful, covering a variety of unique folk arts in Binyang region, and it is also a proof of the integration of Han culture and Zhuang culture. During Guan Gong Broadsword Grinding Festival, Gantang people not only introduced and inherited the Han culture, but also displayed the culture and customs of the Zhuang Ethnic Group in the activities, which made them blend and infiltrate into each other. The activities aim to praying for Guan Gong to bless the living and avoid disasters. The large scale and lively activities reflect Binyang people's affirmation of Guan Gong's integrity, martial arts and other qualities, as well as the worship of Guan Gong's heroic image, which has group characteristics. Festival activities are designed to meet the psychological needs of the people praying for removing ill fortune and for blessing. Binyang Lord Guan Gong's Birthday Festival is of reference value to the study of local history and culture, and of positive social significance to the cultivation of fine moral character. The government of Gantang town listed it as a key cultural project, supported the team to carry out literary and artistic exhibitions, and developed Lord Guan Gong's Birthday Festival into a well-known local cultural brand.

吴门农氏婆祈福祭典

Wumen Nongshipo's Blessing Ceremony

项目名称：吴门农氏婆祈福祭典

别称：无

分布范围：宾阳县王灵镇

入选名录：2015年第六批市级非物质文化遗产名录

保护单位：宾阳县文化馆

代表性传承人：吴耀武

Element name: Wumen Nongshipo's Blessing Ceremony

Alternative name: None

Geographical location and range: Wangling Town of Binyang County

Element inscribed list: In 2015 on the Sixth Municipal List of Intangible Cultural Heritage

Competent body involved in safeguarding: Binyang County Cultural Centre

Representative inheritor: Wu Yaowu

吴门农氏婆祈福祭典是起源于吴氏宗族南顺支系的一项重大祭祀礼仪活动，于宾阳县吴门农氏婆墓园处举行，以崇奉和颂扬良母农妙什的立德、行善、大爱精神为意涵，距今已有近400年的历史。活动于每年农历四月初三子时开始，届时，道师设坛举行谢土法事，第二天各村村民携带各类祭品前去墓园祭祀，各村民俗艺术团队进行游行。

吴门农氏婆祈福祭典分布于南宁市宾阳县、上林县、横州市和贵港市一带。吴门农氏婆墓园区是祭祀祈福大典的主要场所，位于南宁市宾阳县王灵镇辖区，迁移至此已有200多年的历史，这里四季如春，雨量充沛，日照充足，占地面积约25亩。吴氏后裔人口有3万多人，分布于南宁市和宾阳、灵山、邕宁、上林、宁明、都安、隆林、隆安等六十多个县、乡、镇和自然村。据历代族谱等史料记载，农氏太婆生于明洪武二十年（1387）农历七月，是广西永淳县洋额村原住民农氏大户人家的女儿，取名为妙什。她熟读四书五经，聪慧善良，勤劳俭朴，重视家学家风的传承和教育，给世人留下了伟大的良母形象，令人敬仰。明成化三年

舞龙表演
Dragon Dance Performance

Wumen Nongshipo's Blessing Ceremony is an important ritual activity originated from Nanshun Branch of Wu Clan. It was held at Wumen Nongshipo Cemetery in Binyang County. It was to worship and praise the virtue, benevolence and love of good mothers and peasants, with a history of nearly 400 years. The festival begins on the third day of the fourth lunar month every year. At that time, the Taoists sets up an altar for the ritual of giving thanks to the earth. The next day, villagers took various kinds of sacrifices to the cemetery to worship. The folk art groups of the villages marched.

Wumen Nongshipo's Blessing Ceremony is distributed in Binyang County, Shanglin County, Hengzhou City and Guigang City. Wumen Nongshipo Cemetery Park is the main place for worshiping and praying ceremonies. It is located in Wangling Town, Binyang County, Nanning City, Guangxi. It has been migrated for more than 200 years. There are plenty of rains and sunshine in all seasons, covering an area of about 25 *mu*. The descendants of Wu family have a population of more than 30,000, distributed in more than 60 counties, townships, towns and natural villages such as Binyang, Lingshan, Yongning, Shanglin, Ningming, Du'an, Longlin, Long'an and Nanning. According to the genealogy and other historical records of past dynasties, Nongshipo was born in July of the twentieth year (1387) of Emperor Hongwu in the Ming Dynasty. She was a daughter of a large family of aboriginal farmers in Yange Village, Yongchun County, Guangxi, named Miaoshi. She read The Four Books and The Five Classics. Being intelligent and kind, hard-working and frugal, she attaches great importance to the inheritance and education of family traditions, leaving the world a great image of good mother, admirable. In July 1467, the Ming Dynasty, Nong Miaoshi died. In order to commemorate her and spread the virtues of good mother, people further molded her into a respectable, amiable and loving goddess. Wumen Nongshipo's Blessing Ceremony has been inherited from Chenghua in the Ming Dynasty to present the moral and value values of good mother culture, which has had a far-reaching impact on the general public in Binyang over a hundred years.

Wumen Nongshipo's Blessing Ceremony mainly includes: sacrificial Blessing Ceremony, Taoist treading hall, folk art performance, folk opera and folk song duet and other activities. At the time of sacrifice, an altar was set up to sacrifice pigs and sheep. The ceremony of sacrificial prayer is presided over by one chief priest, several priests, one master of ceremonies, one master of incense, one master reading jot scripts, as well as the deacons such as drum priests, music priests and bureaucrats. The ceremony begins with the firing of cannons and the playing of music. The main sacrificial offerings and sacrifices are all in place. The sacrificial offerings are piety, incense, kneeling three times and nine kowtows, followed by "first offering", "second offering" and "final offering". Taoist ritual step on the hall, the wizard dances in the rhythm of witch songs. Dancers wear divine crowns, divine clothes, priest's orders in left hand, priest's sword in right hand, singing and dancing, and followed by many people. The sacrificial dance is divided into three chapters: Purifying the altar, inviting God and stepping on the dead. Although it deduces the pictures of daily life and production activities, it contains primitive mystery and presents strange dancing postures. Folk art performances include double dragon dance, group lion entrance, martial arts team performance and dance lotus phoenix, Maniang performance, etc.

Wumen Nongshipo's Blessing Ceremony prayed for god's blessing through sacrificial activities. It originates from folk beliefs and has a strong religious color, reflecting the long history and deep origin of Zhuang folk culture. It was born under the influence of Confucianism and Taoism and carried forward and inherited the good mother culture of the Zhuang Ethnic Group. On the one hand, it is connected with the traditional world view being handed down from ancient times. Sacrifice and performance activities are to pray for favorable weather and abundant crops. On the other hand, they are closely related to people's daily life. They have developed from traditional sacrificial rituals to folk customs and cultural festivals, attracting the surrounding masses to flock to them. Studying and protecting Wumen Nongshipo's Blessing Ceremony is of important academic value for studying the culture and folk customs of good mothers, satisfying people's psychological need to eliminate disasters and pray for good luck. With the attention and protection of the relevant departments in Binyang County, the Museum of Culture of Nongshipo was established. Binyang Wumen Nongshipo's Blessing Ceremony was inscribed on the Municipal List of Intangible Cultural Heritage in 2015.

（1467）七月，农妙什去世，人们为了纪念她，传扬良母美德，便进一步将其塑造成一位可敬可亲、慈悲博爱的女神，每年缅怀祭祀。吴门农氏婆祈福祭典自明代成化年间传承至今，展现出良母文化的道德观与价值观，对宾阳地区广大民众影响深远。

吴门农氏婆祈福祭典主要包括：祭祀祈福仪式、道家法式踩堂、民俗艺术表演、师公戏和山歌对唱等活动。祭祀时设祭坛，以猪、羊作为牺牲献祭。祭祀祈福仪式由主祭一人、与祭若干人、司仪、司香、读祝文等各一人主持，还有司鼓、司乐、司僚等执事。祭典在鸣炮、奏乐中开始，主祭、与祭等各就各位，虔诚上香、行三跪九叩大礼，接着行“初献礼”“亚献礼”“终献礼”。道家法事踩堂中，巫师需踏着巫歌节奏起舞。舞者头戴神冠，身着神衣，左手执法令，右手执法剑，且歌且舞，后有众人追随。祭祀舞蹈分净坛、请神、踩罡三个章节，虽演绎日常生活和生产活动的画面，却蕴含着原始神秘色彩并呈现奇特舞姿。民俗艺术表演包括双龙狂舞、群狮入场、武术队表演和舞彩凤、马娘表演等。

吴门农氏婆祈福祭典通过祭祀活动祈求神灵庇佑，源于民间信仰并具有浓厚的宗教色彩，体现了壮族民俗文化历史之悠久和渊源之深厚，受儒家思想和道教精神的影响孕育而生，且弘扬和继承了壮族良母文化。它一方面联系远古时期流传下来的传统世界观，祭祀与表演活动是为了祈祷风调雨顺、五谷丰登，另一方面与民众日常生活息息相关，从传统祭祀仪式发展至祭祀和民俗风情文化节，吸引周边群众蜂拥而至。研究、保护吴门农氏婆祈福祭典，对研究良母文化和民俗风情具有重要的学术价值，满足了人们消灾祈福的心理需求。受宾阳县有关部门的重视与保护，农氏婆良母文化博物馆建立。宾阳吴门农氏婆祈福祭典于2015年列入市级非物质文化遗产名录。

横县民间“无人售卖市场”习俗

Market without Salespersons Custom in Hengxian

项目名称：横县民间“无人售卖市场”习俗

别称：无

分布范围：横州市、贵港市、上林县、灵山县、浦北县等周边地区

入选名录：2017年第七批市级非物质文化遗产名录

保护单位：横县文化馆

代表性传承人：温复明、陈本志

Element name: Market without Salespersons Custom in Hengxian

Alternative name: None

Geographical location and range: Hengzhou City, Guigang City, Shanglin County, Lingshan County, Pubei County and the surrounding areas

Element inscribed list: In 2017 on the Seventh Municipal List of Intangible Cultural Heritage

Competent body involved in safeguarding: Hengxian Cultural Centre

Representative inheritor: Wen Fuming, Chen Benzhi

罗凤村“无人售卖菜市”全景
Luofeng Village Market without Salespersons

买菜人自己付钱
The Man who Buys Vegetables Pay by Himself

"Market without Salespersons" is a unique folk trading custom in Luofeng Village, Hengzhou City. "Without Salespersons " means buyers buy goods by themselves without the presence of a seller. Over 100 years ago, "Market without Salespersons" already existed. Although there was no one to supervise the collection of money, there was no shortage of money, which was one of the folk customs with the most ethnic characteristics in Luofeng Village.

Hengxian folk "Market without Salespersons" is located in Luofeng Village, south of Baihe Town, Hengzhou City. The area has abundant sunshine, mild climate and abundant rainfall, which is suitable for crop growth. There are small plains, hills and mountainous areas in the territory, with high-quality rice and tea planting as the economic pillar. The majority living here are Han people. Luofeng village, also known as Luofeng polder, is one of the village-level market polders in Hengzhou City. It is also a distributing centre for import and export of materials and polders for villagers within a hundred Li (fifty km), such as Hengzhou, Lingshan, Guigang and Pubei. The polders have always been busy and the business is booming. There are hundreds of pawnshops. In the feudal era, the social and economic development of this area was relatively closed, and the surrounding areas were surrounded by Baiyue Ethnic Group residences in a large extent, thus constituting a special geographical environment for the growth and inheritance of folk culture. Since ancient

横县民间“无人售卖市场”是横州市罗凤村独有的民间买卖习俗，“无人售卖”，即卖家不在场的情况下由买家自行购买物品。100多年前，“无人售卖市场”就已存在，尽管无人监督收钱，但钱从不缺少，是罗凤村最具民族特色的民间习俗之一。

横县民间“无人售卖市场”位于横州市百合镇南部的罗凤村，该区域日照充足，气候温和，雨量充沛，适宜农作物生长。境内有小平原、丘陵和山区，以优质水稻和茶叶种植为经济支柱，汉族人居多。罗凤村又名罗凤圩，是横州市村级集贸大圩场之一，是当地横州、灵山、贵港、浦北等方圆百里村民进出口物资、赶圩集散地，历来圩场热闹，生意兴隆，当铺上百间。此地汉族先民居多，在封建时代，此地社会、经济发展较为封闭，且周边很大范围内都被百越民族住地所包围，从而构成了民俗民间文化生长和传承的特殊地理环境，自古以来民风淳朴。

在远近闻名的横县民间“无人售卖市场”中，菜市只占一小块空地，摆卖的各类蔬菜经过精心挑选，扎成一捆捆，整齐地摆放于菜篮中，品种丰富，干净新鲜。菜农将几十个菜篮子挂在竹竿上，标好价格，一字排开，不用守在菜摊边贩卖，村民挑选好蔬菜后，就自觉在菜篮子里留下菜钱。尽管整个买卖过程无人监督，但钱从不缺少。在罗凤村，人与人之间相互信任、友好和睦，“无人售卖市场”的交易正是依靠这种信任得以存续的。

“无人售卖市场”是罗凤村先民智慧与美德的集中体现，在村民们代代繁衍生息的人文环境和历史变迁中发展，表达了人们日常生活的理想和愿望，体现了崇尚真、善、美的价值观。无人售卖的交易行为，无须人为组织或指授买卖货物的品种和数量，在民间自然形成，百年以来，不受时代变迁的影响，存续至今。无人售卖交易过程总是以自觉约束、公平守信的理念和方式进行，充分体现了中国的传统美德和当地民众的自律精神。这种村民自发形成、自觉交易，无须其他人员监督管理的买卖行为，节约了交易的劳动成本和管理成本。发掘和保护该习俗，对研究百越民族历史和民俗具有重要价值，也将促进中华民族优秀文化遗产的弘扬和传承，为促进精神文明建设、提高人民群众综合素质树立起良好的榜样。

times, the folk customs here were simple and honest.

In the well-known “Market without Salespersons” in Hengxian, the vegetable market only occupies a small space. All kinds of vegetables are carefully selected, tied in bundles, and placed neatly in the basket, which is rich in varieties, clean and fresh. Vegetable farmers hang dozens of vegetable baskets on bamboo poles in a line, marked the price, and did not have to keep at the side of the vegetable stall selling. After the villagers selected vegetables, they consciously left money in the basket to buy vegetables. There was no shortage of money, even though there was no one to supervise the whole process. In Luofeng village, people trust among other and they are friendly and harmonious. The “Market without Salespersons” trade depends on this kind of trust to survive.

“Market without Salespersons” is the concentrated embodiment of wisdom and virtue of the ancestors of Luofeng Village. It develops in the cultural environment and historical changes where the villagers reproduce from generation to generation, expresses people’s ideals and aspirations of daily life, and embodies the values advocating truth, kindness and beauty. Transaction without salespersons, in which no variety and quantity of goods need to be organized or instructed, has naturally formed among the people. It has not been affected by the changes of the times for a hundred years and has survived to present day. The process of sales and trading without salespersons is always carried out in the concept and way of self-conscious restraint, fairness and trustworthiness, which fully reflects the traditional virtues of China and the self-discipline spirit of local people. This kind of buying and selling behavior formed by villagers, spontaneously and without supervision and management by other personnel, saves labor cost and management cost. The discovery and protection of this custom is of great value to the study of the history and folk customs of Baiyue Ethnic Group, and will also promote the promotion and inheritance of the excellent cultural heritage of the Chinese nation, and set a good example for promoting the construction of spiritual civilization and improving the comprehensive quality of the people.

市场上摆卖的青菜
Vegetables on Sale in Market without Salespersons

横县青桐壮族圩逢

Qingtong Country Fair of Zhuang Ethnic Group in Hengxian

项目名称：横县青桐壮族圩逢

别称：无

分布范围：横州市校椅镇青桐村及周边地区

入选名录：2018年第七批自治区级非物质文化遗产名录

2017年第七批市级非物质文化遗产名录

保护单位：横县文化馆

代表性传承人：陈永锐、谢永长

Element name：Qingtong Country Fair of Zhuang Ethnic Group in Hengxian

Alternative name：None

Geographical location and range：Qingtong Village of Xiaoyi Town in Hengzhou City and the surrounding areas

Element inscribed list：In 2018 on the Seventh Autonomous Region List of Intangible Cultural Heritage

In 2017 on the Seventh Municipal List of Intangible Cultural Heritage

Competent body involved in safeguarding：Hengxian Cultural Centre

Representative inheritor：Chen Yongrui, Xie Yongchang

民间庆祝活动
Folk Celebration

童男童女巡游
Boy and Girl Parade

青桐壮族圩逢是横州传统民间歌圩，每年农历五月十三日依托关帝庙会举行，已有300多年的历史，文化内涵深厚，形式丰富多彩，在横州及周边壮族地区影响深远。

横州山水秀美，风光旖旎。青桐村位于横州市校椅镇北部，交通便捷。横州青桐的关帝庙，于300多年前建造，圩逢也于当时应运而生。每年农历五月十三日是青桐关帝庙会之日。庙会期间，青桐周边民众多达数万人前来赶圩。1971年，关帝庙被拆，圩逢也随之停顿，直到1981年以后才得以恢复。每年庙会当日，全市各乡镇的群众纷纷前去上香祈愿、赶“圩逢”，最为兴旺的时候有100条龙狮进行表演。2010年关帝庙重建，圩逢得以持续稳定地发展。

横县青桐壮族圩逢有山歌对唱、文体活动、祭祀仪式和百家宴席等活动。山歌对唱用壮话或客家话来唱，一般为五言壮欢、七言壮欢两个调。歌手们在唱歌时根据环境、场面、对象等临时发挥，转换内容，有贺酒堂歌、情歌、赞歌，谈生产的、谈生活的、倾诉情感的，内容极其丰富。文体活动则包括狮龙队表演、大鼓表演、舞凤凰、舞麒麟、上刀山下火海、武术、师公戏、文艺演出等民俗表演项目。祭祀仪式盛大隆重，师公在搭建起的道场上做法事，并举行祭拜关帝仪式。百家宴席则为村民们齐赴筵席，享用土鸡、土鸭、鱼生、玉米等当地美食，相互交流，增进感情。

Qingtong Country Fair of Zhuang Ethnic Group is a traditional folk singing festival in Hengzhou. It is held every year on the 13th day of the 5th lunar month on the basis of the Guan Gong Temple Fair. It has a history of more than 300 years. It has a profound cultural connotation and rich forms with far-reaching influence in Hengzhou and surrounding Zhuang areas.

Hengzhou has a beautiful scenery. Qingtong Village is located in the north of Xiaoyi Town, Hengzhou City with convenient transportation. Guan Gong Temple in Qingtong, Hengzhou, was built more than 300 years ago, and Country Fair came into being at that time. The 13th day of the 5th lunar month is the day of the Qingtong Guan Gong Temple meeting. During the temple fair, tens of thousands of people from Qingtong came to the fair. In 1971, Guan Gong Temple was demolished, and the Country Fair stopped. It was not until 1981 that the Country Fair was restored. Every year on the day of the temple fair, people from all towns and villages in the city go to worship incense and pray for the “Country Fair”. At the peak of prosperity, there are 100 dragons and lions performances. In 2010, the Guan Gong Temple was rebuilt, and Country Fair continued to develop steadily.

The County Fair of the Qingtong Zhuang Ethnic Group in Hengxian has folk songs, cultural and sports activities, sacrificial ceremonies and hundred banquets and other activities. Folk songs are sung in Zhuang dialect or Hakka dialect, usually in two tunes, five-character and seven-character. Singers improvise and change the content according to the environment, scenes, objects and other temporary plays. There are hall songs, love songs, hymns, sings talking about production, talking about life and talking about emotions. The content is extremely rich. Sports activities include lion and dragon team performance, drum performance, phoenix dance, kirin dance, various kinds of opera, martial arts, literary and artistic performances and other folk performances. The sacrificial ceremony was grand and solemn. Tao Masters conducted a religious rite on the built pavement and held a ceremony to worship Lord Guan. Hundreds of banquets were held for the villagers to enjoy local delicacies such as home-kept chicken, duck, fish, corn and so on. They exchanged with each other and enhanced their feelings.

Historically, Country Fair is an occasion for people to make friends and an important opportunity for young men and women to be concerned with love and romance. It plays a unique role in the spiritual life of local people and is an indispensable part in the life of Zhuang people. Qingtong Country Fair of Zhuang Ethnic Group is rich in content, including folk songs, cultural performances, sacrificial ceremonies and so on. It shows the local folkways and customs in many ways. The activities include religious beliefs, culture and art, etc. Since its birth, Qingtong Country Fair of Zhuang Ethnic Group has a strong vitality. Except for a few years, it has been continued for hundreds of years. The folk songs of Qingtong Country Fair of Zhuang Ethnic Group are graceful and melodious in tune, easy to sing and remember. The lyrics are improvised according to the scene situation and rhyming freely. They are of high artistic value. With the strong support of leaders at all levels of county and town governments, development of Country Fair is in good condition on the whole.

圩逢在历史上是民众交朋结友的场合，也是男女青年谈情说爱的重要机会，在当地民众的精神生活中发挥着独特的作用，是壮族人生活中必不可少的一部分。青桐壮族圩逢内容丰富，有山歌对唱、文体表演、祭祀仪式等，从多方面展现了当地的民风民情。活动包含宗教信仰、文化艺术等多项内容。青桐壮族圩逢自诞生之日起即具有顽强的生命力，除少数年份暂停举办外，数百年来一直延续。青桐壮族圩逢的山歌，曲调婉转悠扬，易唱易记，歌词依据现场情况即兴创作，押韵自由，具有非常高的艺术价值，是研究壮族传统音乐的重要素材，体现出横州市民歌的艺术特色以及民间艺人的才华。在县、镇政府各级领导的大力支持下，圩逢总体开展情况良好。

壮族婚俗

Marriage Custom of Zhuang Ethnic Group

项目名称：壮族婚俗

别称：无

分布范围：隆安县

入选名录：2013年第五批市级非物质文化遗产名录

保护单位：隆安县文化馆

代表性传承人：无

Element name: Marriage Custom of Zhuang Ethnic Group

Alternative name: None

Geographical location and range: Long'an County

Element inscribed list: In 2013 on the Fifth Municipal List of Intangible Cultural Heritage

Competent body involved in safeguarding: Long'an County Cultural Centre

Representative inheritor: None

Marriage Custom of Zhuang Ethnic Group refers to the marriage customs of Zhuang Ethnic Group in Long'an County, which develops from the marriage custom of the ancient Zhuang Ethnic Group. It was developed when the human society was turned from the matriarchal to patriarchal society. Up to now, it has formed a set of complete marriage custom ceremony. Marriage Custom of Zhuang Ethnic Group is distributed in Long'an County, Youjiang Valley in the southwest of Guangxi. The farming industry here is prosperous; over 90% of residents of the county are from Zhuang Ethnic Group, who live in the stockade house. Marriage Custom of Zhuang Ethnic Group in Long'an derived from the marriage customs after the ancient Zhuang Ethnic Group entered the patriarchal society. According to *Long'an County Record*, "in the Qing Dynasty and the Republic of China, the marriage was determined by parents and the parties could only obey it." "Deciding marriage with songs and selecting spouses by singing", and "taking a son-in-law to home and inheriting the family" have become the special activity in the wedding ceremony of Zhuang Ethnic Group.

The ceremony of Marriage Custom of Zhuang Ethnic Group is roughly divided into seven parts. 1. Select the spouse for marriage. First of all, they select the spouse by singing songs. On March 4 and 5 of the lunar year, hundreds of male and female youths look at each other by crossing the street and sing the folk songs. In the process of singing songs, they convey their feelings with eyebrows and eyes and seek for the one they like. Then they follow the commands of parents and matchmaker for marriage. And some families take in a son-in-law and inherit the family. 2. Exchange the date of birth and give the bride-price. Before marriage, male and female youths of Zhuang Ethnic Group must exchange the date of birth. With no inter-restriction, they may get married. Two or three months before the marriage, the male needs to select a lucky day to invite the matchmaker to send the bride-price to the female and prepare for dowry. 3. Fetch the bride. One day before fetching the bride, the male sends the pork, rice and wine of a stipulated amount to the female's family. On the day of fetching the bride, the male feasts guests and friends; the bridegroom wears red ribbon and rides on the horse to fetch the female along with the team composed of ten people, including the groomsman, matchmaker, little girl, music player and sedan-chair bearers. 4. Go downstairs and go to the bridal sedan chair. After the bridegroom goes to the bride's family, the dressed-up bride is supported by her sisters-in-law to hold the ceremony of "going downstairs", then a person holds the umbrella to rapidly rotate it for the bride; another person

出嫁，散花仪式
Scatter Blossoms at Wedding Ceremony

壮族婚俗是隆安县壮族男婚女嫁的习俗，由古壮族的婚姻习俗发展而来，在人类社会从母系走向父系的时候便产生，延续至今形成了一套完整的婚俗仪式。壮族婚俗分布于广西西南部右江河谷的隆安县，这里农耕业兴旺，全县居民百分之九十以上为壮族人，多住木栏式房屋。隆安壮族婚俗源自古壮族进入父系社会以后的婚姻习俗。据《隆安县志》记载："清代及民国时期，男婚女嫁全听父母之命，媒妁之言，当事人只能听从依顺。""以歌联婚，对歌择偶""招赘上门，传承香火"成为壮族婚礼中的特色活动。

壮族婚俗仪式内容大致分为七部分：1.择偶联婚。首先对歌择偶，以歌联姻，每年农历三月初四、初五，几百男女青年整日隔街相望，对唱山歌，并在对歌的过程中眉目传情，寻觅心仪伴侣；接着按照父母之命，媒妁之言联姻；然后一些人家招赘男青年上门，传承香火。2.换年庚，送聘金。结婚前，壮族男女青年必须交换年庚八字，无相克才能成婚。婚前两三个月，男方就要择吉日请媒人送聘金到女方家给女方置办嫁妆。3.迎亲。迎亲前一日，男方将约定数量的猪肉、白米、白酒等送到女方家。迎亲当日男方家宴请宾朋，新郎身挂红绸带，骑马，与伴郎、媒婆、接新娘闺女、八音手、轿夫等组成数十人的迎亲队到女方家迎亲。4.下楼梯，上花轿。新郎到了女方家，梳好妆的新娘由姑嫂扶出闺房举行“下楼梯”仪式，再由一人为新娘手撑雨伞快速旋转，另一人手提装有爆米花和铜钱、硬币的花篮“散花”，散花结束后，新娘上花轿跟随新郎回家。5.拜堂。新娘、新郎叩拜家公家婆。6.新婚贺词仪式。有钱人家会邀请歌手前来演唱结婚贺词。7.回娘家，俗称“回门”。拜堂后第二天早上，新娘由接新娘的人一路陪同回娘家。

隆安县壮族婚俗礼仪内容丰富且复杂，在长期传统礼俗活动中形成了较为固定的模式，一方面与汉族某些地区婚俗相近，如接新娘、拜堂、回门等，又有壮族特色，如“散花”“下楼梯”。“下楼梯”习俗与隆安县民众特殊的居住环境——木栏式房屋相关，由人离住房必须下楼梯的习惯而成。新娘在歌声中步步下楼，涕泪声声，将对父母的不舍与感恩之情淋漓抒发。发掘、抢救和保护壮族婚俗，对丰富壮民族民间风俗文化具有极为重要的意义，同时也是研究壮族历史文化必不可少的部分，有利于传统美德的广泛传播，对精神文明建设、丰富民众的文化生活具有重要的促进作用。2013年，壮族婚俗列入第五批市级非物质文化遗产名录。

picks up the basket filled with popcorn, copper cash and coin to "scatter the flower". After the flower is scattered, the bride goes to the sedan and follows the bridegroom to home. 5. Perform the formal wedding ceremony. The bridegroom and the bride kowtow to the bridegroom's parents. 6. Wedding congratulation ceremony. The rich family will invite singers to sing the wedding congratulations. 7. Return to the bride's family. On the morning of the second day after the formal wedding, the bride returns to her own family with the accompaniment of the bride-fetching man.

The etiquette contents of Marriage Custom of Zhuang Ethnic Group in Long'an County are abundant and complicated, which has formed a fixed mode in the long-term traditional etiquette activity. On the one hand, it is close to the marriage custom in some regions of Han Ethnic Group, such as fetching the bride, holding the formal wedding and returning to the bride's family. On the other hand, it is of the characteristics of Zhuang Ethnic Group, such as "scattering the flower" and "going downstairs". The custom of "going downstairs" is related to the special living environment of the residents in Long'an County, namely the stockade house; for they have to go downstairs in order to leave the house. The bride goes downstairs in the song and weeps, thus fully showing her gratitude to the parents. To explore, rescue and protect Marriage Custom of Zhuang Ethnic Group is of extremely important meaning to enriching the folk customs of Zhuang Ethnic Group, and meanwhile an indispensable part of studying the historical culture of Zhuang Ethnic Group. It helps widely spread the traditional virtues, promote the construction of spiritual civilization construction and enrich the cultural life of the public. In 2013, Marriage Custom of Zhuang Ethnic Group was inscribed on the Fifth Municipal List of Intangible Cultural Heritage.

散花
Scatter Blossoms

布泉天王庙会

Buquan Tianwang Temple Fair

项目名称：布泉天王庙会

别称：无

分布范围：隆安县布泉乡

入选名录：2015年第六批市级非物质文化遗产名录

保护单位：隆安县文化馆

代表性传承人：无

Element name：Buquan Tianwang Temple Fair

Alternative name：None

Geographical location and range：Buquan Town of Long'an County

Element inscribed list：In 2015 on the Sixth Municipal List of Intangible Cultural Heritage

Competent body involved in safeguarding：Long'an County Cultural Centre

Representative inheritor：None

仙婆们正在写神符
Female Priests are Writing the Talisman

布泉天王庙会是每年农历九月二十一日（即长春公诞辰纪念日）于隆安县布泉乡天王庙举办的大型庙会。庙会包括求神拜佛、唱戏、杂技、龙狮表演、物品交流等，届时场面热闹非凡，人山人海。

布泉乡位于隆安县西南部，属于典型的大石山区，旅游资源丰富，自然生态原始古朴。由于自然条件相对恶劣，这里自古以来生产力低下，百姓生活较困苦，有些年景甚至因遭受自然灾害而颗粒无收。因此，这里的百姓自古以来便希望得到神灵护佑，消灾除难。于是，拥有神力并保佑百姓的奇人马世明诞生了，布泉天王庙会也因此诞生。布泉天王庙位于隆安县布泉乡岑山村上礼屯，庙会始于清代光绪年间，距今已有130多年的历史。据有关经书记载，奇人马世明通过观音帮助，修炼成佛，神通广大，专为当地百姓消灾解难，被人们尊称为“长春仙公”。清光绪年间，人们为其建庙，名为“天王庙”。每年农历九月二十一日被传为长春公诞辰，来自隆安县各相邻乡镇的民众前来烧香祈福，另有各种演艺活动举行。

庙会当天，数百位来自各地的道公与僧人诵经于此。因传说求财求福求平安者十求九灵，人们便纷纷远道而来祭

Buquan Tianwang Temple Fair takes place annually at Buquan Village of Long'an County's Tianwang Temple on the 21th day of the 9th lunar month, and it is also the date of ceremony for the birth of Lord Changchun. This huge festival ceremony includes praying for god, worship Buddha, performing Chinese opera, dragon and lion performance, exchange of goods, which would attract huge crowds of people.

Buquan Village is situated at southwest of Long'an County with an abundance of travel resources and original simple lifestyles. The area is an example of typical rocky mountain geography. Due to its harsh natural environment, productivity has been historically low, thus it is harder for locals to make a living. At bad times, when there is a natural disaster, nothing is harvested from the fields. Thus, natives have longed for god's protection from natural disasters since ancient times. Then, a personage named Ma Shiming who is gifted with the power of god has born to protect the natives, along with the establishment of Tianwang Temple. Buquan Tiamwang Temple is located at Shangli in Censhan Village of Buquan Town of Long'an County. Its history could be traced back to Emperor Guangxu of the Qing Dynasty with a history over 130 years. According to relative record, Ma Shiming managed to attain Buddhahood and gained great power through the help of Guanyin Bodhisattva. Using his magnificent power, he helped the natives through disasters.

On the day of the temple fair, hundreds of Taoist priests and monks from all over the country chanted sutras here. It is said that people who seek wealth, happiness and peace seek nine spirits, and people come seek wealth, happiness and peace seek nine spirits, and people come seek wealth, happiness and peace seek nine spirits, and people come singingopera, commodity exchange and other activities. More than 10000 people came, and Buquan Tianwang Temple was also named "Temple Street". From 1966 to 1976, Buquan Tianwang Temple was destroyed. Only some stone carvings, wood carvings and 28 volumes of scriptures by Ma Changchun survived. In 1986, the masses raised more than 90000 yuan to repair Tianwang Temple. Today, Tianwang Temple has become one of the six major tourist attractions in Long'an County.

Buquan Tianwang Temple Fair, due to its special geographical location and its ancient history, is well known around the area. The very creation of this temple fair originates from natives' appreciation toward a rescuer Ma Shiming and their genuine wishes for blessings and peace. It adds on the usual tradition of ritual sacrifice: despite burning incense, god worship, acrobatics, exchange of agricultural goods (grain seeds, farming tools and so on) also takes place in Tianwang Temple Fair as it has become a unique communal platform for the sale of agricultural goods. Every year, more than 10,000 people would gather here, making it a lucrative location for the travel industry. Thus, the research and protection of Tianwang Temple Fair bears great significance for the development of cultural history and travel industry and economic growth of Long'an County. The 28 volumes of scriptures that survived were all written with brushes, which were precious. They covered many aspects of social life, such as scholar, farmer, worker and businessman. They encouraged people to be kind and educated. Their protection and research had great academic value for understanding the history, culture and ancient social life of the Zhuang people. In 2015, Buquan Tianwang Temple Fair was inscribed on the Sixth Municipal List of Intangible Cultural Heritage.

拜长春公。除了一般的烧香祭拜活动，庙会上还举行杂耍、唱戏、商品交流等活动，来者逾万人，布泉天王庙也得“庙街”称号。1966至1976年间，布泉天王庙被损毁，只有部分石雕、木雕以及马长春的28卷经书幸存于世。1986年，群众筹资9万余元修复天王庙。如今，天王庙成为隆安县六大旅游景点之一。

布泉天王庙会源于特殊的地理环境，因“那文化”而名扬四方，历史悠久。庙会之产生，源于民间对救世主马世明的感恩心理与祈求平安多福的美好心愿。民俗活动与一般庙会祭祀不同，除烧香祭拜、表演杂耍，还有稻谷种子、农具等农产品交流活动，成为农作物传播与销售的特殊渠道，贴近民众生活。每年上万游客相会于此，使这里具有极大的旅游开发价值。因此，研究、保护布泉天王庙会对进一步研究“那文化”的历史发展极为重要，对推动隆安县商品经济发展、旅游开发等具有十分重要的实践意义。幸免于难的28卷经书全部以毛笔写就，弥足珍贵，内容涉及士、农、工、商等社会生活诸多方面，劝人向善，教化一方民众，对其保护与研究对了解壮族历史文化和古代社会生活具有极高的学术价值。2015年，布泉天王庙会列入第六批市级非物质文化遗产名录。

上林县二月二卢於春社

Shanglin Luyu Eryue'er Spring Sacrifice

项目名称：上林县二月二卢於春社

别称：无

分布范围：上林县木山乡

入选名录：2018年第七批自治区级非物质文化遗产名录
2015年第六批市级非物质文化遗产名录

保护单位：上林县文化馆

代表性传承人：无

Element name：Shanglin Luyu Eryue'er Spring Sacrifice

Alternative name：None

Geographical location and range：Mushan Town of Shanglin County

Element inscribed list：In 2018 on the Seventh Autonomous Region List of Intangible Cultural Heritage
In 2015 on the Sixth Municipal List of Intangible Cultural Heritage

Competent body involved in safeguarding：Shanglin County Cultural Centre

Representative inheritor：None

上林县二月二卢於春社场景
Scene of Shanglin Luyu Eryue'er Spring Sacrifice

祭拜仪式之九：踩花灯
The Ninth Worship ceremony: stepping on the Lantern

Luyu Eryue'er Spring Sacrifice is a traditional festival activity organized by residents living in and around Shanglin County. It includes activities like ploughing-starting ceremony, cultural and sports activities, and economic and trade activities.

Luyu Spring Sacrifice is held in Mushan Town of Shanglin County. It is a junction of two counties and two cities, because it is adjacent to Laibin City in the east, Xincheng County and Heshan City in the north, Sanli Town in the south and Qiaoxian County in the west. Mushan Town covers 124 square kilometers with 72 natural villages. It has both dry land and paddy field, but dry land is relatively more. Sugarcane is the main commercial crop of this place. As early as in pre-Qin period of China, the ancient Chinese expressed their good wishes of reducing natural disasters and obtaining bumper harvest through various lively activities, such as collective feasts and sports competitions. According to *Shanglin County Annals*, during the reign of Emperor Qianlong of the Qing Dynasty, people living in Mushan would organize temple fairs in the Spring Festival every year. With the development of economy, these temple fairs have become large and Luyu Spring Sacrifice has become an indispensable part of them. Today, this event not only follows the traditional style, but also constantly innovates and enriches its contents, which allows its influence lager and lager. Since 2012, the government of Mushan Town began to

上林县二月二卢於春社是上林县及其附近居民于每年农历二月初二自发组织举行的传统节庆活动。活动包括开犁仪式、文体活动、经贸活动等。

卢於春社举办于上林县木山乡，东临来宾市，北靠忻城县、合山市，南接三里镇，西连乔贤镇，是两县两市的交界处。木山乡面积124平方千米，有72个自然村，旱地水田均有，旱地较多，经济作物以甘蔗为主。先秦时期，古代劳动人民通过举办各种活动表达减少自然灾害、获得丰收的良好心愿，活动形式丰富，有集体欢宴、集体竞技等，场面热闹。据《上林县志》记载，清乾隆年间，木山乡群众就在每年春节自发组织民间庙会，随着经济的发展，庙会规模越来越大，卢於春社活动即为其中必不可少的一部分。直至今日，它不仅沿袭了古风，还不断创新和丰富，影响力不断扩大。自2012年以来，该活动由民间自发举行转为由木山乡政府组织举办。

上林二月二卢於春社的基本内容大致包括三部分：开

犁仪式、文体活动和经贸活动。开犁仪式即由理事会选出5位农民、5头牛和5把犁一字排开，在附近的甘蔗地里同时开犁，后面10人跟着播种蔗种，寓意一年春耕的开始。5位师公、道公绕蔗地起舞，祈求风调雨顺、五谷丰登。文体活动包括在戏台举行的开幕式演出以及在各场地举行的拔河、搬运甘蔗、打陀螺、摄影、斗牛、斗鸡、打乒乓球、猜灯谜、山歌比赛等多种民间竞技游戏。经贸活动即四面八方的人们带着各类农副产品、手工艺品、日常生活用品在活动场地展示并交易。

上林县二月二卢於春社是当地居民代代相传的传统习俗，具有深厚的民族文化内涵，是当地群众文化信仰的外在体现，内容丰富多彩。文化、艺术、民间体育活动共同举办，将宗教、民间文娱活动与商业活动相结合，共同展现了壮民族节日的独特性、包容性，成为多种民俗活动竞相展示的平台，并吸引八方群众来此聚会，对研究民族传统文化具有较重要的价值。发掘、抢救、保护上林县二月二卢於春社，不仅有利于丰富人民群众的文化生活，还有利于弘扬南宁及其周边地区民族文化的传播和弘扬，也对带动地域经济发展、促进旅游业繁荣产生积极的作用。为保护卢於春社的传承及发展，当地群众自筹资金，重修佛像，坚持每年例行举办活动，上林县政府为弘扬民族民间传统文化，致力打造“木山乡卢於春社文化旅游”品牌。

hold this event, replacing its history of holding by the people spontaneously.

Shanglin Luyu Eryue’er Spring Sacrifice mainly consists of three parts, that is, ploughing-starting ceremony, cultural and sports activities, and economic and trade activities. On ploughing-starting ceremony, with five cattle and ploughs, five famers selected by the board will line up in the nearby sugarcane field to plough at the same time, followed by ten people to sow sugarcane seeds, symbolizing the beginning of the spring ploughing of the year. Meanwhile, five clergy-like persons will dance around the field to pray for good weather and golden harvest of the year. Cultural and sports activities include the opening ceremony performance held on the stage and other activities held in various venues, such as tug of war, sugarcane-carrying competition, gyro playing, photo contest, bullfighting, cockfighting, table tennis, lantern riddles, folk song contest and other folk games. Economic and trade activities refer to displaying and trading of agricultural and sideline products, handicraft and daily necessities by people from all directions.

Luyu Spring Sacrifice in Shanglin County is a traditional custom inherited by the local residents from generation to generation, which bears the profound connotation of national culture, reflecting the cultural beliefs of the locals. With colorful activities covering culture, art and folk games, this event has combined religion, folk cultural activities and commercial activities together, jointly representing the uniqueness and inclusiveness of Zhuang festivals. It has become a platform for folk activities and also has attracted people to come here from all directions, which is of great value for the study of ethnic traditional cultures. To discover, save and protect Luyu Spring Sacrifice is not only beneficial to enrich people’s cultural life, but also good to carry forward national culture of Nanning and its surrounding areas. It also plays a positive role in driving the development of both regional economy and tourist industry. To protect the inheritance and development of Luyu Spring Sacrifice, the local people have raised funds to rebuild Buddha statues and insisted on holding activities every year. At the same time, in order to promote traditional folk culture, the government of Shanglin County also has made efforts to build a brand of “Mushan Town Luyu Spring Sacrifice Cultural Tourism”.

上林县祭冬民俗

Shanglin Winter Sacrifice Folkways

项目名称：上林县祭冬民俗

别称：无

分布范围：上林县巷贤镇磨庄、黎村、渌洛村、苏村、张磨村，宾阳县思陇镇、欧塘村，马山县周鹿镇、林圩镇

入选名录：2017年第七批市级非物质文化遗产名录

保护单位：上林县文化馆

代表性传承人：无

Element name：Shanglin Winter Sacrifice Folkways

Alternative name：None

Geographical location and range：Mozhuang Village, Licun Village, Luluo Village, Sucun Village, Zhangmo Village of Xiangxian Town in Shanglin County; Silong Town, Outang Village of Binyang County; Zhoulu Town, Linxu Town of Mashan County

Element inscribed list：In 2017 on the Seventh Municipal List of Intangible Cultural Heritage

Competent body involved in safeguarding：Shanglin County Cultural Centre

Representative inheritor：None

磨氏祖堂正堂
Main Hall of Mo's Ancestral Hall

上林县祭冬民俗是上林县冬至祭祖习俗，每年由民众自发组织，由上林县巷贤镇磨庄群众创办，于乾隆年间初期形成，世代相传。

上林县位于广西中南部，大明山东麓，县境地处低纬度地区，属亚热带季风气候。巷贤镇位于上林县东南部20千米处，是上林县主要产粮区之一。上林县祭冬民俗于乾隆年间初期形成，当时磨庄先祖磨弘积、磨弘培两兄弟互相资助、勤奋读书，在祖业中设置了以稻谷助学的“帮学谷”规定，每年冬至敬祖合议，给读书的子孙按科级发放，以后演变为惯例和传统。光绪八年（1882），磨氏祖堂建成，全庄孩子集中在祖堂上座房屋读书，并接收外庄求学子弟。随着本庄子弟外迁，该民俗广泛分布于上林县巷贤镇磨庄、黎村、渌洛村、苏村、张磨村，宾阳县思陇镇、欧塘村，马山县周鹿镇、林圩镇。

上林县祭冬民俗不仅有祭祀仪式，还有各类表演和聚餐。祭祀仪式由村干部做司仪，由德高望重的长辈做主祭，

Shanglin Winter Sacrifice Folkways is a custom of ancestor worship on the winter solstice in Shanglin County. It is organized by people living in Mozhuang Village, Xiangxian Town, Shanglin County spontaneously. This winter ceremony is formed in the early reign of Emperor Qianlong of the Qing Dynasty and passed on from generation to generation.

Shanglin County is situated in the east foot of Daming Mountain in South-Central Guangxi at the low latitudes with subtropical monsoon climate. Xiangxian Town is located 20 kilometers southeast of Shanglin County, which is a major grain producing areas of Shanglin. Shanglin Winter Sacrifice Folkways is formed in the early reign of Emperor Qianlong of the Qing Dynasty. The ancestors of Mozhuang Village, brothers Mo Hongji and Mo Hongpei supported each other and studied hard, later setting a regulation of “Grain Study Subsidies”, which means helping others to go to school with grain. On the winter solstice every year, people here would worship ancestors and consult the distribution of subsidies according to the grade of children, which gradually evolved into a custom and tradition. In the eighth year of Emperor Guangxu in the Qing Dynasty, the ancestor's hall of Mo was established, providing a studying place for children in Mozhuang village and allowing children from other surrounding villages to study here. With the emigration of people of Mozhuang Village, this custom has widely spread over other villages, including Mozhuang Village, Licun Village, Luluo Village, Sucun Village, Zhangmo Village of Xiangxian Town of Shanglin County, Silong Town and Outang Village of Binyang County, and Zhoulu Town and Linxu Town of Mashan County.

Shanglin Winter Sacrifice Folkways has not only sacrificial ceremony, but also various performances and dining parties. On sacrificial ceremony, the village head will be the host and the elders of high prestige and universal respect will lead the villagers to offer incense and light, knock chime stone and fire cannons in salute. According to the seniority in the village, people will worship ancestors in turn by bowing three times and reading oration. Then, they will distribute red packets to people over 60 years old, families with new birth and students admitted by universities so as to carry forward the traditional virtues of respecting the old and caring for the young, studying hard and diligently and being loyal and filial to their families. Ladies in traditional Zhuang costumes will provide self-made sweet wine to welcome guests and friends. Under the century-old banyan tree, special dances and folk songs will be performed to celebrate the arrival of guests and friends. After the performance and sacrifice process, dining party will begin, providing an opportunity for people to communicate the family situation of the past year and improve the relationship between family members.

The distribution of "Grain Study Subsidies" has promoted the upsurge of culture and education in the whole village. Taking Shanglin Winter Sacrifice Folkways as the source, the custom has been shaped in the past hundred years among Zhuang ancestors in Shanglin County and Han ancestors in Mozhuang Village, forming a relatively fixed and perfect mode and with wide mass base. The traditional worship ceremony and the plain villages carry the rich political, historical and cultural connotations of Shanglin and its surrounding areas, that are of great value to the study of local historical development. Shanglin Winter Ceremony Shanglin Winter Sacrifice Folkways is the epitome of the history and culture of Mozhuang village, which reflects the production and life of Shanglin County in the past hundred years. As a folk custom of praying for good luck and helping students to learn, it sustains the good vision of local people and plays a positive role in promoting traditional cultures. Through teaching by words and deeds with a silent transforming influence, the distribution of "Grain Study Subsidies" and red packets can encourage loyalty and filial piety, and promote the traditional virtues of respecting the old and caring for the young and studying hard and diligently, which is more easily accepted by people. With a long history and rich contents, the traditional winter ceremony has integrated the Zhuang and Han cultures with distinctive features, which can not only enrich and inherit excellent traditional culture, but also have typical ethnic and regional characteristics, providing a significant value for the study of folk beliefs, literature and art. In 2017, Shanglin Winter Sacrifice Folkways was inscribed on the Seventh Municipal List of Intangible Cultural Heritage.

带领乡亲敬香、上灯、敲罄、鸣炮，按照辈分长幼依次祭拜，行三献礼，读祭祖文，依次给花甲老人、添丁的庄户和考上高校的学子派发红包，以弘扬敬老爱幼、勤于耕读、忠孝持家的传统美德。由身着壮族传统服饰的壮家妹为宾朋献上自家酿制的甜酒，举行迎宾仪式。在庄里的百年高山榕树下，表演独具特色的舞蹈和山歌，庆贺宾朋的到来。在表演及祭祀流程结束后便开始聚餐活动，交流一年以来的家族情况，联络兄弟姐妹间的情感。

“帮学谷”的发放促进了全庄文化教育的兴起，上林祭冬民俗以此为源头，在上林壮族先祖与磨庄汉族先祖历经百年的生产生活中形成，逐渐发展成比较固定和完善的模式，具有广泛的群众性。传统的拜祭仪式和古朴的村落，承载了上林及周边地区丰厚的政治、历史、人文内涵，对研究当地历史发展具有重要的价值。上林祭冬民俗是上林磨庄历史和文化的缩影，反映了上林县百年以来的生产生活，并作为一种祈福、助学的民间风俗，寄托了当地民众的美好愿景，起到了宣传传统文化的作用。“帮学谷”的发放和红包的派发弘扬忠孝持家、尊老爱幼、勤于耕读的传统美德，以言传身教、潜移默化的方式进行道德教育，更易于被人接受。传统的祭冬民俗历史悠久、内容丰富，壮族与汉族文化互相交融，不仅能丰富和继承了优秀传统文化，且具有典型的民族和地域特征，对研究民俗民间信仰、文学艺术具有重要的参考价值。2017年，上林县祭冬民俗列入第七批市级非物质文化遗产名录。